A HISTORY *of*
ANCIENT GREECE

A HISTORY *of* ANCIENT GREECE

CLAUDE ORRIEUX
Professor at the University of Caen

PAULINE SCHMITT PANTEL
Professor at the University of Picardy Jules Verne

Translated by
JANET LLOYD

Blackwell
Publishing

© 1995 by Presses Universitaires de France
English translation © 1999 by Janet Lloyd
This edition © 1999 by Blackwell Publishing Ltd

BLACKWELL PUBLISHING
350 Main Street, Malden, MA 02148-5020, USA
9600 Garsington Road, Oxford OX4 2DQ, UK
550 Swanston Street, Carlton, Victoria 3053, Australia

First published in French by Presses Universitaires de France as *Histoire Greque* in 1995
First published in English 1999 by Blackwell Publishing Ltd

3   2006

Library of Congress Cataloging-in-Publication Data

Orrieux, Claude, 1928–
    [Histoire grecque. English]
    A history of Ancient Greece / Claude Orrieux and Pauline Schmitt Pantel.
        p. cm.
    Includes bibliographical references and index.
    ISBN 0-631-20308-7 (hbk. : alk. paper). — ISBN 0-631-20309-5 (pbk. : alk. paper)
        1. Greece—History—To 146 B.C. I. Pantel, Pauline Schmitt.
    II. Title.
    DF214.07713 1999
    938—dc21   98–56267
                                                                        CIP

ISBN-13: 978-0-631-20308-7 (hbk. : alk. paper). — ISBN-13: 978-0-631-20309-4 (pbk. : alk. paper)

A catalogue record for this title is available from the British Library.

Set in 10½ on 12 pt Galliard
by Graphicraft Ltd, Hong Kong
Printed and bound in the United Kingdom
by TJ International, Padstow, Cornwall

The publisher's policy is to use permanent paper from mills that operate a sustainable forestry policy, and which has been manufactured from pulp processed using acid-free and elementary chlorine-free practices. Furthermore, the publisher ensures that the text paper and cover board used have met acceptable environmental accreditation standards.

For further information on
Blackwell Publishing, visit our website:
www.blackwellpublishing.com

CONTENTS

ACKNOWLEDGEMENTS

The publishers and the translator wish to express their gratitude and appreciation to Professor Daniel Tompkins of Temple University, Philadelphia, for his advice and contribution to the English edition of *A History of Ancient Greece*. We are particularly grateful to him for his expert comments on the draft script and for providing the guide to further reading. We should also like to thank Dr Graham Speake for his advice on the guide to sources.

TRANSLATOR'S NOTE

I have used the following English translations of Greek texts:

Loeb Classical Library, Cambridge, MA, and London
Aeschines, *Speeches*, 1988, translated by Charles Darwin Adams
Aristotle, *Politics*, 1972, translated by H. Rackham
Demosthenes, *Speeches*, 1964, translated by J. H. Vince
Hesiod, *Works and Days*, *Homeric Hymn to Apollo*, 1970, translated by
   H. G. Evelyn-White
Plato, *Laws*, 1926, translated by R. G. Bury
—— *Epistles*, 1929, translated by R. G. Bury
Plutarch, *Lives*, 1967, translated by Bernadotte Perrin

The Penguin Classics, Harmondsworth
Herodotus, *The Histories*, 1954, translated by A. de Selincourt
Hippocratic Writings, 1978, translated by J. Chadwick and W. N. Mann
Homer, *The Iliad*, 1950, translated by E. V. Rieu
—— *The Odyssey*, 1946, translated by E. V. Rieu
Thucydides, *The History of the Peloponnesian War*, 1954, translated by
   Rex Warner

FIGURES

FOREWORD

As this *History of Ancient Greece* follows a certain tradition, a brief historiographical survey will serve to pick out the principal themes that need
to be mentioned in a foreword.

In 1862 Victor Duruy published his *Histoire des Grecs*, writing in his
introduction as follows:

One thing I have never been able to understand is how it is that in France, where
the learning, religion, arts and archaeology of Greece have been studied for so
many years, nobody has yet thought of constructing a general picture of the
historical life of the Greek people. We have plenty of specialist books to consult,
but not a single history to read. I have tried to fill this regrettable lacuna.

In the course of the following twenty years that lacuna was further filled
by a number of books and translations, including one from the English of
G. Grote's *A History of Greece*, as well as several editions of Victor Duruy's
own synthesis. 1864 saw the appearance of Fustel de Coulanges' *La Cité
antique* (*The Ancient City*), which was not a 'Greek history' but, as its
subtitle indicated, 'a study on the religion, laws and institutions of Greece
and Rome', and which soon became a work of reference. The next period
of relatively active publication was not until the 1920s, which saw the
appearance of the works of J. Hatzfeld, G. Glotz, M. Croiset, P. Cloché
and R. Cohen. The third period of activity began twenty years ago and
still continues. It has produced two kinds of books on Greek history:
those in one group are addressed to readers already familiar with the ancient world and comprise both syntheses and monographs; those in the
other group are addressed to readers discovering the Greek world for the
first time. The present *History of Ancient Greece* falls into the second
category, which already includes some excellent predecessors such as *Le
Monde grec antique* by M.-C. Amouretti and F. Ruzé, which appeared in
1978 and was the first synthesis resolutely aimed at this type of reader.

In the meantime, gaps between new productions were filled by reprints
and paperbacks. In the sixties, for example, Jean Hatzfeld's *Histoire de la
Grèce ancienne* (*History of Ancient Greece*, Edinburgh, 1966) appeared in
paperback form, having originally been published in 1926, as did G. Glotz's
La cité grecque (*The Greek City and its Institutions*, London, 1929), first
published in 1928. Students of history in the sixties were often aware of a

certain mismatch between the points of view adopted by the authors of those books, which reflected the learning and theories of thirty years earlier, and those adopted by the teachers of the courses they were following. It was not a bad introduction to historical criticism.

The urgent need to rewrite major syntheses that is felt from time to time is justified in a variety of ways by their authors, in prefaces and forewords that, in their own way, closely reflect the currently prevailing discourse on education and culture of a more general nature (which it would take too long to go into here). V. Duruy, who had thrown himself into an *Histoire des Grecs,* was a General Inspector of secondary education, soon to become Napoleon III's Minister for Public Education (1863–9). He coordinated the programmes and textbooks for *Lycée* pupils. The official programme of 23 July 1874 introduced Greek history in year 5, and V. Duruy himself produced an *Abrégé d'histoire grecque* (*Abridged Greek Hitory*), published by Hachette, the second edition of which (1877) comprised pictures and maps 'to try to bring the museum into the classroom'. During this same period, a student at the École Normale, Salomon Reinach, wrote a *Manuel de philologie classique,* which was published in 1879. Throughout his life, this scholar strove to bring learning to a wider readership. In 1899, while working as a curator in the Musée des Antiquités Nationales in Saint-Germain-en-Layè, he translated and adapted another short survey from the English, James Gow's *Minerva,* an introduction to Greek and Latin studies for schools.

Authors are, of course, prone to speak of their potential readers. They usually tend to imagine them as 'educated but not specialists in the study of classical Antiquity', as J. Hatzfeld put it, or as 'men of the world, or even girls if the day ever comes when France acquires *höhere Töchterschulen* worthy of them', to quote S. Reinach. But they also assumed that some would be students, young teachers or, where school textbooks were concerned, children. In short, knowledge of the ancient world involved a variety of strata of the public and these authors were clearly determined to instruct them.

One theme that tends to recur in prefaces is the lack of originality of books or virtual translations based on the works of 'scholarly experts'. As S. Reinach resignedly observed in the preface to the second edition of his *Manuel* in 1883: 'The fate of a book such as this is to be useful to all yet to seem inadequate to all, because specialists only consult it to find out what they do not know and only judge it according to what they do know.' But such modesty is misleading. All these authors stress that they are keen to present 'the existing state of knowledge relating to Greek history' and above all to introduce some order into 'the sometimes uncertain and frequently contradictory opinions of the scholars of today, to select those most likely to be correct, and to set them out clearly' (J. Hatzfeld). Emphasis is definitely laid on the task of selection and synthesis, and quite clearly the concept of 'what is most likely to be correct' is

extremely contingent. That task even seems to be considered the top priority and one detects the rise of a repressed but ferocious trend of criticism
directly aimed at academics, 'professional scholars, the myopic explorers of
tiny domains who appear much in need of relearning the basics of their
profession', to quote S. Reinach, who went on to remark: 'teaching those
basics is a very good way of relearning them oneself.'

Many authors assign another function to the Greeks: that of reflecting
our own image. R. Cohen's preface to his *Athènes, une démocratie* is a fine
case in point, in which the author declares, even before enumerating them:
'We have faults that are strangely like the faults of the ancient Greeks.' The
image that usually emerges is one in which the Greeks are 'the teachers of
lessons', the inventors of a civilization and the actors in a history that is at
once the crucible and the model of our own civilization and history. It is,
perhaps, no longer the image that we have today of the Greeks. They are
less close to us than they seemed to be one or two generations ago,
more distant and more strange. Nevertheless, the disorientation that their
history produces is productive in that it also raises questions about our
own societies.

In any event, behind the modest utility that all these authors claim for
their endeavours, one can sense a definite pleasure, the pleasure of writing,
of telling a story in one's own turn.

This textbook tries to keep a balance between the different periods of
Greek history and so allots the Hellenistic period the space that is its due.
Chapters 1, 2 and 3 were written by P. Schmitt Pantel, chapters 4 and 5 by
C. Orrieux, but the two authors were in a constant dialogue.

We should like to thank all those who have at some point told us the
story of Greece, and we shall be referring to them in due course. We
should also like to thank all those who have been so good as to listen to us
telling our story, that is to say our own students. This book is for them.

A COUNTRY

How did the Greeks describe their country? This is how Odysseus described his beloved island, Ithaca:

'I am Odysseus, Laertes' son. The whole world talks of my stratagems and my fame has reached the heavens. My home is under the clear skies of Ithaca. Our landmark is the wooded peak of windswept Neriton. For neighbours we have many peopled isles with no great space between them, Dulichium and Same and wooded Zacynthus. But Ithaca, the farthest out to sea, lies slanting to the West, whereas the others face the dawn and the rising sun. It is a rough land but a fit nurse for men. And I, for one, know of no sweeter sight.' (Homer, *Odyssey*, IX, 19–28)

'I grant that it is rugged and unfit for driving horses, yet narrow though it may be it is very far from poor. It grows abundant corn and wine in plenty. The rains and fresh dews are never lacking; and it has excellent pasturage for goats and cattle, timber of all kinds, and watering places that never fail. And so, my friend, the name of Ithaca has travelled even as far as Troy; and that, they say, is a good long way from Achaea.' (*Odyssey*, XIII, 242–9)

And here is the Pseudo-Dicearchus' description of the city of Thebes, in Boeotia, in the fourth century:

The city (*polis*) of Thebes is situated in the middle of the Boeotian territory, with a perimeter of seventy stades, entirely in the plain. It is round in shape, and the ground is black. It is an ancient city, but has been newly planned because, according to works of history, three times already it has been utterly razed to the ground as a result of the intolerable pride of its inhabitants. It has good horse-raising farms. Everywhere is well irrigated, with hills bare of woods. Of all the cities of Greece, it has the greatest number of gardens, for two rivers run through it, watering the entire plain dominated by the town. (Pseudo-Dicearchus, fr. 59, 12–20)

These two texts, of different kinds and from different periods, show that the only landscapes the Greeks described were those marked by the hands of men. Mountains, plains and streams were of no interest in themselves, but only in so far as they related to human beings. The sea was what could not be harvested; the plain could be used for horse-breeding. So it is hard for us to form an accurate picture of the ancient Greek landscape or to discover how it differed from the landscape of today. But before considering the ancient landscape fashioned by human hands, let us remind ourselves of the major features of the relief and the climate of Greece.

THE RELIEF

The Balkan peninsula is bordered to the north by two mountain massifs: the Stara Planina and the Rhodope mountains, which peter out in the Chaldice peninsula. To the west, high massifs form the two parallel lines of mountains that make up the Hellenides chain, extending through Illyria right down to the southern Peloponnese, but interrupted by the Gulf of Corinth. It rises to peaks of about 2,500 m. in the north (Pindus, Parnassus) and to over 2,300 m. in the south (Kyllini, Taygetus). To the east, the lofty, isolated massif of Olympus (2,917 m.) overlooks the coast of the Aegean Sea, prolonged further south by less lofty mountains (around 2,000 m.) alternating with wide valleys. In the Peloponnese, the highest region is the northern edge; the western coast is low-lying. The predominance of limestone rocks accounts for the formation of vast, closed-in inland depressions both in the north and in the Peloponnese. Crete features three limestone massifs: the White Mountains, the Psiloritis mountains and the Lasithi mountains, interspersed by similar depressions and sinkholes. The Aegean islands prolong the Balkans' main axes of relief. The west coast of Asia Minor features a succession of massifs rising to over 2,000 m., plateaux of between 800 and 1,000 m. and valleys occupied by alluvial plains.

Three geological zones account for the characteristics of the natural landscape. The rare plains of silt and alluvia are easy to cultivate, but sometimes marshy. The hills of soft rock (marl, schist, lava) are terraced for cultivation. The areas of hard rock (in particular, limestone) are not cultivable and are severely eroded.

One other feature leaps to notice from a glance at the map: the omnipresence of the sea, which insinuates itself into every coastal inlet and surrounds the many islands. To the west is the Ionian Sea, to the east the Aegean Sea, to the south the Sea of Crete, three relatively distinctive zones of the Mediterranean, to the north-east the Black Sea, known as the Pontus in Antiquity. The Greeks' attitude towards the sea was ambiguous. They feared it and tried to do without it, preferring to live turned towards inland Greece; but at the same time they did know how to domesticate it when they had to, aboard their frail, square-sailed ships, in which they travelled keeping within sight of the coastline.

THE CLIMATE

The Mediterranean climate has two distinct seasons, one cold and wet, during which between 400 and 1,200 mm. of rain fall in violent storms during the autumn and winter, the other hot and dry. However, a sharp contrast distinguishes the Ionian coastline, which is wetter, from the Aegean side of Greece, which is dryer. Most of the cities are situated in the dryer zone.

Although the relief may not have changed much since Antiquity, whether or not the climate has is a more controversial question. Nowadays, scholars tend to agree that the climate of the classical period was not very different from today's but that the climate of Greece was probably wetter in earlier times, before the neolithic period. The climate of the period of the cities was thus a Mediterranean one, but the rainfall in some regions was three times as high as that in others and, furthermore, varied from one year to another.

The natural *vegetation* consisted of medium-sized trees (conifers, chestnuts), evergreen bushes (holm oaks, Aleppo pines, bays, junipers), with a variety of plants, including succulents, in the undergrowth and open spaces.

THE LANDSCAPE: A HUMAN CREATION

The Greek world was characterized by two main types of landscape: the urban and the rural. The former is quite well known, the latter less so. In the ancient texts descriptions of towns predominate, and the traditional archaeological techniques of excavation have provided us with information relating mainly to urban sites, sanctuaries and cemeteries. The onesidedness of this knowledge has been somewhat redressed over the last twenty years by the development of archaeological prospection. The technique is to collect all the surface material present by dividing an area of terrain into the smallest possible squares and at the same time analysing all the plants, animal remains and metals found within each square. In several areas of Greece such prospections of small surface areas have already been carried out. In Boeotia, for example, 1.5 per cent of the surface of the region has been studied in this fashion. Although a very limited area, it has already revealed the density of sites in the countryside and has given the archaeologists some idea of their function. Archaeological prospection is the only systematic source of new information about the ancient rural landscape and it enables us to gain more understanding of a city's outlying territory.

The ancient city (*polis*), the history of whose formation we shall be considering further on, was composed of a number of elements: on the one hand, groups of dwellings, the largest of which would develop into an urban centre, on the other a surrounding territory. The dimensions of these city territories varied greatly, from a few dozen square kilometres (Aegina had 85) to several hundred (Corinth had 880 square kilometres). Athens, with 2,650 and Sparta, with 8,400 square kilometres, seem to have been exceptional. The Greeks thought of their territory as composed of three parts. The town (*astu*) was where the people lived and where most of the political activities in which the whole community was involved took place. Some people also lived in villages, known as *komai*. The second part of the territory consisted of the cultivated land (the *chôra*). The third part was the border zone (the *eschatia*), described by L. Robert as follows:

This was the region beyond the cultivated fields, land that was relatively unproductive or difficult to use or that could only be exploited intermittently, out towards the mountains that always surrounded a city's territory. This land would lie along side the frontier region, merging into it, a region of mountains and forests that separated two city territories and that was left for the use of shepherds, woodcutters, and charcoal burners.

The separation between cultivated territory and territory left fallow was one of the characteristic features of Greek social practice and thought. The *eschatia*, seemingly a world's end of mountainous, remote terrain, which marked out the frontiers of a Greek city, was a place for hunting, for training young men during their period of military service (the *ephebeia*) and for shepherds pasturing their flocks. It was also where the Greeks set the action of many of their myths, the place where Oedipus was exposed as a baby, where the Bacchae roamed, where heroes such as Melanion and Hippolytus went hunting, as did heroines such as Atalanta and Cyrene. In contrast to the *eschatia*, the cultivated space (the *chôra*) was valued extremely highly. It was the *chôra* that a hoplite had to defend in times of war and what he described in his hoplite's oath, when he called upon 'the boundaries of the country, the wheat, barley, vines, olive trees and fig trees' to witness his pledge. It was the *chôra* that was at stake in all military operations. The looting of the territory and the sacking of its crops were more than economic and social disasters, for they affected the very identity of the civic community. The land held a central place in the Greeks' representation of the origins of the members of their community, for they liked to claim to be 'autochthonous', born of the very soil of their country. In mythical narratives and already in Homer, the absence of cultivated land was the mark of a world beyond humanity, a world of Cyclopes and Lotuseaters. In Herodotus' description of non-Greek peoples, for example, the absence of agriculture is a recurrent characteristic of barbarian peoples. The world of the cities was definitely a world of wheat fields, and the peasant was the citizen *par excellence*.

A Greek geography Geographein means 'to write the land', and it is the word the Greeks used to designate both describing and drawing the land. Throughout their history, they constructed coherent images of the world that closely associated seeing, through drawings, and remembering, through a descriptive text. Unfortunately, no Greek map has come down to us, but several Greek texts describe how to make maps and criticize earlier ones. A whole geographical tradition evolved that endeavoured to distinguish between, on the one hand, information that was worthy of belief and, on the other, mere fables. The known world (the *oikoumene*) of the Greeks was a product of real knowledge as much as imaginative representation.

1 / THE GREEK WORLD'S EARLIEST TIMES

The paleolithic period The most ancient vestiges of human occupation in Greece go back to the middle paleolithic period, to 40 000 BC, in a region situated in the north-west of Greece: Epirus. Paleolithic sites have been discovered in Epirus, Macedonia, Thessaly, Elis, Corfu . . . but for the moment the exact extent of human habitation in the paleolithic period escapes us.

The neolithic period in Greece began in about 4500 BC and neolithic sites are scattered throughout the territory. This period is characterized by populations becoming settled and by the beginnings of agriculture. Settlements consisted of groups of a few, very simple, single-roomed houses. The population seems to have been growing and new regions were occupied. It is extremely difficult to assess social evolution on the basis of the archaeological data of those very early periods. However, tools and weapons

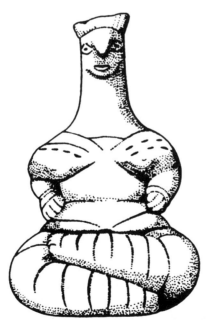

Figure 1 A Neolithic feminine figure from Crete (from R. Treuil, *Les Civilisations égéennes*, Paris, PUF, 1989, p. 139, fig. 7d)

were diversifying and taking specific forms, which would seem to indicate the earliest beginnings of specialization in human activities.

THE BRONZE AGE

The bronze age began in Greece in about 3000 BC. It owes its name to the appearance of metallurgy, learned from the civilizations of the Near East. Items made of metal, such as arms and prestige objects, were rare and possession of them was a sign of high social status. Many questions are raised by this period. Some relate to trade: where did the metals necessary for the production of bronze (an alloy of copper and tin) come from? Others relate to the social structure: who was capable of forging these metal objects? Was there a category of specialists in this domain? Settlements by now comprised more houses and were sometimes protected by encircling stone walls. The latest archaeological discoveries make it possible to construct a picture, albeit one that remains, for the moment, extremely sketchy, whose chronology depends upon the study of pottery. It is not possible, for example, to tell either what kind of political structures these communities developed or what kind of relations existed between them. But one thing is certain: at this period, Greece had not yet developed structures comparable to those of the civilizations of Egypt, Mesopotamia or the great kingdoms of the Near East. Its history was more modest although, as we shall see when we come to study the Cyclades and Crete, distinctions need to be made between one region and another.

The end of the third millennium saw the arrival of new peoples, speaking a different language, one of them connected with the family of Indo-European languages. These people were Hellenes, or Greeks, to give them their Latin name. The inhabitants of the region before their arrival are conventionally known as 'pre-Hellenic peoples', peoples who were there before the Hellenes, before the Greeks.

THE INDO-EUROPEANS

Who were the Indo-Europeans? A precise and detailed answer to that question would require considerable space, but let us sketch in a few simple points. The term *Indo-European* is a linguistic one: it refers to people who spoke languages with morphology, syntax and vocabulary sharing similar features that make it possible to track them back to an original, common, reconstructed form, probably never spoken as such, that we call the Indo-European language. The family of Indo-European languages is extremely extensive. It includes the ancient languages of India (Sanskrit) and Persia, Armenian, the Slavic languages, several Baltic languages such as Lithuanian, the Celtic and Germanic languages, Greek, Albanian, the Italic languages (including Latin) and dead languages once spoken in the

Balkans, such as Illyrian, and in Asia Minor (Hittite, Phrygian). Disagreement still exists over whether the people who spoke these related languages shared a common geographical origin, thought by some to be the steppes lying between the Caspian Sea and the Black Sea, and also over the date at which the movement of migrations began, possibly some time between 6000 and 4500 BC. But one point is certain: the notion of the Indo-European peoples has absolutely no racial connotations, and the Nazis were altogether wrong when they used it in Germany, under the Third Reich, in their racist propaganda, which made the Aryan people, claimed to have belonged to an Indo-European branch, into a superior race that was the paragon of all the values promoted by the national-socialist ideology.

Common features   The civilizations of these peoples speaking related languages also shared certain common or close characteristics. Georges Dumézil was one of the first scholars to show this. He was particularly interested in the forms taken by religion among these peoples. Thanks to his research, we know that one and the same theological structure, which associated the functions of sovereignty, physical strength and fecundity, served to classify the gods throughout the Indo-European area, and that it is possible to detect the same tri-functional structure in many of the domains relating to institutions, justice, mythology and so on. Continuing the work of G. Dumézil, later historians have demonstrated the importance of similarities between Indo-European peoples in agricultural production, craft techniques, habitats, society, the family, royal power, the exercise of justice, systems of gift-giving . . . in short, in very many of the domains that characterize these societies. However, the existence of common Indo-European origins does not suffice to explain how particular practices came to develop in particular societies. As always in history, it is often more interesting to ponder upon particular transformations in particular cultures than upon the origins of particular practices, as the case of Greece will frequently show.

What changes occurred?   Did these new peoples introduce great changes into what now became the Greek world? Our only evidence is that of archaeology, and it does not show conclusively that the period of troubles that checked the momentum of the early Bronze Age civilization resulted directly from the arrival of new populations. In other words, with all due respect to the generations of historians who learned and then taught history based on a theory of invasions and their consequences and who, in this particular case, have made much of the Indo-European invasions, it must be said that our sole source of evidence – archaeology – tells us nothing on this point, or else it is so difficult to interpret that any hypotheses favoured today are likely to collapse tomorrow. A consensus of agreement is emerging in a recognition of indications suggesting that new elements were already present in the Bronze Age culture by the turn of the second millennium (rather than later, in the sixteenth or even thirteenth

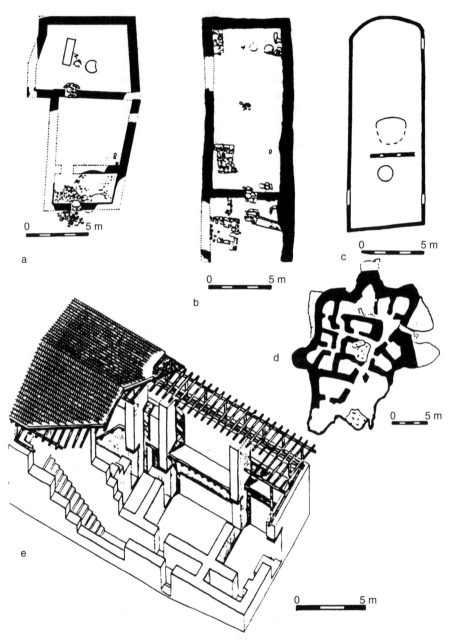

Figure 2 Early Bronze Age dwellings: (a) Eutresis, house; (b) Troy, building; (c) Rachmani, house; (d) Panormos (Naxos); (e) the White House of Kolonna (Aegina) (from R. Treuil, *Les Civilisations égéennes*, Paris, PUF, 1989, p. 175, fig. 11)

Table 1   Bronze Age changes

Before: Early Bronze Age	After: Middle Bronze Age
– populations in villages with fortifications;	– on the same sites, no surrounding walls;
– dwellings: small, wooden, clay-daubed houses, with an irregular design, underground granaries, collective facilities;	– dwellings: houses scattered in anarchical fashion, apsidal design, no grain storage;
– monumental constructions: proto-palaces;	– disappearance of such constructions;
– diversified agriculture;	– no change;
– donkeys, dogs, domesticated animals, hunting, fishing;	– appearance of horses;
– tools;	– new tools;
– cemeteries separated from settlements, burial: graves or cist tombs (beginning);	– burial within settlements, many cist tombs;
– modest funerary furniture;	– funerary furniture rare, or non-existent; children buried in jars, tumuli outside settlements, beginning of tholos tombs;
– pottery: techniques of incised decoration.	– grey, monochrome pottery, known as 'Mynian', potter's wheel.

century BC). It is also generally agreed that populations continued to arrive in the region for a century or two, but it is important to avoid exaggerating the changes that were occasioned by these new immigrants.

The principal changes are summarized in table 1.

The new culture began to develop at the beginning of the second millennium. We know more about it from 1600 on, which is when what is called the Mycenaean civilization began. Before noting its principal features, let us examine what was happening in other regions of the Aegean world, outside mainland Greece, in the Cyclades, Cyprus and Crete.

THE CYCLADES

This group of islands in the middle of the Aegean Sea was already occupied before the Bronze Age. The forms of culture that characterized it during the third millennium are known as the 'Cycladic civilization' (3200–2000). The villages, at first of mud huts, then of stone-built ones, were situated along the shores, frequently perched on hills. The cemeteries lay close by, on the hillsides. The dead were buried along with a variety of objects: pots, bronze daggers, obsidian blades, useful objects and carved marble figurines.

The inhabitants practised agriculture, hunting and fishing, worked with bronze, marble and obsidian, and went to sea aboard strange, high-prowed ships without sails, propelled by oars.

The most spectacular and best-known products of the Cyclades are *marble figurines* of a variety of types at different periods: some are 'violin-shaped' and are of figures with crossed arms or seated figures holding a musical instrument. Most were discovered in tombs. Much has been written about their meaning, the most fanciful hypotheses being that they were used as substitutes for human sacrifices or to satisfy the sexual needs of the deceased in the afterlife. They have also been said to represent ancestors, to be toys, to be figures from Cycladic mythology (nymphs and heroes) or to represent deities. None of these interpretations is satisfactory. In the absence of any informative texts, we are bound to accept that the meaning of this important aspect of the daily life of the Cycladic communities totally eludes us.

The Cycladic civilization reached its peak in the Early Bronze Age, after which its importance waned.

CYPRUS

This large island of 5,500 square kilometres, situated at the extreme east of the Aegean Sea, was inhabited as early as the neolithic period and continued to be settled from 4000 to 3000 BC. In the Bronze Age, the development of the original civilization there can be explained by its position on the sea routes connecting the Near East with the rest of the Mediterranean world, as well as the presence of copper ore in its soil.

As early as the *Early Bronze Age* (2100–1900), settlements on the north coast (Vounous, Lapithos) and the south coast (Limassol) of the island created large necropolises in which very distinctive kinds of pottery have been discovered: vases with human faces, animal and bird heads, jugs with long necks, double bowls. There are earthenware statuettes that evoke rural life: a group in which two teams of swing-ploughs drawn by oxen are guided by ploughmen, two helpers carrying in a trough the grain that a third man is about to sow, women working at milling or kneading. There are also scenes of religious life: an earthenware model from Vounous represents a sacred precinct with a double or triple deity. It was in this same period that the first written texts appeared. The characters resemble those of the Cretan Linear A, and this writing is known as Cypro-Minoan. At least three different syllabaries can be distinguished in it. The problem is what language they were being used to transcribe. It would appear that each type of writing corresponds to a different language.

In the *Middle Bronze Age* (1900–1600), inhabited sites multiplied and fortified settlements such as those at Krini and Dhikomo were built.

The *Late Bronze Age* (1600–1200) began with a period of destruction. Then a number of sites close to the sea developed: in the east Enkomi,

Hala Sultan Tekke, further to the south Kition, and in the west Ayia Irini, Morphou, the 'old' Paphos. A number of peoples of different origins came together in Cyprus, with different cultures and different skills. Craft techniques from Syria, Egypt, Babylonia and Mycenae all seem to have been practised here.

The religious influence of Syria was strong. Temples of an imposing size were to be found in the towns. An eastern temple was a huge architectural complex comprising a large pillared hall, with one or two rooms at the side of the hall, a square, an open-air altar, tables for offerings and libations, statues, and workshops and storerooms, for it also constituted an economic unit. Cults involved the sacrifice of various animals. The temples at Enkomi and Kition were both constructed on this model.

Tombs, often used by the same families over several generations, were grouped some way away from the settlement and marked by earth tumuli. They were tombs with deep graves or *tholoi* (*tholos*, plural *tholoi*) cut into rocks and approached through a corridor (*dromos*) leading to the entrance of the tomb, where funerary rites may have taken place. At Enkomi, horses harnessed to a chariot were found in one corridor. They had been sacrificed in honour of the deceased.

After a period of peace that seems to have lasted for several centuries, a little before 1200 BC the island became the scene of many bouts of destruction. After this, settlements were surrounded by walls. The destruction is attributed to 'sea peoples' whose identity has been hard to establish. They may have come from Mycenae or Anatolia, migrating along the coasts of the Aegean Sea. Between 1220 and 1180 they went as far as Egypt. Cyprus lay on their route.

CRETE

In size, the island of Crete is comparable to Cyprus: 5,200 square kilometres. It lies in the south of the Aegean Sea, not far from the Peloponnesian coast. It is a mountainous island, the highest point being Mount Ida: 2,500 m. The rainfall is adequate for the sufficiency of the island's agricultural land. It too was already inhabited in neolithic times, and in the Bronze Age it went through a period of exceptional development. This is known as the Minoan civilization, named after Minos, a mythical king of Crete. As in Cyprus, this period is divided into three phases: early, middle and late Minoan. Let us rapidly consider these three chronological phases, then attempt a synthesis of the characteristic features of the Minoan civilization.

Early Minoan (2800–2000 BC)   presents no outstanding particular characteristics, so the above description of the beginnings of the Bronze Age in Greece also applies to Crete. The most heavily populated regions of Crete were the south and the north-east of the island.

11

Middle Minoan (2000–1600 BC)   was the period during which the Palace civilization was established, that is to say a political, economic and social organization centred around a palace. Settlements until then consisting of agricultural villages were now replaced by new groups of dwellings surrounding a complex of monumental constructions of variable designs: palaces. Each palace was a centre of power. Crete comprised several regions, each under the influence of a palace. The principal palaces were Knossos, Phaistos, Mallia and Zakros. A long period of peace made it possible for this new type of civilization to develop. In about 1700 some destruction took place, the cause of which is not known (earthquakes? internal unrest?), but without catastrophic consequences.

Late Minoan (1600–1450 BC)   Reconstruction was rapid, opening the time in which the Minoan period reached its peak. By now the island was highly populated and wealthy. The role of the palace of Knossos seems to have been even more important than before, but many other palaces also exercised political power. Links with the rest of the Mediterranean world multiplied and Crete's influence was felt by other civilizations.

In about 1450 almost all the Cretan sites were destroyed, with the exception of Knossos, which was similarly affected a little later, in about 1375. After 1450, populations from the Greek mainland (who must have been Mycenaean) established themselves more or less everywhere in the island. Historians disagree over the cause or causes of the spate of destruction. The explanation that linked the end of the palaces with the volcanic explosion on the island of Thera (Santorini) has now been abandoned on both chronological and geological grounds. Earthquakes, internal disturbances and a real Mycenaean invasion are all suggested causes, but none of those explanations is altogether satisfactory. The great palaces disappeared, but life went on under Mycenaean influence.

THE MINOAN CIVILIZATION

Our evidence for the Minoan civilization is provided by numerous rich archaeological sources and written texts, some of which have unfortunately still to be deciphered. The earliest Cretan writing used ideograms and was thus of a hieroglyphic type. Then came writing of a syllabic type, which took two different forms, conventionally known as Linear A and Linear B. The language transcribed by Linear A is still unknown, so it is impossible to understand its signs, but Linear B transcribes Greek and it is now possible to read the texts written in it (see p. 19). They are transcribed on small clay tablets and are short and often fragmentary. They consist of inventories and documents of an economic nature (accounts, lists, etc.). Thanks to archaeology and these texts, it has been possible to form a better picture of the palace civilization.

Figure 3 A document in Linear A: a stone pot (from R. Treuil, *Les Civilisations égéennes*, Paris, PUF, 1989, p. 245, fig. 23)

The palace Disposed around a central, rectangular courtyard were rooms on one or two floors, served by stone stairs. In Knossos, for example, there are three complexes, known as the official apartments, the private apartments and the royal workshops, covering an area of close on 2 hectares. However inaccurate these descriptions may be, inspired as they are by those that apply in our own seventeenth-century castles, they at least indicate that the space was organized according to specific functions: public, private and economic. The monumental aspect of the palace, with its entrance (*propylaea*), halls with pillars (*hypostyle*), portico, grand staircase and many constructions of chiselled stone, contrasted sharply with the ordinary houses, constructed on stone foundations with mud walls. The interior decoration of the palace was equally grandiose. The walls of its rooms were coated with a surface on which it was possible to paint. The reconstructions for which the English archaeologist Sir Arthur Evans was responsible, consisting of painted columns and rooms in the palace of Knossos, are certainly not accurate, but they at least have the merit of recalling the sumptuous nature of the setting. The size of the surrounding buildings, stores, warehouses and workshops gives some idea of the importance of the economic role of the palace, a subject to which we shall return. Finally, the palace was unfortified, not surrounded by protective walls, as if self-defence was not a major preoccupation. The 'open' character of the Minoan palace tallies with the unwarlike nature of the whole of this civilization, which in this respect differed greatly from the Mycenaean world.

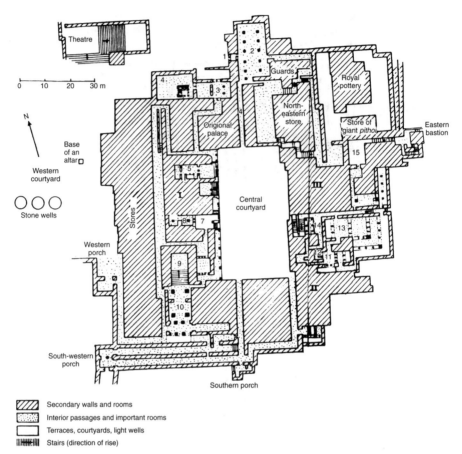

Figure 4 Plan of the palace of Knossos: I official apartments; II private apartments; III royal workshops; 1 propylaea; 2 hypostyle hall; 3 north-western portico; 4 purification hall; 4a lustral basin; 5 throne room; 6 sanctuary; 7 anteroom to the stone throne; 8 and 8a pillared crypts; 9 great staircase; 10 southern propylaea; 11 queen's apartment; 12 baths; 13 Hall of the Two-headed Axes; 14 the colonnaded hall; 15 the hall with a stone gutter (from P. Lévêque, *Nous partons pour la Grèce*, Paris, PUF, pp. 220–1)

'*Towns*' Clustered around the palaces were large complexes of dwellings, with roads and alleyways, which could accommodate a large proportion of people engaged in a variety of types of economic activity. This was the case not only in locations far from the sea, such as Knossos, but also in both slightly inland plains, such as the site of Phaistos, and seaports such as Zakros.

The forms of power We know little about the exact form of political power: one or several kings exercised an authority that seems to have extended to all domains, economic, social and also religious. Similarly, the precise structure of society eludes us, and it is by analogy that the hypothesis has been advanced that there was a group of people close to the 'king', similar to an aristocracy and sometimes called 'the Cretan nobility', a group of artisans specializing in a variety of skills, and peasants, about whom virtually nothing is known.

The system of production Everything originated in the palace and returned to the palace. It directed the agricultural and craft production, distributed land and the raw materials needed by the craftsmen, and organized the workforce; and it then redistributed the harvested crops, the produce from raising animals and the tools that were needed. Everything was recorded by scribes on clay tablets that were then preserved in the palace archives: measures of cereals, the size of the herds of domesticated animals, different groups of men. The seals affixed to merchandise and the marks stamped on container jars indicated that they were the property of the palace. In this way we know the details of, for instance, the system by which the palace of Knossos ensured its monopoly over the production of wool, with about 100,000 sheep in its possession.

Outside Crete The Cretan presence was felt far beyond Crete itself. Archaeo-logical evidence of Cretans (Minoan pottery) has been found in many places in the Mediterranean world, above all in the Peloponnese and Attica, but also in the Near East and Egypt. In one island close by, Cythera, the Cretans seem to have been permanently established. Elsewhere we should imagine Cretan seafarers making temporary visits, either to trade for raw materials not to be found on their own island, or as pirates, piracy being a Cretan speciality. Such signs of a Cretan presence have long been interpreted as proof of the existence of real Cretan power extending be-yond the island, or even of a maritime Cretan empire, known as a Minoan thalassocracy (sea power), which is the term used by fifth-century Greek historians such as Herodotus and Thucydides to refer to the time of King Minos. The hypothesis of this thalassocracy in truth rested upon the myth recounted by the Athenians of the classical period: that of Theseus (the mythical king of Athens) and the Minotaur, according to which Athens was at that time a vassal of the kingdom of Minos.

The myth of the Minotaur is well-known. Minos, the king of Crete, had a wife, Pasiphae, who fell in love with a bull and gave birth to the Minotaur, a monster half-human, half-bull. To shut it away, the architect Daedalus built a labyrinth in Knossos, from which it was virtually impossible to find an exit. Each year Minos demanded, as tribute from the Athenians, that seven youths and seven girls be sent to Crete, to be fed to the Minotaur. One year, Theseus, the son of Ageus, the king of Athens, was a member of this group and, thanks to the advice of Ariadne, the daughter of Minos, managed to kill the monster and escape from the labyrinth alive. This brought Athens' vassalage to Crete to an end.

This was a myth told for the purposes of explanation and legitimation. It was a matter of ascribing to the hero Theseus, the ancestor of the Athenians, a whole cycle of exploits (the slaying of the Minotaur is but one of many) to rival those of another famous hero, Heracles, who was claimed as founder by a number of other Greek cities, in particular, Sparta. However, we should beware of making direct historical use of myths, as their interpretation is far more complex. They are certainly not historical chronicles. It is perfectly possible to recognize how extraordinary the presence of Cretans outside their island was at this period, without going so far as to assume the existence of an empire.

Social and religious life Excavations have brought to light many pots, frescoes and stone seats, the ornamentation of which makes it possible to learn a little more of the social and religious life of the Minoan period. However, we should beware of over-interpreting images from a context unknown to us and about which there is not a single explanatory text, since all the texts that have come down to us are of a quite different nature.

In the religious domain, the Cretans had no built-up cult sites such as the temples that were constructed later on. They used open spaces, terraces and vast palace halls to perform religious rituals that included sacrifices. No details of their rituals are known. One fresco on a sarcophagus discovered on the Haghia Triada site shows, for example, a file of figures of varying sizes carrying animals and other objects in the direction of a static, larger figure. This scene is generally interpreted as a procession of devotees taking offerings to a deity. Even more enigmatic are the relatively numerous scenes depicting figures somersaulting over bovine animals, like acrobats or performers of certain modern bull-ring exploits. Do they represent some ritual? Not many objects used in religious cults have been found: figurines of gods or goddesses (one old and vain question that arises in the history of religions is whether, in Crete, goddesses were more numerous and more highly honoured than gods), two-headed axes, horns and pots in a variety of shapes. Many aspects of the Cretan cults elude us, as does the essential nature of their beliefs, for no texts exist to enlighten us. It has been possible for many widely differing chapters on Minoan religion to be written, for the very reason that it is, perforce, all a matter of interpretation.

The Minoan civilization centred on palaces puts one in mind of civilizations of the same period in the Near East (Ugarit in Syria, Mari on the Euphrates), but in Crete the territory involved was smaller and its monumental splendour was more modest. The 'kings' of the Cretan palaces really seem to have been more like village chieftains than pharaohs. And even while the Minoan civilization lived on, rather on the margins of the Greek world, another region was growing in importance: mainland Greece and the civilization known as Mycenaean. The star of Minos waned, making room for Agamemnon.

THE MYCENAEAN WORLD

The site of Mycenae, in Argolis, in the north-eastern Peloponnese gave its name to a historical period that lasted from the sixteenth century BC to the twelfth, for this site was then one of the most important in mainland Greece. The name in no sense implies that the Greek world was at that time unified around Mycenae or that this centre played a preponderant political role. In terms of the chronological scale used in archaeology, the Mycenaean period began at the end of the Middle Helladic or the end of the Middle Bronze Age.

To date, the only evidence at our disposal for the phase of transition between the Middle Helladic and the Late Helladic periods takes the form of tombs, in particular in Messenia and Argolis. Among the latter are the two circles of tombs discovered at Mycenae, the first (circle A) by Schliemann in 1876, the second (circle B) by Greek archaeologists in 1952.

The tombs (at the foot of the acropolis of Mycenae) are surrounded by a wall constructed of stone slabs, which marks out the space reserved for the dead.

Circle B contains the most ancient tombs (1650–1550). These twenty-four shaft tombs have an entrance and a built-up funerary chamber. They were reused, possibly over several generations, by the same family groups. The material objects found in them include ceramic and metal vases, arms, jewels, gold ornaments for clothing, seals, etc. The archaeologists also discovered traces of certain funerary ceremonies, rituals for the dead such as meals, libations and offerings of food placed around the tombs.

Circle A comprises six shaft tombs dating from 1570 to 1500. These too were reused over several generations. The material objects found in them were exceptionally rich: they included the famous gold masks now exhibited in the Archaeological Museum of Athens, but tombs also contained jewellery of all kinds (necklaces, crowns, rings, bracelets), swords with ornamented pommels, daggers, amber beads. In short, the whole collection was regarded by Schliemann and his contemporaries as a fabulous treasure that justified calling the anonymous dead princes. Ever since, these have been known as the princes' tombs, suggesting that such riches probably indicated that this was a group of individuals who possessed at least some degree of power. Again, historical interpretation is a difficult matter, but the picture of a handful of families sharing power and burying, along with their dead, tangible signs of their wealth is general enough to be universally accepted.

These tombs mark the beginning of the Mycenaean civilization, which was to continue to develop after 1400 and is known to us thanks to both the discoveries of archaeology and the deciphering of texts written in Linear B.

ARCHAEOLOGY

The archaeology of *necropolises* shows that beehive (*tholos*) tombs were spreading in Argolis at the same time as in Messenia. They were composed of a cicular chamber reached by a corridor or *dromos* and formed imposing tumuli that stood out in the landscape. The tomb known as the treasure store of Atreus, in Mycenae, comprises a chamber 14.50 metres in diameter and 13.20 metres high. These were the tombs of personages definitely above the common run. Many less spectacular tombs with non-circular chambers have also been found. All these tombs were used for a number of dead over several generations. The corpses were placed in graves dug in the funerary chambers, or sometimes in wooden or earthenware coffins. Offerings of many kinds were left in the tombs: 'funerary furniture' (the name given to all such deposited objects) was more or less opulent, depending upon the wealth of the family. However, it is not easy to deduce from the tombs many clues as to the society of the living (in particular regarding their social differences) or their beliefs about death.

More and more of these *inhabited sites* are now being discovered. Several hundred have been identified in mainland Greece, in the form of modest groups of peasant settlements.

Fortified palaces constitute the most spectacular signs of the Mycenaean civilization. They first appeared in the second half of the fourteenth century BC and comprised extremely vast precincts and buildings of various kinds, including the type of monumental dwellings that have been dubbed 'palaces'.

THE LINEAR B TEXTS

Since the beginning of the twentieth century, archaeologists have been discovering clay tablets, accidentally baked, which bear texts. They are quite small (one of the largest measures 27 by 16 cm). They were made of ordinary clay, then inscribed with a stylus, dried and arranged in a kind of box or basket. The first tablets were found at Knossos in Crete by Sir Arthur Evans in about 1900: a batch of 3,000 tablets baked in a house fire in about 1370. In Greece itself the most ancient tablets preserved go back only to about 1250 BC. In 1939 over a thousand were discovered at Pylos in Messenia, and since then excavations at a wide range of sites (Mycenae, Tiryns, Thebes, Eleusis, Orchomenus) have turned up more of these tablets.

The deciphering of the tablets Only those written in Linear B could be deciphered. This syllabic writing was deciphered in 1952 by two English scholars, Michael Ventris, an architect, and John Chadwick, a philologist, whose working hypothesis had been that the writing served to transcribe an archaic form of the Greek language. The documents that can now be

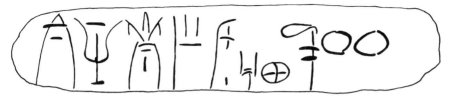

Figure 5 A tablet in Linear B (from R. Treuil, *Les Civilisations égéennes*, Paris, PUF, 1989, p. 389, fig. 43)

read are mostly inventories of palace possessions. They constitute lists of forms of agricultural produce, for example, and make up what may be called the palace archives. The writing, which called for great skill, was the responsibility of a specialized group of scribes and was certainly not known to most of the population. The documents in Linear B cannot be compared to the epigraphic or religious texts to be found in other civilizations at the same period, and provide us with no more than a very partial view of the organization and civilization of the Mycenean world.

FEATURES OF THE MYCENAEAN CIVILIZATION

The fortress-palace The essential features of the fortress-palace can be seen from the plans of Mycenae (figure 6) and Tiryns. The surrounding ramparts are constructed of enormous blocks of stone ('Cyclopean walls') with bastions, and they are pierced by several gates, such as the 'Lion gate' at Mycenae. At Mycenae these surround an area of close on 4 hectares (at Tiryns, over 2 hectares). The heart of the palace, the *megaron*, comprises three parts: an external vestibule, an internal vestibule and the main room, in which was a hearth. All around, various buildings served as storage places. The space left free of buildings could temporarily shelter the whole population. In Argolis, the palaces are more strongly fortified than in Messenia, where the palace of Pylos is hardly fortified at all.

More than 400 Mycenaean sites have been discovered in Greece proper, corresponding to a large number of communities, all independent of one another, ruled from the palace by a chieftain who acted as a protector in times of war. Some palaces, such as those of Mycenae and Tiryns in Argolis, Pylos in Messenia, Thebes in Boeotia and Iolkos in Thessaly, were larger than others, although it is not possible to deduce that any of them wielded any political supremacy.

Political power The tablets tells us what some of the figures in leading positions in these palace societies were called. There was a *wanax*, for which our translation is 'king', and a *lawagetas* or 'leader of the troops'. Each was the owner of an estate, *temenos*, and had a staff of people attached to him: servants, craftsmen, peasants and herdsmen. Also named are *telestai*, whose function may have been religious, and *heketai*, companions,

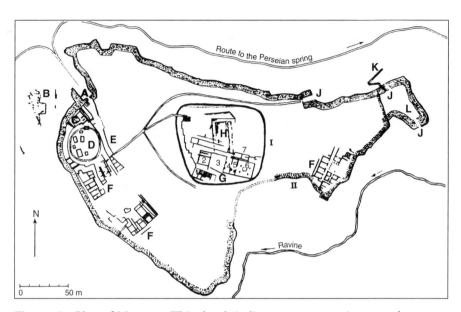

Figure 6 Plan of Mycenae. This sketch indicates two successive sets of fortifications of Mycenae: I the first precinct walls (seventeenth (?) century BC); II the Cyclopean walls (mid-fourteenth century). A the Lion Gate; B prehistoric cemetery; C granary; D the circle of Schliemann's tombs (circle A); E ramp; F Mycenaean houses; G palace: 1 great staircase, 2 throne room; 3 central courtyard; 4 *prothyron*; 5 *prodomos*; 6 *megaron*; 7 domestic quarters; H archaic and later Hellenistic temple of Athena; J posterns; K tank; L storage hut added in the thirteenth century. NB – According to G. Mylonas, the throne was situated not in Room 2 but in the *megaron* (from P. Lévêque, *Nous partons pour la Grèce*, Paris, PUF, p. 142, fig. 30)

linked with the military organization. Other titles are cited sporadically, such as the figures responsible for local village administration. The remainder of the population consisted of the *damos*, the people, and 'servants of the god', probably slaves. A social hierarchy was certainly in place but how it worked remains obscure.

Economic organization The tablets compose a picture similar to that already described for the Minoan world and relatively uniform from one palace to another. Subsistence agriculture and raising animals were the principal activities, the products of which went to the palace, which redistributed them. The products of diversified craft workshops – tools, arms, pots and fabrics – were also organized by the palace.

The Mycenaeans in the Mediterranean The quest for metals took the Mycenaeans to Cyprus for copper, to Portugal, Brittany and Cornwall for tin, to Attica for silver and lead, and to Thrace and the East for gold. Traces of their passing take the form of pots made by them, which are present more or less everywhere in the vicinity of the Mediterranean, sometimes in great numbers. As with the Minoans, whom they succeeded on many sites, it is not easy to determine the extent of their implantation. Although more or less permanent in some places, it does not appear to have involved any political subjection. The principal reason for it was trade.

The material culture   The Mycenaeans built palaces and tombs that still strike the imagination of travellers to Greece; they created new forms of earthenware pottery and were master goldsmiths; in short, they left traces of a civilization that was at once unified (although not politically) and original – dazzling, when one thinks of how many centuries were to pass before such artistic splendour was to recur.

Religion   In this domain, the tablets reveal the names of most of the deities who were later to be honoured in the classical Greek pantheon. Even gods who were thought to be late arrivals in Greece, such as Dionysus, are mentioned on the tablets. We are therefore bound to recognize that the Mycenaean religion already took the form of a complex polytheism. Cults were performed out in the open air or in places not specially reserved for rituals, such as certain palace rooms. Cult objects range from rhyton-shaped vases to earthenware figurines. Blood sacrifices were made but, in the absence of any texts describing them, it is hard to make out any details in the rituals. As with the Cretan world, objects and names are not enough to enable us to reconstruct the beliefs of religious life or those relating to the beyond. Mycenaean funerary customs have been described above, with the aid of archaeology.

THE END OF THE MYCENAEAN WORLD

A phase of destruction on the sites lasted for a century and a half. Most of the palaces were destroyed for the first time at the end of the thirteenth century. Afterwards, life resumed on a more modest scale; but at the end of the twelfth century the destruction was such that the sites were abandoned. Many explanations for this collapse have been suggested and can be mentioned briefly here, without going into details.

First there was the possibility of warfare: either wars between the Mycenaean princes or civil wars within the separate palatial units, sparked off by revolts on the part of the oppressed social categories, or else wars against external enemies, invaders coming to settle in Greece: sea peoples whose action in Cyprus has been noted above, and Dorians, believed to be a new branch of the Indo-Europeans.

Secondly, natural phenomena had some effect, either a change in the climate, with disastrous agricultural effects, or an earthquake.

Faced with these hypotheses, all that archaeology can do is invalidate that of invasion by outsiders, given that the postulated new peoples left no specific archaeological traces. In truth, not one of the above hypotheses on its own suffices to provide a satisfactory explanation of this general but gradual decline, which took different forms in different places and led to the total ruination of the palace civilization only after a long period of instability. Local power struggles, of which we know nothing at all, probably combined with endemically precarious means of subsistence to allow all kinds of social, economic and military violence to gain the upper hand in this easily isolated world. Even today, the rapidity of the collapse of whole countries into uncontrollable violence and famine perhaps makes it possible for us to understand that any over-systematic explanation is to be avoided.

The Mycenaean world is no more. Archaeology and texts enable us to sketch in the scene, a magnificent but rather empty one, like any scene in the theatre bereft of characters to give it life. Some historians have added figures to the ramparts of Mycenae, those of Clytemnestra and Aegisthus, on the lookout for Agamemnon's return from Troy or, in the *megaron* of Pylos, the figure of old Nestor greeting Telemachus, the son of Odysseus. Should we follow them? Or is it better to accept that the famous golden mask never did cover the face of Agamemnon? These are questions that we shall tackle in connection with the use of Homer's epics, the *Iliad* and the *Odyssey*, when we come to consider 'the world of Odysseus'. First though, we must plunge into a period that has long been regarded as mysterious by historians, the period of the eleventh to the eighth centuries.

THE IRON AGE

With the collapse of the Mycenaean world the use of writing disappeared, so that for several centuries our only evidence comes from archaeology. The period, about which very little was known for a long time, is therefore traditionally known as the 'Dark Ages' or the 'Greek Middle Ages'. Over the past twenty years, however, the increasing number of excavations undertaken have enabled archaeologists to produce a number of works of synthesis the conclusions of which are periodically challenged. There can be no question here of following the details of these extremely controversial demonstrations, taking account of all the archaeological material upon which the various studies are based, but it should be pointed out that in this domain any historical synthesis is still bound to be fragile.

Two phases can be distinguished in this period: the eleventh and tenth centuries, and the ninth and eighth centuries.

THE ELEVENTH AND TENTH CENTURIES

At the beginning of the eleventh century, Greece seems to have been a depopulated country. The number of known inhabited sites drops appreciably from 320 sites in the thirteenth century to 40 sites in the eleventh century. However, this depopulation – a loss of three-quarters of the population – did not affect all regions of Greece in a uniform manner. Argolis and Messenia seem to have lost more inhabitants than Attica and Euboea, for example. The few Greeks who remained now lived in rudimentary dwellings in which stone was used only occasionally, for the construction of foundations. The walls were built of unfired bricks, the roofs were of thatch. The houses were apsidal in shape. But even as early as the eleventh century, changes were taking place in several domains.

Pottery in the style known as proto-geometric (1050–900) made use of new techniques and created patterns of circles and semicircles drawn with a compass, and motifs consisting of many lines painted with a multiple 'comb brush', which produced an overall geometric effect.

Iron gradually replaced bronze in the manufacture of tools, arms and objects such as *fibulae*. Zones where iron ore could be extracted existed in Greece itself, so supplies were more readily available than for metalwork using bronze. The latter did not disappear, but was now used mainly for precious objects such as tripods with studded basins and perforated supports. Attica, Argolis and Lefkandi in Euboea were among the new centres of iron metallurgy.

Funerary practices also changed. Corpses were now incinerated rather than buried, except in the cases of young children, who continued to be buried in cist-tombs and in jars. The tombs are frequently individual and the material used is usually poor, although there are some exceptions. One, for example, is the great oval edifice (50 by 10 metres) discovered at Lefkandi in Euboea, dating from the tenth century. Here a man and a woman were first incinerated, then buried, four horses having been sacrificed during the funeral. This set-up and ritual are reminiscent of those of the tombs found at Enkomi in Cyprus and also call to mind Homer's descriptions of the funerals of heroes. However, archaeologists are more inclined to regard Lefkandi as a cult site or a royal edifice.

Greeks were emigrating in small groups from mainland Greece from the end of the eleventh century on, and settling along the coasts of Asia Minor. Their arrival does not appear to have provoked clashes with any local powers. From this period on, both coastlines of the Aegean Sea were thus populated by Greeks.

All these were important innovations, and they suggest that a totally dark and negative view of these centuries would be inappropriate. The tendency today is to rehabilitate this period and emphasize its elements of continuity rather than those indicating a break. In some regions that appear to have been deserted because of the scarcity of archaeological data there, cultural elements in fact did survive, as if dormant, to reappear at the beginning of the archaic period. To account for the contradictory evidence of, on the one hand, severe depopulation and, on the other, cultural continuity, some historians now put forward the hypothesis that the Greeks of this period switched to a pastoral mode of life. It is suggested that the settled cultivators of the Mycenaean period became a people of herdsmen and shepherds, disinclined to build dwellings to last, which is why archaeologists have discovered few traces of their presence. It is a hypothesis that does provide an explanation as to how it was that there was not a total break between the Mycenaean and the archaic worlds. At present there is much discussion on the subject of the extent of the area affected by such a switch (for some regions do not appear to have gone through a pastoral phase at all) and the size of the populations concerned. However, the hypothesis does little to resolve what remains the principal puzzle: what kind of a society and what kind of structures of power existed? It is a puzzle that raises the question of the legitimacy of making historical use of the Homeric epics in order to fill in the gap. Were the men of the dark ages like Homer's heroes? Before attempting to tackle this question, we should note the new elements that characterize the end of this period, that is to say the ninth and eighth centuries.

THE NINTH AND EIGHTH CENTURIES

This is often called the Geometric period, after the name given to the style of pottery that developed at this time.

The depopulation halted and the demographic tendency was progressively reversed, leading to a positive increase in the eighth century. The extent of this reversal continues to be much debated, for the evidence for it is based upon the number of tombs characteristic of eighth-century necropolises. To some, an increase in the number of tombs is a sign of a larger population; to others, it is a sign of a change in funerary customs, resulting in more of the dead being given built-up tombs. One point is certain: the countryside was becoming repopulated, as indicated by the appearance of small villages, sometimes enclosed by walls, and by signs of more crops being cultivated (the presence of silos, barns for storing grain and receptacles for oil) and traces of textile and pottery production. In several sectors, these two centuries are characterized by the introduction of new agricultural features.

The *pottery* in what is known as the geometric style (900–700) became progressively complicated in its designs and eventually produced representations of human figures. The earliest of these paintings represent certain phases in the funerary ritual, such as the *prothesis* (the laying-out of the corpse at home), or scenes of warfare, or processions of warriors and chariots. Scenes such as these adorn in particular pots of the *pythoi* and *loutrophores* types, which are typically found in tombs in the necropolises (see figure 7).

Figure 7 A *prothesis* scene (laying-out of the corpse) on a geometric amphora from Dipylon (National Museum, Athens) (from J. J. Maffre, *L'Art grec*, 2nd edn, Paris, PUF, 1989, p. 38, fig. 6)

Religious life Signs of religious life are once again detectable in the earliest sanctuaries of this period: there were offerings and indications of the cult of certain heroes, all features that were to become characteristic of Greek religion.

It was at this time that real sanctuaries made their appearance. Particular spots recognized as sacred were marked out and became places where offerings were left and sacrifices were made, as can be seen from the animal bones and ashes found there and the occasional presence of altars. In the ninth century the phenomenon was common to northern and central Greece: Dodona, Thermon, Delphi, Eretria, Eleusis and Perachora; to the Peloponnese: Olympia and Argos; and to the islands: Delos, Samos (the Heraion). Within these spaces, little by little buildings came to be erected. Their function continues to be a subject of debate among archaeologists. The buildings may have been where the necessary banquets were held, in which the meat of sacrificed animals would have been consumed, or they may simply have been meeting places.

It seems likely that their function was linked with the cult, even though they were not as yet proper temples, that is to say, the places where religious statues of the gods were housed. Temples in the strict sense of the word did not appear until about 800. One of the first was the temple of Hera (the Heraion) in Samos, a rectangular construction 37 by 9 metres, surrounded by a wooden colonnade.

Rituals in honour of the principal deities of the pantheon gradually became established, in particular, the custom of presenting the gods with offerings. These took many different forms, ranging from modest earthenware figurines to tripod basins of bronze. The quantities of offerings testify to how many people visited the sanctuaries and to their devotion to the gods; and their nature and value provide clues as to the occupations and status of their dedicators, whether these were peasants and shepherds or the high and mighty of this world.

The gods in their sanctuaries were not alone in prompting religious gestures. In this period it also became customary to leave offerings and make sacrifices at tombs that were extremely ancient, some of them dating from the Mycenaean period. The anonymous dead (whose identities were unknown) thus became heroes who were given names and would be attached to particular territories or families; they would then become the objects of cults. It was a way for the local population to create a past and a history for itself (the hero could become their own glorious ancestor) and to root themselves in the territory, demonstrating the legitimacy of their presence there. Most historians agree with this presentation of the phenomenon. However, they differ over the questions of who it was who promoted such cults – free, modest peasants or aristocratic families – and to what extent the movement to do so was linked with the recitation of epic (in particular Homeric epic) in these societies. Once again, the interpretation given to the archaeological data depends largely upon the historian's own particular view of eighth-century society.

Whether they involved gods or heroes, these religious practices indicate that it now seemed right, even efficacious, to devote part of one's wealth to procuring such protection as divine beings might provide; it was now that religion, the symbolic system *par excellence* of Greek societies, was organized. In this domain too, the supporters and adversaries of the theory of continuity between the Mycenaean world and the archaic period find cause for disagreement. The remains from the Mycenaean period found on sites of sanctuaries are seen by some as evidence showing that these places were already cult sites in the second millennium, by others simply as indications that Mycenaean shards never did constitute proof of the existence of a cult but at the very most testified to a human presence. The fact that the Linear B tablets refer to the Greek pantheon is not evidence that cults themselves had persisted in the same form ever since. This debate is far from over, and every new archaeological discovery is a potential reason for restarting it.

Alphabetic writing is another important feature of this period. Syllabic writing of the Linear B type disappeared from Greece and was no longer used, except in Cyprus, in this period. However, we are in possession of graffiti on vases and inscriptions dating from the second half of the eighth century, which suggests that this new system of Greek notation had already been in use for some time, probably since the late ninth or early eighth century. The signs for consonants in this alphabet were borrowed from the Phoenicians, but the Greeks invented letters for vowels as well, which have never existed in Semitic languages. It is not known which region of the Greek world first adopted this system, nor what its reasons for doing so may have been, but its use spread rapidly throughout the whole of Greece and was from the start applied to a wide range of functions. Many kinds of

Archaic alphabet

Greek names	Semitic	Old Attic
Alpha		
Beta		
Gamma		
Delta		
Epsilon		
Vau (digamma)		
Zeta		
Heta		
Theta		
Iota		
Kappa		
Lambda		
Mu		
Nu		

Figure 8 Alphabetic writing

materials were used, but not clay tablets. The consequences of the reinvention of writing by the eighth-century Greeks were not solely of a practical nature. This writing altered their way of thinking and made it possible to adopt a different form of memorization, verification, criticism . . . Such changes of mental attitudes have been carefully studied by anthropologists; and similar methods could well be applied in a study of the phenomenon in Greece.

These four centuries seem to have been a time for the elaboration of techniques, social practices and modes of thought that were to find expression in the archaic period. Then, at least, it is slightly easier to seize upon them, thanks to the appearance of written documents. Foremost among these were the Homeric poems, which might also tell us something of the men of the Iron Age.

THE WORLD OF ODYSSEUS

The two most ancient literary Greek texts that have come down to us are two epic poems: the *Iliad* and the *Odyssey*, attributed to Homer.

Homer is the Greek world's poet *par excellence*. A bust of him represents him as an old man, blind, in accordance with the tradition. Nothing is known of his life, or indeed whether he ever existed. In particular, it is unlikely that the same person wrote both poems, but that does not really matter. The figure of Homer and the place that he came to occupy in the civilization that followed are more interesting to study than the detailed circumstances of his hypothetical life. His was a place of central importance, for Homer is situated at the heart of the whole Greek system of *paideia* (education); he really was 'the educator of Greece', as Plato called him (although Plato then went on to challenge his right to that title). Generations of Greeks learned part or all of the Homeric poems by heart. Greek banquets and festivities resounded to the Homeric poems being sung by professional reciters, known as *rhapsodes*. The adventures of Achilles and Odysseus, the tears of Andromache and Penelope, the beauty of Helen and Nausicaa, the glorious death of Hector on the field of battle beneath the walls of Troy and the shameful deaths of the suitors slaughtered in the banqueting hall of the palace of Ithaca, the society of the gods with its vendettas, its injustices and the rites due to it: all these, young Greeks under the eye of their teacher and adult Greeks at their banquets would make their own, then transpose them into the system of values of their own day.

THE POEMS OF THE *ILIAD* AND THE *ODYSSEY*

It seems likely that these poems were set down in writing between 750 and 700 BC, at the time when Greece was mastering the new mode of transcription constituted by the alphabet. The text, first written down on rolls of papyrus, was subsequently copied on to papyrus and parchment many times over, as long as it remained famous. Many commentaries on it were produced, and it was organized in the form in which we know it during the Alexandrian period. At this point, each poem was divided into twenty-four books. But the transcription of the poems was merely the last stage in a process of composition that must have begun much earlier.

An oral poetry Homeric epic belongs to the genre of oral poetry. The poems were originally composed orally by bards and were sung before an audience. Studies on this type of practice, which is still alive in some parts of Europe, have shown that the reciter built up his work in the course of each recitation, on a basic canvas that always remained the same, a canvas of events, descriptions, rituals and formulae. He did not recite lines learned by heart but on each occasion re-created the story for a different audience. The manner of this creation explains the presence in Homeric poetry of many formulae that recur constantly in identical forms, ranging from 'rosy-fingered dawn' to 'the boiling Achilles', punctuating the text. It likewise accounts for many other characteristics of this epic poetry that was probably diffused orally over several generations before eventually being fixed in writing. But the last recomposition of the texts took place when they were written down. It was probably the work of several poets, since the *Iliad* seems to have been set down in writing in the second half of the eighth century, the *Odyssey* one or two generations later.

The subject of the *Iliad* is the wrath of Achilles and, more widely, the exploits of the Greek and Trojan heroes beneath the walls of Troy. The subject of the *Odyssey* is Odysseus' return to his native island, Ithaca, which he eventually reaches after ten years of wandering. No sooner is the theme of the poems stated than one particularly burning question rises to one's lips: did the Trojan War really take place, and does the *Iliad* give an account of it? This raises the question of the degree of historicity of these poems, or rather that of their relation to history.

Epic and history In the mind of the German archaeologist Heinrich Schliemann, the discoverer of Mycenae, there was not the slightest doubt that Troy had existed and that the Greeks had sailed off one day to conquer it. From 1870 onwards, on the site of Hissarlik, five kilometres from the Dardanelles Straits in Asia Minor, he excavated a settlement whose earliest archaeological strata dated from 3000 BC. He baptized the seventh stratum Troy VIIa and decided that this corresponded to the town destroyed in the Homeric narrative. Archaeology thus authenticated Homer. However, we must reject this tempting reconstruction. There is no evidence to connect Troy VIIa with Mycenaean Greece, nor is the existence of Troy or the Trojan War mentioned in any contemporary document (for example, any Hittite text). Of course, some of the names of the places cited in the *Iliad* do coincide with those of the Mycenaean civilization, but that is all. The world described by the poems bears no resemblance to the Mycenaean world as described above on the basis of the evidence of archaeology and the Linear B tablets. Homer had never known that world, and if his epic does have some link with it, it was through transmission by generations of bards who transformed some insignificant events of the past and their actors into high deeds of glory and heroes, in much the same way as the skirmish in which the tail end of Charlemagne's army was involved at Roncesval in AD 778 was turned into the unforgettable exploit described in the twelfth-century *Chanson de Roland*.

Forget Mycenae. Do the *Iliad* and the *Odyssey* depict the worlds of the eighth and ninth centuries, the periods when they were set down in writing and when the cities were first established? The question has aroused considerable disagreement. M. I. Finley (*The World of Odysseus*) points out the absence in the poems of any allusions to Ionia, writing, iron weaponry or colonization, all of which were features of the eighth and seventh centuries, that is to say, the end of the 'Dark Ages'. C. Mossé (*Le Monde archaïque*) collects together all the features that prove the existence of communities and shows that the *Odyssey*, in particular, assumes the existence of forms of political organization. The dominant type of power, which in the poems is the power of kings, was probably also that of many of the cities of the late eighth century. Besides, today everyone agrees that the primary function of the epic is definitely not the transcription of historical facts of any kind, and that the world that it creates derives part of its originality from the combination of very different periods. The world of Odysseus is also a world of poetic creativity and one in which societies are given to inventing for themselves a past and creating for themselves particular value systems whenever their history demands this. What are the characteristics and values of the world of Odysseus?

THE CHARACTERISTICS OF THE HOMERIC WORLD

The world of the best Foremost in the poems are 'the best' (*aristoi*), the ones who fight beneath the walls of Troy, reign over their kingdoms in the *Odyssey* and are, in truth, the only heroes in these stories. Almost all the talk is of them; the epic is designed to glorify them. They are defined by the families to which they belong, which in some cases can be traced right back to divine ancestors, and blood relationships dictate where their duty of solidarity lies: Agamemnon places himself at the head of the Trojan expedition because it is his brother Menelaus who has been insulted by the abduction of Helen, his wife. The principal activity of these people is warfare, usually war between two kingdoms, sparked off by a raid in which herds are stolen or human beings are kidnapped. The Trojan War, which produced an alliance between many different peoples, is an exception. In warfare a hero fights in the front rank, as a matter of honour, and owes it to himself to seize as much booty as he can: his own survival and that of his *oikos* depend upon it. Single combat between two warriors on foot and heavily armed, who shout challenges and insults at each other and fight without quarter until one of them is killed, is one of the major themes of the *Iliad* stories. One example is the duel between Achilles and Hector. Warfare is the noble activity *par excellence*, the activity that Nestor, the king of Pylos, recalls nostalgically in his old age. Between fights, the heroes sacrifice to the gods and feast together, which is also what they do upon returning to their palaces. We seldom find them occupied in any other tasks unless it be attending councils or activities required by the gods. As well as being related by blood or marriage, these nobles are linked together by strong bonds of hospitality. To be somebody's guest, living under his roof, eating at his table and accepting his gifts, commits one to total reciprocity. In this way, relationships are forged that overstep territorial and generational boundaries.

The rest of this world   The major division runs between 'the best' and the rest, about whom the epic has virtually nothing to say. Yet there are many of them, both free and non-free. They make up most of the community. Free men, herdsmen or peasants, constitute 'the people' (*laos*) at war. The free also include men with special skills of one kind or another, healing, woodwork, effecting contact with the gods: carpenters, blacksmiths, diviners, bards, doctors . . . are all known as 'those who work for the people' (*demiourgoi*).

Scenes of Homeric life depicted on the shield of Achilles

'Next [Hephaestus] depicted a large field of soft, rich fallow, which was being ploughed for the third time. A number of ploughmen were driving their teams across it to and fro. When they reached the ridge at the end of the field and had to wheel, a man would come up and hand them a cup of mellow wine. Then they turned back down the furrows and toiled along through the deep fallow soil to reach the other end. The field, though it was made of gold, grew black behind them, as a field does when it is being ploughed. The artist had achieved a miracle.

He also showed a king's estate, where hired reapers were at work with sharp sickles in their hands. Armfuls of corn fell down in rows along the furrow, while others were tied up with straw by the sheaf-binders. Three of these were standing by, and the boys who were gleaning behind came running up to them with bundles in their arms and kept them constantly supplied. And there among them was the King himself, staff in hand, standing by the swathe in quiet satisfaction. Under an oak in the background his attendants were preparing a feast. They were cooking a great ox that they had slaughtered, and the women were sprinkling the meat for the labourers' supper with handfuls of white barley.

The next scene was a vineyard laden with grapes. It was beautifully wrought in gold, but the bunches themselves were black and the supporting poles showed up throughout in silver. All around it he ran a ditch of blue enamel and outside that a fence of tin. The vineyard was approached by a single pathway for the pickers' use at vintage time; and the delicious fruit was being carried off in baskets by merry lads and girls, with whom there was a boy singing the lovely song of Linus in a treble voice to the sweet music of his tuneful lyre. They all kept time with him and followed the music and the words with dancing feet.' (*Iliad*, XVIII, 541–70)

At the bottom of the hierarchy of free men are those who possess nothing and work for wages: the *thetes*. Their unenviable status is a consequence of their being attached to no *oikos*. There are also many non-free people, more women than men since at this time it was still customary to kill all the men after a battle, rather than take them prisoner and reduce them to slavery. Women, on the other hand, constituted part of the booty, so when Troy was taken by the Greeks, the wives of the Trojans were taken off to be slaves in the various Greek kingdoms. Anybody could one day find himself or herself a slave: Eumaeus, Odysseus' swineherd, would tell anyone who cared to listen that he had been a king's son when he was captured by pirates and sold as a slave.

The oikos   Whatever their status, with the exception of the thetes, all those who belonged to this world were attached to an *oikos*, a collection of possessions and people, a household. Such a unit afforded people security and supplied their material needs. It set out the norms, both social and religious, that were to be respected. Membership of an *oikos* no doubt carried with it certain obligations, but outside such a framework an individual had no existence. Every household possessed a territory and a degree of wealth in the form of both material goods and manpower. The chiefs of the most powerful of them might claim authority over the whole local community, royal power.

Power belonged to the king (*basileus*), who was simply the first of 'the best'. His power was not hereditary; he did not necessarily hand it on to his son. In a case of prolonged absence, such as that of Odysseus, who was away from Ithaca for ten years, royal power was at stake in the competition between the other nobles, the 'suitors' or 'claimants' in the case of Ithaca, and neither Odysseus' son, Telemachus, nor his father, Laertes, could claim power. Odysseus would have to impose himself by force and slay the claimants before he could become king once more. In Mycenae, the titular king Agamemnon, for all that he was the leader of the Greek expedition against Troy, was assassinated upon his return. In short, power was a personal attribute, exercised by force. It depended upon the wealth of the *basileus' oikos*, the extent of his land and the size of his herds. However, a king did have certain prerogatives: an estate (*temenos*) attached to his function, the right to an extra share in the distribution of booty, and many presents. What was the nature of his power? Essentially, it was taking the decision to go to war, and directing the latter; also, that of convoking the assembly.

The *assembly* would have been the second cog in the machine of political power, had its existence been anything more than formal. The king convoked it when he saw fit to do so, proposing the subject for discussion. It neither voted nor took decisions. In principle, the function of the assembly was to make it possible for the opinion of the *laos* to be expressed (within strictly fixed limits, as is shown by the episode in the *Iliad* in which

Thersites, a Greek who spoke up to express his disagreement with Odysseus' proposal, was promptly beaten and ordered to be silent). The king could take decisions without consulting the assembly. Finally, there is no suggestion that the exercise of justice was one of the king's functions.

Forms of wealth The world of Odysseus was also a world of riches that were produced, accumulated and exchanged. The basis of wealth was land, and it was this that determined the hierarchy of households. This land was devoted more to the pasturage of horses and herds of domesticated animals than to agriculture, the cultivation of cereals, vines and orchards. An *oikos* was almost self-sufficient: it produced most of its needs, except in one domain, that of metal objects, tools and weaponry. Foodstuffs and manufactured products were stored in the house of the head of the *oikos*, in a cellar, and were redistributed between members of the household when and where need arose. The surplus of goods was recorded and preserved, to be used later as the gifts that always accompanied hospitality. Each *oikos* thus had a treasure store, more or less well stocked, particularly by objects made of bronze, iron or gold (cups, tripods, basins, weapons . . .), or fabrics.

The lists of gifts exchanged by the epic heroes give some idea of the contents of such treasure stores. For example, Agamemnon gave Achilles seven tripods never touched by fire, ten talents of gold, twenty shining basins . . .

Exchanges A treasure store was clearly used to supply the *gifts* and *counter-gifts* that families would present to one another. But the system comprised a wide range of different categories of gifts: the presents (*hedna*) that a youth would offer the family of his future wife, and the dowry that the girl's family would give the husband, for example. The act of giving was always understood as the first move in an exchange that presupposed reciprocity, a present given in return. There are many Homeric texts that reveal the principal means of exchange in this world, exclusively within the category of 'the best'. Riches were accumulated on a temporary basis for the purpose of ensuring the social exchange that first created, then reinforced links between families, both within a single political community and in different political groups. Such a system is typical of societies that do not use money and attach more value to the gesture of giving than to the object given.

It is easy to see that in such a context *other forms of exchange* are likely to be devalued, as they do not establish any social link. Barter and trade thus tend not to be regarded as honourable activities, since the exchange is an end in itself. For this reason, in epic, trade with the external world is left in the hands of non-Greeks, particularly Phoenicians, and mistrust is evinced towards the stranger-merchant, who is easily assimilated to a pirate. One more feature of these exchanges is worth noting: the unit of value for goods was constituted by a domesticated animal. Laertes, for example,

Figure 9   The duel between Achilles and Hector: a vase painting (© British Museum, London)

had bought Euryclaea, Odysseus' servant-nurse, in exchange for goods worth twenty head of cattle. The world of Odysseus has a number of features in common with that of the Nuer herdsmen of Africa studied by Evans-Pritchard. Their world too was found to be steeped in values that reflected a heroic ethic.

HEROIC VALUES

G. Nagy's *The Best of the Achaeans*, J. Redfield's *The Tragedy of Hector* and J.-P. Vernant's *L'Individu, la mort, l'amour* are among many recent books that have pondered the question of the essence of heroism in the heroic world, taking as their guides Achilles the Greek and Hector the Trojan, the *Iliad*'s heroes *par excellence*.

The first of the heroic values is of a religious nature: respect for the world of the gods and the numerous and demanding rituals that are their due, ranging from sacrifice to the consultation of diviners, from prayers to libations, from offerings of booty to funerary rituals. When a pause in the hostilities occurs, the time is devoted to the gods, already imagined as a highly organized, hierarchical family, subject to both quarrels and passions. The gods' anger constitutes a threat to the stability of both communities and individuals, and the heroes of epic are well aware of this.

The second value is a social one. A hero only exists in the eyes and the memory of a community. And his status largely depends upon his conforming with the norms as a courageous warrior, a diligent head of his *oikos*, a generous host and an honourable competitor in all contests. But there is more to it: for a hero, courage and honour are more important than any other values and, in a context of war such as that of the *Iliad*, they may lead him to death in order to acquire the eternal glory that is the very stuff of the epic song. The exploits of Achilles and Hector will outlive time, outlast centuries, as models of the heroic life, the life of very ancient times, thanks to the songs of the bards and the attention of their listeners. Therein, perhaps, lies one of the keys to the heroic ethic: 'Achilles chooses to die young because he wants to reside forever in the world of the living, to survive amongst them, in them, and remain there forever himself, distinct from all others, through the indestructible memory of his name and renown' (J.-P. Vernant).

2 / THE ARCHAIC WORLD

THE BIRTH OF CIVIC COMMUNITIES

The two main forms of political organization evolved by the Greeks were those of a people (*ethnos*) and of a city (*polis*).

A people (*ethnos*) was a population dispersed over an extensive territory, living essentially in villages, united by weak and intermittent political links. Many regions of the Greek world were organized in this fashion: northern and western Greece (Macedonians, Thessalians, Epirots, Phocidians, Locrians, Aetolians, Acarnanians), and part of the Peloponnese (Arcadians, Achaeans). Not much is known of these political communities in the archaic period, when they do not seem to have played a very active role.

A city (*polis*) was an autonomous political community of people inhabiting a particular territory that included both rural zones with villages and in many cases (but not all) also a more developed, settled zone that can be called a 'town' (*astu*). The term city thus designates an abstract concept: the sovereignty and independence of a group of men, very close to what is meant by the modern term 'State'. To emphasize that political sovereignty, some historians use the expression 'city-state'. But in the Greek language cities were designated not by an abstract entity (Athens, Megara), but by the name of their citizens (the Athenians, the Megarians).

It is very easy to define what a city was in the classical period, but very hard, or even impossible, to say precisely how this type of political community came to be formed. Discussions on the origins of the cities revolve around two major questions that are clearly linked: the question of the date of the appearance of the first cities, and the question of the process of the formation of this new political system.

THE DATE OF THE APPEARANCE OF THE CITIES

The date postulated for the appearance of the first cities varies from one historian to another. Some favour a very early date. For example, the French historian Henri Van Effenterre (*La Cité grecque*, Paris 1985) dates the origins of the city to the Minoan period in Crete, roughly 1700 BC). He bases this theory in particular upon the structures revealed by the excavations at Mallia, in Crete, and believes that the public square was used as a place to assemble a political community and that a hall equipped with seats was where a council met, indicating, along with other signs, a mode of life in which the political features of the city may well have evolved.

At the beginning of the twentieth century the subject occasioned a major debate between two German historians, H. Berve and V. Ehrenberg. In Berve's view, the city did not exist until the establishment of a political regime that had totally and definitively eliminated power entrusted to the hands of a single person (a king or a tyrant). In that case, the city did not make its appearance until the beginnings of democracy, at the end of the sixth century BC, and the model for it was Athens.

For Ehrenberg, the city first came into being when the people, as a community, tried to establish its political sovereignty. The existence of some kind of collective authority – an assembly, a magistracy – thus constitutes the birth certificate of the *polis*, in which case it can be traced back to the early eighth century. This is the more widely accepted view, but the debate is by no means over.

Many historians today, in particular P. Manville (*The Origins of Citizenship in Ancient Athens*, Princeton, NJ, 1990) for example, advocate linking the beginning of the existence of the city with the point at which the rights of citizenship were definitively fixed, that is to say sixth-century Athens.

Faced with all these arguments, it is worth remembering that 'the city' is an ideal model elaborated by historians and then projected on to a reality that is complex or even impossible to seize, as H.-I. Marrou pointed out.

THE PROCESS OF FORMATION

Reflection on how cities came into being to a large extent overlaps with thinking on the origins of the State, particularly that of the nineteenth century.

As Fustel de Coulanges (*The Ancient City*, translated by W. Small, Garden City, NY, 1956) saw it, family groups preceded the city, which was formed when they cohered together. The city was founded upon a close link between social institutions, land ownership and religion. G. Glotz then produced a clear formulation of the pre-existence of family groups before the creation of the city (*The Greek City and its Institutions*, translated by N. Maltinson, London, 1927). Nowadays, however, following the radical criticisms of D. Roussel (*Tribu et cité*, 1976) and P. Bourriot (*Recherches sur le génos*, 1976), that thesis has been abandoned.

Friedrich Engels (*The Origin of the Family, Private Property and the State*, translated by A. West, London, 1972), influenced by the theses of Karl Marx, regarded the genesis of the Athenian State as a creation that was connected with profound changes in economic structures. He stressed the relation between, on one hand, the formation of the State and, on the other, the appearance of private property and the division of society into classes. In his eyes, the Athenian State provided a model for the formation of States in general.

Max Weber (at the end of the nineteenth century and the beginning of the twentieth) put forward an extremely complex typology of the city, but above all he drew a fundamental distinction between the ancient city and the medieval town, suggesting that the former was based on a political unit incorporating both town and countryside and gave rise to 'political man', while the latter was based on a legal distinction between town and countryside and gave rise to 'economic man' ('The City', chapter 16, Part II of *Wirtschaft und Gesellschaft*, translated by D. Martingdale and G. Neuwirth, London, 1960). Max Weber emphasized the political criteria upon which the definition of the Greek city is founded.

These are three examples, among others, of different ways of interpreting the process of the formation of cities. On one point all three agree, namely that it was the members of the city who owned the land.

It is important to be aware of the existence of these disagreements over the origins of Greek cities, even if their arcane arguments are hard to follow, for as we consider all the different ways of writing the history of these very early periods, we learn to distinguish the points of historians who interpret the past in a global fashion. Writing history is by no means a neutral business and, as this particular example reveals, quite simply, in the course of successive intellectual generations it evolves.

THE ANCIENT EVIDENCE

If rival theories on the origins of Greek cities have flourished, that is partly because we possess so little evidence for the earliest days of the cities.

The texts In the Homeric epics, particularly the *Odyssey*, we find descriptions of communities that act as such not only in their social relations and religious life but also in their relations with others, as in warfare. And the space occupied by such a community includes both a town and a surrounding area of countryside. When Odysseus finds himself among the Phaeacians, Nausicaa tells him of the fields and the various crops that they will pass before reaching the town, and goes on to say, 'Our city is surrounded by high battlements; it has an excellent harbour on each side . . . Here is the people's meeting place, built up on either side of the fine temple of Poseidon with blocks of quarried stone bedded deeply in the ground.'

In the work of Hesiod, written in about 700 BC, the village communities of Boeotia seem relatively loosely structured, with the *oikos* still the basic unit of agricultural production and social life. Mention is made of a town, Thespies, the abode of 'the devourers of gifts', but we are told nothing of its functions. On the basis of the texts of Hesiod, it is impossible to tell whether or not the city already existed in its later form.

The earliest text to have come down to us that shows that the city existed as a political community dates from the second half of the seventh

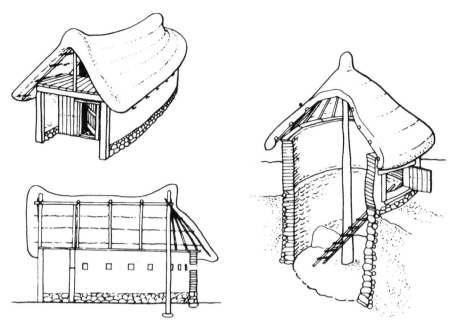

Figure 10 Reconstruction of a house (a) and a barn (b) in Smyrna in the seventh century BC (drawing by R. V. Nicholls from *The Cambridge Ancient History*, III.3, Cambridge University Press, 1975)

century. It is an inscription from Dreros, in Crete, that starts off as follows: 'The city (*polis*) has decided . . .' Then follows a decree setting out the regulations concerning the conditions for exercising a magistracy in the city.

Archaeology, another source of evidence, testifies to *urban development*, but such development is not necessarily synonymous with the form of a civic community. One of the most ancient examples is that of Smyrna, in Asia Minor (see figure 10). The excavations there reveal that the site had been occupied since about 1000 BC and that the settlement had been surrounded by ramparts for the first time in the mid-ninth century. One century later, between 400 and 500 houses built of unfired bricks were sheltered by the town ramparts. The houses were rebuilt in about 700, when the town was redesigned with a regular plan. That life was lived as a community, once the town walls were first constructed, is patently clear. But did the community have the characteristics of an autonomous political entity ever since that early date, or only from the time of its reorganization in 700? It is a question that archaeologists and historians continue to debate and it is a hard one to answer.

Archaeology also testifies to *population growth*, thanks to the study of cemeteries, as we have seen in the case of earlier periods. According to some archaeologists, in a region such as Attica, the population quadrupled in half a century, between 800 and 750. This population growth accompanied the creation of cities, but it is impossible to tell whether it was a cause or a consequence of the latter.

The foundations of cities The most certain proof of the existence of cities in the world of the Greek mainland and islands is provided by the creation of new communities outside this original hub, in the eastern and western Mediterranean, from the early eighth century onward – communities which, as excavations have shown clearly, possess all the structures by which a city is defined. Now, these new communities were the daughters of more ancient ones, their metropolises. So, *a contrario*, it is fair to assume that the mother communities were already organized as cities, that they themselves were cities.

Large numbers of communities One striking thing about these new political communities is how very many of them there were, which means that part of the Greek world was fragmented into numerous tiny independent units. Geography has been invoked to account for this, but wrongly, for there is not necessarily any connection between geographical isolation, due in particular to the mountainous relief of several regions of Greece, and the arrangement of the boundaries of city territories. Some city territories – Sparta, for example – comprised several geographical units. Other cities shared a single plain, as Chalcis and Eretria did in Euboea, or a tiny island such as Amorgos in the Cyclades, which accommodated three cities, Arkesine, Aigiale and Minoa. Of course, that does not mean that cities did not make use of natural geographical boundaries (hills, rivers, coasts) when these existed to mark out their frontiers. But just because geography could be used by cities does not mean that it determined their shape from the start. At the beginning of the *Iliad*, the catalogue of ships and the list of kings and their peoples who took part in the expedition to Troy already indicates the extreme fragmentation of centres of political power. By the classical period there were several hundred cities.

Finally, the formation of cities affected the Greek world over several generations, although not uniformly in all regions. Because the establishment of some cities was slow and regions differed considerably, it is not possible to present a unified picture of this phenomenon. Nevertheless, it was certainly to be one of the distinguishing features of the Greek civilization.

A NEW ART OF WAR

In the eighth century BC a new art of war developed. In Homeric epic two types of combat coexist: one for the compact mass of foot-soldiery (the *laos*), the other for the Greek and Trojan champions, who would leap down from their chariots and fight their duels, one hero pitted against another. These two modes of combat may be a reflection of two different periods, the Mycenaean age with its chariot battles, and the end of the

dark ages with their close-knit battalions that prefigured the fighting formation of the early years of the cities: *the hoplite phalanx.*

The hoplite, the infantryman of the Greek armies, owed his name to
the round shield (*hoplon*) that protected him. The shield was 1 metre in
diameter, with a wooden or wicker frame covered by wood or bronze and
decorated. On the inner face were two devices by which it could be held:
a central ring that surrounded the forearm at the elbow (*porpax*) and a
strap that could be grasped by the hand (*antilabè*). His other defensive
equipment consisted of a helmet, a metal breastplate and greaves (*cnemides*).
His offensive weapons comprised a wooden spear 2 to 2.5 metres long,
with an iron or bronze tip, and a short sword with either a straight or a
curved blade. Some pieces of this panoply had already appeared by the end
of the eighth century (725 is the date of a breastplate and helmet found in
a tomb at Argos, 700 the date for round shields and 675 that of the
greaves to be seen in paintings on proto-Corinthian pots). The hoplite
panoply was not an invention that struck the entire Greek world all at
once, like a flash of lightning. It was a gradual creation that took place in
a number of different cities, a development phased out in time and dispersed throughout the Greek space.

The panoply of hoplite arms implies a change in the art of war and the
adoption of a particular form of combat, that of the *phalanx*, which is
shown on a proto-Corinthian pot, the Chigi Vase, of the seventh century.
Fighting took place in a tight formation, with the hoplites disposed in
ranks, elbow to elbow, several rows deep. The shield protected the left
side of the hoplite, while his right flank was covered by the shield of his
neighbour next in line. Such a formation required and testifies to a sense
of solidarity and discipline. War had certainly become a collective affair
in which it was more important to keep in line than to engage in indi-
vidualistic exploits.

Was there a 'hoplite revolution'? Historians link the appearance of the
hoplite panoply with the extension of the civic body that went hand in
hand with the birth of the cities. However, it is impossible to say which
was the motivating force in the evolution: the new technique of warfare, or
a change in the relations between different social groups. It seems reasonable to suppose, along with Yves Garlan (*War in the Ancient World*, London, 1975), that the hoplite phalanx was both a cause and a consequence
of the social mutations that provoked a progressive expansion of the citizen
body. This new technique of fighting, using infantrymen all of equal status,
dispossessed the small group of 'the best' of their monopoly over the
defence of the community and, at a stroke, also of their sole claim to the
power of political decision. It is in this sense that the expression 'hoplite
revolution' is used.

Given the dearth of textual sources already mentioned, it is impossible to
give a detailed account of the social structures and the mechanism of the

power of decision, that is to say the political power of the earliest civic communities. Rather than project upon this early archaic period all that we can deduce from the Homeric texts and learn from the Greek texts of the next period, it is preferable to wait for a century and then present examples of the cities about which most is known. Even if the assembly, the council and the magistracies were the key organs of city government in the sixth century, it is not necessarily the case that this was likewise so two centuries earlier in communities with different economic and social structures. So before describing the internal structures of particular cities, let us take a look at how they were dispersed around the Mediterranean world, following the trail of those explorers, the Greeks of the archaic period.

EMIGRATION AND THE NEW CITIES

The movement of Greek emigration from Greece proper, the islands of the Aegean and Asia Minor, to other regions in the Mediterranean world began in the second quarter of the eighth century BC (775), at a time when the city (*polis*) was still in an embryonic state in Greece. The Greeks' word for a newly created community was *apoika*, describing the phenomenon as a departure from one settlement to go to another, a move to a new place of residence, an emigration. This general movement began during the initial phase in the constitution of civic communities, when human groups were acquiring a fixed territorial base, a place to worship and shared institutions. In English and in French, such a movement is generally called 'colonization', but this was very different from the movement of colonization of modern and contemporary times, characteristic of States (such as England and France) that are extremely advanced both economically and politically.

In ancient Greece the situation was quite different. The movement of colonization was not the product of a mature, adult society with a desire to expand. So it was not 'colonies' in the modern sense of the term that the Greeks went off to found, but simply new cities which, from the moment of their creation, were independent, sovereign States. The movement was organized to the extent that it would include men all dependent on a particular city or region of Greece, who would go off together to create a new community. Greece was their point of departure, but it would be mistaken to imagine Greece as a monolithic block. The movement of Greek 'colonization' was characterized by a wide diversity of situations, partly – of course – by reason of the diversity of indigenous traditions that confronted the various new arrivals, but also by reason of the diversity of the traditions of all the regions in Greece from which the travellers hailed. To dwell on the general characteristics of the movement would be to do scant justice to the specificity of each case. So, after indicating a few generalities, let us consider a selection of individual cases from each of the regions of the Mediterranean world organized in this Greek fashion.

Table 2 Chronology of the principal colonial foundations

	Date of foundation	Colony	Metropolis
First wave, up to 675			
– To the West:	770	Pithecussae	Chalcis
Sicily and the straits	757	Naxos	Chalcis
of Messina (people	?	Leontini	Naxos (Sicily)
from Euboea and the	?	Catana	Chalcis
isthmus of Corinth)	750	Megara Hyblaea	Megara
	740	Cumae	Chalcis
	734	Syracuse	Corinth
	?	Zancle	Chalcis
	730	Rhegium	+ Messenia
Gulf of Tarentum	late eighth	Sybaris	Achaea + Troezen
(Peloponnesians)		Croton	Achaea
		Tarentum	Sparta
Various	680	Locris	Ozolian Locris
(new colonists)	about 675	Gela	Rhodes + Crete
	about 675	Siris	Colophon
	late eighth	Spreading of colonies:	
		Zancle, Cumae, Naxos, Sybaris	
	early ninth	(Metapontion), Croton, Tarentum	
To Thracian		Torone, Mende	Calchis
Chalcidice and the		Scione, Methone	and Eretria
Thermaic Gulf			
Second wave, after 675			
Northern and	about 682	Thasos	Paros
north-eastern	then	Thasian Peraea	Thasos
Aegean: Thasos and	about 650	Numerous	Aeolians,
the Thracian		foundations	Chios, Andros
coast			
	600	Potidaea	Corinth
	560	in Chersonese	Athens
	545	Abdera	Teos
Hellespont,	Late eighth	Parium	Miletus et al.
Propontis, Bosphorus	About 687	Chalcedon	Megara
		Selymbria	Megara
	Before 675	Astacus	Megara
	676	Cyzicus	Miletus
	Soon after	Abydus	Miletus
	About 660	Byzantium	Megara
	654	Lampsacus	Phocaea
	About 600	Perinthus et al.	Samos
	600	Sigeum	Athens
	Seventh to sixth	Many small settlements	Miletus

Table 2 (cont'd)

	Date of foundation	Colony	Metropolis
– Black Sea: south and west shores	About 650	Sinope	Miletus
	About 650	Istrus	Miletus
	564	Amisus	Miletus
	560	Heraclea Pontica	Megara
	540	Callatis	Heraclea Pontica
	510	Mesembria	Byzantium Chalcedon
		Sesamus, Tieum	Miletus
	Sixth	Trapezus and small trading ports	Sinope
West and north-west shores	646	Olbia	Miletus
	?	Tyras	Miletus
	610	Apollonia	Miletus
	575	Odessus	Miletus
	550	Tomis	Miletus
		and also small foundations by Miletus, Apollonia and Mesembria	
North and north-east shores	600–550	Cimmerian Bosphorus	Miletus + Teos
	seventh–sixth	East coast	Miletus
– Africa	650–625	Naucratis	Miletus + Samos et al.
	630	Cyrene	Thera
	560–520	Barca + Euhesperides	Cyrene
– West: Phocaeans in far west	600	Massilia	Phocaea
	565	Alalia	Phocaea
	540	Elea (Velia)	Phocaeans of Alalia
	?	Emporiae	Phocaeans
		Hemeroscopeum, Mainake	
	Sixth	Theline (Arles)	Massilia
Last foundations in Sicily and Magna Graecia	about 675	Posidonia	Sybaris
	663–592	Acrae, Casmenae, Camarina	Syracuse
	650	Selinus	Megara Hyblaea
	648	Himera	Zancle
	580	Agrigentum	Gela
		and other minor foundations by Selinus, Cnidus, Rhodes and Samos	
– Adriatic	627	Epidamnus	Corinth
	600	Apollonia	and Corcyra

Source: M.-C. Amouretti and F. Ruzé, *Le Monde grec antique*, 2nd edn, Paris, 1990.

THE GENERAL FRAMEWORK

Greek colonizing expeditions continued to set out regularly from the second quarter of the eighth century down to the end of the seventh, but these departures can be classified into two phases.

Phase I: from 775 to 675 For a century the movement was limited to a small number of cities in Greece proper: the cities of the island of Euboea, Chalcis and Eretria, and also Megara and Corinth. The destinations of these migrations were Sicily and southern Italy (known as Magna Graecia) and the Thracian Chalcidice.

Phase II: from 675 to 600 Now a more extensive geographical area was involved: to the north Thrace, the Hellespont, the Propontis, the Bosphorus, the Black Sea; to the south Egypt, Cyrenaica; to the west not only southern Italy and Sicily but also Gaul and Spain. The origins of the 'colonizers' were also more diverse, for Megara was joined by cities in Asian Greece, the Aegean islands, Athens and certain newly founded cities which, in their turn, now sent out founding expeditions. The table (pp. 43–4) showing the chronology of the foundations give some idea of the complexity of the movement.

CAUSES OF THE DEPARTURES

What caused the first departures? As has been pointed out, we know nothing of the history of the cities at the time of the first departures, so answers to that question depend upon the accounts of the origins of cities written by mythologists or historians many years later. These are concerned in particular with the characteristics that the new cities forthwith adopted, characteristics that seem to correspond to certain precise preoccupations of the colonizers.

The need for cultivable land was the principal cause. It was hunger that prompted the Greeks to leave their native cities (the people of Chalcis and those of Thera, for example). Their native soil could not produce enough cereals to feed the entire population. This is sometimes attributed to the inefficient way in which the land was divided among the inhabitants, with some fields fragmented through inheritance to such a degree that they could not support a family, and others monopolized by a few. Poor agricultural methods and the ups and downs of the climate no doubt also played their part. The upshot was that Greeks went off in search of agricultural land to exploit. This was the goal of the foundation of most new cities, and on that account they are known as 'settlement colonies' or 'agrarian colonies'.

The fact that cities were unable to provide for all the needs of the community out of their resources prompted some of them to make contact with regions that could provide whatever it was that they needed – wood, mineral ores, particular foodstuffs – in exchange for which the Greeks would offer pots, oil, possibly tools or weapons. Such contacts might be limited to purely commercial exchanges but sometimes led to the creation of temporary or lasting trading posts, and some of these eventually developed into cities. They are known as 'commercial colonies' but the expression is not intended to suggest that trade was their sole activity.

Local causes must have prompted some departures, but we can only learn of these from whatever chroniclers saw fit to record. Rivalry between aristocratic families may have led to the enforced exile of some of them. The impossibility of integrating new social groups as citizens was no doubt the cause of the departures of some men who were not prepared to accept an inferior status.

Migration, certainly a risky undertaking, given the conditions of navigation and people's very imperfect knowledge of the Mediterranean world, must have received encouragement from the experience of earlier expeditions and above all from the knowledge of foreigners who were skilled navigators, such as the Phoenicians. The eighth-century Greeks did not sail away completely blind, but the fact remains that they needed the souls of true adventurers to leave their own cities one fine spring morning, with no prospect of return, as they launched themselves upon what Hesiod called 'the wine-dark sea'.

THE FOUNDATION OF NEW CITIES

Consultation of an oracle   Once a city had decided to send a group of its inhabitants off to found a new city, it consulted the oracle of Apollo at Delphi to discover, for example, what would be the most propitious place for a foundation. When the people of Chalcis in Euboea came to consult it, the oracle's advice was as follows: 'There where Aspias, the most sacred of rivers, pours into the sea, you will find a female clasping a male; there, build a town, for the god will give you the Ausonian land.' The colonists reached the extreme tip of Italy where, on the banks of the Aspias, they found a viper entwined around a wild fig tree and understood that the oracle had been accomplished. So they founded the city of Rhegium there. It is clear from this that the function of the oracle was not to guide the movement of departing Greeks with precision and premeditation, but rather to provide a religious guarantee for an undertaking for which, in the last resort, the human beings concerned were responsible: everything depended on how they interpreted the oracle.

A leader: the oikiste   An expedition would have a leader, known as the *oikiste*, and he would probably become the first authority in the new city. His role was primarily religious. He was, for example, expected to take with him fire from the original city's hearth (*hestia*) and use it to light fire in the hearth of the new city, thereby marking the link between the two communities. The subsequent history of the two cities would in many cases turn this *oikiste* into a hero for whom a cult would be set up, as the founder, *archegète*, of the city.

In most cases the colonists all came from the same city, but sometimes they would be joined by the inhabitants of another one. Thus the people of Chalcis and those of Eretria founded Pithecussae together. They were a small band, perhaps only a hundred or even fewer on the first expedition, but others may have joined them later. All, or the great majority, of the group were male.

The choice of a site would be dictated by a number of criteria: the need for a fertile territory, an anchorage, a good defensive position. Before marking out the boundaries of the settlement and planning the future town, there would be sacrifices and prayers. The problem of the distribution of land and sites on which to build houses must have been one of the first to be tackled. In many towns it is possible for archaeologists to determine which spaces were allotted for building and which zones were residential, which for temples and which for public buildings. Of course, these little towns took some time to develop and it might be a century, or even two, before the zone reserved for residential buildings was densely occupied. In some cities, such as Metapontum in southern Italy, the cultivable land was also divided up with an eye to equality. The parcels of land, on which isolated houses, called 'farms' by the archaeologists, were built, formed parallel strips of the same size, stretching out from the gates of the urban settlement. This suggests that all the colonists received equal plots of land, possibly after drawing lots, and thereby found a remedy for the land-hunger (*stenochoria*) that had driven them from their native city. The daughter-cities were ahead of their mother-cities in finding a solution to one of the greatest problems of the archaic world: growing enough food to survive, by operating according to a principle of equality towards which people in Greece proper were still feeling their way.

The indigenous peoples   It might appear from this description of the installation of the new arrivals that they had made their way to virgin, uninhabited lands. That is not the case at all. Wherever the Greeks set foot, the land was inhabited by peoples who had been living there for a very long time, speaking non-Greek languages and with civilizations of their own. In short, the arrival of Greek colonists upset these indigenous peoples more or less profoundly. Because of the wide diversity of these autochthonous peoples and their modes of organization, in this domain, even more than in some others, generalizations are bound to produce false impressions. Another problem is that our knowlege of these peoples is extremely uneven. Numerous studies have been made of the new Greek cities and monographs exist on all the sites. But study of the indigenous cultures is much more recent: although very advanced on some regions, on others it has only just begun. On that account, the best thing to do is to discuss the relations between the new arrivals and the local populations on the basis of specific cases where studies have been made of the effects of colonization on the surrounding region.

It is, however, possible to make a few general remarks. The nature and quality of the first contacts between the Greeks and the autochthonous populations depended upon a number of factors:

- the size of the territory that the new city wished to acquire. Where it did not seek to spread by taking over land on which the local population was already living, it posed no threat to the original occupants. When the reverse was the case, conflict was likely;
- the degree of organization of the local populations. The better they were organized, the more promptly they reacted to the Greek occupation;
- the type of exchanges that were established between the two communities. Both the Greek and the indigenous community might, or might not, be advantaged by the new situation in which they lived side by side. It should be remembered that it was not just a matter of exchanging products; people were also involved. There is one point that is difficult to assess but was certainly of considerable importance, at least in the early days of relations between communities: the natives provided wives for the mainly masculine group from Greece. Another factor may have been at the root of conflicts: attempts by the Greeks to make serfs of members of the indigenous community. In short, relations between the Greeks and the local peoples were affected by a whole variety of factors.

Hellenization? It is also simplistic to speak of a gradual, uniform Hellenization of the regions of the Mediterranean world where the Greeks established themselves. In several places the indigenous cultures reacted and survived, albeit at the price of a measure of acculturation. Because most of the sources at our disposal emanated from the Greeks, we often tend to underestimate the clout and vitality of the local civilizations. Recent archaeological work suggests that we should think again about the forms and limits of what has long been believed to constitute a single model of Hellenization and perhaps consider the various influences of the 'colonizers'.

THE RELATIONS BETWEEN MOTHER-CITIES AND DAUGHTER-CITIES

There is one other general feature that reveals the difference between this movement of colonization and modern ones: the new cities' independence of their mother-cities or metropolises. Although relations of a cultural or religious nature may have been maintained, all political and economic links were severed at the time of the foundation.

The political institutions all have an air of resemblance to the extent that the whole of the archaic Greek world produced similar aristocratic institutions. But there is no evidence of the colonies systematically adopting the same institutions as their metropolises. In fact, sometimes the daughter-cities created a constitutional model that was then copied in Greece proper. The first legislators appeared in southern Italy, Zaleucus in Locri and Charondas in Rhegium. They elaborated detailed constitutional laws and made them public, thereby indicating a path that reformers such as Solon and Cleisthenes were to follow in Athens.

No relation of political dependence existed between the new cities and their metropolises. Nor did the one interfere in the management of the other's affairs or recognize any obligation to provide mutual aid in times of conflict. There is no evidence of metropolises coming to the aid of their daughter-cities, or indeed of metropolises themselves calling for help.

The picture is similar in the economic domain. Of course, it is hard to determine the degree of economic relations that obtained between two cities, since the archaeological documentation, which constitutes our only evidence, does not always tell us enough. For example, a total absence in the territory of city B of pottery produced by city A proves only that city A was not in a position to export pottery; it cannot be concluded that no links at all existed between the two cities. Later on, the same applies to coins. The trading links set up in the course of Greek expansion in the Mediterranean were established quite independently of any filial relations between one city and another. A small group of 'old' cities, Corinth, Phocaea, Miletus and Athens, exerted considerable trading influence without being 'metropolises', as can be seen most clearly in the case of Athens, which at this point had founded no new cities. Conversely, the city of Chalcis, a particularly active founder of new cities, played no role in trade.

The *culture* that the colonizers brought with them certainly bore the mark of their origins in one domain at least, that of language, reflected in their writing and their particular dialect of spoken Greek. For example, the inhabitants of Tarentum spoke a Dorian dialect, those of Cumae an Ionian one. But apart from their language, new cities do not seem to have preserved the characteristic cultural features of their cities of origin for very long. In the domain of thought, they were so innovative that it is impossible to detect traces of influence from elsewhere. It was in Magna Graecia that schools of philosophy and medicine first made their appearance (Croton and Elea). Nor are filial links in evidence where the arts are concerned (architecture, sculpture, pottery). Doric temples were built in Chalcidian cities, Ionic ones in Syracuse and Megara Hyblaea. In the western Mediterranean world, at least, a civilization at once homogeneous and original rapidly developed as a result of the penetration of a wide variety of influences.

Religion is the only field in which the tradition of the metropolis unquestionably did maintain its rights. As will be remembered, the *oikiste* founded the new city around the hearth fed by the fire from the hearth of the metropolis. And, as well as Hestia, the principal deities of the original city were honoured in the daughter-city. For example, the Spartan pantheon was also to be found in Tarentum, and the heroic cults of the two cities were likewise the same. The rituals, myths and priesthoods were similar. The religious embassies sent from one city to the other on the occasions of festivals renewed links that remained solid throughout those cities' histories. It was through religion that these cities expressed their family relationship, even if new cults gradually added on in the new cities gave the latter a distinctive air of their own, as they assimilated local deities honoured by the natives into the civic pantheon.

Such were the general features of the Greek expansion in the Mediterranean world in the archaic period. Now let us consider its geographical diversity.

Four regions can be distinguished: the eastern Mediterranean, the north-east and the Black Sea, southern Italy and Sicily, and the western Mediterranean.

THE EASTERN MEDITERRANEAN

Here the Greeks occupied three principal sites: Al Mina in northern Syria, Naucratis in Egypt and Cyrene on the coast of Libya (Cyrenaica). Al Mina and Naucratis did not have the status of independent cities but were permanent settlements without political sovereignty. Cyrene was a city.

AL MINA IN SYRIA

This was sited at the mouth of the Orontes river, in northern Syria. The region was dominated first by the Urartu kingdom, then, after 740 BC, by the Assyrians, two important civilizations the Greeks could not rival.

The first Greeks to settle at Al Mina came from the island of Euboea and the Cycladic islands. They were looking for iron and copper ore, needed for the manufacture of both tools and weapons. They maintained a continuous presence here from the middle of the eighth century until the beginning of the seventh century, at which point Al Mina was destroyed by the Assyrians. During the seventh century trade started up again, most of the Greeks involved now being from the cities of Asia Minor, in particular Miletus. In the sixth century activity on this site slowed down, but it picked up again at the end of the sixth century, when the Athenians became involved in trade there.

Al Mina was not a *polis* but rather a trading post based on a port, where business was done between a number of communities all organized in different ways. It was what the Greeks called an *emporion*. Its existence depended upon the good will of the local powers. The *emporion* had no political autonomy.

NAUCRATIS IN EGYPT

This was sited in the Nile delta. The Greeks – seafarers and traders – are said to have been established there by one of the twelve kings of the delta, Psammetichus I, at the end of the seventh century BC, but Naucratis was granted its special status under the reign of the Pharaoh Amasis, in the mid-sixth century. The Greeks had the right to trade and also to have their own sanctuaries. We know that the Milesians had a temple of Apollo, the Samians a temple of Hera, the Aeginetans a temple of Zeus. A sanctuary known as the *Hellenion* was dependent on the representatives of nine different cities, all situated on the coasts of Asia Minor: Chios, Teos, Phocaea, Clazomenae, Mytilene, Rhodes, Cnidus, Halicarnassus and Phaselis: a relatively rare example of a pan-Hellenic sanctuary.

The representatives of those same nine cities chose nine officials to supervise activities in the port. The Greeks came for cereals, which Egypt was then producing in great abundance, and, to a lesser degree, also for papyrus, linen and ivory objects, bringing in exchange pottery, wine, oil and silver. Naucratis was an *emporion*, a place for trade between two societies with different economic systems. We do not know precisely how this trading was organized but, if we are to believe Herodotus, the *emporion* seems to have enjoyed a monopoly:

Naucratis was the only port in Egypt, and anyone who brought a ship into any of the other mouths of the Nile was bound to state that he did so of necessity, and then proceed to the Canopic mouth; should contrary winds prevent him from doing so, he had to carry his freight to Naucratis in barges all round the Delta, which shows the exclusive privilege the port enjoyed.

The question outstanding is whether Naucratis had the status of a *polis*. Probably not, but the site continued to develop throughout the sixth century, its prosperity attracting craftsmen, artists, writers and poets. Naucratis became a town renowned in the Greek world for its luxury, up until the Persian conquest of this part of Egypt in 525.

CYRENE

The case of Cyrene was altogether different. It was a *polis* founded by the people of Thera, one of the Cycladic islands: Cyrene was situated in a region where the local power was not strong enough to oppose the creation of a sovereign city. It lay on the coast to the north of what is now Libya. The region was inhabited by African and Berber peoples organized

Oath of the founders of Cyrene

(This inscription found in Cyrene was carved in the fourth century BC. It reproduces the much more ancient text of a Theran decree.)

It has pleased the assembly. Given that Apollo has himself ordered Battus and the Therans to colonize Cyrene, it has pleased the Therans to decide to send Battus to Cyrene as founder and king; that the Therans will set sail with him; that they will sail in conditions of complete equality for every family; that one son will be chosen from every family; that those who sail shall be in the prime of life; that among the Therans any free man may, if he wishes, accompany them; if the colonists become masters of the colony, that those of their compatriots who land later on shall share the rights and honours of citizenship and receive a parcel of land taken from vacant fields; if the colonists do not become masters of the colony and the Therans cannot send them help and if within five years they are forced to, they may return from that country to Thera to their own estates and recover their rights of citizenship. Whoever refuses to sail when the city sends him shall be liable to the death penalty and have his possessions confiscated. Whoever takes him in or protects him, be he a father to his son, or a brother to his brother, shall be punished in the same way as the one who refuses to sail. According to these conditions, oaths have been exchanged by those who are remaining here and those who are sailing away to found the colony and they have cursed those who ever transgress these conditions and do not obey them, whether they be among those living in Libya or those remaining here. Having made wax statues, they burned them, pronouncing the following curse in the presence of all gathered together, men, women, boys and girls: whoever does not honour these oaths and transgresses them, let him melt and dissolve like these statues, he and his race and his property. Whoever does honour these oaths, let much good come to him and his descendants. (*Suppl. Epigr. Gr.*, IX, 3)

into tribes. They were herdsmen, with a few settlements in the oases. The history of the foundation of Cyrene is not exceptional, except that it is better documented than many others, thanks to the ancient sources. It provides an example of the kind of tentative procedures that must have preceded the creation of any new city. Around the mid-seventh century the city of Thera consulted the Delphic oracle, following a period of famine, and Apollo advised it to found a new city in Libya. The people of Thera engaged the services of a Cretan sailor, as they did not know the region, and set off under a leader who was later to take the name Battus. At first they settled on an island not far off the coast, then moved on to a first spot on the mainland before eventually discovering the definitive site of Cyrene.

The *oikiste* became the first king, Battus, and was succeeded by his son Arcesilaus. If the texts are to be believed, under the reign of the latter the Greeks of Cyrene were all descended from the first 200 emigrants, and relations with local peoples were good. The first religious edifices (temples) and civic ones (agora) were built. A second group of Greek emigrants, not solely from Thera, arrived in about 580, at the request of the new king Battus II, who promised each of the newcomers a plot of land. But this time the land was taken from the territory of the local natives and this provoked the first conflict between the Libyans, supported by the Egyptian Pharaoh, and the Greeks, who were victorious (in the Battle of Iasa, in about 570). The early years of the city of Cyrene provide a good example of the difficulties inherent in the creation of any new city, the role of the oracle, the loosening ties with the metropolis, the initially good then deteriorating relations with the natives, and the principal aim of such foundations: the agricultural exploitation of new land, distributed equally between the Greek emigrants in such a way as to escape from the endemic cycle of unequal possession of the land, overpopulation and famine.

THE NORTH-EAST OF THE AEGEAN SEA AND THE BLACK SEA

A very large number of new cities were founded in this region. It is not possible to list them all or to describe their foundations in detail. However, it might be useful to take this chance to locate cities that will be repeatedly mentioned in the history of the archaic, classical and Hellenistic periods. Three geographical regions can be distinguished.

THE NORTHERN COAST OF THE AEGEAN

This region, with a heavier rainfall and a cooler climate, possessed fertile plains and mineral resources. It was inhabited by a number of peoples, all classed as Thracians. In the absence of documentation, it is impossible to discover the precise details of the foundation of the new cities in Thracian Chalcidice (the three-pronged peninsula that juts into the Aegean Sea), established as early as the eighth century by Chalcis and Eretria (Torone, Mende, Scione, Methone). The island of *Thasos* was occupied by Thracians at the time when the people of Paros created a city there in about 680, then established themselves on the Thracian coast opposite the island in the region known as Thasian Peraea. Samos founded the city of *Samothrace* on a large nearby island in the sixth century. Potidaea in Chalcidice was the daughter-city of Corinth and dated from the time of the tyrant Periander (about 600).

The smallest of these cities had a hard struggle establishing themselves in the face of well-organized local peoples.

THE PROPONTIS

This is the region between the Black Sea and the Aegean Sea, contained to the north by the Bosphorus straits and to the south by the Hellespont straits (now the Dardanelles). Here two Greek cities, Miletus and Megara, played major roles, for different reasons. Miletus was a very powerful city on the coast of Asia Minor, whose development inland was thwarted by the presence of the Persian Empire. It accordingly turned to the Propontis, where it founded *Cyzicus* in about 750, *Parium* in about 700 and *Abydus* in about 675. Megara, squeezed between Athens and Corinth, had insufficient agricultural resources and was unable to extend its territory. Hence its presence in the Bosphorus region. It founded *Byzantium* in about 660, *Chalcedon* in 687, and *Selymbria* and *Astacus* before 675. Miletus, already an active sea-power, was the principal trader in this part of the Greek world.

THE BLACK SEA

Its ancient name was the Euxine Sea. All its coasts were occupied by Greek cities founded during the second wave of expansion, from 650 BC onward, mostly by Miletus (except for *Heraclaea Pontica* and *Messembria* founded by Megara, and *Phanagoria* founded by Teos). For a long time it was thought that these cities were founded for purely commercial purposes, particularly for the sake of obtaining supplies of products much needed by the Greek world: wheat, wood, fish, metals. If that was so, these cities would have started as simple trading posts, of the same *emporion* type as Al Mina and Naucratis, described above, and would have developed only later as autonomous entities. Nowadays, scholars tend to stress the complementarity of agriculture and trade right from the earliest days of these cities. That they were new population centres just as much as trading posts has been shown clearly in, for example, the case of Olbia.

For geographical and climatic reasons, new cities were more numerous on the west and north coasts of the Black Sea, situated at the mouths of rivers that provided them with both protected ports and also access by river to the interior. Working along the Black Sea coast from the south-west to the south-east, the peoples already living here were the Thracians, the Getae, the Scythians, the Tauri, the Colchians in the Caucasus and the Maryandinians. Herodotus describes them as warrior peoples, nomads, with very different customs from the Greeks, who forced the Greek cities to remain constantly on their guard although, as the centuries passed, contacts did develop between the different civilizations and peoples.

On the south coast   Sinope was the principal and most ancient city founded by Miletus (on an isthmus between a peninsula and the mainland) in about 650. On this site, as on others (Istrus, Berezan), Greek pottery of a much earlier date has been found, but the first Greek contacts did not necessarily take place when the new cities were founded. The Greeks may have been frequenting the site for close on a century before deciding to establish themselves there definitively.

Heraclaea Pontica was the only city in this zone founded by Megara and the people of Boeotia, in about 560, on a site that had the makings of a good port and also a fertile hinterland. This city reduced the local population of Maryandinians to a rural slavery similar to that imposed upon the helots by the Spartans, but promised not to sell them on abroad. The very earliest political regime of this city is said to have been a democracy, a notable exception in the archaic period.

Amisus and *Trapezus* were two other cities of importance on this coast.

On the west coast   Working from the south to the north, one finds the cities of *Apollonia* (610), *Messembria* (510), *Odessus* (575), *Callatis* (540), *Tomi* (550) and *Istrus* (650). The most ancient of these, Istrus, founded by Miletus, was destroyed by the Scythians at the end of the sixth century. When it was rebuilt, in the fifth century, it was surrounded by ramparts.

On the north coast   Working from the west eastward, we find *Tyras, Olbia* (646) and *Berezan, Chersonese* (about 550), *Theodosia, Panticapaea* (600), *Tanais* (600) and *Phanagoria* (545). The case of Olbia, better known than most thanks to recent excavations there, will serve as an example to help us to understand the development of cities in this region.

Olbia was founded not far from the double estuary formed by the Borysthenes (Dnieper) and the Hypanis (Bug) rivers. A *liman* was the name given to such a river estuary with lagoons partly closed off by the coastline. Milesians also settled on the small island of Berezan, at the mouth of the Borysthenes, and in several spots on the estuary shores. The combination of these settlements made up the city of Olbia, named after one of those sites, and for a long time the Greeks continued to speak of the 'men of the Borysthenes' when they meant the citizens of Olbia, a fact that in itself indicates that the city comprised several settlements in the area. The land between the various estuaries formed the city territory.

Olbia proper started as a village and only very gradually took on the aspect of a town, in the course of the sixth century. There were two parts to it: an upper area on a plateau 40 metres above sea level, and a lower area on the banks of the Hypanis estuary, now partly submerged by the sea. The public zone of the town (agora, sanctuaries) in the upper part was built in the second half of the sixth century. In the fifth century the town was surrounded by ramparts. A city such as this could only survive if it came to a suitable understanding with its powerful neighbours, the Scythians.

The river valleys made it possible for Greek products to be carried further inland (pottery, weapons and other metal objects, wine and oil) and exchanged for cereals, salt, fish and slaves, as later texts testify. One of the functions of Olbia and the other cities in this region was to serve as trading posts, but the archaeological discovery of granaries for cereals, animal bones and fish skeletons proves that agriculture, hunting and fishing were also practised. There are also signs of handicrafts. Olbia and its neighbours were thus cities with multiple activities and functions, as was to be expected in a world in which self-sufficiency was the principal mode of survival.

The Greeks settled in the extreme east of the Mediterranean world later than in the west, where many cities date from the first movement of Greek expansion in the Mediterranean.

SOUTHERN ITALY AND SICILY

Before the Greeks settled definitively in these regions, certain sites were visited by them on an occasional and temporary basis which, however, does not really justify a label of 'pre-colonization'. The most ancient Greek settlement dates from the mid-eighth century, on the island of Ischia, off the coast of Campania, opposite the entrance to the Gulf of Naples. Let us consider the new cities of southern Italy first, then those of Sicily.

PITHECUSSAE

Situated on the island of Ischia (in what is now known as the Gulf of Naples), Pithecussae was the most ancient Greek settlement in the region. According to the literary tradition, the island was rich in both agricultural products and goldsmiths' work. The founders came from Chalcis and Eretria in Euboea. The excavations carried out by the archaeologist Buchner reveal a community of the early archaic period, which is very rare. The occupations of this community, whose settlement has been excavated, were craftsmanship and trading. The craftsmen worked with metal (iron and precious metals) and locally produced pottery with geometric ornamentation in which human figures are sometimes represented, showing seafaring and shipwreck scenes. One of these vases bears the most ancient potter's signature known. The tombs of the nearby necropolis contain objects from every corner of the Mediterranean. Pithecussae's status was that of an *emporion* where foreign products as well as foreign merchants circulated. Pithecussae was governed by groups of aristocrats, shipowners, craftsmen, even pirates: an aristocracy whose lifestyle was already characterized by the importance of banquets.

Among the funerary furniture found in the tomb of a young boy or girl, aged about 10, a wine cup of Rhodian origin was found. (The island of

Rhodes is situated off the south coast of Asia Minor.) It dates from the third half of the eighth century and is engraved with the most ancient verse inscription known in the Greek world. It runs as follows: 'It is agreeable to drink from Nestor's cup, but whoever drinks from this cup is instantly seized by the desire of Aphrodite with the fine crown.'

A quarter of a century later, Chalcidians and Cumaeans (probably from Kyme, in Asia Minor) founded the city of Cumae on the mainland. The site was already occupied by native populations and the establishment of the city was not peaceful. In this case, the foundation bears all the marks of a *polis*, with an *oikiste*, boundaries marked out for an agricultural territory and the establishment of civic institutions.

There are a number of possible ways of classifying the rest of the Greek cities of southern Italy: by the provenance of the first colonists (essentially Euboea, the Peloponnese, Phocaea in Asia Minor); by the chronology of the foundations; or by the regions of southern Italy. The commentary that follows will be fuller for some than for others, where their history incorporates elements that help to throw light on the phenomenon of Greek expansion generally.

THE COAST OF THE TYRRHENIAN SEA

In the Iron Age, the Sele plain was inhabited by indigenous peoples, particularly around the sites of Pontecagnano and Arenosola. Upon the arrival of Greeks from the city of Sybaris (Sybarites), the natives withdrew further inland. The Sybarites established an *emporion* at *Agropoli* and founded a city, *Posidonia*, at the beginning of the sixth century. The frontiers of its territory were marked out by three sanctuaries: a sanctuary of Poseidon to the south (at Agropoli), a sanctuary of Hera to the north (at the mouth of the Sele river) and a sanctuary of Artemis inland, on the edge of the agricultural territory (the *chora*). That is worth noting, for it illustrates the role played by the establishment of sanctuaries in the constitution of a city's territory. The gods marked out the limits of the territory, legitimated it and guarded it.

Elea, further to the south, was founded by people from Phocaea in Asia Minor, in about 540, at a spot theoretically inhabited by the Oenotri. This city was to become the refuge of philosophers known as the Eleatics: Xenophanes in the sixth century, later Parmenides, Melissus and Zeno (around 490–445).

Pixus and *Laus* were both founded by Sybaris, and the south of the Tyrrhenian Sea was settled by cities founded by Locri, which was no more than a day's march away. Its territory was poor and mountainous and its aristocracy of a few hundred families was very closed. There were reasons enough – economic, political and topographical – for them to settle on more fertile land in three new cities: *Metaurus* (before 650), then *Medma* and *Hipponium* (early sixth century).

At the southernmost tip of the toe of the Italian boot was the city of Rhegium, founded by Chalcis (in 730). Its history is inseparable from that of Zancle, also a Chalcidian foundation, on the opposite side of the Straits of Messina, in Sicily. The unity of the straits was above all commercial. The ports here were visited by first Chalcidians, then Etruscans, then eventually Phocaeans, all in quest of commodities and objects to trade in the Far East. But these straits also marked the dividing line between the Ionian Sea, which was Greek, and the Tyrrhenian Sea, which for a long time remained a foreign sea. The intermediary position of the two cities, particularly Rhegium, produced fortunate consequences so far as civilization was concerned. Chalcidian pots from the workshops of Rhegium, bronzes (possibly including the Vix Vase) and motifs of earthenware decoration all testify to the synthesis of a variety of influences. In the field of legislation too, Rhegium played a pioneering role when it adopted the laws of the legislator Charondas (of Catana) as early as the late seventh century, and also an oligarchic constitution in which power was shared by the richest.

THE COAST OF THE IONIAN SEA

Locri, on the east coast of Calabria, was founded by the Ozolian Locrians of central Greece (in about 680). The position of the classical city is known, but not that of its archaic site. Moving northward up the coast, the next city is *Caulonia*, founded by the inhabitants of Achaea in the Peloponnese (around 650), who also founded *Croton* (709). The coast here offered a potential site for a port and, right from the start, the town was built according to a regular plan and the plain to its south was exploited agriculturally. *Sybaris*, to the north, was situated further inland, in a rich agricultural plain bordered by two rivers. It had a tragic history: after being founded in about 720, in 510 it was totally destroyed by its neighbour Croton. Its inhabitants nevertheless remained forever famous for their luxurious lifestyle, as the adjective 'sybaritic' testifies. *Siris* was further to the north, founded by people from Colophon in Ionia (Asia Minor) between 680 and 650. Its precise site in a plain that is still fertile and well-irrigated is not certain.

Metapontum, between the Bradano and Basento rivers, founded by people from Achaea after 650, is a city where excavations have made it easier to understand how the new arrivals divided up the urban and rural space. In the town, the first signs of a grid-system date from the mid-seventh century. The whole of the area enclosed by ramparts was divided into squares by great avenues 12.60 metres wide, running from east to west, and secondary streets 6 metres wide marking out rectangular blocks of 35 by 160 metres. As soon as the city was founded, a public zone was reserved for sanctuaries and the agora. The plan shows four large temples, one smaller one and a number of altars. The temples, all dating from different periods, were built alongside one another, without it being necessary to knock an old one down to make room for a new one. Clearly, an extremely large space had from the start been left available. To the east the sanctuaries adjoined the agora and the theatre, also elements of the public space for common use. Two temples were consecrated to Apollo (one built in the seventh century, the other at the end of the sixth) and two to Hera (one built in the sixth century, the other in the fifth).

In the territory, the *chora* (cultivated land), which lay between the two rivers, was divided into regular bands separated by ditches that formed boundaries 210 metres apart. Many farms were situated in the *chora*, which had clearly been carefully allotted, just as the town land had. The separate parcels of land show up very clearly on the aerial photographs that played a role of capital importance in the study of the space of Metapontum. Each allotment was of about 5 or 6 hectares. This constitutes archaeological proof of an egalitarian division of land among the city's first inhabitants, a division that answered the same purpose as the very foundation of a new city, namely to make sure of enough agricultural land to avoid famine.

Tarentum was the only city to have Sparta as its metropolis, along with a foundation history that in itself constitutes a whole novel. The founders of Tarentum are supposed to have been a minority that was regarded as undesirable in Sparta: the Partheniae. According to one of the several coexisting traditions, the Spartans who went off to wage war against the Messenians swore not to return until the war was won. It dragged on for so long that a problem arose as to the renewal of the generations. The youths who had been too young to swear the oath at the beginning of the war were sent back to Sparta under orders to sleep with all the girls, who thus produced children who had no idea who their fathers were. Their name, the 'Partheniae', drew attention to the fact that their only known affiliation was with whichever girl (*parthenos*) was their mother. Different Greek authors give different accounts of the status of the fathers of these children. According to some they were Spartan youths, as in this version; according to others they were slaves (helots) or citizens who had lost their rights as a result of showing cowardice in war. But all the versions have one point in common, which is that the fathers were marginals in the city of Sparta. When they grew to adulthood, the Partheniae were not integrated among the citizens of Sparta. They had no choice but to go into exile. This foundation story, which presents an upside-down world in which women play a dominant role alongside men who are not citizens, was a way for the Greeks to show how very difficult beginnings could be. The same theme reappears in a variety of forms in several other stories about the foundation of new cities.

Callipolis seems to have been the last city situated on this coast.

SICILY

In Sicily, as elsewhere, the Greeks founded new cities in two phases. As many of the later cities here were founded by the earlier ones, we shall be following a chronological order rather than a geographical one as above.

In the eighth century Naxos, on the east coast of Sicily, was founded by the people of Chalcis in 734 (texts and archaeology are in agreement on the date), on a peninsula site to the north of Etna, where there was scant scope for agricultural exploitation. For that reason, the *oikiste*, Theocles, soon created another city further to the south: *Leontini* (in about 726), inland from the coast on a site comprising six hills. The third Chalcidian city to be founded was sited in between the first two. This was *Catana*, in a plain that was extremely fertile, thanks to its deposits of lava from the volcano of Etna.

This region was inhabited by Sicels, who continued to live there after the arrival of the Greeks, apparently without conflict. Historians stress the pacific nature of the Greeks' installation in this spot. Things went differently in Syracuse.

Syracuse was founded by people from Corinth in 733, led by Archias, who belonged to the Bacchiad family then in power in Corinth. The site included an island, Ortygia, which made it possible to build two well-protected ports. The plain bordered by the Anapus river was fertile. There the Greeks installed themselves, controlling a large territory seized from the Sicels who, in this case, were pushed further inland. Gradually, the Greeks also pushed inland, setting up the city of *Acrae* overlooking the Anapus valley. Its function was no doubt to keep an eye on the emplacements of the Sicels, including that of Pantelica, which seems to have been abandoned at about this time.

Megara Hyblaea was situated on the same coast, to the north of Syracuse. It was founded by Megarians who seem not to have been citizens of Megara, around the mid-eighth century. Legend has it that it owed the second part of its name to the Sicel king, Hyblon, who ceded the place to the Greeks. After a few hesitations, a site was chosen on the edge of a well-irrigated coastal plain that had no defensive features and afforded no possibility of building a protected port. Right from the start the city adopted a systematic and well-organized plan, as excavations carried out there have revealed. Major axes 5 metres wide and secondary ones 3 metres wide ran from north to south, carving out blocks 25 by 125 metres, where houses were built. In the seventh century the empty spaces were gradually filled, and in the second half of this century an agora was created, bordered on the east and the north by porticoes, on the south by two temples, and on the west giving on to various buildings of a religious or civic nature (such as the *prytaneum*). The whole complex testifies splendidly to these new cities' determination right from the start to perform certain political, religious and economic functions.

Finally *Zancle*, already mentioned in connection with Rhegium, was established on the northern tip of the island between 750 and 725. Its first inhabitants came from Cumae and from Chalcis, as is reflected in its tradition of two *oikistes*. It was a good site for a port but lacked cultivable land. Zancle's position on the Straits of Messina (the name that it adopted a little later) led it to play an important role as an intermediary in trade between the East and the West.

After 700 a number of other cities were established on the southern coast of Sicily.

Gela was founded by the Rhodians and the Cretans in about 680. It immediately found itself in conflict with the local populations installed on the rich plain that it intended to take over. To protect its territory, Gela embarked upon the conquest of the interior and established a number of fortified strongholds that were gradually to turn into cities. In about 580 Gela and Rhodes together founded *Agrigentum*, 60 kilometres further west, on a hilly site 3 kilometres from the sea.

Selinus, still further to the west, daughter-city to Megara Hyblaea, built its settlement on a hill bordered by two rivers, right on the sea coast. It appears to have been on good terms with the Elymi, the natives of the region, and even – if we are to believe Thucydides – concluded an agreement of intermarriage with the people living in Segesta. At this date, this region of Sicily was controlled by the Carthaginians, and only one other city made its appearance, on the north-western coast: *Himera*, where Chalcidians from Zancle settled, along with a noble family exiled from Syracuse, in about 625. The town comprised an upper part on the hills overlooking the Himera river and a lower part on the river mouth, with a port. It was an advantageous position for both agriculture and trading, both by sea and with the interior by way of the river valley.

Most of the cities founded in southern Italy and Sicily were essentially agricultural, and concern to defend their territories sometimes brought them into conflict with local populations also accustomed to cultivate the fertile coastal plains. This general model was very different from that of the cities of the Far West, for the most part founded by the city of Phocaea in Asia Minor.

THE WESTERN MEDITERRANEAN OR THE 'FAR WEST' . . .

The two principal cities here were *Massilia* (Marseilles) and *Emporiae*, on the coast of Spain. They should be considered within the wider context of the Phocaean cities as a whole. Phocaea, a city of Asia Minor, destroyed by the Persians in 545, had no inland territory and was mainly active at sea. By the end of the seventh century, but even more decisively after its destruction, it was founding settlements in the western Mediterranean such as Aleria (Alalia) in Corsica, Gravisca in Etruria, Elea (Velia) in southern Italy, and was also playing an increasingly important part in sea trade. In the Gulf of Lyons, trade had until this time been in the hands of the Etruscans (the wine trade, for instance, as is proved by large quantities of wine amphorae in the area) and the Carthaginians (more amphorae). For the next few decades a number of different trading currents existed until the Phocaeans gained the upper hand between 580 and 550, depending on the regions.

MARSEILLES

The city, Massilia, was founded at the turn of the seventh and sixth centuries.

A foundation myth Three texts, by Strabo, Athenaeus and Justin, recount the myth of the foundation of the city, of how a Phocaean married the daughter of a local king, who picked him out to be her husband by offering him a cup of wine (or water, depending on the version of the story) during a banquet. The guest thus became the king's son-in-law and was given a piece of land to found a town. This story, like so many other parallel ones, represents a way of telling of the implantation of the Greeks in an indigenous land and of thinking through how two communities came together. We should not look for historical authenticity in these stories. Myths are not condensed versions of historical happenings. But stories such as these may also help in the writing of history, or at least of the history of the modes of thought of those who created them. Nothing is random in these texts: the Greeks, in a group, faced with the king; the bonds of hospitality; the moment chosen (a wedding banquet); the way in which the choice is made, with the amazing freedom left to the girl, in a manner totally contrary to Greek custom. At the origin of the city there is a marriage and a political agreement: the story is a way of legitimating the arrival of the Greeks and generating a mixed population that is half Greek and half indigenous.

The territory of Marseilles was not very large. It was defended by fortified bastions such as those in the present quarter of Saint-Blaise and Saint-Marcel. Recent excavations in the town have revealed its Hellenistic topography mainly, but the limits of the archaic city have also been determined.

A study of the pottery found there has made it possible to work out a detailed chronology and the destinations of traded goods, for trade was the real cause of the city's prosperity in the sixth century.

Maritime *trade* with the coasts of Spain, *Emporiae* in particular, with Languedoc and with Etruria, which in the sixth century was at first prosperous, declined around 500. Overland trade with the Celtic countries was also developed in the sixth century, by way of the Rhône valley as far as Burgundy, and in the Jura. But this too came to a halt in about 500, and at this point Marseilles sank into a definite decline. The causes of this halt in trade can be traced to the disturbances that affected the Celtic world at the end of the Halstatt civilization, which disorganized exchanges with northern Gaul. It was in this period that Mount Lassois, the site of Vix, was abandoned, after being an important centre for trade between natives and Greeks. The great bronze crater possibly made in the workshops of Rhegium was found in a princely tomb in Vix. The interruption of trade

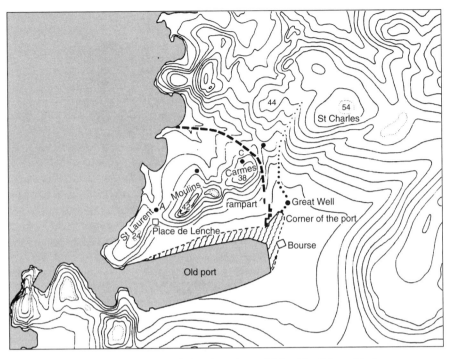

Figure 11   Plan of the situation of Massilia (Marseilles)

seems to have affected, among other products, the tin that was indispensable for the manufacture of bronze, for the people of Marseilles had opened
up an overland route for fetching tin from Cornwall (by way of the Channel, the Seine valley, upper Burgundy and the Sâone–Rhône axis). The
more ancient maritime route by way of the Straits of Gibraltar and the
Atlantic coast of the Iberian peninsula was in the hands of the Phoenicians
and the Carthaginians. But other goods were also exchanged with inland
regions: iron, spices, wheat and slaves, although such trading links were
not necessarily regular.

The Phocaean city of Marseilles presents an example of a different type
of new city, whose prosperity depended not so much on cultivating the
land but rather on trading with neighbouring and more distant peoples. It
played an intermediary role that made it possible for the Greek world to
acquire regular supplies of products indispensable to it and to export the
products characteristic of Hellenism to peoples far away, who were not
direct neighbours of the Greeks.

From Al Mina to Emporiae and from Cyrene to Olbia at the end of the
archaic period, such were the limits of this world peopled with Greek cities.
There were, of course, considerable differences between on one hand isolated cities that were, so to speak, the outposts of Hellenism, on the coast

63

Figure 12   The Vix Crater (Musée de Châtillon-sur-Seine;
photo: Roger-Viollet, Paris)

of Africa or in the 'Far West', and cities cheek by jowl in the Peloponnese
or on some tiny Cycladic island; because of the nature of our sources, the
history of the following two centuries has most to say about the old cities.
But the archaic adventure had lasting consequences for the history of the
Greek world, not least upon the archaic world itself.

THE CONSEQUENCES

The first and possibly the most important consequence was *the discovery
of different peoples*, speaking other languages and with other civilizations,
and learning how to coexist with them. A few years ago all that would
have been expected at this point would have been a few remarks about
Hellenization, as if there could not have been any real exchange between
the Greeks, the bringers of culture, and other peoples, reputed to be barely
civilized. Since them, more emphasis has been laid on the unfortunate

consequences of the Greek models imposed upon indigenous cultures, as a result of which local societies seem to have lost their own cultures in the process of becoming 'acculturized'. Today, because more is known now about some of the features of the non-Greek civilizations, the tendency is to underline the variety of local situations by reason of the diversity of the indigenous and Greek traditions, and the overall enrichment that resulted not only for the indigenous peoples but also for the Greeks when their cultures met. Within the confines of the present work, it is not possible to describe those indigenous cultures, but the bibliography indicates a number of possible lines of reading in that domain.

The second consequence was *the extension of the 'city way of life'*, that is to say both the diffusion of a particular form of political organization and a predilection for an urban form of life that was new to the indigenous societies and that the Greeks brought with them, along with all the social customs inseparable from it. But in the new cities nothing could be exactly the same as in the mother-cities and, plunged as they were into different circumstances, the new cities naturally enough were innovative. It was a new world.

The third consequence was *a capacity for invention*: in this respect it was the new cities that now led the way in a number of areas. There are many examples, as has been pointed out. The first legislators, men who set down laws in writing and tried to create a social and political equilibrium, put their knowledge to work in the new cities: Zaleucus in Locri, Charondas in Catana. The division of land, both out in the city territory and in the town, and the first attempts at what we should call 'town planning' took place at Metapontum, Megara Hyblaea . . . etc. What is particularly interesting about this town planning is the distinction observed right from the start between a public zone, for sanctuaries and collective institutions, and a private zone left for dwellings. The Greek cities of the West were constantly innovative in a whole number of fields: in philosophy, with Pythagoras and the Eleatics, in lyric poetry with Stesichorus of Himera, in textual criticism with Theagenes of Rhegium – one could give many more examples – and in religious life with the importance acquired by Orphism . . . Even if Greece proper was the geographic hub of the Greek world, it was on its periphery that the motivating centre of the Greek archaic world was to be found, particularly in Magna Graecia, as has been stressed by the historian E. Greco, in *Archeologia della Magna Graecia* (1992).

Following the expeditions of the first colonists, this new world established communications between East and West; trading routes were consolidated and goods circulated. *The creation of Greek trade* in the Mediterranean was the most immediate consequence of these migrations. Although the products exchanged, the overland and the sea routes, and the origins of the cargoes are quite well known, thanks to archaeology, the structures of all this trading are more difficult to seize: the exact volume, rhythm and modalities of trade, the men who were in charge, the respective volumes of trade in useful products and luxury goods, the switch from aristocratic self-sufficiency trading to trading effected by professional merchants. Here is one example of the problem: bartering was the rule, but according to what laws? It is impossible to understand the forms taken by these exchanges without relating them constantly to the groups of men involved: the history of archaic trade is also a history of piracy, of luxury and of the practice of gift-giving and counter-giving by which the aristocratic elites were welded together.

The indirect consequences of all this trading are also important for our understanding of the way that the archaic Greek societies evolved in a wide range of sectors ranging from the vitality of craft workshops to the acquisition of wealth by slave-traders. A study of the internal history of the cities will provide a more accurate picture of the economic consequences of the opening up of the Mediterranean world to Greek ships, but two factors are immediately obvious: it was the foundation of new cities that stimulated trade and, in consequence, also craftsmanship, not the reverse, and even the cities most deeply involved in trading, such as Corinth, Phocaea and Athens, did not acquire a trading supremacy. Their originality lay elsewhere. The time has come to trace the historical evolution of the regions and cities of the archaic world about which most is known.

THE FORMS OF POWER

ARISTOCRATIC OLIGARCHIES

Because of the nature of the sources at our disposal, essentially not much is known of the social and political evolution of the Greek cities in the archaic period. As we have seen, archaeology makes it possible to come to recognize an urban landscape, the evolution of a sanctuary, the changes that affected necropolises, and to trace the movements of the products of a particular city around the Mediterranean, but it tells us nothing about the institutional structures, the status of individuals, or the events that took place from day to day. The archaic literary texts are for the most part lyric poems that provide indications as to the historical context only in an allusive and episodic fashion; and epigraphical texts are rare. Essentially, our sources consist of the testimony of authors writing after the archaic period. From Herodotus to Strabo, and including Aristotle, none of these authors is trustworthy, for frequently they use the archaic period as a means of explaining and justifying the history of their own times or, in the case of the philosophers, their own constitutional theories. Today's historians read these testimonies with a critical eye that leads them to question the truth of what, only a few years ago, were presented as unquestionable elements of archaic history; they wonder, for example, how sweeping Solon's reforms in Athens really were. These same historians now tend to sift out the information in our possession, separating what seems to them to be plausible – data concerning the political, economic and social life – from what appears to them to be total invention – anything to do with the behaviour of individuals. But even if the Greeks of later centuries did reconstruct the history of the archaic period, there is no reason why their work should not have touched upon the entire range of historical domains. These preliminary remarks are not intended to lead to an absolute pessimism claiming that nothing can be said for certain where archaic history is concerned, for that would be an exaggeration. All the same, we should bear in mind the very real problems and the many dead ends that historians encounter in this territory, as a result of which the archaic history of the Greek world is neither continuous nor all-encompassing. It can only proceed in a succession of flashes of perception, and it raises more questions than it provides certain answers.

By the time the Greek archaic communities were being established in the eighth century, the power of decision no longer rested with a single individual, the king or *basileus*, but lay in the hands of the landowning families that also provided the community with its armed defenders. Legendary accounts tell of how power shifted from a single individual (monarchy) to a small number of men (oligarchy), but it is not possible to put a date to that shift, which also varied from one city to another. There is very little known historical data, but the documentation regarding Corinth is exceptional.

CORINTH: THE BACCHIAD FAMILY

At the end of the eighth century the territory of Corinth extended to the north of the isthmus, to the detriment of that of Megara. Already in 740 the Corinthians were building a temple to Hera in the sanctuary of Perachora, and by about 700 they had ports on both the Gulf of Corinth (Oenoe) and the Saronic Gulf (Crommyon), and were building a temple to Poseidon on the isthmus. Corinth thus controlled this waterway on both sides, both the north–south route between central Greece and the Peloponnese and the route passing from east to west. There was only a short distance of overland porterage to be covered between the ports situated on the two gulfs where ships unloaded their cargoes. The city also possessed both agricultural land and pasturage and, in the seventh century, it was regarded as the most prosperous city in Greece. As we have seen, it founded new cities such as Corcyra and Syracuse. It built battleships and it also played an important part in the trade that developed following the first phase of Greek expansion in the Mediterranean. Corinth diffused models from the East; it was the creative centre of art of eastern inspiration and produced high-quality pottery that was traded everywhere from Al Mina across to the West.

From the mid-eighth to the mid-seventh century, power in the city was held by one family, one *genos*, the Bacchiads. One of our sources here is Herodotus (V, 92): 'The government of Corinth was once an oligarchy: one clan, the Bacchiadae – who intermarried only among themselves – were in power there.' We know from other sources that this family comprised 200 members, that each year it elected to the principal magistracy one of them who, according to the texts, then bore the name of 'king' or '*prytanis*', that the family monopolized all the city responsibilities, including the post of polemarch, and that it practised a strict endogamy. Presumably the '200' formed an assembly, but nothing is said about this. The Bacchiads may have been just one of the families that made up the aristocracy of Corinth, but it should be pointed out that the figure 200 certainly comprised only the adult males, so the entire family community must have numbered over a thousand individuals. Nothing is known of the exact forms of the city's institutions and government or of the status of the rest of the town's inhabitants.

The power of this family depended upon wealth still mostly in the form of real estate. E. Will (in his *Korinthiaka*, Paris, 1955) has shown that the Bacchiads were neither shipbuilders nor traders, let alone industrialists, but landowners who made a profit out of the trade for which the city territory was the centre, in particular by levying tolls. Like any other aristocratic family, it took part in the movement of Mediterranean expansion: as we have seen, the *oikiste* of Syracuse was a Bacchiad.

The Bacchiads of Corinth were thus in the same mould as other aristocratic families about which we know nothing but the names derived from their status: the Hippeis (knights), the Hippobotai, the Geomoroi ('those who divide the land between them' or, as the poet Hesiod calls them, the 'Fat Ones'). Politically, the powers held by these oligarchies are ill defined and it is only through assimilation with what happened later on that the terms council, assembly and magistracies are used. Citizenship was not yet an abstract category that could be extrapolated from collective practices. As we shall see later, it was a particular lifestyle that marked out the status of citizen, rather than the other way about.

There are, however, two cities about which more is known, although their examples cannot be generalized to the archaic aristocratic regimes as a whole. They are Sparta and Athens.

SPARTA

Sparta's territory in the Peloponnese was put together gradually, starting from the plain of Laconia and the synoecism of four villages (Pitana, Mesoa, Limnai, Kynosoura), in the course of successive annexations of territories all the way out to the plain of Messenia, beyond Mount Taygetus, at the end of the eighth century. A bellicose process of conquest marked the internal history of the city right down to the day when, at the beginning of the fourth century, the people of Messenia recovered their liberty and set about refounding the city of Messene. Sparta thus had a larger territory than most Greek cities and the fact that it did not enjoy easy access to the sea (the port of Gytheum was 35 kilometres south of Sparta) made it a city turned essentially inward on to its lands and the exploitation thereof.

The history of Sparta poses particular problems: first, by reason of the nature of the sources. Most of the literary sources are not of Spartan origin and many are decidedly partisan, either ferociously for or ferociously against Sparta, very seldom neutral. Hardly any inscriptions have been found and archaeological research so far has been concerned with only a small number of sites, where sanctuaries were built. The excavations now in progress will perhaps bring new revelations.

Secondly, because of the peculiar fascination that Sparta has exerted upon Ancients and Moderns alike, that is to say, what has been described as 'the Spartan mirage'. As early as the classical period, Sparta became a model for fourth-century authors such as Xenophon and Plato, a model that was reinforced in the Hellenistic period by the experimental reforms of the Spartan kings Agis IV and Cleomenes III. For the Moderns, Sparta is the point of anchorage for three Utopian legends: that of the importance of the Dorian invasions as an explanation for the characteristics of the city of Sparta and its successes; that of the communism supposed to have been represented by the Spartan division of land and the city's control over the possessions of its citizens; and that of the education whose austerity and regimentation so fascinated the Nazis of Hitlerian schools (Sparta was the subject of a textbook studied in the Adolf Hitler Schulen) and, by the same token, revolted anti-fascists. In short, it is a city that stirs violent passions.

The history of Sparta in the archaic period, however, is the history of *a city like any other*. Its extensive territory (the plain of Laconia covered 1,100 square kilometres, that of Messenia 4,100) included land that was fertile enough for it to be self-sufficient in food products. Little is known of its political regime until the late seventh century, but its civilization was brilliant. It was home to poets (including Tyrtaeus and Alcman between 650 and 590), goldsmiths and potters; its temples were built by the most famous of artists. The city experienced social difficulties characteristic of the early archaic period, prompted by a struggle within the community for rights to cultivate the land and for access to the power of decision. It clashed with the neighbouring cities of Argos (which won the battle of Hysiae in about 669) and Tegea. It founded a new city in southern Italy in about 700, namely Tarentum, which has been mentioned above. None of this is at all exceptional. However, a series of changes strung out over a century was to give the city a look all its own. That, at least, is the explanatory schema of the archaic history of Sparta proposed by M. I. Finley and C. Mossé.

What were the important factors that led to the change? They included:

- the hoplite reform, described above, which promoted equality and cohesion in the group composed of those who defended the city;
- the existence of a constitutional law, known as the *Rhetra*, attributed to the legislator Lycurgus, a text the contents of which we shall be examining later;
- the division of land, a principle recognized by all archaic cities but which found some sort of realization in Sparta;
- the existence and increase, following the Messenian War (730–710), of dependent rural peoples, the helots;
- the establishment of an educational system, the *agogè*, inseparable from citizenship;
- the creation of a body of magistrates, the ephors, to be the guardians and guarantors of the new social order.

The change was no doubt gradual, and it was only when the process was completed that Sparta shut itself off from the outside world. At this point we can describe the structures of the city of Sparta, structures that were to remain unchanged right down to the end of the classical period.

Lycurgus and the 'Rhetra' In his *Life of Lycurgus*, Plutarch describes the circumstances in which this legislator, of whose existence we cannot be certain, took action. Faced with the disturbances by which the city was affected following the Second Messenian War, Lycurgus consulted the Delphic oracle which, by way of reply, produced a *rhetra*, or constitutional law. Here is the text, as cited by Plutarch:

When thou hast built a temple to Zeus Syllanius and Athena Syllania, divide the people into *phylai* [tribes] and into *obai* [residential quarters], and establish a senate of thirty members, including the *archegetai* [the two kings], then from time to time *appellazein* [assemblies of the people] between Babyca and Cnacion, and there introduce and rescind measures, but the people must have the deciding voice and the power.

The second measure attributed to Lycurgus was the division of land. Plutarch writes as follows:

A second and a very bold political measure of Lycurgus [was] his redistribution of the land. For there was a dreadful inequality in this regard, the city was heavily burdened with indigent and helpless people, and wealth was wholly concentrated in the hands of a few. Determined, therefore, to banish insolence and envy and crime and luxury, and those yet more deep-seated and afflictive diseases of the State, poverty and wealth, he persuaded his fellow-citizens to make one parcel of all their territory and divide it up anew, and to live with one another on a basis of entire uniformity and equality in the means of subsistence . . . Suiting the deed to the word, he distributed the rest of the Laconian land among the *perioeci* or free provincials, in thirty thousand lots, and that which belonged to the city of Sparta, in nine thousand lots, to as many genuine Spartans.

The terms used in both these texts have been the subject of commentaries that it is not possible to reproduce in the present work but they do condition the importance of each of these institutions. Let us attempt a synthesis of the political institutions and social structures that were set in place.

POLITICAL INSTITUTIONS

The kings   Royalty was double. The kings were chosen from two different families, the Agiadae and the Eurypontedae. The succession remained within these two families but was not invariably in a direct line of descent. The powers of the two kings were limited by the very facts that there were two of them and both submitted to the city constitution, which they swore to uphold. There were frequent conflicts, either between the kings or with the elders and the ephors, the most frequent complaint being that the kings were abusing their power, in particular by acting with too much independence in their dealings with other cities. The powers of the kings were given the most freedom of expression in the military field. In times of war only one of the kings acted as commander of the armies and he exercised great authority over the troops. As members of the *gerousia*, the kings took part in political decisions. They enjoyed special honours: each owned an estate (*temenos*) taken from the land of the *perioikoi*; they were allowed double rations in the common meals and a greater share of war booty than the other warriors, all of which provided each of them with the means to run a 'household' far superior to those of other Spartan families. Finally, the royal function was of a markedly religious nature. The kings were responsible for most of the city rituals, and their funerals, the grandeur of which exceeded all Greek norms, underlined the exceptional nature of a royalty regarded as sacred.

The assembly, apella, regularly summoned on the occasion of the festivals of Apollo, was composed of all Spartans of free birth and met once a month in the open air, in an unidentified spot. The extent of its authority has been the subject of much discussion. In general, historians do not credit it with much power. In particular, they maintain that it could not discuss the propositions put to it, but could only accept or reject them. However, the interpretation suggested by F. Ruzé for the text of the *Rhetra* (the French translation of which is the basis of the above English rendering), on the contrary restores total sovereignty to the assembly. He claims that it was not simply a recording chamber but a place in which real debates took place. All the same, if it took decisions contrary to the constitution, the kings and the other members of the *gerousia* could dissolve it. It decided on when to seek peace and when to go to war, and elected magistrates and members of the *gerousia*.

The council of elders or *gerousia* comprised twenty-eight members, elected for life by the assembly, plus the two kings. To become a member, a man had to be 60 or over. The *gerousia* drafted laws which were then put to the vote in the assembly. This was the function known as 'proboulematic'. It also acted as a high court of justice in criminal cases. Both its prestige and its powers were considerable. Its method of election elicited a few smiles from the Athenians of the classical period: candidates for the *gerousia* presented themselves, one by one, before the assembly. The level of applause that greeted them decided whether or not they were elected.

The *ephors* constituted a college of five magistrates elected for one year. Eligibility was subject to no census or birth conditions: the ephors were recruited from the citizen body. Whatever the date of their creation, their role definitely seems to have been to thwart any tyrannical evolution of the royal power. Their powers were wide. The president of the college of ephors was an eponymous magistrate (the Spartan year of his office was named after him) and he presided over the *apella*. The ephors decided which political questions should be submitted to the assembly. In times of war, they organized mobilization, and two of them accompanied the king on the campaign, acting as generals. On a day-to-day basis, they supervised the social life of the city, in particular education, and the administration. They also held judicial authority, even over the kings. Their very considerable power was, however, tempered by the short duration of their responsibilities.

SPARTAN SOCIETY

The citizens These were known as the Equals: *homoioi*. To be a citizen, you had to have been born a boy, from a citizen father, and to have been through all the stages in the collective education, the *agogè*. You had to be 30 years of age and capable of making the required contribution to the daily common meal, the *syssition*.

In accordance with the legislation attributed to Lycurgus, every citizen was allotted a parcel of land known as a *kleros*, put at his disposal by the city, along with a number of dependent peasants responsible for cultivating it: helots. Both the *kleros* and the helots were the city's property, not the citizen's, and would normally revert to the city at the citizen's death, to be subsequently redistributed. The plots were carved out of the fertile land of Laconia and Messenia. According to Plutarch's text cited above, initially there were 9,000 of these parcels of land, which gives some idea of the size of the citizen body. Although in principle fair and egalitarian, the system soon became open to abuse (when a son succeeded his father, for instance, the parcel of land would be kept in the family instead of reverting to common property). By the fourth century, real estate inequality was rife among the citizens.

The homoioi worked neither on the land nor as craftsmen; they were primarily warriors for, as we have seen, their political role was a limited one.

The perioikoi, literally 'those who live round about', were the free inhabitants of Laconia who did not have citizenship. They lived in small towns and villages in an autonomous fashion, except with regard to any relations with other cities. They were peasants, craftsmen, traders. They served in the Spartan army in separate contingents.

The helots were rural dependents, hence non-free. They belonged to the civic community and worked on the estates of the citizens, to whom they handed over a predetermined proportion of the harvests. They lived in the countryside, on the land that they cultivated, or in villages. The helots of Messenia were the former people of Messenia, who had been deprived of their liberty when the Spartans conquered Messenia between 730 and 710. They were the descendants of local populations who had also been reduced to slavery, but the exact process of their enslavement is not known. They may have included both autochthonous peoples who had been living in Laconia before the arrival of the Dorians and also people who had lost their freedom as a result of extreme poverty. But whether their enslavement was a consequence of conquest or of economic inequalities, the helots formed a homogeneous group of enslaved Greeks, speaking the same language, employed at the same tasks, and – in the case of the helots of Messenia, at any rate – with the same aspirations.

Sparta was exceptional not only with regard to its constitution and its social structure, but also from the point of view of its institutionalization of education and its collective aristocratic practices, such as its banquets.

The agogè As we have seen, no one could become a citizen without having passed through the various stages of the *agogè*, an education organized by the city. This was altogether exceptional in the Greek cities, where families were normally responsible for the education of their own children. Plutarch tells us that Lycurgus considered 'the *paideia* to be the most important and finest work of the legislator'. And, as the *paideia* involved far more than simply instruction, the legislator first concerned himself with the girls, the future mothers of citizens, with a view to giving them robust bodies, well suited to procreation; and next, with love between boys and girls, and marriage for, according to Lycurgus, the obligations of marriage 'united husbands and wives when their bodies were full of creative energy and their affections new and fresh' and preserved 'in their hearts . . . mutual longing and delight'. All this with but a single aim in mind: the birth of children, upon whose survival or suppression the community as a whole immediately decided. The infants whom the 'elders' did not condemn to die by being hurled from the Apothetai precipice were left in the care of their mothers until the age of 7, then taken in charge by the city, under the responsibility of a *pedonome*, one of the magistrates, and divided into age groups (*agelai*) in which they lived together. Physical games and training

> ## *The* krypteia *in Sparta*
>
> 'The secret service [*krypteia*] was of the following nature. The magistrates
> from time to time sent out into the country at large the most discreet of
> the young warriors, equipped only with daggers and such supplies as were
> necessary. In the day time they scattered into obscure and out of the way
> places, where they hid themselves and lay quiet; but in the night, they
> came down into the highways and killed every Helot whom they caught.
> Oftentimes, too, they actually traversed the fields where the Helots were
> working and slew the sturdiest and best of them.' (Plutarch, *Life of
> Lycurgus*, XXVII, 3–5)

of an increasingly stringent kind, hunting practice, training in the use of
arms, music and choral singing, under the supervision of older boys, filled
their days until adolescence. In the course of the last stage in this education a small number of hand-picked young Spartans underwent the trial of
the *krypteia*: each of these youths had to leave the town, live in the mountains, always on his guard, even when sleeping, remaining unseen by anyone for a whole year. A number of historians compare the *krypteia* to the
episode of living alone in the wilderness that is a feature of other cultures,
and regard it as a period of initiation before a boy's definitive entry into
the life of a citizen. Even setting aside the *krypteia*, which seems to have
been a trial reserved for a limited number of future Spartan citizens, the
agogè's function certainly was to educate a boy in the values of endurance,
courage, sobriety and unselfishness – all requisites for citizenship – and at
the same time to teach him his real profession, that of a hoplite. It is not
hard to see why it was one of the conditions of citizenship. But Sparta's
uniqueness lay in its prolongation of the *paideia* so that its collective values
continued to be accepted by all citizens throughout their lives. One of the
occasions on which the civic community expressed itself was the famous
syssition, the daily meal that assembled all adult citizens and to which each
had to bring his own contribution in order to preserve his citizenship.

The *syssition*, the meal, was not simply a peacetime transposition of a
warriors' feast. It was an institution whose three main aspects summed up
the qualities needed to be a Spartan: the economic aspect, since to bring
one's own contribution to the common table showed that one possessed
a *kleros* worked by helots; the political aspect, since daily participation, that
is, putting oneself at the service of the city, was synonymous with citizenship; and the ideological aspect, since the *syssition* was a place of education
through example, through the recollection of the high deeds of citizens
that took place in the course of the banquets, and a place where the
community of the *homoioi* was daily cemented. The *syssition* was at the same

time a tangible mark of the segregation of the other groups in the population, who were excluded from the banquet, not admitted to the practice that each day reminded the citizens of their membership of the group. The *syssition* symbolized the exclusiveness of a civic community on the defensive, which had irrevocably decided to reserve equality for just a small number of the population.

The *agogè* and the *syssition* are practices of great interest when it comes to trying to understand how citizenship was defined at the time in question. Sparta was, of course, unique in that it carried the institutionalization of these practices to an extreme, but the fact that it did so suggests that similar practices were also important in other cities.

Spartan equilibrium, *eunomia*, was thus achieved in both the domain of political institutions and that of social structures. And even if this city subsequently refused to evolve to such a point that by the fifth century it had already become an object of curiosity to the Athenians, in the archaic period it was certainly one of the foremost laboratories experimenting with the application of the notion of equality to a number of sectors of city life. If Plutarch is to be believed, it was a city 'where there was neither wealth nor poverty, where the resources were equal for all and life was made easy by the simplicity of the customs. Throughout the land there were to be seen nothing but dancing, festivals, banquets, hunting parties, physical exercises, and conversation in places where people met together, at least, that is, during the times that the Spartans did not devote to military expeditions.'

EIGHTH- TO SEVENTH-CENTURY ATHENS

The territory of Athens, that is to say Attica, covered an area of 2,600 square kilometres. It incorporated a number of mountainous zones: to the west the mountains of Citheron and Parnes (1,400 m), to the east the Pentelicus and Hymettus mountains (1,000 m); the valley of the Cephissus river; several large plains, those of Eleusis, Marathon and Mesogaea; and in some places a narrow coastal strip. Its position on a peninsula jutting out into the Aegean Sea gave it wide access to the sea.

The historical process of the formation of this territory is unknown. Already in the *Iliad*, Athens is represented as a unified entity. It must have become so between the end of the Mycenaean period and the beginning of the eighth century. The Acropolis of Athens was occupied by a palace in the Mycenaean period. After this, isolated communities survived in a number of regions of Attica, and in the course of the eleventh century populations went off and settled on the coast of Asia Minor in the movement of Ionian migrations. The city of Athens produced its own version of those very early times: the Athenians had always been there, they were autochthonous. Ion, the ancestor of the Ionians, divided them into four tribes; King Theseus gathered these scattered communities into a single city, thereby effecting what is called a *synoecism*. After that, all the small towns of Attica lived under a single authority. Eleusis and Salamis were annexed later.

The evolution of forms of power also escapes us. Even the Atticographers were very hard put to it to draw up a list of the first kings of Athens and were unable to link the various legends together chronologically. It is therefore not possible to describe or date the stages in a process that saw the collapse of royalty and the establishment of an aristocratic, oligarchic regime. The names of a number of legendary kings lived on, Cecrops, Erechtheus, Theseus, Ion, Codrus and Acastus, who is supposed to have swapped royalty for a magistracy for life (an archontate). After several archontates had been held for life, the duration of office is believed to have been cut to ten years, and the list of yearly archons seems to have begun in 682–681.

The power of decision in communal affairs was shared by nine magistrates, the nine archons (one of whom was always given the title of 'king', *basileus*), but the most important was the *eponymous archon*; the archon in charge of the army was known as the *polymarch*. The council of the Areopagus, of which membership was for life, was composed of former archons no longer in office.

The population was made up of four *tribes*, called after the legendary sons of Ion: Geleon, Aegicores, Argades and Hoples. Each tribe was divided into three *trittyes* and was headed by a *phylobasileus*: 'the king of the tribe'. Another type of unit, the precise function of which is unknown, was the *naucraros*. Because the term *naucraros* means the head of a ship, it has been suggested that this was a unit connected with the financing of the navy, but we cannot be sure of this. There seem to have been forty-eight *naucraroi*, twelve for each tribe.

The aristocratic families, the names of sixty or so of which are known, made up a group called the *Eupatridai*, the well-born. In all probability, they alone were eligible to serve as archons. They pronounced on day-to-day rights and played an important role in the settlement of litigation between members of the community. They also held the posts of priests. In short, their power extended to every sphere of city life.

In connection with *the history of events of the seventh century*, we know of two names: Cylon and Draco. In about 630, Cylon, a member of an aristocratic family, known for his victory at the Olympic Games, tried to seize power in Athens, Surrounded by a group of other aristocrats and possibly aided by his father-in-law Theagenes, the tyrant of Megara, he installed himself on the Acropolis. But one of the serving archons, Megacles, a member of the Alcmaeonid family, had the Acropolis besieged. The insurgents gave themselves up, after being promised that their lives would be spared. They were nevertheless massacred. This sacrilege was the cause of a defilement that thereafter attached to the Alcmaeonid family, who were obliged to go into exile from Athens. This episode illustrates both the constant struggle for the control of power between the aristocratic families, and also the temptation, characteristic of this period, to seize power illegally through a coup, in short, to become a tyrant.

Draco is credited with the first attempt, in about 620, to legislate on criminal justice. Only a few fragments of a law on murder survive, showing that a distinction was drawn between premeditated murder and accidental murder. The rest of Draco's code, reputed to have been very severe (hence our use of the term 'Draconian') has not come down to us, but it is clear that it was not a matter of constitutional law comparable to that attributed to Lycurgus and other legislators. Apart from these two emblematic figures, the history of this century remains obscure. Athens is, however, known to have been the scene of a number of *conflicts.*

It clashed with the city of Aegina, with Megara over the possession of the island of Salamis, and with the city of Mytilene at the end of the seventh century. At the very beginning of the sixth century, Athens also became involved in a conflict known as 'the sacred war', as it broke out over the sanctuary of Delphi. Athens took the side of the Thessalians and the city of Sicyon and fought to liberate Delphi from the domination of the city neighbouring the sanctuary, Cirrha. As a result of doing so, it obtained a seat in the *Amphictonia,* responsible for the administration of the sanctuary. All these events are difficult to date with any precision, the more so because tradition tends, wrongly, to date them to the time of the great man of the sixth century: Solon.

LAND PROBLEMS AND LEGISLATION

THE SHORTAGE OF LAND

The seventh and sixth centuries were periods of internal troubles in the cities, and the aristocratic institutions described above had difficulty resisting the social and political claims being made by certain sectors of the city populations. The fundamental problem was always the shortage of cultivable land, caused both by the small area of fertile land available and also by the inadequacies of the system for distributing it fairly and the custom according to which, at the death of a father, his land would be divided up between all his sons, a measure that soon resulted in a severe fragmentation of real estate. This *stenochoria* (shortage of land) had been one of the causes of the movement of emigration among the Greeks and it remained the principal source of conflicts and complaints in the archaic cities. One possible solution was to divide the land equally between the citizens and to redistribute it for every new generation: this was what Sparta tried to do with Lycurgus' reforms, mentioned above. But most cities drew back from so radical a solution. There was one man, Hesiod, who in his *Works and Days* described the situation in which most small-scale peasants of this time found themselves: a situation of poverty and dependence *vis-à-vis* larger landowners, those whom he called 'the gift-eating kings'. Hesiod was writing of Boeotia, but the scene was a general one. However, for a description of the aspects and mechanisms of what is generally called 'the agrarian crisis', the case of Athens is the best documented.

In response to the shortage of land, the inhabitants of a city would first seek to increase the cultivated area, soon coming up against the mountainous configuration of its territory, which made it impossible to extend the area to be cultivated. The cultivation of terraced mountain slopes was practised as much as possible, to the detriment of zones of pasture land and always with the risk of provoking clashes between the *aristoi* owners of herds and the small-scale peasants intent upon extending their cultivated fields, as is testified by references to the massacres of flocks at this time. In short, attempts to extend the cultivated area produced few results and failed to improve the agricultural yield. The peasants were not even able to harvest enough to feed their families all the year round and were forced to turn to the richest among them to borrow grain both for sowing and for eating. We know nothing of the system for obtaining loans in kind. But such debts had to be repaid, also in kind, out of the next harvest. If this was good, the small-scale peasant could wipe out his debt, but if it was poor the peasant would fall ever deeper into debt until he found himself obliged to farm both his own land and that of his creditor, purely for the benefit of the latter. This process came about in two stages:

- in the first, the poor peasant would have to make repayment in kind (grain) for his debt, to the tune of a fixed proportion of his harvest (the *hectamoroi* of Athens, for example, had to hand over one-sixth of their harvest to the larger landowner);
- the second stage came when the poor peasant, unable to make the repayment, was reduced to slavery. This happened because the large landowner could not become the proprietor of the land of his debtor, since land was inalienable (it could not be sold or ceded to anyone else). He therefore seized all its agricultural products. In Attica, the material indication of such a situation was the presence of markers in the fields to show that the harvest belonged to such or such a person. The rich landowner also had the use of the manpower represented by the peasant and might also press into use the labour of the members of his family.

This logical schema is a reconstruction worked out by historians on the basis of scattered, fragmentary and sometimes contradictory evidence, so on all these points considerable debate continues between specialists.

When the Greeks founded new cities where the primary activity was agriculture, the cereals produced on the more fertile land of these cities could be transported elsewhere and traded. But this did not resolve the inequality of land distribution and the problem of endemic famine, since the poorest peasants had no surplus cereals to exchange for other goods.

Here again, inequality increased between the poor on one hand and, on the other, large landowners who had been able to set aside part of their land for the cultivation of olive trees and thus had olive oil that could be used for trading. The situation seemed insoluble and social tensions mounted.

On the one side were the 'haves', growing steadily richer, on the other the 'have-nots', peasants denied even the income from their own land and growing steadily poorer; on the one hand an aristocracy that held the political power, on the other a population of peasants seeking clarification of the rules of citizenship. It would seem that the claims of the small-scale landowners were at once economic (redistribution of the land), social (the freedom of individuals) and political (changes in the civic legislation), each of these aspirations being inspired by the ideal of equality. However, the response of the legislator, Solon in the case of Athens, did not take equal account of those three types of aspiration.

SOLON, THE MEDIATOR

This is what I have done, through the power of the Law, by dint of both force and justice; I have done it, going right to the end of the road, as I promised I would. I have set out rules, identical for the wicked and the good, giving straight justice to each one. If someone else had been spurred to do this, a fool or a greedy man, he could never have contained the people. For if I had wanted what those in revolt wanted then or even what the other party wished for them, the city would soon have been widowed of many men. That is why, using all my strength, I fought on every side like a dog surrounded by wolves.

That is how Solon sums up his actions in one of the elegies of which a few fragments have come down to us. The work of this legislator is known not only from many much later texts, including those by Aristotle and Plutarch, but also through one or two of his own poems. Solon was elected archon in Athens in 594–593. Later Greek tradition ascribes to him reforms in many domains, but several of them were wrongly attributed to him at a time (the fifth and fourth centuries) when people wanted to turn Solon into the founding father of democracy. It is accordingly necessary to pick out what was unquestionably the work of the archaic legislator, namely all that related to land problems.

The problem of land   Solon himself describes his solution as follows:

I have torn up the markers that were in many places stuck in the black Earth. Once it was enslaved; now it is free. I have brought back to Athens, their country founded by the gods, men who had been sold, some legitimately, others not, some forced into exile by debt, who no longer spoke the Attic tongue – in so many places had they wandered – and others, even here, who had been subjected to unworthy servitude and who trembled at the behaviour of their masters. I have made them free.

And in another fragment he explains what he had denied them:

They came to pillage, being possessed by infinite hopes, each of them hoping to find great wealth and thinking that, despite the sweet seduction of my words, I would manifest an intractable spirit. Vain were the words they used then, and now, angered against me, they look at me askance, like an enemy. Quite wrongly. What I had said I would do, with the help of the gods I achieved. As for the rest, there was no question of acting lightly, I take no pleasure in accomplishing anything through the violence of tyranny, nor in giving equal portions to the good and the bad in the sharing out of the rich land.

Solon's solution had been to annul all debts, and this was done by removing the markers indicating the rights of creditors over the harvests in the fields (this was what Aristotle called the *seisachtheia*: throwing off the burden) and also by doing away with slavery for debt and, at a stroke, with the status of *hectemoroi* (sixth-parters). On the other hand, Solon denied the share of the land claimed by those he called 'the bad' and did not challenge the property of those whom he called 'the good', that is, the members of the aristocracy. The limits thus set on his reforms have frequently been pointed out. Although it may have warded off the civil war that was threatening, it did not get to the roots of the crisis and had the effect of displeasing both the large landowners, deprived of their manpower and part of their income, and also the poor peasants, who could no more live off their land now than they could before. That is all that can be attributed to Solon with any certainty. We should probably abandon the eminently logical historical reconstruction which, on the strength of Aristotle's and Plutarch's claims, presented various other economic and institutional reforms attributed to this legislator as complementary pieces of the same pattern. Those pieces certainly do not date from the early sixth century. What are they?

The laws attributed to Solon   They affect every domain: the economy (measures concerning craftsmen, the system of weights and measures, the ban on the export of all produce except oil); justice (the constitution of a court open to all citizens, the *Heliaea* and the right of any citizen to lodge a legal complaint); social mores (regulations on marriage, the luxurious lifestyle of women, funerals); and kinship and the place of the *oikos* in the city.

Did he introduce institutional changes? Solon is often credited with having divided the citizen body into four census classes that determined who could accede to the magistracies (the *archai*). Income from the land, expressed in measures (*medimnoi*) of cereals, was a factor in determining the classes. The *Pentacosiomedimnoi* were those with an income of 500 *medimnoi* of wheat or more, the *Hippeis* (knights) those with between 300 and 500, the *Zeugites* (possessors of a plough and so also of a team of oxen) those with between 200 and 300, and the *Thetes* those with even less. The major novelty as compared with the earlier system, which divided the Athenians into *Eupatridai* (the well-born, aristocratic families), the *geomoroi* (owners of land, peasants) and the *demiourgoi* (those who lived on payment for their work), was that account was now taken of the level of land wealth in the attribution of political power. Yet this reform seems anachronistic. It calls to mind the Athenian city's clashes at the turn of the fifth and fourth centuries. The same applies to the creation of a council of 400 members (the *boulè*), which is also attributed to Solon.

The stringent critical examination to which the work of Solon has been submitted for the last few years, and which now inclines historians to recognize his paternity only in the case of the measures directly affecting Athens' agrarian problems, is one example of the constant rereading and re-evaluation of the sources that are undertaken by historians. Aristotle's *Constitution of the Athenians* was long considered to be a key source describing Greek institutions generally. Now, however, this too is viewed with a critical eye. Aristotle frequently represented the political work of the archaic period in the image of that of his own century (the fourth), and it is interesting to see to what extent this may have distorted our own view and understanding of the archaic world.

In his poems, Solon on several occasions claims glorious credit for not having agreed to become a tyrant. 'I do not like to accomplish anything through the violence of tyranny,' he wrote. Plenty of archaic cities did, for one or two generations, have at their heads men who held on to power illegally and tried in their own particular ways to control certain aspects of the crisis affecting the cities.

THE TYRANNIES

It should immediately be pointed out that what we refer to as tyrants and tyranny in our modern vocabulary, namely the absolute and coercive power of a single individual, has very little to do with the nature of the archaic tyrannies. But it should then also be said that by the classical period the Greeks had already constructed a negative image of this type of government, an image which was essentially very close to our own description of tyranny. If we do not bear those two points in mind, we shall understand nothing of the archaic tyrannies.

Tyrant (*turannos*) and its derivatives were probably terms that the Greeks borrowed from some other language (from Asia Minor?). They are used for the first time in the mid-seventh century by Archilocus, with the neutral sense of 'to rule'. By the sixth century, Solon was associating tyranny with cruel violence and dishonour. Yet tyrants such as Pittacus of Mytilene and Periander of Corinth also figure in the list of the Seven Sages, men supposed to have made pronouncements full of good sense. Already in this period, then, a tyrant had two faces, one of a monster, the other of a sage.

Let us first note the general characteristics of the archaic tyrannies, then examine the two examples of Corinth and Athens, before finally considering how the Greek image of a tyrant came to be constructed.

GENERAL CHARACTERISTICS

Tyrannies appeared in the seventh century, not everywhere in the Greek world, but in cities that were the most developed both institutionally and socially. A tyrant came from an aristocratic family and was neither an upstart nor a foreigner. In many cases he would first serve, in legal fashion, as a magistrate (*archon*), but would then retain his power beyond the permitted date, this time illegally. Alternatively, he might seize power by force. Either way, he would certainly retain it by force. From a political point of view, a tyrant would, at best, suspend the existing aristocratic institutions (assembles, magistracies) and govern on his own, surrounded by a few close supporters. At worst, he would pursue a systematic policy aimed at levelling the rest of the aristocracy, which might go so far as forcing the great families into exile or contriving the deaths of some of their members, then seizing their property. Tyranny was a telling sign of the inability of aristocracies to govern the cities in times of mounting tensions resulting from social inequalities. Although of aristocratic origin himself, a tyrant clearly governed without and against his own relatives, as many lyric poets testified. So did he seek support from the rest of the free population?

The image of the demagogue tyrant (literally, one who led the *dèmos*, the citizen people), who depended upon the *dèmos* and favoured it, is not well substantiated historically. So far as political power was concerned, tyrants never delegated any of their authority to the rest of the community. Sometimes, as in Corinth, they would try to relieve the poverty of the peasants by distributing among them some of the land that they had themselves seized from the aristocrats. And, through the spreading influence in the Greek world that they acquired from their cities, indirectly they favoured those engaged in trade and the artisans. But as a rule this was not as a result of any systematic policy. So the idea, often expressed, that tyranny was a phase that was helpful to the *dèmos* in its progress towards greater political involvement calls for strong qualification. Once a tyranny disappeared, the aristocratic government would recover its legitimacy and its rights.

One feature common to many tyrannies was their military aspect. The tyrant would surround himself with a guard and would wage war against other cities. In many cases he, or his descendants, would be assassinated. A tyrannical interlude tended to be short, a mere parenthesis interrupting a sequence of aristocratic governments for the space of one generation, or possibly two. Sometimes a tyranny would succeed where an oligarchy had failed: avoiding civil war or bringing it to an end, creating general conditions that gave the peasant population a chance gradually to escape from their poverty, or forging an impressive image of the city *vis-à-vis* the outside world, for example, in the religious and cultural domain – an image that helped to create the city's identity. But the very illegality of the power that the tyrant claimed and of all the measures that he promulgated in order to hang on to that power ran totally counter to the evolution of a society increasingly concerned with equality. As has frequently been underlined, tyranny was an ambiguous parenthesis rather than one that was indispensable to the survival of the archaic cities – as the example of Sparta, which never experienced this type of regime, clearly shows.

It is not easy to enumerate the archaic tyrannies, for in many cases the dividing line between the power of a king, that of a legislator and that of a tyrant is far from clear. Only the manner in which the power was exercised could help to decide the matter, but in many cases these archaic figures are no more than names to us. Table 3, constructed by M.-C. Amouretti and F. Ruzé (in *Le Monde grec antique*, 2nd edn, Paris, 1990), sets out the available data very clearly and is reproduced below.

Some of these tyrannies are more famous and better known than others. In Sicyon, a city in the north-eastern Peloponnese, a certain Cleisthenes (600–565 BC), who belonged to a veritable dynasty of tyrants, the Orthagorids, who ruled the city from the seventh century down to 510, diminished the power of the other aristocrats by taking the symbolic step of saddling the three other tribes of the families descended from the Dorians with ridiculous names (the Pigs, the Donkeys and the Piglets), keeping for his own tribe the prepossessing title of 'Leaders of the People'. Under the tyrant Polycrates (around 530), Samos was a maritime power of the first order, capable of treating with both the king of Egypt and the king of Persia. Tyrannies eventually also developed in Magna Graecia and in Sicily, but those about which we know the most date from around the turn of the sixth and fifth centuries. The great diversity of local situations makes it advisable to add a measure of detail and qualification to this general picture of the characteristics of tyrannies. The tyrannies of Corinth and Athens will provide examples of two individual cases.

CORINTH AND THE TYRANNY OF THE CYPSELIDS

As has been noted, in the seventh century Corinth was ruled by an oligarchy whose members all belonged to the Bacchiad family. This was undermined by social imbalances that the government could no longer control. The first tyrant, Cypselus, was himself a Bacchiad on the side of his mother, Labda, but on his father's side he belonged to the Lapith family. Since the rule was that Bacchiads always intermarried, in normal circumstances Cypselus could not have acceded to power, on account of his irregular birth. Nevertheless, he held the post of *polemarch* (responsible for war, so he was the leader of the hoplites) at the moment when he seized power. Cypselus' government lasted for thirty years (657–627). Many measures are attributed to him.

Table 3   Principal tyrants, *aisymnetai* and legislators

Place	Known names (assumed dates)	Nature of power	Previous regime	Subsequent regime
Mainland Greece				
Corinth	Cypselus (657–627)	Tyrant	Oligarchy Bacchiads	Tyranny
	Periander (627–585)	Tyrant	Tyranny	Tyranny
	Psammeticus (585–584 or 583)	Tyrant	Tyranny	Moderate aristocracy
Sicyon	Orthagoras (about 650)	Tyrant?	Aristocracy	Tyranny?
	Myron?	Tyrant?	Tyranny?	Tyranny?
	Aristonymus?	Tyrant?	Tyranny?	Tyranny?
	Myron II and Isodemus (600)?	Tyrants	Tyranny?	Tyranny?
	Cleisthenes (about 600 or 565)	Tyrant	Tyranny	Moderate oligarchy or tyranny?
	Aeschines (?–510)	Tyrant	?	Oligarchy?
Megara	Theagenes (650?–600?)	Tyrant	Plutocracy	Moderate aristocracy
Argos	Pheidon (about 650)	Tyrannical monarchy	Monarchy	?
Athens	Cylon (about 630)	Failure	Aristocracy	Aristocracy
	Draco (about 620)	Legislator	Aristocracy	Aristocracy
	Solon (594)	Legislator	Aristocracy	Moderate aristocracy
	Pisistratus (561–528/527)	Tyrant	Aristocracy	Tyranny
	Hippias	Tyrant	Tyranny	Troubles then *isonomia*
Asia Minor and the islands				
Miletus	Amphitres (Late 8th or 7th)	Tyrant	Meleides	Monarchy, civil war
	Epimenes (7th)	*Aisymnetes*	Troubles	Aristocracy?
	Thrasybulus (late 7th–8th)	Tyrant or *prytanis*	Aristocracy	Tyranny
	Thoas, Damasanor (6th)	Tyrants	Tyranny	Plutocracy/troubles
Mytilene	Melandrus	Tyrants or oligarchic leaders	Penthilid	Monarchy
	Myrsilus (late 7th)			Aristocracy
	Pittacus (590–580)	*Aisymnetes*	Aristocracy/ troubles	Moderate aristocracy?

Table 3 (cont'd)

Place	Known names (assumed dates)	Nature of power	Previous regime	Subsequent regime
Samos	Demoteles (7th)	Tyrant	Oligarchy	*Geomoroi* aristocracy
	Syloson? (early VIth)	Tyrant?	Aristocracy	Aristocracy?
	Polycrates (532?–522)	Tyrant	Aristocracy?	Troubles/Persians
Ephesus	Pythagoras (about 600)	Tyrant	Basilid Oligarchy	Tyranny
	Pindarus (about 560)	Tyrant	Tyranny	Lydian conquest
	Aristarchus	*Aisymnetes*	Troubles	Tyranny
	Pasicles	Tyrant?	Tyranny	Monarchy or Persians
Naxos	Lygdamis (about 550)	Tyrant	?	Plutocracy

Note: The mention of 'Persians' in the last column indicates a tyranny set in place by the Persians. 'Troubles' means either rivalry between aristocratic factions or struggles between the aristocracy and the rest of the *dèmos* (From *Le Monde grec antique*, by M.-C. Amouretti and F. Ruzé, 2nd edn, Paris, Hachette, 1990).

In the domain of real estate, Cypselus is reputed to have expelled the Bacchiads, taking their property and also in some cases their lives. But it is not known precisely what use was made of this confiscation of land. There are three possible hypotheses: either the tyrant kept the estates for himself, or he made them public property or, alternatively, he distributed them among the landless peasants. The last of these hypotheses is the one generally favoured. But even if it is correct, it would imply only a very partial division of the land, which despoiled only one aristocratic family (the Bacchiads), not the entire mass of large landowners. In the field of taxes, Cypselus is supposed to have consecrated the annual dime (one-tenth) of the real-estate revenue of the Corinthians to the sanctuary of Zeus. This seems to be the first example of what the Greeks called an *eisphora*, an extraordinary tax, usually levied in times of war. The first Corinthian coinage (of staters) is also attributed to him.

He was succeeded by his son, *Periander* (627–585). Periander, far better known in Antiquity than his father, had an execrable reputation. According to Herodotus,

it was perfectly plain to him that [what was] recommended was the murder of all the people in the city who were outstanding in influence or ability . . . and from that time forward there was no crime against the Corinthians that he did not commit, indeed anything that Cypselus had left undone in the way of killing or banishing, Periander completed for him.

He had a personal guard of 300 spearmen (the *doryphoroi*). He is said to have passed measures to stamp out laziness (making work obligatory), to have prohibited the buying of slaves and to have passed many laws against luxury, repressing the ostentation that was characteristic of aristocratic life and the effect of which was to draw too much attention to social inequality.

During this period, Corinth founded a number of new cities (Epidamnus, Apollonia, Potidaea), maintained relations with Asia Minor, exported its pottery throughout the Mediterranean world, extended its sanctuaries and created the Isthmian Games. In short, it was one of the foremost cities of Greece. Nevertheless, the tyranny was toppled soon after Periander's death, while one of his nephews was in power (in 583). The Corinthians then restored an oligarchic regime, in which power was no longer concentrated in the hands of a single family, but was shared between all the city's richest men.

ATHENS AND THE TYRANNY OF THE PISISTRATIDS

Tyranny was established in Athens in about 560, at a time when its aristocratic families were fighting among themselves. They were split into three groups, each named after the region of Attica from which their leader hailed:

- the Pedians ('people of the plain'. The Pedium plain lay to the south-west of Athens, at the confluence of the Cephissus and Illissus rivers), under Lycurgus, of the Eteoboutadae family;
- the Paralians ('people of the coast'), under Megacles of the Alcmaeonid family;
- the Diacrians ('people of the hills'. Diacria was to the north-east of Attica, close to Mount Pares and the Boeotian frontier), under Pisistratus.

The differences between these three groups do not seem to have been of a political nature nor to have had anything to do with economic activities, but Pisistratus is presented as a leader who was followed both by the poor peasants of the villages and by the craftsmen living in town, who had no political rights.

The tyranny of Pisistratus falls into *three periods of power*. He first seized power in 561–560, following a fantastic scenario that is described by Herodotus. Pisistratus, then *polemarch* and famous for his victory in the war against Megara, got himself assigned a guard of 300 club-bearers, seized the Acropolis and governed the city for six years. He was then forced into exile. Eleven years later he returned, with the support of Megacles and the Alcmaeonids. Pisistratus made his entry into the city of Athens riding in a chariot alongside a magnificent woman disguised as Athena. He governed for a few years, then was again forced into exile, but this time beyond Attica, first in the Thracian region of Mount Pangaeus, then in Eretria in Euboea, for three years.

For his third seizure of power, Pisistratus employed the services of mercenaries, landed in the plain of Marathon, overcame his enemies and gained possession of the Acropolis. He remained in power until his death, in 528–527.

The measures taken by Pisistratus According to Aristotle, Pisistratus showed moderation in every domain. He temporarily exiled some of his opponents, in particular, members of the Alcmaeonid family, but did not lay a finger on their property.

Where the peasants were concerned, Pisistratus did not proceed to any distribution of the land among them but he did lend the poorest enough for them to cultivate their land, possibly using the dime that he began to levy at the same time on the harvests (of the richest?). The judges who were established in the demes brought justice closer to the peasants and no doubt diminished the power of the powerful families. Anecdotes tell of the tyrant visiting the countryside to assess just how precarious the life of Athenians was.

The first Athenian coins (showing an owl on one side and Athena's head on the other) were minted either under Pisistratus or under his son, Hippias.

But the most spectacular aspect of his policies was the construction of monuments that gave Athens a really urban air, a great temple of Athena with, at its foot, a temple of Zeus (the Olympeion, not completed until the Roman period) and on the agora the altar to the twelve gods and a fountain known as the fountain with nine mouths: the Enneacrounos, connected to the first network of pipes supplying water to the town. Without going so far as to call this a systematic policy of major public works, as some historians do, it is only fair to point out that these building sites called for a large workforce and did provide work for many of the town's inhabitants, as well as calling upon the skills of specialized craftsmen and thereby hastening social changes for the Athenian population. Artists forgathered from all over Greece to produce the temple sculptures, for example. They also sculpted many a male figure (*kouros*) and many a female one (*korè*) to mark the locations of particular tombs in the cemeteries. The pottery workshops produced vases signed by potters and painters as famous as Exechias, the Amasis painter, and the Antimenes painter; and, alongside the black-figure vases, red-figure vases were produced, using a new technique that allowed for more variation in the designs. This period, which was so creative in every artistic domain, was also concerned to transmit the culture of the past: an edition (in the technical sense of the term) of the Homeric poems was produced; and Ionian poets such as Anacreon and Simonides came to live in Athens.

The monumental constructions show that Pisistratus organized several cults that were to give Athens its particular religious character: the first was that of Athena, its tutelary deity, whose Panathenaea festival was set up at this time, which, thanks to the creation of a panathenaic competition,

attracted visitors from all over the Greek world. The second was the cult of
Dionysus, in honour of whom the first tragedies were performed on the
occasion of the Dionysia. The third was the cult of Demeter, in the sanctuary at Eleusis. The civic tone that these cults took on had both an
internal and an external function: to weld the community together, as its
members attended rituals that were open to all citizens; and also to show
other cities how splendidly Athens honoured its gods, and so to compete
with the cults of those other cities.

Hippias and Hipparchus   After the death of Pisistratus, his two sons Hippias
and Hipparchus succeeded him. Hipparchus was assassinated in 514 by two
Athenians, Harmodius and Aristogeiton, and Hippias was toppled in 510.
The assassination of Hipparchus was later celebrated as Athens' reaction to
tyranny, the two assassins became heroes and their descendants enjoyed
special privileges. At the time, however, the murder, the real motives of
which are not clear, did not bring about the collapse of tyranny. For that
the aid of Sparta was needed, and this was given by its king Cleomenes,
who besieged Athens at the request of the Athenians, led by the Alcmaeonid
family. Here, as in other cities, the collapse of tyranny left the way open for
the return of the oligarchic government and an immediate resumption of
infighting among the great families.

THE IMAGE OF THE TYRANT

Tyranny is described above as a historically dated form of power (that existed
in the seventh and sixth centuries) and, along with many other historians, we
have emphasized certain aspects noted in the texts that seem to have a more
historical explanation than certain others, that is, those to do with political
power, economic organization and social problems. It is, of course, an arbitrary
way of sifting the data and leaves out of account a whole mass of other
remarks about tyrants, particularly their social mores, which, far from being
mere anecdotes, might help us to form a better idea of the archaic world's
system of representations, as Louis Gernet has long since demonstrated.

Furthermore, the Greek texts that speak of tyrants are never neutral.
They fabricate images of the tyrant that vary with the passing of the years
and had a very particular function at the time those texts were written. To
look no further than the classical period, from Herodotus to Aristotle and
taking in the tragic poets and Plato, the discourse on tyranny is in a constant state of transformation, for the subject of tyranny produces ideas about
political power and the figure of the anti-tyrant *par excellence*, the citizen.
It is not hard to appreciate how difficult it is for a historian to construct
a coherent history of the archaic tyrannies, for anything written on the
subject of the tyrant may be part of a subtle campaign conducted against
anything contrary to the civic norm, whether it be a matter of the abuse
suffered by women and young boys, or laws designed to regulate luxury.

If all the characteristics attributed to tyrants are suspect, that makes the historian's investigation all the more interesting, but at the same time all the more contingent: in between the positive assessments of the archaic tyrannies written twenty years ago and the syntheses on offer today, it is possible to discern that many historians are paying increasing attention not only to what the documents of that period actually say but also to the particular way in which they present history.

THE PEOPLES AND CITIES OF GREECE: AN IMPRESSIONISTIC PICTURE

The predominance given to Athens and Sparta and the communities particularly affected by them primarily reflects the state of the ancient sources. Herodotus, for example, only touches in an allusive and occasional way upon many of the Greek communities and only in so far as they fit in to the general plan of his book, whereas he goes into considerable detail about the customs of non-Greek peoples. Archaeological studies in Greece as a whole have been anything but systematic, and it is only recently that a number of investigations and excavations have improved our knowledge of many sites that, until now, have been little more than names to us. This perhaps explains how it is that modern historians, in their turn, have taken some time to begin to tackle the peoples and cities of Greece as a whole and, when they do so, often find the history of the archaic and classical periods the hardest to reconstruct. That is why I have decided to present the past of a number of peoples only at the point when they became involved in the events of Greek history in general, in the fourth century BC and later (in the cases of Epirus and Macedonia). The present picture is essentially geographically oriented, very dependent on maps. Its historical elements are no more than fleeting flashes that leave most of the period and the Greek space in the shadows.

NORTHERN GREECE: THESSALY

This region of plains was governed by 'kings' (*basileis*) belonging to great noble families, a few of whose names are known to us: the Aleuadae, the Scopadae, the Echecratids and their descendants. They exercised control over the towns, in particular Larissa, Crannon, Pharsalus, Pherae. Their wealth came from their land and their herds, and they were famous for their ostentatious lifestyle: banquets, horse-racing, the patronage of poets (such as Simonides, Anacreon, Pindar) and offerings in the sanctuary of Delphi. The nobles governed without sharing power with the other free men, the peasants and the craftsmen. When they first arrived in the region, they had reduced the earlier local population, the *Penestai*, to servitude. The *Penestai* cultivated the land and presented a contribution in kind (a large proportion of their harvests) to their masters. Their status was similar to that of the helots, except that they belonged to individual masters, not to the community as in Sparta.

There is no way of knowing how unified Thessaly was in the archaic and classical periods. In the fifth to fourth centuries Thessaly was a federal State, but how long had it been so? At that time it was divided into four regions: Hestiaiotis in the north-west, Pelasgiotis in the north-east, Thessaliotis in the south-west and Phthiotis in the south-east. In 511 the Thessalians sent an army to help the tyrants of Athens, having made a common decision to do so: this implies the existence of some kind of common institution, such as a council. Later, it seems that the four regions, ruled by four *tetrarchs*, were each divided into smaller units with a military function, namely to provide a contingent for the common army. The leader at the head of the army was known as the *tagus*. It was a fragile, federal organization because the 'kings' were constantly clashing as rivals.

The peoples in the surrounding regions were, depending on the period, either subjected to Thessaly or allied to it, and were known as the *perioikoi*. To the east of Mount Pindus were the people of Dolopia, on the northern frontier the people of Perrhaebia, on the eastern coast the people of Magnesia and in the southern region the people of Achaea Phthiotis.

Thessaly played an important role in the administration of the sanctuary of Delphi, for it belonged to the group of cities and peoples that formed the *amphictionia* and helped to defend the sanctuary from the greed of neighbouring cities (the first Sacred War ended in 590).

CENTRAL GREECE: LOCRIS, PHOCIS, MALIS, DORIS

The mountainous regions to the west of Thessaly and Boeotia included Malis, in the valley of the Sperchius river, Doris where the Cephissus river rose, Phocis surrounding Mount Parnassus, and Locris, which was cut in two by Phocis: Opuntian Locris, to the east, extended as far as the shore facing the coast of Euboea, while Ozolian Locris, to the west, stretched as far as the Gulf of Corinth. The population was grouped and organized politically, either as a people (*ethnos*) or as a city (*polis*). These were wild regions, with robber bands lurking in the inland countryside, but on the coasts towns developed, each with its own institutions. For example, the city of Naupactus, on the coast of western Locris, had magistrates, an assembly, a council and another institution called the Hundred Households (*oikoi*), the role of which is not known. Phocis was frequently at war with Thessaly, in particular over the sanctuary of Delphi (the Phocidians of Cirrha appropriated the sanctuary's wealth).

We know very little of the history and organization at this period of the peoples of Aetolia and Acarnania, still further to west. It would appear that vast areas gradually became Hellenized, but life there seems to have been very insecure, to judge by the local custom of always bearing arms.

BOEOTIA

In the archaic period, Boeotia comprised a dozen or so cities, including Orchomenus, Chaeronea, Thespiae, Haliartus, Thebes, Acraephia, Plataea, Tanagra and Oropus. The city of Thebes dominated southern Boeotia except for Plataea, and in about 519 tried unsuccessfully to get all the cities to enter a confederation.

In his *Works and Days*, Hesiod, himself a native of Ascra, paints a picture of peasant life in Boeotia at the end of the eighth century. It was dominated by the need to work: 'Work, high-born Perses, that Hunger may hate you and venerable Demeter, richly crowned, may love you and fill your barn with food'; work, which averted hunger and created wealth; the duty of hospitality: 'Call your friend to a Feast, but leave your enemy alone; and especially call him who lives near you'; and the duty to seek purity in relations with the world of the gods: 'Never pour a libation of sparkling wine to Zeus with unwashen hands, nor to others of the deathless gods; else they do not hear your prayers but spit them back.' All these duties composed a life for which the rhythm was set by the agricultural calendar. In this farming region, changes in the city governments were few; oligarchic regimes predominated. At the time of the Persian Wars, most of the Boeotian cities treated with the king of the Persians, in retaliation for which Thebes was destroyed by the Greeks after the battle of Plataea (479).

Notwithstanding their reputation for lumpishness, much spread about by their sarcastic Athenian neighbours, the Boeotians in truth excelled in every domain of archaic and classical culture: music, architecture, sculpture, bronzework, pottery and poetry. Pindar was a native of the Thebes neighbourhood. They were also innovative in the sphere of institutions, setting up a constitution for the Boeotian confederation (for the period 447–368).

EUBOEA

This large island extending along the coasts of Boeotia and, in particular, Attica, boasts three prestigious sites: Chalcis, Eretria and Lefkandi.

Lefkandi was situated halfway between Chalcis and Eretria. Its importance for our knowledge of the early archaic period has already been noted. But Lefkandi began to decline in about 825 and by a century later was totally abandoned.

Chalcis, as we have seen, was actively involved in the foundation of a number of new cities. It compensated for its agrarian difficulties with its bronze-work and the activities of its seafaring traders. The only fertile plain on the island, known as the Lelantine plain, was fought over by Chalcis and Eretria in a war that lasted for close on a hundred years. Other Greek cities also appear to have taken part in this conflict, which was a novelty in the history of archaic wars. Chalcis was finally victorious but not long after, in 506, it was defeated by Athens, which installed 4,000 Athenians on the land that had previously belonged to the great landowning family of the Hippobotae.

Eretria's rise coincided with the abandonment of Lefkandi. Nothing is known of its internal development. Like Chalcis, it played an active part in the Greek movement of expansion throughout the Mediterranean world and in the diffusion of pottery known as Euboean. The archaeological excavations undertaken at Eretria have revealed an extremely prosperous city. In 700 it entered upon a programme of urban construction that included the building of town walls complete with a defensive bastion known as the West Gate, and public buildings such as the temples of Dionysus and Apollo Daphnephoros in the sixth century, as well as many private houses. Its tombs contained articles that testified to the wealth that the city had enjoyed before it was worn down by the Lelantine War.

In the fifth century Chalcis and Eretria belonged to the Delian League, but apart from a number of attempted revolts followed by the installation of cleruchies (groups of Athenian citizens) on their land, little is known of their history.

THE PELOPONNESE

The archaic history of Corinth and Sparta has been summarized in the context of our study of the various types of Greek political regimes, and our account of the events of the fifth century will be concerned with most of the cities of the Peloponnese. But at this point it is worth drawing attention to the diversity of the political units in this southern region of Greece, for in several regions of the Peloponnese both the types of political organization produced by the Greek world coexisted: the people (*ethnos*) and the city (*polis*).

Virtually nothing is known of Achaea and Elis, in the northern regions of the Peloponnese, in the archaic period.

ARCADIA

Slightly more is known of Arcadia, although it is very difficult to disentangle myth from history in the stories that concern it. According to Herodotus, the Arcadians had always occupied Arcadia; they were autochthonous. However, they had to defend themselves agianst Indo-European invaders, and not until the fifth century were the frontiers of Arcadia firmly established. In this period most of the country was divided into villages grouped together in communities of the *ethnos* type. But between the late sixth and the early fifth centuries two urban centres developed synoecisms with neighbouring communities in their respective regions, and in this way engendered the two first Arcadian cities: Tegea and Mantinea. These two were not followed by any other cities until the fourth century, when the Arcadian League was set up, along with the creation of a third city, Megalopolis.

Although politically fragmented, on a few occasions the Arcadians did demonstrate a real unity. For example, just before the battle of Salamis, they marched as one to the isthmus of Corinth in order to defend the Peloponnese against the advance of the Persians; and in the fifth century they united and fought together against Sparta.

Arcadia was a land of poor and very dry soil, and agriculture was by no means predominant there. Its principal resource was herding; large herds of horses, sheep, goats and their herdsmen (and their god Pan) occupied a position of great importance, unlike most Greek cities. Arcadia was also a land of swamps and marshes on account of the geographical configuration of valleys deep in the mountains, where it was impossible for the water to drain away. These zones were unsuitable for agriculture, but a paradise for birds, and they constituted splendid hunting grounds. The Arcadians lived in a harsh environment but, if we are to believe a unanimous Greek tradition, they set great store by developing institutions of a kind to soften their lifestyle. They learned music and produced it, above all choral singing, in religious festivals and all suitable social occasions such as banquets. On account of their great courage in battle, from the fifth century on they were greatly sought after as mercenaries. Finally, by the classical period, the Arcadians were playing a role of central importance in the Greeks' representations of the origins of man and civilization.

ARGOLIS

This region to the north-east of the Peloponnese was bordered by the Gulf of Argolis to the south and the Saronic Gulf to the north. Several small cities, Prasiae, Nauplia, Asine, Hermione, Calauria, Troezen and Epidaurus all cowered before Argos, which in fact destroyed Asine (in about 725–700) and annexed its territory, then that of Nauplia, having already proceeded in the same fashion against Mycenae and Tiryns.

Argos could depend on fertile agricultural land and its craftsmen produced pottery and bronze objects. Here too, the tombs testify to the wealth of a small proportion of the population, while the construction of sanctuaries (the *Heraion* at some distance from the town, and that of Apollo actually in the town) indicate the affluence of the community as a whole. As to the city's social organization, it is known to have been divided into four tribes. A category of dependent peasants, called the Gymnetes (*gumnos* means someone without arms) is known to have existed.

What is known of the political history of Argos revolves around Pheidon, an enigmatic figure since there is considerable disagreement as to the exact dates of his period in power and the form and results of his rule. (The schema suggested below will accordingly in all likelihood be challenged!) Pheidon appears to have been the leader of Argos at the end of the seventh century and the beginning of the sixth (rather than fifty years earlier, as is sometimes suggested). If that is the case, he cannot have been the victor

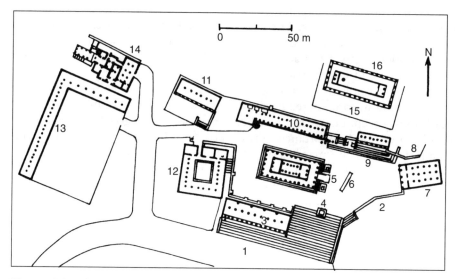

Figure 13 Plan of the Heraion sanctuary (in the territory of the city of Argos). 1 southern *analemma* wall (fifth century); 2 transverse *analemma* wall; 3 south portico (mid-fifth century); 4 altar; 5 new temple; 6 altar; 7 hypostyle hall (fifth century); 8 archaic *analemma* wall; 9, 10 archaic porticoes; 11 archaic propylaea; 12 west building with a central courtyard (with banqueting halls); 13 gymnasium; 14 Roman baths; 15 *analemma* wall of the old temple; 16 old temple (from P. Lévêque, *Nous partons pour la Grèce*, p. 152, fig. 32)

over Sparta at the battle of Hysiae (669), nor can it have been he who helped the people of Pisa to gain control of Olympia and its games in 668. However, he may have played a part in founding the games of Nemea. He is presented as a classic figure of a reformer; in particular, he is supposed to have introduced a system of measures for both solids and liquids that greatly facilitated the trading of agricultural products and made it much fairer.

Argos was the greatest rival of Sparta in the Peloponnese. It never entered any system of alliance dominated by Sparta and the two cities were frequently at war. Although victorious at the battle of Hysiae in 669, Argos was conquered in 546 and thereafter lost its claims to the Thyreatis. It was beaten again at the turn of the sixth and fifth centuries, at the battle of Sepeia. The antagonism between these two cities directly influenced the systems of alliance set up in the fifth century, particularly during the Peloponnesian War, in which Argos was a natural ally for Athens.

THE ISTHMUS REGION

Apart from Corinth (see p. 67), the cities of Sicyon and Megara occupied this region bridging the Peloponnese and central Greece.

Megara sent men to found new towns in Sicily and in the Bosphorus region, as we have seen above. Its regime was oligarchic, interrupted by a period of tyranny in the days of Theagenes' power. According to Theognis, there was violent conflict between the landowners and new citizens. In about 540 Theognis, a supporter of the aristocracy, virulently attacked any idea of a shift towards greater equality before the law (*isonomia*): 'Our city is still a city, but its inhabitants have changed; those who once knew nothing about rights and laws, and were only just capable of clothing themselves in their goat-skins and pasturing beyond the city walls, like deer, are now the good ones; and the respectable folk of yesteryear are now considered as nothing.' Relations first with Corinth, then with Athens, two cities with common borders with Megara, deteriorated. The conflict with Athens turned to the latter's advantage when it annexed the island of Salamis, but the hostility between the two cities continued to smoulder until it found expression again during the events leading up to the Peloponnesian War.

Sicyon   The history of Sicyon emerged from obscurity thanks to Herodotus who, writing of the family of the legislator Cleisthenes of Athens, recorded the story of his grandfather Cleisthenes, the tyrant of Sicyon. This tyrant belonged to the Orthagorid family, who governed the city from the end of the seventh century until 510. He came to power at the beginning of the sixth century and Herodotus attributed to him the measures taken in the struggle against the local aristocracy. To pour ridicule upon the great families who were split into three Dorian tribes, he is supposed to have given the latter the demeaning names of 'Pigs', 'Donkeys' and 'Piglets', meanwhile honouring his own tribe with the name 'Leaders of the people' (*archelaoi*). This action, along with a prohibition against the aristocrats practising the cult of Adrastus, the hero of Argos, seems to have been part of a systematic policy designed to put down the aristocracy, attributable to the tyrants rather than to an impulse on the part of the non-Dorian population to take their revenge against the Dorian families. Cleisthenes of Sicyon is also known for the offerings he made at Delphi (where he constructed several edifices) and, of course, for the lavish wedding celebrations that he organized for his daughter Agarista, which involved offering hospitality for a whole year to the flower of the entire Greek aristocracy. Sparta took a hand in toppling Aeschines, the last of these tyrants. Sicyon then, in accordance with the usual pattern of events, reverted to an oligarchic regime.

THE AEGEAN ISLANDS

Most of the Aegean islands boasted one or several cities. These were isolated communities, cut off by the sea that surrounded them. Ships were untrustworthy and sailors feared pirates as much as storms. Yet the sea constituted their only link with the outside world and encouraged the inhabitants of these cramped territories to travel elsewhere to found new cities. A list of them all would be of little interest, but it is worth noting their geographical situations and a few scraps of the history that is known of a small number of them.

In the Cyclades, the cities of *Paros* and *Thera* founded Thasos and Cyrene respectively, and are better known on that account. *Naxos* was situated on the largest of the islands, which was also the richest thanks to the relative fertility of its soil and the presence of marble quarries. It sent offerings not only to the nearby sanctuary of Delos, but also to Delphi. Virtually nothing is known of its internal history except that in the mid-sixth century it was ruled by a tyrant by the name of Lygdamis.

On the island of Delos, the sanctuary of Apollo was, under the influence of first Naxos, then Paros, crowded with buildings and statues, outstanding among them the lions lined up at the entrance to the sanctuary of Leto. From the mid-sixth century on, Athens took an interest in this sanctuary. Pisistratus proceeded to purify the island (by having its tombs removed). In about 525 the tyrant Polycrates of Samos took possession of the nearby island of Rheneia and consecrated it to the Delian Apollo. The sanctuary, now the proprietor of the island, drew its income from cultivating the land and also used Rheneia as a cemetery. Meanwhile religious life was developing, in particular, processions to mark the Delian festivals, in which Greeks from many of the Ionian cities took part. Thus, *The Homeric Hymn to Apollo*, written in about 700, addresses Apollo as follows: 'Phoebus . . . in Delos do you most delight your heart; for there the long-robed Ionians gather in your honour with their children and their shy wives.'

Several other cities are known through the offerings they consecrated in the sanctuaries of Olympia and Delphi, which testify to their considerable wealth. *Siphnos*, for example, built one of the most beautiful treasure-stores in Delphi.

CRETE

To the south of the Aegean Sea, between Greece and the coast of Egypt, lay Crete, the intersection of influences from the East and influences from Greece as a whole. During the archaic period its history was eventful. At first it was prosperous and full of innovations, but in the early sixth century its material culture began to crumble, although at the same time its cities were setting up institutions that were to endure for a very long time. When one reads the laws that its communities were giving themselves at the end of the archaic period and the turn of the classical period, it seems unfair to lay all the emphasis on the decline of Crete at this period.

We know of close on a hundred sites on the island, dating from the second half of the eighth century and the seventh century. Those of Knossos, Arkades, Gortyn, Dreros and Praisos are still visible. And new sites are appearing, such as Axos, Lissos, Lato and Kato Symne. The island was heavily populated and its people spoke a number of different dialects, which may have originated with different strata of settlers. The later Greek tradition tells us that during the period when legislators were setting to work in various parts of Greece, it was not uncommon for them to come to Crete to draw inspiration from the laws already in place there. Crete was reputed, at least in the fourth century, to be the place of origin of many social and religious rules and political institutions. In the archaic period several Cretan cities had a code of laws, as is testified by a number of archaic and, above all, classical inscriptions, for it was in the fifth century that these laws were recomposed and set down in writing.

The most extraordinary example is the *Gortyn code*, elaborated by a city to the south-west of Knossos. The inscription that records this text of 600 lines was carved in the early or mid-fifth century on twelve columns, using an archaic alphabet. In truth it is not exactly a code, but rather a compilation of laws, some of which are more ancient than others. They concern the status of both people and property and constitute an irreplaceable source of information about the city institutions and its system of justice, one that has no equivalent in any other Greek city of this early period.

Power was held by an aristocracy. It was exercised by magistrates known as *cosmes*, a council of elders and an assembly. Other figures, judges (*dikastai*) dispensed justice. An inscription of an unknown city (around 500) mentions the contract of a scribe by the name of Spenthisios, who was responsible for the community memory (his title was the *mnamon*). This text records both the remuneration (in kind) to which the scribe was entitled for his work and also his status in the city. He possessed the full rights of a citizen, in particular, that of participating in the *andreion* (literally 'the men's place', where all the citizens ate together), a Cretan equivalent of the Spartan *syssition*.

The life of the Cretan citizens, like that of the Spartans, was indeed of an extremely communal nature. The daily common meal was one feature of it, the education of the young, organized by the cities, was another. The citizens formed a minority group. Alongside them existed other free men known as *apertairoi*, but these held no political rights. Each dependent (known sometimes as a *dolos*, sometimes as an *oikeus*) belonged to a master but had privileges that slaves did not usually enjoy, such as the right to own domesticated animals and a house, to found a family and to defend himself before the law. The Cretan institutions served as the starting-point for the constitutional thinking and theories of the fourth-century philosophers, Plato and Aristotle in particular. They present another example of the care with which the earliest civic communities legislated in numerous domains that reached far beyond the institutions described as political.

THE CITIES OF THE COAST OF ASIA MINOR

The Greeks settled in this part of Asia – the coast of Anatolia – very gradually, from the eleventh century onward, founding cities all along the coast. Three major regions can be distinguished, according to where the Greeks who established themselves there originated and the type of Greek dialect that they spoke. To the north of the Hermus river was *Aeolis*, settled by Aeolians from Thessaly and Boeotia; in the centre was *Ionia*, settled by Ionians who had come from Attica and Euboea (as far south as the Meander river); to the south was Doris and the Dorians. Each city had its own particular history, but the Greeks of Asia Minor as a whole had to face up to several invasions and dominations: by the Lydians in the early seventh century, the Cimmerians in 650 and the Persians from 546 onward.

As in mainland Greece, the earliest form of power in these cities was monarchy, soon replaced by oligarchic government. However, these cities then suffered veritable civil wars waged between their major families, and by the end of the seventh century tyrants were ensconced in power more or less everywhere. A number of figures stand out. The poet Alcaeus, for instance, inveighed against the tyrants of his city, Mytilene, on the island of Lesbos. In the early sixth century the Penthelids, the royal family, were dethroned and the tyrants Melanchrus, Myrsilus and Pittacus, who succeeded them, forced Alceus into exile. The last of these, Pittacus (in power from 590 to 580) behaved as a good legislator, however, and after ten years even laid down his powers.

Herodotus tells of a tyrant of Miletus, Thrasybulus (late seventh, early sixth century), who gave Periander of Corinth a useful lesson in tyranny:

[Periander] sent a representative to the court [of Thrasybulus], to ask his opinion on the best and safest form of constitution, and Thrasybulus invited the man to walk with him from the city to a field where the corn was growing. As he passed through this cornfield, continually asking questions about why the messenger had come to him from Corinth, he kept cutting off all the tallest ears of wheat which he could see, and throwing them away, until the finest and best grown part of the crop was ruined . . . Periander seized the point at once; it was perfectly plain to him that Thrasybulus recommended the murder of all the people in the city who were outstanding in influence or ability. (Herodotus, V, 92)

Herodotus also followed the fortunes of the tyrant of Samos, *Polycrates* (about 532–522). According to tradition, having come to power following a civil war, Polycrates (literally 'he who has great power') turned the city into a sea power, combining the methods of piracy (used against the islands of the Aegean Sea) with those of diplomacy (used with the pharaoh of Egypt, Amasis, and the king of Persia, Cambyses). A number of Samians opposed to the tyrant managed to persuade Sparta to lay siege to Samos, but in vain. In this period the city of Samos – possibly spurred on by the tyrant himself, possibly not – had built itself a complex of mammoth constructions, the gigantic proportions of which won the admiration of all Greeks: a tunnel covered a canal that brought water to the town; a jetty protected the port; and the temple of Hera in the Heraion sanctuary was constructed by Rhoicus, the architect of Samos. In short, Samos was one of the foremost cities in the archaic world by the time Polycrates' successor, Maiandrus, 'proclaimed *isonomia* for the city'.

Among the cities of the coast of Asia Minor, the twelve cities of Ionia (Miletus, Myus, Priene, Ephesus, Colophon, Lebedos, Teos, Clazomenes, Phocaea, Samos, Chios and Erythraea) formed *a league* and observed a common cult of Poseidon Heliconios in the sanctuary of Panionion, close the Cape Mycale, on the occasion of the festival of the Panionia. However, the union was not strong enough for the cities to succeed in banding together to defend themselves against the Persians.

Some of these cities owed their prosperity in the seventh and sixth centuries to their relations with the cities they had founded elsewhere, in particular in the Bosphorus and round the Black Sea (see p. 53f.). Some of the trade in products needed by the cities of the Greek mainland and the coasts of Asia Minor passed through their hands. As a consequence of their wealth, these cities became extraordinary centres of culture in all domains, in particular that of philosophy (see p. 109). The Persian conquest, followed by the failure of their revolt against the new power, was to have disastrous consequences for most of them.

The expansion of the Persian empire as far as the coast of the Aegean Sea was the major event of the second half of the sixth century in this region of the world (see p. 181f.). Soon it was also to affect the rest of Greece and force its cities to mobilize for a war which, for the Greeks, fast became a symbol of their resistance to despotic power.

An Aristocratic Power

The men of the eighth, seventh and sixth centuries were now peasants, now warriors, now nobles, sometimes all three at once. In the normal way of things, one would try to produce a differentiated picture of the life of each category, according to its status, but that is not possible. One particular way of life dominates all that we know of the archaic period: it is that of the 'best ones', the *aristoi*, simply because it was the subject of more poems, stories and paintings than the others. What were the forms of wealth, the lifestyle and the values of this aristocratic society?

Wealth

Land constituted the major form of property and for three centuries remained the most valuable: agricultural land, where the principal crop was that of cereals but where, in the course of this period, the cultivation of vines and olive trees also developed; and pastoral land, where herds were raised. It is hard to make out the exact size of real-estate properties. One characteristic of the period was the unequal distribution of land between free men. It was an inequality so great that a small number obtained surpluses from the cultivation of their land while the majority either survived

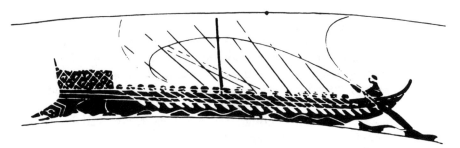

Figure 14 A penteconter: a detail from a late sixth-century Attic *dinos* (Musée du Louvre, Paris; drawing from *The Cambridge Ancient History*, III.3, Cambridge University Press, 1975, p. 336, fig. 48)

in a most precarious fashion or slipped gradually into a state of first economic, then personal dependence *vis-à-vis* the larger landowners.

Livestock was also an important form of wealth, above all cattle and horses. Sheep for wool and goats for milk, the donkey for transport, and farmyard animals – chickens were introduced into Greece at the end of the eighth century – complete the list of livestock.

A rural *house* was very simple: one or two rooms, mud walls, a thatched roof, and in some cases an outhouse used for storage. The same was true of most of the houses grouped into small towns. However, evidence of more spacious and better-built houses has been found in, for example, Smyrna, dating from the seventh century. These dwellings had brick walls set on stone foundations and some had an upper storey. Different plans were used in different regions: in eastern Greece the houses opened on to a portico; in Athens the rooms gave on to an inner courtyard.

A workshop Artisans had always existed but in the seventh and sixth centuries their numbers were on the increase. A workshop belonged to a single individual and essentially housed the tools that he needed: a forge for a bronze craftsman, a kiln for a potter, raw materials and finished products. Signatures of potters and painters first began to appear in the sixth century. Sculptors too sometimes signed their statues before consecrating them to the gods. Offerings of this kind testify to a measure of affluence among craftsmen.

Ships While craftsmen appear not to have been landowners as well, the status of shipowners and traders is less clear. Two categories seem to have coexisted: large landowners who used their surpluses for the construction of ships and, having built them, went off to trade their cargoes; and, alongside these, men who were professional merchants and made trade their principal activity. Ownership of one or two vessels was clearly a sign of great wealth. Aegina was one of the most powerful and prosperous cities in the archaic world, and most of its wealth depended on the activities of its fleet.

Slaves Greek society always included slaves, but from the sixth century on slavery assumed altogether new proportions. The ranks of hereditary rural dependants, such as the helots of Sparta and the local peasants whose poverty had driven them into dependence in other cities, were now swollen by 'chattel slaves', that is, bought slaves who came from elsewhere (other Greek cities or barbarian peoples) and were sold in the same way as any other commercial commodities. According to Theopompus, the people of the the city of Chios were the first to buy slaves in this way. It now became common to own a slave who could be put to various types of work.

Movable chattels As in the Homeric poems, objects of great value still made up the bulk of a family's treasure store. Tripods, basins of bronze, arms, roasting spits, jewellery, ornaments for clothes, belts and painted vases were used as the obligatory gifts to be given on many social occasions, and also as offerings for the gods.

THE INTRODUCTION OF COINS

To be able to trade two different objects, it is necessary to have some point of reference or standard. The Greeks used a variety of standards in different periods and in different cities. The value of Odysseus' nurse, for example, had been estimated at a certain number of head of cattle. Tripods, basins, roasting spits and metal weights could also be used as standards. Coins constituted a more reliable and accurate means of determining values, for a coin was a piece of metal which, whatever its type, always weighed the same and was guaranteed by the authority that had minted it.

The earliest coins came from Lydia and King Gyges is credited with having invented the idea. At the end of the seventh century the king of Lydia, Croesus, replaced a currency of electrum (an alloy of gold and silver) with two kinds of coins, one of gold, the other of silver. The Greek cities of Asia Minor were also, at this time, minting coins of electrum of various standards and types. These coins have been found in treasure stores in Asia Minor itself, but they do not appear to have circulated further afield. Coinage spread through Greece proper from the mid-sixth century on. At this point Aegina was minting silver coins (staters) stamped with the effigy of a turtle. By 500 most Greek cities were minting coins. Two monetary standards emerged: that of Aegina (the Aeginetan standard) and that of Euboea (the Euboean standard), which Athens and Corinth adopted. The cities of southern Italy and Sicily had their own monetary standard.

The minting of coins was the prerogative of civic communities and soon became a sign of the independence of the city. The cities used this new instrument for public purposes: shipbuilding, the payment of mercenaries (in the case of tyrants), levying taxes on commercial goods, fines and the construction of public buildings. The use of coins by private individuals, for trading for instance, took longer to spread and was not common before

Figure 15 Coins: (a) coin from Knossos in Crete (mid-fifth century BC): silver stater (weight 11.4 g), representing the Minotaur (BN 83); (b) coin from Gela in Sicily (fifth century BC): silver tetradrachma (weight 17.43 g) representing the Gelas river in the form of a bull with a human face (BN 478); (c) coin from Athens (reverse side, 470–465 BC): silver tetradrachma (weight 43.01 g) showing an owl with spread wings (Bibliothèque Luynes 2037); (d) coin from Agrigentum (420–415 BC): silver tetradrachma (weight 16.81 g) representing a crab, the emblem of the city (BN 88A) (photo: Bibliothèque Nationale de France)

the fifth century, by which time smaller monetary units had been introduced, in particular, coins of bronze. Monetary circulation thus began slowly and the hoarding of coins was rare. Very few treasure hoards in the form of money date from the sixth century.

This poses the problem of why money in the form of coins appeared in Greece. Today it is no longer thought that it was the development of trade that made it necessary to create the instrument of money. Instead, following Edouard Will, the creation of this instrument is associated with the vast movement characteristic of the archaic period, which tended to promote greater equality in social relations. Coins made it possible to fix the value of an object or a piece of work and to use a reference recognized by everybody, thereby avoiding the arbitrary element in exchanges, particularly when these were effected between individuals of unequal status. At the origin of the adoption of the instrument of money there would appear to have existed a moral aspiration similar to that which prompted the setting down of laws in writing. Once diffused, this instrument soon came to be seen as a means of facilitating distant trade, and by the fifth century it was certainly playing an important economic role.

Wealth thus took many forms, and these made possible the type of life that the aristocracy led, a type of life dictated by the values that this society recommended.

THE LIFESTYLE

The initial framework of reference was the *oikos*, the household. Starting from this and spreading far beyond it, a network of social links was created through the various social practices that set the tone for life in the earliest cities.

The *oikos*, or household, was both an economic unit and a unit of kinship. People from the same family all belonged to the same *oikos*, so several generations might be living together, the rule in general being that men remained in the *oikos* of their birth, while women switched to a different *oikos* when they married. A household also performed various cults and ritual obligations, such as keeping alive the memory of the dead. An *oikos* would die when there was nobody left in it to perform the rituals in honour of the dead.

One of the preoccupations of aristocratic households was precisely to ensure the survival of the lineage, if possible increasing its wealth at the same time. From both points of view one practice in particular was important: marriage. *Greek marriage* consisted of the giving of a woman, along with gifts. The notion of gifts was central, but in different periods and different cities the gifts given along with the woman varied, as did the status of the givers. In the archaic period two different systems existed. In Sparta and certain Cretan cities, such as Gortyn, a daughter inherited land just as her brothers did, and she passed it on to her children; she was thus mistress of both her person and her possessions. In Athens and most of the other cities, a daughter inherited no land but received a dowry in the form of movable chattels; her husband then managed this, so the woman was not mistress of her own possessions. From this it is clear that the status of a woman was linked with the nature of the goods that she could possess: only the possession of civic land gave her a measure of independence.

This produced consequences affecting the preferred type of marriage. In a city where daughters could inherit land, almost all marriages took place within that community, and in particular between kin, as this made it possible to increase the family's land. In a city where daughters brought no land with them when they married, marriages could equally well take place outside the community. They could serve to cement links between great aristocratic families from different cities. One of the most famous examples is the marriage, in about 575–570, between Agarista, the daughter of Cleisthenes, the tyrant of Sicyon, and Megacles, an Athenian belonging to the Alcmaeonid family.

But marriage was not the only means by which households (*oikoi*) could forge links with other groups.

Hospitality (*xenia*) was a means of turning a stranger into a friend and forging links between two people or two families who were not of the same kin. Sometimes it was formalized by an announcement such as 'I make you my *xenos* (guest),' by an exchange of gifts or by the presentation of a *symbolon* (an object broken into two, of which each party retained one piece: fitting the two pieces together exactly could later on be a way of proving the relationship of *xenia*) or else by a meal. The obligations of hospitality were numerous, ranging from simple material assistance (food and board) all the way to mutual aid in times of conflict. But hospitality only operated in this way between people of the same rank or status. It was

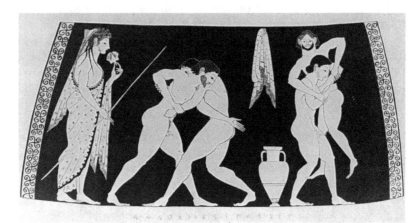

Figure 16 A wrestling scene: detail from an Attic amphora by the painter Andocides (National Museum, Berlin; Bildarchiv Preussischer Kulturbesitz)

a horizontal structure of solidarity that excluded all inferiors. In the archaic period it cemented links both between aristocratic families within the same city and between families belonging to different cities. Before cities took to drawing up agreements of mutual protection for their respective inhabitants, hospitality constituted a means of protection, whereby a host would guarantee the safety of his guest.

The concept of an *agon*, a competition or contest, was also central to social relations and in particular explains the ever-increasing success in this period of the athletic and musical competitions organized on the occasions of festivals held in honour of the gods. These competitions, quite inaccurately known as 'games' (776, the Olympic Games in honour of Zeus at Olympia; 582, the Pythian Games in honour of Apollo in Delphi; 581, the Isthmian Games, in honour of Poseidon, in the sanctuary of the Corinthian isthmus; 573 the Nemean Games in honour of Zeus in Nemea, in the northern Peloponnese). The manner and nature of the trials were fixed in this period. The central idea was that a man had to pit himself against others in order to prove his own worth. Victory in one of these contests brought great prestige for both the individual and his city. There was great rivalry to obtain a crown of leaves and hear one's exploits celebrated in song by a poet specially appointed to do this. At the beginning of the fifth century Pindar performed this task.

Along with these competitions, the necessary training areas were created, such as the *palestra* and the *gymnasium*, which were also used as places in which to train in the techniques of hoplite warfare, throwing the javelin, running, marching to the strains of the double flute and singing. It was in these places too that the athletes' bodies were on show, helping to create the canon of physical beauty to which sculptors and painters were to give figurative expression, while poets celebrated it in verse and lovers dreamed of it: the words 'So and so is beautiful' could be read on many a cup circulating at a banquet.

HUNTING

Hunting served as a school of both endurance and sociability and was another way of obtaining meat, to supplement that obtained by sacrificing domesticated animals. There were two kinds of hunting: hunting on one's own for small game, and hunting in a group for deer or wild boar, and each called for qualities that were also required of a citizen. The physical training involved also prepared a man for combat; in fact, the Greeks represented hunting as a war against the animal world and, more generally, as the art of acquiring mastery over wild nature. 'The best and most necessary of wars is the war between men as a group against the savagery of beasts. The next best is war waged by Greeks against Barbarians and those who are by nature their enemies,' wrote Isocrates. However, hunting and warfare did not respect the same laws, and to confuse them was a crime.

Hunting also served to strengthen links between members of the same community, for it defined the rules of what was more than a sport, a way of behaving with one's equals. The archaic aristocratic society passed much of its time in hunting, as is testified in particular by the frequent use of the theme in vase paintings. It was also around this activity that the Greeks elaborated many stories about heroes, myths that in various ways defined the limits set on the activities of men.

Finally, hunting was connected with the erotic world. The hunted game would often be presented as a love token; and the metaphors of hunting are also those of love, love between men and women, and also love between men – another important part of social life.

BANQUETS

Banquets, in the sight of the gods, constituted one of the centres of social and cultural life and one of the occasions in which archaic citizenship found expression.

A banquet fell into two successive phases. First those present would eat meat previously sacrificed in homage to a god, and cereals; then they would drink a mixture of wine and water, consecrating it to Dionysus. Both the food and the drink were made sacred by the ritual fashion in which they had been prepared and their consecration to the gods.

The second phase of a banquet was called a *sympósion*, and in it men drank together. Both texts and paintings testify to its importance, for this was the key moment of sociability. It took place according to precise rules decided by the group and presided over by the leader of the banquet, the

Figure 17 A banquet scene: detail from an Attic crater, early sixth century (Musée du Louvre, Paris; © Photo RMN)

symposiarch. The rules concerned in particular the series of libations that were to be offered to the gods, the proportions of wine and water to be mixed in the crater, the circulation of the wine cups among the participants, and who should speak when. Their purpose was to establish equality between all present.

As can be seen in the detail from an Attic crater (figure 17), the men reclined in pairs on couches arranged all round the banquet hall, the *andron*, or room for men. Alongside each couch was a table on which dishes and cups could be set. The picture is not designed as a realistic snapshot of a particular moment in the banquet, but represents a combination of important points in it, as is suggested by the various objects portrayed. Young men, without beards, alternate with older, bearded men. Such a mixture of age groups was a common feature of aristocratic sociability.

Other activities, not represented on this pot, took place during banquets: the *kottabos* game (a game of skill which consisted of projecting a drop of wine into a cup held by another drinker), music and singing, the recitation or improvisation of poems. Most archaic poetry was designed to be sung in the course of banquets, which on that account became the place in which the values and norms of society were affirmed.

The Greeks present at a banquet all shared the same culture, belonged to the same social group and had access to the same form of power. Without being as strictly regimented as in a Spartan *syssitia*, participation in a banquet was synonymous with citizenship. When a man acceded to citizenship he could also take part in these banquets, in which discussion might turn on constitutional law as well as on the pleasures of love and warrior exploits. In a banquet the rules of equality applied. An aristocratic banquet was an expression not just of a way of life, but of the archaic way of being a citizen.

FORMS OF CULTURE

WRITING AND READING

The adoption of the alphabet around the mid-eighth century made it possible to develop writing. What were its various social uses? The civic community was very soon making use of writing to set down the laws proposed by legislators; these amounted to veritable constitutions and codes of justice. These texts were inscribed in writing on stelae that were then set up in the most frequented places of the city so that the rules of power were made public and were thereby shared by all. Writing was also used by a magistrate with the special skills of a scribe or secretary, a kind of public writer, whose task was to transcribe all decisions concerning public affairs, in particular, those adopted by the assemblies.

But writing was not used solely by the political authorities. Individual citizens could use it for other purposes. Here are two examples: the in-scriptions made by merchants on the bottom of pots served to indicate quantities and prices; and formal recognitions of debts inscribed on lead tablets (the most ancient of which, discovered in Corcyra, date from around 500) attest to the use of writing in relations of an economic nature.

Finally, and perhaps most important, writing made possible the devel-opment of a whole new way of thinking in every domain. Philosophers, geometers, doctors, geographers, and historians, equipped with their tab-lets and a stylus, explained, described, verified, reported and transmitted a body of knowledge that was itself a product of writing. The introduction of writing thus gave rise to new forms of knowledge and new intellectual disciplines.

But writing was nothing without reading, and the practice of reading developed simultaneously. It was reading aloud, put at the service of the written text, to give it life and enable it to be known and diffused. The practice of reading aloud established, as it were, a bridge between the oral culture of the early archaic period and the gradual establishment of a culture dependent upon writing, up to the point, towards the end of the sixth century, when silent reading made its appearance.

Archaic culture took many forms. But, having just noted the role of writing and reading, we should first remember that it was also in this period that both lyric poetry and philosophy were born.

Figure 18 Alceus and Sappho as rhapsodes: detail of a vase in Munich (drawing by F. Lissarague)

LYRIC POETRY

The adjective 'lyric' stresses one particular characteristic of archaic poetry, namely that it was designed to be sung or declaimed to a musical accompaniment, usually played on a lyre or a flute. These poems, many of them quite short, came in a wide variety of rhythms and themes. The language in which they were composed also varied according to local dialects: lyric poetry was produced in absolutely all regions of the Greek world. As well as themes considered timeless, such as love, these poems would frequently tackle subjects peculiar to their own time, such as political conflicts. The texts would either be sung by a single singer – in which case they are known as monody – or else by a choir, in which case they are known as choral poetry. The choirs were formed of young people and there was dancing as well as singing, particularly at festivals held to honour the gods. Another function of choral lyric was to honour the victors in the great competitive games. These poems, or *epicinia*, would be recited in the course of the celebration arranged by the victor's city, to welcome him on

Table 4   The most famous archaic poets

Poet	Date	City	Themes
Iambic poetry			
Archilocus	650	Thasos	War, love, fables
Semonides	7th	Amorgos	'On Women', misogyny
Elegiac poetry			
Tyrtaeus	7th	Sparta	War, hoplite heroism
Solon	7th–6th	Athens	Politics, morality
Theognis	6th	Megara	Defence of the *aristoi*
Individual lyricism			
Alcaeus	630–580	Mytilene	Politics, drinking songs
Sappho	7th–6th	Mytilene	Marriage, emotional love
Anacreon	6th	Teos–Athens	Banquets, wine, love
Choral lyric			
Alcman	7th	Sparta	Choirs of girls
Stesichorus	6th	Sicily	Mythical stories
Simonides	6th–5th	Ceos	Epicinia
Bacchylides	5th	Ceos	Epicinia
Pindar	5th	Thebes	Epicinia

his return. Then there was also iambic poetry (the iambic was a satirical poem recited to the accompaniment of stringed instruments) and elegiac poetry (declaimed to the sound of flute music).

The table above sets out the names of the most famous archaic poets, but most of their works have come down to us only as fragments. That is the case with Sappho, the only known female author, who, in Mytilene on the island of Lesbos, taught music and singing to girls, so that they could perform in a chorus.

Lyric poetry, in which the author wrote in the first person, addressed its audience directly and spoke of contemporary themes, marking a definite break with the epic genre of earlier times.

PHILOSOPHY (THE PRESOCRATICS)

By the late seventh century already, first in Ionia, then southern Italy, men were exploring new ways of explaining the world (*cosmos*), to the extent

Table 5 The Presocratics

Philosopher	Date	City	Themes
Thales	640–550	Miletus	Astronomy, mathematics
Anaximander	7th–6th	Miletus	Enquiry into nature (*phusis*)
Anaximenes	mid–6th	Miletus	On the properties of air
Heraclitus	540–480	Ephesus	Mobility and conflicts in the world
Pythagoras	7th–6th	Croton	Mathematics, individual religious beliefs
Xenophanes	570–475	Colophon then Elea	Against an anthropomorphic view of the gods, notion of a single god
Parmenides	515–450	Elea	Being and non-being
Zeno	489	Elea	Inventor of dialectic
Anaxagoras	500–428	Agrigentum then Athens	Close to Pericles
Democritus	5th	Abdera	Atomist
Empedocles	490–?	Agrigentum	'On nature', 'On purifications'

that they were distancing themselves from the explanations until then given by myths. This development was to have crucial consequences for ideas on the political organization of cities. It is quite impossible to summarize in a few sentences the complex and subtle theories elaborated during this period, theories of which we know thanks to the few fragments of works that have been preserved and, above all, the ancient philosophical tradition, which continued to be based on the writings of those archaic philosophers, in that it either criticized them or attempted to perpetuate them. One of the major features, for a historian at least, as J.-P. Vernant has shown (in *The Origins of Greek Thought*, London, 1982) is the emphasis placed upon equality, and the symmetry of the principal powers that form the world, which was perceived as the result of a balance between equal powers, not as the product of a hierarchy and the power of a single individual (monarchy). This egalitarian way of conceiving of the way that the universe works is closely connected with the establishment of new institutional practices in the world of men, which were trying to introduce *isonomia* (equality before the law).

THE ARTS

Between the eighth and the seventh centuries, techniques and designs from the East were adopted in major artistic fields such as work in gold or bronze and pottery, to such an extent that the seventh century is often said to be the period of 'orientalizing art'. The archaic period was a time of

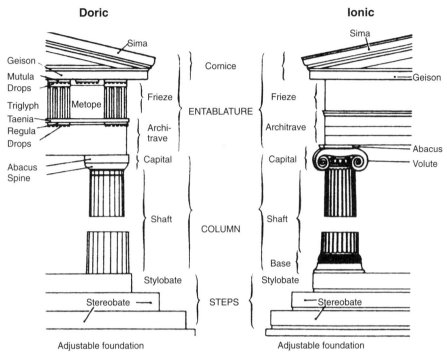

Figure 19 The orders of Greek architectural (from J.-J. Maffre, *L'Art grec*, Paris, PUF, 1986, p. 72, fig. 9)

innovations and the best way to learn about its creations is to plunge into the major syntheses of Greek art that now exist.

It is now believed that, in the field of architecture, the first temples built of stone appeared right at the end of the eighth century (which is the date of the most ancient state of the temple of Artemis in Ephesus). Earlier constructions were of clay and wood. In the seventh century a particular design of temples became established in two major styles: Ionic and Doric. In the sixth century temples proliferated throughout the Greek world, from Asia Minor to Italy. Also in the sixth century, the presentation of offerings to the gods, in particular in the pan-Hellenic sanctuaries of Olympia and Delphi, prompted the construction of smaller buildings, known as treasure stores. Some of their ornaments in the form of sculptures and earthenware objects have been preserved.

In the field of *sculpture*, all kinds of materials were used. Hammered bronze was used to make the great basins placed on conical supports (instead of tripods, as previously), decorated with the heads of exotic animals, and for ornaments on belts. The earliest bronze statues using hollow moulds appeared in the mid-sixth century. Figurines were modelled

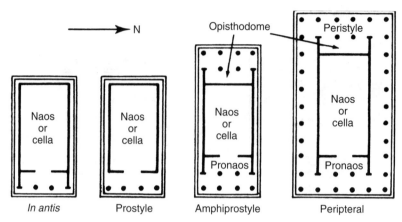

Figure 20 Various plans of Greek temples (from J.-J. Maffre, *L'Art grec*, Paris, PUF, 1986, p. 75, fig. 10)

from terracotta, but it was stone that became the material *par excellence* for sculpture, with the production of large statues of standing figures in the late sixth century: statues of nude men (*kouroi*) or clothed girls (*korai*), which were destined to be offerings in sanctuaries or to mark tombs in the cemeteries.

Pottery For a historian, all these objects constitute precious documents. On a number of counts their manufacture forms one aspect of the history of technology, and the phenomenon of their production is an aspect of social history in that, in the archaic period, it was accompanied by the appearance of artisan quarters in Greek towns and workshops close to the sanctuaries: the circulation of these objects provides one of our best means of learning about trade in this period, as we have already noted with regard to bronzes and pottery. The hoarding of them and, in particular, their being deposited in tombs provide insights into the wealth of their owners, their clientship and its prevailing tastes. The part they played in the sealing of alliances between men and the gods, when they were used as offerings, was a major feature in religious life. Finally, their ornamentation and the extraordinary diffusion of figurative representation constitute a major source for the understanding of, not so much the customs of daily life, but rather the imaginary representations of the archaic societies. For their sculpted or painted scenes, like their poems, are the creations of artists who, although they may take reality as their starting-point, then transpose it in their own way. One of the tasks of a historian is to try to understand how those imaginary representations came to be created.

Figure 21 Types and shapes of vases: (a) pithos; (b) amphora;
(c) pelike; (d) crater with scroll handles; (e) dinos; (f) stamnos; (g) hydria;
(h) loutrophoros; (i) oenochoe; (j) cantara; (k) cup; (l) skyphos; (m) aryballos;
(n) alabastron; (o) lecythos; (p) pyxis (from H. Metzger, *La Céramique grecque*,
2nd edn, Paris, PUF, 1964, pp. 15, 18, 20)

The lifestyle and the culture of the archaic society were exceptionally
rich, but they no doubt owed their vitality to the coherence of the social
group that produced them: here we are provided with a rare example of an
aristocratic culture.

3 / THE CLASSICAL PERIOD THE FIFTH CENTURY

New Institutions in Athens

The reforms of Cleisthenes

After the fall of the Pisistratids, the government in Athens reverted to an oligarchy, a small number of great families in competition for power. It was at this point, in 508–507, that a member of the Alcmaeonid family, Cleisthenes, got the assembly to adopt a series of measures that were to provide the Athenian institutions with a general framework that was to remain unchanged throughout the classical period (the fifth and fourth centuries). Two texts constitute our principal sources for an understanding of what are traditionally known as 'the reforms of Cleisthenes': one is a passage from Herodotus' *Histories*, the other a passage from Aristotle's *The Constitution of the Athenians (Athenaion Politeia)*.

The general context of the reform has been described above: it comprised the end of tyranny, the return to power of the aristocracy and the clash between aristocratic families, particularly the Alcmaeonid family and the family of Isagoras. The Alcmaeonids had played a political role of importance ever since at least the end of the seventh century. One of its members, Megacles, had been involved in the assassination of Cylon. Now allies of the tyrants, now exiled by them, the Alcmaeonids were a strong presence in Delphi, where they financed the reconstruction of the temple, which had been burned down; and they had used their influence to persuade Sparta to intervene to overthrow the tyranny, thereby making it possible for them to return to Athens. The family of Isagoras had originated in Ionia, and was part of the Eupatridae clan.

In the immediate context, Isagoras was archon when 'Cleisthenes, who was getting the worst of it, managed to attach the people to his *hetairia*' (Herodotus, V, 65). This is a cryptic statement and, if considered as a description of Cleisthenes' seizure of power, fails to explain both the nature of that power and upon what it depended: The term 'people' (*dèmos*) is vague; *hetairia* meant an informal group of companions; Cleisthenes does not appear to have become *archon*. The result of the manoeuvre is clear, however: Cleisthenes was able to propose a series of reforms to the assembly and to get them passed. He then disappeared from the political scene.

THE DEFINITION AND DISTRIBUTION OF CITIZENS

These reforms established a new definition and distribution of the part of the population that was to have the right to participate in the political institutions, in other words, those who qualified for citizenship. They spelt out how a number of political institutions should function and created new ones.

The origin of the new citizens is not clear. They were either Athenians who had been banished by the tyrants and had now been recalled to Athens, or part of the population domiciled in Athens who had so far had no political rights. In both cases the bestowal of citizenship no longer appeared to be connected with the possession of real estate, as it used to be. As a result, the citizen body was definitely increased.

Tribes, trittyes, demes The citizen population was now divided into ten tribes instead of four. These tribes took the name of their founding hero; they were names selected by the Delphic oracle out of a list of a hundred heroes. For example, the Erechtheid tribe bore the name of the founding hero Erechtheus. Each tribe comprised a population that lived in three different parts of Attica, and all these territorial divisions were known as trittyes. Each tribe thus consisted of three *trittyes*, one situated in the zone called *Paralia* (the coastal zone), one in the zone called *Mesogeia* (the internal zone) and the third in the *Astu* (the town zone). Finally, each tribe comprised a number of *demes*, that is, villages, each with a surrounding agricultural territory or urban quarters. Each citizen was from now on known by the name of his deme, in which he had to be registered if his rights were to be recognized. Tribes, trittyes and demes represented the bases for the recruitment of members for all the institutions of political life.

This reorganization was represented in Antiquity either as the result of Cleisthenes' desire to emulate his ancestor Cleisthenes, the tyrant of Sicyon, who had introduced a new system of classification for the population of his city, or of his concern to integrate new citizens who were not members of any of the old tribes. But Aristotle already spotted Cleisthenes' determination to intermingle all the Athenians. His system did indeed mix people with a variety of activities (cultivators, fishermen and sailors, craftsmen, merchants . . .) and had the effect of limiting the clientship of the major families, which rested upon local territorial roots. From now on, none of them could hope to dominate the decisions of the tribe, given that its members came from demes that were geographically distant from one another, and the tribe comprised people with a wide variety of daily occupations. The reforms for this reorganization were above all political, the purpose being to create frameworks within which a greater number of people could take part in political decisions.

Most of the institutions of the classical period stemmed, in the way that they functioned, from the system of tribes, trittyes and demes created by Cleisthenes, as we shall see (p. 119f.).

Figure 22   The monument of the eponymous heroes in the agora of Athens. This drawing reconstructs the appearance of the monument on which official documents were posted. The heroes are the eponymous heroes of the ten tribes created by Cleisthenes: Erechtheus, Aegeus, Pandion, Leo, Acamas, Oineus, Cecrops, Hippothoon, Ajax, Antiochus (from J. M. Camp, *The Athenian Agora*, London, Thames and Hudson, 1986, p. 98)

The new creations existed alongside more ancient institutions, as Aristotle reminds us: 'Cleisthenes allowed the *genè*, the *phratries* and the *priesthoods* to remain in their traditional forms.' The role of the families (*genè*, singular *gènos*) was essentially religious. Some of them held priestly functions throughout the entire classical period. Similarly, the phratries continued to exist: groups of people all of whom recognized a common ancestor ('those with the same father'). Their role is revealed in the Athenian religious festivals such as the *Apatouria*, in which the phratries welcomed into their ranks the young men who were about to become citizens.

THE ESTABLISHMENT OF *ISONOMIA*

Cleisthenes' reforms pose two categories of questions: what were the models from the past that he followed; and, looking into the future, how far, exactly, were these measures to effect the future elaboration of a democratic regime? To draw attention, as Herodotus did, to the reforming tradition of Cleisthenes, the tyrant of Sicyon, the grandfather of the Athenian Cleisthenes, was, apart from its anecdotal interest, to emphasize

116

the similarities between all archaic legislation. From this point of view, Cleisthenes' reform fitted into the tradition of legislators who tried in a variety of ways to resolve the social and political crises of the archaic cities. There can be no doubt that those examples were known to Cleisthenes, but he was probably also affected by developments in sixth-century thought which, as has been noted above, in a number of domains set at the heart of the organization of the world a respect for balance, *isonomia*, equality before the *nomos* or law (in the sense of 'that which regulates'). It was a concept that was also used in the political domain. A banquet song (*scolion*) thus glorifies the assassins of the tyrant Hipparchus for having restored *isonomia* to Athens. Similarly, according to Herodotus, the successor to Polycrates, the tyrant of Samos, whose name was Maiandrus, rejected tyrannical power, declaring 'I, for my part, place power at the centre. I proclaim *isonomia* for you.' As P. Lévêque and P. Vidal-Naquet point out in their book *Cleisthenes the Athenian*, *isonomia* stood in opposition to tyranny; a city with *isonomia* was one in which those who took part in public life did so as equals. However, to create institutions of a kind to make this kind of equality possible was to take a further step forward, a step that avoided the necessity to have recourse to the providential legislator or to a tyrant. Seen purely from the point of view of the ideas that characterized the end of the archaic period, the importance of Cleisthenes' reform lay in having institutionalized *isonomia*. But the Greeks of the classical period perceived Cleisthenes' reform as a significant step in the direction of democracy. Both Herodotus and Aristotle describe the reform as, respectively, 'democratic' and 'much more democratic than Solon's reform'. It is on this account that Cleisthenes' reform is often said to mark the start of Athenian democracy, despite the well-known fact that it was to take several generations for the institutions to take on a truly democratic character. So Cleisthenes can be seen both as the last of the archaic legislators and also as the first politician of classical Athens.

THE DEVELOPMENT OF INSTITUTIONS IN THE FIFTH CENTURY

A number of new institutions adopted during the first forty years of the fifth century were to give the *dèmos* more weight in the constitution of Athens.

The law on ostracism was the first new measure. It was adopted either at the same time as the Cleisthenian proposals or at the beginning of the fifth century and was applied for the first time in 488–487. The procedure of ostracism consisted in designating, by a secret vote in the assembly, the names of the citizens whom one wished to condemn to *atimia*, that is, to to be stripped of their political rights and exiled for a period of ten years. Once a year, at the sixth prytany, the assembly of the people voted with a show of raised hands on whether it wished to proceed to a vote on ostracism. If it did, the next step was a secret ballot on the name of the man to

Figure 23 Examples of *ostraka*. An *ostrakon* was a shard of pottery on which a citizen inscribed the name of the man he chose to exclude from political life for a period of ten years. On these fifth-century *ostraka* the names that appear are those of Aristides, the son of Lysimachus, and Cimon, the son of Miltiades, both of whom were, in effect, ostracized.

be condemned. A quorum of 6,000 citizens was necessary for the ballot to take place. The name of the procedure was derived from the manner in which the ballot was conducted: the name of the man each citizen wished to condemn was written on a fragment of pottery called an *ostrakon*. Many such inscribed shards have been discovered in the course of excavations of the agora. They bear the names of many of the famous statesmen of Athens. The aim of this procedure was to rid the city of any figure whose political influence became too great and who might be tempted to act as a tyrant. The ballot proceeded in a contradictory fashion. The assembly had to choose between the names of two citizens. Presumably the purpose of this was to defuse the conflicts and rivalries by exiling one of the two most prominent figures of the moment. It was a radical, and sometimes unjust, procedure and it underlines the importance ascribed to the judgement of the *dèmos* in political life.

The oath of the bouleutes At some unknown date, the members of the *Boulè* were required to swear an oath when they took office. It consisted of an undertaking not to favour any illegal manoeuvre and to respect the law. The spirit of this oath was also to prevent any return to tyranny.

The role of the strategoi The *strategoi*, who were the army chiefs placed under the control of the *polemarch* archon, quite suddenly acquired greater autonomy. Once they were elected, each was assigned to one of the ten tribes and together they formed a college. Their power became resolutely political, for their legitimacy stemmed from their election by the *dèmos*. It was as *strategoi* that most of the statesmen of the classical period governed.

The role of the archons This magistracy was one of the most ancient in Athens; there were nine archons and one thesmosthete. The way in which they were designated was altered in 487–486. At first they had been elected; but now they were selected by lot from a list of 500 names of members of the *dèmos*, all of whom belonged to the two highest census classes (the *pentacosiomedimnoi* and the *hippeis*). After this the power of the archons appears to have declined: for example, the *polemarch* lost all his military power, although he retained his religious and judicial responsibilities. The decline of the archons' power is often considered to have coincided with the rise of the *strategoi*.

These various measures all marked the weakening of the archaic aristocratic institutions, a process rounded off by the laws attributed to Ephialtes.

Ephialtes' laws limiting the power of the Areopagus The Areopagus was a council that dated from the time when the aristocracy was in power. Its sessions took place on the hill of Ares, hence its name. It was composed of all ex-archons, that is, men from the two highest census classes, and they held office for life. Its powers, both judicial and political, were considerable, and it seems to have acted as a brake upon evolution in the direction of greater participation of the *dèmos* in political power. The laws proposed by Ephialtes transferred the powers of the Areopagus, with the exception of those that were of a religious nature, to the *Boulè* and the *Heliaea* (the people's court of law). The *Boulè* now interviewed magistrates when they took up their responsibilities and when they left them, at the *eisangelia*, and ensured that the constitution was being respected. We know nothing of the opposition provoked by these measures, except that Ephialtes was assassinated.

As a result of a series of institutional amendments, the Cleisthenian *isonomia* acquired more content, but it was not until around the mid-fifth century, with the creation of the *misthos* and the redefinition of the civic body under Pericles (see p. 148) that a real place was made for the *dèmos* in the functioning of the institutions. However, there was of course a background to this evolution in the institutions: political events had brought about a number of social changes that made it essential to give access to political power to a wider range of strata in the *dèmos*.

A PICTURE OF THE INSTITUTIONS IN THE CLASSICAL PERIOD

There are certainly practical reasons for presenting a picture of the Athenian political institutions in the classical period, but it should not obscure the evolving historical context and the developments to which these institutions testify directly, which are described in other chapters of this book. In *The Constitution of the Athenians*, Aristotle (or more probably a member of his school) prefaces his static description of the Athenian institutions with a historical overview. Even in the course of the two centuries known as 'the classical period' (the fifth and the fourth), the content, organization and function of several of these institutions changed.

The state of the institutions described below is, by reason of our sources, that of the period of Demosthenes, so the present account might have been expected to appear in the section of this book that is devoted to the fourth century. However, in order to understand the political life of fifth-century Athens, it seemed necessary to describe at this point how the various institutions functioned. For lack of space, it is not possible to provide a detailed history of each of the institutions within the framework of the present book. The work by M. Hanson, *The Athenian Democracy in the Age of Demosthenes* (Oxford, 1991) provides all the chronological details necessary for an in-depth study of each of them.

Let us take as our guideline the rubric of an Athenian decree in order to understand, step by step, how these institutions underpinned a formulary every bit as complex as that of our own modern decrees: 'It has pleased the council and the people, the Acmantis tribe exercised the prytany, Onasippus was secretary, Eumedes was *epistates*, Leon made the proposal.'

THE COUNCIL OR BOULÈ

Since Cleisthenes, the *boulè* had comprised 500 members, recruited by lot from the lists made up in the demes of all the citizens over 30 years old. Each provided fifty *boulè* members. Anyone could be a member and his responsibilities lasted for one year. Each tribe's fifty members held uninterrupted power in the council for one-tenth of the year. This portion of the year was called a prytany and the members of the *boulè* who held the power were known as the *prytaneis*. The above-mentioned rubric states: 'The Acamantis tribe held the prytany.' When a prytany came to an end, it was the turn of another group of *boulè* members to exercise their authority. Lots were drawn to decide on the order to be followed. Furthermore, each day lots were drawn to decide the name of the *prytaneus* who was to be the *epistatès* of the *prytaneis* for that day, that is, the president of the council. In our example the *epistatès* is called Eumedes. It seems that from 487 on the *epistatès* also presided over the sessions of the assembly and held the keys of the treasury and the archives. The fifty *prytaneis* represented the permanence of the city. They lived together, and some slept in the round building known as the *Tholos*, at the side of the agora, for the duration of their prytany.

Before taking up his responsibilities, a member of the *boulè* would undergo a *dokimasia*, an examination to verify that the candidate fulfilled all the required conditions for this post (citizenship, age, respect for the family cults, no criminal record . . .). Before every meeting in the building known as the *bouleterion*, at the side of the agora, the *boulè* made sacrifices and poured libations and the citizens present donned wreaths of myrtle. The *boulè*'s powers were extensive: it was an organ that was at once legislative, executive and judicial.

Its first function was to prepare the laws that were to be submitted to the assembly. This was known as the proboulematic function (the *proboulema* being the preliminary project). Secondly, it supervised the application of

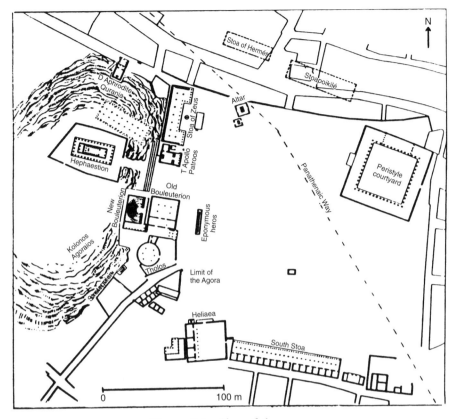

Figure 24 Plan of the agora

laws; it was also responsible for the *dokimasia* of certain magistrates and for hearing an outgoing magistrate's account of his period of office; it ran the city's administration (public works, supplies of wheat, the construction of triremes, public thoroughfares . . .); and it received embassies (*theoroi*) from other cities.

The people (dèmos) This was how decrees referred to the assembly of the people, the *ecclesia*. But now let us see who composed the *dèmos*.

THE *ECCLESIA*

The assembly brought together all the Athenian citizens. To belong to it, the sole qualification was citizenship. It was an assembly elected or selected by the drawing of lots, simply a general assembly of the civic population. There was no delegation of power in this *ecclesia*; it held power directly. In theory, it could bring together 30,000 people, if we accept this figure for the number of Athenian citizens. Of course, that is a matter of speculation,

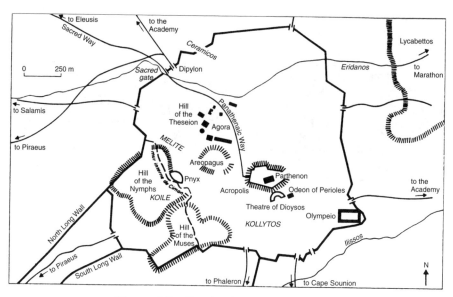

Figure 25   Sketch of the site of Athens

but we know that for grave decisions such as ostracism the required quorum of persons present was 6,000.

The *ecclesia* met on the Pnyx, the hill opposite the Acropolis, and sat from sunrise to sunset. The citizens sat on the ground, on the slopes of the hill, and a tribune for orators and an altar for sacrifices to the gods were set up there. The organization of the *ecclesia* changed over the years. In the fifth century, it met ten times a year, once every prytany; in the fourth century it met forty times a year, four times in each prytany, and one of those assemblies was known as the principal assembly. The *ecclesia* was convoked by means of a signal hoisted above the temple of the Thesmophorion. When this was lowered, the session began. It is hard to give a precise figure for the number of people present at an assembly.

A session began with a sacrifice. Then the texts on the agenda, prepared by the *boulè*, were read out. Any citizen could propose the text of a decree to be put to the vote, but he was held personally responsible for whatever he said. In the rubric of the decree that we are using as an example, the proposer's name is Leon. If a citizen made a proposal that was contrary to the existing laws, he could be charged for having violated the law. The orator mounted the tribune wearing a crown of myrtle, a sign of the sacred function upon which he was engaged. Voting was by a show of raised hands (*cheirotonia*), except in a case such as ostracism. The *prytaneis* counted the votes. Once a decree (*psephisma*) had been voted upon, it was written down on tablets or papyri that were then stored in the city archives, and was also engraved on a stone stele erected in a public place.

The subjects dealt with in the assemblies were very carefully organized. In Aristotle's day, there was a principal assembly and three legal assemblies in each prytany. The principal assembly confirmed the appointment of magistrates, deliberated on the stocks of grain, on defence and on accusations of high treason, made up lists of confiscated property and dealt with the marriages of *epikleros* girls (girls who inherited a *kleros*). The ballot on ostracism was held in the sixth prytany; magistrates were elected in the seventh. The second assembly dealt with supplicants. The third and fourth dealt with other business (sacred matters, matters to do with embassies, secular matters).

The assembly deliberated on extremely important matters, so first the relevant information needed to be efficiently circulated, and then the choices involved needed to be explained simply and clearly to the citizens. Sometimes an assembly would change its mind from one day to the next. Those who explained to the *dèmos* what exactly was at stake in its decisions thus came to acquire more and more political influence: these were the orators, who dominated the political life of the fourth century.

THE *DÈMOS*: THE CITIZENS

The term *dèmos* designated the entire body of citizens. Sometimes it is translated as 'the people', an expression that can cause confusion, for the Athenian *dèmos* did not comprise the whole of the Athenian population.

Did the citizens form a homogeneous body? Yes and no. Yes, to the extent that professional divisions played no role with regard to access to political power. No, in that throughout the classical period people were divided into four different census classes (possibly created by Solon, although this no longer seems certain), according to the amount of real estate that they owned: the *pentacosiomedimnoi*, the *hippeis*, the zeugites and the thetes (see p. 80). These distinctions did condition access to the magistracies, but gradually their discriminatory role in this domain disappeared. From 457 on, for example, any citizen could become an archon. Other divisions sometimes became noticeable between citizens, such as those between men of the town and men of the countryside, between the old and the young, or between the rich and the poor. But although these divisions are detectable in the assembly debates and voting patterns, they did not affect recruitment to institutional posts of authority.

The *dèmos* also excluded certain citizens, those condemned to *atimia*, who were deprived of their political rights and became as it were passive citizens, such as those proved cowards at war, prostitutes, city debtors and those who mistreated their parents or who had squandered the family patrimony, but also traitors, conspirators, the authors of proposals for laws that ran contrary to the *politeia* (the constitution). But the great mass of the *dèmos* were honest citizens.

A citizen was a male born from a citizen father, who had reached the age of eighteen. In virtually all cases, citizenship was acquired by birth, through descent.

In 451, when Pericles was archon, a law specified and restricted the criteria for citizenship. To be a citizen, a male now had to have both a citizen father and a mother who was the daughter of a citizen. This measure ruled out citizenship for the children of couples in which the mother was foreign to the city or came from a family of metics. It is not clear why this law was passed (perhaps the number of citizens was increasing too rapidly; perhaps it was particularly aimed against the major Athenian families, who traditionally found their wives outside the city . . .). At any rate, its consequence was to reserve citizenship for natives of Athens. However, during the Peloponnesian War this law seems to have been applied quite loosely. And under the archontate of Euclid (403–402) the law was revoked, although specifically without retroactive effect.

Athenian citizenship was closed. One could easily be excluded. The lists of citizens were periodically revised and we know that in 445–444 this led to close on 5,000 people being sold as slaves for having usurped citizens' rights. Conversely, it was virtually impossible to acquire Athenian citizenship. Known cases in which individuals were granted citizenship amount to no more than ten or so for the whole of the fifth century. However, it sometimes happened that the Athenian city granted citizenship collectively to particular groups of citizens of other cities. Two famous instances occurred in the fifth century. In 427 the city of Plataea in Boeotia, Athens' ally ever since the late sixth century, was razed to the ground by the neighbouring city of Thebes. The Plataeans who took refuge in Athens obtained the rights of citizenship. At the end of the Peloponnesian War a decree granted citizens' rights to the people of the city of Samos, who had been unswervingly loyal to Athens throughout. But apart from those two instances the granting of citizens' rights was extremely rare, and participation in political power remained jealously guarded. At several points in Athens' history attempts were made to limit the number of citizens, for example, in 411 and 404.

However, birth was not enough to become a citizen. A man also had to get the city to recognize his right to citizenship. How? By having his name inscribed on the deme register, the *lexiarkhikon grammateion*, at the age of 18. At this point the boy would be presented by his (natural or adoptive) father to the members of his deme. A twofold vote then took place, first to establish whether the boy was old enough: since there were no official registration documents, an oral enquiry would be held; secondly, to establish whether he was truly the legitimate son of a citizen and the daughter of a citizen. The name was then inscribed on the deme list. Only then could he become the member of a *trittye* and a tribe. After two years of military service (the *ephebeia*), the young citizen's name would be entered on the Assembly register. Men were sometimes rejected for having the status of metic. It was possible to appeal against such a decision before the court of law, the *Heliaea*, but if the latter ruled against the man bringing the appeal, he could be sold as a slave for having tried to usurp the rights of citizenship.

Let us return to the wording of our decree: 'The Acamantis tribe held the prytany. Onasippus was secretary, Eumedes was *epistates*, Leon made the proposal.'

The secretary took a copy of all decrees that were passed; the rest of the terms have already been explained. Of course, this rubric does not mention all the Athenian institutions. Athens also had at its disposal a number of other assemblies.

THE AREOPAGUS AND THE HELIAEA

The *Areopagus* comprised archons who had stepped down from their responsibilities. Since Ephialtes' reform (see p. 119) this council had wielded very little power. It passed judgement on crimes involving bloodshed and on certain religious matters.

The *Heliaea* was the people's court of law and comprised 6,000 citizens of over 30 years of age, known as heliasts. These were selected by drawing lots for 600 volunteers from each tribe, and they were required to swear an oath. Their judgement was sovereign. They held their session close to the agora in a building called the Heliaea, and operated on about 200 days each year. They formed a number of courts or *dikasteria*, with a variety of responsibilities, each presided over by a magistrate, and passed judgement on a wide variety of affairs. Once the reason for bringing legal action had been explained, they heard the evidence of witnesses and the pleas of the prosecution and the defence, then decided upon the innocence or guilt of the defendent in a secret ballot, using counters such as those represented in figure 26. Political lawsuits were also brought before the Heliaea and it could furthermore overrule a law passed by the *ecclesia*, following a charge of illegality (known as a *graphè para nomen*), which could be brought by any citizen (from 415 on). The importance of the Heliaea in political life increased in the course of the classical period, as can be seen clearly by the fourth century. The heliasts were the first to benefit from Pericles' creation of the *misthos*, a payment introduced in about 450 for services rendered to the civic community. The payment was initially two obols, later raised to three.

Other law-courts of an extremely specialized nature also existed, such as the Palladion and the Delphinion, but little is known of their roles except that they do not seem to have been very important. By reason of its composition, the frequency with which it met, and the wide range of its powers, the Heliaea was considerably more than a court in the modern sense of the term. It was one of the city organs that regulated political life.

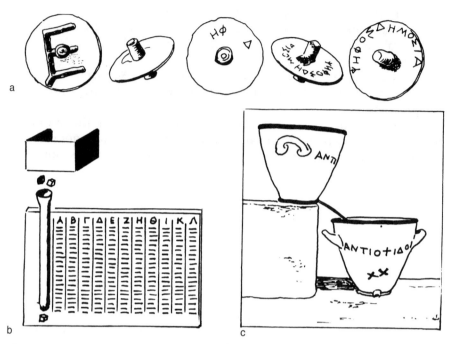

Figure 26 The functioning of the Heliaea court: counters used by the heliasts, a machine for drawing lots and a clepsydra. (a) Each counter carried the inscription *psephos demosia*, public counter. The letter in relief (e.g. E) may have indicated the section of the court's jury. The stem of the counter indicated the verdict: a level stem indicated acquittal, a projecting one condemnation. Each member of the jury held both kinds of counters, deposited the one indicating his verdict in the voting urn and placed the other in a basket. (b) This machine was used for drawing lots for the names of the judges who would preside over the court for the day. Each citizen had a wooden or bronze ticket inscribed with his name and also with the section of the Heliaea in which he was to serve. These tickets were slipped into the notches cut in the marble. A throw of the dice decided whether or not a horizontal row of names would sit in the court. (c) A clepsydra worked on the same principle as a sand-timer, but used water instead of sand. It served to measure the time allowed for speeches in the Heliaea: forty minutes for the prosecution (enough time for 33 litres of water to drip away) and twelve minutes for the defence (10 litres of water).

THE MAGISTRACIES

The assemblies needed men to execute their decisions and this task fell to 'those in command, those who held the *archè*', those whom we refer to as 'the magistrates', knowing full well, however, that they were not only officers for judicial affairs but also exercised executive power. In the classical period there were 700 magistrates, either elected or selected by the drawing of lots, and frequently grouped into colleges of ten, one magistrate for each tribe. They were subjected to a *dokimasia* (see p. 121) before they took up their responsibilities and had to give an account of their actions when they were discharged from them.

The archons   There were nine archons and one secretary: the eponymous archon (who gave his name to the year and whose functions were judicial and religious), the king-archon (*basileus*, who organized certain religious ceremonies), the polemarch (who presided over the Palladion court and ceremonies to honour those who had fallen in battle), the six *thesmothetai* (who verified laws) and the secretary to the *thesmothetai*. The conditions of their recruitment varied in the course of the fifth century. Originally, they were elected, then from 487–486 on they were selected by lot, for a period of one year. Originally they came from the two highest census classes, then in 457 the zeugites also became eligible.

The strategoi   There were ten *strategoi*, one for each tribe, elected for one year but eligible for re-election, and they belonged to the first census class. They were in command of the army. However, their power was gradually extended to foreign policy, finance and Athenian politics generally. In the fourth century they were elected without regard to their tribe and their respective functions were specified. There was a *strategos* for hoplites, one for the territory, two for Piraeus, one for the *symmoriai* and five with no fixed duties. The principal Athenian statesmen all held strategic posts: Themistocles, Aristides, Pericles (for fifteen years), Nicias, Alcibiades and Cleon in the fifth century, Timotheus, Iphicrates, Phocion, Chabrias and Chares in the fourth century.

The rest of the magistrates all had specialized functions. The little table below names them and indicates their tasks.

These political officials were not paid for their services, but the *misthos*, once introduced, was extended to some of these posts. However, the fact remains that essentially power was exercised by the citizens who belonged to the city's wealthiest families. This was a constant feature of political life, as studies on a combination of prosopography and wealth have shown clearly. But that does not mean that all these statesmen from the same social category necessarily advocated the same policies.

The respective weight given to each of these institutions changed in the course of the fifth and fourth centuries, but two of the features that characterize them seem today, if not particularly democratic, at least to have afforded a large number of citizens access to the city's affairs. Those features are the drawing of lots and the rotation of responsibilities (the latter were annual and it was normally forbidden to occupy the same post several times in succession). Both practices were based on the idea that the exercise of political functions called for no particular skills or, to be more precise, that anybody who was a citizen was by the same token capable of

Table 6 Some of the magistracies

Selected by lot:

Ten *poletai*:
   the sale of property confiscated by the city;
   adjudication on mining concessions;
   location of sacred zones.

Ten *apodectai*:
   reception and distribution of funds for the magistracies.

Ten *astynomoi*:
   maintenance of order in the town and Piraeus;
   upkeep of public thoroughfares.

The *agoranomoi*:
   supervision of markets.

Ten *metronomoi*:
   supervision of weights and measures.

Ten *sitophylakes*:
   supervision of the selling price for grain and flour;
   treasurers of Athena;
   magistrates with judicial functions.

Elected:

Magistrates with military functions: *strategoi, phylarchoi, taxiarchoi, hipparchoi*; in the fourth century, the magistrate responsible for the administration of the *theorikon* funds.

administering a sanctuary one year and taking command of troops another year. Another feature of these Athenian institutions was the omnipresence of civic safeguards (the *dokimasia*, the accountability of magistrates, ostracism and the charges brought for illegality, among others) with regard to those who exercised authority – safeguards that were designed to avoid malpractice, usurpation and the confiscation of power. This code of political deontology, sometimes forgotten by our modern democracies, is most clearly summed up by the oath that the Heliasts were required to swear. It seems fitting to close this overview of the Athenian institutions by quoting it.

The oath of the Heliasts
'I shall vote in conformity with the laws and decrees of the Athenian people and the *boulé* of the Five Hundred, and shall not cast my vote for either a tyrant or an oligarchy. If anybody topples the Athenian democracy or makes a proposal or submits a decree to that end, I shall not follow him. Nor shall I vote for the abolition of private debts or for the redistribution of the land and houses of the

Athenians. I shall not call for the return of exiles or those condemned to death. I shall not eject those who live in this country in conformity with the law and the decrees of the Athenian people and the *boulè*; I shall neither do so myself nor allow anyone else to. I shall not grant the right to hold a magistracy when this has been designated to someone who has not rendered his accounts for a previous magistracy . . . I shall not twice entrust the same magistracy to the same man nor two magistracies to a single citizen for the same year. I shall accept no gifts as a heliast . . . I am not less than thirty years old and shall listen with equal attention to the accusers and the accused and shall make my decision solely on the basis of the affair itself.'

GREEKS AND PERSIANS

THE GREEK WAR

War is the principal theme of the historians of the classical period, Herodotus, Thucydides and Xenophon. The fact is that for close on two centuries Athens was at war for two years out of every three. So, to understand the history of the Greek world in the classical period, we need to be aware of some of the essential features of Greek warfare.

To the Greeks, war was something perfectly natural, an expression of the spirit of competition (*agon*) that fuelled most social processes (lawsuits, debates in the assembly, competitions). Besides, combat had its place in rituals. It was quite common to see bare-fisted and also stone- and cudgel-wielding fights in the festivals held to honour the most civic of the deities. Warfare was the exact counterpart to the ideal of self-sufficiency: the city endeavoured to be self-sufficient internally and it entered into conflict with anyone who threatened the fragile balance of its autonomy.

If one adds to external warfare the warfare that took place within a single city, what the Greeks called *stasis*, civil war, one realizes the extent to which whole sectors of social life were understood in terms of confrontation.

War was a city responsibility, and in general military organization tended to be confused with civic organization; citizens were warriors. The cities had no professional armies; the *strategoi* in Athens and the ephors in Sparta were magistrates with no particular military experience, yet they commanded the army. Preparation for war was part of the education of every future young citizen. It took the form of exercise in the gymnasium, followed by the final apprenticeship for young men between the ages of 18 and 20, when they completed a kind of military service, known in Athens as the *ephebeia*. The ideal was certainly that of the citizen-soldier. But by the end of the fifth century there were no longer enough citizens and the cities were forced to turn to mercenaries, a development that speeded up in the fourth century. It was the people's assembly, the *apella* in Sparta, the *ecclesia* in Athens, that decided between war, truces and peace, following a public debate.

THE MANNERS OF WAR

Warfare was limited in time, for fighting took place only in the fine season. It was also limited in space: it was a matter of proving one's superiority on the battlefield. Normally, the purpose of the war was not to annihilate the enemy. But scorched-earth tactics were frequently employed: the enemy army would invade the countryside at harvest time, burn the crops and withdraw without doing battle. This weakened the powers of resistance of the city they were attacking and also its economic potential, since the city in question could not survive without adequate food supplies. It also affected its psychological potential in that the peasants, who constituted the majority of the city's inhabitants, were seriously afflicted by their land being ravaged. It was a tactic that was exploited to the full during the Peloponnesian War.

Warfare could bring in profits partly from the army's looting the countryside, and above all from the war booty. After every battle the victors divided up the spoils. In many cases, even when the gods' share had been set aside, considerable riches would still remain to be seized, distributed, then sold, as we can see from Herodotus' description of the booty captured by the Greeks from the Persian camp after the battle of Plataea.

The booty captured by the Greeks after the battle of Plataea

'Pausanias [the king of Sparta] . . . issued an order that everything of value which had fallen into their hands as a result of the battle should be collected by the helots, and that nobody should touch it. The helots accordingly went over all the ground previously occupied by the Persians. Treasure was there in plenty – tents full of gold and silver furniture; couches overlaid with the same precious metals; bowls, goblets, and cups, all of gold; and waggons loaded with sacks full of gold and silver basins. From the bodies of the dead they stripped anklets and chains and golden-hilted scimitars, not to mention richly embroidered clothes which, amongst so much of greater value, seemed of no account . . . When all the stuff had been collected, a tenth was set apart for the god at Delphi, and from this was made the gold tripod which stands next the altar on the three-headed bronze snake; portions were also assigned to the gods at Olympia and the Isthmus, and from these were made, in the first case, a bronze Zeus fifteen feet high and, in the second, a bronze Poseidon nine and a half feet high. The rest of the booty – the Persians' women, pack animals, gold, silver, and so on, was divided among the troops, every man receiving his due.' (Herodotus, IX, 80–1, translated by A. de Selincourt)

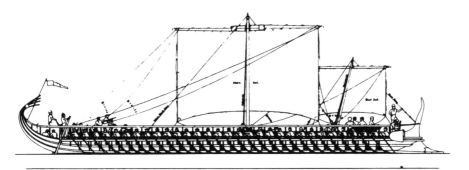

Figure 27   A trireme. A warship with a crew of 200 men, a trireme could transport 30 hoplites. The sails were seldom used, and never in battle. The maximum dimensions of a trireme were 37 by 6 m. There were three categories of oarsmen: 62 thranites, 54 zeugites and 54 thalamites, seated on three different levels. Their oars were between 4 and 4.2 m. long (drawing from *The Cambridge Ancient History*, plates to vol. IV, Cambridge University Press, 1980, p. 144, fig. 181a)

Finally, it was in warfare that the omnipresence of religion in the life of the cities best found expression. Rituals of every kind had a part to play in warfare, as did beliefs of all kinds, and the sanctuaries were full of offerings from men grateful for the victories the gods had granted them. The offerings ranged from shields hung on the temple walls to statues of great value financed by the gods' dime from the war booty.

TYPES OF COMBAT

Fifth-century warfare mainly took the form of hoplite combat. As we have seen, a hoplite was a heavily armed infantryman. He paid for his own arms, so citizens who were too poor – in Athens, the thetes – were not able to fight as hoplites. Other fighters might also take part in the battle: horsemen, who served mostly as scouts, and lightly armed men such as archers. In the Peloponnesian War a new type of fighter appeared: *the peltast*. He carried a Thracian shield (a *peltè*, a crescent-shaped framework of wood or wicker covered with sheep- or goat-skins), which was lighter than the hoplite's shield, and he fought mainly with javelins. But hoplite combat remained the model of warrior confrontation. Even when the war shifted to the sea, hoplites boarded the ships and fought on triremes just as if they were on land.

The use of ships, to carry the war into enemy territory, and sea combat appeared at the time of the Persian Wars. The instrument used by the fleet was the *trireme*, a ship with three levels of oarsmen (see figure 27). It was a vessel with a long, narrow hull (35 to 38 metres long, 4 to 5 metres wide), of shallow draught, with no bridge, which could be protected by a kind of palisade fixed to the sides. The texts distinguish between three categories of oarsmen: the thalamites (at the lowest level), the zeugites (at

Table 7 The organization of the Athenian army

Hoplites:	men between 18 and 40 years of age; 42 different classes.
Mobilization:	by means of an order posted by the taxiarchs on the monument of the eponymous heroes, in the agora, designating the classes to be mobilized.
Divisions:	a *taxis* commanded by a taxiarch (10 in all); a *lochos* (company), under a *lochagos*, was a subdivision of a *taxis*.
Cavalry:	96 cavalrymen, under the command of 2 hipparchs and 10 phylarchs.
Bowmen.	

the middle level) and the thranites (at the top level). The crew consisted of 170 oarsmen.

A trireme would be built by the city. But in Athens a trierarch (the man responsible for the liturgy called a trierarchy) equipped the ship, gave it a name and decorated it. Combat tactics at sea were at first identical to those on dry land; then innovations were introduced, such as passing at high speed in between two enemy ships and breaking their oars, or circling round them, gradually closing in, thereby forcing the enemy ships to squeeze closer together and terrifying them. Superiority usually depended on technique rather than numbers. Sometimes the techniques evolved at sea in naval battles also came to be applied in land warfare. But above all, naval warfare engendered a new sense of solidarity, since it integrated into the ranks of the oarsmen categories of citizens who could not afford a hoplite panoply.

A state of war was suspended when a truce was called, followed by a treaty between the belligerents. The peace was usually contractual: it would be agreed to make peace for ten or twenty years, by means of a treaty, for example. In general, the signing of a treaty was accompanied by an alliance with the former enemy. The treaty itself was placed under the sanction of the gods. It was preceded by libations and sacrifices, and it involved the swearing of oaths. A treaty only became valid once it had become an internal law of the city, passed by its assembly.

The two main conflicts of the fifth century were the Persian Wars (490–478 and 448) and a war fought between Greeks, the Peloponnesian War (431–404).

The first of these was fought against a powerful adversary, which ruled the greatest empire of the day and was heir to civilizations far more ancient and more highly developed than the Greek civilization at that time. The fact that it was a *Greek* history of these wars that was written affects the light in which this clash between the Persian empire and a handful of cities in the Greek world is presented. For the Greeks, it was a major event. Was it likewise for the Persians? Before deciding, let us take a look at this empire.

THE PERSIANS

The Persians were a people with an Indo-European language who originated in the Iranian province that still bears its name (Fars; its chief town
is Shiraz). The Medes, whose name is used in French to refer to these wars
(*les guerres médiques*), belonged to the same civilization, which extended as
far as India. Both the Persians and the Medes first appear in our documentation in the ninth century BC. The founder of the Persian empire, Cyrus
the Great (557–529), was descended from the dynasty of the Achaemenids,
who governed a small principality that was a vassal subject of the Medic
kings of Ectabana (Hamadan). These dominated Asia Minor up as far as
the Halys (Kizil-Hirmak) river, which was the frontier of the kingdom of
Lydia, whose king Croesus was sovereign over the coastal Greek cities of
the Aegean Sea. In 549 Cyrus united the Medes and the Persians under
his authority. Croesus allied himself with Babylon and Egypt against him.
Cyrus annexed Lydia, after capturing Sardis in 546. The cities on the
mainland of Asia Minor were subjected in 540. In 538 Cyrus occupied
Babylon, probably thanks to treachery, and declared himself heir to the
Mesopotamian kingdoms: 'King of the universe, King of Sumer and Akkad,
King of the four regions (the cardinal points)'. His son Cambyses (529–
522) conquered Egypt. With Darius the Great (522–486), the Achaemenid
empire reached the height of its powers, covering about 5,000 kilometres
from east to west and an area of 3 million square kilometres.

The common Indo-European origins of the Greeks and the Persians
('sisters of the same blood', according to Aeschylus) should not obscure
the fact that, ever since Homer, the Hellenic civilization had distanced
itself from the cosmic vision that continued to be exalted on Achaemenid
monuments: 'The hierarchical submission of the world to the man who
governs it, of men to the king, of the king to the supreme god' (H. Van
Effenterre). The cities had long since rejected the sacredness of a sovereign
mediating between gods and men, and by now regarded such a system
simply as despotism. From this point of view, the gesture that most intri-
gued the West was the one reported in the Bible: Cyrus authorized the
Judaeans deported to Babylonia to return home. His predecessors had
sought to integrate peoples with different languages and religions, heirs to
the most ancient literate civilizations, by deporting their ruling classes from
one extremity of their empire to another. Cyrus, in contrast, granted them
internal autonomy: provided they made no trouble, they were free to conduct their affairs as they wished, to follow their own customs, and to
worship the gods of their ancestors. The best proof of the originality of the
Persians was their choice of a Semitic language, Aramaic, as their official
language.

There has been much speculation on the 'secret' of the Achaemenids.
Attention has been drawn to their 'tolerance'; but perhaps a better way of

putting it would be their sense of administration, which is an art of what is possible that they had inherited from Sumer, where bureaucracy was invented, and from Akkad, the first Mesopotamian empire. Their major innovation could be compared to what, in the context of decentralized regions, is now called the deconcentration of State functions. The Great King delegated his supreme authority to satraps (the word in Iranian means 'the protectors of royalty'). These were empowered to take emergency measures in provinces of sizes that varied according to the principal ethnic groups living there, and then they had to explain those measures to the central authorities. The latter were in this way given time to mobilize the royal army and intervene to suit the circumstances. Herodotus and his successors did not really understand the satrap system: they regarded it simply as a fiscal organization designed to accumulate fabulous riches and an irregular, ill-equipped army that it would be easy to vanquish.

According to the cuneiform texts (so called by reason of the characters used, which are formed of corners and dots), Cyrus himself issued the founding charter. It could be summed up as 'Peace through arms'.

The Chronicle of Nabonidus Babylonia presents the capture of Babylon as a liberation: 'Cyrus proclaimed a state of peace for the whole of Babylon . . . so the inhabitants of Babylon now have joyful hearts, like captives when their prisons are opened.' The *Cylinder of Cyrus* explains the nature of this peace: 'The kings of all the countries between the upper sea [the Mediterranean] and the lower sea [the Indian Ocean] . . . brought me their heavy dues and kissed my feet in Babylon.' The formula used suggests that a corrective might be in order, as Herodotus, a native of Halicarnassus, was quick to see: 'tribute in return for peace'. For most of these peoples, the identity of their conqueror was a matter of indifference; but others practised passive resistance and, sooner or later, when the possibility arose, revolted and obtained their liberty (Egypt and Babylonia, for instance, and the Greek cities).

Darius' contribution seems to have been his overall vision of territorial continuity. Herodotus tells how in 499 the tyrant of Miletus, Aristagoras, presented the Spartans with 'a copper tablet on which was engraved the circumference of the whole earth, with all the sea and all the rivers'. Out of all the peoples whose territories bordered one upon another, the commentary named only the Ionians and Susa, the capital, and the only river mentioned was the one that flowed from the capital to the Persian Gulf. This Ionian map, which made Herodotus smile, was inspired by a Babylonian tablet on which the earth was represented as a circular continental area surrounded by sea. It was clearly quite the opposite of what Herodotus, writing of Polycrates the tyrant of Samos, describes as a 'thalassocracy', a sea empire.

The concrete meaning of the word translated as 'circumference' that is used by Herodotus is a fortified precinct. As Darius saw it, every empire had a limit, and this the central authority had to defend. Upon his orders, the Carian Skylax of Caryanda explored the Iranian and Arabian coasts from the Indus delta as far as the canal recently dug to join the Red Sea and the Nile, that is to say, the Mediterranean. In similar fashion, Democedes of Croton, also on behalf of the Persians, 'spied out' the European coasts as far as southern Italy. But to the north of Iran, the Achaemenid frontier was not protected by sea. The Scythians of Europe and Asia were raiding the borders of the eastern satrapies. Cyrus had died while leading an expedition against the Scythians of Asia. According to Herodotus, in 513 Darius decided to intimidate the Scythians of Europe to the north of the Danube, which he crossed by means of a bridge of boats built by Greeks from Asia who had travelled there by sea, among them Miltiades, the tyrant of Thracian Chersonesus. That was a strategic piece of luck for Darius. Upon his return, he ordered one of his generals to turn Thrace into a satrapy extending from the Danube to the Strymon. For defensive reasons of dubious efficacy, the coastal Greek cities on the straits were subjugated, in particular Byzantium, which was the key to the Black Sea, where the early colonies of Miletus were situated. The Ionian revolt was sparked off by Miletus, so it is tempting to make a connection here. Was Aristagoras of Miletus fearful for his commercial interests? Herodotus tells us that, on the contrary, the city had never been richer than under Persian domination. But why revolt at this particular point? Nothing in Herodotus' account provides any answer to this question.

THE PERSIAN WARS

The earliest origin of the Persian Wars was thus the revolt of the Ionian cities of Asia Minor against the Persians. The city of Miletus and Aristagoras, who had just given up the tyranny, were the instigators of an uprising against the Persian authority represented by the satraps, at the very beginning of the fifth century. The cities of mainland Greece, from whom the Ionians requested aid, either refused to become involved (Sparta) or sent no more than a few reinforcements (twenty ships from Athens, five from Eretria).

In 498 the cities of Asia Minor banded together to form a league with its headquarters at the Panionian sanctuary, advanced as far as Sardis, the capital of the satrapy, and burned the town to the ground before returning home.

In 494 the Persians captured all the cities, including Miletus (the town was razed to the ground and the population was deported) and defeated the Ionians at sea, at Lade. King Darius imposed treaties on the cities: they retained their internal autonomy but had to pay tribute. This regime was, however, more favourable than the earlier one had been. In Athens, the news of the capture of Miletus came as a shock. No doubt it was suddenly realized how powerful Persia was and what a threat it represented.

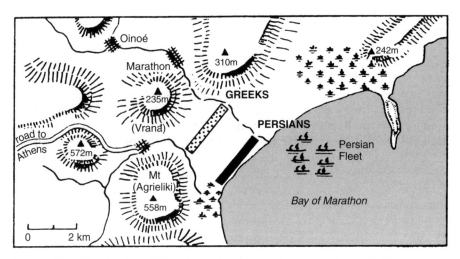

Figure 28 The battle of Marathon (from *Historiens grecs*, Paris, Gallimard, p. 1837, fig. IX)

In 493 Themistocles, who belonged to the Lycomid family, became an archon. He set about constructing a port at Piraeus. His political opponent was Miltiades, from the Phylaïdae family, whose support came from the traditional landed aristocracy. He, in his turn, became an archon in 490.

THE FIRST PERSIAN WAR

The Persians continued to settle in the area of the straits connecting the Aegean Sea and the Black Sea (the Hellespont) and in Thrace, where they set up regimes favourable to themselves. In 490 they launched an expedition to the Cyclades and Euboea: the city of Eretria was taken and its population reduced to slavery. From Euboea the Persian troops crossed the arm of sea separating them from the mainland and proceeded as far as the plain of Marathon, in northern Attica. One man in particular urged them to march on Athens. This was Hippias, the last tyrant of Athens and the son of Pisistratus, who had taken refuge at the Persian court and was trying to create a group favourable to the Persians in the Athenian *ecclesia*. However, Miltiades' advice to resist the Persians won the vote and the Athenians decided to fight. They requested aid from Sparta (which arrived too late), but did receive the help of the people of Plataea.

Marathon A passage in Herodotus makes it possible to follow the events of this battle (490 BC) in detail (VI, 102–19). After several days with the armies drawn up face to face, the battle commenced, with 9,000 Athenians and 1,000 Plataeans on one side, and almost double the number on the Persian side. Miltiades was the *strategos* responsible for the Athenians' victorious tactics. The hoplites performed marvels, and Greek casualties were light. The Persians, under the command of Datis, suffered heavy losses. Legend has it that after the battle the messenger sent to carry the news of the victory to the assembly ran the entire 42 kilometres from Marathon to Athens, where he died of exhaustion from the effort. The Athenians then managed to prevent another Persian landing and the Persians beat a retreat. Marathon was no doubt no more than a skirmish to the Persians, but for the Greeks this battle came to symbolize Greek resistance in the face of the barbarians.

THE PERIOD BETWEEN THE WARS (490–481)

On the Athenian side, in 489 Miltiades led an expedition against the Persians in Paros. It failed and he was killed. The war against Aegina meanwhile continued. In 483–482 Themistocles suggested using the revenue from the Laurion silver mines, in Attica, to build a fleet of warships. Until then, this income had been divided between the Athenian citizens. The assembly agreed to the proposal and the city treated itself to a fleet of 200 triremes. This was an event of crucial importance, not only for the conduct of the war but also because it integrated into the army citizens who were too poor to be hoplites (the thetes), who now became oarsmen. The Marathon army is estimated at 10,000 hoplites; from now on, however, Athens would be able to mobilize many more soldiers.

On the Persian side, King Darius died in 486 and his son Xerxes succeeded him. He quite soon decided to resume the war, but preparations for it took several years. He arranged for the Persian army's communications and supplies by constructing two bridges of boats across the Hellespont straits and depositing stocks of food and equipment along the Thracian coast. According to Herodotus, he mobilized over 100,000 men and a fleet of 1,207 ships. Xerxes was keen to subdue the Greek cities, but not necessarily to annihilate them. First he sent ambassadors to them, seeking to obtain a peaceful capitulation, and there were plenty of cities that chose this solution.

In 481 war was imminent. The Greeks were not united on the question of the attitude to adopt *vis-à-vis* the Persians: some chose submission and alliance (above all, those in Thessaly and Boeotia), others decided upon resistance (first and foremost Athens and Sparta). A similar disunity existed within individual cities, with some in favour of war, others against it. The Greeks who were determined to fight met in 481 on the Isthmus of Corinth, decided to suspend hostilities among themselves (such as the war between Athens and Aegina), concluded an alliance and entrusted command of the Greek army to Sparta. They also decided where to make their stand against the Persians: on land, at the Thermopylae pass linking Thessaly to central Greece; at sea, off Cape Artemision, to the north of Euboea.

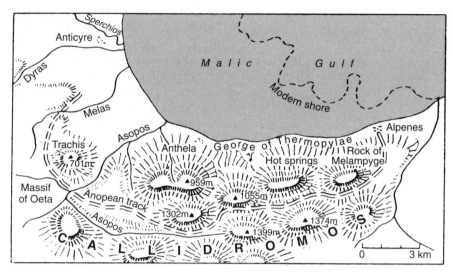

Figure 29   Thermopylae (from *Historiens grecs*, Paris, Gallimard, p. 1837, fig. X)

THE SECOND PERSIAN WAR

In the spring of 480, the Persian army marched through the regions to the north of the Aegean Sea without a blow being struck and reached southern Thessaly.

Thermopylae   As planned, the Greeks defended the Thermoplyae pass, but were too few (about 7,000) to block the huge Persian army. Following an act of treachery, the Persians attacked the Spartans left to defend the pass with their king, Leonidas, from the rear. However, most of the Greek army had had time to pull back to the south.

Artemision   The sea battle was indecisive and both fleets withdrew, neither the victor.

The route to the south was now open to the Persians, and they crossed Boeotia and reached Attica. As the Greeks had decided to block the Persian army at the Isthmus of Corinth, even further south, there was no battle to defend Attica. The very town of Athens was taken over and the Acropolis there was burned down. Most of the population had taken refuge in Troezen, Aegina and Salamis. Only the most stubborn had remained, convinced that they would be safe behind the 'ramparts of wood', which they considered the defensive walls of Athens to be. They were all massacred. Mention of the 'ramparts of wood' that were to save the city had been made in the Pythian oracle delivered at Delphi at this time. But Themistocles had persuaded the assembly to interpret this as an allusion to the ships of Athens, and had organized resistance to the Persians from the fleet, which was anchored out to sea off the island of Salamis.

The oracle delivered to the Athenians before the battle of Salamis

Prepared as they were to listen to the oracle's advice, the Athenians had sent their envoys to Delphi, and as soon as the customary rites were performed and they had entered the shrine and taken their seats, the Priestess Aristonice [the Pythia] uttered the following prophecy:

> Why sit you, doomed ones? Fly to the world's end, leaving
> Homes and the heights your city circles like a wheel.
> The head shall not remain in its place, nor the body,
> Nor the feet beneath, nor the hands, nor the parts between;
> But all is ruined, for fire and the headlong God of War
> Speeding in a Syrian chariot shall bring you low.
> Many a town shall he destroy, not yours alone,
> And give to pitiless fires many shrines of gods,
> Which even now stand sweating, with fear quivering,
> While over the roof-tops black blood runs streaming
> In prophecy of woe that needs must come. But rise,
> Haste from the sanctuary and bow your hearts to grief.

The Athenian envoys were greatly perturbed by this prophetic utterance; indeed they were about to abandon themselves to despair at the dreadful fate which the oracle declared was coming upon them, when Timon, the son of Androbulus and one of the most distinguished men of Delphi, suggested they should re-enter the shrine with branches of olive in their hands and, in the guise of suppliants begging for a better fate, put their question a second time. The Athenians acted upon this suggestion and returned to the temple. 'Lord Apollo', they said, 'Can you not, in consideration of these olive boughs which we have brought you, give us some kindlier prophecy about our country? We will never go away until you do; indeed no; we'll stay here till we die.'

Thereupon the Prophetess uttered her second prophecy, which ran as follows:

> Not wholly can Pallas win the heart of Olympian Zeus
> Though she prays to him with many prayers and all her subtlety;
> Yet I will speak to you this other word, as firm as adamant:
> Though all else shall be taken within the bound of Cecrops
> And the gold of the holy mountain of Cithaeron,
> Yet Zeus the all-seeing grants to Athene's prayer
> That the wooden wall only shall not fall, but help you and your children
> But await not the host of horse and foot coming from Asia,
> Nor be still, but turn back and withdraw from the foe.
> Truly a day will come when you will meet him face to face.

Divine Salamis, you will bring death to women's sons
When the corn is scattered, or the harvest gathered in.

This second answer seemed to be, as indeed it was, less menacing than the first; so the envoys wrote it down and returned to Athens. (Herodotus, VII, 140–1, translated by A. de Selincourt)

Salamis (late September 480)   Through a cunning ruse, Themistocles managed to force upon the Persians both the time and the place of the naval battle that was fought between the island of Salamis and the Attic coast, which was a space far too cramped for the Persian fleet to be able to manoeuvre (see figure 30). The result was carnage. It is described by Aeschylus in *The Persians* (412–28):

> First the floods of Persians held the line,
> But when the narrows choked them, and rescue hopeless,
> Smitten by prows, their bronze jaws gaping,
> Shattered entire was our fleet of oars.
> The Grecian warships, calculating, dashed
> Round and encircled us; ships showed their belly:
> No longer could we see the water, charged
> With ships' wrecks and men's blood.
> Corpses glutted beaches and the rocks.
> Every warship urged its own anarchic
> Rout; and all who survived that expedition,
> Like mackerel or some catch of fish,
> Were stunned and slaughtered, boned with broken oars
> And splintered wrecks; lamentations, cries
> Possessed the open sea, until the black
> Eye of evening, closing, hushed them.

Much of the Persian fleet was destroyed. King Xerxes returned to Asia, leaving Mardonius and part of the Persian army in Thessaly.

During the winter of 479 Mardonius tried to negotiate a treaty with Athens, but failed. Sparta assured Athens of its aid. In the spring Mardonius invaded Attica and the Athenian political authorities went off to Salamis. The Spartans, once again delayed by their observance of a religious festival, eventually arrived from the Peloponnese.

Plataea   Mardonius had withdrawn from Attica and was encamped on the border of Thebes and Plataea, in Boeotia. The Greeks, close on 40,000 hoplites under the command of Pausanias, the king of Sparta, gathered near by, on the lower slopes of Mount Cithaeron. The battle was fought in

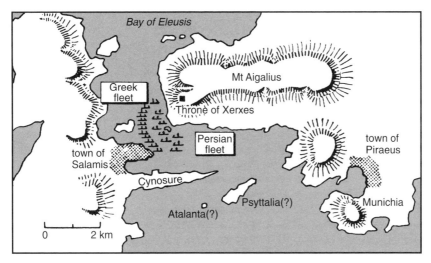

Figure 30   The battle of Salamis (from *Historiens grecs*, Paris, Gallimard, p. 1838, fig. XI)

September and lasted three weeks. Despite their numerical superiority and the excellence of the cavalry, the Persians were eventually defeated and Mardonius was killed. Then it was time to divide up the booty (see Herodotus' text, p. 130). Next, the dead were buried. The Persian leader Artabazus withdrew northward in a retreat that looked very much like a rout. He crossed Thessaly, Macedonia and Thrace, concealing the gravity of his defeat from his hosts, and returned to Asia.

Mycale Meanwhile the Greek fleet pursued the Persian fleet through the Aegean Sea and attacked it at its base close to Cape Mycale, destroying many Persian ships.

The Persian Wars brought the Greeks into conflict with an empire far more powerful than themselves. Their victory seemed all the more re-sounding on that account and continued to be celebrated throughout the classical period, while at the same time a whole corpus of discourse was elaborated, first and foremost by Herodotus, to explain the reasons for Greek superiority. The Persians, the most refined representatives of the barbarian world, lost the wars quite simply because they lacked the expert-ise of city life and its principal characteristic: its egalitarian sharing of power. Underlying the Persian disaster was the disaster represented by all absolute power, all tyranny, blind to the virtues of dialogue, the cut and thrust of differing opinions, and collective decision. The hoplites of Marathon (more than the oarsmen of Salamis, whose exploit is much less fêted by Greek history) owed part of their valour to the excellence of their city. This

141

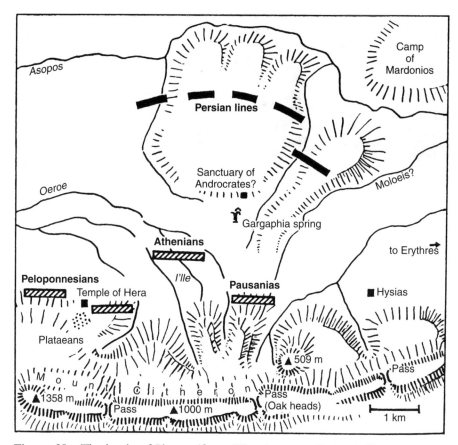

Figure 31 The battle of Plataea (from *Historiens grecs*, Paris, Gallimard, p. 1838, fig. XII)

was certainly the great lesson that Athens, for its part, learned from the Persian Wars.

HEGEMONY AND DEMOCRACY

THE DELIAN LEAGUE

After the Greek victories of Plataea and Cape Mycale (479 BC), the Persians were no longer a threat to the Greek mainland, but the war was not yet over. The cities along the coast of Asia Minor and the Aegean Sea were seeking reliable allies to prevent a return of Persians on the offensive. Sparta, temporarily preoccupied with internal problems of its own (King Pausanias' aspirations to unshared power), and external ones too (its relations with its Peloponnesian allies) succumbed to its traditional temptation to withdraw into its own territory and refused to play a federating role in the anti-Persian struggle. Athens, on the other hand, did take up the challenge and so became the major partner in an alliance with the cities of the Aegean and Asia Minor, to continue the fight against the Persians. This *symmachia* was formed in 478.

Our own name for this *symmachia* is the Delian League, as its centre was the island of Delos, where the federal sanctuary of the Ionians was situated. From the moment of its creation, the rest of the cities recognized Athens' leadership: Athens was its *hegemon*. However, each of the cities possessed a vote in the council (the *synedrion*) that met once a year in Delos. The League's principal function was to maintain a common army and, above all, a fleet prepared to intervene wherever necessary against the Persians. To this end, each city supplied a contingent of soldiers and ships or, if unable to do so, paid a contribution (*phoros*) instead. Initially then, this alliance was egalitarian. Under the leadership of the Athenian Aristides the fleet was built up, and under that of Cimon (between 477 and 461) the first decisive victories over the Persians were won, in particular the victory of the Eurymedon (Pamphylia) in 469, over the Persian fleet.

Athens and the other League cities also suffered reverses, as can be seen from the bloody disaster of the expedition to Egypt. In 463 a Libyan leader, Inarus, heading an insurrection against the Persians in Egypt, appealed to the Athenians for help. The allied fleet, which was bound for Cyprus, set sail for Egypt, and the Greeks then advanced victoriously as far as Memphis. But in 456 a Persian expedition defeated the Athenians, who found themselves besieged on an island in the Nile delta. The dispatch of reinforcements (fifty triremes) in 454 could not save them, and the Greek army was annihilated.

In the mid-fifth century three events emphasized the weight that Athens carried in the League. First, in 454, following a crisis and a series of defections by the other cities, possibly connected with the defeat in Egypt, the treasure store of the League was transferred from Delos to Athens, where it was housed in the temple of Athena on the Acropolis. Athens reckoned that it would be safer there.

In 448, the *Peace of Callias* (so called after the name of the Athenian negotiator) was signed with the Persians, bringing the war to a definitive end. The Aegean Sea was from now on forbidden to the Persian fleet, the autonomy of the coastal cities of Asia was recognized by the Persians, a band of land one kilometre wide was demilitarized, and Athens promised never again to interfere in the affairs of Egypt and Libya. The *symmachia* no longer had any *raison d'être*. Nevertheless, Athens considered that the League should remain in existence in the name of the common interests of all the cities (in particular, security on the high seas). It stamped out revolts in some of the cities, which wanted to leave the alliance, such as Euboea in 447–446 and Miletus in 446–445. The conditions imposed upon the defeated cities were tough. For instance, all the citizens of Chalcis in Euboea had to swear the following oath:

I shall not separate myself from the Athenian people through any ruse or manoeuvre, either in words or in deeds, and I shall not obey any who separate themselves from them; if anyone counsels defection, I shall denounce him to the Athenians. I shall pay the Athenians tribute to whatever value I persuade them to fix it and I shall be the best and most loyal ally possible. I shall come to the aid and defence of the Athenian people if anyone wrongs them, and I shall obey the Athenian people.

In 446–445 a peace of thirty years was agreed between Sparta and Athens. It brought to an end a long series of battles (see p. 156) and recognized Athens' supremacy over the Aegean and Sparta's over the Peloponnese.

From this point on, Athens not only headed the League (*hegemonia*) but also assumed command of it (*archè*). We know rather more about how the League functioned at about this time thanks, in particular, to the preservation of accounts engraved on stone year after year, relating to the sums levied for the goddess Athena (one-sixtieth of the tribute paid by the allied cities). One such document concerns the years 454 to 439 and lists the names of 275 cities. It is not possible here to provide details of the extremely complex functioning of this league, but let us at least make a note of its structures.

The phoros The levying of the tribute (*phoros*) that provided Athens' financial resources was of fundamental importance. The cities were grouped into first five, then four geographical districts: Thrace, the Hellespont, Ionia, Caria (later joined to Ionia) and the islands. Each district comprized dozens of cities (ranging from 29 in the islands to 81 in Caria). The sum to be paid as tribute was fixed every four years for each city (having been drafted by the *boulè*, the decree would be voted through by the *ecclesia*) and varied considerably depending upon the supposed wealth of the community and also the degree of its allegiance to Athens (ranging from less than 1 talent, as for Caunus in Caria, to over 5 talents, as for Phaselis in Lycia, and 15 talents for Byzantium and Abdera). The overall total remained stable from one year to the next (about 400 talents), except during the Peloponnesian War, when it rose to over 1,000 talents. The *phoros* was collected each year at the time of the Great Dionysia in Athens, and *hellènotamai* were made responsible for its management. Normally, it was used to finance the common army, but from 450–449 on the Athenians claimed for their own city sums to the tune of half the *phoros* total.

Relations between the cities Normally these were regulated by agreements known as *symbolai*. Disputes between citizens from two different cities were judged in the city of the defendant. But Athens took to having all cases in which an Athenian citizen or a supporter of Athens was involved judged in Athens itself (before the Heliaea), thereby dispossessing allied cities of a number of their judicial prerogatives. Similarly, all litigation concerning League affairs, in particular, refusals to pay the *phoros* and any city's revolt, were judged in Athens. And the *ecclesia* decided on the penalty to be imposed upon such a city, for example, the dispatch of a garrison.

Garrisons, cleruchies, expulsions Athens established garrisons (*phrourai*: contingents of Athenian soldiers) in allied cities in times of war and wherever a city had tried to secede. The cleruchies were groups of Athenian citizens (*cleruchs*) who lived in allied cities and made a living by farming confiscated land. In this way the allied city was kept under surveillance. This system was applied on a number of occasions in the course of the fifth century (in 450 in Andros and Naxos, in 447–446 in Thracian Chersonesus and in Euboea, and in 427 in Mytilene, involving a total of 6,000 cleruchs). It was a measure that was less radical than expelling the whole local population and replacing it with Athenian citizens, which was the worst punishment imposed upon cities that revolted (in 446 for the city of Hestiaea in Euboea, in 431 for Aegina, in 429 for Potidaea, in 421 for Skione and in 416 for Melos). The treatment that any city conquered militarily (such as Thasos in 463 and Samos in 440) could expect was to have its walls razed to the ground, its fleet seized, hostages taken and payment for the costs of the war extorted. In times of peace Athenian surveillance was less Draconian.

A form of surveillance Some Athenian magistrates lived permanently in the allied cities (the *episkopoi*, the supervisors or 'archons in the cities'). The *proxenoi* in Athens were, on the contrary, natives of the allied cities, but ones who were devoted to Athens' policies. Through these two categories of men, Athens was apprised of the internal policies of its allies. However, Athens does not appear to have attempted to impose a political model upon the cities as a whole. Oligarchies and democracies both existed in the League. In some cases, Athens seems to have secretly favoured the advancement to power of not so much democrats as simply the men most inclined to tolerate its crushing alliance.

ECONOMIC ASPECTS

The Athenian *archè* has often been presented as an annexation of the cities, comparable to modern forms of imperialism, that is to say, dictated above all by economic considerations, primarily a quest for commercial outlets. We shall be studying features of the Greek economy elsewhere (see p. 196f.). At this point we should simply be aware of the chasm separating the system of modern, and in particular capitalist, economies from the ancient system. So far as can be seen from the documentation available to us, Athenian strategy was not dictated by economic expansionism – something totally foreign to the thinking of the time; but, on the other hand, there were some aspects of it which, though not clearly formulated, were undeniably economic, and these should not be minimized. Its aim was *to assure the city supplies* of basic necessities: cereals and all the raw materials used by craftsmen and in shipbuilding, so as to give it the economic autonomy indispensable for political supremacy. Athens' eagerness to attain this goal explains its concern, throughout the fifth century, to ensure free circulation for its ships in the Aegean. It achieved this first by wiping out the Persian fleet, then by fighting against pirates and any other enemy fleets and by securing alliances with cities which, by virtue of their position, controlled strategic routes: stopovers in the Cyclades, the routes to the north of Euboea, along Thracian Chersonesus and through the straits between the Black Sea and the Aegean Sea.

Particularly sensitive were zones that produced supplies of cereals, since Attica was very deficient in these. Wheat could be brought in from Egypt, from the coastal towns of the Black Sea and from southern Italy and Sicily, and a sufficient quantity of it needed to find its way to the port of Piraeus and the Athenian markets. At the time of the Peloponnesian War, Athens seems to have strengthened its control to the point of denying non-Athenian ships access to the Bosphorus straits and forcing all ships to unload and sell their wheat in Piraeus. These drastic measures could be explained by the fear of asphyxiation of a city whose agricultural territory was annually ravaged by war.

Another measure, likewise connected with both the economy and politics, was Athens' attempts to *standardize all weights and measures* on the basis of the Attic system (the Decree of Clearchus in about 437). The economic aspect of this was that it facilitated trade; the political aspect was that the other cities lost a little more of their traditional sovereignty, which had been partly expressed through the minting of their own particular currencies.

Add to all this the tapping of the *phoros*, which enabled Athens to finance the reconstruction of its own monuments and probably also expenses such as the *misthos*, which enabled more of the *dèmos* to take part in the mechanisms of political life, and it will be seen that the economic consequences of the Athenian *archè* were certainly not negligible. But it is important that our modern analysis should also take into account the Greeks' own attitude to these phenomena: for them, what was essential was the correct functioning of the *politeia*, the political regime, both internally and externally, so it was in political terms that they analysed all their strategies. Recognition of this is fundamental to any understanding of how the city functioned ideologically.

The system briefly described above without the slightest doubt made it possible for Athens to develop and run a political regime that was more egalitarian and that was described as democratic. The debate on the very nature of this *archè* and hence also on the value we should ascribe to Athenian democracy is not a vain one, although it is insoluble to the extent that, depending on the light in which the measures taken are interpreted, it is possible to fasten in particular either on the positive aspects or on the negative ones, on liberty or on tyranny. The same applies to other criteria by which democracy is defined, such as the liberty of citizens, which was founded upon slavery and the exclusion of most of the population. Far from presenting a utopian vision of an ideal democracy that respected all forms of liberty, the way in which the Athenian *archè* functioned provides an extremely clear historical example of the price that has to be paid for the exercise of any power, even democratic.

DEMOCRACY AND FAMOUS MEN

It may seem paradoxical to juxtapose on the one hand a term that lays emphasis on the collective power of citizens and, on the other, some of the individuals who left their mark on the political life of the fifth century. We have already considered the institutional aspect of democracy (see p. 119f.). In the sources, the history of events is regularly punctuated by the names of its principal magistrates. This makes it possible to sketch in a chronological framework.

ARISTIDES AND THEMISTOCLES

Two men stand out in the political scene of the first twenty years of the fifth century: Aristides (540–468), a friend of Cleisthenes and a member of an aristocratic family, and Themistocles, born of an Athenian father and a foreign mother. The ancient texts present them as opposites, both by temperament and in their political choices, but that is probably just a way of constructing history. Both men were active in the Persian Wars. Aristides was a *strategos* at the battle of Marathon, along with Miltiades. Themistocles proposed using the revenue from the Laurion mines to construct a fleet, and persuaded the Athenians to abandon the town in 480 and to engage the Persians in battle at sea, off the coast of Salamis. Both were ostracized, Aristides in 483, Themistocles in 471. But that is where the resemblance between them ends. Aristides was soon recalled from exile and thereafter was active in Athenian political life right up to his death. In particular, he helped to fix the sum of the *phoros* and allocated the contributions to be paid by the various cities in the Delian League. He died with the reputation of a moderate and wise man. Athens never recalled Themistocles, and after a few years of wandering he ended his days as a sumptuously rewarded councillor to the Great King of Persia. His bad reputation (changeable, corrupt, vain, boorish) is typical of that ascribed to any man who advocated change. It was he who, by steering Athens towards the sea, opened up a space in political life to accommodate social categories other than the landowning peasants.

CIMON AND PERICLES

The second opposed pair consists of Cimon and first Ephialtes, then Pericles. Tradition represents the former as a member of the arisocracy not much inclined to change, the other two as advocates of greater access to political power for the whole of the *dèmos*. *Cimon* (510–449) was the son of Miltiades (of the Philaïdae family). He fought at Salamis, then, in 478, entered political life as a *strategos*. He was extremely active in the Delian League, emerged as the victorious *strategos* from the battle of Eurymedon against the Persians in 468, and fought against Thasos, which was in revolt, in 463. He was ostracized in 461 after unwittingly causing Athens to suffer an insult (the Spartans sent him back to Athens when he arrived in Sparta with an Athenian contingent to help them in their struggle against the helots). He was recalled to Athens, and died during the siege of Kition, in Cyprus. It was in his absence that Ephialtes (495–461) managed to get his reform passed (see p. 119), and he is presented as Pericles' main political opponent at the beginning of the latter's career.

Pericles is so famous that the fifth century bears his name: it is 'the age of Pericles', despite the fact that he really dominated Athenian political life for only twenty or so years, from 450 onward. Through his birth he was connected to two of the greatest Athenian aristocratic families, the Bouzygae through his father Xanthippus, the Alcmaeonids through his mother Agariste. It is hard to assess how much in his policies was prompted by a desire for democratic change and how much was simply part of the usual rivalry between the great families. He opposed first Cimon, then *Thucydides, the son of Melesias*, Cimon's son-in-law. Thucydides was ostracized in 443. In was during this period that a split, in the *ecclesia* at least, developed between the 'elites' (in other words, the aristocracy) and the 'people', and Plutarch, to whom we owe that observation, goes on to say: 'The clash and rivalry between these two men caused a deep rift that separated the two groups, which from that time on were known as the people and the minority.' But this does not mean that a veritable democratic party formed around Pericles. It was more a matter of a political expression of the difference between two social groups with different interests, on the one hand the landowners, on the other the townsfolk. However, our interpretation is heavily dependent on the Greek texts, which *a posteriori* tried to rationalize actions that may in truth have been extremely empirical. Consider, for example, the creation of the *misthos*.

The misthos was an allowance paid to citizens who devoted their time to the service of the city. The first *misthos* was given to the citizens who sat in the Heliaea in about 450 (the *misthos heliasticos*). It amounted to 3 obols. Later a *misthos* was introduced for the *bouleutai* and for certain magistrates, and eventually, at the very end of the fifth century, also for the *ecclesia*. Aristotle and Plutarch, who both describe the conditions in which the *misthos* was created, say that it was Pericles' way of rivalling Cimon in generosity, for Cimon use to hold open house for the citizens of his deme. Looking beyond the anecdote, we should see this as an opposition between two ways of allowing for the material subsistence of the citizen people (the *dèmos*). The favourite method of the aristocracy was to create

Figure 32 Bust of Pericles (Vatican Museum; from J.-J. Maffre, *Le Siècle de Périclès*, Paris, PUF, 1994, p. 122, fig. 10.)

links of dependence between a benefactor and those beholden to him, links that might later be exploited in political life. The other method was designed to marginalize all links of personal dependence by having the civic community pay an allowance that made it possible for citizens too poor to take a day off work to take part in the sessions of the law-court. However, what constituted the abandonment of a whole earlier tradition and seems to us a gesture that was typically democratic, since it aimed to disentangle political participation from economic contingencies and from relations of clientship, was presented – and probably genuinely regarded – by the ancient authors as simply a ploy in the interplay of political rivalries.

Another measure attributed to Pericles was the 451 reform of the quali-fications for citizenship, making these somewhat more stringent (see p. 124). Then, in 450–499, Pericales proposed, and succeeded in getting voted through, a decree that decided to use part of the funds of the Delian League to rebuild the Acropolis (the construction of the Propylaea and the Parthenon), a decree that Thucydides, the son of Milesias, opposed in the name of the interests of the allies. There are other decisions too that bear the mark of Pericles, even if there is no explicit evidence that it was actually he who proposed the decrees.

Pericles was re-elected as a *strategos* without a break from 443 to 431. This was, as we have seen, an important magistracy, for the ten *strategoi* sat in the *boulè* and thus played a part in the preparation of drafts for the laws that were then submitted to the *ecclesia*. In the institutional field, he seems to have managed and perpetuated previous reforms. His originality lay elsewhere: in a lifestyle somewhat marginal to the traditional life of citizens (with his own circle of friends, his companion, Aspasia, who was a foreigner, and his lack of enthusiasm for the places and practices of citizen sociability), in his skill at winning over assemblies and a manner of exercising power that remains a mystery to us. Thucydides' famous remark: 'Theoretically the people was sovereign, but in reality the State was governed by the city's first citizen' simply increases our perplexity.

Pericles died of the plague in 429, shortly after the outbreak of the Peloponnesian War. One of his last political actions was delivering the funeral address in praise of the Athenians who died during the first year of the war, and this famous speech, in the form in which Thucydides reports it, is one of the rare documents justifying the democratic regime.

In the course of the Peloponnesian War, other statesmen came to the fore. The opposition between them was expressed above all in the ways that they wanted to conduct or stop the war.

CLEON, NICIAS, ALCIBIADES

Cleon, the son of Clainetus (?–422) was in favour of waging war until Athens won a complete victory. He was one of the first statesmen who did not belong to an aristocratic family. He was a tanner. For seven years he dominated Athenian political life, was present at all the debates (for example, on the fate to mete out to the city of Mytilene in 427) and on many battlefields (such as Sphacteria in 425). Aristophanes painted a most scurrilous portrait of him as a demagogue at once ambitious and incompetent (in his play, *The Knights*, Cleon is a Paphlagonian tannery slave, 'a kind of genius in the field of cheating and calumny'). Nevertheless, Cleon was an excellent orator who retained the support of the *dèmos* right up to his death, fighting at Amphipolis in 422. During Cleon's lifetime there was one man who seemed to gather around him those who were opposed to the extremism of the policies of the day: Nicias.

Nicias (before 469–413) was a *strategos* several times both before and during the war, in which he led a number of actions that were crowned with success: he took the island of Cithera in 424, then captured Mende, in Chalcidice, in 423. He was one of those who negotiated with Sparta for a halt to the war (the Peace of Nicias, in 421). He then opposed Alcibiades, warning against the Sicilian expedition, in which he nevertheless had to take part as a *strategos*. He delayed the attack for too long and was caught in a trap by the Syracusans, taken prisoner, and put to death in 413. Plutarch portrays him as a very wealthy man, always ready to take on liturgies for the city, but at the same time over-hesitant and lacking in charisma. In this respect too, he was the exact oppoosite of both Cleon and Alcibiades.

Alcibiades (450–404) was the son of Cleinias (killed at the battle of Coronea). Through his mother, he was connected to the Alcmaeonid family, through his wife to the Kerkyes family. Pericles was his guardian, and he was a friend of Socrates. From 420 on, the year in which he became a *strategos*, he was the leader of those who supported the war, in opposition to Nicias, who had just negotiated a peace and was trying to make it last. After a famous oratorical duel against Nicias, reported by Thucydides, he persuaded the assembly to send a fleet to Sicily. The *dèmos* saw this as a chance for an easy victory, with an immediate pay-off for the soldiers, and were hoping for a success 'that would assure them of a permanent wage'. Although initially appointed as one of the leaders of this expedition, Alcibiades deserted from the Athenian ranks in order to avoid two accusations of sacrilege for two consecutive acts of impiety: the mutilation of the hermes of the agora and a parody of the Mysteries of Eleusis. Having been condemned to death in Athens, he took refuge in Sparta and acted as this city's adviser in its conflict with Athens, but was ejected in 412. He later returned from Lydia (where he had found refuge with the satrap Tissaphernes) and fought for the Athenians. He was then, in 407, authorized to return to Athens. Not for long, however. Forced into exile once again, in 404 he died in Phrygia, under the protection of the satrap Pharnabazus. His life was a veritable adventure story and the opportunism of his politics leaves room for doubt as to the sincerity of his desire to advance the cause of democracy. At that time the rifts in the city were those not of a parliamentary regime, but of a direct democracy in which the aspirations of the majority really could lead to political action; and in this instance continuing with the war seemed the only way of ensuring the revenues necessary for the survival of the citizens.

The *dèmos* was therefore inevitably in favour of the war. The only means of halting it and allowing a hearing to those who advocated peace seemed to be to remove the *dèmos* from public life. A number of Athenians had for years been thinking of doing exactly that, and in the space of less than ten years they were to make two attempts to establish an oligarchic regime in Athens. The circumstances linked with external politics and the Peloponnesian War are discussed on p. 163f. At this point, let us follow the events that led to these seizures of power within the city, and examine the programmes that were advocated.

THE REGIME OF THE FOUR HUNDRED

'The fine and the good' (*Kaloikagathoi*), who were hostile to the clout acquired by the *dèmos* in political life, met almost daily in banquets held in turn in each other's houses, and they formed groups of friends and companions that are sometimes likened to the archaic aristocratic *hetairiai*.

There was much criticism of the political system, while their drinking songs exalted the charms of the Athens of the beginning of the century, the Athens of the fighters of Marathon. The normal forms of aristocratic sociability took on a political tonality. This hotbed of unrest generated the idea of constitutional reform, to impose which it would be necessary to seize power. The concrete modalities were complicated. Very briefly: in the winter of 412, Athenian *strategoi* in command of the fleet at Samos made contact with Alcibiades to discuss the possibility of his return to Athens. One of the *strategoi*, Pisander, was sent to Athens to propose entering into negotiations with Alcibiades and the satrap Tissaphernes. The *ecclesia* was eventually persuaded to accept the principle of these negotiations, but they then broke down. The partisans of oligarchic power at this point moved into action by having a number of democrat leaders assassinated; and when Pisander had returned to Samos, an assembly was convoked at Colonus (a deme situated outside the town) to ratify their proposals.

The constitution proposed to abolish all forms of the *misthos*, to alter the conditions of eligibility for magistrates, and to replace the *boulè* of the Five Hundred by a *boulè* of 400 members designated by being co-opted (not by the drawing of lots). This new *boulè* was to draw up a list of 5,000 citizens who alone would enjoy all political rights. The proposal was accepted by the *ecclesia*, and the *boulè* was dissolved. The oligarchic regime was installed without a single blow being struck in Athens. But the plotters had reckoned without the reaction of a large part of the *dèmos*, the part that was a long way away from Athens, serving with the fleet lying off the coast of Samos. When they learned the news, these sailors demoted their leaders, elected new ones, and decided to return to Athens to topple the oligarchic regime. On the advice of Alcibiades (who now made a timely reappearance), they called for the abolition of the new regime. Meanwhile in Athens itself, dissension among the oligarchs and a disastrous military situation (the defeat of the Athenians at Eretria in September 411) gave the *ecclesia* the chance to regain the initiative, under the influence of Theramenes. It began by demoting the Four Hundred and handing power to the Five Thousand. But soon after (in the summer of 410) the previous system was totally restored.

That first attempt to establish oligarchic power brought to light the social rifts that divided the citizens. Until then, they had been expressed in the *ecclesia*. Now they found expression in the streets, with the risk (narrowly avoided in 411) of plunging the city into a veritable civil war. The reaction of the soldier citizens in Samos has greatly impressed modern historians, who have seen in it the sign – disturbing for some, exalting for others – of a real seizure of power by the people. Much less is said about the assassinations of democrats that preceded it and paved the way for the ballot in the assembly of the new *politeia*; yet it was they that carried the seed of the violence that was to characterize the second attempt at an oligarchic regime, in 404.

THE REGIME OF THE THIRTY

Athens had just been forced to accept the conditions for peace laid down by Sparta, but the treaty did not specify what kind of political regime it was to adopt. Among those who advocated an oligarchy there were both moderate men, such as *Theramenes*, and men who were all for a radical change of power, such as *Critias*.

In April 404, with the support of the Spartan general Lysander, a citizen by the name of Dracontides of Aphidna put before the *ecclesia* a proposal to designate thirty individuals to draft a new constitution. The decree was approved by vote and the Thirty were selected from among the friends of Theramenes and Critias. A Spartan garrison was encamped on the Acropolis and the Thirty embarked upon a reign of terror. They executed not only citizens suspected of being democrats but also rich metics, in order to seize their fortunes for themselves. That was how Polemarchus, the brother of Lysias the orator, met his end. Then dissension among the Thirty began to grow. Theramenes favoured a return to greater legality and a government based upon landowning citizens, 'those who are capable of defending the city either with their horse or with their shield'. Critias had him excluded from the list of 3,000 citizens, which made him an outlaw, and he was obliged to die by drinking hemlock. The government of the Thirty forced many citizens and metics into exile, but many of them regrouped in Piraeus. It was from there and from the fortress of Phyle that the democrats, led by Thrasybulus, set out on their reconquest of power. In the end, the Spartan king Pausanias mediated between the Thirty and the followers of Thrasybulus, persuading the latter to agree to declare a total amnesty for all Athenians compromised with the oligarchs, except for the Thirty themselves. A democratic regime was thus restored in 403. After this bloody episode of civil war, the order of the day from Thrasybulus himself was to forget all the disagreements of the past. Would Athens now be able to become a united city?

A DEMOCRACY?

Now that we have sketched in the sequence of events in Athenian political life, let us in conclusion reflect not upon the nature of the political regime, for in the present work we cannot possibly tackle the huge historiographical debate about the nature of democracy, but rather upon the characteristics of Athenian democracy. The trouble is, once again, that it is impossible to come up with any answers if we limit ourselves to the study of a single domain of Athenian practices. To form some idea of the character of the regime it is necessary to take into account features of many kinds – institutional, economic and social, and cultural – and also what effect they had, in other words, both the internal history of Athens and the external history, without necessarily giving priority to its political institutions, as some recent works propose (for example, M. H. Hansen, *The Athenian Democracy in the Age of Demosthenes*, Oxford, 1991). Cleisthenes' reforms created institutional frameworks that made direct political participation possible, affected the social conditions of that participation, and bestowed an essential value upon political life. The reforms that followed strengthened the powers of the majority, at the same time restricting access to citizenship. The limits of this institutional democracy were of an economic, social and ideological nature. As our litany of great men has just served to remind us, political power remained in the hands of a small number of citizens who were members of the greatest Athenian families, even when access to political responsibilities was no longer conditioned by any reference to census classes. The external political history of Athens reveals the crucial role played by war in opening up politics to a larger proportion of the *dèmos* (the thetes, for example, who acted a oarsmen in the triremes at Salamis, by the end of the century constituted the basis of every *ecclesia* and every Heliaea) and also by the fragile balance of the workings of democracy, which depended to some extent upon the prosperity brought by hegemony.

Fifth-century Athenian democracy was also characterized by a strict system of exclusions (foreigners, slaves and women; see p. 183f.) that made it possible to achieve greater equality within the restricted group of citizens. Finally, it also created a particular lifestyle and a culture, an urban way of life in which the discussions of the assembly were continued in the little stalls on the agora, in the gymnasia, between two sets of exercises, and at banquets in private homes. It was a culture in which debate about the bases of the democratic regime found its way into the widely differing genres of history, theatre and philosophy.

RELATIONS BETWEEN THE CITIES: WARS AND TRUCES

From the day in 479 when the Persians shook the soil of the Greek mainland from their feet as they departed, to 404, when the Peloponnesian War came to an end, the cities never ceased to be in conflict. What is known as 'the Peloponnesian War', that is, the clash between on one hand Sparta and its allies, banded together in the Peloponnesian League, and on the other Athens and its allies of the Delian League, was in fact the last episode in virtually non-stop hostilities. It would almost be more accurate to speak of the Peloponnesian War*s*, in the plural, when attempting to describe relations between the cities in the fifth century. So, before chronicling the course of this great war, we need briefly to recall the bellicose episodes and occasional truces, or even periods of peace, in the run-up to 431, in order to situate this major event of the end of the century within the constant cycle of clashes.

HALF A CENTURY ON THE QUI-VIVE (478–431)

In Greece For fifteen years the relations between the cities of the two hegemonic systems remained tolerable, possibly because Sparta was obliged to establish order in the Peloponnese. What fighting there was took place between Sparta on one side and Argos and the Arcadians on the other. Sparta won two victories, first at the *battle of Tegea* in 469, then at the *battle of Dipaia* in 468 or 464. The Arcadians then joined the alliance.

Shortly after, in 464–463, Laconia was the victim of an earthquake that killed many people and appears to have given the signal for a revolt on the part of the helots of first Laconia, then Messenia. The Messenians withdrew to the mountainous regions of *Mount Ithome* and continued to defy the Spartans until 459. Sparta asked for aid from other cities in the Peloponnese and even from Athens. Cimon persuaded the *ecclesia* to send them 4,000 hoplites under his own command. But, for reasons that remain unclear, the Spartans sent the Athenians home at the end of 462, which Athens considered an insult. As a result of this, Cimon was ostracized. The war against the helots continued for several years until, in 459, the Messenians were forced to capitulate and leave the Peloponnese for ever. However, Sparta continued to live under the threat of another internal secession.

The year 462 marked the end of cordial relations. Athens repudiated its alliance with Sparta and formed new alliances with the latter's enemies: Argos, the Thessalians and even Megara. At first the open conflicts were fought out between the cities of the Peloponnesian confederation and Athens, without Sparta intervening. Athens' purpose was to implant itself in zones until then reserved for Corinth, Epidaurus and Sicyon . . . It won some of the battles and lost others (it was defeated at the *battle of Haliae* and victorious at that of *Kekryphalaia* in 459–458). Relations deteriorated even further when Athens *laid siege to Aegina* in 459–458. The siege continued until late 457 or early 456, and ended with defeat for Aegina. The city was obliged to raze its walls to the ground, surrender its fleet and agree to pay the *phoros*: in other words, it was forced to switch over into the Athenian alliance system.

In the meantime, in 457, Athens completed the construction of a system of fortifications that would assure the town of supplies even when the enemy invaded the territory of Attica. The fortifications consisted of the Long Walls, a pair of parallel walls that connected the fortifications of the port of Piraeus with those of the town of Athens. That same year the Spartans and the Athenians joined battle for the first time.

In the summer of 457, while returning from an expedition in central Doris (where they had helped the Dorians in their struggle against the Phocidians), the Spartans clashed with the Athenians in Boeotia, in the *battle of Tanagra*, won by the Spartans. Later that same summer, the Athenians beat the Boeotians at the *battle of Oenophyta*, which made it possible for them to extend their influence over Phocis and the sanctuary at Delphi.

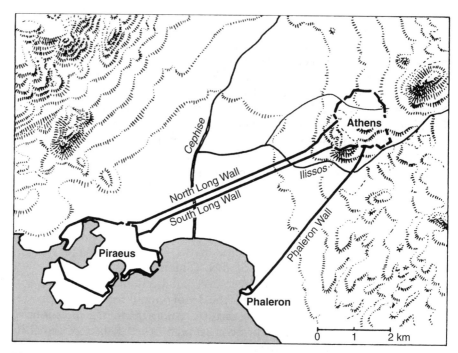

Figure 33 The fortifications of the Long Walls linking Athens and Piraeus (from E. Will, *Le Monde grec et l'Orient, le Ve siècle*, 3rd edn, Paris, PUF, 1990, p. 157)

In 456–455 the Athenians, under the command of Tolmides, launched raids on the coasts of the Peloponnese (at Gytheion in Laconia, and in Messenia) and also in the Gulf of Corinth, where they captured the city of Chalcis in Aetolia, founded by Corinth. In 454–453 they continued with the same tactics, attacking Sicyon and attempting, without success, to take Oeniadae in Acarnania. Then a five-year truce was concluded with the Peloponnesians, at the end of which the fighting became even heavier.

In 448–447 the Spartans clashed with the Athenians and the Phocidians, close to Delphi. In the following year, 447–446, Boeotians who favoured an oligarchy gradually regained control of the cities of Boeotia. The Athenians supported the democratic regimes and suffered a defeat at the *battle of Coronea*. A federal system of oligarchic inspiration was then established between the cities of Boeotia.

In 446 the cities of Euboea and Megara rose simultaneously against Athens. Luckily for Athens, the Peloponnesians, led by Sparta's king Pleistoanax, abandoned the struggle in Megaris without a fight, and Athens was thus able to throw all its forces against Euboea, which it overcame. This was the situation when Sparta and Athens came to an agreement.

In 446–445 the two cities decided on a *Thirty-year Peace*. It was a bilateral agreement and made no mention of the other warring cities. The peace provided for arbitration in the case of clashes and each city recognized the other's system of alliance. The past thirty years or so of conflict in the Peloponnese and central Greece, now temporarily interrupted by the Thirty-year Peace, had naturally scarred the cities' memories, and the resulting hostility encouraged the resumption of the war, which then dragged on for even longer and was fought in a more systematic fashion.

In the mid-fifth century another area of conflict became identifiable. It was to play an important part in the Peloponnesian War. This was in the west, in southern Italy and, above all, in Sicily.

In southern Italy   The cities of southern Italy shared common enemies, the Samnite peoples to the north and the Iapyges to the south, who, having become better organized than before by the fifth century, did not hesitate to sally forth from their territories and raid those of the cities. However, the latter were above all at war with one another, as is shown by the total destruction of Sybaris by Croton in 511, and Tarentum's attempts to limit the implantation of Thurii by founding the city of Heraclea.

The foundation of Thurii   In the hollow of the foot of the boot of Italy, the former inhabitants of Sybaris had made two attempts to refound their city, but without success. In 446–445 a new city, Thurii, was founded near its former site. The Athenians floated the idea of an *apoika*, which attracted many Greeks from various different cities and peoples to take part in its leadership. The *oikiste* was an Athenian, Lampon, and the design of the city was the work of Hippodamus, the famous town-planner responsible for the layout of both Miletus and the Piraeus, while the constitution was drafted by Protagoras of Abdera, a philosopher who was a member of Pericles' circle of friends. The city did not maintain close links with Athens once it was founded, which shows that Athens was not really particularly interested in this part of the Greek world.

On the isthmus, Rhegium, under the tyranny of Anaxilas at the beginning of the fifth century, had seized Zancle and settled it with Greeks from Messenia, who gave it the name of Messina. It is not certain when and in what conditions Athens concluded its first *alliances with the cities of Rhegium and Leontini* (around 440–439?), but the alliances were renewed in 433–432. This was not done upon the initiative of Athens. It was simply responding to a request from these cities, which were worried by the excessive influence acquired by the city of Syracuse in Sicily. The west was not yet regarded by the Athenians as an Eldorado.

In Sicily   The Greeks were no longer the only ones coming to terms with the indigenous population, for the Carthaginians now controlled the western part of the island of Sicily. Most of the Greek cities here went through episodes of tyrannical government that lasted for varying periods of time at the end of the archaic period and during the early fifth century.

In *Gela* the first tyrant, Cleander, was assassinated in 498. He was succeeded by his brother Hippocrates. The tyranny then passed into the hands of another family, the Deinomenidae. Gelon became the tyrant of Gela (in 485) with the support of the knights (the largest landowners) and also took control of the city of Syracuse, with the help of the proprietors of the largest estates, the *gamoroi*, and left his brother Hieron to rule the city. Since 489 the city of *Agrigentum* had also been ruled by a tyrant, Theron, who adopted aggressive policies and ejected Terillus, the tyrant of the city of Himera. Terillus appealed to the Carthaginians for help, but the allied armies of Gelon and Theron defeated them at the *battle of Himera* in 480. Gelon died in 478, having acquired control of the whole of eastern Sicily. Hieron succeeded him and continued the war against the Etruscans, whom he vanquished at the *battle of Cumae* in 474. He turned Syracuse into a town of sumptuous buildings, which offered a welcome to a number of poets from elsewhere (Pindar, Aeschylus, Simonides). At his death, the power passed to his brother Thrasybulus, who was toppled and replaced by a democratic regime, as happened in many other cities in Sicily.

Before Athens made its intervention in Sicily, the cities there had had to put down a revolt by the Sicel peoples, led by Donketius. Around 420 Syracuse seems to have been by far the most powerful city in the island.

After half a century of strained relations between the two hegemonic systems, that of Sparta and that of Athens, in the space of a few months war became inevitable.

THE PELOPONNESIAN WAR (431–404)

We are able to follow the progress of this war thanks to two main sources. The work of Thucydides, *The Peloponnesian War*, is almost entirely devoted to it, and the beginning of Xenophon's *Hellenica* takes up the story of the war where Thucydides left off, in 411. These texts are worth reading over and over again.

Three very different events, each concerning a different part of the Greek world, were at the immediate origin of the war:

- In 433 Corcyra requested and obtained Athens' aid in a conflict with its metropolis, Corinth, over one of Corcyra's foundations on the Adriatic coast: Epidamnus. Corinth accused Athens of thereby breaking the Thirty-year Peace (445), which recommended recourse to arbitration in the event of any conflict.
- In 433 Potidaea in Thracian Chersonesus, a city founded by Corinth but which belonged to the Delian League and paid the *phoros* to Athens, rejected an increase to this *phoros*. Athens laid siege to Potidaea, which requested Corinth's help.
- In 433 an Athenian decree denied the neighbouring city of Megara access to its markets and to the markets of the cities of the Delian

League. This was a particularly grave blow for a city that lived essentially on its trade with the outside world, for it threatened to stifle it.

These three affairs involved Athens in conflicts with cities of the Peloponnesian League. If Sparta decided to support them, war would be inevitable. Neither side could afford the slightest upset in the equilibrium between the two hegemonies.

The outbreak of war In the autumn of 432, Corinth and Megara tried to persuade Sparta to declare war. The debate before the Spartan assembly was contradictory and the Athenian defence obtained a hearing. However, the assembly decided that the treaty of 446 had been broken and that the Athenians were at fault. A similar vote was taken by the Peloponnesian League as a whole.

In Athens, the Spartan demands (to dismiss Pericles from public life, to lift the siege of Potidaea, to abrogate the decree against Megara and to respect the autonomy of allied cities) were rejected.

The two camps Sparta and the Peloponnesian league could muster 40,000 hoplites, Athens and the Delian League only 13,000, to which could be added 12,000 Athenian reservists, who could be called up. The Boeotians provided most of the Peloponnesians' cavalry. Athens could count on 1,200 knights. Sparta and its allies had very few warships; the Delian fleet was 300 triremes strong. Finally, Athens had greater financial resources than its opponents. As can be seen, the respective strong points of the two camps encouraged one to wage a traditional hoplite war, the other a war that made the most of the mobility made possible by a fleet.

The tactics of the two camps differed, but their goal was the same: to carry the war into the enemy's territory and lay it waste. That is what the Peloponnesians systematically did in Attica for several consecutive years. Athens also organized raids on enemy territory from the coastline, where it would land forces from its triremes. Right from the start, however, Athens' defensive strategy was unexpected. Pericles decided to abandon the territory of Attica to the invaders and to gather the entire population of Attica within the defences of the town of Athens and Piraeus. A passage in Thucydides gives a realistic picture of this shake-up of rural customs:

The Athenians took the advice he [Pericles] gave them and brought in from the country their wives and children and all their household goods, taking down even the woodwork on the houses themselves. Their sheep and cattle they sent across to Euboea and the islands off the coast. But the move was a difficult experience for them, since most of them had always been used to living in the country . . . It was sadly and reluctantly that they now abandoned their homes and the temples time-honoured from their patriotic past, and that they prepared to change their whole way of life, leaving behind them what each man regarded as his own city. (Book II, 14–16)

It was indeed asking a lot of the peasants, who lost all their means of subsistence and had to look on helplessly as 'the land of their fathers' was laid waste.

431–421: FROM THE OUTBREAK OF WAR TO THE PEACE OF NICIAS

The war was fought on several fronts at once, which makes it difficult to give a continuous account of the conflict. In an attempt to give a clear account of its evolution, the emphasis here is laid upon the chronology of events.

431   The war began in the spring. Thebes attacked Plataea unsuccessfully, and the latter executed all prisoners. The war thus began with an act of barbarity. It was to be the first of many.

Archidamus, the king of Sparta, invaded Attica and laid the crops waste; the Athenians took refuge in the town.

The Athenian triremes landed their troops in Elis and Laconia, and they invaded Megaris.

The people of Aegina were ejected from their island and replaced by Athenians.

430   Operations similar to those of 431 were carried out by both sides.

An epidemic in Athens (typhus or the plague) killed between a quarter and a third of the population.

Winter, 430–429: Potidaea was taken by Athens.

429   In the autumn, Pericles died in the epidemic. The usual kind of operations continued in 429 and 428.

Plataea was taken by the Peloponnesians after a two-year siege. The town was destroyed. The refugees were given Athenian citizenship, which – as already noted – was quite exceptional.

Mitylene (Lesbos), which had seceded, capitulated after a long siege. The Athenian assembly initially decided to put all the inhabitants to death (as proposed by Cleon). It then changed its mind and decided to reduce them all to slavery instead. Thucydides brings the assembly's bitter debate to life.

An Athenian expedition was sent to Sicily to lend support to Rhegium and Leontini against Syracuse (twenty triremes).

425   In Corcyra, the civil war that had raged since 427 between the poor, who favoured Athens, and the rich, who favoured the Peloponnesians, came to an end.

On their way to Sicily, on a second expedition, the Athenians stopped in Pylos (in Messenia), under the *strategos* Demosthenes. The Spartans tried

> ### Description of the plague in Athens in 430–429
>
> 'At the beginning of the following summer the Peloponnesians and their allies, with two thirds of their total forces, as before invaded Attica, again under the command of the Spartan king Archidamus, the son of Zeuxidamus. Taking up their positions, they set about the devastation of the country. They had not been many days in Attica before the plague first broke out among the Athenians. Previously attacks of the plague had been reported from many other places in the neighbourhood of Lamnos and elsewhere, but there was no record of the disease being so virulent anywhere else or causing so many deaths as it did in Athens. At the beginning the doctors were quite incapable of treating the disease because of their ignorance of the right methods. In fact, mortality among the doctors was the highest of all, since they came more frequently in contact with the sick. Nor was any other human art or science of any help at all. Equally useless were prayers made in the temples, consultation of oracles, and so forth; indeed in the end people were so overcome by their sufferings that they paid no further attention to such things . . .
>
> A factor which made matters much worse than they were already was the removal of people from the country into the city, and this particularly affected the incomers. There were no houses for them and, living as they did during the summer in badly ventilated huts, they died like flies. The bodies of the dying were heaped one on top of the other, and half-dead creatures could be seen staggering about in the streets or flocking around the fountains in their desire for water. The temples in which they took up their quarters were full of the dead bodies of people who had died inside them. For the catastrophe was so overwhelming that men, not knowing what would happen next to them, became indifferent to every rule of religion or of law.' (Thucydides, II, 47 and 52, translation by Rex Warner)

to dislodge them but were not successful. Instead they themselves were trapped on the small island of Sphacteria and were forced to surrender when Cleon captured the island. Sparta relaxed its pressure on Attica.

424 Many defections from the Athenian camp were provoked by Athens trying to raise the *phoros* contributions so as to increase its financial resources.

Athens suffered a severe defeat at the hands of the Boeotians at Delium, on the north coast of Boeotia. Over a thousand hoplites were killed.

Amphipolis, on the Thracian coast, was besieged by the Spartans under general Brasidas. It surrendered in 423, the Athenian *strategos*, Thucydides, having arrived on the scene too late. He was condemned to exile (and wrote his work of history . . .).

423   A one-year truce.

422   Athens launched an offensive operation in Thrace, under Cleon, who was killed while trying to recapture Amphipolis. Brasidas was also killed.

Negotiations began between the Spartan king Pleistonax and the Athenian Nicias.

421   The Peace of Nicias included the following clauses: peace was concluded for fifty years; all captured places and prisoners were to be returned; the cities of Thrace were to be evacuated by the Peloponnesians; future quarrels were to be settled by arbitration and negotiation.

Several cities refused to sign this peace treaty (Corinth, the Boeotians, the Eleans, Megara).

Athens and Sparta now concluded a defensive alliance, according to which Athens promised to come to Sparta's aid in the event of an uprising by the helots.

This fifty-year peace lasted but a few brief years. Right from the start, both sides failed to honour their undertakings: Sparta did not return Amphipolis and the Athenians remained in Pylos. In 418 hostilities were resumed.

421–404: FROM THE PEACE OF NICIAS TO THE END OF THE WAR

418   In the Peloponnese an attempt was made to organize a new Peloponnesian confederation, under the leadership of Argos. Athens allied itself with Argos, Mantinea and the Eleans and, after a number of military campaigns, these new allies clashed with Sparta and the Arcadians at the *battle of Mantinea*, in which they were defeated.

416   Melos, an Aegean island, had remained outside the Athenian alliance. Athens laid siege to it, insisting on its submission, in the name of the law of the strongest. Melos surrendered, the men were killed, the women and children sold into slavery, and cleruchs were installed on the soil of Melos. As Thucydides represents it, the debate between the Athenians and the Melians opposed the rights of law to the rights of nature, in the finest tradition of sophistic debate.

415–413: the Sicilian expedition   The cities of Sicily were becoming less and less amenable to the hegemony of Syracuse. Athens had already intervened once, in 427–425, to help Rhegium and Leontini. Now it was Segesta that requested its aid. In the spring of 415 the Athenian assembly, caught between the reasoning of Nicias, who was hostile to any intervention, and the bellicose arguments of Alcibiades, initially voted to send sixty triremes,

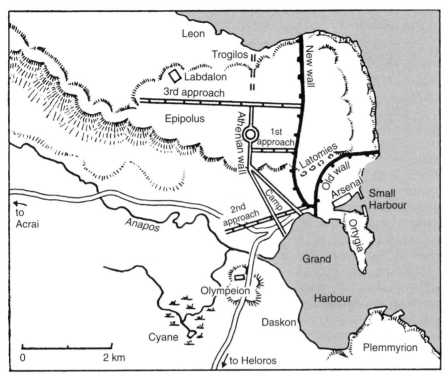

Figure 34 Sketch map of the battle around Syracuse (from *Historiens grecs*, Paris, Gallimard, p. 1847, fig. VIII)

then doubled that number. The expedition to provide aid took on the look of an expedition of conquest. Its leaders were Alcibiades, Lamachus and Nicias.

- June, 415: the fleet left Piraeus and anchored at Catana.
- Spring, 414: Nicias and Lamachus surrounded Syracuse but were then, in their turn, encircled by Syracuse's allies, the Spartans and the Corinthians. Lamachus was killed.
- Spring, 413: seventy-three Athenian triremes arrived as reinforcements, under Demosthenes' command. Realizing that it would be impossible to take Syracuse, Demosthenes was in favour of evacuating the Athenian troops by ship. Nicias hesitated, influenced by an omen. The Syracusans then attacked the Athenian fleet in the bay of Syracuse and destroyed it. The 40,000 Athenian survivors tried to escape by land. Some were captured, others gave themselves up. Very few escaped either immediate death or a slow death in the infamous Syracusan quarries, the Latomia. The captured leaders, Nicias and Demosthenes, were executed in the autumn of 413. This was the worst disaster Athens had ever known.

- In Attica, things were going just as badly. The Spartans were encamped in Attica itself, at Decelea. They ravaged the *chôra* and allowed the slaves employed in the Laurion silver mines to escape. The Athenians became short of funds.
- Athens gradually lost control over the east Aegean coast and the Straits. The Spartans, thanks to money lent them by the Persians, had at last built themselves a fleet, and persuaded Chios, Clazomenae, Erythraea and Teos to switch to their side.

411 After the failure of the oligarchic *coup* in Athens, Athens lost Euboea, but won a victory at sea at *Cynossema*.

410 Athens recaptured Perinthus, Byzantium and also Thasos. Alcibiades returned as a conqueror to Athens.

406 The Athenian *strategos* Conon was hemmed in off Mitylene by the Spartan navarch, Lysander. An Athenian fleet that arrived with reinforcements destroyed part of the Spartan fleet at the *battle of Arginusae* (summer, 406). However, the victorious generals had committed a religious transgression: they had not picked up the sailors who had been shipwrecked in a night storm. When they returned to Athens, they were tried and condemned to death.

405 In August the Athenian fleet was crushed by the Spartan fleet, commanded by Lysander, off *Aegospotami*.

In the autumn the Spartans laid siege to Athens. Many of the population died of starvation. It became imperative to negotiate. Theramenes was entrusted with this task.

404 The congress of the Peloponnesian League debated the question of Athens' fate. Some favoured total destruction (Corinth, Thebes); others declared themselves content with the destruction of the fortifications and the Long Walls (Sparta), and it was the latter decision that prevailed.

In Athens, the *ecclesia* agreed to the conditions: to destroy the fortifications of Piraeus and the Long Walls, to evacuate all the cities, to be content with the territory of Attica, to recall those in exile, to keep no more than twelve triremes; and it voted for peace – external peace, that is. Civil peace was another matter, as we have seen.

The fifth century was dominated by war, first against the Persians, then between the Greeks; and war made itself felt in a thousand ways in the history of the cities. In the first place, it dictated a community's priorities: the war effort consumed much, if not most, of the available wealth; the choice of statesmen often depended on their ability as tacticians or even as leaders of men on the battlefield; the debates in the assemblies turned endlessly on the conduct of the war. Warfare also left its mark on the demography of the cities, for each year hundreds of citizens died in battle or in its aftermath or were taken prisoner, all representing manpower sorely needed by the cities. But the cities were loath to enrol non-citizens. In Sparta, the helots formed separate battalions placed under the command of *homoioi*, but in Athens the slaves were never enrolled and it is doubtful whether metics were, except very occasionally. So recourse to the use of mercenaries progressively came to be regarded as the solution. But it was not just soldiers who died in times of war. The civilian population also suffered and died. We have already noted the fate meted out to the populations of defeated cities, but it was even worse when the cities destroyed themselves from within, in interminable civil wars. In short, warfare stamped itself upon the minds of the Greeks. Not only was it omnipresent in the works of historians; it was also the theme of plays, both tragic and comic, of the figurative representations painted on vases and, no doubt, of daily conversations in the agora. When speeches were made in honour of the war dead, this provided an opportunity to remember the valour of ancestors and the virtues of present political regimes. Warfare, as much as democracy, provided the essential context of fifth-century culture.

A DEMOCRATIC CULTURE

It is, of course, reductionist to treat the culture of the archaic cities as a homogeneous whole, but it is possible to do so, given that what the sources available to us reveal are essentially the features of a culture that belonged to the dominant social category, the aristocracy, which was not only present in each one of the cities but was, moreover, in power there. But such a way of proceeding is impossible for the fifth century. Because we possess so much more information for this period, we really ought to aim to present a picture that reflects the differences between regions, between types of political regimes and between periods. However, even more than in the case of the earlier period, the 'Athenocentrism' of our textual sources is a very real handicap. For that reason, the present work will be tackling a number of aspects of the classical civilization taking Athens as its sole example. Yet, although Athens may be better known, this does not mean that it can really serve as an example for the whole of Greece; quite the reverse. To the extent that many features of its culture were connected with the political regime that it progressively established, namely a democracy – an altogether minority regime among the fifth-century cities – it could almost be said that Athens was, in truth, an exception. History, the theatre, philosophy and art are the domains that we shall be examining in our discussion of the major aspects of this culture founded upon the links constituted by society.

HISTORY

As has been mentioned, we owe our knowledge of the Persian Wars and many aspects of the history of the cities of the archaic period to Herodotus, and that of the inter-war period and the Peloponnesian War up to 411 to Thucydides. Both historians lived in the fifth century; Thucydides was himself an Athenian, and Herodotus spent much of his life in Athens. It is with them that a new way of thinking about the past, if it did not begin, at least started to be constructed, namely the historical genre, or what we call history.

The Greeks did not wait for historians to create their representations of the past. Epic, myths and lyric poetry all in their own particular ways served a function indispensable to the identity of any community: that of situating it in time, in particular, in relation to the past generations. However, these epic or mythical accounts did not constitute what the Greeks themselves called *historiè*, an enquiry. The mission of one who called himself a *histor* was to preserve the actions of men from oblivion by recounting them. He picked up where the bard and the archaic poet left off, but was distinct from them in that he used writing, composition in prose, a subject that concerned contemporary or very recent happenings, and a method that depended on enquiry and not upon the inspiration of the Muses. After Hecataeus, who lived in Miletus around 550 and whose works, a *Periegèsis* (a description of the world) and some *Genealogies* have been almost entirely lost, the most ancient of the historians is Herodotus.

HERODOTUS

Herodotus was born in Halicarnassus in about 485. As an opponent of its tyrant, Lydamis, he was forced into exile. He lived in a number of Greek cities, including Athens, and also travelled in non-Greek lands; eventually, in about 444–443, he settled in the new city of Thurii. The exact date of his death is not known. His work, the *Histories,* has been presented, ever since the Alexandrian period, divided into nine books, each named after one of the nine Muses. The heart of the work concerns the Persian Wars, and around this theme Herodotus writes of whatever, directly or indirectly, may help us to understand the great clash between the Greeks and the Persians. His book thus contains not only the history of the past of a number of Greek peoples and cities in the archaic period, but also the history of non-Greek peoples and an account of their ways of life.

After being known by generations of historians as 'the father of history', today Herodotus is regarded just as much as one of the earliest of geographers and ethnographers. The three facets of his work are, of course, inseparable, each one a product of his desire to understand the world in which he lived.

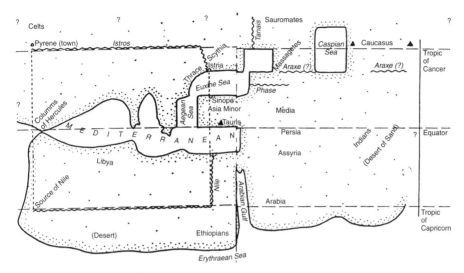

Figure 35   Map of the world according to Herodotus

A geography? The first thing to note is that Herodotus' world's limits are drawn well beyond where the unknown began. To the south-east the edge is the Erythrean Sea (the Indian Ocean), to the north-east the Caspian Sea, to the extreme east India; the north and the west of Europe are surrounded by sea, as is Libya in the south. This early fifth-century view of the world is that of a circular space divided in half by a median line that is imagined to pass through the Mediterranean. The centre of this circle is Delphi, that is, Greece. The further out towards the edges of this world, towards its limits, the more extreme the climates and the stranger the landscapes. This construction of space constitutes an ordering of the known world that makes it possible to apprehend it and render it intelligible. The same applies to Herodotus' description of its peoples.

Ethnography? At the centre there are the Greeks, and the further a traveller ventures from that centre, the more the peoples encountered differ from the Greek norms. Herodotus' account does not consist of an exact catalogue of the customs and habits of non-Greek peoples, 'an enquiry into the terrain', as modern ethnologists might put it. What he sets out to do is to classify the various peoples according to a scale in which the degree of their distance from the Greek world coincides with the degree of their strangeness: strangeness in every domain – politics, religion, food, sexual behaviour. Every aspect of their ways of life is assessed in relation to a norm, Herodotus' norm, the norm of the Greeks. For example, if the Greek norm for eating is to consume sacrificed meat, a people that makes no sacrifices, or eats no meat, or eats human flesh, or honours its parents by eating their corpses, is outstandingly different. Herodotus' travels tell us less about the real customs of the barbarian peoples of his day than about the pattern of behaviour as a whole that the Greeks would recognize as being civilized.

History? Here too a deliberate construction is patently obvious. What Herodotus wants to prove is the superiority of the regime of cities over that of monarchies, and the superiority of decisions reached in common, on the basis of dialogue, over despotic authority; and the events that he relates, whether those of archaic history or those of the Persian Wars, are organized to that end. His history is more or less contemporary; it was written less than thirty years after the events, and its author was deeply committed to his work. It was read aloud to an audience of Greeks, sometimes even to Athenians, and was composed with a view to convincing them. These *Histories* reflect the values of the Greek world, of life in the city, sometimes even of democracy.

THUCYDIDES

Thucydides was an Athenian citizen, related to Miltiades. He was born in abut 460 and died around 400. In 424 he was a *strategos*, at the time when Amphipolis had to be defended against the Spartans, commanded by Brasidas. His failure in this affair caused him to be ostracized and to live in exile until 404, when he returned to Athens. During that time he had composed his great work, *The Peloponnesian War*.

Thucydides did not wish to be someone who wrote down stories he had been told, in order to please an audience, as – he claimed – was the method of his predecessor, Herodotus, whom he criticized. His own ambition was to discover the factual truth. First, he had to establish the facts in the surest way possible, fixing the precise chronology of events and comparing evidence; then he had to interpret those facts and understand them. So for Thucydides, the only possible true history was that of the present time, since this allowed for verification. At the same time though, the historian was not a passive witness. He reasoned, illuminated, presented the facts in what seemed to him the most intelligible way possible for an understanding of the political behaviour of the cities of his time. For Thucydides too, history meant construction, and his work provides a magnificent example of this.

The Peloponnesian War was divided into eight books in the Hellenistic period. The first is devoted to the history of the early years of the Greek world, a rapid survey designed to set in place the historical context of the war. Thucydides then explains his method. Next, he reflects upon the origins of the war, then embarks upon tracing its development from one year to the next, up to 411, at which date his account stops. The account of the events themselves is punctuated by long citations from speeches delivered by the principal protagonists, in particular, in the city assemblies that had to decide on how to pursue the war. These speeches are clearly reconstructed, their principal function being to explain the positions of each of the parties involved and the reasons for their decisions, – in short, to explain the history of these extraordinarily complicated years of the fifth century. The explanations endeavour to be as rational as possible. Recourse to religious and psychological motivation is avoided. Economic causes are not explained as such; the major axis of Thucydides' explanations is the political will of those involved. The historian also passes judgement on the actions of his contemporaries, so his work is frequently that of a moralist. Thucydides' talent as a writer makes him one of the very foremost writers of the classical period.

The differences between these two major fifth-century historians are often, quite justifiably, underlined, but sometimes they are set in opposition in somewhat rhetorical dichotomies. They did not belong to the same intellectual generation and their respective visions of the world were affected by this, quite apart from their personalities, which are hard to gauge. Only by reading their works can you decide whether you succumb more easily to the charm of Herodotus or to that of Thucydides. Between the two of them they generated the historical genre in Greece, and that was a major achievement. The cities now had at their disposal a form of discourse that enabled them to reflect upon the past in order to reconstitute the events of the present and gain a better understanding of them, without resorting to any overall explanation that rested upon a divine will. This reflection on time sprang from the cities' need to get a grip on the present, particularly in the case of Athens. It is as if opening up political debate to a larger number of citizens, combined with the hegemony Athens had assumed over part of the Greek world, increased the urgent need for a history. To what extent was this history accessible to a wide public? Although Herodotus is reputed to have given public readings or recitations of his work, nothing of the kind is known of Thucydides. In this respect, the case of the theatre is quite different, as there can be no doubt as to the public nature of its reception.

THE THEATRE

In the Greek world, the civic institution of theatre was one element in the cult of a deity. The comedies and tragedies were presented in competitions that took place during major religious festivals, the rural Dionysia, the Lenaea and the Great Dionysia. The latter incorporated performances of many kinds: comedy, tragedy, satyr plays and dithyrambs. The city organized the entire festival. The eponymous archon was responsible for the Great Dionysia. The *choregoi*, the poets, the plays to be performed, the actors, and the competition judges were all chosen by the city. The *choregia* was an expensive liturgy and *choregoi* were designated from among the richest citizens, those whose fortunes amounted to over three talents. The *choregos* organized a chorus that took part in the competition and had it trained.

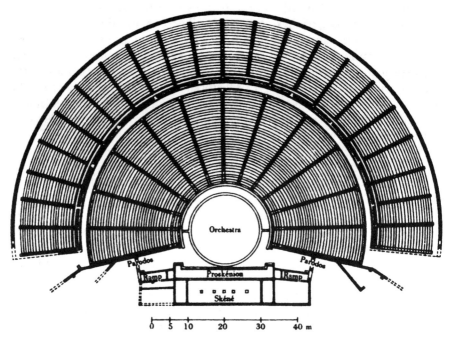

Figure 36 Plan of the theatre of Epidaurus (from J.-J. Maffre, *L'Art grec*, Paris, PUF, 1986, p. 104, fig. 12)

In the fifth century there were three *choregoi* for the tragedies, five for the comedies and ten for the dithyrambs. In the tragedy competitions, three tragic authors were engaged, each of whom had to produce four plays: three tragedies (a trilogy) and one satyr play. In the comedy contest, five comic authors competed.

Apart from the members of the chorus (*choreutai*) under its leader (the *koryphaios*), the play was performed by three actors (the protagonists), each of whom played several roles. All the chorus and actors were men, and they wore masks representing the characters they were playing. In each competition the judges awarded three prizes, to the best poet, the best *choregos* and the best actor. The prizes were crowns of ivy.

At the Great Dionysia the competition took place on the day after a procession and a sacrifice, in the sanctuary of Dionysus, on the southern slopes of the Acropolis. It lasted three days. A theatre, the steps of which were of wood in the fifth century, then in the fourth were built of stone, accommodated the crowd of citizens and foreigners who came to watch the plays (see figure 36). The spectacle lasted from dawn to dusk. The statue of Dionysus stood on the *orchestra*, and the day began with the sacrifice of a piglet and libations, poured by the magistrates, for whom seats of honour were reserved. The public paid a two-obol entrance fee, but from 355 on a special coffer, the *theorikon*, was introduced, which made it possible to hand out to every poor citizen the coin that was necessary to get into the theatre. At the end of the fourth century, a stone-built theatre could accommodate 17,000 spectators.

The theatrical productions of the Great Dionysia gave the Athenian city a chance to demonstrate its political influence. This was the occasion on which the allies brought their tribute, which was put on show, it seems, on the *orchestra*, before the whole *dèmos*. Before the performance of the plays, a proclamation was made in the theatre, naming those whose actions had brought glory to the city and to whom the assembly had voted a crown, and the herald then presented the orphans whose fathers had died in battle. It was a way of reminding all present of the glorious past and present of Athens.

A theatrical production, a moment of unique civic ritual (a play was performed only once) was very different from what it is today. What of the themes tackled by these plays?

The theatre, like the assembly, was a place for debating questions of interest to the whole body of citizens, and so was a place where social thought was forged and expressed. The spectator participant witnessed a clash of opinions and ideas on problems that currently affected the city, and the theatre provided him with food for thought and the means of forming an opinion of his own. For that reason, the tragic and comic texts are an essential source for any historian seeking to understand the systems of representation and the modes of thought of classical Athenian society. The theatre makes it possible to study how a human group thought about its practical and religious policies and its customs, and that reflection in its turn either reinforced or changed those practices.

For a long time historians made use of the tragic and comic texts in a reductionist fashion, combing them for individual passages that could throw light on certain aspects of Athenian political or institutional history (for example, the passage in Aeschylus' *Persians* describing the battle of Salamis, the passage in Sophocles' *Oedipus Rex* evoking the plague of 430 and the passage in his *Ajax* that was read as a protest against the 451 law that excluded from citizenship all those not born from both a citizen father and a mother who was the daughter of a citizen); but in so doing, they failed to take into account the specifically literary character of the text. Meanwhile, specialists in Greek literature gave priority to a study of the authors and their texts, treated and sometimes explained without any reference at all to their times. But they too have changed and now proclaim their interest in everything that provides a context for the texts, and themselves tackle many questions such as the audience, the places in which the plays were performed, and the interaction between theatrical conventions and the civic body. In short, the adoption of new methods of reading the texts on the part of both literary scholars and historians explains how it is that present-day research on comedy and tragedy attracts such interest.

Figures 37 to 40 Aeschylus (Naples Museum); Sophocles (Musée du Louvre, Paris); Euripides (Capitol Museum, Rome); Aristophanes (Musée du Louvre) (from J.-J. Maffre, *Le Siècle de Périclès*, Paris, PUF, 1994, p. 89, fig. 4)

TRAGEDY AND COMEDY

Tragedy succeeded epic and lyric poetry, and faded away as philosophy became established. It thus belongs to a precise historical moment: fifth-century Athens. The stories treated in the tragedies were known by all the ancient Greeks. The public came to the theatre not to discover new stories but to see how, in that particular year, the old stories would be told. The themes are the legends of heroes, the subject-matter the contemporary social, political, juridical and religious thought of the city at that time. Here is one example, that of the characters of Antigone and Creon in Sophocles' *Antigone*. They argue about the values of the *oikos* (the household) and those of the city; about the best kind of power, that of a single individual or that of the community; about the limits that need to be respected for fear of falling into excess (*hubris*); and about many other subjects too. Neither character is in possession of all the right answers, and both are blind and fail to see the fatal end to which their behaviour is leading them (a constant feature of tragedy). *Antigone* dramatizes problems that interested the public, as a group of citizens who elsewhere, in the assembly or the law-courts, were expected to decide on questions of a similar type. The play proposed no solution but, in this particular case, it provoked thought about the content of democratic powers just as, in other domains, history and philosophy did.

The comedies Those of Aristophanes are the best preserved. They are usually considered to allude more directly and openly to the political world. Attacks against statesmen of the moment are frequent, as we have noted in the case of Cleon. However, most modern commentators refuse to regard this as true political discourse. Some think that humour and laughter cannot convey real political messages and refuse even to consider the

Aeschylus 525–456

Born in Athens, a citizen.
He belonged to the generation that fought at Marathon and himself fought at Salamis and at Plateau.
He wrote 73 plays, of which 7 tragedies have been preserved, as well as numerous fragments. He was 13 times victorious in the competitions.
The Persians (427)
The Seven against Thebes (467)
The Suppliants (463)
Prometheus
A trilogy: *The Oresteia* (458): *Agamemnon, The Choephori, The Eumenides*

Sophocles 497–405

Born in Athens, in the deme of Colonus, a citizen and a statesman: a *hellenotamias* (treasurer of the Delian League) in 443; several times a *strategos*; a commissioner of the Council in 411.
He wrote 123 plays, 7 of which have come down to us intact.
He was 24 times victorious in the tragic competitions. The dates of his plays are a subject of considerable controversy.
Ajax
Antigone (441)
The Trachinean Women
Oedipus Rex
Philoctetes (409)
Oedipus at Colonus (401)
Electra

Euripides 484–406

Born in Athens, a citizen. Nothing is known of his public life, but he knew all the intellectuals of his day.
He wrote 92 plays, 19 of which have been preserved, as well as numerous fragments. He was 4 times victorious in the competitions. *Alcestis* (438), *Medea* (431), *The Heracleidae* (430–428), *Hippolytus* (428), *Andromache* (425), *Hecuba* (424), *Suppliants* (423), *Ion* (418–414), *Electra* (417–415), *Heracles* (417–415), *Iphigenia in Tauris* (413), *The Pheonician Women* (412–408), *Iphigenia in Aulis, The Bacchae* (performed after his death), one satyr play, *The Cyclops,* and one tragedy the authenticity of which is challenged: *Rhesus.*

Aristophanes 445(?)–388

Born in Athens, a citizen. He wrote 44 plays, 11 of which have come
down to us intact, as well as numerous fragments.
The Acharnians (425)
The Knights (424)
The Clouds (423)
The Wasps (422)
The Peace (421)
The Birds (414)
Lysistrata (411)
The Thesmophoria (411)
The Frogs (405)
The Assembly of Women
Plutus

The structure of a comedy

Prologue
Parados: entrance of the chorus (24 men)
Parabasis: the *koryphaios* introduces himself
Agon: the scene of a debate between two theses
A variety of scenes
Exodos: tumultuous exit of the chorus.

---

possibility that comic humour might have been a means of persuasion.
Others emphasize the carnivalesque world that comedy constructs, a world
of fantasy, without the slightest impact on the places where decisions were
taken. But by dint of making precise analyses of a number of different
comedies, it has been shown that the above views are mistaken. Obscenity,
parody, disguise and reversals of fortune (all characteristic of comedy) are
imbued with a dynamic that has a definite persuasive effect. The comic
poets did want 'to give the *dèmos* good advice' and to discuss serious
matters; and by championing the underdogs and broadcasting minority
views they did influence the formulation of civic ideology. Comedy certainly was a way of confirming the sovereignty of the *dèmos*, in that it
ridiculed statesmen and laid the responsibility for every evil at their door.

Theatre, both as a collection of texts and as an institutional practice,
gave the citizens as a whole a chance to reflect upon their beliefs and
practices, to pass judgement on them, perhaps even to modify them. It was
an essential element in a democratic culture organized around debate.

The Hippocratic oath

(Hippocrates is supposed to have composed this oath when accepting as students under his instruction foreigners who were not members of the family of the Asclepiadae.)

'I swear by Apollo the healer, by Asclepius, by Health, and all the powers of healing, and call to witness all the gods and goddesses that I may keep this oath and promise to the best of my ability and judgement.

I will pay the same respect to my master in the science as to my parents and share my life with him and pay all my debts to him. I will regard all his sons as my brothers and teach them the science, if they desire to learn it, without fee or contract. I will hand on precepts, lectures, and all other learning to my sons, to those of my master and to those pupils duly apprenticed and sworn, and to none other.

I will use my power to help the sick to the best of my ability and judgement; I will abstain from harming or wronging any man by it.

I will not give a fatal draught to anyone if I am asked, nor will I suggest any such thing. Neither will I give a woman the means to procure an abortion.

I will be chaste and religious in my life and in my practice.

I will not cut, even for the stone, but I will leave such procedures to the practitioners of that craft.

Whenever I go into a house, I will go to help the sick and never with the intention of doing harm or injury. I will not abuse my position to indulge in sexual contacts with the bodies of women or of men, whether they be free men or slaves.

Whatever I see or hear professionally or privately, which ought not to be divulged, I will keep secret and tell no one.

If, therefore, I observe this oath and do not violate it, may I prosper both in my life and in my profession, earning good repute among men for all time. If I trangress and forswear this oath, may my lot be otherwise.'

(*The Hippocratic Treatises*, translated by J. Chadwick and W. N. Mann, Pelican Classics, Harmondsworth, 1978)

MEDICINE AND PHILOSOPHY

Already by the beginning of the century, philosophers such as Alcmeon and Empedocles, on the basis of their knowledge of cosmological systems, were constructing theories that were then applied to the art of healing. But it was in the mid-fifth century that, centred on the sanctuary of Asclepius in Cos, there appeared a school of doctors whose leader we know as *Hippocrates*. However, even if Hippocrates was a real man who lived from

Figures 41 and 42 Hippocrates (Naples Museum); Socrates (Naples Museum)
(from J.-J. Maffre, *Le Siècle de Périclès*, Paris, PUF, 1994, p. 12, fig. 1.

460 to 377, the writings that bear his name ('the Hippocratic corpus')
group together over fifty treatises, which date from the fifth century, the
fourth and even later. 'Hippocrates' marks the beginning of a rational
concept of disease and its treatment that breaks away from the temple
medicine practised in their sanctuaries by priests who attributed both the
cause and the cure of sickness to divine action. The authors of these
treatises won acceptance for the idea that disease is a natural phenomenon,
an effect of natural causes, and that treatment for it must be based upon
detailed and methodical observation of the symptoms. Their opinions differed as to the explanation of causes for here, with insufficiently accurate
anatomical and physiological knowledge, philosophical theories once again
came into their own. However that may be, the beginnings of this medicine all stem from the kind of thought that we have noted in the historical
genre, thought that rejected arbitrary presuppositions and looked for proofs
in a new quest for the truth.

Socrates (470–399) was the predominant figure in the fifth century, but
we know of him only through what Aristophanes, Plato and Xenophon say
about him. He was an Athenian citizen who assembled around him a circle
of disciples that included young men from the aristocracy such as Plato and
Xenophon. Convinced that man is capable of knowing himself by developing a method of rational thought that can assess a variety of hypotheses
against one another in order to discover the truth, he taught his disciples
to do without masters. This quest of his, to which he set no limits, was to
come into conflict with the city which, for its part, considered one of its
functions to be precisely to define limits. The pretext was impiety and the
punishment was death (in 399; see p. 228). Socrates' philosophical ideas
are known to us only through Plato (see p. 250), but he was clearly

opposed to the mode of thought in vogue with the majority of his day: that of the sophists.

The sophists were itinerant teachers whose primary concern was to train citizens involved in the cut and thrust of political debate. They perfectly suited the needs of a society in which the art of persuasion in the assembly was playing an increasingly important role in the acquisition and maintenance of political authority. Their pupils belonged to the great, wealthy families who continued to provide most of the cities' statesmen. The sophists not only taught the art of speech, rhetoric; they also pressed for a reassessment of the social, political and religious rules upon which the city was founded, demonstrating their contingent and conventional aspect.

The names of some of the sophists have come down to us, but none of their writings. The best known is Protagoras, since Plato sets him on stage in the dialogue that bears his name and also in the *Theatetus*. He was born in Abdera at the beginning of the century, moved to Athens and became close to Pericles. During this same period Athens was also home to Prodicus, Hippias, a native of Elis, and Gorgias, from Leontini. The next generation of sophists, in the last quarter of the fifth century, took a more direct part in political action. Among them were Antiphon, Thrasimachus and Critias. Critias, a fervent supporter of oligarchy, was a member of the government of the Thirty.

The work of an unknown writer (known as the Pseudo-Xenophon), entitled *The Constitution [Politeia] of the Athenians*, follows the same line as this sophistic thinking that was so critical of democracy. It is a virulent pamphlet that attacks all the democratic features of the city's government. Once again, one sees clearly how much the very regime of the city stirred up debate and prompted attitudes which, by the turn of the fourth century, were openly hostile to democracy.

ART

The fifth century is considered to represent the peak of classical art. This took so many forms that it would be impossible to mention them all here, except in an uninformative list. Besides, any description of the evolution of architecture, sculpture, vase painting and bronze-work would be pure rhetoric in the absence of the evidence itself. The best thing for the reader to do is to consult the works on Greek art indicated in the bibliography, for these contain many illustrations. Quite deliberately, only one example will be mentioned here, that of Athens, and it revolves around a question that it is perfectly legitimate for a historian to ask, but for which an answer may well not be found: is there any connection between the Athenian art of the fifth century and the nature of the city's political system? The days are gone when the history of art devoted itself to a study of the evolution of various forms of art without setting them in a historical context. Nevertheless, it seems risky to attribute the dominant characteristics of classical art to particular historical causes. Today, the interpretations suggested by specialists in ancient art try to steer a course between the two above-mentioned reefs, in what is sometimes a passionate debate, of which historians have high hopes.

At this point a few preliminary remarks seem called for. A fifth-century work of art was, of course, bound to constitute a response to whoever commissioned it and in that sense would be bound to tally with mental attitudes of the period. But in fifth-century Athens, commissions of a new kind appeared: *most came from the civic community.*

One of the new characteristics of the fifth century was the appearance of works of art that commemorated a historical or political event. The most ancient example in Athens was the group of statues representing Harmodius and Aristogeiton, the two Athenians who assassinated the tyrant Hipparchus in 514, during the festival of the Panathenaea. A first group of statues had already been sculpted in the late sixth century, in 510, by Antenor. It was carried off as booty by the Persians in the course of the Persian Wars. In 477–476 a new bronze monument was sculpted by Critius and Nesiotès, and was placed in the agora. It represents Harmodius as a beardless youth pointing a horizontally held sword, ready to be plunged into the tyrant's body, while Aristogeiton is depicted as a man of more mature years brandishing above his head a sword that is about to smite the tyrant's skull. The tyrant is not represented. These two statues were known as the 'monument to the *tyrannoktonoi* (tyrant-slayers)'. The construction of the monument was decided upon officially by the assembly and it had no particular religious function – which was a new feature. It was the first monument set up in the political centre of the city with the primary function of keeping alive the memory of a doubly founding action: one that had founded both liberty and democracy – at least, that was the interpretation that fifth-century Greeks put upon the assassination of the tyrant.

In similar fashion, mythical episodes such as the battle against the Amazons (*Amazonomachia*), the capture of Troy (*Iliupersis*) and the fights against the Centaurs and the Giants became events that could be set alongside the high deeds of contemporary times. The *Stoa Poikilè*, the portico built on the edge of the agora by the Athenian Peisianax between 475 and 450, was ornamented with paintings representing the victories over the Amazons and Troy, and these were flanked by pictures of victories over the Persians at Marathon and the Spartans at Oenoe, thereby conferring upon the latter as great an exemplary value as that of the mythical episodes. Representations of collective exploits were now preferred to those of the individual exploits of heroes such as Heracles or Theseus, which had been popular with the preceding generation. Another example of the self-representation of the Athenian people was the frieze representing the

Panathenaea sculpted on the Parthenon. But this too belonged to a series of works all commissioned officially by the civic authorities.

THE RECONSTRUCTION OF THE ACROPOLIS

The buildings on the Acropolis were destroyed by the Persians in 480 and 479. In particular, the temple of Athena built by Pisistratus and his sons was badly damaged by fire.

For over a generation, the Athenians were confronted with this scene of devastation, for it was not until 449 that it was decided to rebuild the sanctuaries of the gods. The first stage took place while Pericles was a *strategos*, and the texts emphasize the predominant part he played in pushing ahead with the plan of reconstruction. The necessary funds were found by dipping into the treasury of the allies and into those of other deities as well as Athena, and the produce of one of the Laurion mines was also diverted into this building operation. The overall plan included the construction of a monumental entrance, the Propylaea, the renovation of the south-eastern zone with the construction of a temple to Athena Nike, the refurbishment of the Erechtheion, the demolition of the old temple of Athena and the construction of the Parthenon, and the restoration of the sanctuaries of Artemis Brauronia and Athena Ergane. Only the Parthenon (447–432) and the Propylaea (437–431) were completed before Pericles' death. Work on the rest of the monuments was slowed down by the Peloponnesian War, and the programme was not completed until 406. The sculptor Phidias supervised the operation as a whole, aided by the architects Callicrates, Ictinus and Mnesicles.

Of course the coherence of the programme as a whole, its relatively rapid realization, the great expenditure devoted to it in both human and financial terms, and the fame immediately acquired by this exceptional building project all testified to the power of the Athenian city. The sculpted decoration of the Parthenon, in particular the frieze of the Panathenaea, was a very tangible sign of the city's role in the operation.

Right around the peristyle ran sculpted metopes alternating with triglyphs. On the façade they represented a Gigantomachia, with Athena in the middle, battling with the giant Encelades; on the west side they represented an Amazonomachia, which also symbolized the Athenians' struggle against the Persians in the Persian Wars; on the north, the capture of Troy; and on the south a Centauromachia, under the leadership of Theseus. The sculptures on the pediments represented on the east the birth of Athena, on the west the dispute over Attica between Athena and Poseidon. It has been shown that each of these themes, although a part of the common Greek patrimony of mythology, is treated in such a way as to emphasize the importance of the past of the city of Athens and its glorious exploits. As for the frieze, it was a representation of the *dèmos* itself, taking part in one of its religious activities: a procession.

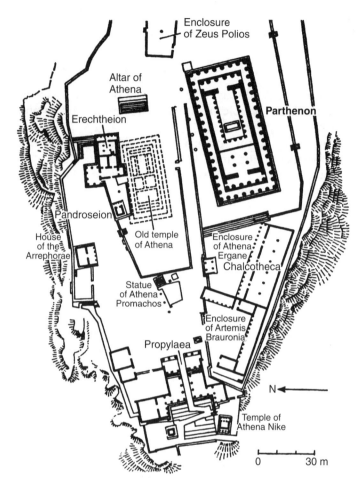

Figure 43 Plan of the Acropolis of Athens (from J.-J. Maffre, *Le Siècle de Périclès*, Paris, PUF, 1994, p. 102, fig. 8)

THE PANATHENAEA FRIEZE

This sculpted frieze was situated inside the colonnade, at the top of the wall of the *sekos* of the Parthenon. It ran right around the monument (almost 160 metres), and incorporated over 200 figures of people and animals. Arguments still continue about the exact order in which the figures in the frieze were arranged and its precise subject. Clearly it represented a *pompe* (procession), and the most generally accepted theory is that this was the procession that took place every four years, at the Great Panathenaea. The figure at the centre of the façade is usually identified as Athena Polias. Flanked by two women carrying cushions, she is presiding over the bestowal of the *peplos*. Deities and men (magistrates) look on while young girls approach the scene from either side, leading processions that ran parallel along the south and the north faces of the temple and that comprise sacrificial animals, people carrying offerings, musicians and citizens on foot, riding in chariots or on horseback. In short, the frieze represents a summarized version of the Athenian population usually present in the procession. One important factor is the novelty of this representation of a civic group on a monument consecrated to the gods. The sculpted ornamentation of the Parthenon reinforced the exceptional character of this monument on which its dedicator, the *dèmos*, presented itself both as the heir to a glorious past and as the actor in a present characterized by a serene opulence that was naturally offered up to the gods.

These few Athenian examples show how the plans of a civic community could leave a lasting mark on the monumental and artistic landscape of a city. By the fourth century the classical style was already being identified with the age of Pericles and Phidias, and from that time on it has been regarded as a norm. Without indulging in value judgements that would be partial and contingent, it is worth observing, along with E. La Rocca, that the quest for balance and harmony that characterized this art corresponded to a moment when the artists identified themselves with their client, the *dèmos*, so in this sense the technical advances of their art are inseparable from the political, social and spiritual triumphs of the city of Athens.

A single group, the Athenian *dèmos*, 'carried' the work of Phidias, as it did that of Sophocles and Thucydides. That, at least, is what these works from such different domains seem to tell us, as they set out before us what it seems fair to call a democratic culture. This democratic culture forges an image of the Athens of the fifth century at a moment when there was room in debate for a measure of political consensus, when the sense of community (*koinonia*) won out over dissension, and when a daily pattern of behaviour shared in the agora, in the assembly, in the ranks of the hoplite phalanx, in religious processions and in banquets restated and prolonged the civic *paideia*. Behind that image the historians of today, like those of yesterday, continue to seek for the real democratic Athens.

Temples built in the fifth century outside Athens

Aegina	490	Temple of Aphaia
Selinus	490–460	Temples A and E
Syracuse	480	Temple of Athena
Agrigentum	470	Temple of Hera Lacinia
Olympia	460	Temple of Zeus

Paestum	450	Temple of Hera II
Agrigentum	440	Temple of Concord
Delos		Temple known as the Temple of the Athenians
Segesta		
Bassae		Temple of Apollo

Monuments constructed in the fifth century in Athens

Acropolis	447–432	Parthenon
	438–432	Propylaea
	427–424	Athena Nike
	421–406	Erechtheion
Eleusis	450	Telesterion
South of the Acropolis		Odeon of Pericles
West of the Agora		Temple of Hephaestus
Agora		Bouleterion, porticoes
Sunium		Temple of Poseidon
Rhamnonte		Temple of Nemesis
Brauron		Portico

Sculptors (fifth and fourth centuries)

Myron of Eleutherae	fifth	The *Discobolos* (Discus Thrower)
Polycletes of Argos	fifth	The *Doryphoros* (Spear-bearer)
Phidias of Athens	fifth	Athena Promachos, Athena Parthenos Olympian Zeus
Scopas of Paros	fourth	Pediments of Tegea
Praxiteles	fourth	Hermes carrying Dionysus
Lysippus	fourth	Heracles Epitrapezios

Painters (fifth century)

Polygnotes of Thasos	fifth	Leschè of the Cnidians in Delphi and Stoa Poikile in Athens
Micon of Athens	fifth	Stoa Poikile

Vase painters: Hermonax, and anonymous painters known as 'the painter of the Niobidae', 'the painter of Penthesilea', 'the painter of Achilles', 'the painter of Colophon', 'the painter of Eretria', 'the painter of Meidias'

SOCIETY AND THE ECONOMY IN THE CLASSICAL PERIOD

Citizens and non-citizens, the free and the non-free, the rich and the poor, men and women, adults and the young: all these constituted important divisions in the societies of classical Greece, divisions more often superposed than juxtaposed. Depending on individual historians and historiographical trends, priority tends to be given to one particular division in their overall explanations of the social system and how it evolved. For instance, the emphasis may be laid almost exclusively on the division between free men and slaves, or on the differences between those with the power of political decision, the citizens, and all the rest. But no system of explanation can be pushed to the total exclusion of all others without risk of contradiction and without turning the Greek reality into a caricature that is bound soon to be rejected. In the interests of clarity, let us consider each of these divisions in turn, where possible evaluating the relative importance of their effects, as we go along.

THE LEGAL ASPECTS OF SOCIAL STATUS

The citizens   The first division in any classical Greek society was between those with citizens' rights and those without. The status of *citizen* (*politès*), with its attendant rights and duties, has already been described (see p. 123). The fifth and fourth centuries marked the end of an evolution: the rights of citizenship were defined little by little in the course of the archaic period and were made more precise, in a negative rather than a positive fashion, that is, by definitely excluding from citizens' rights a number of categories of people who might otherwise have been able to claim them, by abolishing intermediary categories, by prohibiting changes of status, and by limiting the prerogatives of those qualified to enter the political domain and to own land.

Foreigners   The Greek term translated as 'foreigner', *xenos*, may designate either an enemy or a host/guest. A choice between two relationships was open to two foreigners: either to become linked by the bonds of friendship or to do battle. Very few rules regulated relations with foreigners before the classical period, when this status became more common: whoever ventured beyond the frontiers of his own city became a foreigner, a Megarian in Athens, an Athenian in Plataea, to take examples from the cities closest to Athens. In the fifth and fourth centuries a distinction gradually came to be drawn between foreigners passing through and foreigners living for a long time in a city. The former had no particular status; in some cities the latter acquired one.

A few rules concerning foreigners as a whole   The existence of *proxenoi*: a *proxenos* was 'a citizen who, quite apart from any relationship such as an alliance between the two cities, assumed for all the citizens of a particular foreign city the functions and duties offered by a *xenos* (host) to a foreign individual or family' (according to the definition given by P. Gauthier). In this capacity, he welcomed and assisted these foreigners and would stand as a witness or guarantor for them, but only as a purely private individual. The *proxenos* for Spartans in Athens was an Athenian who had established city links, as an individual, with the Spartans, and his functions continued whatever the circumstances. For example, in times of war, the *proxenos* for the Spartans in Athens looked out for the welfare of the Spartan prisoners of war. As time passed, the numbers of *proxenoi* in a single city increased (whereas intially a given city would have only one *proxenos*, from the fourth century on whoever had been helpful to that city could become a *proxenos* for it), as did the number of cities whom a single *proxenos* took under his protection (in the Hellenistic period, a man could be *proxenos* for dozens of different cities). A *proxenos* was designated by decree.

The existence of agreements between cities facilitated the protection of foreigners. A number of different types of agreements were possible:

- *Symbola* were agreements, attested in the fourth century, that protected the citizens of the two contracting cities against arbitrary actions. They provided protection against violence, checking the right to take reprisals (the *sylon*) that normally applied in peacetime and wartime alike. Little is known of the precise wording of these agreements in the classical period.
- *Dikai emporikai*: commercial lawsuits. In about 350 the Athenians drew up legislation for commercial litigation involving foreigners. *Thesmothetai* now presided over these legal actions, instead of the *epimeletes* of the *emporion* (one of the ten port magistrates appointed by the drawing of lots), as in the past.
- Agreements designed to facilitate commercial activity and provide certain guarantees for foreigners in transit existed between certain cities, in the fifth century (for example, the agreement between the two Locrian cities, Oeanthea and Chaleion, in the mid-fifth century).

The fourth century saw the appearance of the first agreements on *isopoliteia*. Each city granted the citizens of the other city the possibility of obtaining citizenship in its own territory, in the event of their settling there.

During the classical period, agreements between cities concerning foreigners thus affected both commercial litigation and the basic security of individuals.

Resident foreigners   These were foreigners who lived for a long time in the same city. Athens is the best-known case. Here these people were known as *metics*. A metic was a free foreigner who lived and worked in Attica. After residing there for a certain time (about a month), he had to find himself a *prostatès*, who would answer for him in any judicial affair. He registered as a metic on the register of the deme in which he lived, and paid the tax on metics (the *metoikion*: 12 drachmas per year for a man, 6 drachmas for a woman). A metic was protected by the laws, was liable for liturgies, had to serve in the army, but possessed no political rights. He could not own real estate, but was allowed access to all movable forms of wealth and could practice any profession he chose. The precise number of metics in Athens is not known. At the time of Demetrius of Phalerum (late fourth century) the figure of 10,000 is mentioned, but it is not known whether this covered only men or the whole metic population. In the course of two centuries, the numbers fluctuated according to the political ups and downs and wars: the eventual accumulation of economic difficulties had the effect of forcing many metics to leave Athens for more prosperous cities.

The attitude of citizens towards foreigners is hard to assess. According to the Pseudo-Xenophon, at the end of the fifth century there were no distinctions between a metic and a citizen in Athens, a fact that he deplored. The only city known for its hostility towards foreigners was Sparta.

Sparta systematically expelled all foreigners (*xenelasia*), a measure that Plutarch attributed to Lycurgus:

[Lycurgus] actually drove away from the city the multitudes which streamed in there for no useful purpose, not because he feared they might become imitators of his form of government and learn useful lessons in virtue, as Thucydides says, but rather that they might not become in any wise teachers of evil . . . He thought it more necessary to keep bad manners and customs from invading and filling the city than it was to keep out infectious diseases. (*Life of Lycurgus*, XXVII, 3)

Plutarch goes on to say that for this reason there were no merchants, rhetors, diviners or *proxenoi* to be found in Sparta. It was certainly not an attitude shared by cities whose wealth was derived from contacts with various other parts of the Greek world, in particular, seafaring cities.

A distinction also seems to have been made between foreigners who spoke Greek and the rest, those who expressed themselves in an incomprehensible language and were on that account called 'barbarians' (The term *barbaros* is said to translate an onomatopeia imitating the strange sound, to Greek ears, of non-Greek languages.) Despite their different dialects, Greeks could understand one another, had a common way of life, shared the same religious beliefs. A Greek foreigner in a city was still close to it through his culture. His presence was more than tolerated, for it testified to the city's prosperity, its ability to attract Greeks from all over the Mediterranean world. Certain controls were imposed, but freedom of movement was the general rule. The number of non-Greek foreigners (barbarians) increased in the course of the fourth century. Their manners (physical appearance, style of dress, religious beliefs) clashed with those of the Greeks, and whenever one comes across an expression of hostility towards them, it is primarily prompted on that account.

In a comparison, Aristophanes described the citizens as the flour made from Athenian wheat, foreigners as the chaff that is easily rejected and the metics as the bran 'that cannot be distinguished from the milled grain and that, so far, is a part of it'. He thereby called attention not only to the differences between the various statuses but also to the radical separation of citizens from the rest. It would be impossible to overemphasize the fact that, for the Greeks of the classical period themselves, the fundamental dividing line was drawn between citizens and non-citizens. It was an opposition that informed their system of values, their discourse, their ideology. In most texts, a slave is conceived of primarily as an anti-citizen.

THE SLAVES

Several forms of slavery existed in classical Greece, but until the fourth century Greek authors did not perceive any real difference between rural servitude and chattel slavery. All such subjected people were non-free. None of them could dispose freely of their own persons. One of the terms used to designate them was *doulos*.

Rural servitude was the most common form of slavery. An entire rural population would have been deprived of its liberty for one reason or another, and would work on the land of the citizen landlords. The best-known case is that of the helots of Sparta (see p. 73), but the position was more or less the same for the *clarotai* of Crete, the *penestai* of Thessaly, the *gymnetes* of Argos, the Marandinians of Heraclaea on the Black Sea and the Kyllirians of Syracuse.

Chattel slavery developed in cities where the reduction to slavery of the natives in the community had been forbidden, as in Athens, for example, from the time of Solon, who abolished slavery for debts. A workforce would only be imported from outside when the internal workforce became inadequate. So this type of slavery was first introduced in cities that protected their own natives from servitude, these being also the cities that evolved more rapidly towards a democratic political regime. Such cities resorted to buying slaves from elsewhere, either from other parts of the Greek world or from barbarian countries. These slaves were bought and sold in special slave markets, like any other chattels, hence the expression chattel slavery used to designate their status.

A slave was a living instrument, and would be listed in inventories and wills along with parcels of land, furniture and jewellery. He had no rights at all, neither political nor civil, and was legally deprived of any personality (even his evidence was only valid if it had been extorted under torture). His master had total power over him, the power to sell him, the power to beat him . . . In Athens a slave's murderer would be judged before the Palladion court, provided a complaint was lodged. The penalty would consist of a fine. But if a master killed his own slave, there would be no charge to answer.

Ancient judgements on slavery

'The slave is no easy chattel. For actual experience shows how many evils result from slavery, – as in the frequent revolts in Messenia, and in the States where there are many servants kept who speak the same tongue, not to mention the crimes of all sorts committed by the "corsairs", as they are called, who haunt the coasts of Italy, and the reprisals therefor. In view of all these facts, it is really a puzzle to know how to deal with all such matters. Two means only are left for us to try – the one is not to allow the slaves, if they are to tolerate slavery quietly, to be all of the same nation, but, so far as is possible, to have them of different races; and the other is to accord them proper treatment, and that not only for their own sakes, but still more for the sake of ourselves.' (Plato, *Laws*, VI, 777)

'Some thinkers hold that . . . for one man to be another man's master is . . . unjust, for it is based on force . . . Property is part of a household . . . for without the necessities even life, as well as the good life, is impossible . . . so the manager of a household must have his tools, and of tools some are lifeless and others living . . . and a slave is a live article of property . . . If every tool could perform its own work when ordered, or by seeing what to do in advance, . . . if thus shuttles wove . . . masters would have no need of slaves . . . Therefore all men that differ as widely as the soul does from the body and the human being from the lower animal (and this is the condition of those whose function is the use of the body and from whom this is the best forthcoming) – these are by nature slaves . . . and for these slavery is an institution both expedient and just.' (Aristotle, *Politics*, 1253b–1255a f.)

How many slaves were there? This is a controversial question. Historians overestimate or understimate their number according to their own overall view of classical society, for the ancient sources provide hardly any information to go on. The figure of between 60,000 and 80,000 slaves for Athens in the fifth century is generally accepted but, depending on various authors, it can oscillate from 30,000 to 400,000. Rather than wrangle over figures, it is perhaps more useful to note that the price of a slave was low enough for any free man to own one, and that a large proportion of both agricultural production and the production of crafts and workshops was the fruit of slave labour. There can be no doubt at all that classical Greek society was a society based on slave labour and that it was so used to this form of man's exploitation of man that it no longer even questioned it.

Very few slaves were born and reared in a family, for masters preferred to forbid their slaves to reproduce, or else abandoned any babies born into servitude, who for years would have been non-productive. Most slaves thus came from foreign lands where they had been either carried off from their homes by pirates or else taken prisoners after a battle, or even rounded up by their own sovereigns. In any event, they would then be sold on to merchants who specialized in the slave trade. They hailed from every part of the Greek world but, increasingly, also from barbarian lands: Thrace, Scythia, the Caucasus, Anatolia, Syria. The largest slave markets were those of Thasos, Ephesus, Delos, and Athens.

Slaves were used for all kinds of tasks: domestic slaves in households, agricultural slaves in the countryside, and craft-workers in the workshops. The largest concentration of slaves was in the Laurion mines. Thucydides reports an escape of 20,000 slaves from these mines in 421. Female slaves made up the bulk of the prostitutes working in both public and private Athenian brothels. A few, rare slaves did not live in the house of their master (they were known as *choris oikointes*), but possessed a measure of autonomy in their daily work, the product of which they turned over to their masters. Usually a master would make direct use of his slaves, but there were some slave-owners who hired out the services of their servile chattels, on demand. The civic community also employed slaves in public functions: they would assist the magistrates, maintain the roads, even ensure the maintenance of order (these were known as Scythians, on account of their origin, and in the mid-fifth century they formed a force 300 strong). All slaves were deprived of their liberty, but day-to-day living conditions no doubt varied according to the tasks that they performed and their more or less close relations with their master.

There were only two means of escaping from slavery: flight or affranchisement. *Flight* was common, either individual or collective, when circumstances were favourable and, in particular, in times of war or city disturbances. Thucydides does not tell us whether the 20,000 slaves who escaped from the Laurion mines in 421 were recaptured or returned to their countries of origin, but from an economic point of view the flight of slaves could be a disaster. *Affranchisement* could take a number of forms. A master could decide to free his slave. If so, he would be more likely to do so at his death, specifying his desire in his will. A slave could buy his liberty: this happened in the rare cases of slaves known as *choris oikointes*, who had managed to amass a sufficient sum from their labour (two fourth-century bankers, Pasion and Phormion, were former slaves). A slave could also be sold fictitiously to a sanctuary, where the god hastened to affranchise him, a quite common gesture of piety. Finally, in very exceptional circumstances, a city could liberate slaves, as Athens liberated those who were present at the battle of Arginusae. Whatever the mode of affranchisement, links remained to bind the former slave to his master: he would become a metic and his master would be his *prostatès*. In the classical period, not many slaves were touched by affranchisement. It was certainly not a social phenomenon comparable to what it was to become in the Roman world.

As has been noted, slavery was not questioned by anyone in the classical period. Xenophon, Plato and Aristotle made room for slaves in their ideal cities and showered their contemporaries with advice as to how to avoid the most obvious drawbacks of slavery, such as their slaves taking to flight or rebelling, and how to use their labour in a rational fashion. Aristotle clearly justified slavery on natural grounds: some are made to command, others to obey. In the fourth and fifth centuries nobody could even imagine a society without slaves, not even in the most Utopian of worlds, such as that which Aristophanes represented when, in *The Assembly of Women*, he set women in power.

The terms of the debate   Now that the mechanisms of slavery have been briefly described, it is worth at least mentioning the place held by this theme in the debates between historians since the nineteenth century. Important books have been written on the subject, such as M. I. Finley's *Ancient Slavery and Modern Ideology* (London, 1980) and Y. Garlan's *Slavery in Ancient Greece* (Ithaca, NY, and London, 1988), and it is advisable to read them and form one's own opinions. The debate concerns the validity of a Marxist approach for an understanding of the place of slavery in ancient Greece, and it hinges upon two questions: can Greek Antiquity be described as a society based on slavery? And did the Greek slaves constitute a social class? As Y. Garlan points out, to claim that a society is based on slavery is to say that it was 'founded' on slavery from a socio-economic point of view. For this author, the cities that practised chattel slavery, Athens in particular, certainly were, in this precise sense, slavery-based societies at certain points in their history. In my own opinion, it would be hard to deny that a large proportion of Athenian wealth was indeed founded upon servile labour.

The question of whether the slaves formed a social class in the Marxist sense deserves a more nuanced discussion than is possible within the framework of the present textbook. The article by P. Vidal-Naquet, 'Were the Greek Slaves a Class?', reprinted in *The Black Hunter* (Baltimore, MD, and London, 1986) and Y. Garlan's response in his book cited above are essential reading on this subject. Like all great historiographical debates, this one involves tendencies in contemporary thought and cannot be resolved with just a few remarks.

The priority that the Greeks ascribed to political status is also evident in the domain of slavery. The Greek classical texts that have come down to us do not regard slavery and the separation between the free and the non-free as the sole principle organizing social life. They lay far more emphasis on the importance and privileges that attach to citizenship and, by the same token, on the chasm separating citizens from non-citizens. Access to political power, to decision-making, seems to them by far the most important thing at stake. So they establish a hierarchy between the two opposite pairs of groups mentioned above, ranking the division between citizens and non-citizens as more important than that between the free and the non-free.

DIFFERENCES OF SEX AND AGE

WOMEN AND MEN

Ever since Hesiod and the gods' fabrication of Pandora, the first woman, one thing was taken for granted: woman was 'a beautiful evil', sent to earth by the gods to avenge Prometheus' theft of fire. Her portrait, flattering so far as appearance went but disastrous as to character and behaviour, was refined by generations of Greek authors, and the cities themselves invented many fine stories to justify their definitive exclusion of women from political life and from the transmission of names and inheritances. Although Athena watched over the fortunes of Athens as its tutelary deity, women were subjected throughout their lives to the authority of their master and guardian (*kurios*), now their father, now their husband, now their brother, and had no legal identity. As the daughters of citizens they could not inherit land, only movable chattels. However, when a citizen died without a male heir, his daughter could pass on real estate (the *kleros*) to her first male descendant and such a young Athenian woman was declared to be *epikleros*. Marriage, around the age of 15, marked a girl's entry into the adult world, when she moved from her father's house to that of her husband. Yet her new status was precarious: her husband could repudiate her or claim that she was not his legitimate wife and refuse to recognize her children as his heirs. A woman who was repudiated or widowed returned to her father's house to be remarried as quickly as possible.

Little is known of the lives led by women. As babies, they were exposed more often than infant boys. As little girls, they received no education except from the example of traditional society. The circle of women in a household would be a wide one: mother, female relatives, elder sisters, concubines, servants. The picture of women confined to household quarters reserved exclusively for them, a *gynaikeia*, has been rejected by modern scholars. However, women had few contacts with the outside world and with people beyond their own kin. They worked all day long at various household tasks, mainly preparing food and making clothes, and only a few wives of rich Athenians had the role of overseer rather than housekeeper. In the *Oeconomicus*, Xenophon describes how tasks and roles should be divided between the men and women of the household, and Isomachus teaches his extremely young wife what her duties are. Nothing, from the way to give orders to slaves to the way to turn down the bedcovers, is left out of the compendium of masculine expertise with which he complacently inculcates his wife. This text has inevitably been taken quite literally by many historians, who have seen in it a division of roles with which they are perfectly familiar. But perhaps it should rather be regarded as reflecting a moment when attempts were being made to construct a theory of masculine/feminine relationships, a theory strictly related to the delimitation of the public and the private domains.

The fabrication of the first woman: Pandora

'Forthwith he [Zeus] made an evil thing for men as the price of fire; for the very famous Limping God (Hephaestus) formed of earth the likeness of a shy maiden, as the son of Cronos willed. And the goddess bright-eyed Athene girded and clothed her with silvery raiment, and down from her head she spread with her hands a broidered veil, a wonder to see; and she, Pallas Athene . . . put upon her head a crown of gold which the very famous Limping God made himself and worked with his own hands as a favour to Zeus his father. On it was much curious work, wonderful to see; for of the many creatures which the land and sea rear up, he put most upon it, wonderful things, like living beings without voices: and great beauty shone out from it.

   But when he had made the beautiful evil to be the price for the blessing, he brought her out, delighting in the finery which the bright-eyed daughter of a mighty father had given her, to the place where the other gods and men were. And wonder took hold of the deathless gods and mortal men when they saw that which was sheer guile, not to be withstood by men. For from her is the race of women and female kind: of her is the deadly race and tribe of women who live amongst mortal men to their great trouble, no helpmeets in hateful poverty, but only in wealth . . . Zeus who thunders on high made women to be an evil to mortal men, with a nature to do evil. And he gave them a second evil, to be the price for the good they had: whoever avoids marriage and the sorrows women cause, and will not wed, reaches deadly old age without anyone to tend his years, and though he at least has no lack of livelihood while he lives, yet, when he is dead, his kinsfolk divide his possessions amongst them. And as for the man who chooses the lot of marriage and takes a good wife suited to his mind, evil continually contends with good; for whoever happens to have mischievous children lives always with unceasing grief in his spirit and heart within him; and this evil cannot be healed.' (Hesiod, *Theogony*, 1. 570– 610, translated by Hugh G. Evelyn-White)

The types of images of Greek women on vases show that, as in the texts, the representation of the world of women is to a large extent coded. These are not so much scenes of daily life as examples of the various ways in which men represent the feminine world to themselves and assign roles to women, ranging from the dutiful wife to the maenad.

   The retiring place of women in social life (except in religious life, see p. 207f.), the absence of writings by them (apart from Sappho) and the silence that they are enjoined to observe by the men, Pericles first and foremost, contrast forcefully with the importance of men's reflections on

Figure 44 Women at a fountain: an Attic hydria. Five women, out of doors, are coming and going at a fountain, each carrying a full or empty hydria on her head. The fifth women is filling her pot (Musée du Louvre, Paris; © Photo RMN)

women in every area of Greek culture. It is as though the supposedly natural hierarchy between the sexes was in constant need of justification, and all this reflection on the masculine and feminine domains was one means of tackling and understanding the fundamental divisions in the city. This has become the orientation in recent research, rather than attempts to describe the condition of women realistically, an area in which the documentation is very incomplete. (What is really known, for instance, of the condition of the wives of foreigners or of female slaves?)

THE YOUNG AND THE ADULTS

The above remarks may serve to remind us that the history of representations is inseparable from social history. The same applies when it comes to attempting to understand the place of the young.

Age was an important factor in determining a man's political role. At the age of 18 the son of an Athenian citizen would himself become a citizen and have his name inscribed in the register of his deme. In the fourth century he had to wait until he was 20 and had completed his *ephebeia*. At this point he could join only the assembly and the *boulè*. Not until he was 30 could he be sworn into the Heliaea court, become a legislator (*nomothetès*) or a magistrate. According to what we know of ancient demography, it would seem that one-third of the citizens were aged between 18 and 30, while two-thirds were over 30. This means that one-third of the citizen body did not have full political rights because they were too young.

In Greek society, as in most traditional societies, age was considered to guarantee temperance and wisdom. In Sparta access to the council of elders (the *gerousia*) was reserved for citizens of over 60 years of age. In Athens there was no similar rule, but in the assembly men of over 50 were invited to speak first, and the average age of the Areopagus council was 55. Sometimes political life betrayed a certain antagonism between the old and the young. The most famous episode illustrating this is the clash between Nicias and Alcibiades on the eve of the Sicilian expedition, in Thucydides' account, in which the dash of Alcibiades is set in contrast to the prudence of Nicias' riper years.

Youth was also the time for apprenticeship, and every city was committed to teaching its young men in such a way as to make citizens as good as possible. Some cities, such as Sparta, took charge of the education of boys at a very early age (see p. 73, on the Spartan *agogè*). Others, such as Athens, left it to their families and were content simply to organize (for youths of 18 to 20) a two-year course of military and ideological training for their future citizens, within the framework of the *ephebeia*. But the Greek *paideia* (education) consisted of more than what we would call instruction. It was a training in the mechanisms and values of society and was a more or less permanently on-going process that took place within the fabric of the social and political life.

Much was at stake here, for it was a matter of reproducing the city, not just as a civic body – although of course it was essential for the young men to become soldiers, magistrates and the fathers of families – but also as the crucible of norms and of an ideology that marked out the specificity of one city as opposed to another: what Thucydides, in Athens' case, called its 'inimitable character'. The Greeks were acutely aware of the dangers of youth rejecting those norms, and in both their mythical narratives and their tragedies they set on stage young people who tried to avoid becoming adults. There was no future for those fierce, touchy, young hunters: Hippolytus is not a model; but they were certainly present in the imaginary representations of the city, as extreme cases that helped one to think about normality.

THE SOCIAL CLASSES

A third type of classification took into account the economic level of individuals both from the point of view of definite legal status (the rich citizens and the poor citizens) and within the framework of the entire social group living in the same city (rich citizens and metics on one hand,

Figure 45 The education of the young: music, writing, reading; details from the Delos Cup. This famous cup shows a boy engaged in 'school' activities. From left to right: a teacher shows him how to play a double flute or *aulos*, another teaches him writing; the youth is then taught the *cithara* and has to learn the letters inscribed on a scroll unrolled by the teacher. These were the bases of any literary education. Physical education was equally important. Exercises at the *palestra* and the *gymnasium* enabled a youth to master the throwing of a javelin, wrestling, running races . . . all feats included in competitions such as those of the Olympic Games and that also prepared boys for hoplite combat. Hunting constituted a school of endurance and taught the youths to accepts collective discipline. In Xenophon's view, this exercise, practised above all by the aristocracy, constituted the basis of every good education.

The world of boys was also a world of seduction and love between the youths and their elders – important elements in a culture sometimes described as 'bisexual', meaning that it accommodated both homosexuality and heterosexuality, but all within a framework of strict rules. Quite apart from such stories as, for example, that about the abduction of a young Cretan by an older man, followed by his return to the city, which symbolized his accession to citizenship, figurative representations often treat the themes of gifts (often of hunted game) and of lovers' meetings. (National Museum, Berlin; Bildarchiv Preussischer Kulturbesitz).

all the poor on the other). So these divisions do not coincide exactly with any others.

Between the fifth and the fourth centuries, the criteria according to which social groups were classified changed. In the fifth century, income from real estate determined both the military functions of individuals and, as we have seen, their eligibility for public posts. The fourth century took more account of overall sources of wealth in order to construct the bases for a taxation system.

In the fifth century the system of census divisions that Solon had established still existed in the background (see p. 80). Citizens belonging to the first two census classes (*pentacosiomedimnoi* and *hippeis*) provided the cavalry for the Athenian army. These knights, as portrayed by Aristophanes, formed the aristocratic elite of the city. They nurtured a deep sense of their own superiority and tended towards conservatism in both their style of life and their political attitudes. The citizens of the third census class, the zeugites (*zeugitai*), were enrolled as hoplites. They were landowners who were rich enough to pay for their own military equipment and to have a slave to accompany them as a military orderly. Some historians refer to them as the 'hoplite class', by which they mean a middle class, which was probably in the majority in the first part of the fifth century but then lost its economic stability as a result of the wars. As for the thetes, the last of the census classes, who received no income from the land, they served in the ships both as soldiers and as oarsmen and also in the units of light-armed troops who fought as bowmen. With the arrival in town of part of the population of Attica, this last group expanded in the course of the century, and its economic importance increased, along with the role that it played in the defence of the city. As warfare was essentially a matter for the citizens, such a classification leaves out one section of the free population, some of whom were extremely wealthy, namely the metics.

In the fourth century the classes created by Solon lost virtually all their significance, from the point of view of both eligibility for magistracies and the part that they played in warfare, and also from the point of view of taxation. They fell into disuse. The Greek terms that were now used distinguished between the 'haves' (*euporoi*) and the 'have-nots' (*aporoi* or *penetes*). The 'haves' were those with a large enough fortune to be liable for liturgies and for payment of the *eisphora* tax. At the time of Demosthenes, they are believed to have numbered about 1,200, 300 of whom were considerably richer than the rest: within the framework of the administrative divisions responsible for paying taxes (the *symmoriai*), these were expected to advance whatever sum was necessary. The 'have-nots' included people with just enough to live on and also people who were really poverty-stricken. In the fourth-century texts, the opposition between the rich and the poor is often presented in political terms, with the philosophers assimilating the 'have-nots' to the majority and the crowd, and the orators turning the 'haves' into oligarchy sympathizers. In this way an economic division slipped into the domain of politics, which was the chief concern of public life. It should be pointed out that metics were to be found among the *euporoi* (and were liable for liturgies), just as they were, of course, among the *aporoi*.

Clearly, these pairs of oppositions never functioned in isolation. The identity of each individual was compounded by his or her juridical status, sex, age and social class. However, the Greeks of the classical period still represented membership or non-membership of the city body as the most important factor in a person's identity.

THE PLACE AND FUNCTION OF THE ECONOMY IN THE CITIES

In our contemporary world, the term 'economy' covers a concept and sectors of activity that are well defined, but that was not the case in Greek Antiquity. So before describing the activities of the Greeks, we should consider the place and function of the economy in the Greek cities and ask ourselves what the economy meant for the Greeks, whether the cities had economic policies and what was their concept of work. Once again, the nature of our documentation obliges us to focus upon Athens.

The Greek term *oikonomia* has two meanings: a restricted sense, the management of the family estate; and a wider sense, the management of the city. A number of treatises written in the fourth century are entitled *Oeconomicus*. Xenophon's, for example, concerns the management of the family estate and the role of the head of the *oikos*. Only one economic activity is tackled: agriculture, and the book is full of advice that does not really concern the economic domain but is more to do with how a good citizen should behave. Another treatise, attributed to Aristotle's School, returns to the same themes as Xenophon's, but is also lavish with advice aimed at rulers on matters such as taxation. They do not testify to the existence of any abstract concept of the economy together with all the elements that we consider to depend upon it (work, production, capital, investment, revenues, circulation, demand). To put that another way: the Greeks practised agriculture and craftsmanship, exploited mines, minted money and made loans, but they never associated all these activities in one conceptual unit that might be called 'the economy'.

We are consequently faced with a methodological problem. The use of modern economic concepts might distort any description of the ancient reality. So we shall have to seek other, more suitable ones.

One last, fundamental, point: the Greeks were not unaware of the importance of economic factors in their history, but for them these existed only in so far as they related to others to which they ascribed far greater importance, political factors, for example.

One good example of the difficulties encountered by modern historians attempting to describe the ancient economy is the great historiographical debate that has been continuing ever since the nineteenth century between 'primitivists' and 'modernists', with the primitivists out to demonstrate the archaic nature of the economic activities of the Greeks, and the modernists on the contrary emphasizing the rapid evolution and modern character of plenty of those activities. Neither of those extreme positions is defended today, but the debate on the place of the economy in the Greek world is far from over.

DID THE CITIES HAVE ECONOMIC POLICIES?

Finances The cities did not work out a budget in the modern sense of the term, but they certainly knew what their resources and their expenses amounted to. Their treasuries constituted, as it were, a woollen sock stuffed with a mass of coins and kept, in Athens, for example, in the temple of Athena. The city saved hardly anything: when an unexpected need arose, it simply resorted to imposing extra taxes, such as the *eisphora*, which was first levied in wartime. There were no regular taxes on wealth until at least the fourth century.

A city's revenues came from the aftermath of war (booty, ransoms extracted for the return of prisoners), income raised from public assets and from mines, direct taxes levied on non-citizens, such as the *metoikion* in Athens, and taxes on trade (in Piraeus, one-fiftieth was levied on all imported and exported products, and taxes were imposed on all merchandise sold in the agora and also on all foreigners who came there to trade). The collection of these taxes was often farmed out and special magistrates were responsible for overseeing the operation. In fifth-century Athens another source of revenue was the tribute paid by the allied cities in the Delian League. But even this was not enough to cover all the city's expenses, so it also appealed to private generosity through the allocation of liturgies.

A *liturgy (leitourgia)* was a commitment by a private individual to bear the cost of a project in the public interest. The city relied upon liturgies in three main domains: for financing the war fleet, for organizing religious festivals and, in the fourth century, for covering the *eisphora. Leitourgoi* were chosen from among the most wealthy citizens and metics, and those who were selected could not decline. The details of the system were complex and were based on the division of the citizens into ten tribes. Two liturgies were particularly famous: the trierarchy, which consisted in equipping a trireme and paying the costs of its crew; and the *choregia*, which covered all the expenses of the theatrical productions put on for the Dionysia. A liturgy was a heavy burden for whoever took it on, but might lead to his being loaded with honours if the city was satisfied with his services. By these means the city financed activities of collective interest and at the same time helped to establish a better balance between the social classes, since the small number of rich men placed their fortunes at the disposal of the poor.

The city's expenses increased particularly in times of war. On top of these, part of the treasury was immediately redistributed to the *dèmos* in the form of *misthoi*, distributions of cereals were made and animals had to be supplied for sacrifices . . . The city would also launch itself into major enterprises, such as the reconstruction of the Acropolis, and would invest in projects that reinforced the city's identity. It is difficult for us to pass judgement on its choices, given our own ideas on economic rationality. Spending money on the gods, for their rites and temples, was certainly regarded as a priority by a community which, at every step, reaffirmed the intangible link between the religious and the political domains.

Money   All the cities minted money. It was a sign of independence and was the monopoly of the city. Many different currencies thus coexisted. Bronze coins were used in local trade; silver coins circulated more widely and their value was well established. In the fifth century an Athenian decree attempted to impose the use of Athenian currency throughout the empire, but it was unsuccessful.

Supplies   One of the major concerns of cities was to provide regular food supplies for their inhabitants, for the ancient world was often on the edge of starvation. The city kept a careful watch on the delivery of cereals to its ports and on the selling price of grain, flour and bread. In fourth-century Athens thirty-five magistrates, the *sitophylakes*, were responsible for supervising prices. In times of shortages, the city appointed commissioners, *sitonai*, whose duty it was to buy grain in the city's name. It sometimes happened that kings, such as the Pharaoh of Egypt in 445 BC, or cities such as Cyrene in the late fourth century, would make gifts of grain. If this happened it was distributed free among the citizens.

Procuring supplies of other materials important for building the fleet of warships, such as wood and metals, was also supervised by the cities, which regarded all these economic preoccupations as elements in the political endeavour: namely internally to maintain social peace and externally to preserve the city's supremacy.

THE CONCEPT OF WORK

Some of the judgements that the Greeks passed on one or other type of economic activity stemmed from their attitude to work, or rather, to be more precise, from their lack of a unified, abstract concept of work such as we have. Work was usually only considered in concrete forms, as so many different activities.

The Greeks had a hierarchy of occupations: at the top was work on the land, agriculture, in particular, the cultivation of cereals. To work on the land was to live at peace with it and with the gods. Agriculture was also the best means of attaining the ideal of self-sufficiency, that is, for an *oikos* to produce everything that it needed in order to survive. Other activities, such as craftsmanship and trade, were depreciated, because they did not bring those who practised them independence, since they were always obliged to sell what they produced and also because they did not develop the physical qualities of a citizen, but on the contrary atrophied them.

According to Xenophon, subjection of the body led to subjection of the soul. The judgement passed on the work of craftsmen had nothing to do with its economic importance to the city, but was prompted by its relation to political activity.

Manual labour was not despised, provided it was practised under absolutely no constraint (an example frequently cited is that of Odysseus constructing his own bed). Of course, the existence of slavery had a great deal to do with the depreciation of labour, since the hardest tasks were reserved for slaves. But there was more to it. Some cities reserved citizenship for those who did not work, arguing that taking part in political affairs took up a great deal of time. And in the fourth century philosophers such as Plato and Aristotle insisted on the need for leisure in order to perform well as a citizen.

Athens presents a good example of the ambiguity of attitudes towards work. Some of its deities, such as Athena Erganè and Hephaestus, were the patrons of craftsmen, and Pericles reminded his listeners: 'In our city, it is not shameful for anyone to acknowledge his poverty but it would be not to seek to escape from it by working. It is perfectly possible for men to busy themselves both with their private affairs and with public affairs, just as it is possible for those who work hard to know enough about political matters.' There were laws to discourage idleness. Yet on stage in the theatre of Dionysus, Aristophanes made people laugh at Euripides, whose mother sold vegetables, and also at Cleon, the tanner.

A VARIETY OF ECONOMIC ACTIVITIES

THE PEASANTS

In the fifth and fourth centuries most of the Greek population lived off the land, but ever since the archaic period production had failed to feed the entire population and, except in newly Hellenized regions, the cities were dependent on the outside world for their food, in particular for cereals.

The geographical and climatic conditions, which have already been decribed (see p. 2f.), only allowed a limited area of the Greek territory to be cultivated. Vast spaces, used as pastures for the herds, were left fallow. Agricultural tools were simple: mattocks, hoes, sickles, ploughs. The only type of mill known, with which women milled grain, dated from neolithic times. Crop rotation was biennial, with fields left fallow every other year. Ploughing teams were composed of two animals, either mules or oxen. The land was ploughed three or four times a year, sowing began in November, harvesting in the early summer. Vines and olives were planted in among other crops.

Ploughing and sowing

'Hew also many bent timbers, and bring home a plough-tree when you have found it, and look out on the mountain or in the field for one of holm-oak; for this is the strongest for oxen to plough with when one of Athena's hand-men has fixed in the share-beam and fastened it to the pole with dowels. Get two ploughs ready and work on them at home, one all of a piece, and the other jointed. It is far better to do this, for if you should break one of them you can put the oxen to the other. Poles of laurel or elm are most free from worms, and a share-beam of oak and a plough-tree of holm-oak . . .

So soon as the time for ploughing is proclaimed to men, then make haste, you and your slaves alike, in wet and in dry, to plough in the season for ploughing, and bestir yourself early in the morning so that your fields may be full. Plough in the spring; but fallow broken up in summer will not belie your hopes. Sow fallow land when the soil is still light; fallow land is a defender from harm and a soother of children.

Pray to Zeus of the Earth and to pure Demeter to make Demeter's holy grain sound and heavy, when first you begin ploughing, when you hold in your hand the end of the plough-tail and bring down your stick on the backs of the oxen as they draw on the pole-bar by the yoke straps. Let a slave follow a little behind with a mattock and make trouble for the birds by hiding the seed; for good management is the best for mortal man as bad management is the worst.' (Hesiod, *Works and Days*, lines 427–35 and 458–72)

plough-tree: a long piece of curved wood connecting the share-beam to the pole or plough-share.
share-beam: the part in which the pole or plough-share was held.
plough-share or pole: a long piece of wood, the axis for the pulling of the plough, which connected it to the yoke.
mattock: a kind of hoe.

The land belonged to the citizens. It was inalienable and could be neither sold nor bought, at least until the fourth century. At each inheritance it was, in principle, divided between the male heirs, and the disparities between landowners were great, even in Sparta where land was distributed on an egalitarian basis. Little is known of the size of properties: an average one might be 25 to 30 hectares, but many were smaller. In Athens, a landowner might have estates in different parts of Attica. Parcels of land could have different status: some belonged to sanctuaries, others to religious groups, particular demes or the city; yet others were private.

Work on the land was not the sole preserve of citizens. There were many slaves in the fields. Large landowners would have several dozen and a steward, possibly himself a slave, to manage them. A small landowner would have at least one slave, with whom he would share the daily tasks. Shepherds too were frequently of servile status.

The agricultural calendar was also a religious calendar, punctuated by numerous festivals. The rural space was dotted with sanctuaries, sacred woods and rivers, and the cultivation of the earth was deeply felt to be a sacred action, hence its pre-eminent position in the hierarchy of human activities. The cultivation of cereals was described in myth, first and foremost in that of Prometheus, as the human activity *par excellence* right from the day when men became separate from the gods.

The peasant citizen was the norm. How was he integrated into political life? In Athens, a peasant would come into contact with political life at the level of his deme, where he could take part in the local assembly and in magistracies. In the context of his tribe he would come across town-dwellers. It is hard to tell what the part he played in the assembly might amount to. The fact that he lived some distance away from the town and the consequent loss of working days entailed by attending assemblies no doubt limited a country-dweller's participation in debates until the institution of the assembly *misthos* (early fourth century). However, many inhabitants of the town and its immediate neighbourhood were landowners too. The split between town-dwellers and country-dwellers became sharper at the time of the Peloponnesian War. Pericles' decision in 431 to abandon the defence of Attica and assemble all the peasants within the town walls marked the start of a development that grew as the war proceeded. The peasants could not earn their living in the town and they criticized the continuation of the war, for which they, as hoplites, provided the essential effort and which deprived them of their fields; so they supported the peace party. This split found expression in clichés that represented the peasants as tight-fisted, thereby setting a countryman (*agroicos*) in opposition to a townsman (*asteios*).

The peasant citizens supported Nicias and the peace that he negotiated in 421, and at the end of the fifth century they belonged to the nostalgic and conservative movement that recommended a return to the old days of Marathon and a 'republic of peasants'.

The town and the countryside were complementary, and although the Greeks set a high value on the work of the peasants, they also regarded the urban centre as the hallmark of Hellenism. A town was not a village, nor was it simply a cluster of dwellings with 'neither official buildings, nor theatre, nor agora, nor water brought to the fountain, where people live in hovels like mountain shacks on the edge of some ravine' (Pausanias). Rather, it was a place that was both political and cultural. The countryside produced the agricultural goods that were consumed in the town, but the town-dwellers were not mere consumers. They were producers and merchants too, for many of them were crafstmen or traders.

The accounts of the building site of the Erechtheum

Inscriptions provide us with the accounts relating to the construction of the Erechtheum in Athens. On the basis of the accounts for the year 408–407, it has been possible to construct the following table showing the distribution, according to status, within each of the professions represented on the work-site.

Distribution according to status within each of the professions represented

	Citizens	Metics	Slaves	Status unknown	Total
Architect	2				2
Secretary	1				1
Guard				1	1
Mason	6	9	24	5	44
Sculptor	2	6		1	9
Wood carver	1	5		1	7
Carpenter	4	10		3	17
Sawyer		1		1	2
Joiner		1			1
Wood turner				1	1
Painter		2		1	3
Gilder		1			1
Labourer	1	5		3	9
Work unknown	2	3		2	7

(according to work-site contracts)

An extract from the accounts: wages paid for the fluting of a column of the Erechtheum:
Ameinades (citizen), inhabitant of the deme of Koile: 18 drachmas
Aeschines: 18 drachmas
Lysanias: 18 drachmas
Somenes (slave): 18 drachmas
Timocrates: 18 drachmas

See R. H. Randall, 'The Erechtheum Workmen', *American Journal of Archaeology*, 57 (1953), pp. 199–210.

THE CRAFTSMEN

This rapid survey of the craftsmen's domain will consider the structure of this sector and the exploitation of raw materials, the types of activities and the place of technological work within the city.

Figure 46 A potter's workshop: detail from a red-figure hydria. Two *Nikai* (Victories) are helping Athena to crown craftsmen who are decorating craters and *kantharoi*. The representation of a woman employed in a workshop (on the extreme right of the painting) is exceptional (Milan, Torno Collection; drawing from *La Cité des images*, Paris, 1984, p. 6)

Structure   Citizens, as well as foreigners and slaves, were craftsmen, and in Athens ownership of the goods produced was restricted to free men, either citizens or metics. In no sector did the work of craftsmen acquire an industrial character. The norm was a workshop with a boss and two or three slaves. The workshop of an arms-maker, Cephalus, who had a hundred or so slaves working for him, was quite exceptional. Plenty of craftsmen worked on commission, at home, in their workshops or out in the street. In some cases the customer would provide the raw material and would pay only for the craftsman's labour. Craftsmanship provided a living for a large propor-tion of the population, but only just above the poverty line.

The mines   In Attica, the exploitation of the silver-bearing lead mines of the Laurion massif constituted a particular case. The city owned the land and leased out the exploitation of seams for either three or seven years in return for a sum that varied between 20 and 6,000 drachmas, depending on the size of the concession. As we have seen, the miners were slaves. Exploitation of these mines fluctuated. Very active in the fifth century, it then suffered from enemy invasions in the Peloponnesian War and, by the beginning of the fourth century, it was vegetating. In the mid-fourth century (350–338) production picked up, but only for a while. The silver extracted

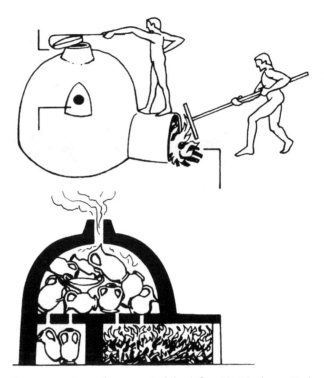

Figure 47   Reconstruction of a potter's kiln (after H. Hodges, *Technology in the Ancient World*, London, 1970)

was used to mint Athenian coins and supplied the workshops of gold- and silversmiths, but it was also exported to cities that possessed no mines.

Building sites   Our information on these comes solely from the accounts for public buildings approved by vote in the assembly or by the body responsible for a sanctuary. In Athens, part of the accounts for the construction of the Erechtheum on the Acropolis in 409–407 have been preserved, as they have for the reconstruction of the temple of Eleusis in 329–328. Elsewhere, the accounts for the construction of the temple of Asclepius at Epidaurus and the temple of Apollo at Delphi, in the fourth century, constitute sources that tell us about the various professional teams who worked on the temples. In Athens, the work to be done would be approved by vote in the people's assembly; then commissioners would set out the details in a notebook and see that it was respected by the entrepreneurs, who were assigned precise tasks, to be completed within a time limit. The workmen would be from one of several social groups: citizens, foreigners and slaves worked side by side on the Erechtheum site and were paid either by the day (one drachma a day) or for piece-work. Everyone doing the same work received the same wage, whatever his legal status.

Pottery Vases are probably the best-known product of the Athenian crafts-men, as thousands of them have been preserved. One quarter of Athens, known as the Ceramicus, situated between the agora and the Dipylon gate, concentrated all the potters' workshops. The master of a workshop was generally a potter, not a vase-painter. He had one or several assistants, most of them slaves. Some vases were signed with the names of the potter and the painter, but most were anonymous. However, pottery experts are able to identify the various workshops, thanks to their painting styles. The shapes of the vases and the themes of the paintings varied according to the use of the pot and the taste of the customer. The early fifth century was the high point for red-figure paintings, when Athenian pots were exported throughout the Greek world. Production is impossible to quantify. It slack-ened in times of troubles and wars; but that was not at all the case with metalwork.

Metalwork This was closely connected with warfare, the primary activity that required objects made of metal: helmets, greaves, armour, weapons. The Athenian craftsmen supplied the Athenians in the first instance, but also their allies. Throughout these two centuries the demand was constant and the market assured: a citizen had to equip himself as a hoplite and the equipment of the fleet was a liturgy. The largest workshops known in the fourth century served this sector and were owned by metics.

Leatherwork This too was linked with warfare, ranging from the manu-facture of sandals to that of shields. The animal skins came from sacrifices; the sanctuary priests did a brisk trade in their sales to tanners, who treated the skins, then sold them on to craftsmen who worked on a commission basis. You could watch your pair of sandals being made before your eyes, in the agora.

Textile work This was essentially domestic. In the *oikos*, the women spun, wove and made clothing that, for the most part, was not sewn but con-sisted of draped swathes of material, fixed in place by pins, *fibulae*. Only the dyeing was likely to be done outside the home, in some workshop. The end of the fifth century saw the dawning of the idea that the women might produce more than was needed in the *oikos*, and the head of the family could thus make a profit from his feminine workforce by selling the surplus on the outside market. That, at any rate, was the advice that Socrates gave one of his friends.

From the *oikos* to the workshop, the town thus hummed with craftwork performed by people of every kind of status, without the slightest indica-tion of competition between free and servile labour. The production of the work of craftsmen could undoubtedly be a source of wealth, but only for a very few individuals, for example, the owners of workshops or the exploiters of mines. Most citizen-craftsmen were poor and, rightly or wrongly, regarded Athens' hegemony over the other cities as the guarantee of their employment. For that reason they supported the continuation of the war, and in the assembly were receptive to the arguments of the demagogues.

THE MERCHANTS

Peasants and craftsmen could easily sell the fruits of their labour directly, in their village or town market. But alongside them there were merchants, who acted as intermediaries between producers and consumers: small-scale commerce existed everywhere and affected every sector of life, but we know nothing of its rules. In ports such as Piraeus, men sold products from distant lands. Wholesalers such as these would seek out associates in the form of shipowners and bankers, whose loans would be guaranteed by the merchandise and the ship. It is impossible to go into detail here, but some of these activities, such as slave-trading, were certainly very lucrative.

As we have noted, the city played a part in this trade, levying taxes on all imported and exported merchandise, and all transactions.

Throughout these two centuries, Athens' imports and exports, which varied little in kind, affected every part of the Mediterranean world. Athens imported two-thirds of its cereals, and all its iron, copper, wood, ivory, precious stones and slaves. It exported oil and wine, silver in the form of ingots and coins, and the products of craftsmanship, above all, pots.

The texts of the fourth-century orators and especially the speeches in the courts of law describe the life of some of the citizens and metics who lived in Piraeus and had business contacts with other parts of the world. They were among the wealthiest men of Athens and their lifestyle and culture set the tone, as those of the aristocracy had in the archaic period. However, their prosperity was precarious and in the course of the fourth century, in the space of one generation, Piraeus declined from being the best port (in about 380) to the worst (in about 356), so closely was its prosperity linked with the external political context. The decline of commercial activity produced direct consequences for the internal politics of Athens, threatening both the regularity of supplies and its finances, since a large proportion depended on taxes. But did all this really amount to 'a crisis'?

The activities described above are for the most part known to us from fourth-century texts, such as Xenophon's on agriculture and those by the Attic orators on craftsmen and merchants. So it is hard to tell how much things changed between the fifth and the fourth centuries. In recent years there has been much debate over the question of whether the fourth century experienced a crisis in all these domains. At first it was believed that it did; but now that view has undergone considerable qualification. What had appeared to be an agrarian crisis was in fact an increase in the *political* conflicts between the rich and the poor and the result of land being to a certain extent concentrated in the hands of the rich. Agriculture does not seem to have declined in the fourth century, but it was affected by climatic changes, and a lack of rain brought catastrophe close in about 361–360, and then again between 330 and 326. Large landowners were forced to learn how to calculate their expenditure according to long-term planning. The craft sector changed hardly at all, and the largest profits came from commerce. The general schema as regards the economy of the fourth century seems to have been as follows: the Athenian economy was certainly damaged as a result of the Peloponnesian War: silver was in short supply; but the conditions for agriculture were good. In about 388–387 overseas trade began to make large profits; a return to a dynamic economy then followed. Only at this point did major difficulties arise.

Between 1950 and 1980 debate – even polemical debate – between historians centred largely on the interpretation of data concerning the classical economy and society. Probably in reaction, present-day analyses of the classical world are more inclined to focus on its institutions and politics. This presents another example of Greek history's permeability to the major swings that affect the writing of history in general, in particular, in this case, to the hesitant methodological experiments that have followed upon the rather too rigid schemata dictated by ideological convictions that are no longer valid today.

POLYTHEISM AND RELIGIOUS LIFE

The Greeks worshipped a number of different deities: theirs was a polytheistic religion. Most of the rites were precisely fixed by tradition and by new laws that the cities passed. Religious life thus had its own particular characteristics in each of the cities, but these were grafted on to a basis of common beliefs. The various cities were very attached to their own religious particularities and these found expression in myths, in the grouping (pantheons) of deities peculiar to each city and in festivals reserved for their own cities, from which all other Greeks were excluded. But the Greeks also practised pan-Hellenic cults that were common to them all and were open to the entire Hellenic community, such as those identified with the famous sanctuaries of Olympia and Delphi. What with local particularism and pan-Hellenism, their religion made itself felt in even the smallest manifestations of social and public life. One of the principal features of this religion was the part it played in activities that, for us today, would have absolutely nothing to do with religion: an assembly meeting or a battle, for example, had to be preceded by a sacrifice and libations. For this reason, the boundaries between what we, in our culture, call the sacred and the profane, the religious and the secular, did not exist in the same way in the Greek world, so that at first sight Greek religion is very disorientating.

Figure 48   The assembly of the gods: a red-figure cup, signed Oltos, about 510 BC (Tarquinia). From left to right: Hebe, Hermes, Athena, Zeus, Ganymede, Hestia, Aphrodite, Ares (drawing by F. Lissarague)

DEITIES AND MYTHS

The large number of divine powers is something that strikes anyone looking at the sculptures on the pediment of a temple or reading a chapter of the *Iliad*. The names of most of these deities were already to be found on the Mycenaean tablets, and in the great early texts of Homer and Hesiod each has a clearly defined place and functions. In his *Theogony*, Hesiod even provides a history full of conflicts that ultimately lead to the establishment of the deities of Olympus, grouped around the figure of Zeus. The gods and heroes were the principal powers to whom the Greeks devoted cults.

The gods   The gods were immortal: once born, they never died. Their immortality was reflected in their way of life: they fed on ambrosia, nectar and even the smoke from the sacrifices that men offered up to them. In their veins flowed *ichor*, instead of the blood of the mortals. Greek thought organized the gods and classified them according to their powers, which were perceptible from their modes of action and the various domains in which they intervened.

Each god had a name, particular attributes, and a history; but he or she was only fully meaningful in relation to the overall divine system. The names of the gods were more or less the same throughout the Greek world, but their attributes varied more from place to place and were conveyed by a whole series of religious titles (*epiklèseis*). Zeus could be Soter (saviour), Poleius (city protector), Boulaios (of the Council), Ktesios (property protector), Astrapaios (thunderbolt-flinger), Hoplosmios (who overcomes with weapons), to name but a few examples.

A list of twelve gods, known as the Olympians, was drawn up in the fourth century and later taken over by the Romans: Zeus, Hera, Poseidon, Demeter, Apollo, Artemis, Ares, Aphrodite, Hermes, Athena, Hephaestus and Hestia. But each city with a pantheon could, of course, have its own version of the list of the twelve gods. Furthermore, depending on the circumstances, a city might also call upon different groups of gods. On examining the deities represented on the Parthenon frieze in Athens we notice, for example, that Eros has slipped in among the Twelve, displacing Hestia. And reading the oath taken by ephebes in Athens, we find that they swear by Aglaura, Hestia, Enyo, Enyalius, Ares, Athena Areia, Zeus, Thallo, Auxo and Heracles, a mixture of deities known throughout the Greek world and deities peculiar to Attica. The 'twelve gods', and the deities that compose various pantheons, are not always the same because there were no obligations in this matter, no dogma that fixed beliefs definitively. In some parts of the Greek world some very strange deities combined human with animal features (theriomorphic deities); for instance, Demeter Melaina at Phigalia in Arcadia had the head of a horse.

The diversity of polytheism also stemmed from its capacity to integrate new gods. Very often cities would officially welcome in new deities and decide to establish a cult for them. In fifth-century Athens the Arcadian god Pan, the Thracian goddess Bendis and the god Asclepius were officially recognized, while the cults of the eastern Sabazios and Adonis were no more than tolerated.

The heroes The heroes differed from the gods through their history. In principle, they were mortals who had served the community so well that a cult was set up for them when they died and they were raised to the level of divine powers. The centre of a hero's cult would be his tomb: the *heróon*. Heroes were for the most part honoured locally, their fame confined to their village or city, as in the case of the heroes chosen by the Delphic Pythia to become the eponymous patrons of the tribes created by Cleisthenes in Athens. But some heroes, such as Heracles, were known throughout the entire Greek world. The fields of intervention of the heroes were as varied and vast as those of the gods. They pronounced oracles, healed, protected and punished. They had sanctuaries and festivals; and their stories were told in cycles of myths, such as that of the twelve labours of Heracles, that were known throughout the Greek world.

The appearance of heroic cults was linked with the establishment of cities in the eighth and seventh centuries. These new cults helped the civic community to create itself an identity, a past, by honouring their founding hero. At the same time, they marked out their domination of a territory by setting up sanctuaries for their heroes on the city frontiers. The heroic cult conferred legitimacy on the city by rooting it in history and in the soil.

A highly organized system For a long time scholars maintained that Greek polytheism indicated very confused religious thinking. But that was incorrect. Rather, it marks a highly elaborated symbolic system that classified the deities and their powers and gave them a place within the ordering of communities. Ever since the work of G. Dumézil, scholars have been studying pantheons to work out how they are structured, that is, by seeing how the various deities stand in relation to one another. For example. J.-P. Vernant does not study Hestia and Hermes separately, but seeks to discover how the functions, modes of intervention, myths and rituals of these two deities resemble or are opposed to each other, so as to understand the logic behind their cults. In this way the particular characteristics of each deity stand out clearly, making it possible to understand the intellectual reasoning that determined a city's particular choice of a pantheon.

Greek religion also provided an explanation of the world, conveyed through a corpus of stories: mythology.

MYTHOLOGY

When you read the story of Heracles killing the lion of Nemea or gathering the golden fruit of the garden of the Hesperides, or when you contemplate a vase painting representing the same Heracles bringing the monstrous dog Cerberus back from the Underworld, you are confronted with a mythical narrative and its pictorial representation. Etymologically, myth (*muthos*) means 'formulated speech', and at first mythical stories were diffused orally. But for us, today, the Greek myths are all transmitted in written form, in a wide variety of texts from different periods. The most ancient collections of myths are the Homeric epics and Hesiod's works, the *Theogony* and the *Works and Days*. These stories and others were then taken over by the lyric poets, the authors of tragedy and comedy, the chroniclers, the philosophers and the compilers, all of whom transformed and reinterpreted them. What we now call 'Greek mythology' is the entire mass of data in this huge corpus of texts.

As in the case of the pantheon, the way to study this type of story raises problems and in this domain, as in that of the Greek pantheon, the method adopted can be important. Suffice it to point out the diversity of the possible approaches represented by the work of scholars such as J. G. Frazer, M. P. Nilsson and W. Burkert. Following the studies of C. Lévi-Strauss on the myths of the peoples of America and of G. Dumézil on the myths of the Indo-European peoples, myth has come to be considered as a symbolic system that makes it possible to organize or classify human experience in all its diversity and to render it intelligible. The Greeks had myths that explained the reason for animal sacrifices, the origins of marriage and the hierarchy of the gods. This kind of thought on the world is vibrant: as it passes from one generation to the next it changes. It is not so much a matter of belief: no myth is regarded as a dogma: in the Greek world, for example, several concurrent theogonies existed. Rather, it is an explanatory way of setting things in order. Greek mythology presents a whole world which, quite apart from the pleasure to be derived from reading its fascinating stories, allows us, step by step, to follow labyrinthine paths leading into a particular culture.

A perusal of a dictionary of mythology will enable anyone to discover the stories of the principal myths. Let us concentrate here on just one of the narratives, Hesiod's *Theogony*, in which he sketches out the history of the gods and constructs their extremely complex genealogy. First he describes the birth of the world (*cosmos*), hence the term 'cosmogony' that is applied to the beginning of the narrative. In the beginning there were three powers: Chaos (the yawning Gap), Gaia (Earth) and Eros (the power of renewal). Chaos and Gaia each independently gave birth to other powers. Then Gaia united with Ouranos and engendered the Titans, the three Cyclopes and the three Hundred-Arms. But Ouranos prevented his children from seeing the light of day, as he continuously covered Gaia, obliging her to keep her children deep inside her. Gaia then devised a cunning ruse. She made a sickle and gave it to the youngest of the Titans, Cronos, who thereupon castrated his father. From that time onward, Ouranos was separate from Gaia, fixed in his place at the top of the world. The generation of the primordial beings was over and the world could become organized; and with this the struggle for power between the gods began.

The children of Ouranos and Gaia in their turn engendered more divine powers. And history repeated itself. Cronos, the spouse of Rhea, swallowed his children as soon as they were born, to prevent any one of them from becoming king: Hestia, Demeter, Hera, Hades and Poseidon. The last of them, Zeus, eluded him, for Rhea gave him a stone to swallow instead. Zeus grew up and forced Cronos to vomit forth his children. However, before becoming master of Olympus, Zeus and the gods of his generation had to overcome the Titans and Typhon. Their victory ushered in peace and justice in the kingdom of the gods. All that remained was for Zeus to deflect the misfortunes of his ancestors. To avoid being dethroned, he swallowed his wife Mètis (Cunning Intelligence), who was pregnant, and himself gave birth to Athena. The cosmos and the world of the gods were in place; as was the world of men.

At the heart of the *Theogony* lies an important episode: the appearance of the hero, Prometheus, the institution of blood sacrifice, and the definition of the status of man, now separated from the world of the gods and obliged to reproduce himself (hence to take a wife: Pandora is created), to feed himself (and so to cultivate the land) and to die. The time of rituals now began for men, for this was the only means left to them to communicate with the gods.

VARIOUS ASPECTS OF GREEK RELIGION

THE RITES

The Greeks observed many rites, ranging from the simplest kind, such as individual prayer, to the most complex, such as festivals lasting several days, held in honour of a deity. The observance of the rites made for the permanence of tradition and the cohesion of the community; and both public and private life provided opportunities for many kinds of rite, many of them performed daily. There was no need to be a specialist to perform most of them and, although the presence of priests is often attested in sanctuaries, it was certainly not necessary when libations and sacrifices were made. However, for the performance of every rite a state of purity was required, purity of both body and mind, without which it was not possible to make contact with the divine world. The Greeks followed a number of procedures to expunge defilement, ablutions, for example, before entering a sanctuary, or the sacrifice of a piglet when it was necessary to purify a house after a birth or a death. Other far more complex procedures were adopted when the defilement was particularly grave, such as that left after a murder or that which affected a large community. The quest for the guilty one, the person whose defilement had unleashed the scourge that was decimating the city by making everyone sterile is, for example, the theme of Sophocles' tragedy, *Oedipus Rex*.

Prayer Prayer, pronounced aloud by an individual standing up, more often than not took the form of a request addressed to the gods, who listened and heard. It might be accompanied by a promise, to be fulfilled if the prayer was granted. Before a battle, it was quite common for the combatants to promise to set up a trophy to the god who brought them victory. Prayers accompanied everyday activities such as eating meals and working in the fields. But the civic community as a whole would also pray at the beginning of every session of the assembly in Athens, for example, or before setting out on an expedition. Prayers were often accompanied by libations.

Libations A libation involved pouring some liquid on to an altar or on to the ground, announcing for whom and why the offering was being made. The liquid would be either wine or wine mixed with water, milk or a mixture of water and honey. A little liquid would be poured from a ewer (*onochoe*) into a flat-bottomed cup (*phiale*), then from the cup on to the ground. Sometimes the entire libation would be used, sometimes only some of it, the rest then being drunk. There were an infinite number of occasions when libations would be made. They were customary before banquets (when they would be offered to Dionysus) and before every sacrifice. They were obligatory in funerary rituals: libations (*choai*) would be poured on to the tomb; and also on the occasion of the signing of a treaty, when they were called *spondè*, and would set the seal on the alliance concluded between the two parties. Many vases display representations of the peaceful scene of offerings being made by men or women.

Sacrifices There were many kinds of sacrifice. The first distinction to make is between blood sacrifices and *non-blood sacrifices*. The latter consisted of offerings of foodstuffs of every kind, except animals, which were burned on an altar: bread, cakes, fruit, vegetables or perfumes. These were without doubt the most frequent kinds of sacrifice and are attested to have taken place daily in family cults. They were also particularly prescribed in the cults of certain deities such as Demeter Melaina at Phigalia, whom we have already encountered. Moreover, Greeks who rejected blood sacrifice, such as the disciples of Pythagoras and Orpheus, also practised this kind of sacrifice.

There were two types of *blood sacrifice*. The animal victim was sometimes consumed entirely in the flames: this type was called a *holocaust*. It was rare where deities were concerned, but more frequent in the cult of heroes and the dead. The more usual type was blood sacrifice in which the meat would eventually be eaten. The animal would be slaughtered in ritual fashion, some parts (the bones and the fat) would be reserved for the gods and burned on the hearth; then the greater part of the meat would be pre-pared, cooked and eaten by men. The first distribution, between the gods and men, commemorated the foundation of sacrifice by Prometheus and underlined the radical difference which, from that time on, distinguished mortal men, who ate meat, from the immortals. Very often the meat would then be divided up again, this time among the men themselves. In some periods the most prestigious parts were reserved for the bravest of the warriors (in Homeric times) or for the city magistrates (in Athens, in the classical period), testifying to the existence of a social hierarchy. The remainder of the meat could then be distributed in an egalitarian fashion, each share being of the same weight. Thus, at the sacrifices of the Panathenaea in Athens, the magistrates were entitled to particular portions at a preliminary distribution, after which each citizen would receive an equal share of what remained of the sacrificed animal. This second distribu-tion excluded all non-citizens: foreigners, slaves, young people and women. Sacrifice was a way for the city to define the strict limits of the civic community.

The rules regulating blood sacrifices were at once similar as regarded the ritual procedure and particular for each individual deity. For example, while the general rule was always that only domesticated animals should be sacrificed, certain deities in certain cults expected goats, others sheep or even oxen, rather than any other animal. It is not possible here to describe the entire ritual in detail, but two vase paintings (figures 49 and 50) show the essential elements.

Figure 49 A scene of sacrifice, before slaughtering the animal: a red-figured crater, about 440 BC (Boston). The scene represents the moment before the slaughter. The victim, a sheep, is being brought to the cubic altar (*bomos*) by a youth. The sacrificer, an adult (bearded) man, holds out his hands to a receptacle held by a young acolyte. This is the *khernips*, the basin containing the water with which the victim is to be sprinkled. When it shook its head, this was taken to be its agreement to the sacrifice. In his other hand the young man holds a basket, the *kanoun*, filled with grain that conceals the *màchaira*, the sacrificial knife, lying at the bottom. The grain would be tossed over both the animal and the people present, thereby symbolically indicating the close link between the cultivation of cereals and sacrifice. On the right is a priest, on the left a flautist (drawing by F. Lissarague)

THE PERSONNEL

As has been mentioned, rites could be performed by a wide range of individuals, but some cases were bound by restrictions. For example, sacrifices could only be made by individuals who were at once male, adult and citizens. The Greek religion was not in the hands of a Church and its clergy. Nevertheless, cities did delegate religious functions to particular citizens, and in the sanctuaries sacred affairs were run by special individuals, the priests.

Many civic magistracies included some religious task, which was very natural given that, as we have seen, civic life and religious life were intertwined. Thus, in Athens, the king-archon, the eponymous archon and the polymarch were all responsible for, among other things, organizing sacrifices and festivals. The cities also annually elected citizens to take charge of religious matters generally: the *epimeletai*. Finally, all sanctuaries had their

Figure 50 A sacrifice scene, roasting the meat: a red-figured vase, about 470 BC (Naples). The scene depicts the sacrifice after the animal's slaughter and takes place still around the altar over the flames of which the meat is roasting. On the left a bearded man is pouring a libation over the meat from a cup. On the right a young man holds the meat on spits to be roasted. Behind the altar, to the left, a Hermes pillar can be seen, front view. The picture shows the moment after the animal's death and the cutting-up of the carcass, when the participants consecrate the viscera and the meat and cook them before eating them.

There are other vase paintings that show the cutting-up and preparation of the pieces of meat and the banquets in which it is eaten. Conspicious by its absence is the moment of the animal's death. This is never represented.

priests and priestesses (this being one of the rare responsibilities entrusted to women), who were selected according to a variety of procedures. Their function was to assist in sacrifices or, frequently, to perform them and to take charge of the entire running of the sanctuary, from the upkeep of the statues down to the cleaning of the buildings, and to administer all sacred property. Certain cults required more specialized functions, such as, in Delphi, the interpretation of oracles or, in Epidaurus, care of the sick. The priests received a fixed share of all sacrifices and also had other sources of revenue, such as the sale of the victims' skins. Their social status and wealth was very variable, depending on the importance of their sanctuary.

SITES

There were numerous cult sites, ranging all the way from a domestic altar in the middle of a house's courtyard to the complex sanctuary of Olympia. Any spot could become a sacred space, a *hieron*. All that was necessary was to mark it out, that is, to surround it with boundary posts, a wall or a fence . . . to separate it from secular space. A wood, a spring or a field could be chosen as a *hieron* if the presence of the divine made itself felt there in some way, and many Greek sanctuaries were very modest, with no prestigious buildings at all. Both the countryside and the towns were full of them. A city such as Athens had several hundred sanctuaries scattered throughout the territory of Attica. Certain prohibitions attached to them, such as being born or dying there, and privileges too, such as the right to asylum.

Sanctuary constructions, where they existed, related to the needs of the cult. Thus, the most indispensable was *an altar* (*bômos*) on which to make sacrifices. The altar, whether of stone or simply an accumulation of ashes, as at Olympia, was always out in the open, in front of the temple, if there was a temple.

The temple was not a place in which rituals (sacrifices or prayers) took place. It was the building that sheltered the statue or statues of the god and all the objects dedicated to him. However, some temples were built close to particularly sacred sites, such as the Erechtheum on the Acropolis of Athens or the temple of Pythian Apollo at Delphi, and certain rites, such as consultations with the oracle at Delphi, might in that case take place there, but they would be exceptional. The most ancient temples were constructed of wood. The first stone temples date from the early eighth century, as we have seen in the chapter on the archaic world, and it was then that their plan and ornamentation became fixed (see the schemata on p. 112 and the plan of the Acropolis, p. 180).

Other buildings were also sometimes to be found in a sanctuary. A treasure store would frequently be built in the form of a small temple and would be used to store the offerings made to the god by cities (in which case the treasure house bore the name of the city) or by private individuals. Fountains would provide the water for the necessary ablutions that preceded every ritual act. Porches and covered halls offered shelter for those visiting the sanctuaries, where they could rest or refresh themselves. Finally, some constructions were connected with the competitions held there: a theatre, a stadium, a gymnasium.

As well as these constructions, the sanctuaries contained masses of *offerings* of every kind, brought by pilgrims: statues, vases, shields won from the defeated in war, but also earthenware figurines, clumsily modelled, and dozens of ex-voto plaques. Everybody, from rich barbarian princes to anonymous peasants, gave what he could to the god; this was one of the elementary marks of Greek piety, and the sanctuaries became huge stores filled with all kinds of different objects. The inventories kept by the priests and the dedications inscribed on offerings tell us something of the donors of objects, most of which have by now disintegrated and disappeared.

When great gatherings, known as *panegyria*, were held, the sanctuaries were surrounded by activities of all kinds, veritable fairs brought into being by the great crowds attracted there. Nor was it uncommon, despite the inviolable nature of any sacred place, for a sanctuary to become a battle-field. One famous scene, described by Xenophon, was that of a pitched battle between the Eleans and the Arcadians in the sanctuary of Olympia. Arrows flew from the porches and even from the great temple itself, barricades were built, and men clambered on to be the temple roofs in pursuit of their opponents . . . Clearly, sanctuaries were also a part of everyday life.

SOCIAL FRAMEWORKS

Given that religion was not confined to any particular domain, it was to be found at every level of social life, and to trace it wherever it appeared would be a project far beyond the scope of the present work. Here instead are a few reminders of general characteristics.

The life of an individual was punctuated by rituals that allowed him to become gradually integrated *into the world of the family*: rites at the time of his birth; then city rites: at adolescence, when a youth was about to become a citizen. Marriage was also a time for purificatory baths, sacrifices, processions and songs in honour of numerous deities. Finally, death was also an occasion for very strict rites: the exhibition of the body at home (the *prothesis*), taking it to the cemetery (the *ekphora*) to the sound of ritual lamentations and the dirge (*threnos*), cremation or burial, followed by the erection of a *sema*, a stele, for example, to mark out the tomb, and the placing of offerings on the tomb. All these rites were essential if the corpse was to accede to the status of the dead. The cult of the dead was both a family and a civic matter.

The household (*oikos*) was one place for rites. Here, offerings and sacrifices were made to the gods who protected the house, first and foremost Hestia, the goddess of the hearth, under whose care every new member of the household would be placed: a new-born baby, a wife, a slave. Extended families would sometimes have parties, such as the festivities of the Apatouria, celebrated by Ionians who recognized common ancestors.

Within the framework of the village, for example, an Athenian deme, there were also many religious obligations. Calendars have come down to us listing the sacrifices and offerings to be made to the heroes and deities honoured by the deme, and these lists enumerate several rites, at different sites, for every day of the month. Then, some cults were common to all the members of the same tribe in Athens: that of its eponymous hero, for example. Greeks would also belong to religious associations, groups of the devotees of a particular deity's cult, and within this framework would also celebrate sacrifices and share meals. Finally, everyone could take part in the *festivals common to all members of the city*.

Here again, we are in possession of religious calendars that give precise details of these festivals, month after month. Sometimes the calendar had to be reorganized to accommodate new festivals that had been added to

Calendar of the festivals in Athens

Festivals	Months and days	Deities
Kronia	Hekatombaion 12	Kronos
Synoikia	Hekatombaion 15 and 16	Athena
Panathenaia	Hekatombaion 28	Athena
Eleusinia	Metageitnion (?) 4 days	Demeter
Niketeria	Boedromion 2	
Plataea	Boedromion 3	
Genesia	Boedromion 5	Gè
Artemis Agrotera	Boedromion 6	Artemis
Democratia	Boedromion 12	
Mysteries of Eleusis	Boedromion 15–17, 19–21	Demeter
Pyanopsia	Pyanopsion 7	Apollo
Theseia	Pyanopsion 8	Theseus
Stenia	Pyanopsion 9	Demeter
Thesmophoria in Halimus	Pyanopsion 10	Demeter
Thesmophoria	Pyanopsion 11, 12, 13	Demeter
Chalkeia	Pyanopsion 30	Athena
Apatouria	Pyanopsion (?)	
Oschophoria	Pyanopsion (?) (Maimakterion)	Athena
Haloa	Posideon 26	Demeter
Theogamia	Gamelion 2	Hera
Anthesteria	Anthesterion 11–13	Dionysus
Diasia	Anthesterion 23	Zeus
Asklepeia	Elaphebolion 8	Asclepius
Dionysia (town)	Elaphebolion 10–14	Dionysus
Delphinia	Mounichion 6	Apollo
Mounichia	Mounichion 16	Artemis
Olympeia	Mounichion 19	Zeus
Thargelia	Thargelion 6–7	Apollo
Bendideia	Thargelion 19	Bendis
Plynteria	Thargelion 25	Athena
Arretophoria	Skirophorion 3	Athena
Skira	Skirophorion 12	Demeter
Dipoleia or Bouphonia	Skirophorion 14	Zeus

To these days must be added the festivities on the 1st, 2nd, 3rd, 4th, 6th and 8th days of each month. This brings the total of festival days to 120.

The dates of certain festivals are not known. We know, for example, only that the Apatouria took place during the month of Pyanopsion. In the above table, such uncertainties are indicated by question marks.

the old ones. Thus, in Athens, the citizen Nicomachus, at the request of the assembly, drew up a new calendar of festivals at the end of the fifth century. It was engraved and then put on public view in the Stoa Basileia, on the agora. Civic festivals were celebrated on a scale beyond the means of individual families or demes. They lasted for several days, attracted hundreds of people, were the occasion of major sacrifices ('hecatombs' were sacrifices of a hundred animals) and even of competitions. They were extremely costly, so however many herds a city possessed and however many sacred estates the incomes of which could be used to finance cults, they would try to find other expedients. One would be to entrust the organization of festivals to rich individuals, as Athens did with its system of liturgies. We know that the theatre competitions held at the Great Dionysia were paid for by the *choregoi* and that the banquets at the Panathenaea were offered by 'public hosts'.

RELIGIOUS PECULIARITIES

Every city and every people integrated religion into its public institutions and did all it could to secure the protection of as many deities as possible. At the same time, every community had its own particular pantheon, its own poliad deity, its own founding myths, and would sometimes exploit this religious identity to affirm its own political superiority.

The close link between public institutions and religion is constantly evident. From the moment a city was founded, the gods would have their place in it, as we have noted in connection with the emigration of Greeks in the archaic period. An oracle would be consulted as to the siting of the new city, and before marking out its new boundaries a sacrifice would be made. A large area of the new city's territory would be reserved for its sanctuaries. The heart of the city constituted the common hearth, the *hestia koina*, a symbol, connected with the cult of Hestia, of all the hearths of family groups. The prytaneum was one of the first public buildings to be constructed in the vicinity of this hearth and served as a meeting-place for the city magistrates. Many features of Athenian institutions testified to the collusion between the political and the religious: the sessions of the assemblies, councils and courts, all preceded by libations and sacrifices; the decisions on religious issues, put to the vote in the assemblies; the trials of those charged with impiety; the oaths required from new citizens (at the time of the *ephebeia*) and from magistrates; the treasure of the city, which was in fact the treasure of Athena, stored in the Parthenon.

But the gods were also the city's protectors in times of crisis, and more and more procedures for ensuring their support were introduced. Themistocles, it will be remembered, consulted the oracle at Delphi before the battle of Salamis; before every military campaign or battle the auspices were taken by examining the livers of sacrificed animals, diviners were asked to interpret dreams and, above all, prayers were said. In Aeschylus' *Seven against Thebes*, Eteocles speaks as follows:

May our ramparts repulse the enemy army: that is the prayer to make to the gods. Besides, that would be in the interests of the gods themselves. Is it not said that the gods desert a captured city? . . . Before the gods, the masters of this land, I declare that if all turns out well, if our town is saved, I will make the blood of ewes run on the divine altars, to celebrate our victory; and I will turn the clothes of our enemies into offerings hanging on the walls of their holy dwellings.

Eteocles is almost cynical about it: the destiny of the gods is linked with that of men. What indeed would a city be without their support, but also, what would the gods be without the sacrifices that mortals offer them?

Every civic community had a deity as its patron, hence the epithet *poliad* for Poseidon in Corinth, Hera in Argos, Athena in Sparta and in Athens. And through a series of myths, each city rewrote its origins. One of the important points for the Greeks, during the classical period at any rate, was to be able to prove that they had always occupied the same soil, the same land, so as to legitimate their claims to hegemony there. For example, through the myth of Erechthonius, the first king of Athens, born from the Earth, the Athenians declared themselves to be autochthonous, born from the soil, and so to have been the inhabitants of this land from the beginning of time. With the myth of Theseus, the son of Aegeus (or of Poseidon) and Aethra, they invented a civilizing hero capable of rivalling the hero revered by the Spartans, Heracles, and created a moderate king who brought people together (the synoecism of Athens was attributed to him): the very image of what the fifth-century city wanted for itself. A city's political identity was thus forged by reappropriating myths, heroes and even cults. This element of religious life fitted in perfectly with the constant antagonism manifested between the cities in the classical period. Yet however much a city was attached to the altars of its own gods, it was equally concerned to take its place in the great communal festivals that were open to all Greeks.

THE PAN-HELLENIC CULTS

These were cults that were open to the whole body of Greeks, over and above the framework of cities and confederations. Some were organized on strictly international lines, certainly those of the four sanctuaries that celebrated with competitions. But the consultation of oracles, cults of healing, and mystery cults could also bring a pan-Hellenic clientele to sanctuaries.

THE PAN-HELLENIC COMPETITIONS

In the classical period, four sanctuaries organized festivals and competitions to which the cities sent religious ambassadors (*theoroi*) and which had an international status that they all recognized. The competitions (*agones*) of what was called the *periodos* (a four-year cycle) were the Olympic Games celebrated at Olympia in honour of Zeus every four years, the Pythian Games at Delphi in honour of Pythian Apollo every four years, the Isthmian Games close to the Isthmus of Corinth in honour of Poseidon and the Nemean Games at Nemea in honour of Zeus, the latter two held every two years. The first 'games' were held in 776. This marked the beginning of a system of dating that was common to the whole of the Greek world and which divided time into periods of four years, or Olympiads, the first Olympiad being 776. Before the date of each of these Games a sacred truce was declared, to allow the pilgrims to travel to the sanctuaries without risk of reprisals.

The competitions constituted the second part of the festivals, which always began with processions and sacrifices. The pattern taken by the competitions varied, but in general the contests would be gymnastic, equestrian or musical. The victors received crowns of laurel (bay) at Delphi, of olive at Olympia, and of wild celery at the Isthmus and Nemea. These *stephanitès* competitions, for which the prize was purely honorific, namely a crown, not a sum of money, were by far the most prestigious. They conferred great glory upon the victor and his native city, fame that would sometimes be sung in poems known as Epicinians, several of which were composed by the Boeotian poet Pindar. The victors also had the right to erect statues to commemorate their victories, either in their own cities or in the sanctuary at Olympia.

The competitions gave the cities a chance to measure themselves against one another, but not on a battlefield, and also presented a fleeting opportunity to test the unity of a civilization of peoples who never achieved political unity. Both confrontation and common values were reflected in the very topography of the pan-Hellenic sanctuaries, where the offerings consecrated by rival cities would be lined up opposite one another, as they are along the first part of the sacred way at Delphi.

ORACLES

Divination (*mantikè*), of which oracles constituted a particular form, was one of the means by which men could make contact with the gods and learn their opinions on all sorts of matters in both private and public life. One form of divination consisted in the manipulation of various objects and the observation of certain signs (the flights of birds, the viscera of sacrificial animals . . .) entrusted to a specialist, the diviner. Another form, more highly valued by the Greeks, was listening to the god's words, the oracle, and interpreting what was said. There were a number of oracular sanctuaries that were famous in the classical period, that of Zeus at Dodona, that of Apollo at the Didymeion, near Miletus, and that of Apollo at Delphi, for example.

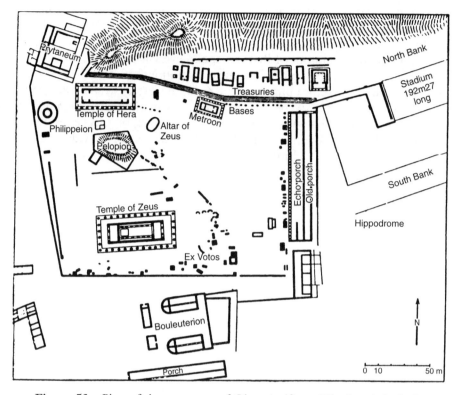

Figure 51 Plan of the sanctuary of Olympia (from *Histoire générale des civilisations*, vol. 1, p. 354, fig. 24)

We are particularly well informed about consultation of the Delphic oracle. Initially, this took place once a year, but later it was allowed once a month. The person consulting the oracle had to follow strict rules: purify himself, pay a tax, the *pelanos*, and offer up sacrifices, before he could present himself at the place of consultation, the *adyton*, somewhere in the temple of Apollo (exactly where we do not know). The question put to the god required not a prediction on the future but specific advice as to what to do or not do. 'Should I marry?' or 'Should such-or-such a city go to war?' The Pythia, the priestess whose job it was to pronounce the oracle, would give a reply that was then transmitted to her questioner by the priests of Apollo. The reply would sometimes be ambiguous; it was up to the individuals or the city to interpret it correctly. That was, for example, the onerous task that fell to the Athenians gathered in the assembly on the eve of the battle of Salamis, who had to decide on the meaning of 'the rampart of wood'. An oracle was a safeguard requested from the gods in order to come out on top in an action whose successful outcome lay in the hands of men, as the Greeks were all too well aware.

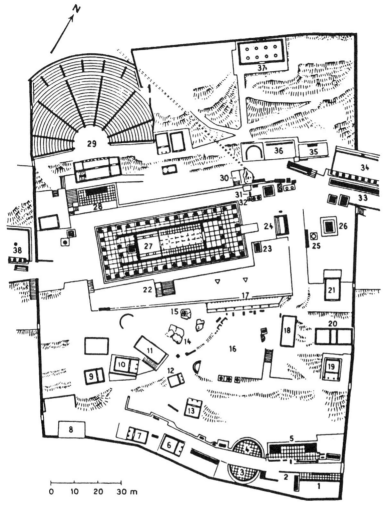

Figure 52 Plan of the sanctuary at Delphi: 1 the Navarchs, ex-voto from the Spartans; 2 ex-voto from the Athenians; 3 the *Epigonoi*, ex-voto from the Argives; 4 the Kings, ex-voto from the Argives; 5 anonymous Hellenistic niche; 6 Sicyon's treasure house; 7 Siphnos treasure house; 8 Thebes' treasure house; 9 Potidaea's treasure house; 10 Athens' treasure house; 11 Bouleuterion; 12 Cnidus' (?) treasure house; 13 anonymous Aeolian treasure house; 14 the rock of the Sibyl; 15 the Sphinx of the Naxians; 16 open area; 17 porch of the Athenians; 18 Corinth's treasure house; 19 Cyrene's treasure house; 20 Prytaneum (?); 21 treasure house of Brasidas and Acanthus; 22 fountain; 23 pillar of L. Aemilius Paullus; 24 Chios' altar; 25 Plataea's tripod; 26 chariot of the Rhodians; 27 temple of Apollo; 28 Craterus' offering; 29 theatre; 30 Cassotis' fountain; 31 pillar of Prusias; 32 the Eurymedon palm; 33 monumental foundation from Attalus I; 34 porch of Attalus I; 35 enclosure of Neoptolemus; 36 Thessalian ex-voto from behind; 37 *Leschè* from the Cnidians; 38 western porch (from P. Ginouvès, *L'Art grec*, p. 86, fig. 6)

CULTS OF HEALING

Many heroes and local gods were credited with powers of healing and their sanctuaries attracted people from the surrounding area. One was the hero Amphiaraos, on the border of Boeotia and Attica. But in the late fifth and early fourth centuries the cult of Asclepius, a hero who had become a god, spread throughout the Greek world, as did the fame of his sanctuaries, one in Cos, the other in Epidaurus. People would travel a long way in order to lie under the sanctuary porches and wait, in a state of *incubation*, for a dream through which the god would indicate the means of healing the complaint from which they suffered. The sanctuary priests played a by no means negligible role as advisers on the treatments to be followed, and even if their 'obscurantism' clashed with the early advances being made by a more rational type of medicine centred on the Hippocratic school, they nevertheless did treat many sick people, as the ex-votos testify, sometimes with a certain humour.

MYSTERY CULTS

These were characterized by two features: they were devoted to the spiritual transformation of the individual, who was required to go through a veritable initiation (*telete*); and the rituals that they performed had to be kept secret. A number of cults answered this twofold description: the cult of the Cabiri, close to Thebes in Boeotia, that of the Great Gods at Samothrace and that of the Great Mother, for example. But the cult of Demeter and Kore, in their sanctuary at Eleusis (an Athenian deme) was the one that was the best known in the Greek world.

At Eleusis the status of the devotee was of no importance. One of the most original features of the mysteries was that they were open to individuals of all social conditions: free men, slaves, women, foreigners, all could be initiated and become *mystai*. In the classical period most of the rare cults that permitted unrestricted participation were eastern cults that were not always recognized by the cities and that took place within the framework of special religious associations, but the cult of Eleusis was a civic one. The ceremonies of the Mysteries passed through a number of different stages, the Small Mysteries in the spring, the Great Mysteries six months later, in the autumn. The Great Mysteries lasted ten days. A procession guided the bodies constituted by city officials, on one hand, and the faithful on the other, from the sanctuary of the goddesses at the foot of the Acropolis, the Eleusinion, to the Telesterion of Eleusis, passing along the Sacred Way and making ritual halts, in particular, for a major purification in the sea. The mysteries proper, in which only the *mystai* could take part, lasted three days. Three priests directed the rites, sharing the tasks between them. The function of the *hierophantes* was to display the sacred objects (the *hiera*). He was always chosen from the Eumolpid family. The priestess of Demeter

Figure 53 Scene from a Dionysiac cult: maenads dancing round the statue of Dionysus, a detail from an Attic cup, about 490 (Berlin, Antikenmuseum; drawing by F. Lissarague).

came from the Philleid family. The *dadouchos* (torch-bearer) came from the Kerykes family. Little is known of the details of the rituals apart from an enigmatic formula that was spoken by the *mystai*, which suggests the manipulation of sacred objects: 'I have fasted, I have drunk the *kykeon* [a mixture of water, barley seeds and mint], I have taken from the *ciste* [basket] and after working I have replaced in the *calathos* [large basket], I have taken from the *calathos* and replaced in the *ciste*.' Perhaps this rite also commemorated the founding myth of the Mysteries, the story of Demeter seeking her daughter Kore and being offered shelter by the king of Eleusis. It is a myth that is known to us thanks to the *Homeric Hymn to Demeter*.

The mystery cults testify to the wide variety of the religious experiences available to the Greeks, affording means of expression and satisfaction to different types of piety.

THE CULT OF DIONYSUS

In conclusion, the cult of Dionysus was both a city cult and a cult of elsewhere. It blithely combined processions, sacrifices and competitions, organized in an extremely official fashion by the civic community, the festival of the Great Dionysia in Athens, and marginal rites, described mainly in myths, that involved both male and female Bacchae who, when possessed by the god and in a state of rapture, would no longer be themselves. However, the city made no choice between the two forms of the cult but integrated them both, as being equally necessary aspects to religious and social experience. This figure of Dionysus, so often regarded as the antithesis of the regulated, responsible city, is surely in truth a symbol of the extraordinary richness of a religion that welcomed, transformed and diversified all kinds of experiences, a religion that also worked itself into even the most withdrawn pockets of social life and that, to borrow the words of J.-P. Vernant, 'forces us to think simultaneously about religion and politics, anthropology and history, morality and daily life'.

4 / THE CLASSICAL PERIOD: THE FOURTH CENTURY

Around 400 BC

408 – The return of the Persians

After being so deeply involved in the Persian Wars, the Athenians had in 425 covered themselves *vis-à-vis* the Persian threat by signing a treaty of friendship with the new Great King, Darius II Ochos (425–404). But the Sicilian disasters, the machinations of Alcibiades, and the Ionian War presented the Persians with the chance of their dreams to take their revenge by backing Sparta against Athens. Three successive bouts of negotiation in 411 resulted in the Spartans, in exchange for Persian gold, recognizing the Great King's sovereignty over Asia. In 408, Darius II gave full powers to his younger son, Cyrus the Younger, to coordinate the action of the satraps in support of the Peloponnesians. What followed showed that the only winners in the Peloponnesian War were the Persians. In their eyes, the situation prior to the Persian Wars had been restored.

403 – Forgetting, in the city

In 403, all the Athenians swore 'to forget the evils of the past'. The city ejected war: the fact that there had been two camps was forgotten. It was the victors themselves who resolved that it should be so, and there were not too many hitches. Majority rule was re-established; the laws were revised; the civic body and the courts were reorganized. Athens' defeat produced comparable results in the other cities: their former regimes were stablized.

    The speech that Xenophon (*Hellenica*) ascribes to Thrasybulus recognizes the social realities that had resurfaced with the loss of the empire: the 'townspeople' were richest, with their ramparts, their arms, their money and their Peloponnesian friends; the ordinary people were poor, with none of those advantages. Like many of the cities exhausted by the war, Athens, divided against itself, witnessed the return, under the cover of ideological debate, of what before Solon had been, in Aristotle's words, 'the most intolerable and bitter of political evils'. Docked of its income from an empire that was now beyond its reach, how could Athens avoid the inequality between the rich and the poor from once again degenerating into civil war?

399 – The return of religion

The misfortunes of war had revived traditional piety: the citizens turned to their protector gods, hoping they would give them peace, and they adopted foreign gods who seemed more suited to their needs (in Athens, Asclepius after the plague, Bendis imported from Thrace, Cybele from Asia Minor, Sabazios from Phrygia and Adonis from Phoenicia). They also prosecuted the sacrilegious and impious. Public opinion suspected the sophists who, among other things, spread philosophical criticism of mythology that went back to the sixth century, of having lost belief in the tutelary gods and of corrupting the young. It was an accusation that Aristophanes brought against Socrates in 423, in his play *The Clouds*, despite the fact that Socrates himself vigorously refuted the sophists.

In 415 it was discovered that certain aristocrats were deliberately indulging in sacrilege (mutilating the pillars of Hermes and parodying the mysteries of Eleusis), thereby proving that they no longer feared gods who (according to Critias, a future leader of the Thirty) had been invented simply to frighten credulous people into obeying the laws. Reconciliation between the citizens was achieved at the cost of a scapegoat; and it was Socrates who, although scrupulously observant of the laws, openly passed a negative judgement on democracy in the presence of his disciples. In the spring of 399, accused by the entourage of Anytus (a former Theraminian, now rallied to the new regime) and condemned to death for impiety, Socrates insisted upon accepting this majority verdict.

The fourth century thus opened with a defeat, a political compromise, and a philosophical misunderstanding, sealed by a legal crime.

THE END OF THE CLASSICAL HEGEMONIES

AROUND THE AEGEAN SEA (404–355)

THE PEAK OF SPARTAN POWER: PERSIAN GOLD

Peloponnesian propaganda had promised liberty (that is, independence) to the cities subjected by the Athenians. But in fact, from 405 on Lysander applied a policy of military occupation in the Aegean, which in some cases Sparta was later to relax but in others, on the contrary, would extend even to include some of its former allies: an 'autonomous' executive power would be entrusted to oligarchs, supervised by a military governor (a *harmost*) and a garrison. Once the euphoria provoked by the influx of massive booty in the form of silver had worn off in this city still attached to the austerity of its collective education and its own iron coinage, the Spartans soon realized that their domination depended upon subsidies from the Great King.

Darius II had died in 404, leaving the throne to his elder son Artaxerxes II Mnemon (404–359), to whom Plutarch devoted a churlish biography in his *Parallel Lives*. On the strength of his past cooperation with the Peloponnesians, Cyrus the Younger set about attempting to usurp the power of his elder brother, with the aid of an army reinforced by a strong contingent of Greek mercenaries (the 'Ten Thousand'), one of whom was Xenophon, who wrote an account of the expedition in his *Anabasis*. Cyrus the Younger was killed at Connaxa, near Babylon, in 401. Harassed by the troops of the satrap Tissaphernes, the 'Ten Thousand' retreated in the depths of winter across Armenia to the Black Sea. The 5,000 who survived, led by Xenophon, got back to Thrace, where they were soon recruited in the service of Sparta.

Immediately after this victory, Artaxerxes ordered Tissaphernes, equipped with the extended powers that had been held by Cyrus the Younger, to impose his suzerainty over the Greek cities of Asia. At this point the Greeks of Ionia wrung a few promises from the Spartans, who sent some small contingents to Asia, playing off one satrap against another but soon finding themselves reduced to pillaging the countryside in order to find food supplies. Sparta, by now on frosty terms with its principal allies, was fearful of open war against the Persians at a moment when the ephors had only just put down a conspiracy led by a certain Cinadon (with a force that for the first time included 'inferiors', citizens who had been demoted, *perioikoi* and helots). A Peloponnesian congress nevertheless decided to send a proper army to Asia, led by the young king Agesilaus, the successor of Agis. Xenophon, who served under him, gives a somewhat exaggerated account of his exploits, which included the execution of Tissaphernes, who was accused of treason.

Pharnabazus, the satrap of Phrygia, ordered by Artaxerxes to deal with the Spartans once and for all, then embarked on a diplomatic campaign, buying off his enemies with Persian gold, using as his intermediary the Rhodian Timocrates and the Athenian Conon (earlier defeated by Lysander with the aid of this very satrap!). Discontent being rife, the operation was soon so succesful that Athens and Thebes formed an alliance. After an unsuccessful expedition in Boeotia, where Lysander was killed, the coalition won over Corinth, Argos and many of the cities of central Greece. Hastily recalled, Agesilaus defeated the coalition forces at Coronea (394). However, the key power, Corinth, continued to resist. Not long before, a Graeco-Phoenician naval squadron had destroyed the Peloponnesian fleet off the coast of Cnidus. After this, the satrap and the Athenian *strategos* ejected the Spartan garrisons from the Aegean islands and the coastal cities, promising the Greeks there autonomy. Conon entered Piraeus in triumph at the head of the Persian fleet, with enough money to complete the reconstruction of the Long Walls that had been begun the previous year. It was the Persians who profited: as soon as they came out on Athens' side, Sparta was forced to recognize that it was unable to fight on two fronts.

Peace and liberty

The King's Peace (386)

'The king Artaxerxes rightly judges that the cities of Asia shall be his, together with the islands of Clazomenae and Cyprus, and that the other Greek cities be left autonomous, whether small or large, except for Lemnos, Imbros, and Skyros which, as in the past, belong to the Athenians. As for all those, on whatever side, who will not accept the clauses of this peace, I shall myself wage war on them, accompanied by those who do accept them, on both land and sea, using all my ships and my wealth.'

Alliance between Athens and Chios (384)

'Given that the citizens of Chios have decided faithfully to observe . . . the existing treaties, as the king, the Athenians, the Spartans and the other Greeks have sworn to . . . the people decrees that the citizens of Chios are our allies, in liberty and autonomy, without violating any of the undertakings inscribed on the *stelai* concerning the peace.'

Ratification of the alliance between Athens and its allies (377)

'Good luck to the Athenians and the allies of the Athenians! So that the Spartans leave the Greeks in peace and quiet, free and autonomous, secure in their own territories . . . the people decrees: if any among the Greeks or the barbarians living on the mainland or the islands, unless they belong to the King, wishes to become an ally of the Athenians and their allies, let them be so yet remain free and autonomous, with whatever political regime they want, without having a garrison or governor imposed upon them, without having to pay tribute, under the same conditions as Chios, Thebes, and the other allies.'

Athens' oath of alliance with Corcyra (375)

'I shall come to the aid of the Corcyran people with all my strength, so far as is possible on both land and sea, if anybody invades the Corcyran territory and the Corcyran people request it; I shall work for war or for peace in accordance with what is decided by the majority of the allies; I shall do this according to the decrees of the allies.'

THE 'KING'S PEACE'

The return to warfare between Greeks reawakened the pan-Hellenic aspirations that had appeared during the Peloponnesian War. In *The Peace* (421) and *Lysistrata* (413), Aristophanes had evoked the (legendary) union of the Greeks of all countries (pan-Hellenes already in the *Iliad*) during the Persian Wars. At the Olympic Games of 392, the sophist Gorgias of Leontini urged all the Greeks to turn their arms against the Barbarians. In 391 the Spartans proposed, without success, recognizing the 'autonomy' of the cities in the coalition, in return for a 'common peace' (Andocides, *Speech on Peace*).

That they failed was understandable: the word 'autonomy' was by no means synonymous with 'liberty'. (The autonomy guaranteed to the people of Aegina by the Thirty Years' Peace, for example, in effect set the seal on their submission to the Athenians.)

Having decided to support Egypt and Evagoras, the dynast of Salamis in Cyprus, in their revolt against the Great King (Isocrates, *Evagoras*), the Athenians quarrelled with the Persians. Short of funds, Thrasybulus resorted to a number of new expedients (a toll on the Bosphorus, port taxes, enforced taxation, the pillaging of the countryside). He was assassinated by the inhabitants of Aspendus, in Pamphylia. The time had come for Artaxerxes to change his tactics. The special powers of Pharnabazus, recalled by the king to become his son-in-law, were transferred to the satrap of Lydia, Tiribazus, with whom the Spartan Antalcidas had been negotiating ever since the collapse of the exploratory talks between the Greeks.

In 386 a 'common peace' was imposed upon the members of the coalition, convoked to Sardis. The right to autonomy left any dominant city of the moment free to prevent any hegemony other than its own, on the pretext of protecting small cities against large ones. At a congress organized in Sparta, the members of the coalition bowed to necessity: the Boeotian League was dissolved; and the 'autonomous' cities of Asia submitted to the satraps. Evagoras did likewise in 380. The mercenaries on the Athenian payroll, who had been supporting the Egyptians, now switched to the Persian side. The last great independent pharaoh of Egypt, Nectanebo I, repulsed the invaders. The Athenians held on to their islands settled with cleruchs and remained allied with Thebes and the king of the Odrysians of Thrace and, unopposed, entered into alliance with Chios in 384. But as soon as Olynthus resuscitated the Chalcidian League, the Peloponnesian League intervened in the name of autonomy. After three years of war, Olynthus capitulated and gave up its ambitions (in 379).

A NEW DEFINITION OF PEACE

That same year a bold strike by the Thebans ejected their Spartan garrison. The reconstituted Boeotian League, with the aid of Athens, repulsed the counter-offensive of the Peloponnesians, accusing them of imperialism. In a *Panegyric*, believed to have been declaimed at the Olympic Games of 380, Isocrates blamed Sparta for the poverty that was spreading through Greece, on account of its having readmitted the Persians to the Aegean Sea. He proposed uniting once again, as in the good old days, to resume the struggle against the Barbarians, under the hegemony of Athens, a hegemony that would respect the liberty of the Greek cities. All Barbarians would be made *perioikoi* of all the Greeks, who could then exploit the resources of Asia free from risk, thereby restoring prosperity to Europe. In this manner, both social and international peace would be restored.

In 377 (one century after the foundation of the Delian League), the Athenians created a veritable 'confederation' against the Peloponnesians, in which the cities remained 'free', that is, independent. Each of the guarantees formulated under oath constituted a reaction against their former errors. The cities would be autonomous and free; there would be no occupying troops, no governor, no tribute, no cleruchs, no diplomatic decisions without consultation and the agreement of the Council of Allies, in which each city, regardless of size, had an equal say on resolutions put to a majority vote; and the Council controlled the common treasury. Athens would therefore have to depend solely upon its own resources to balance its budget. A new generation, grouped around Callistratus of Aphidna, made this their business. The levying of the war tax (*eisphora*) was reorganized: those liable (excluding the thetes) became members of a taxation unit, a *symmoria* (a sharing together); each *symmoria* paid the same fraction of the overall estimated contribution; the three richest citizens advanced the fixed sum, then were responsible for recouping it in a benevolent fashion.

In 376 the Athenian *strategos* Chabrias destroyed a Peloponnesian naval squadron off Naxos. The Chalcidian League reformed, under the cover of the Athenian federation, and was soon joined by the Thessalian League (which had passed out of the control of the aristocrats of Larissa, allies of Sparta, and into that of Jason, the tyrant of Pherae). Apart from the Asian coast, the new *symmachia* was not far off covering the same area as the old one.

THEBAN REVENGE: THE RISE OF THEBES

However, in 373 the Boeotians destroyed Plataea, resurrected from its ruins fifteen years earlier by the Spartans (Isocrates, *Plataicus*). The survivors took refuge in Athens where, like their predecessors of 427, they were granted 'Plataean' citizens' rights (Pseudo-Demosthenes, *Contra Neaira*). This time the 'common peace' had been directly violated. A congress met in Sparta in the presence of Persian ambassadors. The tyrant Dionysius of Syracuse and the king of Macedon, Amyntas III, also took part. The King's Peace was renewed. The Thebans, who had not been allowed to swear the oath in the name of the whole Boeotian League, rejected the agreement (in contrast – a sign of the times, this – each member-city of the Athenian confederation had taken the oath on its own account).

The Peloponnesian army which, under orders from King Cleombrotus, was protecting Phocis against the Boeotians, now entered Boeotia from the south, after advancing along the Gulf of Corinth. It took up position at Leuctra, to the south-east of Thespiae. Here the Peloponnesians suffered a defeat from which Sparta was not to recover. The victory of the Thebans, under the leadership of their *strategos* Epaminondas, was the fruit of a tactical innovation. A classical phalanx attacked from the front, with a depth of eight to twelve rows of hoplites, the best of whom would be positioned on the right wing. In this battle, Epaminondas inaugurated his new, oblique tactic: massing his best troops on the left, to a depth of fifty rows, with the idea that by opening up a breach in the strongest wing, his hoplites would then overcome the rest of their opponents, attacking them from the rear. Given the slenderness of its civic body, the high death toll spelt disaster for Sparta: out of 1,000 citizens (according to Aristotle), 700 had fought in the battle; of these 400 had been killed (according to Xenophon). The Athenians had decided too late to take the Spartan side.

At the invitation of the Arcadians, who were trying to form a League, Epaminondas invaded Laconia during the winter of 370–369. He camped before Sparta, now depleted of ramparts. The king Agesilaus improvised a defence and recruited 6,000 helots into the army, promising them their liberty. The Boeotians contented themselves with laying waste the country-side all the way to the sea. Then they liberated the Messenian helots who, with the aid of the Messenians of Naupactus, were to build their capital, Messene, at the foot of Mount Ithome. The Arcadian League organized itself by creating a federal capital, Megalopolis, by means of a synoecism. In 368, finding his authority challenged by the aristocrats of Larissa who were supported by a Macedonian garrison, Alexander of Pherae, the successor to Jason (assassinated in 370) and the leader of Thessaly, appealed to the Boeotians. Pelopidas ejected the troops sent in by Alexander II, king of the Macedonians, who then gave up the idea of intervening in Thessaly and handed over, as hostages, a number of adolescent nobles to be educated in Thebes. One was his youngest brother, the future Philip II (368). In 365, in exchange for a formal alliance with Thebes, his younger brother and successor, Perdiccas III, negotiated the return to Pella of Philip, then 17 years old.

FRAGMENTATION

The new situation created by the rise of Thebes had not escaped the notice of Artaxerxes II. He entrusted to the satrap of Phrygia, Ariobarzanes, Pharnabazus' brother and successor, the mission of conciliating the Boeotians and Spartans on the basis of a common peace. The negotiations, which foundered over the Messenian question, were transferred to Susa, where the Great King himself presided over them and this time played the Theban card. The Spartans were to allow Messene its autonomy and the Athenians were to recall their war fleet to Piraeus. At the congress that met in Thebes for the swearing of the new treaty among Greeks, both the Spartans and the Athenians refused to commit themselves (366). The *strategos* Timotheus at this point abandoned the Aegean Sea policy inaugurated in 377. He seized Samos and Sestos, where he established a cleruchy (365); then he occupied Pydna and Methone (364); the little island of Ceos, close to Attica, which had seceded, was reintegrated into the confederation by force (363). Athens in this way provisionally restored safe communications with the Black Sea, but did so at the cost of a perjury for which it was to pay dearly. In 362 Cotys I, king of the Odrysians, in protest at the reimplantation of cleruchies on his territory, broke off the long-standing alliance with Athens and reoccupied Sestos.

The Theban hegemony was fragile. Pressed by the complaints of the Thessalians, Pelopidas was forced to fight Alexander of Pherae at Cyno-scephalae, close to Pharsalus. The new hoplite tactics won him a victory, but he died in the battle (364). A second campaign proved necessary to force the tyrant of Pherae to restore autonomy to the Thessalian cities and their *perioikoi* peoples (363). Meanwhile, what with the distant protection of the Boeotians and the close hostility of its neighbours, Elis and Sparta, the Arcadian League was splitting apart. Tegea sided with Thebes, Mantinea with Sparta. Epaminondas confronted Agesilaus and his allies close to Mantinea: although tactically victorious on his left wing ('like a trireme, with the spur of the prow out in front', Xenophon wrote), he suffered a fatal blow (362). So it was that the three hegemonic cities one by one lost 'their illusions of grandeur' (G. Glotz), the kind prompted by military superiority when this was not supported by reasonable policies and assured funding. For the Greeks who (with the exception of Sparta) had just agreed among themselves to a common peace that confirmed the independence of the Messenians, the shadow of the Great King was enough to deter any attempts to exploit a revolt on the part of the satraps (361).

Artaxerxes II had entrusted the satrapy of Phrygia, situated on the coast of the Hellespont, to his grandson Artabazus, the nephew of the previous incumbent Ariobarzanes, who had been recalled to the court. The satraps of Asia Minor, all closely or distantly related to the royal family, formed the impression that the Great King was thereby making an advance designation of his successor. They supported Ariobarzanes in a revolt that spread as far as Cappadocia. Artabazus, for his part, had at his disposal the royal army, reinforced by Greek mercenaries under the command of two Rhodian brothers, Mentor and Memnon, whose sister he had married. In Phoenicia the insurgents joined forces with the army of the Pharaoh Tachos, which was also reinforced by Greek mercenaries led by Agesilaus and the Athenian Chabrias. Artaxerxes took his time and had little difficulty splitting up his opponents. Toppled by his kinsman Nectanebos, Tachos found refuge in Susa. Those who, opportunely, had wavered, now rallied and recovered their satrapies. Ariobarzanes was handed over by his own son and was executed. Agesilaus ended his long career as the leader of the mercenaries in the service of Nectanebos II (359–341). The crisis over the succession was resolved in favour of Artaxerxes III Ochos (358–338) who, on the death of his father, acceded to power without encountering any resistance.

THE WAR BETWEEN THE ALLIES

The aggressive policies adopted by the Athenians were beyond their means: they could not simultaneously maintain their communications with the Black Sea with no Thracian alliance, lay claim to Amphipolis and repress secessions, as they had in the good old days (in Byzantium, Lesbos and Chios in 364, Cyzicus in 362, Corcyra in 361) and meanwhile also defend their own territory (Alexander of Pherae raided Piraeus in 361). The assembly attributed these reversals to *strategoi* whom it judged guilty of high treason and who were either executed or went into exile, and to its foremost statesmen, such as Callistratus of Aphidna who, although condemned to death, found refuge in Macedon. The *coup de grâce* was delivered by the hereditary satrap of Caria, Mausolus, whose family had long since become Hellenized. In 357 he initiated an alliance, clearly directed against Athens, with Rhodes, Cos, Chios and Byzantium. Faced by Chios and Byzantium, the Hellespont fleet, commanded by Chares, was helpless. Despite reinforcements brought by Timotheus, the Athenians suffered a decisive defeat off Embata, near Erythrae (356). Although militarily responsible for this disaster, which was due to his own imprudence, Chares contrived to get the blame laid on Timotheus. Then, in order to obtain the financial means that his fellow-citizens could no longer provide, he placed himself at the service of Artabazus, who had refused to submit to the Great King. This 'war between the allies' was finally stopped by a Persian embassy despatched to draw attention to the clauses of the 'common peace': the Athenians had to recognize the independence of their former allies. The confederation was reduced to a handful of naval bases in the Aegean Sea (355). Chares returned to Athens, and Artabazus eventually went off to Macedon to join up with the mercenaries of Memnon (352).

Artaxerxes III at last had his hands free to carry out his great plan. Having subjected Cyprus and Phoenicia, he conquered Egypt with the aid of many mercenaries, some of whom were commanded by Mentor. Egypt once more became a satrapy. Artabazus and Memnon's mercenaries returned to the service of the Great King; order again reigned in Asia. But not in Thrace, where the Achaemenid frontiers were still those established by Darius the Great (341). There was no way of foreseeing that nine years later the Egyptian priests would be wecoming Alexander as a liberator. But the supposed Persian decadence does not explain everything.

AT THE FRONTIERS OF HELLENISM

The peripheries of the Hellenic world seem marginal only because of the nature of our literary sources, which are all centred on the Aegean Sea. Epigraphic discoveries have shown that in reality the fate of the Greeks was played out on its borders, where the political regimes and the cultural contacts that were developing would dictate the future. A phenomenon that our documentation's strong focus upon the central zone of Hellenism partly obscures emerged clearly in the fourth century: the great hegemonic cities were fighting over a space that had been occupied for a very long time and whose frontiers were shrinking in the east and stabilizing in the west. The territorial stagnation of a civilization that remembered its unity only during the brief calm periods of the Olympic Games was encouraging a relative over-population, and this cast upon its highways many mercenaries and robbers. The only people trying to look ahead to see a future that would somehow have to be invented if the world at war was to become a world at peace were men such as Plato, Xenophon and Isocrates. Deeply conservative, they sought for new inspiration in a return to the legendary sources of Hellenism. Naturally enough, they turned their attention to regions that had never ceased to constitute a laboratory for political experiments, the old colonial world in which relations with Barbarians were a part of everyday life.

The problem was the following: what constitutional hypothesis could provide the basis for a city capable of becoming the centre of a vast, polyethnic territorial State in which warfare would be banished to beyond its frontiers, within which social conflicts would, solely through political debate, be resolved by a fair distribution of the communal wealth? During this period, Rome was coping with Gallic invasions and was a long way away from zones of contact with Magna Graecia. But archaeological excavations show that in Italy, and in Celtic, Thracian and Scythian countries, as well as in Asia and Africa, the cultural influence of Hellenism had already reached many peoples. Their ruling classes, at least, lived in an artistic environment in which Attic pottery was to be found alongside bronze or gold vases inspired by local traditions. These peoples nevertheless preserved their own identities by developing a vigorous reaction of anti-acculturation that initially stabilized cultural frontiers, but later rolled them back. The more their cultural standards rose, the closer they came to perfecting military techniques capable of rivalling those of the Greeks and then of overcoming them through sheer weight of numbers. That is why at this point, as historians, we need to return to the fourth-century colonial world.

AROUND THE BLACK SEA AND THE STRAITS

Our documentation, which stems from the major preoccupations of the Athenians, leads first to the extreme north of the Black Sea. The route for convoys of cereals passed through three groups of city-ports: to the north of the Black Sea (Tanais, Panticapaeum, Tauric Chersonesus, Olbia Pontica); to the west of the Black Sea (Istrus, Tomi, Callatis, Odessus, Apollonia Pontica) and to the north of the Straits (Byzantium, Perinthus, Sestos); and to the south of the Black Sea and the Straits (Trapezus, Amisus, Sinope, Heraclea Pontica, Chalcedon, Cyzicus, Lampsacus, Abydus).

The most northern station, Tanais, at the mouth of the Don, was in the fourth century inhabited by a population that was 'Helleno-Scythian' (an expression that Herodotus uses in connection with the Callipidae, to the north of Olbia), at least to the extent that the pottery and other items of material evidence reveal both Greek and Scythian influences.

The kingdom of the Cimmerian Bosphorus, founded in 438 by Spartocus, who chose as its capital Panticapaeum (Kertch), lies on both sides of the straits leading to the Azov Sea. The Cimmerians had a bad reputation that had been established in the Assyrian annals well before the foundation of Panticapaeum: in the seventh century they had invaded Lydia and Palestine and pushed on as far as Egypt. The reputation of the nomadic Scythians, who had followed them as far as Media, was no better. A good example of the relentless defamation practised by the Athenian orators is provided by Aeschines, who called Demosthenes 'a Scythian barbarian who speaks Greek . . . descended through his mother from Scythian nomads', simply because his grandfather, banned from Athens during the Peloponnesian War, had been given a village by the 'tyrants' of the Bosphorus (*Against Ctesiphon*; *On the Embassy*).

The Spartocids kept out of Greek affairs, but were courted by cities concerned for their food supplies. From Satyrus (393–389) the Athenians obtained priority for the loading of their convoys, which amounted to a monopoly in times of shortages. His son Leucon (398–389) was given the title of citizen by the Athenians and sent them wheat during the famine of 357. His grandsons Spartocus II (348–344) and Paerisades I (348–310) were awarded a decree of praise which gave them the right to enrol crews for their fleet in Piraeus. These titles given to the Bosphorus rulers are revealing, but of what? In Aeschines' eyes they were 'tyrants'. But in inscriptions Leucon is called 'archon of the Panticapaeans', 'archon of the Bosphorus and Theodosia and ruler of the Sindae, the Taurii, the Dandarians, and the Psessae'. Did this reflect the past or the future? It was probably just a sign of the political vocabulary not keeping up with the evolving colonial situation, in which territorial units were to be found that included both Greek cities and Hellenized indigenous populations, under the authority of a hereditary sovereign (the same indecision appears in Caria, where Mausolus is concerned: in the inscriptions of Mylasa he is a 'satrap'; but the Greek authors call him a 'dynast', 'archon' or 'tyrant').

Archaeological exploration at Tauric Chersonesus (Sebastopol) has revealed the regular quadrilinear layout of the streets and the division of the land into civic allotments, quadrangles bordered by low stone walls and reached by roads running parallel to the network of urban streets, each with a farm and a vinyard. The case of Olbia Pontica is quite different: the town plan (acropolis, lower town, agora) follows the irregular layout of more ancient foundations. Roads fan out from the town, leading to villages that were no doubt inhabited by 'Helleno-Scythians'.

IN THRACE

The group of cities along the Thracian coast adapted their external policies to the military ups and downs in the Aegean Sea. Thus Byzantium, occupied in 405 by a Spartan garrison, recovered its liberty in 393, joined the second Athenian confederation in about 378, left it in 364 and sparked off the 'war between the allies' in 357.

Even more remarkable was the role played in the region by the kingdom of Thrace, which had become established between the Strymon, the Danube and the Black Sea following the departure of the Persians in 478. Under the sovereignty of the king of the Odrysians, this Hellenized State incorporated peoples some of which still kept a king of their own, particularly in the mountainous regions and the Danube delta. When the central power was weak, they resumed their liberty. Seuthes I, who became king in 424, levied from the coastal cities and from his own subjects tribute that, according to Thucydides, sometimes amounted to as much as 400 talents (that is, as much as the average tribute levied from the Delian League). Thanks to their silver mines, the Odrysians were already minting coins of the Greek type by the end of the fifth century. The encomium devoted to King Hebryzelmis by the Athenians in 386 praised the beneficence of his ancestors. At this date, with only Lemnos, Imbros, and Skiros left in its possession, Athens was desperately in need of an alliance that would guarantee the safety of its convoys. But when Timotheus regained a footing in Thracian Chersonesus, King Cotys I went to war and installed a garrison in Sestos (362). After his assassination in 360, possibly instigated by the Athenians, who bestowed the rights of citizenship upon his murderers, Thrace split into three kingdoms: one stretching from the Black Sea to the Hebrus, one between the Hebrus and the Nestus, the third between the Nestus and the Strymon. Athens was hoping to play them off one against another. In 357 a treaty concluded with the three kingdoms authorized them to levy the traditional tribute from the cities in their own territory. The cities of Chersonesus, which were now returned to the Athenians, who immediately collected the tribute, were declared free and autonomous. The situation thus created was to be short-lived, but the Athenians did not know that.

IN ASIA MINOR

The Black Sea cities subjected to the Persians witnessed some interesting events. At the time of the retreat of the Ten Thousand, Xenophon had noticed that Sinope had set itself up as a 'micro-empire' composed of a number of cities that paid it tribute (Cotyora, Cerasus, Trapezus). In Bithynia, Heraclea Pontica, despite its modest territory, armed a large war-fleet, with which it was able to go to the aid of Tauric Chersonesus. Its oarsmen were rural dependents. In 364, after a number of political crises, a former pupil of Plato and Isocrates, Clearchus, founded a dynasty there with the support of the *dèmos*, which chose him as *strategos* with full powers. He confiscated the land of the oligarchs who had been executed or exiled, liberated the dependents who had been cultivating it and gave them their former masters' wives and daughters in marriage. He remained loyal to the Great King during the revolt of the satraps. His friend Timotheus obtained him citizens' rights in Athens. His dynasty lasted up until 285.

IN AFRICA

On the Mediterranean coast of Africa two ancient foundations, Naucratis and Cyrene, were flourishing in the fourth century. Naucratis, on the most western branch of the Nile, still maintained its monopoly over exports to Greece. It was a cosmopolitan trading port that had passed without trouble through the alternating periods of Egyptian independence and Persian domination, always useful to its sovereigns, whoever they happened to be. It presents an example of an autonomous pan-Hellenic city that never was free and soon would have no difficulty adapting to the mould of the Hellenistic cities. The cities of Cyrenaica faced all the risks of isolation in a hostile environment. Whether they were paying tribute to the Achaemenid empire or were free, they prospered under the rule of their oligarchies, accepting the hegemony of Cyrene. The successful cultivation of their civic land enabled them to send large quantitites of cereals to a large number of cities during the famines of Alexander's period (between 330 and 326).

IN THE FAR WEST

Marseilles, situated in relatively similar isolation, practised the same neutrality, preserved its Ionian cults and its oligarchic constitution admired by Aristotle, and boasted of the more or less legendary exploits of its bold navigators. Confined within the narrow limits imposed upon the civic territory by the surrounding relief, it survived the ups and downs of the export trade in merchandise either produced in the Celto-Ligurian interior or in transit through it, where Greek acculturation had long since begun to penetrate. In the mid-fourth century it enjoyed a lasting period of increasing prosperity and added to its ancient trading ports of Emporium (Ampurias, in Spain), Alalia (Aleria, in Corsica) and Hyele (Velia, in Lucania) new ones: Olbia (Hyères), Antipolis (Antibes) and Nicaia (Nice).

In Sicily and Magna Graecia

By reason of its size, its agricultural potential and its ancient colonization, Sicily constituted a likely spot for new experiments, and on this point at least, Plato was not mistaken (see p. 241). Apart from its Greek cities and the Phoenician trading posts in the north-west of the island, Sicily was occupied by three autochthonous peoples (from east to west, the Sicels, the Sicans and the Elymians). So the disaster of 413 should not be allowed to mask what was at stake when Segesta made its appeal to the Athenians. Segesta was a Hellenized Elymian town (where one of the most beautiful of Doric temples still stands), which was at war with Selinus and had at first appealed, without success, to the Carthaginians. After its victory, Syracuse was unsuccessful in its efforts at arbitration in the conflict. Segesta, weary of war, offered to pay tribute to Carthage, in exchange for military aid. In an expedition organized from Motye (Marsala), the Carthaginians destroyed Selinus and Himera despite Syracuse's support for them (408), then Agrigentum (406). The Carthaginians' superiority in the taking of towns (*poliorketika* or siegecraft) stemmed from its use of very large iron-tipped rams mounted on mobile assault towers that were capable of overcoming the defenders posted on a city's ramparts.

Dionysius the Elder

The Syracusans now appointed Dionysius, the assistant of the former conqueror of the Athenians, as *strategos* with full powers (*autokrator*). After occupying Gela and Camarina, the Carthaginians agreed to negotiate peace terms: the western half of the island (to the south as far as Camarina, to the north as far as Himera, comprising the territories of the Elymians and the Sicans) would belong to them (405). Within a few years, Dionysius had extended his hegemony over the entire zone left free by the treaty. The resources in terms of both food and money at his disposal were such that no city could compete with him. He recruited numerous mercenaries, some of them Greek, but also Iberians, Celts, Campanians and Lucanians; he governed with the support of the *dèmos*, confiscated the property of his wealthy opponents, liberated their Hellenized rural dependents and made them citizens. How should his power be defined? For Isocrates, he was 'the tyrant of Sicily'; for Aristotle, he was 'a dynast'; in Athenian inscriptions, he is 'the archon of Sicily'. In 367, after their reconciliation with Sparta, the Athenians and his allies awarded him an encomium and allied themselves with Syracuse. The oath of alliance was pronounced by Dionysius in person, the council, the magistrates and the *strategoi* of the Syracusans. As often happened under tyrants, the civic framework was preserved.

Plato's political mistakes

428 – Plato was born in Athens. He received an aristocratic education and at the age of 20 became a disciple of Socrates.

404 – 'I thought that as soon as I should become my own master I would immediately enter political life . . . In the government, a revolution took place . . . Thirty were established as irresponsible rulers of all. Now some of these were actually connections of mine . . . I imagined that they would administer the State by leading it out of an unjust way of life into a just way . . . I saw how these men, within a short time caused men to look back on the former government as a golden age' (Letter VII, to Dion's associates and friends).

403 – 'But in no long time the power of the Thirty was overthrown . . . the exiles who then returned exercised no little moderation. But as ill-luck would have it, certain men of authority summoned our comrade Socrates before the law-courts . . . on the charge of impiety . . . and condemned and slew him . . . So I was compelled to declare . . . [that] the classes of mankind will have no cessation from evil until either the class of those who are right and true philosophers attains political supremacy or else the class of those who hold power . . . becomes, by some dispensation of Heaven, really philosophic' (*ibid.*).

388 – Foundation of the Academy. His teaching had a political purpose.

387 – At the invitation of Dionysius the Elder, whose young brother-in-law Dion was smitten by philosophy, Plato visited Syracuse. He displeased the tyrant, whom he criticized for the immorality of his entourage. Having been expelled on a ship that landed him on Aegina, then at war with Athens, he narrowly escaped being enslaved.

375 – In *The Republic*, he set out his ideal of a perfect city.

367 – Dionysius the Younger succeeded his father and chose Dion as his adviser. Plato returned to Syracuse. But then Dion was suspected of coveting power for himself, and was exiled.

357 – Dion seized Syracuse and became tyrant. After three years of clumsy authoritarianism, he was assassinated.

350 – In *The Laws*, a wiser Plato suggested simply improving the existing regimes.

Three times Dionysius the Elder tried to repulse the Carthaginians. In the first war (397–392), he captured Motya by storming it (using catapults firing arrows and towers on wheels, for the first time) then razed it to the ground. By way of reprisals the Carthaginians, who were supporting the rebellious Sicels, destroyed Messina. Dionysius managed to save Syracuse with the support of the Peloponnesian fleet, and obtained a peace agreement that confirmed his dominion over the Sicels. To reduce irredentism, he expelled the inhabitants of Catana and replaced them by his Campanian mercenaries. A second conflict (382–374), in which Syracuse supported an uprising of Elymians and Sicans against Carthage, ended with the frontier being pulled back to the Halycus river (Platani), to the west of Agrigentum. In the last year of his life, Dionysius tried to eliminate the Punic zone altogether. The peace concluded by his son Dionysius the Younger, in 367, confirmed the existing frontier. Carthage was to retain its hold over about one-third of Sicily until the period of the Punic Wars.

Dionysius' ambitions were not limited to his own island. By repopulating Messina with colonists brought in from Epizephrian Locri (the Locri in Catana) and a few Messenians from Naupactus, he upset the policies of Rhegium (Reggio), which wanted to control both sides of the Straits of Messina. The cities that belonged to the Italiot League, designed to contain the peoples of southern Italy (Samnites and Lucanians) supported Rhegium. Locri sided with Dionysius, who won two victories in Calabria over the Italiot army (389). Eventually Rhegium capitulated; in 378 the Italiot League accepted Syracusan hegemony. At this point Dionysius himself took over the objectives of the dissolved league and laid waste the territory of Agylla (Caere, to the north of Rome), so as to fend off the 'threat' of the Tyrrhenians (Etruscans).

With similar aims, he set about gaining control of the entrance to the Adriatic. The idea of a hegemony established on both banks of the Otrante channel (which was barely 60 kilometres wide at its narrowest point) was justified by geography. The Greeks thought of it long before the Romans. Between Bari and Ancona the Italian coast had no anchorage points and was disadvantaged by shallows. Merchant vessels would put into the Albanian coast at two prosperous cities from which exports penetrated deep inland. One was Apollonia (close to Fieri, at the mouth of the Aoos), the other Epidamnus (later Dyrrachium or Dürres), both founded at the end of the seventh century, by Corinth and Corcyra respectively. They would then follow the Illyrian coastline as far as the islands of the Dalmatian archipelago, where they paused at Corcyra Melaina (Korcula), founded by the Cnidians in the seventh century, opposite the mouth of the Neretva. Eventually they reached the trading ports of the Po delta, Adria and Spina, where the Greeks had long been established. By collaborating with Paros, Dionysius colonized Issa (Vis) and Pharos (Hvar). He then formed an alliance with Bardylis, the king of the Illyrians (whose territory, bounded by Epirus, Macedonia and Thrace, extended as far as the Neretva in Herzegovina). In 385, thanks to mercenaries and hoplite troops provided by Dionysius, Bardylis restored to his throne Alcetas, the king of the Molossi in Epirus, who had taken refuge in Syracuse. Collaboration between Greeks and Illyrians seems to have been a recent phenomenon, the earliest instance having been in Epidamnus, in the years preceding the

Peloponnesian War. Thucydides mentions that, having been reduced to ruins by neighbouring Illyrians, the city was divided by a civil war. Banished by the *dèmos*, the aristocrats joined forces with the Barbarians and laid siege to it by both land and sea, with the support of the Corcyran fleet. The *dèmos* seems to have emerged victorious.

DIONYSIUS THE YOUNGER

When Dionysius the Younger chose Dion as his adviser, it seemed the right moment to establish a Platonic republic in Syracuse (see p. 241). But Dion, suspected of plotting with Carthage, was then exiled. His return in force sparked off civil war and put an end to the Syracusan hegemony. The restoration of Dionysius the Younger in 346 simply increased the bloody conflicts. An old friend of Dion's, Hiketas, the tyrant of Leontini, appealed to the Carthaginians, who sent a fleet to the Straits of Messina. The Corinthians, who up until then had avoided all involvement with their former colony, now entrusted to a member of their oligarchy, Timoleon, ten triremes and several hundred mercenaries. By the time he was greeted in Tauromenium (Taormina) by the tyrant Andromachus (the father of the historian Timaeus, one of Plutarch's sources), Hiketas held the town of Syracuse, Dionysius the citadel. Dionysius abdicated after surrendering the citadel to the Corinthians, who then liberated the lower town. Eventually, after two failed Carthaginian expeditions, Hiketas was captured and executed. A new treaty confirmed the status quo of the frontiers (339).

TIMOLEON

Timoleon established an oligarchy in Syracuse. The direction of affairs was entrusted to a council elected from the highest census class. The army was commanded by a college of *strategoi* who, in the event of invasion from outside, would be placed under the orders of a Corinthian general-in-chief. Timoleon resettled the towns ruined in the war, recalled those who had been banished and recruited new citizens from the Greek world, distributing land to as many as 60,000 of them, according to a source cited by Plutarch. According to Thucydides, Corinth considered settling the affair of Epidamnus in similar fashion, sending new colonists to the besieged inhabitants of the town, where they (the colonists) would be granted equal citizens' rights. Such operations for reinforcing civic bodies were to be called 'politography' in the Hellenistic period.

Making the most of these disorders, the peoples of southern Italy increased their pressure on the cities of Magna Graecia. Tarentum appealed for help first to Phalaecus and the remainder of his Phocidian mercenaries (345), then to Archidamus, the king of Sparta, who fought on in Italy until his death in battle (338). The king of the Molossi, Alexander I, then took his place. For three years he was victorious, defeating the Lucanians, who were allied to the Samnites. But, suspecting him of aspiring to tyranny, the Tarentines dismissed him. He then got himself entrusted with the hegemony over the Italiot League, coming to an agreement with the Romans, who were also at grips with the Samnites, for the control of Campania. He died fighting the Lucanians (330), while his nephew Alexander the Great was finally overcoming the Great King. Fate had decreed that the first contact between Rome and a Greek sovereign should be a missed opportunity.

AGATHOCLES

After Timoleon's withdrawal in 337, civil war soon broke out once more. One of the 'new citizens' of Syracuse, Agathocles, put a stop to it. Having been appointed *strategos* with full powers by Dionysius (317), he re-established Syracusan hegemony in Sicily and found himself at war, yet again, with the Carthaginians (311). Routed by a superior enemy force, he took a chance, landed at Cape Bon, and took his revenge beneath the very walls of Carthage, with no adverse consequences. A final treaty then stabilized the Punic frontier in Sicily (307), after which, to be up to date with the fashion, Agathocles took the title of king, without in any way modifying the Syracusan institutions, then seized Corcyra, which he gave as a dowry to his daughter when she married Pyrrhus, the king of Epirus (295). By the time he was assassinated, in 289, he had restored democracy in Syracuse. Everything reverted to the way it used to be. Greek Sicily continued to prosper. Rome emerged victorious from the Samnite Wars. Following the adventures of Agathocles through to their conclusion, thereby slightly spilling over into the Hellenistic period, has shown the degree to which the western Mediterranean remained preoccupied with its own problems, already distant from the event of crucial importance to history in general, namely the Macedonian conquest of the Achaemenid East.

IN NORTHERN GREECE: EPIRUS

On either side of the Pindus, two 'northern countries still steeped in old traditions' (G. Glotz) defended the frontiers of Hellenism. Not that the cities showed any gratitude. Not until Polybius was their contribution recognized: 'Who is there who does not know that Greece would be permanently exposed to grave dangers were it not protected by the ramparts that the Macedonians constitute for it?' Only from the time of King Alexander (about 343–330) did Epirus become a unified political entity. Before then the Molossi formed a federation of tribes (*koinon*, 'community') led by the Aeacid dynasty. Their mythical ancestor, Neoptolemus, the son of Achilles and a descendant of Aeacus, was believed to have conquered the country. The king swore to govern 'according to the laws' and his subjects swore to support the royal rule, also 'according to the laws', laws supposed to have been made by King Tharpis, following a visit to Athens (at the end of the fifth century). If the king did not abide by his oath, the federal asembly (*ecclesia*, or simply 'the Molossi') could depose him (which is what happened in the case of Alcetas, re-established by Bardylis, the king of the Illyrians, in 385). The king was flanked by the '*prostatès* of the Molossi', a magistrate elected annually by the tribe members, an aristocratic council and a college in which all the tribes were represented. This perfected constitution 'contrasts sharply with the semi-barbarian reputation usually ascribed to this kingdom' (P. Cabanes). The creation of a confederation or symmachy (*symmachia*) of Epirots followed the incorporation of a number of Greek cities situated at the entrance to the Gulf of Ambracia. The three principal components of the confederation, the Molossi to the east, the Thesproti to the south-west and the Chaones to the north-west, were not tribes but allied peoples, who minted their own coins and enjoyed autonomy, just as cities did. Far from constituting a volatile mixture like the symmachies of the classical type, Epirus became a stable state, with institutions that evolved innovative procedures for the pacific integration of new members.

THE CASE OF MACEDONIA: A COUNTRY, A PEOPLE, A MONARCHY

The historical centre of the Macedonian kingdom was the plain crossed by the lower course of the Axius and the Haliacmon rivers. In the classical period its frontiers extended to the point at which they divide to flow into the Gulf of Salonica. The Macedonians spoke a little-known dialect, some peculiarities of which were apparently close to the Thessalian and Boeotian dialects. When he referred to the peoples of Epirus and Macedonia as Barbarians, Thucydides quite wrongly restricted Hellenism to the world of the cities. The Macedonian dynasty claimed to be descended from Heracles via the Temenids, who had moved to Macedonia from Argos. The Macedonians credited them with the initiation of their expansion. Macedonia was thus by definition the territory conquered by the Macedonians under the leadership of the Temenids. In other words, the army was the fundamental institution. It seems to have been organized during the Persian Wars, when a number of Macedonian contingents were integrated into the invading Persian forces. The peasants incorporated into the light infantry were known as *pezhetairoi* ('foot companions'), which according to the lexicographers means that they became the 'warrior companions' of their king. In the absence of more information, it seems reasonable to suppose that, like the army, society was divided into a powerful cavalry, the 'Companions' in the full sense (*hetairoi*) and a peasantry that was free but politically weak, upon whose support the king could call when he clashed with his over-ambitious nobles. The Persian retreat provided the opportunity to annexe the people of Upper Macedonia (from north to south, the Paeonians, the Pelaginians, the Lyncestians, the Orestians and the Elimiots) and eastern Macedonia (the Bysaltians) up as far as the Strymon. According to Thucydides, these vanquished peoples became Macedonian in so far as they were allies and subjects, that is, they paid tribute, meanwhile – as under the Persians – retaining their ethnic autonomy (so that an individual might declare himself to be a 'Macedonian Lyncestian'). Their kings (Xenophon refers to one of them as 'the archon of Elimaea') reasserted their liberty whenever the central power betrayed signs of weakness.

The authority of the monarch depended on the possession of religious and military techniques that ensured victory (a notion that was to be passed on to the Hellenistic monarchies). The sovereign himself performed the functions of priest for his people, offering up daily sacrifices. In times of war he would assume personal command of the army. In order to accede to royalty, a claimant to the throne had to obtain the consent of the assembly (the *ecclesia*, or simply 'the Macedonians') in the manner known to Homer (the assembly would express itself through applause, silence or boos). In the absence of any rules governing the succession, and given a royal family that practised polygamy, the Macedonian assembly would legitimize one of the claimants from the dynasty, designate a regent, or revoke an inefficient sovereign and transfer the royal title to another. In practice it contented itself with acclaiming whoever had managed to get himself accepted by the 'Companions' who sat on the Royal Council (often by force, by having his rivals executed or assassinated). In times of normality the king ruled on his own, assisted by his council (*synedrion*). The assembly possessed no powers (of a legislative or judicial nature) that would limit the hereditary prerogatives of the dynasty. It was useful to the king in times of war, when he needed a concrete demonstration of popular approval. (According to Diodorus, Philip II, in the dire conditions of his accession to power, spent an entire winter building up the trust of the Macedonians. He trained them for combat himself, and frequently convoked assemblies; later, Alexander was to make the army assembly his accomplice in his personal settling of accounts.) The authority of the monarch was thus autocratic, yet the king was not a despot, so long as he conformed with the Macedonian *nomos* (that is to say, with non-written ancestral customs). In so far as a nation is understood in the long run to integrate peoples of different origins, either willingly or by force, you could say that the Macedonian monarchy was 'national' (A. Aymard).

Archelaus (413–399) reorganized the kingdom's defences. He constructed many forts, opened up routes through the forests and trained the infantry in hoplite combat. He attracted to his new capital, Pella, the flower of intellectual Hellenism (Euripides died there). But following an unfortunate expedition to Thessaly, to take aid to Larissa, he was assassinated. The next forty years were dominated by dynastic conflicts. Amyntas III (393–370) was subjected to two invasions by the Illyrians, to whom he was forced to pay tribute. Perdiccas III (368–359) tried to reconquer upper Macedonia from the Illyrians under Bardylis, but the expedition ended in disaster, with the king killed.

PHILIP II

When Philip, at the age of 23, was appointed guardian of his nephew Amyntas IV, proclaimed king while still a child, Macedonia was under threat from all four points of the compass: the Illyrians in the west, the Paeonians in the north, the Thracians in the east and the Athenians in the south. Inside Macedonia he was faced with competition from five rivals, three half-brothers and two cousins, who had earlier been manipulated against Perdiccas III by the Athenians. As the external threat was pressing, Philip was given the royal title (359). He began by buying time in the east and the north by paying tribute to the Thracians and the Paeonians. Then he neutralized the Athenians by withdrawing the Macedonian garrison that had been sent to help Amphipolis against Timotheus. According to Diodorus, it was during the winter of 359–358 that Philip created the Macedonian phalanx. As Polybius describes it, it combined two new techniques: heavy weaponry (the spear, the *sarissa*, was greatly lengthened, from 2 to 7 metres; and a small convex shield was attached to the shoulder by a strap) and the depth of the phalanx was increased to sixteen rows, all bristling with spears.

In the spring of 358, Philip won his first victory, over the Paeonians; their king reverted to accepting Macedonian suzerainty. Then he crushed the Illyrians in a battle that was memorable in military annals, in which he had both his infantry and his cavalry attack the weak points of his opponent, his flanks and his rear. The frontier between Macedonia and Illyria was pushed back to Lake Ohrida (Lychnitis). The combined use, in all seasons, of the war fleet, the cavalry, the phalanx and the light-armed troops and bowmen, together with siegecraft (borrowed from the Carthaginians by Dionysius of Syracuse) was to remain the hallmark of Macedonian tactics, to the immense chagrin of Demosthenes, who did not realize this until too late (*Third Philippic*). The balance of forces was beginning to shift. Philip immediately turned on Amphipolis, the possession of which was strategically crucial for Macedonia. After a few weeks' siege, the Macedonians took this fortified town that had been fending off the Athenians for over sixty years. They then took Pydna. Philip entered into alliance with the Chalcidian League, promising it Potidaea. In that same year he married Olympias, the granddaughter of Alcetas, the king of the Molossi. The two kingdoms from that time on made common cause against the Illyrians.

At this point Crenides, a Thasian foundation in the gold-mining district of Mount Pangaeus, under threat from the Thracians, gave itself to Philip. He reinforced it with Macedonians and refounded it, giving it his own name, Philippi. The Athenians, at war with their allies, improvised a last-minute alliance with the Thracians, the Paeonians and the Illyrians. Philip, who was busy with the siege of Potidaea, sent his second-in-command, Parmenion, to repel the invaders. Anecdote has it that in the very same month that Potidaea fell and was handed over to the Chalcidians, the

Mercenaries and money

The adventures of Agesilaus, who ended his career in the service of the king of Egypt, illustrates the unfortunate lot of Greek mercenaries in the fourth century. In 380 Isocrates, borrowing the expression with which Tyrtaeus, the Spartan poet of warrior courage, had evoked the hopeless destiny of any outlaw, bewailed the plight of the mercenary without employment 'wandering abroad with his wife and children' (*Panegyric*). In the middle of the century Plato cited the very same elegy: 'In the war of which Tyrtaeus speaks, there are vast numbers of Mercenaries ready to die fighting "with well-planted feet apart" of whom the majority, with but few exceptions, prove themselves reckless, unjust, violent and pre-eminently foolish' (*Laws*, Book I, 630B). War was not what it used to be.

Only States with plenty of money could employ mercenaries. Their wages were paid out of the booty that such cities possessed in great abundance. First though, they had to be recruited at great cost (between 1,000 and 1,500 talents were spent in this way during the 'war between the allies', and all for nothing). It has been noticed that certain issues of coins were minted to coincide with military expeditions (Carthage minted its first silver *tetradrachmae* during its struggle against Dionysius the Elder).

Demosthenes produced a lucid analysis of the vicious circle to which some cities committed themselves. The professionalism of troops permanently available, their manoeuvrability in action, in which they could be deployed in successive waves, and their mobility in battle were all advantages that favoured a 'tyrant' such as Philip, who did not have to account for his actions to anybody. In contrast, in cities mercenaries would betray or encourage movements of sedition; meanwhile *strategoi*, forced into financially viable stratagems (the praises of Timotheus were sung for winning victories at very low cost), tended to loosen their links with their city.

In 356 the looting of the treasure of Delphi (estimated at 10,000 talents) enabled the Phocidians to recruit initially 10,000 and eventually 20,000 mercenaries. In 338, 15,000 mercenaries reinforced the 30,000 citizen-soldiers mustered against Philip. In 336, 50,000 Greeks fought against Alexander in the Persian ranks.

young king also learned first of Parmenion's victory, then of the birth of his son Alexander (July 356). The next year he captured Abdera and Maronea, then laid siege to Methone, which capitulated in 354. Traumatized by the failure of their second confederation, the Athenians failed to perceive the danger. Isocrates (*On Peace*; *Areopagitica*) naively declared that in order to live at peace with Philip, Athens had only to give up all its imperialistic aims. It is true that Philip did not present himself as an aggressor: he had the Potidaeans sold into slavery but let the Athenian garrison go free without a ransom.

In this first phase of his political action, Philip had pursued the aspiration of territorial continuity (introduced by King Cotys I in 362, when he had opposed the return of cleruchs in the Thracian Chersonese). Such a strategy depended upon the stabilization of defendable frontiers. The Achaemenid example showed that the geopolitical dominance of a State was ultimately determined by its own resources, that is, its ability to defend the space it occupied against all aggression and to administer it, maintaining the public security and agricultural prosperity of its provinces. From this point of view, Darius the Great's decision to turn Thrace into a satrapy was a mistake. If it was really necessary to protect the northern frontiers of the empire against the Scythians of Europe, it would have been more economical to obtain the neutralization of the cities and peoples on the European shore of the straits by means of a network of unequal treaties, as Artaxerxes II understood perfectly when he created his 'King's Peace'. Territorial continuity simplifies the problems of defence so long as methodical care is taken to strengthen the cohesion of the subject peoples. Philip II had thus returned to the policies of Archelaus. He installed Macedonian garrisons in the strongholds of Illyria, transferred whole populations to resettle devastated cities, and settled in towns mountain peoples previously accustomed to move around seasonally with their flocks. In such conditions attacks from the sea eventually collapse, once the invaders have exhausted their military means and overstretched their lines of communication. Then all you need to do is exploit their divisions. In this respect, the Greek cities had always been ideal stakes.

THE AGE OF ELOQUENCE

In the space of two generations half a century apart, with Lysias, Andocides, Isaeus and Isocrates (born in the 430s) and Demosthenes, Aeschines, Hyperides and Lycurgus (born during the 380s), Greek literature entered the great period of orators (*rhetores*). The audience was still the *dèmos*, but a *dèmos* that had lost its illusions and wanted to hear about its problems. What was the use of the equality of majority voting, recovered at great cost after two oligarchic *coups d'état*, if unfavourable economic conditions precluded converting that into social equality? The primary concern of every citizen was his *oikos*, his household: it was at this point that the word 'economy' (*oikonomia*) made its appearance.

The literary sources that tell us of fourth-century political thinking reflect the disillusionment fostered by both the democrats and the oligarchs, whose ideas had produced such fiascos. In the previous century, the improvised speeches of the great *strategoi* had exalted the hegemonic vocations of their cities (at great length in Athens, tersely in Sparta). But after the Peloponnesian War, a *strategos* was nothing but a tactician, who commanded mainly mercenaries and whose chief concern was how to find the money to pay for their wages (see p. 248). The model of political discourse now became the civil legal speech in which recourse was taken to any means in order to wring a condemnation or an acquittal from the popular jury. Since it was essential at all costs to defeat one's opponent, a statesman was bound to study rhetoric, the technique of argument inherited from the sophists, in lessons that were given in return for a fee. (Isocrates complains of the fall in fees: at the time of the Great Sophists a fee could be as much as 10,000 drachmas, whereas he himself asked for no more than 1,000 and his undermining competitors would go as low as 300.)

The arguments had not changed: they were based on facts known to the entire audience and on legal texts. The obligatory reference to objective data was not a pure artifice, for even a fabrication had to be made credible in the eyes of public opinion, which held sway in the law-courts as it did in the theatre. For example, it is interesting to note that all the contemporary authors whose works have been preserved, whatever their generation and political inclinations, be it Aristophanes or Lysias, Plato or Xenophon, Isocrates or Demosthenes, produce the same diagnosis when faced with the return of poverty: this was the worst obstacle to social coherence and it endangered the very city. None can envisage any remedy except moral renewal. They all come up with the same solution: moral regeneration will come from the education of the young (*paideia*). Since the *dèmos* plays its part in designating more or less all magistrates, it is necessary to give priority to the education of those who will exercise power in its name. The trial represented by Aristophanes in *The Clouds* ends in a non-suit: provided it conforms with the moral and religious traditions of the ancestors, the 'new education', philosophy and rhetoric, can supplement the old. At the price of that general consent, which amounted to considerably more than a simple compromise, philosophers and orators would be left in peace, even as they criticized the democracy that allowed them free expression.

PLATO (ABOUT 427–347)

Plato was not a *rhetor*. He was a philosopher, the greatest of all Antiquity, but one who knew perfectly well how to win over an audience. His bequest to us is the Socratic dialogue that gives pupils the impression that they themselves have discovered the concepts of the truth, the beautiful and the good, on their own, while leaving their teachers with the illusion of their own efficacy. Legend has it that his disciples included a whole constellation of famous men, generals, legislators, tyrants, kings' counsellors, scholars and philosophers, and even a woman from Arcadia, but gives no hint as to how the 'wisdom' that he taught them to love (that is the literal meaning of the word 'philosophy') could have led them and their dependents to the contemplative life of leisure that is the supreme goal. At any rate, after him it was no longer possible publicly to present knowledge as a commercial commodity to be sold to the highest bidder without also raising the question of the responsibility of intellectuals in the city.

Plato demanded from his students a kind of moral perfection that presupposed long years of a communal life spent in his company. Like the Pythagorean sect, the Academy was a private religious brotherhood (a *thiasos*) devoted to a cult of the Muses. Positioned close to the sacred wood of the hero Academus, a place long visited by pilgrims, the Academy was approached along a path bordered by tombs, commemorative monuments and sanctuaries, after leaving Athens by way of the Double Gate (*Dipylon*). There the master, who had remained celibate, would talk with a tiny group of privileged followers in a relaxed atmosphere. In this paradise Plato conceived of an ideal city that conformed with justice, which he described in *The Republic*. For individual virtue was not enough; it would make a philosopher a stranger in his own city, which would then be a cave in which people turned their backs on the sun so as to contemplate the shadows. Those who became capable of looking the sun full in the face, in order to reach Ideas, had a moral obligation to return into the community of citizens. Plato produced a long analysis of the economic conditions of life in society: the need for food, lodging, clothing, producers and intermediaries to store, transport and trade the necessary products. Given that these needs are virtually limitless, society naturally tends not to be self-sufficient: that is why the city must impose a restraint that calms down bellicose instincts and limits the warrior function to the defence of the territory. The problem that then arises is how to discover that restraint and how to supervise putting it to work: hence the institution of the 'Guardians'. Carefully selected and specially trained since infancy, they are to be kept at the city's expense, with no possessions of their own, sharing all wives, children and material goods in common, so that no desires born of possessing things can distract them from their sole purpose. In this way, 'Men will live happily, regulating the number of their children in relation to their resources, for fear of poverty or war.'

Plato was prepared to undertake long sea voyages if there was a chance of converting a single aspirant to the vocation of 'Guardian', and right to the end of his life he remained ready to take political action. In the *Laws*, he imagines founding a Magnesian colony in Crete. The number of colonizers is fixed once and for all at 5,040 citizens (the product of seven prime numbers, divisible without remainders into fifty different quotients), a figure that perfectly expresses the geometric relationship between the means of subsistence and a controlled birth rate; the land is cultivated by slaves; craftsmen, sailors, merchants and poets are all excluded from citizenship. Apart from its detailed minutiae, the plan was not a new one: the oligarchic coups had made provision for a more or less drastic reduction of the civic body. Plato had failed to learn from experience just how dangerous Utopias could be. In the last chapters he envisages instituting a 'Nocturnal Council' that would pass judgement on, among other things, individuals secretly denounced for impieties committed as a result of false reasoning, even when their intentions and morality were above suspicion. Such people would be confined in a 'house of correction' where, for five years at least, they would be re-educated appropriately by members of the 'Nocturnal Council'. If such a person had not come to his senses by the end of this confinement, he would be put to death. 'The philosopher who had turned away from the real city after seeing Socrates, out of loyalty to ideas that the city did not accept, agree to die, thus ended up constructing an ideal city in which no Socrates could have lived' (Claude Mossé).

XENOPHON (ABOUT 430–350)

Xenophon suffers by comparison with Plato. Reading him, you feel he is repeating ready-made ideas. Yet his life taught him a great deal, and his experience enabled him to reach beyond the limited horizons of other Athenian thinkers. In their view, Athens was too big since its territory was not defendable, given that it could not be taken in at a single glance. They imagined the city as a besieged fortress, haunted by the possibility of betrayal. Xenophon, for his part, was a man of strong character, toughened by war, accustomed to handling men, whether they were soldiers or agricultural workers. He was an Athenian by birth, but the misfortunes of the time turned him into the very epitome of an outlaw who, on that very account, was more than usually attached to the Hellenic space as a whole. As a mercenary, under the orders of first Cyrus the Younger, then Agesilaus, he fought against his own country at the battle of Coronea. When banished by his compatriots, he serenely composed his Socratic dialogues in the fine estate of Scillus, in Elis, which the Spartans had given him. When ejected by the Eleans, after they had been liberated from Spartan domination, he settled in Corinth.

The *Hellenica* begins as follows: 'After that, and only a few days later . . .' The narrative picks up where Thucydides (also banished) left off. And the book ends, after a desolate description of the battle of Mantinea, with the following words: 'After this battle, the confusion and disorder in Greece grew even greater than they had been before. At this point I am ending my story. Perhaps another will devote himself to continuing it.' The story of Hellenism thus unfolds from Herodotus on in a continuous interpretation which, as the contemporaries of Xenophon saw it, ought to contribute to the education of future generations. What was needed was a description of a harmonious, albeit totally fabricated, civic past that skipped the intermediary period, which continued to unfold amid divisions, and focused upon an undivided city in a reconciled Greece. That is why, in his 'biographies',

Xenophon puts together a collection of examples aimed at the young, in which his didactic intentions justify the most outrageous manipulations (for example, the portrait of the perfect disciple sketched in the *Memorabilia* reappears, identical in every detail, as a description of Cyrus the Great in the *Cyropaedia*, of Cyrus the Younger in the *Anabasis* and of Agesilaus in the funeral oration that bears his name); and in his *Spartan Constitution*, he imagines the model institutions attributed to Lycurgus and concludes by deploring the existing situation in which the Spartans no longer observe the laws that made them great.

In contrast, when Xenophon tackles the concrete organization of the Persian empire, he writes as an expert: he describes the flexible spread of power in the satrapies, and the local autonomy that respected the peculiarities of each people, balanced by the control exercised by the sovereign himself, thanks to the rapid communications and the special envoys supported by the royal army. Achaemenid inscriptions indicate that his analysis was on the whole correct, even on the ideological level. Xenophon thought of everything: he explains how the Great King behaves *vis-à-vis* his Persian compatriots whom he has established in positions of authority over his empire, as a 'dominant ethno-class' (P. Briant) and how the sovereign himself is bound by a contract for government to the Persian elders and the most important magistrates.

In the *Cyropaedia*, the well-brought-up prince becomes the restorer and guarantor of peace in the lands that he has conquered by force of arms. To be sure, his aim is political dominion over the occupied territories, together with its economic consequence, the levying of tribute: Greeks and Persians are in agreement on that definition. But Xenophon has a longer view. Instead of regarding Cyrus as a despot, he attributes to him the possession of the royal art *par excellence*, as defined in Plato's *Politics*, that is, the ability to take care of the human community as a whole. Cyrus appeals to the goodwill of men, whatever people they belong to, by getting them to understand what is in their interest. He suggests a pact that will be advantageous to both parties, according to which they will pay tribute in exchange for peace. In other words, it is possible to conceive of managing a great, poly-ethnic territorial unit if it is founded on the consent of the subjected people. During the conquest of Babylonia, Cyrus is supposed to have harangued a group of prisoners whose lives he had just spared. He reckoned that the beneficiaries of this favour would appreciate the advantages of tranquillity, the source of economic prosperity (which increased the level of tribute) and would observe with indifference foreign armies settling conflicts that did not concern them:

Your obedience has saved your lives. If you behave like this in the future, you will find that nothing has changed for you except your master. You will inhabit the same houses, till the same soil, live with the same women and exercise the same authority over your children as you do today. The only difference will be that you will no longer fight against either us or anyone else. If you are wronged, it is we who shall fight for you. In order that nobody shall order you to take up arms, you have surrendered those that you possessed. To all those who lay down their arms as you have, we guarantee peace, and they shall enjoy all the benefits that we promise them; but we shall march immediately against all those who refuse to surrender their arms to us.

This was in fact also to be the policy of the Hellenistic sovereigns: switch to the name of the new master; that was all there was to it.

ISOCRATES (ABOUT 436–338)

As a professor of rhetoric and a composer of fictitious speeches, Isocrates probably influenced classical education more than anyone else. He claimed to be the best at writing conventional encomia for great contemporary figures (as found in honorific decrees) and even claimed that he had surpassed Pindar, by producing a work in prose just as artistic as his but more instructive to the young. According to him, a well-educated man adapted his own knowledge quickly to unexpected circumstances and more often than not came up with the appropriate solution, not, to be sure, the best in the absolute sense, but the most effective at that particular time.

In his *Panegyric*, in which he sets out the principles of pan-Hellenism, he has no compunction in claiming that the Athenians surpass other men in respect of thought, speech and nobility. They have not kept the gifts of Demeter selfishly for themselves but have shared them with all the Greeks. Furthermore, they have no qualms about recognizing as Hellenes all those who speak Greek and learn Greek ways, without regard for their ethnic origin. His opening passage on 'the universal' conjures up a picture of Athens, clad in its immutable superiority, just as it was in the good old days when the Areopagus ensured the well-being of all (*Areopagiticus*). If fate decreed that an exemplary Athenian be born (one such as his pupil Timotheus), he would condemn imperialism definitively. The liberated would then understand that their sole enemy was the Great King. They would enter into agreements with the king of Macedonia and the king of the Odrysians and found colonies in Thrace for Hellenes threatened with destitution (*On Peace*, 356; *On the Antidosis*, 353).

He was too patriotic to take a direct interest in Macedonia. But once peace was concluded in 346, he applauded the man of destiny. His long life had taught him that only a victorious and unchallenged *strategos* could lead the great expedition against the Persians, from which he believed the salvation of the Hellenes would come. Philip, a descendant of Heracles, who was the benefactor of the whole of Greece, was not linked specially with the Macedonians or with any city in particular. He was free to consider the whole of Hellas as his country. He would be capable of extending the boundaries of Hellenism as far as a line drawn between Cilicia and Sinope; he would found new cities settled by vagabond mercenaries. And, if he followed enlightened advice, this young man would cease to be distracted by endless wars against the Barbarians of Europe. Then all men would be grateful to him, the Greeks whose benefactor he would be, the Macedonians whom he would govern not as a tyrant but as a king, and all the other races that he would deliver from Barbarian despotism and upon whom he would bestow Hellenic protection (*Philip*). In 338, at the age of 98 according to tradition, he congratulated the king of Macedonia on his victory at Chaeronea. The time had now come to carry the war into Asia. 'When you have forced the Barbarians, apart from those who have fought for you, to become the helots of the Hellenes, all that will remain for you will be to become a god' (*Letter to Philip*).

ARISTOTLE (384–322)

It may not seem very logical now to turn our attention to Aristotle and yet to defer studying the greatest of the Attic orators, Demosthenes, given that, according to tradition, the two of them were born in the same year and also died in the same year. But the message of Demosthenes the orator is inseparable from his political action, upon which he embarked in 354. Aristotle, on the other hand, represents the antidote to the eloquence that triumphed with Isocrates. With his scientific mind, skilled at methodically classifying everything, and able to express Hellenism in formulae just at the moment when the classical period was bequeathing it to the future, he appears in the world of the cities like the Stranger in the Platonic dialogues, introducing into the debate the point of view of 'the other'. His father was a doctor at the court of Amyntas II, the king of Macedonia. His mother was a native of Chalcis, in Euboea. In 349 Philip destroyed Aristotle's tiny native city, Stagira, in Chalcidicus. In 367, he arrived in Athens to attend the courses given by Plato, and remained there until the death of his master. He then settled in Assos, in Troas, at the invitation of Hermeias, the tyrant of Atarneus. In 342 Philip entrusted him for a short period with the education of Alexander, then aged 13. In 335 he returned to Athens, where he enjoyed the protection of Antipater, appointed *strategos* of Europe by Alexander. There he founded the Lyceum, organized as a *thiasos* in the same way as the Academy, but situated on the opposite side of the town ramparts (in an arrangement similar to that of the Jacobins and the Cordeliers in French medieval cities). In 323 he left Athens, which was at war with Macedonia, for Chalcis, where he died the following year.

His immense *oeuvre* touches upon every branch of knowledge except mathematics: two treatises on literature (*Poetics, Rhetoric*), twelve on philosophy (seven books on formal logic); *Physics, Metaphysics, On the Soul, Ethics, Politics*; and many scientific works (*On the Heavens, Meteorology*), and a number of studies on *Animals*). The two works that are the most useful to a historian are the *Politics* (written at the end of his teaching career) and, discovered by chance on a papyrus, part of a *Constitution of the Athenians*, one of the 158 treatises composed under his direction by his students, on the political institutions of Greek and barbarian cities and peoples. He sets out not to captivate the reader but to instruct him. His starting-point is a scrupulous observation of reality; next, he laboriously strives to discover general norms. That is how it is that his *Politics* (followed by numerous other works by the Aristotelian School) presents a historian with the primary documentation for which he can seek in vain from other authors, steeped in rhetoric. The first part of *The Constitution of the Athenians* shows that Aristotle does not manipulate his sources: it is easy to make out which are democratically inspired, which oligarchic (for example, a false one such as the 'Constitution of Draco').

His value judgements are inspired by Socratic morality. He contrasts three 'correct' regimes (royalty, aristocracy, republic) to three 'corrupt' ones (tyranny, oligarchy, democracy). Consequently, it turns out that a tyrant converted to philosophy, such as his host Hermeias, is no longer a tyrant but instead a devotee of the Muses (and his execution, on the order of Artaxerxes III in 342, for betrayal in the interests of Macedonia, converted him into a hero).

Aristotle, like Socrates, was hostile to exclusive government by either the rich or the poor. He condemns Spartan oligarchy in radical terms and declares roundly that Lycurgus was not a good legislator: he had set domination and warfare before his city as the supreme good, whereas one ought to aim for leisure and peace; his laws on helotism were a source of constant trouble, and those concerning property had encouraged social inequality and the love of money; he had not ruled on procreation correctly and the civic body had become dangerously diminished (oliganthropy). In a territory capable of feeding 30,000 hoplites, the number of citizens had never risen above 10,000, and by the time of the battle of Leuctra barely 1,000 remained. Worse still, the governors were in fact governed by women spoilt by luxury, who owned almost two-fifths of the cultivable land.

It was Aristotle who formulated the school definition of a city, a community of men who governed themselves, which was independent and self-sufficient. The question that remained to be answered was who was a citizen and how he related to the centre where the power lay. Here experimentation came in again, taking in a wide range of possible solutions, which for the most part combined elements borrowed both from the three theoretically correct regimes and also, unfortunately, from their opposites. Aristotle inclined in favour of 'the ancestral constitution (*Patrios politeia*)', according to which the assemblies and the law-courts were attended by a 'middle class' of well-to-do peasants, capable of arming themselves at their own expense. Magistracies should be reserved for those who had been able to complete the full cycle of the *paideia* and thereby acquire the skills necessary for governing, under the benevolent supervision of the Elders. In practice, even a good political regime ought never to push its fundamental principles to extremes, for fear of eventually becoming intolerable and thereby sparking off sedition (*stasis*). The quest for a constitution that was absolutely the best in ideal conditions was therefore quite a different matter from choosing one that was the best relatively, in the concrete conditions inherited from each city's own past. From this point of view, what had to be avoided at all costs was civil war, by adapting institutions to suit the desires of the greatest possible number of citizens. In other words, good sense required kings and cities to respect the autonomy of particular communities: that was the essential condition for peace.

The conclusion was clear: the orators and the philosophers of the fourth century reflected different sensibilities, but none of them imagined that it would be possible to live anywhere but in a city, whatever its political regime might be, for any regime could be improved without having its principles radically brought into question. The city as an institution was not in crisis. But we know that it was in danger.

Around 350 BC

359 – Macedonia's rise to power

For anyone who knows what followed, the 350s seem a run-up to armed conflict, the outcome of which vastly exceeded anything that the belligerents of the moment could foresee. We know nothing of Philip's ambitions. His mythical ancestry sufficed to justify to him the dream that Isocrates was one day to set before him. As for the Athenian orators, they lacked the criteria to judge a Greek reigning over a whole constellation of barbarian peoples in the process of being Hellenized. His strategy disconcerted them, for they failed to analyse the realities that impinged upon him just as he himself impinged on them.

As a result of being attacked on all sides, Macedonia was poised to become a novelty in the Greek world, a great territorial State whose dynamism would find expression in the political genius of its sovereign. A glance at the map of mainland Greece brings to mind a tidal wave gathering precisely on the borders of peoples with principally pastoral economies, despised for their 'backward' institutions, but Greek nevertheless. The pressure from the Illyrians, the movement southward of the Epirots and the Macedonians, and the descent of the Aetolians towards the Gulf of Corinth were prompted by a gradual demographic growth that led to spontaneous migrations. Archaeological excavations have revealed a trend in town planning that was to lead, in Asia, to the new form of

Hellenistic cities. After three-quarters of a century on the ebb, this wave was not to break until it had swept forward as far as the Indus. Perhaps we really ought to follow H. Bengtson's (as yet unheeded) suggestion and set the beginning of the Hellenistic period back to the 350s . . .

356 – *The path of realism*

The days were past when the Athenians were split into a 'party of the rich' (oligarchs and pacifists) and a 'party of the poor' (democrats and warmongers), although the old clichés did resurface from time to time. Most of the *dèmos* had now been won over by the 'economists'. Those who were neither rich nor poverty-stricken, who did not leave their fields, stalls or workshops to go to the assembly or the law-court unless they received in recompense the three obols that were paid indiscriminately to all citizens present, were of a mind to profit from the dividends of peace without regrets: just so long as the essential situation remained unchanged and they continued to live off the non-citizens.

Isocrates (*On Peace*) and Xenophon (*Oeconomicus*) told them what they wanted to hear. Pauperization was simply a temporary result of unproductive wars. With peace restored, the city would see passing foreigners and metics returning. Isocrates announced that these would double the revenue from taxes, and Xenophon proceeded to enumerate the latter with great precision: taxes on entries to and departures from the commercial port, on purchases and sales, and on residence for metics. The fiscal revenue from the Laurion mines would be increased by leasing out more concessions, in which the rich would invest their money, since it would no longer be wasted in subsidies for warfare. A balanced budget would ensure that civic fees were paid regularly. All surpluses would be used for defence strategies (*stratiotika*) or put into the fund for spectacles (*theorikon*) designed to pay for theatre seats for the poor. If funds still remained after all this – and they surely would – they would be used for public works and religious festivals.

The credit for the undeniable success of this programme must go to a little-known figure, Eubulus, who, according to Plutarch, was the first to devote himself to public finance. None of his speeches, which were probably all improvisations, have come down to us. His enemies were to insist that he was responsible for the mistakes in foreign policy between 356 and 346. By reorganizing the *theorikon* and channelling all surpluses into it, he managed to impose strict management upon all public expenditure. The sharpest financiers heaved a sigh of relief. This was the hour of the bankers, freedmen who employed a servile workforce (the best known being Pasion and his successor Phormion). They had begun their careers as money-changers, then served as intermediaries for naval loans, charging high interest in view of the high risks (shipwrecks, reprisals, pirates, swindlers). Written contracts became valid evidence in commercial lawsuits, in which citizens, metics and passing foreigners all enjoyed the same legal guarantees. To lighten the load of a trierarchy, the system of symmories was introduced, which shared out the cost between the 12,000 wealthiest citizens (Demosthenes was a trierarch three times).

Result: after years of deficit, direct revenue rose from 130 to 400 talents; the fleet had 300 triremes ready to sail; in 352 the Athenians had no difficulty financing the expedition that halted the Macedonian advance at Thermopylae.

351 – The lessons of the Sacred War

In 356 the Phocidians (the inhabitants of a modest territory to the east of Delphi, the principal city of which was Elatea) occupied Delphi by way of taking reprisals for the heavy fines imposed upon some of them, who had been indicted for sacrilege by the Council of the Amphictionia (the association of the twelve peoples that administered the sanctuary of Apollo, in which the majority was held by the Thessalians and their Boeotian allies). The 'Sacred War' was then declared. In their resentment of the Thebans, Sparta, Athens and their allies took the side of the Phocidians. In the following year the *strategos* Onomarchus managed to halt the Amphictionic troops in the passes leading to Delphi. In 353 he entered Thessaly, where he was supported by the tyrant of Pherae, an ally of Athens. Larissa again requested Macedonian aid. Philip suffered two bloody defeats and retreated to Macedonia. Orchomenus and Coronea fell into the hands of the Phocidians. Cersobleptes, the king of the Odrysians, allied himself with the Athenians, who reoccupied the Chersonese. In the following year Philip, on being elected archon of the Thessalian League, routed the army of Onomarchus, who was slain in battle; 3,000 prisoners, condemned as sacrilegious, were hurled to their deaths from the cliff tops. Pherae capitulated. The Macedonians marched on Thermopylae, but 10,000 allied hoplites, landed in the nick of time, held the pass, with reinforcements from the Phocidians provided by Phayllus, the brother of Onomarchus. Philip did not persist. He led his troops to Thrace (over 1,000 km away) to fight Cersobleptes (352). The next few years marked a pause in hostilities.

It was at this point that Demosthenes learned the lesson of the Sacred War and for the first time designated the king of Macedonia as the enemy (*First Philippic*). His writings, like those of the other rhetors trained to earn their livings as advocates, contain defamation, sophistry and naivety too; but nobody else possessed his bitter lucidity in the face of events over which his country had long since lost control. The Athenians had allowed themselves to be caught off their guard by Philip's skilful manoeuvres.

They had spent the time deliberating while he was taking action, and their under-funded forces had arrived too late. The danger was drawing ever nearer. In the Aegean Sea the Macedonian fleet was waging piratical warfare, and at Marathon it had just captured a sacred trireme setting out for Delos. The Macedonians would never desist unless halted at the right moment, as Thermopylae had shown. The orator then suggested making a modest effort: that of maintaining close to the Macedonian coasts a permanent army (50 triremes, 2,000 hoplites, three-quarters of them mercenaries). In vain: his compatriots who, out of habit, had become unreceptive to new ideas, closed their ears to this one too: 'A man from Macedon, who has conquered the Athenians in battle, now controls the affairs of the Hellenes.'

THE MACEDONIAN PEACE: FROM ONE COMMON PEACE INTO ANOTHER (355–336)

THE YEARS OF HESITATION

The conquest of Chalcidicum   After Philip's failure at Thermopylae, a number of Olynthians seem to have tried to exploit the weariness of the soldiers whom he had submitted to such trials in Thrace. They set up two pretenders to his throne, half-brothers of his who had taken refuge in Olynthus. When they refused to expel these, Philip declared war (349). This time the Athenians did agree to follow Demosthenes' advice and sent off an expedition to come to the aid of the Chalcidians (*First and Second Olynthians*). But the 2,000 mercenaries under the command of the *strategos* Chares were unable to repulse the Macedonians, who captured the Chalcidian cities (beginning by destroying Stagira, Aristotle's native city).

A second front was then opened up in Euboea. Eretria and Chalcis left the already depleted Athenian confederation. The assembly dispatched a small army of citizens commanded by Phocion. After a shortlived success, this expeditionary force capitulated. Bitterly, Athens paid the ransom to liberate the prisoners. Demosthenes continued to stress that the main front was in Chalcidicum. Charidemus holed up in Olynthus with 4,000 mercenaries. Then 2,300 citizens led by Chares arrived on the scene, but too late. The city was destroyed, its inhabitants sold as slaves, their lands distributed among the Macedonian nobility. By now the kingdom of Macedonia, fronted by an uninterrupted coastline, held a territory with a population estimated at one-fifth of the total number of the inhabitants of central Greece, out of which 80,000 constituted a potential force of men in a position to compensate for any military losses. The 'Giant City' of Athens, with its 30,000 citizens, was vastly outnumbered (348).

The peace of Philocrates   Both before and after the fall of Olynthus, Philip
had offered to make peace with the Athenians. At the suggestion of Philocrates, the assembly unanimously decided to send an embassy to Pella. When
accused of illegality, Philocrates was defended by Demosthenes and was
acquitted. The data on this embassy are contained in four slanderous speeches
by Demosthenes and Aeschines, both of whom were members of the
ambassadorial delegation. Two were delivered in 343 (*On the Embassy*) and
two in 330 (*On the Crown; Against Ctesiphon*).

Eubulus, hoping to negotiate from a position of strength, during the
winter got the assembly to send ambassadors (one of whom was Aeschines)
to the cities that were still neutral, to persuade them to enter a defensive
alliance with Athens. Without success, for in the spring of 347 the pace of
events speeded up. Phalaicus, the son of Onomarchus, the *strategos* of the
Phocidians since the death of Phayllus, was deposed for corruption. However, he still controlled Thermopylae and now made contact with Philip.
The new rulers of the Phocidians suggested that their allies attempt to
reoccupy the pass. But Phalaicus refused to surrender the fortresses. At this
point the Spartans pulled out of the conflict.

The Athenians had nothing left to offer in return for the liberation of
their prisoners captured in Chalcidicum, except their alliance; but they
wanted at least to include in the negotiations the last remaining members
of their confederation. The ambassadors hastened to Pella, where the king
received them courteously. He undertook to observe a truce in the Thracian
Chersonese for the duration of the negotiations; if these led to an alliance
agreed in due and proper form, the fate of the Phocidians would then be
decided by common agreement. Demosthenes was the only one to sense a
trap: the sole alternative to simply agreeing was to enter upon a war that
was lost in advance.

Philip's two closest Companions, Antipater and Parmenion, were received
in Athens as plenipotentiaries. Two turbulent sessions of the assembly
discussed, then adopted, a text composed by Philocrates: the Athenians
and their allies would enter into an alliance with Philip and his allies; the
partners would abstain from any naval aggression (April 346). Once the
oath had been sworn in the presence of the Macedonian visitors, a second
embassy left for Pella to settle the Phocidian question. The negotiators,
laden with gifts, waited, along with Philip's allies and the representatives of
the Phocidians, for the return of the sovereign, who was busy fighting
Cersobleptes. Once he was back, the Athenians split. Demosthenes, who
was isolated, warned of treachery. So that nobody should be in any doubt
as to the winner in this affair, Philip and their allies swore their oath in
Pherae. The Athenian prisoners were liberated without a ransom.

The Sacred War still had to be brought to an end. Philocrates got the
assembly to pass an ultimatum ordering the Phocidians to evacuate Delphi,
but without result (July). Philip was already at Thermopylae, where the
fortifications were handed over to him by Phalaicus, who was allowed to

go free with his mercenaries. In a belated reaction, the Athenians refused to fight against their former allies. The Macedonians dismantled the Phocidian cities and liberated Delphi, in the name of the *amphictionia*, which would now decide the fate of those responsible for the sacrilege. These were not massacred, but banished: the Phocidians were dispersed into villages and were required to return the value of the treasure of Apollo (paying 60 talents annually until 337, and thereafter 10). Their two votes in the Amphictionic Council were transferred to Philip and his successors. At the suggestion of Demosthenes, who was already meditating his revenge, the Athenians gave their agreement (*On the Peace*, autumn 346).

THE 'DEMOSTHENES YEARS'

The counter-offensive For the time being, the king of Macedonia's main worry was his northern frontier, once again under attack from the Illyrians, now joined for the first time by the Dardanians (from the Skopje valley). The Macedonians emerged as the victors, but only at the cost of heavy losses (345). Philip then strengthened his links with Epirus by installing on the throne of the Molossi Olympias' young brother, Alexander I, who had been brought up in the Pella court (343). He then formed an alliance with the Aetolians, promising them Naupactus, on the Gulf of Corinth. The common front formed by the peoples excluded from the world of the cities was now complete.

During these years, Demosthenes and his friends were preparing a vigorous counter-offensive. Their plan was simple: at all costs to contain the Macedonian thrust; to that end to form a coalition with the greatest possible number of cities against their common enemy; and first of all to convince the Athenians that the artisans of peace had been corrupted by Philip and had betrayed their interests. Philocrates, the first to be accused, fled before being condemned to death in his absence. Next it was Aeschines, accused of the abuse of authority, who spoke in his own defence against Demosthenes (*On the Embassy*). He was acquitted by a tiny majority of votes. But public opinion had by now been won over. It was in vain that Philip sent a series of delegations to calm down the Athenians. As a pledge of his good will, he offered them the little island of Halonnese, between Lemnos and Skyros, which had been liberated from pirates. Demosthenes persuaded the assembly to reject what would, he said, in any case not be a gift, but simply a restitution: old memories of hegemony were resurfacing. The orator now felt strong enough to move on to the second stage (*Second Philippic*). Between 342 and 340 he pulled off a brilliant diplomatic offensive. Euboea was organized into a federal state; Megara, Corinth, Ambracia, Corcyra, and the Acarnanian and Achaean federations formed a line of defence. Having learned that the Odrysians had revolted, the Athenians informed the Great King that they were attached to the 'common peace', and obtained the support of the satraps in the last remaining independent cities of Thrace.

After an extremely hard campaign that forced him to spend the winter in the Hebrus valley, Philip founded a new city to which he gave his own name, Philippopolis (Plovdiv, in Bulgaria), and annexed Thrace as far as the Black Sea and Mount Hemus (the Greater Balkans). The conquered territories became a Macedonian province governed by a *strategos* and defended by a string of fortresses. The little coastal cities acknowledged their submission, among them Cardia, on the narrow tongue of land that linked the cleruchies of the Chersonese and Thrace. Athens sent reinforcements, but without financial means. To procure the latter, the Athenian *strategos* captured some slaves in the territory of Cardia. The last two independent cities of the region, Byzantium and Perinthus, effected a reconciliation with Athens, which refused to criticize the actions of its *strategos* (*On the Affairs of the Chersonese; Third and Fourth Philippics*).

Philip could never remain inactive. He encircled Perinthus and Byzantium, without result, for they were supported by the satrap of Hellespontine Phrygia. Chares, posted at the entrance to the Bosphorus with forty triremes, was ordered to protect the convoys of wheat leaving the Crimea. The Macedonians made a surprise strike and captured 180 Athenian merchant vessels crammed with merchandise and money. At the instigation of Demosthenes, the Athenian people decided that Macedonia had broken the alliance (autumn, 340). Eubulus' law relating to the fund for spectacles was amended: fiscal surpluses could now be used for military funding. The fate of the Greece of the cities was to be decided in a clash of arms.

In the spring of 339 Philip consolidated his new frontier with the Scythians. He had better luck than Darius, and defeated the Scythian king Ateus at the mouths of the Danube. On the return journey he was surprised by the Triballi of the western Balkans and was severely wounded. Nevertheless, the retreat continued in good order by way of the Strymon valley. Upon his return to Pella, he was begged by the *amphictionia* to take command of another sacred war, this time against the Locrians of Amphissa (to the west of Delphi), accused by Aeschines of cultivating the sacred land of Apollo, on which cultivation was forbidden. The Thebans had taken the side of Amphissa and had ejected the Macedonian garrison from Thermopylae. Philip circled round the defile by way of the passes of Mount Ceta and occupied Citenium, in the upper Cephissus valley. Then, instead of proceeding toward Amphissa, he crossed demilitarized Phocis and installed himself where he was least expected, in Elatea, on the road from Thermoplyae to Thebes.

CHAERONEA

Demosthenes had for some time been seeking to detach the Thebans from the Macedonian alliance. In a famous passage in his speech *On the Crown,* he recounts how he won them over. For the first time ever, Athens recognized their hegemony over Boeotia. In the common struggle, they would be in command on land, but would shoulder only one-third of the expenses. That was not too much for Athens to pay for a rallying that might spread into a general uprising. However, apart from the Achaeans, the Peloponnese remained neutral, including Sparta, whose king Archidamus was away in Lucania fighting on behalf of Tarentum (October 339).

Philip's advantageous position forced the coalition to establish a double line of defence in deep midwinter: an army of citizens would defend the pass that led into Boeotia; mercenaries under the command of Chares would man the defence of the route that led towards Amphissa. An old stratagem led this *strategos*, who had been taken by surprise so many times already, to believe that the king had fallen back to the north, to crush an insurrection on the part of the Odrysians. On the orders of Parmenion, the Macedonians turned off towards the pass that had been left defenceless, crossed it by night, massacred the mercenaries at dawn, then took Amphissa (April 338). They then marched through Locris, captured Naupactus from the Achaeans, and gave it back to the Aetolians.

The allies took up their positions at Chaeronea. The opposed forces were probably of equal strength: the victory would depend on the quality of the command. Philip had entrusted his best troops to Alexander, then 18 years old, who was to concentrate the main attack against the right wing of the coalition members, held by the Thebans. On the left wing the Athenians, not understanding the tactics of the king, who was gradually pulling back, believed victory was theirs (one of their *strategoi* is even supposed to have cried out 'Forward to Macedonia!'). Demosthenes, along with his compatriots, overcome from the rear by Alexander, was swept away in the débâcle. On the Athenian side 1,000 were dead, 2,000 taken prisoner, and over 1,000 Thebans had also been killed (August 338).

Promptly seizing the advantage, Philip in his own inimitable way confirmed the 'news' announced thirteen years earlier in the *First Philippic*: he did indeed now settle the affairs of the Hellenes as their master, taking the elementary precaution of dividing them in lasting fashion. The Athenians were in for an extraordinary surprise. The orator Hyperides was preparing them for resistance behind the Long Walls. He offered to those banished the chance to return, to the metics citizenship, and to the slaves who were willing to join the army their liberty. Technically, this strategy was defensible: the Athenian fleet was intact; Artaxerxes III, more powerful than ever after reconquering Egypt, had forced Philip to raise the sieges of Perinthus and Byzantium . . . However, the king of Macedonia made an even better offer: namely to return the Athenian prisoners, leave them Lemnos, Imbros, Skyros, Delos and Samos, and give them Oropos (taking it away from the Thebans), in exchange for the Chersonese. It did not take the Athenians long to choose. Alexander and Antipater solemnly accompanied the ashes of the dead to Athens; the king and his son were given the rights of citizenship, and it was agreed that a statue of Philip be erected on the agora.

The hand of the victor fell more heavily upon the other members of the coalition. He placed Macedonian garrisons in Thebes, Chalcis and Corinth. In the Peloponnese, despite the fact that it had remained neutral, he arbitrated in a number of old quarrels, to the detriment of the Spartans, forcing them to submit by laying waste Laconia all the way to the sea. After all this, it was in vain that Demosthenes railed against the egoism of the other cities who, according to him, had betrayed Hellenism. Two centuries later, when Rome was victorious, the historian Polybius of Megalopolis produced the riposte: '[Demosthenes] judged everything from the point of view of the particular interests of Athens. He thought that all Greeks ought to keep their eyes fixed on the Athenians; if they did not, he accused them of treachery.'

Carrying on the policy   During the winter, a congress organized in Corinth by Philip brought together all the Greek States, with the exception of Sparta. They concluded a new common peace, theoretically of unlimited duration, designed to provide the permanent framework for their future relations, whatever their size and whatever their constitution (*polis, ethnos* or *koinon*). The instrument of this multilateral peace was to be 'a common council of Hellenes' to which the States would delegate representatives, in numbers proportional to their sizes, who would be under no obligation to justify the decisions taken. Executive power would belong to the commander-in-chief (*hègemôn*), the military man responsible for maintaining the peace, namely Philip and his descendants.

The member States received guarantees even greater than those promised to Athens' allies in 377: against any subversion of their political system, against any judgements that did not conform with their own laws (on death, banishment, the confiscation of property, the distribution of land, the annulment of debts, the affranchisement of slaves in the event of threatened revolution). Clearly, whoever decided upon these clauses were men from the cities. Their ambition was to extend the spirit of 403 to the whole of Greece and to banish warfare to beyond the frontiers of Hellenism. Of course, the former hegemonic cities lost the independence that they had used so badly. They all had to trust the man of destiny who was leaving them their autonomy and promising them a lasting peace. The writing was on the wall.

What was not taken into account in these agreements that froze traditional institutions in their existing forms were the social realities that would not, on that account, desist from evolving. Not, that is, unless Isocrates had been right in declaring that the new colonization that he predicted would be a universal panacea. What did the king of Macedonia really want in the spring of 337 when, at the first meeting of the Common Council, he proposed declaring war on the Persians in reprisal for the profanations, by nature indefensible, that Xerxes had committed on the Acropolis in 480? Our sources, which are so loquacious on other matters, have nothing to say on this point. However, we can at least suppose that his advisers were well primed in the classics, and that he himself had been turning the plan over in his mind for some time. The court at Pella was opulent enough to attract numerous literary men, and the contemporary literature is full of anecdotes and daydreams about the East. Constant contacts with Egypt, Phoenicia and Asia Minor had over the past century been encouraging phenomena of acculturation that we might describe as 'proto-Hellenistic'. Philip had had plenty of opportunities to acquire information from Artabazus and Memnon, who had taken refuge at his court in 352, or from the tyrant Hermias of Atarneus, who had been host to Aristotle in 347. Artaxerxes had acted in a resolutely hostile fashion during the campaign against Perinthus and Byzantium, and he had had Hermias executed in 341 for treachery that served the interests of Macedonia. And now, in the summer of 338, he had himself been assassinated. The customary crisis over the succession was not resolved until the investiture of Darius III Codoman in 336.

Philip was not a man to let slip such an opportunity. The Common Council approved his proposal, decided that the member states would supply him with all the triremes, cavalry and hoplites that he needed, and appointed him general-in-chief with full powers. The declaration of war thus gently turned the common peace into a military alliance against the Barbarians. From this date on, it is fair to speak of a second 'Corinthian League'. In the spring of 336 a vanguard of 10,000 men under the command of Parmenion crossed the Hellespont. Their mission was to follow the Aegean coast, liberating the Greek cities as they went. They had reached Magnesia on the Meander river when Philip was assassinated, during the marriage of his daughter Cleopatra to Alexander I of Epirus (summer 336). Alexander, who, on the proposal of Antipater, was proclaimed king by the Macedonian assembly, was just 20 years old.

ALEXANDER THE GREAT (336–323)

THE HERITAGE

In time-honoured Macedonian fashion, Alexander and his mother Olympias began by setting their house in order. All possible claimants were assassinated (including a new-born baby from Philip's seventh and last marriage). Only one half-brother, Arrhidaeus was spared, as he was feeble-minded. Alexander, at the head of an imposing army, took possession of his heritage. He got himself appointed archon for life of the Thessalian *koinon*, took over the two Macedonian votes in the Amphictionic Council, and received from the Common Council of the Hellenes full powers for the war against the Persians.

In the spring of 335 he appeared on the frontiers of Thrace, which had been annexed in 342, harassed the independent Thracians who had blocked the passes on Mount Hemus, crushed the Triballi who, repulsed eastward by the Celts, had arrived at the lower reaches of the Danube, crossed the river at the point where the delta began, under the protection of a squadron sent by Byzantium, and destroyed the capital of the Getae of Dobroudja. The Triballi, the Getae and the Celts in the neighbourhood all acknowledged their submission to him. (It was on this memorable occasion that a Celtic chief is said to have made the proud declaration remembered in so many school text books: 'Now all we have to fear is lest the sky should fall on our heads.') He then crossed the land of the Peonians to repress a predictable Illyrian invasion to the south of Lake Ochrida. He did no more than re-establish the frontier in its previous position as, following a rumour that he had been killed in Thrace, a general uprising plotted by Darius III was being prepared in central Greece. Already the Thebans were laying siege to their Macedonian garrison.

Thirteen days after receiving the news, the young king confronted Thebes with 30,000 infantrymen and 3,000 cavalry. Figures of 6,000 dead and 30,000 prisoners, including women and children, were recorded. Their punishment was fixed by the League of the Hellenes: the town was to be razed to the ground (except for the temples and Pindar's house); the prisoners were to be sold; the civic territory was to be divided up between the neighbouring cities (October 335). When informed of the preparations made by the Athenians, who now proclaimed their loyalty, Alexander initially demanded the banishment of the ten most deeply compromised orators and *strategoi*, including Demosthenes, Lycurgus and Hyperides; then he decided to content himself with only Charidemus, the old leader of the mercenaries. The Common Council left it to 'the little young man', at whom Demosthenes had once jeered, to decide how many allied troops should take part in the expedition to the East: 7,000 infantrymen and 600 cavalry, supported by 5,000 Greek mercenaries (50,000 Greeks fought on the Persian side). In this symbolically pan-Hellenic War, the number of Barbarian contingents (Odrysians, Triballi, Agrianes and Illyrians) exceeded the number of allies.

Alexander had proved himself as a warrior. But was he a statesman? We shall be examining the (affirmative) answer to that question carefully. It helps to explain how it was that his reign produced something completely new, a Hellenistic monarchy, after the collapse of a Persian empire in full possession of all its means, skilfully managed and led by a competent sovereign, which for two centuries 'had supplied the best overall solution to the complex problems of the ethnic and cultural mosaic of the East' (E. Will). For the lasting achievement of Philip's son radically surpassed the ambitions of the man whom he is said one day to have called his 'putative father'.

A great loss assessed: the sources for the history of Alexander

We know of the career of Alexander the Great through four principal authors: Diodorus Siculus (mid-first century AD), Quintus Curtius (late first century), Plutarch (early second century) and Arrian (early third century). Even the most ancient of them was writing three whole centuries after the events. Only short fragments of the Hellenistic histories have come down to us (apart from Polybius). Why? Two chronological poles were studied in parallel by Plutarch: the succession to Alexander and the succession to Caesar, that is to say, the end of classical Greece and the beginning of the period of the Roman empire. And that is the cause of the loss.

Consider the example of what we call 'Greek tragedy': thousands of tragedies had been composed by the end of Antiquity, but three Athenian authors, Aeschylus, Sophocles and Euripides, are the only ones we read; and out of all their 300 or so works, we know only 32 plays. The trouble is that the series is limited to the 'classics', that is, those taught in class for the instruction of pupils. What pupils and in what period? It was in the Hellenistic period that history became 'a part of the programme' of literary instruction, long after Homer, and as an auxiliary to the art of oratory. But the selection of particular 'authors to be included in the programme' dates from the early Roman empire, so it reflects the tastes of a Romanized public. By that time even the professors were bored with the bellicose racket of the Hellenistic sovereigns. In other words, Rome imposed its own definition of classical Greece on us. We had no say in the matter.

The four historical accounts that we possess are summaries. They condense (at the same time adding supplementary information and commentaries of their own) a second-hand work (the 'Vulgate'), composed by Clitarchus at the beginning of the third century BC, which consisted of a résumé of the 'war memoirs' of the Companions of Alexander. What remains of the primary sources after this triple reworking (for the Companions too had a point of their own to defend)? Very little indeed.

CHRONOLOGY OF THE MACEDONIAN CONQUEST

Spring 334   By the time Alexander landed in Asia, the troops sent there by Philip, who had suffered several reversals at the hands of Memnon's mercenaries, still held only one bridgehead between Abydus and Troy, to which the young king immediately went on a symbolic pilgrimage. He had at his disposal forces the size of which varies from one ancient historian to another: between 30,000 and 40,000 infantrymen and between 4,500 and 5,000 cavalry, along with a large number of non-combatants (baggage trains, military engineers, doctors, caterers, chariots and beasts of burden, all travelling in convoy). He was accompanied by a chancellery directed by Eumenes of Cardia, who not only organized his correspondence and made use of documentation gathered in advance, but also kept a day-to-day record, *Ephemerides*, relating the facts and the doings of the king. He was surrounded by men of letters and scholars, historiographers such as Callisthenes of Olynthus, Aristotle's nephew, who directed the school for the squires, geographers, naturalists, translators capable of questioning prisoners and collecting information from local populations, and topographers, known as *bèmatistes* (the 'counters of paces'), who prepared itineraries. The scientific documentation accumulated during the expedition has sadly sunk without trace (see p. 268). But Alexander's pilgrimage to Troy shows that he intended to do his bit for history and legend (considering this to be an aid to government).

The apparent set-back of the Macedonians had decided Darius III to limit himself to the usual precautions taken in cases of Greek invasion: that is, to contain the troops that landed by means of a local counter-offensive organized by the satraps in the theatre of operations; then to carry the war into first the Aegean, then Europe; and to mobilize the royal army with a view to finishing off the war in a pitched battle.

Summer 334 The first phase of this strategy was a complete failure: the satraps of Hellespontine Phrygia and Lydia were defeated on the east bank of the Granicus river. The chief towns of the two satrapies, Daskyleion and Sardis, surrendered. Macedonian satraps then took the place of the Iranian ones. The village officials continued to collect the tribute, but now it was destined for the king of Macedonia and upon his orders. In Hellespontine Phrygia, for example, 'he ordered the inhabitants to pay the same tribute as they were accustomed to hand over to Darius; he invited the Barbarians who had descended from the mountains to make their act of submission and return home' (Arrian, *The Anabasis of Alexander*). In other words, the tribute-paying peoples, whose basic unit of organization was the village (*kômè*), passed from one dynasty to another without upset, so long as their habits remained unchanged. The apathy engendered by the Achaemenid regimes was one of the causes of its rapid collapse.

That very first decision of Alexander's provided the right solution to all the financial problems earlier encountered by the city *strategoi*. The army had at its disposal just one month's provisions and 70 talents, whereas the tribute from the eastern satrapies alone, even in the event of Asia Minor being lost, were bringing the Great King 5,000 talents each year. Military funding would no longer be dependent on booty, which could be left to the soldiers to divide up. The war would now be financed by the ordinary revenues of the royal estate. But this represented no more than the first item in Alexander's political programme, the Asian panel of which rested upon what were conventionally known as the 'rights of war'. In accordance with good Greek logic, victory occasioned a transfer of sovereignty to the victor. Alexander is said to have hurled a javelin on to the beach where he landed, 'thereby signifying that he was receiving Asia from the gods, like booty acquired at the point of a spear' (Diodorus, *World History*).

The other panel of the diptych related to the Greek cities. One by one they were delivered from their Persian garrisons. Alexander forbade the Ephesians to take their own reprisals against the oligarchs sympathetic to the Achaemenids; he alone would be the judge of the punishment to be meted out or the pardon to be granted to traitors. He ordered that those banished be recalled, and that the taxes formerly paid to the Barbarians revert to the tutelary goddess, Artemis. This regime in every detail resembles the contented, undivided city imagined by the rhetors. In the cities as in the countryside, the Macedonian peace replaced the Achaemenid peace. He then issued a proclamation about which there was nothing rhetorical at all: he had embarked on the war in order to bring the Greeks their liberty; he recognized their autonomy (that is, their free choice of their own laws which, in the course of the Hellenistic period, were to tend towards moderate democracy) and exempted them from royal taxation. In return, the coastal cities would have to recognize his sovereignty. They did so, showering honours upon the king.

Ownership of cultivable land (*chôra*) was another reality that should not be confused with sovereignty, as was proved in the summer of 334 by an edict of Alexander's concerning Priene (situated at the mouth of the Meander), which is partially reproduced in an inscription dating from half a century later. The preserved text establishes the fiscal difference between a civic territory and the royal estate. Evidently the general proclamation on the juridical status of the cities of Asia had been supplemented by individual agreements made with each one of them. Those who lived in the localities dependent on Priene (the town, port, fortified places and villages) were Prienians, that is, autonomous, free, the owners of their houses, their land for building and their *chôra*; they were furthermore exempted from the royal tax (*syntaxis*). In contrast, the inhabitants of other villages, listed by name, were dependent upon the royal estate: 'I know that this land (*chôra*) is mine.' These people paid the tribute (*phoros*). Taxation thus drew a fundamental distinction between two real-estate systems: within the cities, plots of land were bought and sold by the citizens, as property-owners; but the king was the landlord of the former estate of the Achaemenids. Considering the cities' frequent inability to balance their budgets (that is, to finance their expenses in a concrete fashion), it would be interesting to know who advised Alexander on this extremely crucial point. It was too soon to designate the personal status of the 'royal peasants'. To refer to them, the Hellenistic documents revived a Homeric word (*laoi*). Suffice it to say immediately, however, that they were to become neither helots nor rural dependents in the manner of the colonial cities.

On the military level, following the capture of Miletus and against the advice of Parmenion, Alexander committed an imprudence by dismissing his landing fleet (160 ships, as against the 400 Persian vessels that were cruising out to sea). In the short term, this premature decision cost him dearly, but it was inspired by a long-term strategy. Given that he could not hope to overcome the Cypriot and Phoenician ships, he was planning to neutralize them by land, by seizing all the naval bases in the eastern Mediterranean. Philip had proceeded in just such a fashion in the coastal cities of Macedonia and Thrace.

Autumn 334   Meanwhile, Darius was realizing the extent of the difference between a king of Macedonia and a king of Sparta. He entrusted full powers on both land and sea to Memnon of Rhodes. The counter-offensive was centred on Halicarnassus, the chief town of the satrapy of Caria, which had a fortified port. Despite his siege machines, Alexander was not able to take it by assault. He left allied contingents to contain this pocket of resistance.

Winter 334–333   Alexander rallied the last cities of the Lycia–Pamphilia coastline. He then advanced, with reduced troops, towards Gordion, where he was to meet up with reinforcements sent from Macedonia (3,000 infantrymen and 650 cavalry) and the major part of the army, which was wintering in Sardis under the command of Parmenion.

Spring 333   The Macedonians had a hard time crossing Greater Phrygia, where they were not successful in overcoming the Persian garrison in the chief town of the satrapy, Kelainai. Antigonus, until then a *strategos* for the allies, was appointed satrap. With 15,000 mercenaries under his command, his orders were to control a vast area in which there were no Greek settlements.

Memnon's counter-offensive was able to develop unobstructed. He had at his disposal his usual advantages: a large sum of money, 300 ships and Greek mercenaries who, since the battle of the Granicus, were well aware of the fate that might await them (those who escaped death would be sent to do forced labour in Macedonia for having taken up arms against other Greeks). Memnon sent negotiators to Sparta and other cities in mainland Greece. Around the Aegean Sea, Chios, Cos, Rhodes and most of the Cyclades made common cause with the Persians. When Memnon died (of disease), Darius replaced him by his nephew Pharnabazus, who recaptured Miletus. Mytilene fell into the hands of Chares, who was now under the orders of the Great King. Learning of this news in Gordion, Alexander himself recognized his mistake (largely prompted by his erudite advisers' jingoistic talk about the decadence of the Persians). A new fleet in the Hellespont would now assure his liaisons with Antipater.

Summer 333   To avoid the fortified strongholds that protected the Royal Way, Alexander branched off in the direction of Cilicia. Behind him he left most of Asia Minor unconquered (Greater Phrygia, Cappadocia, Bithynia,

Paphlagonia and also the cities of the Black Sea coast were all still under Persian domination). He seized the chief town of Cilicia, Tarsis, which had been left undefended by its satrap, who had reckoned it more urgent to get a warning to Darius.

Autumn 333 The Persian army assembled in Babylon was transferred to Damascus, the capital of the satrapy of Transeuphratene, which commanded the routes leading to the Euphrates and Phoenicia. Learning that the Macedonians were occupying the passes leading to the gates to Syria, Darius devised an audacious plan. He moved around the mountains bordering the Gulf of Iskenderun and, from the north-east, entered the plain of Tarsis, which he then proceeded to reoccupy. Caught off balance and with no chance of escaping by sea, Alexander should logically have stuck to his plan of marching across the plain of Damascus, where he would have confronted an opponent with far more numerous forces. But that was not his way of doing things. Instead, he made an about-turn and attacked the Persians close to Issus, a terrain of his own choice, a narrow coastal plain where the Persians would be unable to deploy all their forces. Darius narrowly avoided having to capitulate (November 333). While the Macedonians looted his abandoned camp, the elite of his troops fell back in orderly fashion. Parmenion took Damascus and captured the heavy convoy carrying away the treasure of the defeated Persian army.

Winter 333–332 Once back in his general headquarters in Babylon, Darius mobilized a new army in the central and eastern satrapies. The generals who had escaped from Issus recruited fresh troops in Cappadocia and Paphlagonia. Greater Phrygia was caught in a pincer movement between a large-scale offensive launched from the east and a number of Aegean bridgeheads. The new satraps, Callias in Hellespontine Phrygia, Antigonus in Greater Phrygia, Balacrus in Cilicia and Nearchus in Lycia–Pamphylia, were to restore the situation at the end of the summer.

Spring 332 The Macedonian army continued its advance along the Phoenician coast. The towns that surrendered without a fight retained their kings and their traditional institutions. Those that resisted held Alexander up for a whole summer. A hundred or so recently rallied Phoenician, Cypriot and Rhodian ships blocked entry to the ports.

Summer 332 After the collapse of Tyr (in August: 8,000 Tyrians were massacred, 2,000 being crucified below the ramparts; 30,000 were sold as slaves), it was the turn of Gaza, defended by an Arab garrison (October: 10,000 men executed; women and children sold into slavery).

Autumn 332 The Persian threat in Asia Minor and the Mediterranean had been definitively eliminated. There was now nothing to stop Alexander, who was well informed of the situation there, from occupying Egypt. The satrap surrendered Memphis, the old capital that Artaxerxes had recaptured nine years earlier. The Egyptian priests welcomed him as a liberator: all they needed to do was change to the name of their new pharaoh for order to be re-established everywhere, until such time as better days arrived.

Winter 332–331 The foundation of Alexandria (January 331). Alexander made another highly symbolic pilgrimage: to the sanctuary of Zeus Amon, on the Libyan frontier. This was an oracle recognized by the Greeks, which made it possible for individuals and cities on cold terms with the Delphic Pythia to consult the king of the gods (the Egyptian priesthood had identified Amon of Karnak in Thebaid with Re, the sun-god, whom the Greeks assimilated to Zeus). The oracle had no difficulty in allotting the title of Pharaoh, 'Son of Re', to the young sovereign – an important step forward for his legend. In the meantime the Aegean islands had rallied, and Miletus and Halicarnassus had capitulated. The principle of territorial continuity was triumphing.

Spring 331 Back in Tyr, Alexander entrusted the military finances to Harpalus (the son of an Elimiot prince and a brother-in-law of Philip's) and organized the levying of tribute from large fiscal constituencies: Cleomenes of Naucratis was made responsible for collecting the royal revenues in Egypt; Asia Minor formed another subdivision, where financial resources were centralized in Sardis; a third included the contributions of Syria, Phoenicia, Cilicia and Cyprus.

Summer 331 Confident of what he was leaving behind him, Alexander turned off from Damascus along the old path that was the scene of former Egypto-Mesopotamian clashes, and crossed first the Euphrates, then the Tigris, despite the delaying tactics employed against him by Darius' son-in-law Mazaeus, the satrap of Transeuphratene. The Great King drew on all his reserves on a terrain of his own choosing, Gaugamela, close to the ruins of Nineveh (not far from Mosul), for a battle that he hoped would prove decisive. It did. Darius, defeated, took refuge in Ecbatana (Hamadan) in Media (1 October).

This was the point at which Agis III, the king of Sparta, mistakenly chose to use funds received from the Persians to settle an old score. At the head of 22,000 men (of whom 10,000 were mercenaries who had escaped from Asia Minor), he laid siege to Megalopolis in Arcadia. Antipater attacked him with 40,000 soldiers. Agis died in the battle. The Common Council left the choice of punishment to Alexander, who opted for clemency: Sparta was to hand over Darius' former mercenaries and fifty hostages. Athens had made no move.

Winter 331–330 The Macedonian army occupied the centres of Achaemenid power without having to strike a blow, first the General Headquarters in Babylon (the biggest town in the ancient world, hostile to the Achaemenids for the past two centuries, which welcomed Alexander as a liberator and recognized him as 'king of the universe'), then the administrative capital Susa (where 50,000 talents were raked off for army funds). The Macedonians were held up for a short time at the Persian Gates, but then entered into the heart of the empire, Persia proper (Fars), and occupied the dynasty's two holy cities, Persepolis (Shiraz) and Pasargadae, where the tomb of Cyrus was located (January 330). Quite apart from all the booty looted by the troops, the military funds were increased by 120,000 talents in Persepolis and 6,000 in Pasargadae.

Spring 330 A general treasure store was established in Babylon, the responsibility of Harpalus, who was in charge of managing both the military funds and the huge fiscal constituencies. Alexander then set fire to the royal palace of Persepolis (May 330). This was a deliberate gesture, a political message aimed at the Greek world: the symbolic goal of the pan-Hellenic war had been achieved: the arson of the Acropolis had been avenged.

The young king had now quite literally reached a crossroads, that of the four royal ways that fanned out across the 'four regions'. He had already passed along those that led to the Aegean Sea and to Egypt. The others wound around the desert depression constituted by the Iranian plateau. One ran north-east towards Gabae (Ispahan) and Rhagae (Teheran), crossed the foothills of the Elbruz at the Caspian Gates, entered via Hecatomplyae (Damgan) into Hyrcania (to the south-east of the Caspian Sea) and continued towards Afghanistan, whence it rejoined the upper valley of the Indus. The south-eastern route, finally, led by way of Karmana (Kerman) to the straits of Hormuz and then followed the edge of the plateau until it reached the Indus delta.

It was now that Alexander the audacious *strategos* showed that he was also a statesman, one capable of conceiving of things that no Greeks from the cities had ever envisaged. In Asia Minor he had assessed the efficacy of the Achaemenid model. From the welcome that he had received in Egypt and Babylon, he had learned something else: the dominant ethnic class should not be replaced by a purely Macedonian one, for fear of provoking similar irredentism. In Babylon he started off by appointing a number of high-ranking Iranians. Darius' son-in-law Mazaeus became the satrap of Babylonia. Others followed. However, he was not a man to risk his power for a symbol: the satraps of eastern origin were each assisted (in reality, supervised) by a Graeco-Macedonian *strategos* and a treasurer.

Summer 330 The royal army reached Ecbatana, but too late to catch Darius. To underline the importance of this moment, Alexander sent home the allied contingents, who would be able to spread his legend, loading them with booty. He then set off in pursuit of the Great King, who fled towards the Caspian Sea with his last faithful supporters, Greek mercenaries.

Upon passing through the Caspian Gates he learned, in Parthia, that the unfortunate sovereign was a prisoner of Bessus, the satrap of Bactria. With the Companions' cavalry, he at last caught up with the chariot in which Darius III had just been assassinated (July). Alexander had the body taken to Pasargadae to be laid in the dynastic tomb. He then, in accordance with Macedonian tradition, in which the heir to the throne presided over the funeral of his predecessor, proclaimed himself Darius' legitimate successor. To prove his point, he avenged him by setting off in pursuit of Bessus, who had proclaimed himself king, taking the name Artaxerxes IV. This time, Alexander's message was aimed at the East.

Autumn 330 There were six eastern satrapies: Hercania (already conquered), Areia, Drangiana, Arachosia, Bactria (respectively to the north-west, the south-west, the south-east and the north-east of Afghanistan) and Sogdiana, which was virtually independent (Kazakhstan). To cut Bessus off from his back-up troops, Alexander occupied the chief towns of Areia and Drangiana, upon which he bestowed his own name: Alexandria Areion (Herat); Alexandria of Drangiana (Farah). It was in Drangiana that the trumped-up trial of Philotas, the son of Parmenion, took place, followed by the assassination of the latter in Ecbatana (we shall be returning to this). After this, Craterus brought back most of the army that had been left in Ecbatana, along with a number of reinforcements from Greece.

Winter 330 After occupying the chief town of Arachosia (Kandahar, Arachosian Alexandria), the army waited for the snows to melt on what is now the site of Kabul (Alexandria-under-Caucasus), at the foot of the Hindu Kush, which the expedition's geographers took to be a prolongation of the Caucasus.

Spring 329 The royal army crossed the Hindu Kush, passing through the high Panshir valley, and came upon the plain of Bactria (Balkh) from the east, whereas Bessus was expecting it to arrive by the customary route from the south. Fearing to be surrounded, the satrap took refuge beyond the Oxus river, in Sogdiana. A noble Sogdian by the name of Spitamenes, no doubt thinking that, having avenged Darius, Alexander would advance no further, offered to hand him over. A strong column under the command of Ptolemy took possession of the usurper. He was condemned to death for treason and was later executed in Ecbatana. Alexander then moved toward the Jaxartes river (Syr-Daria, another tributary of the Aral Sea). This was the ancient frontier of the empire, where Cyrus the Great had constructed a line of strongholds facing the independent Scythians. The largest of these, Cyropolis, resisted. It was destroyed and replaced by Alexandria Eschate ('the Farthest', Khodjend). After a show of strength on the eastern bank of the river, a pact of non-aggression (which was to last) was concluded with the Scythians. By this time it was clear that Alexander had set himself limits, those of the Achaemenid empire.

Three whole years were necessary to subdue Sogdiana, which had been administered for years by native dynasties who, from on high amid their craggy peaks, which the Greeks called 'the Rocks', protected the peasants in return for tribute and recruited extremely belligerent local militias. The first defeats were suffered by the king. Then he took, lost, then re-took not only the chief town, Maracandra (Samarkand), but also a number of strong-holds deep in lost valleys or perched atop steep hills. Five of his 'infernal columns' waged a pitiless war of murderous ambushes and surprise raids. After the death of Spitamenes, in 328, the last 'Sogdian Rock', defended by Oxyartes, capitulated (327). Oxyartes' daughter, Roxane, was to become the hero's first wife.

Spring 326   Since Herodotus, India, for educated people, had been no more than the twentieth satrapy of the Persian empire, conquered by Darius the Great and then lost – that is, the lower valley of the Indus (Sind). The Dekkan, the Ganges Basin, and the Himalayan foothills, let alone Tibet and China, were all completely unknown to them. To conquer this satrapy, whose tribute in gold dust was, according to Herodotus, worth 4,800 talents of silver, Alexander had mustered a mixed army of 120,000 men (Macedonians, Greeks, Iranians and other easterners). He was believed to be responding to an appeal from the prince of Taxila (an important archae-ological site where signs of a brilliant civilization going back to the fourth century have been discovered), who feared invasion by his aggressive neigh-bour, the king Poros. Having neutralized the mountain peoples of the last Himalayan foothills, Alexander met up with the major part of his army again. He appointed a satrap, meanwhile leaving the Indian princes their internal autonomy.

Summer 326   Poros was waiting for the great army on the east bank of the Hydaspes (Jhelum, a tributary of the Indus), with troops three times as numerous and 120 elephants. This was the last pitched battle and, for the Macedonians, the most costly in terms of casualties. Once again, victory resulted from a counter-intuitive manoeuvre (made possible thanks to the discovery of a ford up-river). Poros, treated as an independent king, re-nounced his claims to the land west of the Hydaspes, which would now serve as a frontier. Two new Alexandrias were founded, one each side of the river (the one surnamed Nicaea, in memory of the victory, the other Bucephalus, after the king's horse, killed at this spot). Alexander immedi-ately gave orders for the construction of close on 2,000 warships and transport vessels, designed to descend by river to the Indian Ocean.

In the meantime the king of Macedonia agreed to compensate his new ally for territorial losses to the east that the latter claimed to have suffered. But there was no way of Alexander knowing that he would soon have to confront a vast state coveted by an exile, Chandragupta, who had found refuge in the court of Poros. The kingdom of Maghada had been founded in the early sixth century, at the same time as that of Taxila. Its capital was Pataliputra (Patna, in the present state of Bihar) and the kingdom occupied most of the Indus/Ganges plain, doubtless with a vast population. The 'great army', swelled by Indian contingents (and elephants), encountered stiff resistance and it was only with difficulty that it managed to reach the Hyphasis river (Beas, the right-hand tributary of the Sutlej).

At this point Alexander learned from a prince by the name of Phegeus of the existence of the Ganges and of countless peoples living beyond the Hyphasis. The young king realized that Poros was luring him into trouble, so he turned back. He returned to his headquarters on the Hydaspes river with his soldiers, who sensed that the moment was approaching when they would be able to go home. Having covered about 20,000 kilometres from Amphipolis, they certainly deserved to. Later authors have embroidered with pathos a tale of bitter conflict in which these veterans opposed a king obsessed by the ambition to reach the mouth of the Ganges, the Ocean of Homeric legend, which had been believed to encircle the world. More probably, he was anxious to embark on the last project in his programme: namely to explore the southern front of the Achaemenid inheritance, in order to set up defences there. (With exactly the same aim, Darius I had ordered a survey of Iran and Arabia.) That was a wise policy for a practical fighting man, and it owed nothing to literature.

November 326 The last expedition set out. On either side of the Hydaspes two army units, one commanded by Craterus, the other by Hephaestion, accompanied the fleet, which was placed under the orders of Nearchus (whose journal of the journey was later used by Arrian). On the way they had to take large towns by assault. Alexander was gravely wounded. Although in great pain, he had to show himself to his soldiers, for in the belief that he was dead they were panicking. Eventually the great army reached the Indus, where it split. Most of the troops, led by Craterus, along with the demobilized veterans, the wounded and the elephants, made for Arachosian Alexandria, then moved on to join the king in Carmania. The Sindh was crossed at the cost of many bloody battles. Macedonian frenzy reached such a degree that the prince of Patala (in the Hyderabad region) decided to abandon his town along with all his subjects.

Autumn 325 After resting for a few months, the land army and the fleet separated. Following the example set by Xerxes in the Second Persian War, Alexander was planning to follow the arid coastline of Gedrosia (Baluchistan). He would halt at anchorages where the fleet would put in for supplies. But Nearchus soon fell behind schedule and explored the sea route from the Indus to the Euphrates on his own, while the land troops crossed a desert where the inhabitants inland refused to give them any food. After two months of suffering the survivors spent the winter at Poura, the chief town of the satrapy.

December 325 With reduced forces Alexander reached Carmania, where, as arranged, Craterus met him. Alexandria in Carmania was founded not far from the port of Harmozia (Hormuz), where Nearchus' fleet hove to in January. Thanksgiving sacrifices were performed, and athletic and artistic competitions were held, followed by a triumphal procession to celebrate the conquest of the empire of Darius the Great.

THE METAMORPHOSIS OF THE MACEDONIAN MONARCHY

The restoration of order Herodotus and Xenophon had penetrated the secret of Persian greatness. Thanks to a rapid postal service, the Great King had managed to keep himself personally informed of all the most important events. In that way, Xerxes had continued to govern even while present at the battle of Salamis. On the other hand, the immensity of the empire needed an upper administration that was both competent and loyal to the sovereign, and that meant a hereditary nobility. In Carmania, where he had convoked the civilian, military and financial officers who had been appointed before 327, Alexander realized that his prolonged absence had led satraps and *strategoi* to take initiatives that bordered on felony. Out of hostility towards Parmenion, who had been left in Ecbatana in 330, he had neglected to appoint a *strategos* endowed with full powers in Asia, like Antipater in Europe. By 325 he had learned of the secession of the military colonists installed in Bactriana, where one of the *strategoi* had declared himself king. He now understood that the exercise of authority at the head of such a mosaic of peoples depended upon a metamorphosis of the Macedonian monarchy.

The late sources at our disposal are over-inclined to lay the blame for the disorders on officials who had enriched themselves at the expense of those under their administration. They add that the punishments meted out were excessive, for the king's character had deteriorated under the influence of all the 'eastern' adulation. It is true that the toll taken by the purge is telling. Of the twenty-two satraps known in 325, only four were unaffected: six were executed for treason, others were imprisoned to await judgement, yet others were deposed. The pressure of circumstances was such that the central power had shrunk to the close entourage of the sovereign: the chiliast (an Achaemenid title: 'the chief of one thousand', 'the first after the king'), Hephaestion, the chancellor, Eumenes of Cardia, the 'minister of finances', Harpalus, a few staff-office generals such as Craterus and, finally, the eight who formed the king's 'bodyguard', some of whom, such as Perdiccas, Ptolemy and Lysimachus, were to compete for the succession. In fact, the high command suffered from a shortage of qualified leaders. It was a matter of urgency to establish the bases of a veritable imperial nobility, linked to the monarch through personal allegiance, which would expand the old aristocracy of the Companions and render it more effective.

The most striking aspect of the course adopted by Alexander appears in the composition of the royal army. Since 330 this had lost its national character, which had constituted the basis of Macedonian power in Philip's day. To be sure the king would, as before, call assemblies of the veterans, who would express their views there in the traditional forthright way; and, also as before, he continued to exploit the social rifts between the hoplites and the cavalry. But the reinforcements sent from Europe no longer sufficed (another 30,000 infantry and 6,000 cavalry in 326). Alexander had recruited 30,000 young Asians, trained in the Macedonian fashion and educated as Greeks, the 'Epigoni'. According to Quintus Curtius, by 324 he retained only 2,000 Macedonian cavalrymen and 13,000 Macedonian infantrymen; moreover, many of these were dispersed, together with former Greek mercenaries, among the military colonies. In 323, 20,000 Iranians were incorporated into the hoplite phalanxes.

A number of the Companions had sensed the significance of these changes, whereas later writers discern only their external aspects, the costumes, the court ceremonial, the luxury – in a word, the orientalization. The resistance of the old aristocracy explains, but does not justify, the death sentence for plotting passed by the assembly in January 330 on Parmenion's son Philotas, the leader of the cavalry, followed by the execution of Parmenion in Ecbatana. Those were deliberate political murders. The son-in-law of Antipater, Alexander Lyncestis, was condemned by the assembly on the same pretext. When, in the course of a drinking party in Samarkand, Alexander killed Cleitus, his childhood friend, who had saved his life at the Granicus, the assembly justified the murder, alleging a conspiracy. They even found a philosopher, Anaxarchus, to explain to the sovereign that he had a right to act in such a way: he was the sole master of the world, and his will was law. Whatever the exact date when it was formulated for the first time, this autocratic rhetoric marked a decisive turning-point.

For a while, traditionalist resistance managed to slow down the ineluctable change. After celebrating his marriage with Roxane (spring 327), Alexander planned to standardize protocol by generalizing the practice of prosternation before the sovereign (*proskynesis*). For the Persians this was simply a sign of respect, but for the Greeks *proskynesis* was an honour reserved for the gods. Callisthenes of Olynthus managed to persuade the king to give up the idea. However, as a result of being implicated in a conspiracy among the squires, to whom he gave lessons, this killjoy was thrown into chains and was executed in lamentable circumstances a few years later.

The reconciliation   The restoration of order continued in Susa, where the victorious Great Army had made its solemn entry in the spring of 324. But Harpalus preferred to act on his own account. Despite the fact that, during his stay in Carmania, the king had issued a letter ordering all the *strategoi* and satraps of Asia to dismiss the mercenaries in their pay, Harpalus installed himself in Tarsis with as much money and as many mercenaries as he could gather together. Alexander's decision was perfectly logical: given that the pacification of the territory was considered to be completed, the only remaining military force ought now to be the royal army. Now this army included Asian nobles incorporated into the Companions' Cavalry, and also the 30,000 Epigoni. To demonstrate the role that he was preparing for Hellenes, Alexander held a collective wedding ceremony celebrated with great pomp in which those who so wished were married to their eastern concubines (most of the generals, eighty Companions and 10,000 veteran soldiers). He himself married a daughter and a granddaughter of Darius III. Only one of these unions produced a well-known dynasty, that of Seleucus, a colossus who commanded the elite troops, with Apama, the daughter of Spitamenes, who, like Roxane, was a Sogdian. All this obviously had nothing to do with the grandiose dream that Plutarch describes in the Stoic manner, claiming that the aim was to 'consider all men as compatriots and fellow-citizens'. Alexander's long-term objective was to create a mixed aristocracy, on the model of the army. However, he allowed those who preferred to return to Europe to do so unhindered, led by Craterus.

Realizing that the king would not be returning to Pella, the Macedonian phalanx revolted ('let him go ahead and wage war with his father, Amon . . .'). A single speech to them would have been enough to calm the mutineers. However, their leaders were immediately executed. Then, in early summer, Alexander set sail with Nearchus' fleet, descended as far as the Persian Gulf and made his way back up the Tigris as far as Opis (to the north of Baghdad). A grandiose banquet was held to honour the departure of the 11,500 veterans who had chosen to return home, covered in glory and loaded with booty (July 324). Hellenistic monarchy was born: the king's will was law.

The Greeks had yet to be persuaded to accept this. Our literary sources, once more loquacious, plunge us back into the political life of Athens. After Chaeronea the orator Lycurgus, an aristocrat who was a disciple of Plato's and was hostile to the Macedonians, acquired power by reason of his financial skills. The *ephebeia* was now remodelled on the lines described in Aristotle's *Constitution of the Athenians*. *Strategoi* were allotted particular specialist duties (foreign campaigns, defence of the territory, ports . . .). The arsenal for naval equipment (*skeuthèkè*) was completed in Piraeus. Naval inventories list over 400 warships. The Panathenaeic stadium was inaugurated. The debate on democracy was enough to bring together even the supporters and the opponents of Macedonia. The situation suddenly became explosive. The return of the dismissed mercenaries to Europe filled the place with a mass of footloose adventurers. On top of everything else, a royal letter addressed to Antipater (and solemnly read out at the Olympic Games in August 324 by the herald who was the victor in the elocution competition) enjoined him to persuade the cities to allow all their exiles to return home, with their possessions fully restored to them. This was the

'Macedonian Peace', modelled on the 'King's Peace'. A decree issued in Tegea, dated 324, shows how carefully the cities tried to prevent the perverse effects of a decision which, after all, had simply taken the rhetors' speculations literally. The oath appended to the decree reproduced the terms of the amnesty of 403: 'I shall no longer remember the wrongs committed in the past toward anybody.' But far from setting the seal on pan-Hellenic unity, the combined principles of, on one hand, the internal amnesty and, on the other, the cities' autonomy produced the opposite effect and led to a fragmentation that only an autocrat would be able to federate, by force. And Alexander was a realist.

THE HARPALUS AFFAIR

In the midst of the inevitable agitation provoked by those two measures, Harpalus arrived off the coast of Athens with thirty ships, 6,000 mercenaries and 5,000 talents. Earlier, the Athenians had granted him citizen's rights. Now they prudently refused to welcome his flotilla. The *strategos* in charge of Piraeus allowed him to land on his own (with pocket money to the tune of 700 talents). Antipater pressed for his extradition. Demosthenes had him imprisoned pending Alexander's decision, overruling Hyperides, who wanted to seize the chance to recover independence, making the most of Harpalus' funds and his mercenaries. When counted, the sum confiscated from Harpalus was found to have been depleted by half. Hyperides accused Demosthenes and a few others of corruption. After a long enquiry by the Areopagus, Demosthenes was found guilty, and sentenced to prison and a fine of 50 talents. But he escaped and went into exile (March 323). Before him already, Lycurgus, who had died in 324, had escaped condemnation for corruption only by the skin of his teeth (he had been held responsible for several years of shortages that had resulted from the disruption of convoys in the Black Sea and speculation on the price of wheat imported from Egypt, encouraged by the satrap Cleomenes). It looked as though 'the republic of lawyers' (E. Drerup) was again ripe for a *coup d'état*.

Alexander had taken the Harpalus affair seriously. He considered making an expedition to central Greece in order to have done with the Athenians; but, as it happened, Harpalus escaped and was then assassinated in Crete. In the autumn of 324 the king wrote a letter to the Athenians as a whole in which, according to Plutarch, he dispensed them from having to recall those banished to Samos (whose land had been allotted to cleruchs), since they had received that island in 338 from Philip, 'then my lord and putative father'. Once again Athens had had a narrow escape, and Alexander had scored double points. The expression 'putative father' shows that, in the space of a quite short time, the 'little young man' had become a crafty politician. Did the implicit reference to the title 'son of Zeus Amon', bestowed upon him in 332, mean that Alexander had formally requested divine honours? The Athenians were subtle enough to read the message between the lines. Demosthenes was quoted (by Hyperides, who opposed him a few months later) as saying: 'Well, let him be the son of Zeus, and the son of Poseidon too, if that is what he wants!' He is also said to have suggested erecting a statue to him, dedicated to 'The king Alexander, the invincible god' (the religious title of his 'ancestor' Heracles). Both proposals were rejected.

When seen in proportion, this fiction fits into the game of poker that Demosthenes liked to play, in the meantime hoping for better days. The problem raised was a typically Athenian one, so there is absolutely no call to go looking for 'oriental influences' (as was done as early as the Hellenistic period). For a long time already the Athenians had been showing their gratitude to their foreign benefactors by issuing eulogistic decrees, in particular for the kings of Thrace and the Cimmerian Bosphosus, who protected their imports of cereals. Little by little, they had perfected a barometer of skilfully graded honours (attested by Aristotle and amply illustrated by the epigraphical evidence). But the king of Macedonia had already been decreed all the usual honorific distinctions. What more could be done? Upping the stakes led straight to the summit of the hierarchy of honours, to those that the city reserved for the gods and for heroes deified after their deaths. (Aristotle enumerates the sacrifices, sacred precincts and hymns that were devoted to them.) Like Plato and, after him, Aristotle, Isocrates was of the opinion that it was justifiable to consider an exceptional benefactor of the Hellenes as equal to the gods, even before he passed on to the Islands of the Blessed. But why should the Athenians have felt they should do more? Because it was the least costly way of avoiding the individual humiliation of *proskynesis*: they would offer even more than that, but collectively, so that it really hardly mattered. Once again the Athenians would be 'the first' if they granted 'King Alexander', who had already made so many concessions to them, an honour never before given to anybody. As Demosthenes saw it, it would simply constitute a further mark of derision for the Barbarian who was humiliating his country.

And what was Alexander's view? Plutarch ascribes to him the reaction of a soldier. Seeing the blood flowing from one of his wounds, he is supposed to have declared: 'This is blood, my friends, not the rarefied liquid that flows in the veins of the blessed gods!' And according to Quintus Curtius, he expressed the following wish: 'Let the Indians believe me to be a god, for prestige counts for everything in warfare!' Actually the Indians certainly did not believe him to be a god; that at least is clear, for his name is not cited in any ancient Indian text. As for the Orientals in general, all they asked was that they be left in peace; and their political vocabulary remained unchanged. So, sensitive to reasons of state and steeped in Athenian literature as he was, did Alexander himself complete the transfiguration by launching an idea that was to gain ground in Western culture, beginning with Athens? It seems the most likely of scenarios. The collapse of the

Periclean model at the beginning of the century had first provoked a return to religion, then, among philosophers and orators, a renewal of mythical thought. A myth lasts only for as long as it answers a lasting need. Alexander 'was prone to rush into action, but always wanted it to be symbolic' (P. Vidal-Naquet). If all Hellenistic political theory hangs on his legend, that is no doubt because a need for the legend made itself felt. 'For my own part, I have no means of guessing precisely what Alexander had in mind, nor does it matter to me' (Arrian).

He did not have time to legitimate the imperial nobility that he thought of creating. With his head full of plans that may or may not have have been realizable, he died, probably of malaria, having never missed personally performing the daily religious rites until the day that he lost the power of speech, 10 June 323 BC.

THE FULFILMENT OF DEMOCRACY

By July 323 Alexander's death was unofficially known in Athens. The democrats, led by Hyperides and Leosthenes, a former mercenary leader in Asia, quickly made the most of the opportunity. During the summer Harpalus' fortune became available and was used to recruit mercenaries in the Peloponnese. With this army Leosthenes made for Aetolia, crossing the Gulf of Corinth (the Boeotians remained submissive). The Aetolians joined him and occupied Thermopylae. A decree cited by Diodorus proclaimed that the Athenians would fight for the common liberty of the Hellenes, as in the days of the Persian Wars.

The Lamian War The successive levies of reinforcements for Asia had left Antipater with depleted forces. After an unsuccessful attempt to take Thermopylae, the defection of the Thessalians forced him to hole up in the citadel at Lamia whilst awaiting the arrival of the royal army, which had been summoned to his aid (hence the name 'Lamian War', coined by Diodorus). In the Peloponnese, not yet recovered from the defeat of Agis in 331, only Argolis, Sicyon, Elis and Messenia joined the coalition. On the other hand, most of central Greece aligned itself with the Athenians. Leosthenes, who had been elected commander-in-chief, was soon killed in an ambush. Early in 322 Leonnatus entered Thessaly with large reinforcements. He too was then killed, but first managed to extricate Antipater, who pulled back to Macedonia. It was after these deceptive successes that Demosthenes and Demades were recalled from exile (the latter had previously supported the Macedonians, as had the *strategos* Phocion, now an octogenarian who, according to Plutarch, had been re-elected *strategos* forty-five times, and who loyally took part in the defence of Attica). The Athenians were counting on their 240 warships to win mastery of the sea. But their hopes were dashed. Faced with the royal Hellespont fleet, they lost the first naval battle, off the coast of Abydus; the second, off Amorgos, ended in total disaster for them. During the summer Craterus landed with his veterans. The Macedonian forces consisted of about 50,000 hardened infantrymen trained under Alexander, as against 25,000 allies. The inevitable defeat took place at Crannon, to the south of Larissa (September 322).

The members of the coalition dispersed. Antipater insisted on treating with them separately, without resorting to the mechanisms of the League of Corinth, which had by now virtually dissolved. The Aetolians, who took refuge in their mountains, were saved from being deported to Asia by the first clashes between Alexander's successors. The Athenians, represented by Demades and Phocion, agreed to the following conditions: to hand over the leaders of the anti-Macedonian party, chief amongst them Hyperides and Demosthenes; to repatriate the cleruchs of Samos; to accept a garrison in Piraeus; and to set up a census-based oligarchy that denied political rights to anyone possessing less than 2,000 drachmas (Plutarch cites a figure of 12,000 thus excluded, many of whom went into exile in Thrace, where Antipater allotted them land). Hyperides was arrested in Aegina and was executed. Demosthenes decided to take poison in Calauria (on the island of Poros, November 322).

A STATE OF LAW

The death of the great orator marked not the end, but the fulfilment of ancient democracy. The decisive progress accomplished in the fourth century had produced a State based on law, founded on a written constitution (the 'laws') that guaranteed the civil society's rational control over the public authorities. To be sure, orators and philosophers of all tendencies continued, as in the fifth century, to complain of the abuses committed by the *dèmos*. That happens in all democracies, ancient and modern alike; and in the case of Athens, it was a matter of an incurable sickness that stemmed from ignorance of representative government. But, to judge from the convergent testimony of the orators and Aristotle (who describes the institutions at the time of Lycurgus) the crucial point lay elsewhere, namely in the procedures (the word, which comes from Latin, conveys the idea of gradual progress) designed to stabilize civil peace, which had begun to be elaborated under the archontate of Euclid (403–402). Having charged a committee of 500 nomothetes ('those who establish the law') with the task of recasting the earlier laws, in particular those of Draco and Solon), the assembly decided that thenceforth magistrates would no longer in any circumstances apply unwritten law and that no decree, either from the council or from the people, could overrule a law (Andocides, *On the Mysteries*). Aeschines (*Against Ctesiphon*) and Demosthenes (*Against Leptines, Against Timocrates*) attest that in their time the annual revision of laws by the thesmothetes and, if necessary, the appointment of a committee of nomothetes who had sworn an oath before the heliasts, was a practice that went back to time immemorial (Hyperides and Demosthenes attributed it to

Solon). According to Aristotle, the superiority of written laws (applied by the magistrates and the law-courts) made all the difference between a demagogic regime, in which the people legislated by decrees, and a constitutional regime (*politeia*) in which supreme power lay with the law. The many precautions surrounding the modification of any law, even to improve it, showed that the restored democracy definitively opted for stability, since laws familiar to everyone and observed for many years provided a better guarantee of social peace than did the whims of the assembly (it was in this connection that Aristotle observed that one swallow did not make a summer).

In its legal and abstract form, this ruling constitution represented the completion of a long and painful history that is reflected in thought on the opposition between law and nature. Thucydides, to his great credit, spelt out the significance of this theoretical distinction. Only human nature is common to all human beings; the law is simply a convention accepted by a particular community. That is why laws are different among Greeks and among Barbarians. And even if laws exist that are common to all Greeks (respect for the gods, the dead, relatives and guests or hosts), these carry only a moral obligation, which often turns out to be a dead letter. Only the laws that are particular to a particular State are effectively applied by the public authorities. The gravest consequence of this stark truth was illustrated by the Peloponnesian War. From this Thucydides deduces that international relations are ruled by natural necessity, according to which it is the strongest who calls the shots (ultimately, it was the Persians who tipped the scales in the war between the Greeks). To be sure, treaties attempted to contain inter-state violence, but they were repudiated as soon as national interest so dictated.

The dream of the fourth century was to put a stop to wars between Greeks by promoting the idea of a common peace. In fact, the only power capable of realizing it was, once again, the strongest, first the Great King, then Philip of Macedonia. If the Athenians perforce resigned themselves to this inherent impotence of human nature, they nevertheless learned from the *coups d'état* of 411 and 404 to detest civil war. And it has to be recognized that the maintenance of internal peace up until the death of Demosthenes was their finest achievement in a century in which, in other domains, they met with so many failures. Later, the changes to their regime were imposed from outside, but they returned to democracy as soon as they could (between 281 and 261, and then again between 229 and 86).

The efficacy of the laws naturally depended upon the law-courts (*dikasteria*). Demosthenes addressed a jury of heliasts as follows:

Consider the question, what is it that gives you who serve on juries such power and authority in all State affairs . . . it is due . . . to the strength of the laws. And what is the strength of the laws? If one of you is wronged and cries aloud, will the laws run up and be at his side to assist him? No, they are only written texts and incapable of such action. Wherein, then, resides their power? In yourselves, if only you support them and make them allpowerful to help him who needs them. So the laws are strong through you and you through the laws. (*Against Meidias*, 221–5)

It is probably fair to say that politicians have never been so closely supervised by the courts of law as in fourth-century Athens. As a general rule, before taking up their responsibilities magistrates (who numbered about 700) underwent an examination (*dokimasia*) by a court that they had to satisfy as to their handling of public accounts (*euthynai*). Similarly, the assembly usually passed on to a court cases of high treason (*eisangelia*), which were liable to heavy fines or capital punishment and by which *strategoi* were particularly threatened. Finally and above all, the courts played their full constitutional role when they judged actions for illegality (*graphè paranomion*), which were liable to heavy fines or capital punishment and in which any citizen could invoke the help of the law to oppose whoever had proposed any law or decree, even if this had been passed by the assembly. The proposal would be suspended until such time as it was either confirmed or annulled. The institution of the *graphè paranomion* has been linked with the reforms of Ephialtes (G. Glotz), because it seemed logical to entrust the protection of the constitution, which, according to Aristotle, had at this time been removed from the Areopagus, to some other institution. However, there is no evidence of it functioning before the end of the fifth century.

According to Aeschines, Aristophon of Azenia (who instigated the condemnation of Callistratus of Aphidna in 361 and of Timotheus in 355, but then lost all influence under Eubulus) boasted of having been accused of illegality seventy-five times. The case of Cephalus of Collytos (influential after 368) was just the opposite:

Not so the venerable Cephalus, famous as the truest representative of democracy – not so, but he took pride in the the very opposite fact, saying that although he had been the author of more measures than any other man, he had never been indicted for an illegal motion. (*Against Ctesiphon*, 194)

Here, as with Demosthenes, one detects a fourth-century tendency to tackle political problems in moral terms. In effect, Athenian penal law confronted politicians with their own personal responsibility by constantly reminding them of the risks that they ran if they deceived or betrayed those who had placed their trust in them. It presupposed that the heliasts possessed a political conscience and, correlatively, a margin of action for the verdict that they had to pronounce, which to us seems unthinkable (M. I. Finley). The fact is that the Athenian courts were not government organs as they are in modern States, with powers exercised in the name of the people but strictly limited by the legislative and executive powers. They were the *dèmos* itself which, through the judicial institution, gave itself a chance to redress its own mistakes by referring to the existing laws, which were meticulously revised each year and were abundantly cited in the course of lawsuits. Certainly, when the *dèmos* took a decision on foreign policies, alliances, war, peace or any important matter in the economic or social domain, in the last analysis it was the assembly that decided. But the sovereignty of the laws meant that these were not like decrees, the fruits of fortuitous circumstances and fleeting relations of strength; instead, they constituted as coherent as possible a system for maintaining a balance of powers, and thereby safeguarding peace.

THE FAILURE OF THE MACEDONIAN PEACE (323–281)

The forty years that followed Alexander's death witnessed the collapse of the Macedonian Peace and a return to a period in which constellations of alliances between various cities spoilt the image of a civilization whose cultural union and attraction was even then just being discovered by the oriental peoples. Private wars waged under the pretext of monarchical legitimacy, and plots and counter-plots (too numerous to mention) were setting in opposition those known as the *diadochi* ('successors'), who set about eliminating one another in a bloody and pointless series of massacres. Of these, Antipater, Antigonus and Polyperchon were veterans of Philip's generation; the rest were Alexander's Companions. Apart from the chancellor Eumenes of Cardia (in the Thracian Chersonese), they all belonged to the upper Macedonian nobility. The man who now held the top rank in the administrative hierarchy, having replaced Hephaestion, who had died in 324, was Perdiccas. Alexander had handed the royal seal to him as he died. Next came the members of the General Staff Office, Craterus, Leonnatus, Lysimachus and Ptolemy.

THE BABYLONIAN COMPROMISE

For want of a better system, the succession to Alexander, in every way exceptional, followed the Macedonian tradition, which entrusted the army assembly, following the royal council's recommendation, with the designation of a new sovereign. Given that Alexander and his mother had eliminated all claimants to the throne who possessed royal blood, none remained except one of his half-brothers, Arrhidaeus, who had been spared because he was mentally retarded. The royal council, with Perdiccas presiding, decided to wait for the birth of the child Roxane was expecting. If this was a boy, he would be king. The cavalry approved. But the hoplites did not and proclaimed Arrhidaeus king, under the name Philip III. A wobbly compromise was reached, which avoided a blood bath: there would be two kings, each equally incapable of governing, Philip III and Roxane's son, who meanwhile had been born and named Alexander IV. Now the regency had to be organized. It was constituted as a triumvirate, with ill-defined attributes: Perdiccas, confirmed in his functions as chiliarch, which in principle placed him at the head of all the affairs of a kingdom worthy of the name, albeit without a king; Craterus, the guardian of the kings, and Antipater, the *strategos* of Europe, as before. The other 'Companions' divided the satrapies between them: Lysimachus received Thrace, Leonnatus Hellespontine Phrygia, Antigonus Greater Phrygia, Lycia, Pamphylia and Pisidia, Eumenes Cappadocia (yet to be conquered). The territorial administration remained in place and there was no reaction from the subject peoples (it was a matter of 'peace in exchange for tribute', as Cyrus the Great's formula had put it).

The first eliminatory test of strength was not long in coming. Acting as commander-in-chief of the royal army, Perdiccas ordered Antigonus and Leonnatus to join up with him and occupy Cappadocia, which was to be given to Eumenes. The former refused to budge; the latter decided that it was more urgent to go to the aid of Antipater, besieged in Lamia. Once the Lamian War was over, a first conspiracy united Antipater, Craterus, Lysimachus, Antigonus and Ptolemy against Eumenes and Perdiccas. Perdiccas chanced his arm in Egypt, where he was executed on the decision of the army assembly (May 321). Craterus was killed while fighting Eumenes in Phrygia. Eumenes was then, in his turn, condemned to death by the army assembly. The sentence, the execution of which was entrusted to Antigonus, on account of his title of *strategos* of Asia, was not carried out for five years. A new compromise, agreed at Triparadisus in northern Syria, made Antipater ('the eldest, with the highest rank') the guardian of the kings, who had been transferred to Macedonia. Before he died, in 319, Philip's old companion made the only mistake of his long career: paying no attention to the prerogatives of the royal army which, despite its heterogeneous composition, was the sole guarantor of Macedonian legality, in his will he bequeathed to Polyperchon the full powers that went with the guardianship of the kings, passing over his own son Cassander. Polyperchon appointed Eumenes *strategos* of Asia in place of Antigonus and, in order to win over the cities, restored their constitutions, which Antipater had abolished. In Athens the restored democracy lasted only long enough to perpetrate one act of vengeance: the old *strategos* Phocion was accused of treason, condemned to death and executed.

By 317 Cassander had occupied central Greece and Macedonia, where Philip Arrhidaeus appointed him regent. Polyperchon took refuge in the Peloponnese. The Athenians resigned themselves to negotiating. They accepted not only a Macedonian garrison in Piraeus, but also the appointment of an Athenian governor who, for the form of it, was to be elected a *strategos*. Cassander appointed Demetrius of Phalerum, who for the next ten years administered the city as a philosopher-tyrant. He restored the regime based on a census, but reduced the fortune necessary to qualify for the rights of citizenship from 2,000 to 1,000 drachmas. He organized a new census, which registered 21,000 citizens and 10,000 metics. He was a disciple and friend of Theophrastus of Eresos (Lesbos) and secured for him the privilege of acquiring possession of the place where he was teaching and where his disciples, associated with the cult of the Muses, met once a month to share a common meal. Demetrius also got laws on luxury passed by vote. They banned ostentatious funerals and feminine coquetry, and created a special magistrate, the *gynaikonomos*, to supervise these matters. The triarchy and the *choregia* were abolished. A college of seven *nomophylakes* ('those who protect the laws') enforced respect for the laws (in the place of the heliasts). The Athenian society of this period is described by Menander and other authors of 'New Comedy'. The old queen Olympias made the most of the circumstances to complete the operation of putting her house in order, which she had started when Philip died. She arranged for the assassination of Arrhidaeus. She was herself then condemned to death and executed by the army assembly. Alexander IV and Roxane were placed under secure army guard. In 316 Eumenes, pursued by Antigonus to the neighbourhood of Gabes (Isfahan), was handed over by his own elite troops and was executed.

In order to be the sole master of Asia, Antigonus seized the satrapy of Babylon from Seleucus, who had been appointed to that post by the Triparadisus agreement. He rejected an ultimatum from Cassander, Lysimachus and Ptolemy, demanding that Seleucus be restored to his satrapy (315). He then issued a proclamation from Tyre that was designed to rally the cities: they were declared free, autonomous and relieved of their garrisons. Not to be outdone, Ptolemy made similar promises. Leaving his son Demetrius in charge of the defence of Asia, Antigonus then went to the Aegean to gather the fruits of his initiative. With Delos as its centre, the federation (*koinon*) of the Islanders (*Nesiotai*) was formed. In 312 Ptolemy won a victory over Demetrius in Gaza, which made it possible for Seleucus to recover Babylonia (April 311, the beginning of the Seleucid era). A new arrangement now replaced the earlier scenario: Asia went to Antigonus, Macedonia and the guardianship of Alexander IV to Cassander, Thrace to Lysimachus, Egypt to Ptolemy. The arrangement was immediately undermined. Cassander cleared the little king and his mother out of the way by having them assassinated. The way was now clear for the trial of strength, which took place, fittingly enough, in the Aegean Sea, at the very centre of Hellenism (late 310).

The trial of strength As Seleucus had not been included in the agreements, Antigonus attempted, without success, to overcome him in Babylonia. Determined to become a front runner himself, Seleucus occupied the most distant satrapies and soon managed to settle the question of the Indian frontier. Prince Chandragupta, whom our sources represent as a refugee at the court of Poros in 326, had since then founded the Maurya dynasty, placed himself at the head of the ancient Maghada kingdom, and conquered the Indus valley. Now he was encroaching on territories won by Alexander. At the cost of a few territorial concessions, Seleucus sealed a pact of lasting friendship with Chandragupta.

The confused situation in mainland Greece inevitably resulted in a threatened return of barbarians, forcing Cassander and Lysimachus to defend their frontier against the Celts. Ptolemy seized his chance to gain a foothold in Cyprus, Cos and a number of coastal cities in Asia. But Demetrius acted even faster: in 307 he freed Athens from the Macedonian garrison and, together with his father, was granted 'divine honours' there. In 306 he destroyed the Ptolemaic fleet off Cyprus. On the strength of their victory, Antigonus and Demetrius got themselves jointly proclaimed kings by their armies. Cassander, Lysimachus, Seleucus and Ptolemy followed suit: 306–305 was 'the year of the kings'.

In 305 Demetrius, despite an unprecedented abundance of siege machines (hence his title *Poliorcètes*, the 'taker of towns') suffered a rebuff at Rhodes, an independent city supported by Ptolemy. On this occasion Ptolemy received divine honours from the Rhodians and also his title of *Soter* ('Saviour'). In 302 Demetrius convoked a congress of Greek cities in Corinth, which had also been liberated; and the League founded by Philip in 338 was reformed. The fear of seeing Antigonus reunify Alexander's empire, to his own profit, decided Cassander, Lysimachus, Seleucus and Ptolemy to concentrate all their troops against him in Asia Minor. He was defeated and died in battle at Ipsus, in Phrygia (summer 301). However, Demetrius still rejoiced in his royal title and still had his fleet, with solid naval bases in Corinth, the Cyclades and Asia Minor – quite enough to continue to be feared right up until his death. An unexpected event helped him in 297: Cassander died prematurely. Making the most of the quarrel over the succession, Demetrius got himself proclaimed king by the Macedonian assembly (294). Lysimachus, the Boeotians, the Aetolians and the young king of the Molossi, Pyrrhus, Ptolemy's protégé, banded together against him. He left Macedonia, which Lysimachus and Pyrrhus then divided between them. He was taken prisoner by Seleucus in Asia and died in captivity (283), after bequeathing his royalty to his son, Antigonus Gonatas.

In 285 Lysimachus, in his turn, tried his luck. As master of Asia Minor, Thrace, Macedonia and Thessaly (from which he ousted Pyrrhus), he eventually began to worry Seleucus, who invaded Asia Minor. Lysimachus was defeated at Corupedium (close to Sardis), and died in battle (February 281). Seleucus crossed the straits with the intention of occupying Thrace and, if possible, the rest of Lysimachus' possessions too. But he was assassinated by Ptolemy *Keraunos*, the son of the first marriage of Ptolemy Soter (who had himself died in 282), who had excluded him from the succession in favour of Ptolemy II, born from his second marriage. Ptolemy Keraunos was proclaimed king by the Macedonians (September 281).

All the 'diadochi' were dead. What conclusion can be drawn from their fleeting endeavours?

They restored the map of the oriental world to a pre-Achaemenid schema, that of rival, warlike States with nothing in common except that they lay in the hands of potentates who were foreign to the cultures of the countries under their domination. In other words, the existence of the Hellenistic States represented the liquidation of the only unificatory and pacificatory success in the East ever known in Antiquity. (E. Will)

5 / THE HELLENISTIC PERIOD

281: the last adventure

In the course of the summer of 281 Tarentum appealed to Pyrrhus, the king of Epirus, to help it against the Romans. Apparently there was nothing new in this: Phalaecus, Archidamus, Alexander I of Epirus and, in about 300, Cleonymus, who had been ejected from the throne of Sparta by his nephew Areus, had all gone to the aid of the Tarentines against the Italic peoples (see above, p. 244). But, as it happened, this was the last challenge mounted by the first generation of the Hellenistic kings, a generation of professional fighters who, for the past forty or so years, had enjoyed a free run from India to Italy and from the Arabian desert to the Danube.

In Italy, Pyrrhus began by winning two victories, but at such great cost that, according to Plutarch, he himself remarked: 'If we win another victory against the Romans, we shall be totally lost.' He then liberated Syracuse, which was besieged by the Carthaginians, and withdrew to Campania, where he was defeated at Beneventum (275). During this expedition another tidal wave of Celts swooped down upon Greece. Epirus seemingly had nothing to fear: an alliance with the Illyrians protected it. Instead of using the support of the mountain peoples (the Dardanians are believed to have offered him 20,000 men), Ceraunus allowed himself to be submerged in the very first wave and died in battle (279). Under the command of an ordinary *strategos*, the Macedonians repulsed the invaders. A second wave swept down the Axius river, gave the Macedonians and Thessalians a nasty shock, avoided Thermopylae, which was well defended, and threatened Delphi. The sanctuary of Apollo was saved by the Phocidians (who in consequence regained their seat in the Amphictonia, which they had lost in 346) and the Aetolians (who, admitted as members in 277, soon became predominant). The third wave was halted by a resounding victory won by Antigonus Gonatas, whom the 'Macedonian army thereupon proclaimed king. The Celts (whom the Greeks now called Galatians) suffered a last defeat in Asia Minor, where they were restricted to a territory to be called Galatia (in the Ankara region). Having returned to Epirus, Pyrrhus reoccupied Macedonia, where he was once again recognized as king (274).

Cleonymus boasted that he would rally Sparta and the rest of the Peloponnese to his support, but Sparta could not be won over. Pyrrhus' adventurous career came to an end in Argos, where he was killed in street fighting (272). In that same year Tarentum capitulated and the western limit of the Hellenistic world stabilized temporarily along a line running from the Adriatic to Cyrenaica.

What do we really mean by 'the Hellenistic world'? To the extent that the expression designates a new kind of political regime, it can be applied to the zone of influence of the dynasties that for several centuries played a leading role in the eastern Mediterranean: the Antigonids in Macedonia, with Antigonus II Gonatas (272–239), the Seleucids in Asia, with Antiochus I Soter (281–239) and the Lagids (from Lagus, the father of Ptolemy I) in Egypt, one of whom was Ptolemy II Philadelphus (283–246). These long reigns were to set their stamp on the second century. In default of a universal empire, they inherited the form that Alexander personally gave to the royal title (*basileus*). Their problem, and that of their successors, was – and was to remain – how to maintain around them, in the face of those disputing their right to the terrain, states that were viable, even though their dimensions were constantly changing, depending upon the three criteria that bestowed upon each one its particular physiognomy: their administrative efficiency, their military power and their wealth.

So much was made clear in 281: when Lysimachus disappeared so did his kingdom. Thrace was occupied by the Celts. The northern and eastern cities of the Black Sea remained independent; those on its south coast and along the Straits (Byzantium, Chalcedon, Heraclaea Pontica) became so and formed the kernel of a little-known federation, the Northern League. In Asia Minor, the cities of the north-west, led by Philetaerus, the commander of the citadel of Pergamum, rallied to Antiochus I. The Islanders' League, followed by Miletus, Halicarnassus and several other city-ports in Caria, Lycia and Pamphylia entered the sphere of influence of Ptolemy II. The former Achaemenid territories that Alexander had left under the rule of their Iranian dynasties detached themselves completely from the Macedonian guardianship. Working from west to east, these were Bithynia, the Pontus, Cappadocia, Armenia and Atropatene Media. The Seleucid possessions, beginning in the south-east, formed a belt around Asia Minor, but one that did not contain a wide fringe stretching from the Black Sea to the Caucasus, in consequence of which the Seleucids' access to the old royal way leading from Sardis to Susa was blocked, and instead they were obliged to use the route across Cilicia that had been taken by Alexander.

And what of the cities, both old and new? In a history of Greece (not a history of the Hellenistic world, which would require more attention to be paid to the eastern peoples), it is they that must be of most interest to us, as they were to all the Hellenes scattered through the various Hellenistic states. Short of entering into a federal state, their modest size ruled out any military competition with the large Hellenistic kingdoms. Yet they still had a great deal going for them. Even when a city could no longer make its mark as a warrior power, it still possessed what Aristotle had defined as its very essence: the ability to form a community of free men that was a good place to live in. Instead of foundering amid ruinous foreign ventures as in the past, a city could now concentrate on 'the citizen profession', lucrative enterprises and cultural activities. As soon as a new city reached a sufficiently high level of prosperity, it would tend to behave as the more ancient cities before it had: it would open schools, provide a welcome for artists, philosophers and orators, construct a harmonious architectural framework, whether it was a capital such as Alexandria or a turntable for major international trade, such as Rhodes. Indifferent to their 'benefactors', whom they liked to treat as foreigners, kings who spent their time fighting one another but whom they showered with honorific decrees, the cities lived on and continued to diffuse to the very heart of Asia a civilization that recognized no political frontiers.

THE BALANCE OF POWER: A WORLD AT WAR (281–220)

The expression 'balance of power' designates a relative stabilization of international frontiers that results from the relations of strength that exist between sovereign states that seek a coexistence that favours their interests as much as possible, without any of them claiming hegemony. The political boundary between the two Mediterranean basins established in 281 provides an example: communications between the two shores of the Adriatic continued despite the boundary. But, quite simply, the Greeks no longer possessed the means to cross the Otrante channel and Rome, for its part, was for years kept busy settling its differences with Carthage (First Punic War, 264–241).

CHRONOLOGY OF THE PRINCIPAL EVENTS

The First Syrian War The 'Syrian Wars' were really Mediterranean wars over zones of influence to which both the Seleucids and the Lagids laid claim. The military operations (which are very poorly documented) are only comprehensible in relation to the foreign policies of the ruling sovereigns, and those policies in their turn depended on internal problems. A

simple summary of the events should therefore reflect the material necessary for an analysis of the balance of power.

Antiochus I (whose father had associated him with the royal power as
early as 293, when he had made him responsible for the administration of
the eastern satrapies, just as Darius had used Cyrus the Younger in Asia
Minor) had deployed considerable energy in establishing his authority over
all that it was possible to salvage of his dynastic heritage. At the beginning
of his reign, when threatened by sedition in Seleucis (a particularly strategic region, where Seleucus had founded four cities situated close together,
Apamea and Antioch inland, Laodicea on the sea and Seleuceia in Pieria
close to the coast), Antiochus had agreed to large territorial concessions,
making peace with Philadelphus in 279 and with Gonatas in 278. On the
other hand, no Seleucid was ever to go back on the claim formulated by
Seleucus in 301 to Syria (the former satrapy of Transeuphratene), which in
the eyes of the Greeks extended as far as the Gaza region (the ancient land
of the Philistines, called 'Palestinian Syria' by Herodotus).

Since 277 Philadelphus had been laying claim to Cyrenaica (which shared
its western border with the territory of Carthage), challenging his half-
brother Magas for its possession (Magas had been appointed as its governor by Ptolemy I, and had later proclaimed himself king). Naturally enough,
Magas had entered into alliance with Antiochus. The conflict was resolved
without a battle, and Magas remained king for twenty or so years, with the
understanding that his possessions would then revert to Ptolemy III. Between 274 and 271 Antiochus reckoned himself strong enough to conquer
the Syrian territories occupied by Philadelphus. At first Antiochus gained
the upper hand in the hostilities, but later things went in Philadelphus'
favour. The peace treaty gave no advantages to either side.

The Chremonidean War   Once the Syrian conflict was over, Lagid diplomacy was reactivated in the Aegean. Philadelphus founded an anti-
Macedonian League, in a partnership with Areus I of Sparta that was
then extended to include the Athenians. The Chremonidean decree (August
268), which has been preserved in an inscription, once again recalls the
common struggle of the Athenians and the Spartans during the Persian
Wars and returns to the theme of liberty, as follows: 'King Ptolemy, in
conformity with the policies of his parents (Ptolemy I and Berenice I) and
his sister, demonstrates his manifest zeal for the common liberty of the
Greeks.' This is the first instance of an official document that recognizes
the role played by a Hellenistic queen in affairs of State. The queen in
question was Arsinoë, who had died in 270 and been awarded divine
honours. This woman of forceful character had initially married Lysimachus,
then her half-brother Ceraunus, and finally her full brother (hence the
epithet that they shared, Philadelphus, 'who loves her brother/his sister').

The evolution of the hostilities shows that Ptolemy II's intention was
only to contain Antigonid influence in southern Greece. The list of allies

mentioned in the decree conveys the limits of that influence: neither Thessaly, nor Boeotia, nor Aetolia, nor Argolis, nor Messenia were part of the coalition. To meet up with the Athenians, Areus tried to penetrate the line of strongholds that Craterus, the half-brother of Gonatas, had implanted in order to bar access to the isthmus of Corinth. On his third unsuccessful attempt he was killed (265). The Athenians, assisted by a Ptolemaic fleet with an operational base on the island of Cos, off the coast of Attica (two fortified Lagid camps have also been discovered by archaeologists, one on a small island close to the Sunium promontory, the other on the eastern coast of Attica), were equally unsuccessful at ousting the Antigonid garrison from Piraeus. Alexander II of Epirus, 'to avenge the death of his father, Pyrrhus' (according to Justinian), then created a diversion in upper Macedonia, from which he was repulsed. Gonatas, in his turn, opened a second front by besieging Miletus, where the general staff office of the Ptolemaic fleet was located, commanded by Callicrates of Samos: he was unsuccessful on land but won a naval victory off the island of Cos. Reduced to fighting on its own, Athens capitulated (spring 261). The Athenians were then forced to accept garrisons in all their Attic fortresses. Gonatas made peace with Philadelphus that same year. The Lagid positions in the Aegean remained intact.

The Second Syrian War Ptolemy Philadelphus seized the opportunity provided by the death of Antiochus I (June 261) following a war against Eumenes I of Pergamum, the nephew of Philetaerus, who had seceded. He consolidated his strategic forces along the Aegean coast, which he now controlled from Ephesus to Halicarnassus. Antiochus II (261–246) riposted vigorously on the Syrian front. The peace concluded in 253 stripped the Lagids of their implantations in Ionia and Pamphylia. The Islanders' League collapsed.

Gonatas, who had remained neutral in this conflict, in 253 faced up to the secession of Alexander, who had succeded his father Craterus as the commander of the Antigonid naval bases in central Greece (the efficacy of which had been demonstrated in the Chremonidean War). Having lost part of his fleet, Gonatas negotiated the neutrality of Alexander II of Epirus (272–252) and of the Aetolians. Together these, organized into a federal state since 326, held a territory that extended from the Gulfs of Corinth and Ambracia all the way to the Gulf of Malia, taking in Thermopylae. This was the first time that any sovereign had cut a diagonal swathe right through central Greece, from one sea across to the other. Alexander happened to die in 244, and Gonatas recovered his naval strongholds; but not for long.

The Third Syrian War In 246 Antiochus II and Ptolemy II both died. A third Syrian War immediately broke out (246–241) between Seleucus II

(246–226) and Ptolemy III Euergetes (246–222). At the request of his sister Berenice, known as the 'Bringer of Dowries' (Antiochus II had married her in 253, after repudiating his first wife, the mother of the future Seleucus II), Ptolemy III Euergetes marched to Antioch, where he found that Berenice had been assassinated, advanced as far as Mesopotamia, then returned to Alexandria to repress a revolt. The peace that was then negotiated restored to the Lagids the cities they had lost in Asia Minor and also left them Seleuceia in Pieria, the port that served Antioch (which they retained until 219).

The backlash from this defeat made itself felt at the two extremities of the Seleucid kingdom. In 245, in Iran, the satraps of Bactria and Parthia seceded. The former, Diodotus, proclaimed himself king, but the latter was killed by invading Parni (from the Aral Sea region). These settled definitively in Parthia (hence their name, Parthians). Their leader, Arsaces, had assumed the title of king in 247. To obtain his support in the Syrian War, Seleucus II had ceded the co-regency and Asia Minor to his younger brother, Antiochus Hierax. In opposition to his brother, who was trying to establish his own authority, Hierax formed an alliance with the kings of Bithynia, the Pontus and Cappadocia, recruited a force of Galatian mercenaries, and inflicted a serious defeat upon Seleucus II (in about 239). He then sent his mercenaries to put down the movement of secession in Pergamum. Attalus I, the cousin and successor of Eumenes, fought them off, took the title of king (in about 236) and occupied Asia Minor as far as Phrygia. Hierax then tried to seize what was left of his brother's territory. These two sons of Antiochus II died in the same year (226). The new claimant to the throne, Seleucus III (226–223) was assassinated by a Galatian during a campaign against Attalus I.

Macedonia encircled   Two incidents that began in about 250 show that in the mid-third century, 'if there was a capital in which the threads of worldwide politics crossed, that capital was neither Antioch nor Pella, but most definitely Alexandria' (E. Will). The first was short-lived. At the death of King Magas, his widow, the daughter of Antiochus I, tried to prevent the scheduled return of Cyrenaica to the Lagids. She offered her daughter, Berenice II, promised to the future Ptolemy III, to the brother of Antigonus Gonatas, Demetrius the Handsome, along with the royal title. If this ploy proved successful, the Lagid dynasty would be caught in a pincer-hold between its two rivals. However, Berenice had the new king, who was too flighty, assassinated, and returned Cyrenaica to the Lagids. The second incident involved a young man of 20, Aratus of Sicyon (who, to make sure he was remembered by posterity, took good care to write his *Memoirs*). In a bold, surprise move, he began by liberating his city from a pro-Macedonian tyrant and persuaded his fellow-citizens to join the small Achaean federation (organized as a *koinon* since 280, it extended from the borders of Sicyon to those of Elis). Then he travelled to Egypt and obtained financial aid from Philadelphus. He was elected *strategos* of the Achaeans in 245, and continued to be re-elected every two years (in accordance with the federal rule) until his death in 214. In 243, again by dint of a surprise strike, he seized Corinth, its two ports and the Antigonid fleet sheltering there. At this, Epidaurus, Troezen and Megara all, along with Corinth, entered the Achaean federation, which conferred the title of *strategos* upon Ptolemy III Euergetes.

Gonatas riposted in a devious manner: he promised to share the Achaean territory with the Aetolians, provided they would undertake the necessary military operations. The Achaeans allied themselves with Sparta. King Agis IV (who was attempting a bold social reform, to which we shall be returning) met them with an army composed of young men who were drawn from the poor community. In these circumstances, Aratus preferred to avoid a direct confrontation with the Aetolians, who marched past the walls of Corinth and Sicyon without halting. He then attacked them unexpectedly while they were busy dividing up the booty they had seized in some small Achaean town. After this, the Aetolians and the Achaeans made peace and left things as they were (240).

Antigonus died in 239, aged 80. As soon as his son, Demetrius II, took over, a war broke out. Polybius calls it the 'Demetrian War', because it continued throughout his reign. The hostilities began over a switch in alliances: the Achaeans entered into alliance with the Aetolians against Macedonia. Demetrius II skilfully distracted the members of this coalition with a new front, rallying the Boeotians to himself. The royal family of Epirus, which since the death of Alexander II had been weakened by a succession of female regencies, died out in 232. The Molossian monarchy was replaced by a federal state whose foreign policy was not yet clear. Demetrius now started up another distraction on Epirus' southern frontier: he paid Agron, the king of the Illyrians, to liberate a small Acarnanian city besieged by the Aetolians. The Illyrians, carried there in light craft of the type generally used by pirates, raised the siege (231). Meanwhile Demetrius was called away by trouble on his Balkan frontier. He was killed in a war against the Dardanians. His sole heir, the future Philip V, was only 8 years old.

At this point Thessaly defected to enter the Aetolian federation. Aegina and the Peloponnesian cities still in the hands of pro-Macedonian tyrants joined the Achaean federation. On the payment of 150 talents, partly collected thanks to subscriptions donated by Aratus and other friendly cities, Athens obtained the evacuation of the Macedonian garrisons in Attica. Once free, however, the Athenians refused to bind themselves to the Achaeans. The ideal of liberty, 'the old liberty of our ancestors', as a commemorative inscription put it, on which the Athenians had had no compunction in trampling when it happened to be the liberty of others, still, two whole centuries after the death of Pericles, seemed to them an accessible objective. Only Euboea remained loyal to the Antigonids.

THE BALANCE OF FORCES

This chronological overview reveals the constraints that conditioned the foreign policies of the three kingdoms. The Seleucids were fighting on three excessively widely separated fronts. Their possessions remained a reservoir of wealth and soldiers that far exceeded the potential of their rivals. However, their Aegean façade was occupied by ancient cities that could only be held by gaining control of their access to the sea; and their war fleet (which did not control the arsenals of the Phoenicians, since the Ptolemies held these) was unable to neutralize the fleets of their opponents. In Syria they were defending their frontier that ran from the river Eleutherus (Nahr el-Kebir), the only significant break in the coastal chain of mountains, up as far as the source of the Orontes river, then passed in a straight line eastward, but without taking in Damascus, the chief town of the former satrapy of Transeuphratene. For the moment, their eastern frontier seemed less threatened. The third Mauryan sovereign, Asoka (about 268–236) had converted to Buddhism and was issuing predictive edicts that were diffused throughout his kingdom. Many examples of these have been found, in particular bilingual inscriptions (in Aramaic and Greek) discovered in Arachosia (in the Kandahar region). They record that the sovereign sent ambassadors to teach non-violence to his neighbour Antiochus II and also to Antigonus Gonatas, Ptolemy Philadelphus, Magas of Cyrene and Alexander II of Epirus. It is not hard to imagine the reception they must have received.

The Lagids were the most favoured geographically, for their centre was Egypt, endowed with solid natural frontiers, thanks to the surrounding desert (and also with all the gifts of the Nile's 'golden waters', as Callixenes of Rhodes calls them). The defensive technique established by the first three Ptolemies is described by Polybius with great clarity:

They paid more attention to foreign affairs than to their powers over Egypt itself. They thus threatened the kings of Syria both on land and at sea, thanks to their dominion over Coele Syria and Cyprus. They kept within striking distance of the dynasts of Asia and the island peoples by maintaining their power over the most favourably situated cities, bases and ports along the coast from Pamphylia to the Hellespont and also Lysymacheia and the neighbouring region. They kept under surveillance the affairs of Thrace and Macedonia by remaining masters of Ainus and Maronea and other inland towns too. So as not to have to defend Egypt, they extended their hand of authority a long way and swept their power far before them.

The Lagid possessions thus formed three deep defensive lines. Coele Syria (called 'Syria and Phoenicia' in the Ptolemaic texts) and Cyprus ensured immediate cover for Egypt and had the effect of deterring belligerence on the part of the kingdom opposite from relatively close quarters: from a distance of less than 200 kilometres from Antioch (not to mention the even closer Lagid stronghold of Seleuceia in Pieria) and over 700 kilometres from Alexandria. A string of naval bases in Pamphylia, Caria and Crete, prolonged to the north by fortified outposts, enabled them to wring respect from the independent cities and princes. Lastly, Euergetes had acquired a foothold on the shores of the straits when he had seized Lysimachus' former capital, and also on the coast of Thrace proper: this third circle of defences, on the very doorstep of Macedonia, is reminiscent of the kind of posthumous revenge that Athens was prone to seize.

The Antigonids paid a heavy price for the Macedonian past. Mainland Greece had emerged exhausted from the endless wars and emigration to the East. The scarcity of men was sorely felt. Isocrates had predicted that the spoils taken from the Barbarians would make the Greek cities rich. But what had still been a possibility within the framework of Alexander's empire was so no longer, now that the Greeks of Europe were reduced to their own meagre resources. Gonatas had chosen first to save Macedonia proper, if only demographically. So far as he possibly could he protected the lives of a nation bled dry for which 'a whole generation of convalescence was certainly not excessive' (E. Will). Outside Macedonia, his land troops and his fleet were recruited from mercenaries (Galatians, for example). In the face of the hostility of the old cities, by now traumatized by Macedonian brutality, his defence system was both economical and effective: he simply maintained a large, well-trained fleet, stationed in a few well-situated bases (Polybius called them 'the fetters of Greece: Demetrias, founded by his father on the Gulf of Pasagae, Chalcis, Histiaea, Eretria in Euboea and, when possible, Piraeus), reinforced by a network of frequently shifting alliances with the Peloponnesian cities that were governed by tyrants. But Macedonia was in danger when forced to defend itself on several fronts at once: in that respect, the state of the kingdom in 229 was reminiscent of that at the time of Philip II's accession to the throne in 359.

To summarize: the naval bases maintained by the Hellenistic kingdoms were conceived in a static mode, as a line of defence on land. In other words, in the eastern Mediterranean a 'thalassocracy', in the sense in which Pericles understood the term, no longer existed. The Aegean Sea, once the heart of Hellenism, was no longer a unified area, but rather a kind of 'no-man's land' over which no sovereign State exercised its control. As Thucydides had remarked in connection with Crete under Minos (which was supposed to have been the first power to arm a fleet capable of dominating the Cyclades), without control of the sea, in the long run commercial navigation becomes dangerous. The same went for the Adriatic, now an area open to roaming pirates, to whom we shall have occasion to return.

THE KINGDOMS

THE IMAGE OF A KING

Is it possible to make out a typology of a Hellenistic king, on the basis of this wide variety of personalities and political situations? C. Préaux's view is as follows:

I believe it is, if we look down on the situation from a great enough distance. All those kings had the same concept of warfare, which was their common preoccupation, of diplomacy, in which their respective interests clashed, of their relations with the cities, of their own role as protectors, and of the prestige of victory and wealth, the condition of their power.

Hellenistic royalty was a phenomenon that stemmed from an image inherited from Alexander and based on the heroic model transmitted by Homer's *Iliad* (which was memorized in the very first cycle of the *paideia*). The unanimous preference of the philosophers and the orators of the fourth century was for the regime of the *polis*; but, given the misfortunes of the times, they resigned themselves to that image. In fact, they even rehabilitated it by developing the negative picture of the tyrant, for whom they reserved the odious features of the absolute monarch. Only the characteristics generally expected in a politician were incorporated in the protrait of a true king, which the Greeks of the cities presented as 'a mirror of the prince' to the real kings, in the desperate hope that the latter would be inspired by it in dealings with their own cities.

In other words, this was a literary phenomenon, diffused in a hundred different variants by inscriptions and the works of court poets, and illustrated on coins and by statues and monuments. It would be vain to seek there for new ideas. The schools founded by Plato and Aristotle allotted no more than a marginal place to the study of the institution of monarchy: for their disciples, politics, as the word itself indicated, was a matter for the *polis*. And the later philosophical schools (the Cynics, Epicureans and Stoics) right from the start bypassed the collective framework, whatever it might be, and taught their members that, individually, on their own, they could attain the goal that Aristotle had assigned to the city (living well, wellbeing). The explanation for that lacuna is simple: their teaching was addressed to Greeks living in cities either old or new, cities that wanted to be 'classical', that is to say, cities attached to values that were sure, cities that were resistant to innovations and proud of being so.

The focal point of the royal image was 'qualification through victory' (G. Préaux). The men of the cities fell into the trap created by their own definition of the soldier-citizen. Somehow they crystallized this in the person of the king – which amounted to transforming it into its opposite: all the theoretical effort once deployed around the concept of collective combat, the perfect image of a city undivided, was reduced to nothing but the (still potent) rhetoric of 'the Victor of . . .'. This idealization was reinforced by the scorn felt since the fourth century for the figure of the mercenary soldier, whom New Comedy represented as a braggart and a coward. Of course, a tyrant would 'naturally' use foreign mercenaries whom he would pay at the expense of his fellow-citizens. A true king, in contrast, mobilized his own Hellenic subjects, himself led them to victory, saved them from their enemies and repeatedly, as a benefactor, distributed among them the treasures won from the vanquished. Occasionally it did still happen that a Hellenistic king chanced to defeat Barbarians, in particular the fierce Galatians; but that was all that remained of the pan-Hellenism of Isocrates, who had dreamed of banishing warfare from the world of the cities. Most of the time the war that the kings made was between Greeks. Now, however, that was of little account: all that mattered was victory.

The enumeration of royal virtues, endlessly repeated, stems from that postulate. The vocabulary used in the funeral orations pronounced in honour of the Athenians who died for their country reappears in the eulogies for deceased kings written by the best Hellenistic historian, Polybius, even though he was certainly no crawling courtier and his admiration for the Roman Republic was sincere. Polybius dwells, as an expert, upon the skills required of sovereigns educated since childhood with a view to warfare, and even explains how they may be turned into tyrants by bad advisers: what is required are the classic virtues of the model citizen (courage, tactical skill, prudence, justice, piety and loyalty). The robot portrait thus produced is as abstract and disembodied as the picture of the ancient city imagined in the fourth century. But whether its impact was efficacious is problematical: in the absence of any constitutional controls, the kings (unlike city magistrates) did not have to account for anything to anybody. Fortunately for the cities, other traditional virtues, but of a concrete and self-interested nature, such as benevolence (*eunoia*), a commitment to benefaction (*euergesia*) and humanity (*philanthropia*) also tended to be practised by the sovereigns. By dispensing largesse in the most public places, they reckoned to outshine their rivals in magnificence, boost their reputations and, in return, obtain useful support.

THE CULT OF THE KING

The heroic nature of the virtues required of a 'true king', such as Alexander during his earthly life, revealed his princely nature, which was divine. After Alexander, royal cults took three different forms. The most ancient and also the most general became a part of the civic religion in which, even before their deaths, the kings were associated with the poliad deities. 'Although there were local variants, a quasi-stereotyped schema existed: a *temenos* (sacred precinct), an altar, sacrifices, a yearly procession, games, hymns, the offering of golden crowns, statues, and the dynastic name that would be bestowed upon a particular tribe or month' (C. Préaux). The second form was a dynastic cult of the Greek type, instituted, organized and controlled by the sovereigns themselves, with priests, festivals and so on. Neither the Antigonids nor the kings of Epirus nor the Attalids founded on their own territories cults that revered either their ancestors or themselves, even though they had received divine honours in a number of cities. On the other hand, the Seleucids and the Lagids did found either separate or combined cults of kings and queens: first for their deceased ancestors

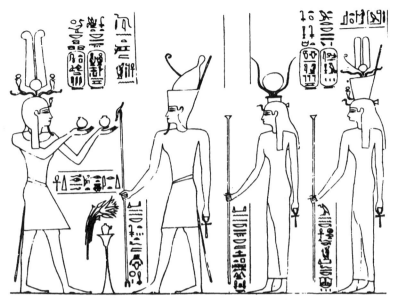

Figure 54 Detail from the carvings on the Pithom stele. King Ptolemy Philadelphus (on the left) offers a sacrifice to the god Atum, 'his father', who is accompanied by the goddess Isis and Arsinoë, deified during her lifetime. The stele was erected in Pithom ('The House of Atum') on 2 January 264 BC to commemorate the fortieth anniversary of Ptolemy I's accession to the throne. The town, known to us from Herodotus and the Bible, was situated on the bank of the canal linking the Nile and the Red Sea (from E. Grzybek, *Du Calendrier macédonien au calendrier ptolémaïque*, Basle, Reinhardt Verlag, 1990)

(for example, Ptolemy I and Seleucus I), then for themselves (for example, Ptolemy II and Arsinoë Philadelphi, honoured in 272 as *theoi adelphoi*, 'brother and sister gods'). Finally, unlike the Seleucids, whose non-Greek subjects had not learned from the Achaemenids the practice of cults addressed to kings 'as if to gods', the Lagids, as the successors to the pharaohs (deified as the sons of Amon-Ra) were the objects of a dynastic cult that was purely Egyptian. The illustrations and hieroglyphic inscriptions that cover the walls of the Egyptian temples repaired or constructed by the Ptolemies are no different from those of the period of the pharaohs.

To help us understand the religious significance of the cult of sovereigns, we have in our possession a hymn in honour of Demetrius Poliorcetes, composed on the occasion of a triumphal visit of his to Athens, in 290:

Like the greatest and most beloved of gods, they make their joyous entry to the city, Demeter and Demetrius, whom a happy chance has brought together and to us. She comes to celebrate the august mysteries of Core; he appears with a fine and handsome face, smiling as befits a god. What an august spectacle! All his friends

303

cluster round him and he is in their midst. Salutations, all-powerful son of the god Poseidon and Aphrodite!

The other gods are too far away, or have no ears, or do not exist, or are paying no attention to us. But as for you, we see you face to face, not wooden or stone, but real!

That is why we pray to you, you the most beloved. First give us peace, for you are our Lord. As for that Sphinx, the Aetolian, who lies in wait on his rock, like the ancient Sphinx, avidly capturing our men, I have no strength left to fight him. Yes, it is typically Aetolian to make surprise raids to loot the goods of neighbours and now even those of people far away. In so far as is possible, you must punish him! If not, find an Oedipus to hurl this bird of prey to the foot of its eyrie or to turn it to stone.

Despite the progress made by Greek science and philosophy, whose earliest efforts in the religious field, taking the form of a criticism of poetic language, date from as early as the seventh century, the 'deification' of living kings does seem quite logical. However, as we have seen in the case of Demosthenes, it was a logic of derision. The tutelary gods had sorely disappointed those who believed in them, for they had repeatedly failed to ward off disasters. The impotence of Athens had revealed the impotence of Zeus himself in the face of destiny. A longing for security did the rest. The poetic representation of the divine was essentially based on the notion of power, a cosmic power constantly intervening in the existence of human beings. As soon as politics stopped being a rational attempt to make citizens themselves responsible for public affairs, and instead turned into submission to the force embodied in a single man, it once again became natural to assimilate the sovereignty of kings to that of the gods. To do so, all that was needed was to cease to pay attention to the scientific concept of the world which, since the beginning of the classical period, had been insisting on the transcendent nature of the divine. Our own modern logic would conclude that, if divinity is identified with omnipotence, gods who are impotent in the face of destiny to not exist. The Hellenistic period chose the opposite solution: if the power that religious feeling attributes to the divine is present in a king, he must be essentially divine.

The hymn to Demetrius Poliorcetes illuminates this phenomenon. The questions relating to the nature of the gods that are expressed in its second section date from Homer and later resurface in the philosopher Epicurus (342–271), an exactly contemporary Athenian. Having experienced the inefficacy of the poliad gods and even of the foreign gods called in to assist them, might it not be more economical to address oneself directly to a god of flesh and blood, in order to obtain peace at last? The most immediate threat in this instance was that of the looting Aetolians, who were in occupation of the sanctuary of Delphi and who, on the strength of their alliance with Thebes, might at any moment invade Attica. Hence the allusions to a new Sphinx (the myth of Oedipus). When Demetrius was defeated by Seleucus the Athenians would, just as logically, cease to accord him divine honours. Clearly, nobody was duped by this game of mirrors; and meanwhile the impotence of the poliad gods had in no way diminished religious practices. The corollary to the cult of sovereigns was a degradation of the notion of the divine that Socrates and Plato had elevated to such a high degree of transcendency. But the poliad cults continued to provide opportunities for festivity; and the royal festivals were the most sumptuous of all.

THE KING'S LAW

It was not only the gods that prompted misgivings among the men of the cities. Their own civic institutions had also let them down. After long years of gradual progress, Athens had given itself a regime placed under the protection of the law, which was sovereign. But what was one to think of a law that was powerless to ensure the survival of the city in its full form, in which liberty was essential? Should that impotence not be attributed to the muddled and sometimes cruel ideas of the *dèmos*? The gravest failing of Greek thought, faced with the twofold evidence of the strength of kings and the weakness of cities, was not the adoption of the cult of sovereigns. Rather, it was the acceptance, as a fundamental principle of law (not simply as a matter of fact, imposed by military might), of the idea that the royal will had the force of law. It is true that Aristotle had accepted, as a working hypothesis designed to illustrate an extreme case, that if there existed in a city a man whose virtue and competence far surpassed those of his fellow-citizens as a whole, it was natural that he should be 'like a god among men'. But he had immediately gone on to explain: 'Against such superior beings, there is no law: they themselves are the law. In truth, it would be ridiculous to try to legislate against them; they would probably riposte in the same way that, according to Antisthenes, the lions responded to the hares that were arguing in the assembly for equality for all.' Aristotle takes it for granted that everyone knew how the lions reacted. According to the founder of the school of the Cynics (early fourth century), they responded by demanding: 'And where are your claws and sharp teeth?' In other words, when the balance of forces is too unequal, anyone who resists is ridiculous. However, under no circumstances was it permissible rationally to assimilate the coercive power of a sovereign to the sovereignty of the law. That would have constituted an intellectual dereliction. Besides, the Hellenistic kings had in fact not forgotten their Macedonian roots: the king of Macedonia was himself subject to the Macedonian *nomos*. Even if that *nomos* did not lay many obligations upon him, it was nevertheless a guarantee of his legitimacy. That was what made him a king, not a tyrant or an Asian despot. But the Hellenistic chancellories reserved the term *nomos* for the laws of cities. A decision of a sovereign would be promulgated in the form of a letter (*epistolè*), an edict (*prostagma*) or a ruling (*diagramma*). For example, the *diagramma* that Ptolemy, at that time still the satrap of Egypt, promulgated in 321, for Cyrene, in sovereign fashion fixed the constitution of that city as an oligarchy, with assemblies that would vote on the laws to be passed. Clearly, since the authority of the satrap of Egypt, and subsequently that of his successors, was superior to the cities, it was also above their laws.

Fortunately, the kings were too busy with other matters to legislate in every domain. That is what saved the Hellenes from sinking into apathy. Those who lived in cities, as most did, governed themselves according to their own laws, meanwhile, as in ancient times, maintaining diplomatic relations with the kings and with other cities. Those who did not live in cities, about whom quite a lot is known thanks to the papyri of Egypt, enjoyed similar privileges. So long as their fiscal interests were not involved (and if they were, lawyers were not even allowed to bring a case against the Treasury), the Lagids left it to the civil courts to pass judgement on disagreements between private individuals by applying the *politikoi nomoi*, that is, the common law that all Hellenes (and Hellenized non-Egyptians) observed. Furthermore (and this may be one of the reasons why the Egyptians of the Thebaid preserved their combativity to the point of rebelling for their independence as early as the reign of Ptolemy IV Philopatur), they allowed a private, purely Egyptian law to develop, the 'laws of the country' (the word translated by 'country', *chôra*, referred to the Egyptian territory outside Alexandria, in the same way as in France 'the provinces' are distinguished from Paris). This law was applied by Egyptian priests, the *laokritai* ('judges of the *laos*') in litigation between Egyptians (and even between Egyptians and Hellenes in instances where the contracts in question had been drawn up in demotic, the popular language).

THE ROYAL ADMINISTRATION

The Hellenistic monarchies introduced a new experiment: they discovered administration, together with its corollary, bureaucracy. The colonial world, fragmented into tiny units, had, as we have seen, already experimented with a number of regional or local solutions to the problems posed by the domination of foreign masters over autochthonous peoples (in particular, various forms of rural dependence, of the helot type). But the Greeks had never had an opportunity to adopt their expertise in lifestyles and organization to the scale of a continental empire. Alexander had immediately adapted to this new situation by deciding to maintain the system of the satrapies. By dint of the very absurdity of their behaviour the *diadochi* had demonstrated the viability of this solution: their armies had spread through the vast world, bringing pillage and massacre with them; yet even in these conditions the administrative infrasctructure had not imploded. The management of the occupied territories proved its own durability. The Macedonians soon learned the administrative methods that had been evolved over several thousand years in the empires of the East. They proceeded to employ them with at least as much success as the barbarians before them.

The upper administration continued to conform with the Macedonian model. The State apparatus rested upon 'ministries' (the etymological meaning of 'minister' being a servant of the king) entrusted to 'friends' (*philoi*: this term replaced *hetairoi*) of the king (that is, men who were chosen and dismissed as the king saw fit). To refer to governmental activities as a whole, the expression 'the affairs of the king' (*basilica pragmata*) was used. The royal council (*synedrion*) was composed and convoked according to the same rules (or rather the same absence of rules) as in the time of Philip II. There were not many 'ministers'. In the Seleucid kingdom an 'official for affairs' held the post of a prime minister, possibly on a temporary basis. In the Lagid kingdom this post was not an official one: it was simply filled by the adviser to whom the king paid most attention or who enjoyed his favour. The upper administration, in the strict sense of the expression, was composed of well-funded offices that used thousands of rolls of papyrus each day. The great chancellery was divided into two services, one headed by an *epistolograph*, who was in charge of the royal correspondence, the other by a *hypomnematograph*, who received appeals (any subject of the Ptolemies could appeal to the king directly) and drew up the 'official journal' of the reign (the *ephemerides*); the royal finances were the heavy responsibility of the *dioikètes* (the 'head of the administration'). The commander-in-chief of the army (the *strategos*) or of a fleet (the *navarch*) would be appointed with a particular military campaign in view and would be invested with very extensive but temporary powers. The highest dignitaries would be on convivial terms with the king when at court or when accompanying him on an expedition. They would try to keep him amused and would provide an appreciative audience for his banquet witticisms.

It is important to distinguish carefully between the central government of the kingdoms and the court (*aulè*, literally the inner courtyard to be found in all Greek houses, that is, a space that was private, as opposed to the public space of the street, the agora and the official monuments). The court was 'the king's home'. The same functions and the same honorific titles attached to the courtiers of both the Seleucid and the Lagid kingdoms. For example, the palace officials would include a High Chamberlain, a major-domo, a chief huntsman, a head of the stables, a private doctor, a chief baker and a chief cup-bearer. Court titles gradually became fixed in a a hierarchy: in the court of Alexandria, in the second century, working from the top to the bottom, there would be 'relatives', 'those assimilated to the relatives', 'head of the bodyguard', 'friends', 'successors' (future courtiers) and 'bodyguards'. These were titles that might be attributed to high officials but they did not correspond to any precise offices (for example, the 'bodyguards' (*somophylakes*) were no longer anything like Alexander's companions, some of whom themselves became kings).

In a large kingdom it was the intermediate grades, in between the central services and the peasant communities, that ensured that royal affairs ran smoothly. In this regional administration a heavy military presence, a legacy from Alexander, was everywhere the major feature. The second place went to Treasury officials, by reason of the need for abundant resources to finance the war effort. The Antigonids seem (according to M. B. Hatzopoulos) to have divided Macedonia proper into four 'divisions' (*merides*), under the authority of a *strategos*, their chief towns being Pella, Thessalonika, Amphipolis and an unidentified city in upper Macedonia. The Seleucids retained the system of satrapies, which was well suited to an extremely extended territory with scattered settlements. Appian refers to the existence of seventy-two satrapies. We know of only twenty or so, but he may have included in that number autonomous territories and districts attached to certain temples in Asia Minor. Each satrapy was placed under the direction of a satrap and a *strategos*, or a *strategos* and a manager (*oikonomos*). The most distant satrapies, known as the upper satrapies, were grouped together under the authority of a kind of viceroy. The Lagids likewise preserved the old Egyptian provinces, 'nomes' (the word came from a verb meaning 'to divide up'), initially defined as irrigation basins. Their number fluctuated around the forty mark. At first the nomes were governed by a nomarch, assisted by a *strategos*, an *oikonomos* and a *basilikogrammate* ('royal secretary'). From the time of Ptolemy Euergetes on, a nome was ruled by a *strategos* who, in the name of the king, held power over all the officials. The nomes of upper Egypt constituted a separate region, the Thebaid, placed under the authority of an *epistrategos* whose main responsibilities were to put down uprisings aspiring to independence and to keep watch over the eastern desert that stretched from the Nile to the Red Sea. All royal officials were Greek; only their assistants were Egyptian. It was only the offensive of Antiochus III, in 219, that forced Sosibius, the chief adviser of the young Ptolemy IV Philipator, to integrate 20,000 Egyptians and 3,000 Libyans into the infantry, a move that turned out to be the salvation of Egypt in 217, at the battle of Raphia.

WAS MACEDONIA THE EXCEPTION?

There is still considerable disagreement over what might be called the Macedonian (and, up to 232, Epirot) exception. What is not known is whether, following the brutal interlude of the diadochi, the monarchy remained as it was at the time of the Temenids. Some clues have suggested that it did (the absence of any cult of the sovereign, the existence of a political entity called 'the Macedonians', the role played by the royal council, the continuity of a landowning nobility, 'the foremost of the Macedonians', that played its own part in any succession crisis. The essential distinguishing feature remained the 'national' character of the kingdom. Unlike the Egyptians, despite the fact that these were a people far more unified by their millennium-old history, the Macedonians (and the Molossi in Epirus too) were not governed by a foreigner. However, that fact has no bearing on the regime: was it an absolute or a constitutional monarchy?

The Antigonids were at first referred to simply by their own names preceded by the royal title (*basileus*). Sometimes their patronyms and ethnic names would be added (king X—, son of King Y—, Macedonian). This titulary system is also attested for the Seleucids and the Lagids. But only in the case of the Antigonids do we find 'King of the Macedonians'. Later, so far as we can tell from the documentation in our possession, from the reign of Antigonus III Doson, the successor to Demetrius II, we find the formula expanded to 'King X—, son of King Y—, *and the Macedonians*' (which may be compared to Pyrrhus' dedication at the national sanctuary of Dodona after his victories in Italy: 'King Pyrrhus, the Epirots and the Tarentines, to Zeus Naios, the spoils of the Romans and their allies'. The mention, alongside the king, of the Macedonians as an entity (sometimes described as a 'community' [*koinon*]) constitutes a reference to a traditional concept that still retained the force of a *nomos* (in the sense of a 'customary right'). However, that glorious heritage, assumed by a 'usurping' dynasty, only set a limit on royal absolutism in circumstances when the regime was weak (when it took the form of sedition, as in the other Hellenistic kingdoms).

THE FEDERAL STATES

'Hellenistic Greece – apart from Sparta before its inclusion in the Achaean League, and Athens – was a Greece of federated states . . . However, one cannot judge it by the Hellenistic experience of federalism, for this came to nothing . . . a chapter with no follow-up and that achieved nothing' (E. Will). The *raison d'être* for the Hellenistic federated states is obvious. For them it was a matter of attaining the 'crucial size' that would enable them to defend their own independence against the three 'powers' of the day. It was all a matter of size, as V. Ehrenberg illustrates with (approximate) figures. Before the Roman intervention, the Hellenistic world knew of only one 'superpower' worthy of the image used in the Bible, 'a colossus with feet of iron mixed with clay': namely, the Seleucid kingdom. At its largest, it covered a continuous area of about 3.5 million square kilometres. The Lagid kingdom, together with its external possessions, reached 150,000 square kilometres (Egypt on its own, about 30,000). Pyrrhus' Greater Epirus incorporated 20,000 square kilometres. One also has to take into account the real military potential of these huge units. The ancient authors attribute to Egypt – whose 'polyanthropy' they regarded as fabulous – about 7 million inhabitants. But until 219 the Lagid army, for reasons of security, only recruited Hellenes. According to the calculations of V. Ehrenberg, the 'critical threshold' was about 20,000 square kilometres. That was the area attained by the Athenian federation after 188. This means that the 'great powers' of the fifth century, Athens, Syracuse and Sparta (respectively 2,650, 4,700 and 8,400 square kilometres) were no longer 'viable'.

THE BOEOTIANS

The first feature of the federated states (and one that strikes us as astonishingly 'modern') is that they set up a prototype of a representative government: the various components of these states ('tribes', 'ethnic groups' or cities) were represented in proportion to their human resources (in concrete terms, their military potential, which would include their financial resources). This was a reasonable solution to the problem posed by symmachies, in which the weaker allies were, according to Thucydides, reduced to 'slavery' by the hegemonic city. The Boeotians led the way here. As early as the mid-fifth century they divided their common territory into eleven districts (*merè*), all with equal rights and obligations. The advantage of this uneven number (which is sometimes described as 'Cleisthenian', because it was designed to promote an equitable distribution of power) stemmed from the fact that it never corresponded to the total of member cities (which oscillated between ten and twenty from one period to another). A district could include a variable number of cities or a single city might incorporate several districts (after the destruction of Plataea in 427 Thebes included four districts, one of which contained five cities). The majority vote (facilitated by the uneven number) in principle made it possible for Orchomenus and Thespiae, each with two districts, to counterbalance Thebes. However, these Theban institutions were no more than a blueprint that might evolve in either of two directions: either towards total unity (fusion around Thebes, similar to Attica's fusion around Athens) or towards a confederacy. The confederal tendency found expression in the creation of common political bodies: the Council, which sat in Thebes, on the Cadmeia (660 councillors – sixty from each district – divided into four sections, which succeeded one another for periods of three months each); and magistracies (eleven boeotarchs, with principally military responsibilities, placed under the authority of one of their number when on campaigns). However, by themselves, good institutions are not enough to produce good policies. (The Athenian confederation of 377 had been developing along similar lines, yet we have seen what that led to.)

The Boeotian League, dissolved in 386, then restored in 379, was definitely evolving towards federalism: it created a common assembly (known as the *damos*) in which all the inhabitants of its member-cities who (in accordance with the census rules) possessed the right to vote could take part; and the boeotarchs, now seven in number) were placed under the permanent authority of an eponymous archon. In the Hellenistic period, the Boeotians even possessed the ultimate essential privilege of a federal state: double citizenship. However, with their 2,580 square kilometres of territory, they could never attain the crucial criterion of power. At least, though, the Boeotian example demonstrated how a quite loosely linked ethnic political community could invent a new kind of political organization (*koinon*, in the strict sense of the word), founded upon truly common citizenship.

THE ACHAEANS

Another example of progress towards 'modernity': in contrast to the hegemony of the symmachies, the transfer of the essential prerogatives of sovereignty (diplomacy, the army, war and peace, arbitration between the federated cities and peoples) to a federal system did not in any way affect the 'liberty' of the federated cities. In the Achaean federation, at any rate, in all matters that had no bearing on common federal affairs they retained their initiative in their relations with other cities, whether or not these belonged to the *koinon*. According to Polybius, who composed an emphatic eulogy of the Achaean federation (which his own city, Megalopolis, along with the other Arcadian cities, joined in 245), common citizenship was regarded by the Achaeans as an extension or reinforcement of their own rights of citizenship. In accordance with his customary method (to his mind the institutions of Rome were the reason for its victories), he regarded the *koinon*, founded on the equality and liberty of all the member cities, as the secret of its rapid expansion at the time of the statesmen whom he admired, Aratus and Philopoemen (in 191 the whole of the Peloponnese belonged to the federation). It is true that, reading of the stormy clashes between the two *strategoi* and the federal assembly, you might indeed think you were back in Pericles' Athens. But Polybius, who himself witnessed the tragic end of the Achaean federation, knew better than most that even the best of laws can produce perverse effects.

The principle of double citizenship brought in its train not only a partial duplication of the civic institutions but also constant efforts at adaptation designed to ensure a fair balance in the prevailing circumstances (which were to prove disastrous). The range of federal institutions included:

- annually elected magistrates; these were led by the *strategos*, who was the head of the federal state and was assisted by military and financial magistrates;
- a small executive college (*demiourgoi* in the case of the Achaeans, *apocletoi* in the case of the Aetolians) which met in secret with the magistrates so as to be in a position to intervene directly in the *koinon*'s relations with the outside world;
- a council (*boulè* or *synedrion*) composed of several hundred delegates elected by the member states in numbers proportional to their respective resources;
- an assembly, the composition of which varied from one federation to another.

THE AETOLIANS

The Aetolians originally had a basic assembly, in which all citizens of the federated states could participate. But they persistently sought to improve their representative system, testing out the respective advantages and disadvantages of voting as individuals and voting as cities. According to L. A. O. Larsen, after 200 a representative assembly (*synodos*) brought together the council and the magistrates in regular sessions devoted to current affairs. The gravest decisions on matters of foreign policy were taken by a specially convened plenary assembly (*synkletos*), which probably included the assembly, the council and the magistrates, in which each city had a vote.

In foreign policy the Aetolians were remarkably innovative, making the most of their reputation as pirates to create a zone of influence for themselves: they concluded agreements of mutual security and asylum with a number of cities (offering protection against *sylai*, violent seizures of both persons and goods on both land and sea), agreements that sometimes also granted *isopoliteia* ('equal civic rights'). For example, one Aetolian decree guaranteed the Delians security 'in so far as this depended upon the Aetolians and the cities [in their federation]'. Clearly, the only pirates over whom the Aetolians exercised any authority were their own. Similar judicial agreements (*symbolai*) were exchanged between the Aetolians and Delphi, Athens and Miletus. In the agreements of mutual security and asylum, the Aetolians guaranteed to return anything seized; in the judicial agreements, they offered the possibility of recourse to their federal law-courts. This was a surprising use of the term *asylia*. Normally asylum meant a cancellation of the right to take reprisals that one city would claim against another that had wronged it. Once the right to reprisals had been proclaimed, any individual could seize persons of goods from the city declared to be liable to reprisals. Acts of piracy, however, were never under any circumstances considered to stem from seizures declared to be licit, since the city that underwent them could not be regarded as guilty. Links of *isopoliteia* combined with guarantees of security were contracted in the Aegean with Chios, Ceos and Mytilene, in Crete with Axos, in Asia Minor with Magnesia on the Meander and Teos, with Lysimacheia in the Thracian Chersonese, Chios on the Asian coast of the Propontis and Chalcedon on the Bosphorus. In all probability these cities were more interested in this cynical protectorate than in any future exercise of federal citizens' rights in Aetolia.

THE CITIES

The Hellenistic cities were all 'true' Greek cities, for the Greek cities did not 'die' at Chaeronea (in 338). They resembled and recognized one another; and they maintained diplomatic relations of the classic type both within and beyond the kingdoms and the federal states, with the approval of the kings and the federal authorities. Thus a stele from the sanctuary of Leto in Xanthos, in Lydia, dating from the reign of Ptolemy IV Philopator, records the visit of an embassy from Cytenion, a tiny city in the Doris region (to the north of Mount Parnassus), which was a member of the Aetolian federation. In 205 the Cytenians asked Xanthos (and probably a number of other cities too) for financial aid to rebuild their town, whose ramparts had been destroyed in an earthquake and whose houses had been burned to the ground by the troops of Antigonus III Doson in 228. A decree from the assembly and a letter from the three eponymous magistrates (the *strategos*, hipparch and secretary) of the *synedrion* of the Aetolians provided the ambassadors with their credentials. They recalled the kinship (*synegeneia*) 'inherited from the gods and the heroes' between the Dorians of the metropolis and the Xantians, reinforced by the (equally mythical)

The decree of Antioch in Persis[1]

'It has so pleased the assembly, at the proposal of the Prytaneis: given that the citizens of Magnesia on the Meander are relatives and friends of the people [of Antioch in Persis] and are famous among the Hellenes for having rendered them notable services; for in the past Antiochus I Soter made it a point of honour to enlarge our city, which bears his name; he had sent them a letter concerning the dispatch of colonists;[2] first they voted a fine and honourable decree; then in their ardour to increase the Antiochean people, after offering up prayers and sacrifices, they sent a suitable number of men known for their valour; since the people reveres gods common to itself and the Magnesians[3] and wishes to confirm its good wishes for its kin[4] . . . Hoping for Good Luck, let it please the council and the people to award a eulogy to the people of Magnesia for their piety toward the deities and for their friendship and their good wishes for King Antiochus III and the Antiochean people; and to recognize the Stephanite competition[5] as the equal of the Pythia instituted by them in honour of Artemis Leucophryene.'

1 Probably Bushehr, on the Persian Gulf; date: about 205.
2 Letters from the Hellenistic sovereigns constituted orders.
3 As in the archaic period, the colonists brought their gods with them to the new foundation (*apoikoi*) and assured themselves of their protection by continuing their cult.
4 The 'kinship' between the two cities meant that the origins of at least part of the civic body lay in the metropolis.
5 The Stephanite Games, in which the prize was a wreath, were very prestigious. Recognition of the games by other cities gave them a pan-Hellenic character. Their equality with the famous games of Delphi had been recognized by a Pythian oracle. Several inscriptions that have survived indicate that *theoroi* (sacred ambassadors) were well received throughout the Greek world, and particularly by Antiochus III, Ptolemy IV and Attalus I of Pergamum.

kinship that linked them with Ptolemy IV and Antiochus III through the intermediary of Heracles, the 'ancestor' of the Macedonian kings. A contemporary decree from Antioch in Persis (see above) also referred to its (real) kinship with the city of Magnesia on the Meander which, on the order of Antiochus I, had sent a contingent of colonists to reinforce its Greek population.

In the face of such a phenomenon, it is customary to represent the Hellenistic cities as empty shells. But the truth was quite the opposite. The legal notion of 'kinship' (whether real or fictitious) conventionally recognized between cities is one of the most striking illustrations of the deeply rooted belief (which was to survive down to the present day) that Hellenism was, first and foremost, and right from the start, a civilization. Its vocation: to integrate polyethnic groups by dint of diffusing the 'humanities', a fine word which, ever since the Renaissance, has been used to designate the *paideia*. And the Hellenistic age was, *par excellence*, the age of the 'humanities': that is how Hellenism became diffused in the East, despite the fact that the diadochi and their successors turned it, for several centuries, into a world at war.

THE ROYAL FOUNDATIONS

The foundation of new cities by Alexander and his successors answered three needs: a strategic one (to keep frontiers and communication routes under surveillance), an economic one (to acquire rich civic territories) and a social one (to secure access to a large, autochthonous workforce).

Let us consider the case of Sogdiana which, alongside mountainous and desert regions, incorporated extremely rich rural areas containing many villages. In 327 Alexander decided to found a city, Alexandria Eschatè, on the banks of the Iaxartes (Syr Daria), on a site (Khodjend) that would make it possible to protect the old Achaemenid frontier against the Scythians, who lived on the other side of the river. Arrian tells us that, in the new walled town, he brought together Macedonian veterans, Greek mercenaries and Barbarians from the vicinity. The 'neighbouring Barbarians' were either the inhabitants of the seven strongholds he had taken by assault or local villagers who had taken refuge there. Quintus Curtius adds that the latter were 'given' to the new colonists. The villagers who had been farming the agricultural territory that surrounded the 'Rocks' for the Sogdian princes thus passed under the dependence of the new arrivals, along with the territory that henceforth constituted the civic territory. 'The transfer of dependence modified the quality of that dependence, even though the level of tribute remained the same,' we are told by P. Briant. However, the texts do not explain how the personal status of the villagers was changed by Alexander. Quintus Curtius was probably thinking of the *deditici*, the enemies of the Roman people who threw themselves on its mercy. But that tells us nothing about their legal status.

Here is another example: the new cities of northern Syria (Apamea, Antioch on the Orontes, Laodicaea on the sea and Seleuceia in Pieria). This fertile region, occupied without a fight and containing no large towns, became a network of communications once the path of the Royal Way was moved to the south so that it ran through the Cilician Gates and the Syrian Gates. The civic land (*politikè gè*) was taken out of royal land. The new citizens were attracted by various material advantages (each being allotted a *kleros*, exempted from taxation and given a consignment of livestock and agricultural tools). The plotting out of the town grid no doubt accompanied the allotment of land: being allotted a plot and being entered on the civic list went hand in hand. In Antioch on the Orontes, the initial civic body (5,300 citizens, according to a late source) was composed of veterans from Seleucus' army and Cypriot, Cretan and Argive mercenaries. Later on, if there was a fall in the numbers of the civic body (which would anyway be small at first: 2,500 to 3,000 men on average, according to V. Tcherikover; 6,000 citizens in Seleuceia in 220, according to Polybius), a 'politography' took place, that is, new citizens of Greek origin were inscribed (Aetolians, Euboeans and, under Antiochus III, more Cretans). It was a procedure that was also adopted by the older cities. In about 224 Smyrna, which had remained loyal to Seleucus II during the Third Syrian War, gave citizens' rights to mercenaries from Magnesia on the Sipylus, 'if they were free and Greek, on condition that they would remain loyal to the royal cause'. Similarly Miletus, probably independent at the time, doubled its civic body in both 227 and 222 by allotting plots of land and citizenship to Cretan mercenaries, who settled down there with their wives, sisters and children. The decree of 222 mentions long-standing relations of kinship between the Cretans and the Milesians. The new city of Antioch in Persis acted in the same fashion under Antiochus I (see p. 313): 'This was not a Hellenism of borderlands, wasting away and suffocating, for it was copiously and freely irrigated' (L. Robert, on the subject of Ai Khanum).

All our documentation is epigraphic, and very few inscriptions mention the personal status of the natives who cultivated the civic land. It is always hard to decide between the two extreme possibilities of 'serfdom' and slavery. The rare relevant texts, analysed by P. Briant, show clearly the difference between *laoi* (an old Homeric word used in the Hellenistic period to designate free natives legally attached to autonomous villages) and rural slaves. When a king decided to 'give' or 'sell' to an individual an estate taken out of the royal land, it was the income (*phoros*) from the villages that was 'given' or 'sold', not the villagers. The change that took place in the Hellenistic period was a major one, as can be seen from the semantic evolution of the word *phoros*, etymologically 'burden'; then 'tribute', 'royal tax'; and ultimately 'rent', 'farm rent' paid to the king or to some other individual on the basis of a written contract. The former rural dependents became legally free (albeit economically dependent) men.

In the new cities of the Seleucid kingdom there seems to have been no 'fusion' between Hellenes and natives: their civic bodies remained exclusively Greek. Either the new foundation would be built next to an ancient town (the Alexandrias of Arie, Drangiana, Arachosia, the Caucasus and Margiana were all definitely separate from the chief towns of the Achaemenid satrapies; Seleuceia on the Eulaeus was next to Susa; the Lagid capital, Alexandria, was even said to be 'next to Egypt'); or else it would incorporate a pre-existing village within its urban perimeter, inside the ramparts (Berioa/Aleppo, for example), where the village would constitute a 'native quarter' inhabited by craftsmen and small-scale merchants. The preference given to Seleuceia on the Tigris even set the seal on a change of policy: Babylon, despite having welcomed Alexander as a liberator, found itself stripped of its rank as the administrative capital in favour of Seleuceia on the Tigris. The Chaldean clerks protested, but to no avail. The new city was settled with Macedonian colonists; and Babylonian peasants were transferred to the authority of the new civic territory. A cuneiform document shows that another deportation of agricultural workers took place in 274, on the order of Antiochus I; the peasants came from Babylon, Nippur and Cutha, all historical towns.

The last and most interesting case is that of the eastern towns of Syria-Phoenicia under Ptolemaic domination. New towns had been founded at the time of the diadochi (as is suggested by their Macedonian names: for example, Pella and Dion in Jordan). Towns destroyed by Alexander (Tyre, Gaza) or by the diadochi (Ace, Acco and Acrae) were resettled with the rank of Greek cities (Ace became Ptolemais; and at the time of Ptolemy II Philadelphus Rabbatammana Amman became Philadelphia). On the other hand, the Mediterranean ports, whose rallying had been crucial after the battle of Issus, retained their existing institutions and were declared Greek cities.

Let us single out the example of Sidon. Having been destroyed in 344 by Artaxerxes III Ochos, it welcomed Alexander and kept its own king, at least to begin with (Philocles, the king of Sidon, became the admiral of the Ptolemaic fleet). A relatively early inscription exists, dated 'Year 14 of the people of Sidon (the Greek translation reads "the *koinon* of the Sidonians")'. However, we know virtually nothing of the Sidonian institutions. On the other hand, a Greek inscription (found in Sidon by Renan) helps to explain how the transition took place. It consists of an epigram inscribed on the base of a statue erected in honour of a Sidonian magistrate, Diotimus, victor in the Nemean chariot race at Argos in about 200:

On the day when, in the valley of Argolis, all the competitors from their seats urged forward their own swift horses in the competition, the people of Phoronis chose to honour you and you received the eternally memorable crown. For, first of all the citizens, you brought back from Hella the glory of an equestrian victory to the house of the noble Agenorids. The holy Cadmean city, Thebes, also exults, seeing its metropolis made famous by your victories. And as for your father, Dionysius, the wish that he made for this competition was fulfilled when Hellas resounded with applause: it is not only with ships that you excel, proud Sidon, but also with horse-drawn chariots that carry off victory.

'The people of Phoronis' were the Argians, 'the holy Cadmean city' was Thebes and, most important, 'the metropolis of Thebes' was Sidon, 'the house of Agenor'. We should not be too surprised by all this. After all, the Romans themselves got the Greek world to acknowledge their Trojan origin. Well before the Macedonian conquest, the Sidonians had stood by their own legend: Agenor, the first king of Sidon (a temple of Agenor was to be found there in the fourth century) was the son of Phoronis, the king of Argos, and fathered Cadmus, the founder of Thebes, whose metropolis Sidon therefore was. 'All this was certainly no puerile game' (E. Bikerman). The cities recognized one another, provided their common origins could be proved. 'The establishment of such links of kinship was a historical task completed thanks to history and mythical history, between which there was no difference' (L. Robert). Admission to the community of the Hellenes conferred the right to take part in the pan-Hellenic games and, as a corollary, to institute similar competitions (in Sidon, a gymnastics competition placed under the patronage of Delphic Apollo).

In other words, recognition of the status of a Greek city was dependent upon four conditions: the presence of a Greek-speaking population, that is, one that had acquired Greek acculturation through a *paideia* (the rulers of Sidon had been bilingual since long before Alexander); a geographical situation in which an urban centre was associated with a civic territory; political institutions that were at least analogous to those of a city; and civic cults addressed to local deities assimilable to the Greek gods (in Tyre, Herodotus considered Ba'al Melquart to be Heracles).

POLITICAL LIFE

Political life in the Hellenistic cities continued, without a break, to follow the old customs. The same civic institutions, organized to fulfil the same needs, were to be found everywhere, under different names: an assembly, a council, a court of law and magistrates. However, the way that they functioned changed between the 'early' and 'late' Hellenistic periods. The break came around the mid-second century, as P. Gautier has shown in his study of what is called 'euergetism' in the decrees passed in honour of city benefactors (*euergetai*). That is one of the reasons why the present work stops at 146 BC. L. Robert describes the 'late Hellenistic period' as follows: 'The evolution of society increasingly removed city business from the sovereign action of the people's Assembly and placed it in the hands of a more or less hereditary minority of elites, who guaranteed many essential services with their wealth and in return received increasingly numerous and dazzling honours.' The epigraphic documents of the 'early Hellenistic period', in contrast, resemble those of the classical period, in both content and style.

As in the past, assemblies passed laws and, as was the custom, delegated their judiciary responsibilities to the popular law-courts; and judgements continued to be based upon the ancestral laws (*patrios politeia*). Cities that felt too weak to defend their own security against their neighbours or against pirates would unite, through treaties, with one or more other cities, in various ways: synoecism (several cities came together to form a single one), *sympoliteia* (two or more cities instituted common citizenship), *isopoliteia* (the citizens of one city were given virtual citizenship in another) or *politographia* (the inscription of new citizens). All citizens concerned would have the right to participate in public affairs. Whether or not a king had intervened in the negotiations made no difference.

Cities were often obliged to appeal to a king in order to defend themselves: from this point of view the 'benefactions' of the kings were certainly not superfluous. They had to be solicited through diplomatic channels (sending ambassadors, or getting influential fellow-citizens to approach the monarch in question), then by expressing thanks by an honorific decree accompanied by 'gifts' (a list of which was drawn up by Aristotle). It should be remembered that, even for a tiny city, entering into relations with a sovereign, a federal state or another city was always a political action from the point of view of any foreign power, so it was a grave decision that had to be approved by the supreme authority, namely the Assembly.

As in the classical period, the cities themselves ran a number of services that stemmed from their internal autonomy. In the first place, they tried to safeguard their food supplies, essentially cereals, taking into account the effects of wars and piracy. (Thus Delos, independent from 314 to 167, maintained good relations with the cities of the Black Sea and the Straits that either produced cereals or controlled the convoy routes, those long used by the Athenians.) Trade expanded and supplemented budgets with import and export taxes, for many of the cereals were re-exported within the Aegean Sea area. To pay for these supplies, it was sometimes necessary to contract public loans (particularly when shortages pushed market prices up), turn again to local or foreign benefactors (who would charge a low price for wheat) and also arrange some means to finance the repayment of loans. Also to be taken into account were the management of civic sanctuaries (the cost of sacrifices, for example), the organization of religious festivals and the arrangements for competitions (centred on the gymnasium whose president, the gymnasiarch, was a figure of the first importance), the maintenance of public doctors (appointed by the Assembly and paid by the city out of the proceeds of a special tax, the *iatrikon*) and finally all public works (roads, the water service, repairs to the ramparts and civic monuments). All these activities organized by the civic society represented heavy responsibilities that mobilized many devoted public servants, many of them unpaid.

The degree of importance ascribed to the people's Assembly, the Council, the method adopted for appointing magistrates, and the insistence on a census threshold to determine access to citizenship all continued to be factors that differentiated between a tyranny, an oligarchy and a democracy. It is clear though that most cities tended to call themselves democratic and imitated the Aristotelian model of participation. Obviously, the problem lies in evaluating that participation. (According to Strabo, the Rhodians considered that they lived in a democracy on the grounds that their ancient traditions required them to take care of the *dèmos* and to distribute food to the poor. Similarly, Polybius asserted that the Achaean federation was democratic, despite the fact that the power was confined to the wealthiest citizens.) But in the first place, we should bear in mind the chronic abstentionism that the orators of the fourth century were constantly deploring, for this helps to qualify certain remarks that are made all too often: 'it is, for example, sometimes suggested that the masses were de-politicized, because they realized that the cities had become mere puppets, with the kings (and later the Romans) pulling the strings' (P. Gauthier). To judge from the inscriptions, which are virtually our sole source of evidence in the third century BC, it was rather the reverse that was true, at least in the early Hellenistic period.

On this point, let us follow the arguments of Philippe Gauthier. The first thing to note is that the idea of democracy was gaining ground in public opinion and tending to be seen as the most desirable form of city life. To be sure, democracy was no longer what it had been in Pericles' day. But the Athenians had themselves renounced that after 403. What was 'called democracy' (Thucydides) now had a much better reputation than it had had in the eyes of Aristotle. From seeing the diadochi and their successors found their power upon oligarchies and tyrannies, the cities learned from bitter experience to consider the two 'as twin regimes that were equally detestable because both were imposed upon impotent communities by external powers or were supported by the latter'. The hatred felt for tyrants and oligarchs had expunged the memory of the misdeeds of the radical democrats. In default of obtaining the independence that remained their stubborn objective, the cities demanded that sovereigns should at least recognize and guarantee not only their 'autonomy' but also their 'democracy', which, in so far as was possible, would limit royal interventionism in their internal affairs.

So what was a Hellenistic city? Essentially a regime in which the citizens selflessly devoted themselves to their little country, expecting no reward apart from an honorific decree. That was, to be sure, an ideal; but so too had the classical city been. And it was an ideal that citizens committed themselves by oath to respect (in cities as diverse and as dispersed as the Taurian Chersonese and Smyrna, or Drerus and Itanus in Crete). The texts closely echo the oath of the fourth-century Athenian ephebes. Here is the oath sworn in Cos (just off the coast of Halicarnassus, the birthplace of Ptolemy II Philadelphus):

I shall remain loyal to the established democracy . . . to the ancestral laws of Cos, to the decrees of the Assembly . . . I shall also be loyal to the friendship and alliance of King Ptolemy and the treaties with allies ratified by the people. I shall on no pretext set up an oligarchy or a tyrant, or any regime other than a democracy; and I shall not allow anybody to set up [such a regime], but shall prevent it in so far as I can. I shall occupy no fort or citadel; I shall not tolerate any diminution of the territory of Cos, but shall on the contrary extend it as far as is in my power. I shall also be a fair judge and an impartial citizen, voting either with raised hand or with a voting chit, without giving way to compliance, on any decision that has seemed to me to be advantageous to the people. (About 200 BC)

The oaths sworn in Crete contain similar commitments to loyalty to the country and its laws. But since the regime there was aristocratic, the citizens had furthermore to promise to oppose any revolutionary *coup d'état* (*stasis*), denounce any conspiracies to the magistrates, and refuse to be party to any redistribution of land or houses or any abolition of debts. In every period there were cities and individuals that went back on their oaths. But what all these oaths reflect, over and above a certain nervousness that is easily explained by the brutality of both foreign and civil wars, is the fact that the citizens themselves feel and wish to be responsible for not only the survival of their country but also the stability of its laws. As was customary, democracies tended to impose heavier responsibilities, in the name of national sovereignty, and insisted that citizens should discharge these to the best of their ability and in the best common interests.

The new procedures for acquiring citizenship have suggested to some scholars that 'the profession of citizen' became devalued (and it is indeed known that in Byzantium, in the early fourth century, in a few exceptional cases individuals did manage to buy citizens' rights). But in fact the changes made the rules even stricter than before. Athens set the example here, and was followed by the cities of the Aegean and Asia Minor: the formalities became more complicated, the decisions slower; an oath of loyalty was required, a *quorum* was introduced and the poll for the definitive vote was kept secret. A similar strictness extended to all decisions considered particularly important (laws, agreements between cities, the granting of privileges). Numerous texts show that the figure for a *quorum*, designed to ensure the presence in the Assembly of a minimal number of citizens, was frequently exceeded (in Magnesia on the Meander, where the *quorum* was 600, the registered figures show that there were between 3.5 and 7.5 times as many people present). So citizen participation in political life does not appear to have diminished.

The Hellenistic cities opened up more to their neighbours in the judicial domain, where in the past only citizens used to have access to the city's law-courts. Here too the Athenians led the way and were imitated. By the mid-fifth century, they concluded bilateral agreements (*symbola*) that gave the members of both cities access to the courts of both cities (the trial would usually be held in the city where the offence had been committed). In about 350 it was decided that trials covered by a judicial agreement would be judged according to a new inter-community code of law, spelled out precisely in the *symbola*. The evidence collected by P. Gauthier is particularly full for the Hellenistic period. However, at the beginning of the second century a change took place: the *symbola* now entrusted trials to foreign judges summoned especially for the purpose. In the absence of even a minimum degree of social concord, many citizens no longer trusted their own courts. (In Boeotia, for example, judicial operations ceased altogether from 213 to 188, according to Polybius). But the many examples of cases where foreign judges were brought in on the grounds that they would be more impartial (except, notably, in Athens, Rhodes and independent Delos) do not necessarily mean that the civic courts were no longer functioning, for they are still attested in the second century. However, it certainly was a sign that the ideal of popular justice was gradually being eroded. Meanwhile, though, the juridical exchanges between cities created a civil law that was common to all Hellenes and that was to be applied throughout the entire Hellenistic world.

Another improvement in the juridical status of foreigners that was introduced by the Athenians was the institution of commercial actions (as mentioned above) in 350. The Athenian law-courts were now accessible to all merchants, regardless of their nationality. This was the origin of a commercial code of law based exclusively on the notion of contractual obligations and the probatory force of a written contract (*syngraphè*). Counterbalancing the advantages that it introduced was the fact that the commercial code of law was the only one to submit the accused to physical constraint, that is, imprisonment, until such time as a fine was paid, following his arrest at the request of the plaintiff. As is proved *ad nauseam* by the papyri of Zeno, this practice was to prove a terrible weapon in the hands of the Greeks of Egypt, when it was used against poor immigrants and Egyptians who had fallen into debt. This immediate detention, which prevented the arrested man from working off his debt, was a patent absurdity, the perverse effect of an innovation that in other ways testified to the inventiveness of the Greek communities that were the heirs to fourth-century Athens.

In conclusion, it seems reasonable to ask the following question, along with E. Will: did the undeniable vitality of the civic spirit and the persistent hope (sometimes fulfilled) of one day recovering from the kings that lost independence defeat the monarchical experiment of the Hellenistic world? The truth is that, as a result of not finding a satisfactory juridical solution to their congenital opposition, both the cities and the monarchies eventually came to grief. Rome was to arbitrate between them.

A WORLD AT PEACE

'A world at peace' is how C. Préaux describes the 'world' of the papyri discovered in their thousands in Egypt. The fragility of papyrus as a writing material has two consequences for a historian, one a drawback, the other an advantage. Humidity, even if slight, has unfortunately destroyed all but a tiny fraction of the Hellenistic world's texts written on papyrus. Only in rural Egypt did they survive. On the other hand, by chance it happens that on the basis of those texts we can fill in a number of chapters of social and economic history from original documents that are exactly contemporary with the details of the daily life that they record. And these concern the very categories that tend to be forgotten in other sources: namely the most deprived sections of the population. Compared to the classical period, whose literary works convey above all the cultural and political history centred on Athens, this seemed such a change to M. Rostovtzeff, one of the pioneers of papyrology, that he felt he was witnessing the birth of a new species, *homo oeconomicus*, which was taking the place of the classical *homo politicus*. Of course, this 'world at peace' was not really another world, rather simply 'the other side of the coin', as C. Préaux has put it. The life of the Greeks in Egypt, as we know it from the papyri, is not as remarkable as M. Rostovtzeff first thought. In reality, there was considerable continuity between their mental framework and that of the classical period; and what we know of Egypt may, to a certain extent, give us an idea of what must have been going on in the rest of the Hellenistic world.

THE HELLENES IN POWER

The cleruchs The new social circumstances of the Hellenistic world as a whole resulted from the large numbers and influence of immigrants who had come from Greece and other regions of the known world. The largest mass of them were soldiers whose only common characteristic was that they all spoke Greek. It is important to recognize this linguistic phenomenon. The soldiers were quartered in rural towns where they lived, initially at least, in lodgings requisitioned from the native inhabitants. The Seleucids and Lagids rewarded each of them, out of their revenues, with a *cleros* taken out of the royal estate, to revert to the king at their deaths: that is why they were called 'cleruchies' (the Seleucids also founded some military colonies that did not rank as cities). The size of the allotment varied according to the rank of the cleruch (ranging from 25 to 6 hectares in Egypt; then, when Egyptians were incorporated in the scheme, from 250 to 1.2 hectares). The cleruchs with the largest allotments (the knights) rented their land to farmers, either Egyptians or foreigners, so that they themselves could go and live 'in town', that is to say in one of the chief towns of their nome.

Did the presence of cleruchs in the countryside contribute to Hellenization? At the time of the New Deal, in the United States, during the thirties, there was much debate about the civilizing influence of the cleruchs. But nowadays nobody believes that their mission was to be part of a plan for the development of agriculture, which – thanks to them – became the basis of a monetary economy. If any economic progress did take place, it was under the impulsion of the royal officials, but this required so much effort that their energies were exhausted by the end of the third century. Nor, most certainly, were the cleruchs 'missionaries' of Hellenism. On the contrary. As Greeks, they kept themselves to themselves, meeting in their gymnasia, which had proliferated throughout the Hellenistic world, even in the country towns. Their barely tolerated presence led to many clashes with the local population. Could it at least be said that linguistic contacts were made? The use of Greek in public documents was obligatory. Inevitably, the Egyptians recruited into the lower echelons of the bureaucratic hierarchy became bilingual. The effects of this one-way acculturation only became noticeable from the second century onward. Polybius' account of the victory won at Raphia (217) is instructive. The Egyptians and Libyans incorporated into the phalanxes remained in national groups. They understood only the few standard commands, given in Greek, that were necessary for manoeuvres on the battlefield (a similar situation obtained in the Seleucid army, which also comprised non-Greek infantrymen recruited from all over the kingdom). Only the junior officers had to be bilingual, so as to understand orders and explain them to their men. E. Will notes that when Antiochus III tried to reconquer Bactria in 208–206, the army of the secessionist king there included 10,000 horsemen. This was the largest known cavalry contingent in the Hellenistic period and must have been recruited among the redoubtable and heavily armed Turanian horsemen (such as the Parthians), which implies that in the more distant satrapies, at least, Graeco-Iranian acculturation was more rapid than elsewhere.

The bureaucracy Apart from the cleruchs, the Greek presence in the countryside was ensured by a vast, ramified bureaucracy. The power of the *strategos* in charge of a nome, the direct representative of the sovereign, was balanced, in matters solely connected with the royal revenues, by the power of an *oikonomos* (dependent upon the *dioketès* of Alexandria), who made frequent tours of inspection in the *chôra*. The *strategos* was assisted by a *basilikogrammateus* (royal secretary). He was furthermore surrounded by subordinate *strategoi*, each in command of one of the military units established in the nome. The civil administration was headed by a nomarch (in some nomes, there were several of these). A group of several villages was placed under the authority of a toparch (from *topos*, 'place'). The basic unit was the country town (*kômè*), managed by a komarch, with the assistance of a village clerk (*kòmogrammateus*, who might be an Egyptian) and a detachment of rural police under the command of a brigadier (*archiphylaktitès*).

The financial administration was an integral part of all sectors of rural life. In the papyri, the expression 'the king' usually means the royal tax (*basilikon*). When a man had done 'what was right with regard to the king', what was meant was that he had paid his taxes. The licence fee of a poor merchant of cooked lentils was paid 'to the king'. The omnipresence of fiscal obligations must certainly have weighed more heavily on the minds of the peasants than the cult of the sovereign. The collection of tax revenues was the responsibility of both tax collectors (*logeutai*) and tax farmers (*telonai*). The royal revenues were collected either in money or in kind (the money would be stored in banks, the contributions in kind in public depots). The whole operation was supervised by an accounts office (*logiterion*) situated in the chief town of the nome. The *oikonomos* managed all the income from the nome: he made sure it was sent to the capital, where everything converged upon depots or, if in the form of statements, upon the accounting offices of the *dioketès*, directed by a commissioner of accounts (*eklogistès*), who recorded the entire budget of Egypt.

Most of these officials were Hellenes. They were powerful, in that they were the servants of the king. Throughout the hierarchy, from top to bottom, the Lagids adopted the principles according to which things used to be run by the pharaohs. The king was, by definition, just, which to oriental minds meant that he re-established justice by punishing those who transgressed it. It was thus to him, in principle, that the extremely numerous complaints against the administration would be addressed. According to the Achaemenid formula, the royal revenues were demanded from the nomes and their subdivisions, not from individuals. All the responsibility was thus borne by the officials, who were caught between two fires: they could be sacked for infractions against the king on one hand, on the other the people under their administration. The penalties were very harsh: pecuniary (fines, the confiscation of property) in the third century; but as from the beginning of the second century even the death penalty was not ruled out.

The law-courts The judicial function of the king, the only one that remained in Egypt since Ptolemy I Soter, the satrap who became king, had ceased to convoke the assembly, was to maintain peace within his kingdom. His essential coercive task was thus to repress criminality in all its forms (from high treason down to burglary and other delinquencies committed in the villages, including tax evasion). Justice was done by, first and foremost, the king in person. He reserved for himself the cases that he considered to be the most grave. He received in audience (or in writing) complaints of every kind, to which he would respond with a decree (*prostagma*) beginning 'On the order of the king . . .'. He appointed travelling judges, *chrematistai*, who would periodically tour the provinces to pass judgement on both Egyptians and foreigners in all cases that concerned his financial interests (*chremata*, resources). At the end of the third century they set up permanent juries in the *chôra*. The *strategos* of a nome possessed extensive coercive powers. It was he who responded to most of the complaints addressed to the king; and he also carried out the functions of our modern administrative courts. Finally, straighforward policing in the towns and villages was the responsibility of the *phylakitai*, supplemented by Egyptians.

The king was also, *par excellence*, the person with the power to lay down the law to be applied in the courts. A *diagramma* issued by Ptolemy II Philadelphus in about 275 organized two networks of law-courts, one for each of the two languages, supervised by a royal official, the *eisagogeus*, who brought the charges. The dicasteries handled cases for the Greek-speaking population, and committees of *laokritai* handled them for the Egyptians. The dicasteries' judges formed juries and were selected by lot (ten for each jury: nine dicasts and one chairman). One papyrus lists the legal criteria that applied to the dicasteries:

The circular (*diagramma*) that Heraclaea has presented to the court orders us, on all points that are known or shown to have been decided in royal circulars, to judge in accordance with those circulars; in others, which have not been decided in royal circulars, but have been by the citizens' laws (*politikoi nomoi*), those laws shall be applied; in all other cases, judgement will be passed in accordance with the most equitable opinion.

The reference to the most equitable opinion was, according to Demosthenes, to be found in the oath sworn by the Athenian heliasts.

The real extent of this [legislative] power [of the Lagids] was limited in many ways: first, by manifestations of legislative activity in the Greek cities, by the survival of local native law, and by the diffusion in Egypt of rules of Greek origin that went back to the tradition of the cities; and also by the tendencies and objectives of royal legislation itself. (J. Modrzejewski)

It was that last point that in practice was the most important. The primary objective of royal legislation was to protect fiscal resources, which were needed for the war effort. Direct interventions in private law were rare (for example, the maximum interest rate was fixed at 25 per cent per year; but moneylenders went so far as to charge 75 per cent). The law for individuals and families escaped the king's attention. This legislative vacuum produced an unexpected effect: it liberated Greeks from the constraints imposed by the laws of their *ethnos, koinon* or native city.

Legally, the Egyptian population had the same rights before the courts as the Greek-speaking population. Some privileges did exist, but they only benefited particular professional groups (soldiers, officials, priests, merchants, the cultivators of royal land and so on). The inequalities were of a social and economic nature. In this domain the judicial system was not neutral, for most lawsuits were over the production and circulation of merchandise. The weakness of royal authority in the second century led to the coercive power of the administration becoming less flexible. In the *chôra* the dicasteries left the field open for the courts of the *chrematistai*. The *laokritai* were still producing judgements in 96 (the last attested case).

I have been careful to use the expression 'Greek-speaking population'. In Egypt, 'Hellenes' came to include all those who spoke Greek or who carried some 'ethnic' proof, that is to say those who, in official business, could (with the help of oral or written evidence) justify their claim to previous membership of a *polis, koinon* or *ethnos*. One remained Athenian, Macedonian, Thessalian, Cretan, Aetolian, Thracian, Galatian, Syrian or Judaean (for example, in 173 BC, in Crocodilopolis, the chief town of the nome of Arsinoë, in Fayyum, an 'Athenian' man married a 'Macedonian' woman). It was forbidden, on pain of death, for any individual resident in Egypt to falsify his name or his ethnic origin (*patris*). His personal status could not be changed, even if all ties with his homeland had long since been broken. Everyone always had to state his place of origin (*idia*). It was an obligation that included Egyptians. The reason for this obligation, and for the heavy sanctions that accompanied it, was clearly fiscal: the administration had at all times to be able to verify the identity of taxpayers, so as to register their tax declarations.

This extension of the idea of a domiciled foreigner that was used to define the Hellenes in Egypt has sometimes been considered as a degradation of the status of a metic in Athens. However, P. Gauthier has shown that the phenomenon had begun, in Athens itself in fact, as early as the fourth century, in response to the needs of taxation. Take the example of the son of a man highly placed in the *entourage* of Satyrus, the king of the Cimmerian Bosphorus. Just before 390, on behalf of his father, he delivered the cargoes of two ships carrying wheat supplies to Athens. During his stay there he, like other metics, had to pay the *eisphora* tax. The following year he was even designated a 'distributor' (responsible for drawing up lists of the taxes to be paid and pursuing those who attempted to dodge them). In the fourth century, any foreigner who was resident for long enough had to pay the financial charges imposed upon metics. What all the Hellenes in Egypt shared in common was that they were considered 'foreigners passing through', even if their 'passing through' took an entire lifetime. What was different in their case, though, was that, whereas the metics in the cities constituted a minority of lower status, who were tolerated simply because they were useful, the Hellenes in Egypt were a minority that was dominant. They exercised power by virtue of their personal link with the king. In this way, every Hellene was either directly or indirectly in the service of the king or of servants of the king (all the way down from Demetrius of Phalerum who, having imposed an oligarchic government in Athens, subsequently took refuge in Alexandria, whose constitution he is supposed to have inspired, to a Greek peasant or shepherd of Fayyum). That development was a consequence of the mobility of the Hellenes in the East, particularly in Egypt, and that mobility was a phenomenon that dated from well before Alexander (for example, Caromemphites are known to have been living in Memphis at the time of the last pharoahs, having first come there as mercenaries from Caria, as are Hellenomemphites descended from Ionians recruited in the same fashion). The Hellenes did not feel lost in this vast world. They shared a common language (*koinè*); and they enjoyed common contractual rights, which J. Modrzejewski calls 'juridical *koinè*'. The term Hellene became synonymous with social status, and they were conscious of their unity as a superior group, totally different from the natives 'subdued at the point of a spear'. J. Modrzejewski concludes that their name and their status were potent factors in maintaining the separation between Greek-speakers and natives in the East for three whole centuries.

THE HELLENES AT WORK

In Egypt, as elsewhere, all the resources of the kingdom could be mobilized, in principle at least. In practice, things were more complicated. In this respect, it is fair to say that Ptolemy II Philadelphus was well advised. 'If the goal of a government was to obtain the greatest possible revenues from a territory, in Antiquity the Lagids were the past masters of political science' (T. Mommsen); which means, among other things, that it was not out of philanthropy that they strove to attract immigrants, but in order to put them to work. As they saw it, 'the profession of citizen' remained a full-time occupation, but in the service of the sovereign; and this left little time for leisure. However, it should not be imagined that the expatriate Hellenes were of a mind to change their ways. Given that they held the key posts in the administration, they were well placed to learn how to get on, how to slip through the net and, with a bit of luck, make their own fortunes. In default of that luck, they simply had to make do with the by no means enviable standard of living of the non-Greeks.

THE RURAL ECONOMY

Alexander and his successors made use of the already existing mode of production in their own fashion. They preserved it because it worked virtually automatically, but they certainly did not regard it as sacrosanct. Its existence did not stop them from remaining attached to the Greek notion of the economy which, ever since Homer, had been based on hereditary landownership. They sapped the Achaemenid system legally at its foundations by granting rural dependents the status of free men, but at the same time they maintained the system of chattel slavery in the same forms as it existed in the cities, that is, chiefly for household slaves but also for growing numbers of specially educated elite slaves, who were free to move about at their own discretion on the business entrusted to them by their masters.

'Royal slaves', that is, those who cultivated royal land, were no longer forced to do so by a binding contract. They became farmers under a lease-contract, not 'serfs', as they are sometimes – anachronistically – described. Their link with the royal land was an economic one: it was their place of work, which enabled them to earn a meagre living to support their families. They did not hesitate to strike or to seek asylum in the temples if they needed to protest against their employer's breaking the lease-contract. (The first known example of such a peasant strike is attested in 257. The employer in question was none other than the *dioketès*, Apollonius, in person, who had been employing the peasants to farm his vast estate of 2,740 hectares at Philadelphia in the Fayyum.) Clearly, these royal slaves were not not without means of self-defence, at least to the extent that they were organized in what constituted a basic cell, that is, their village, which had its own accredited leaders, the elders (*presbyteroi*), who had access to the authorities. The case of the Seleucid *laoi* was similar, for this kind of village autonomy went back to the Achaemenid period. However, when they fell too deeply into debt or, because of having committed some grave offence, they could no longer count on the support of village solidarity, they would take to flight (*anachoresis*). This phenomenon of runaway peasants, which by the third century was already common, would not have bothered the authorities had it simply occasioned a temporary shortfall in the labour force. What was far more serious, for the same reason as that which made the ethnic status of Hellenes so important, was that by leaving their administrative place of residence (*idia*) these peasants could elude the tax-collectors.

As well as royal land, there was 'sacred land', the inalienable property of the temples. The exact area that it covered is not known, but it was certainly considerable. The Lagids needed the Egyptian priesthood because it guaranteed the submission of the natives. The temples were full of sumptuous offerings and were maintained, repaired and built at the Treasury's expense. One example was the temple of Isis at Philae, another the temple of Horus at Edfu. But even this did not prevent a revolt in the Thebaid, around the temple of Karnak, which experienced two Nubian pharaohs between 207 and 186. This episode resulted in new concessions being granted to the clergy. The high priests of Memphis, whose genealogy is known to have remained in the same family for ten generations (from the early third century down to the end of the Ptolemaic monarchy) remained loyal, however. Notwithstanding that loyalty, the High Priest Psentaïs III referred as follows to Alexandria: 'I went to the residence of the king of the Ionians, which is on the shore of the Greek Sea, to the west of Rhakotis.'

The royal estate was divided up without raising any problems of principle, to be turned over to the cleruchs, and in the late second century their holdings became hereditary. Since these foreigners were not their subjects, it was natural enough for the Ptolemies to attach them definitively to a particular plot of land that would serve as a permanent base for the purposes of military recruitment. Little by little, private landownership developed. By the first half of the third century, the Greeks who were planting vineyards and orchards had become their quasi-owners. By the following century they had become fully so: the word *ktèma* (property) even became the term used to designate a vineyard in the language of the papyri.

It is hard to tell whether the Lagids intended this evolution or whether they simply accepted it. At any rate, it was accommodated in their pragmatic taxation system. Here, for interest, is a list of the Ptolemaic revenues. It is taken from Claire Préaux's monumental work, *L'Economie royale des Lagides* (1939; since revised by the author in her *Le Monde hellénistique*, 1978):

- agriculture (cereals, oil-producing crops, textile plants, vines, and orchards;
- stock-raising (agricultural animals, draught animals, domesticated animals, geese, bees);
- craftsmanship (weavers, dyers, fullers, tanners, butchers, baths, river transport);
- trade (oil monopoly; free trade for cereals, fabrics, slaves; licences for small-scale merchants);
- mines (quarries: salt, alum, saltpetre, gold, precious stones);
- customs (import, export) and tolls;
- royal banks (deposits, exchange, loans to consumers);
- taxes on land and homes: registration dues, taxes on changes of ownership and inheritances;
- personal taxes (on cleruchs, priests);
- income from the judicial system (fines, confiscations, legal charges);
- income of an extraordinary nature ('presents' and other contributions from Greek cities, booty, the sale of prisoners of war).

In addition to this long list, we should mention the enormously high rates of taxation. C. Préaux has calculated that, taking into account not only farming dues (often as high as 30 per cent) but also additional taxes, royal taxes absorbed over half the cereal harvests of royal peasants. On wine, there was the 'Philadelphian one-sixth' that financed the cult of Arsinoë; and on certain vines, as much as one-third or even half the harvest was returned as taxation. In the various trades, taxes as high as one-quarter of the produce (of fishermen, bee-keepers, bakers, perfumerers and grocers) are recorded, and even one-third (for baths and dovecotes). Egypt was, quite literally, a colony of exploitation, controlled by a distrustful and hesitant administration that was less concerned to encourage initiative than to track down tax evasion.

It is important to understand the reason for this close surveillance; it was crucial for the king to accumulate all products that could be sold for a profit in order to make the money needed to cover external expenses (the army, the fleet, diplomacy, warfare). This budgetary (or economic, in the ancient sense of the word) goal was pursued concretely by adapting a procedure long favoured by the Greek cities because it was so convenient: tax-farming. The method consisted in getting a particular wealthy individual to guarantee the funds destined to cover public needs. At first sight, the system seems as simple as the relationship that used to obtain between a housekeeper's purse and the purchases that she planned to make in the market: it was a matter of working out how much to spend on the various items before she set out. The 'prognosis of the revenue from taxation' (E. Will) was established for the entire Nile valley on the basis of the agriculture possible in an arid zone. This depended upon the quality of irrigation, which – in turn – depended upon the height of the annual floods and the maintenance of dikes and canals, all of which was – of course – far more complicated than the forecast that would be made by individual Greek cities.

The key factor in this forecast, which has been studied by P. Vidal-Naquet, was the 'sowing schedule'. Each year, in the offices of the *dioketès* of Alexandria, this reviewed the areas to be sown, nome by nome and town by town, with a range of cereal- and oil-producing crops. It is not known whether this document took in other types of land than the royal estate. It would be worked out on the basis of records showing the height of the flooding (which might be low, abundant or violent). It was a synoptic table, compiled from the data available and then adjusted by the local administration in the light of the statistics of previous years (in particular, surveys of the total areas of land to be cultivated and land that was unproductive). Once passed by the *dioketès*, the schedule became an objective, imposed on all officials, who were personally responsible for seeing that required quotas were met (a system that puts one in mind of the Soviet long-term planning that used to be believed to be productive).

This model of budgetary prognosis was no doubt adopted for fiscal revenues as a whole, for it served as the basis for the adjudication of tax-farming at every level. The tax-farmer covered the risks run in the entire process of the production and transformation of crops and taxes into money. He named guarantors who pledged their own wealth. He did not interfere personally in the process of tax collection, but supplemented the surveillance of the officials involved, with a view to defending his own interests. It was the task of the royal banks to act as intermediaries between the tax collectors and the buyers of the contributions in kind and to convert all the collected revenue into money. The banks' accounts were inspected by the offices responsible for the economy. A monthly balance-sheet was sent to the *eklogistès* of Alexandria, who would produce a synthesis and pass it on to the *dioketès*. It was only at the end of the budgetary year that the tax-farmer discovered his fate: either the Treasury returned to him all sums in excess of those that he had guaranteed (for unless the job was made worthwhile, there would have been no candidates to be judged); or else it would embark upon the process of making the accounts balance (by seizing the possessions of the guarantors and punishing the officials responsible).

We are less well informed on the budget of the Seleucids. They had continued with the Achaemenid system of tribute, exacted both in the form of money and in kind, the amounts of which were fixed in advance for each satrap, who was left to organize how the burden should be distributed. The bulk of the tribute was raised by revenues from the royal estate (collected, as in Egypt, within the framework of the villages, from the *laoi* who had to pay a farm-due). Cities that had not received special dispensation, autonomous dynasties and ethnic groups, and temple estates also paid the tribute. And they were furthermore liable to the habitual levies of Greek taxation systems: customs charges and dues, dues on changes in landownership and for registration; taxes on markets and professions. As a result of all these resources, the Seleucids could probably match the Lagids; and their intentions were equally belligerent.

A significant example   It was for a long time believed that the desire to increase production was peculiar to Egypt. In his monumental *Histoire économique et social du monde hellénistique* (1941; French translation, 1989), M. Rostovtzeff exaggerated the significance of the experiments in agricultural development tried out in the great estate (*dôrea*) that Philadelphus ceded to Apollonius (see figure 55). This was not 'an Egypt in miniature', as M. Rostovtzeff claimed. It is true, however, that the Fayyum basin constituted a vast 'pioneering front', where Greek engineers dug two large irrigation channels along the rim of the basin at its highest level, so as to bring the uncultivated land under cultivation. The *dôrea*'s grid of irrigation canals was designed on a geometric plan (that is preserved on a papyrus). The archives of the steward Zeno testify to serious attempts to increase productivity, directly inspired by the sovereign's passion for agronomy: higher-yielding cereals were selected, Greek vines and trees were acclimatized in the royal park of Memphis; on the king's direct orders, attempts were made to produce harvests twice a year; and animal stock of both large and small domesticated beasts was improved. On the other side of the Great Canal, out in the desert, Zeno created a new foundation, Philadelphia, the orthogonal plan of which ran parallel to the layout of the irrigation canals. Luxurious villas were built for high-ranking Alexandrian officials on the more pleasant side, along the banks of the Great Canal, close to the residences of the king and the *diokètès* (the best known of these resembled the type attested in Delos). This area contained many cult sites (probably quite small oratories), a theatre, a *stoa* (portico), a gymnasium and a small *palestra*, frequented by the young and by cleruchs. Everything suggests a deliberate communion with Hellenism. In truth, though, Philadelphia was no more than a show-case to be admired by foreign visitors (such as the ambassadors

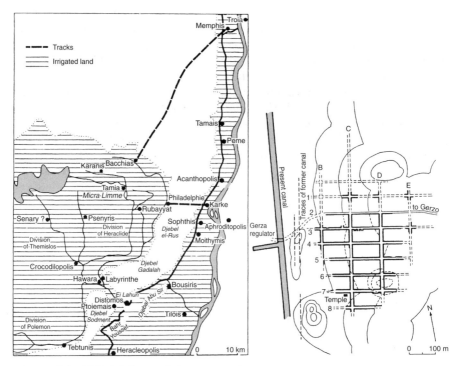

Figure 55 Philadelphia and the surrounding region. The north-eastern edge of the Fayyum depression through which the great irrigation canal passed rose to a height of 20 metres opposite Philadelphia. The water flowed, as a result of gravitation, through the hydraulic network to Lake Qarun, the present surface of which is 45 metres below sea-level (from C. Orrieux, *Zéno de Caunos, parépidémos, et le destin grec*, Paris, Belles Lettres, 1985)

of Pairisades II, the king of the Cimmerian Bosphorus). As soon as the encouragement from Alexandria slackened, the vices of the system became manifest. From the late third century on, the effects of excessive fiscal pressure were clear: agricultural production steadily diminished, provoking increasingly oppressive measures that proved more and more ineffective.

How did the Hellenes settled in the countryside cope with a rural economy organized with the sole aim of making the king ever wealthier? By good fortune, we know of a Carian established in a *kome* that he himself had coaxed out of the land, Zeno of Caunus. His individual case, unlike that of Apollonius' *dôrea*, is representative of the rest of Egypt, even somewhat precursory. Americans classify him as 'middle class', while the French place him in the 'bourgeoisie'. His social rank was indeed midway between Alexandrian high society, which was parasitic on the regime, and the 'poor Greeks' (an expression used here as 'the poor whites' was used in the European colonies of Africa), whose standard of living was not much better than that of the Egyptians. He seems to have risen, by dint of hard work, to the rank of the elite in a large country town, rather as a silkworm surrounds itself by a cocoon that is the right size for it. He was a benefactor of the gymnasium, and had an imposing house built for him (with a wine-cellar that did not escape the attention of burglars and which may have been where his intact papers were preserved). He had a small library, and sent the works of Callisthenes, Alexander's unfortunate historiographer, to a young brother of his who was completing his studies in Alexandria. He also used to lend his books to friends for their enjoyment.

How did he rise to this level? Like anyone else, by living a frugal life. During the years that he spent in the service of the *dioketès* of Philadelphia, he invested part of his salary in the working world. What he set up was not so much a business as a way of getting along. While in Alexandria and in Syria-Phoenicia, he had noticed a general feature of the Ptolemaic economy: the amount of money in circulation was very inadequate for the needs of exchange (Egypt possessed virtually no silver-bearing lead mines). When he arrived in the Fayyum, he found cleruchs settled in the villages close to Philadelphia. They had two main preoccupations: one was to offload their agricultural tasks at little cost to themselves; the other to lay their hands as quickly as possible on the revenues produced by their allotments. But as these were perforce in kind, the income from them only reached them after the long delays caused by the collection of the levies imposed on their harvests. This did not bother Zeno. He proceeded to rent their land-holdings and had them worked by Egyptian or Greek cultivators. His monthly salary enabled him to pay advances in money on the land rent that he owed for the use of the plots of land; at the same time he kept a substantial proportion of the proceeds from the cultivated land for himself. That is only one example. When he retired from the service of Apollonius, he chose the most profitable of investments, the raising of sheep (every property had its own flock; fiscal dues took the form of taxes, but the administration did not interfere with production). He contracted the wool-work out to independent weavers. His domestic slaves were specially trained, trusted men who saw to it that the products, which were sold in the region lying between Memphis and Alexandria, were commercially profitable, by speculating on price differences. The picture presented by his relations in the working world is an interesting one: half his employees were 'poor Greeks' (cultivators, herdsmen, craftsmen and transporters).

By employing a number of different stratagems, he furthermore acquired the reputation of a 'just and good' man, as was noted in papyri in which, for the first time, the term 'patronage' (*skepè*) appears. This was rooted in a custom that was both Egyptian and Greek, namely recommendation. He profited shamelessly from the bane of the countryside, the indebtedness that landed peasants in prison. Whether they were Greek or Egyptian, he would obtain their release and they then became attached to him as their 'benefactor'. For him to act in this way, it was enough for him that they should be recommended by one of his friends. The appeals for help reveal cases of the direst poverty. In what respect was his behaviour precursory? This type of 'benefactor' was unheard of in the cities before the mid-second century, as P. Gauthier has shown. It was a phenomenon that looked forward to the Romans. As J. Andreau has observed, 'There was a topography to patronage; it was by frequenting particular places and practising particular activities that one became a client.' Zeno came upon his 'clients' in their place of work, where Greeks and Egyptians were subject to the same social conditions. It would thus appear that Greek sociability evolved earlier outside the cities. But it was nevertheless a sociability of civic origin, in which all the influence belonged to the 'good', which meant the rich.

EXTERNAL TRADE

U. Wilcken has compared the discovery of the gold of the New World to the economic impact on the Hellenistic world of the flow of precious metals captured from the Persians by Alexander. The sudden increase of the mass of money in circulation and the extension of the Greek monetary economy to Egypt, Asia and as far as India inevitably resulted in a sudden surge of trade in new markets. It was a progress that was represented as normalization. Although some sovereigns continued to mint coins of gold and bronze (the latter was allowed only in subjugated cities), the international monetary system was based on silver and the Attic standard (17 grams of silver to every tetradrachma). The choice of a different standard (in Lagid territories, Rhodes and, later, Pergamum) signalled a political desire to create a separate trading zone. However, whatever the increase in money generally, the quantity of coins in circulation never sufficed to cover all the needs of commercial trading and, despite the presence of banks in country regions, a 'natural' economy (in which payments were made in kind) continued to exist in rural regions.

In Seleucid Asia the intensification of trade and commercial prosperity was linked with the proliferation of cities, which resulted in a rising demand for consumer goods. A civic territory could seldom satisfy its citizens' need of foodstuffs. Hence, throughout the Hellenistic world, there was a tendency to plan production to meet the demand for supplies in kind, a demand that was obviously Greek. The Ptolemies made the most of their ability to export cereals. However, it is noticeable that the Alexandrians, despite prohibitive customs duties, continued at great cost to import foodstuffs that suited Greek tastes. To cover such expenses, they exported the products of local craftsmanship (fine textiles, pottery, silver and gold ware, and perfumes) at extremely high prices. Taking this crucial factor into account, it turns out that the list of long-distance traded articles of merchandise, both exports and imports included, remained unchanged from the classical period (it consisted of cereals, oil, wines, dried fruits and seasonings for meat and fish; wood, metals, textiles; luxury products; slaves), quite simply because the needs and tastes of the Hellenes remained constant.

The explorations of Alexander (undertaken, as we have seen, for purely strategic reasons) did not have the secondary effect of opening up new commercial routes. Ever since Herodotus, the Greeks had known that the Scythians' gold came from Siberia, but, for them, the area to the north of the Caspian Sea nevertheless remained a legendary land. The Lagids' relations with the Sudan and Ethiopia, via the canal linking the Nile to the Gulf of Suez and the Red Sea (used for captured elephants and other exotic animals) simply renewed the links maintained earlier by the pharaohs. They did not develop maritime communications with southern Arabia until they had lost access to the spice route that led to Gaza. The possibility of making the most of the monsoon to reach India was discovered only at the end of the second century. In the end it was the Chinese who made contact with the West, after the collapse of the Greek kingdom of Bactria.

The only important change was the eastward shift of the major Mediterranean trading routes. Alexandria and Rhodes came to supplant Athens. Alexandria was protected against the wind by the island of Pharos (where the famous 'Pharos' (lighthouse) tower, three storeys high, was built in about 285). Its advantages as a port were threefold: to the east, there was the commercial port (*emporion*); to the west the military port and the naval dockyards, separated by the jetty that linked up with the island of Pharos; and to the south the river port of Lake Mareotis, which was linked to the Nile by canals and eventually to the Red Sea via the canal of the Ptolemies (which ran from the start of the delta, not far from Memphis). The traffic using the river port was greater than that of the sea port: supplies had to be brought in to feed the capital's population, which G. Husson estimates to have totalled about 500,000 people. According to Strabo, the city was shaped like a cloak, 30 stades (5.3 kilometres) long and 7 to 8 stades (1.3 kilometres) wide, in all 75 stades (in perimeter). It was not the largest town in Egypt: according to Diodorus, the perimeter of Memphis was 150 stades. The orthogonal plan conceived by Deinocrates of Rhodes respected the principles of specialized zones. The royal quarter (*basileia*) was the administrative capital, containing the king's palace and gardens, the museum, the library and the central offices. A wide, straight street, bordered by porticoes, crossed the town from east to west, separating the village of Rhakotis from the new town (Neapolis), where the city's public monuments were to be found (agora, *boulè*, law-courts, theatre, gymnasium). The sanctuary of Sarapis overlooked the town on the south-east, and the temple of Arsinoë was situated on the coast (see figure 56).

If Alexandria held pride of place as a port for exports, one of the few truly independent cities in the great kingdoms, Rhodes, operated as the turntable through which many types of merchandise passed in transit between Egypt, Syria-Phoenicia (via the old coastal route which, after following the eastern coast of the Mediterranean, made a detour to Cyprus, so as

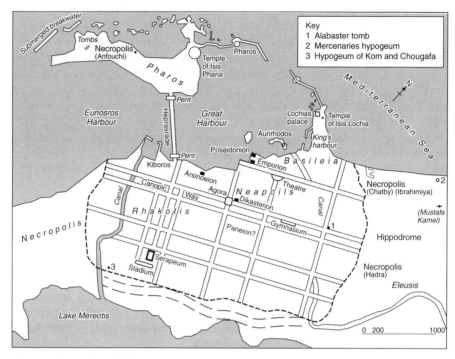

Figure 56 Plan of Alexandria (from C. Jacob and F. de Polignac (eds), *Alexandrie, IIIe siècle avant J.-C.*, Paris, Autrement, 1992)

to avoid the Seleucid ports), the islands and the Aegean coasts, the free cities of the Straits and the Black Sea, and finally the distant kingdom of the Cimmerian Bosphorus. On the mainland, the city of Rhodes exploited the agricultural resources of an annexed territory (Peraea) the area of which varied according to political circumstances (Caunus, of which Zeno was a citizen, bought in 197 for 200 talents from the Lagid *strategoi*, and Stratoniceia in Caria, opposite Rhodes, between them paid an annual tribute of 120 talents, according to Polybius, making the situation extremely viable economically). The Rhodians, bold seamen who were prepared, even in winter, to sail directly to Alexandria, did not themselves carry many cargoes. On the other hand, their fleet of battleships did protect their merchandise from pirates. They set themselves up as wholesalers, shipbuilders and bankers in the principal ports of call, making the most of their neutrality. But they were always ready to go to war (as, for example, against Byzantium in 220), to defend the freedom of maritime trade (which the Ptolemies never made any attempt to control).

Hellenistic commerce projected an impression of prosperity that fascinated the Romans in the second century. Delighted though they were to rake in the proceeds of the booty taken by their legions, in the name of Republican austerity they nevertheless deplored the softness (*tryphè*) engendered by the extravagant luxury of kings and private individuals alike. For the high-risk loans necessary for long-distance sea journeys came from private individuals, so some of them at least must have possessed huge fortunes. The Greek cities profited greatly from this prosperity, not only to improve their material standard of living, but also to develop their educational institutions and to encourage letters, arts, sciences, philosophy and religious thought, in a word, all the humanities. However, we should beware of forgetting what the Egyptian papyri tell us of the poverty of life in the countryside, which tallies with Polybius' observations on the poverty of mainland Greece in the second century. That prosperity represented only one side of the coin.

THE AGE OF THE HUMANITIES

The culture (*paideia*) of the great aristocratic families was transmitted spontaneously, through social mimesis ('breeding will out'). In the fifth century, the *paideia* became a stake in the game of politics, as can be seen from Aristophanes' *Clouds* and *Frogs*. The battle between the old and the new types of education was brought to an end in the fourth century, thanks to a mutual amnesty. The word *paideia* had initially had the full, wider meaning of our term 'civilization', whose contents combined all that our own disciplines methodically separate (even religion). But in the Hellenistic period it took on the dryer sense of 'educational system'.

It is important to emphasize its systematic and classificatory spirit (a legacy from Aristotle). However, this should not be confused with rationality: it amounted to no more than a spirit of 'geometry', to borrow Pascal's expression. For things were all of a piece: for example, take another phenomenon, the fiscal and judiciary system set up by Philadelphus. This concealed 'a fundamental disorder' (P. Vidal-Naquet): the absence of economic, social and cultural exchanges between the capital and the provinces (in spite of the fact that the founding notion of secularity paid no attention to the division between town and country). Historians such as C. Préaux, who prefer at this juncture to use the term 'town' rather than 'city' do have a point: they recognize the gap that, in the course of the Hellenistic period, came to separate 'city dwellers' and 'country folk'. Even more important is the fact that Hellenistic man played a double game. From the courtier down to the 'poor Greek', everyone lied yet no one seemed to. The royal cult was itself the height of hypocrisy. Survival depended upon an eye to the main chance and resourcefulness: the threat among the courtiers of systematic denunciation and possible disgrace gave rise to a complicated game of 'cops and robbers' in which roles quite frequently came to be reversed. 'Men of letters' concealed their servility with skill. Like all Hellenes, they tried to fit in with the present circumstances, while hoping for things to change. Thus, because it was both a means of earning a living and also a personal passion, Callimachus put together a carefully devised catalogue of the Library of Alexandria, *Lists of the Authors who have won Fame in their Particular Sector of Culture and of the Works that they have Written*. It ran to 120 volumes! Over 500,000 rolls of papyri were arranged on the library shelves, labelled, summarized and classified according to discipline (poetry, rhetoric, medicine . . .). In his poems, which contain many erudite references, Callimachus sang above all the praises of the Greek past, not forgetting that of his own city Cyrene, the home of Queen Berenice, who had recently married Ptolemy III Euergetes. In *Berenice's Lock*, a lock of the queen's hair is carried up to the heavens, where it becomes a constellation. And in the *Hymn to Delos*, Apollo, while still inside the womb of his mother Leto, advises her to give birth to him in Delos, so as to reserve the island of Cos for the birth of Ptolemy Philadelphus . . . But in all (possibly excessive) fairness,

the true heir to the ancient city is not the individual, as is so often claimed, with somewhat pejorative implications, but human personality which, liberated from the collective conditioning and totalitarian constraints that had been imposed upon it by city life, now became aware of itself . . . More than ever, Greek man thought of himself as the measure of all things. (H.-I. Marrou)

Perhaps that is why Cicero translated *paideia* as *humanitas*.

THE EDUCATIONAL SYSTEM

From Solon to Hippocrates, the Ancients divided life into 'weeks of years'. The *paideia* (our 'basic education') began at the age of 7 and lasted for the following two 'weeks' (that is to say fourteen years), including the time of the *ephebeia*. It was entrusted to private institutions, some of which even admitted girls and domestic slaves.

For the seven years of primary schooling, the child was taken to school by a slave, the 'pedagogue'. The teacher was called a grammatist (from *gramma*, 'letter'). The child learned to read (the alphabet, syllables, words, texts, recitations), to write (on wax-coated tablets or on papyrus) and to count (using his hands: units, tens, hundreds, thousands).

For the seven years of secondary schooling, physical training held pride of place. It was received in the gymnasium, which was also used by adults. This was the place where Hellenes not domiciled in cities would meet together. For them, gymnastics were the surest criterion of Hellenism. A gymnasium formed a complex consisting of a palestra (from *palè*, 'wrestling'), surrounded by various amenities including the stadium running track (the word *stade* designated a unit of length, 600 feet). The Olympic stadium measured 192 metres, 200 yards. Ephebes received special, military-oriented training under the direction of a gymnasiarch. A *paidotribès* ('trainer') taught the five exercises of the pentathlon (wrestling, running, long jump,

2

discus throwing, javelin throwing), boxing and the *pankration* (in which any kind of blow was allowed). Special trainers taught the ephebes fighting manoeuvres (*hoplomachia*), archery and how to use war machines. The *ephebeia* was designed for a minority of rich young men, all of whom the cities accepted, even if they were foreign, providing they were Hellenes.

Artistic education incorporated the teaching of drawing, the playing of musical instruments (lyre, flutes), choral singing and dancing. The teaching of mathematics included arithmetic and geometry (from *The Elements of Geometry* by Euclid, who was brought to Alexandria at the invitation of Ptolemy I), astronomy (from the *Phainomena* of Aratus of Soli, resident at the court of Antigonus Gonatas, who had transposed into verse the astronomical system of Eudoxus of Cnidus, one of the greatest scholars of the fourth century) and musical theory (of the Pythagorean school). Literary education, which tended to become predominant, was entrusted to a 'grammarian'. He would produce commentaries on the 'classics': essentially Homer, but also Hesiod, Pindar, Herodotus, Thucydides, Euripides, Xenophon and even Menander and Callimachus. First one would study the grammar of the text (morphology, syntax), then its literal meaning (exegesis), all crowned by aesthetic and moral appreciation and complemented by practical writing exercises.

At this point the *paideia* was complete. Higher education, which Plato believed should continue up until the seventh week of years, that is to say up to the age of 50, took the form of a 'continuous training'. At the risk of becoming too personal, it is hard to resist calling to mind the education of Ptolemy II Philadelphus, whose tutors were hand-picked by his father: Philetas of Kos, grammarian and poet; Strato of Lampsachus, physician and mathematician, a former pupil of Aristotle's successor in Athens, Theophrastus (he developed a theory of the vacuum that is believed to have inspired the construction of the famous pneumatic machines of Philon of Byzantium); and finally Zenodotus of Ephesus, the author of the first critical edition of Homer's poems and the first director of the Library of Alexander. None of them was really creative, but they provided a balanced diet of classical scholarship as a whole.

MEN OF LETTERS AND SCIENTISTS

The Hellenistic period produced two social types who are still with us today, one 'literary', the other 'scientific' (the 'jurist' was essentially Roman and did not appear until Cicrero's time). These were professional men who, to earn a living, entered the service of their 'benefactors', either kings or private patrons. Consider the case of Theocritus, born in about 300, probably in Syracuse (in his *Idyll 11*, which is a typical example of his style, he describes as his 'neighbour' Polyphemus, the Cyclops of Etna, whom he disguises as a love-sick shepherd led astray by the nymph Galatea). In Cos, Philetas was his teacher in literary studies. He then tried to place himself

339

under the protection of Hieron II, Pyrrhus' former second-in-command who later proclaimed himself king (268–215) and, by signing a treaty of friendship with Rome, saved Theocritus' city from destruction in the First Punic War. In this endeavour Theocritus was not successful. He then entered the service of Ptolemy II Philadelphus, whose blonde locks he praises in the most mediocre of his compositions (*Idyll 17*). Theocritus and Callimachus, both of whom could have 'done better', were in this way forced to become aesthetes who cultivated the minor genres of 'Alexandrian poetry', the idyll (a 'short form' in which Theocritus imitated Sappho and Alceus) and the epigram ('an inscription, dedication for a statue, or epitaph'). It was a type of poetry designed to please city-dwellers with a nostalgic fondness for nature, provided it was unsullied, not the nature of uncouth peasants but that of shepherds and ox-herds (*boukolos*, hence 'bucolic'); and who were not averse to decrying their own type of petit-bourgeois life by lampooning comical figures (such as two gossipy old wives from Syracuse, visiting Alexandria to see the festival of Adonis, *Idyll 15*). It was a genre that was not beneath the notice of Theophrastus, who composed the *Characters* by which La Bruyère was inspired.

A cynical critic might suppose that the vogue for brief genres among busy people was simply a healthy reaction against the *longueurs* and grandiloquence of post-classical drama, the memory of which was by now kept alive only by the magnificent theatres in which it had been performed. However, to do so would be to overlook a work as characteristic of the new style as the *Argonautica* of Apollonius Rhodius, an impertinent student of Callimachus': an epic about half the length of the *Iliad*, crammed with erudition, which recounts the quest for the Golden Fleece in Colchis undertaken by Jason and his companions aboard the *Argo*. It presents a relaxed picture of Jason, who is portrayed as a kind of anti-hero, and a touching representation of Medea. It would also be to overlook the Athenian Menander (about 340–292), who refused to enter the service of Ptolemy Soter but has been rediscovered thanks to the research of papyrologists. He has a masterly grip on the art of intrigue and comic situations. As C. Préaux has commented, 'A comedy by Menander is a microcosm of the Hellenistic world, shut up in its towns and fearful of taking chances, yet also a world in which it is possible to travel and in which distant lands inspire dreams of escape.'

We need not dwell on the sad loss of the greater part of Hellenistic historiography (see the passage on p. 268). All that has survived is part of the *Histories* of Polybius of Megalopolis (about 210–125), the last great Greek historian. His father Lycortas was a *strategos* in the Achaean federation, and he himself served as a hipparch. Sent as a hostage to Rome in 168, he mingled there with the circle that revolved around the circle of the Scipios. He witnessed the Roman sack of Carthage and that of Corinth in 146. The man's natural reserve makes his passion the more moving. (Read the pages in which he describes Archimedes determinedly constructing machines to defend Syracuse, which was being besieged by Claudius M. Marcellus in 212. Polybius saw Archimedes as a symbol of Greek resistance.) He analyses the unfolding of events as an organic and coherent movement the sole result of which, as he saw it, was to be Rome's triumph, and he traces the decisive turning-point to the 140th Olympiad (220–216), when the Second Punic War began, leading to the alliance between Hannibal and Philip V of Macedon. He is tempted to explain that sole result by a sole cause, namely the institutions of Rome (in the same way as Thucydides had explained Athenian imperialism). However, he was too much like the scientists of his day, who liked experimentation allied with reason and accuracy in the establishment of facts, not to recognize that in the last analysis there was no necessity linking the chain of events. He was therefore forced to admit that gods and men alike are ruled by chance (*tychè*), a conclusion that elicits a long quotation from Demetrius of Phalerum's treatise *On Fortune*:

Do you think that if, fifty years ago, a god had foretold what would happen either to the Persians and their king or to the Macedonians and their king, they could have believed . . . that the Macedonians, whose very name had thitherto been unknown to most people, would become the masters of the world? Fortune, who makes us no promises in our lifetimes, foils all our forecasts with constant new ploys and delights in manifesting her power by making the most unexpected moves.

That is how the men of this time were: they drew close to their fellows, seeking shelter from the blows dealt by fortune. 'Poets gathered in literary groups; workshop traditions played a preponderant role in the development of art; philosophy and science evolved in highly orgnized schools. Even mystics could only find their gods from within their brotherhoods' (P. Lévêque). It was in Alexandria, in the entourage of Ptolemy I Soter, that the idea of an international scientific community germinated. It was to be a brotherhood devoted to the Muses (hence 'Museum'), which the first Ptolemies were to endow with means of an unprecedented lavishness (as well as the Library, an astronomical observatory, a botanical and zoological garden, and a laboratory of pathological anatomy). The whole institution, directed by a priest appointed by the king, was reserved for 'philologists' of the highest level (the word, nowadays applied to 'literary specialists', at that time designated all those who reached knowledge through discussion, *logos*, so also included 'scientists'). It had at its disposal a whole mass of funds to meet its expenses, and a specially appointed area in the Palace zone (*Basileia*), with shady paths for walking (*peripatos*, from which came the name 'Peripatetics', given to Aristotle's followers), an exedra (meeting hall) and a vast building (*syssition*) in which the scholars ate together. The Museum was thus not a teaching establishment, as our universities are. It was a research centre, where experimentation and research pursued in common was the general rule in all disciplines. Seen from the outside, it appeared a closed institution. In the eyes of one (jealous?) sceptic philosopher, Timon of Phlius, it was full of well-fed individuals 'who spent their time twittering in the aviary of the Muses'.

The Museum enjoyed its heyday in the third century and remained active until 145, at which date Ptolemy VIII ejected the scholars in retaliation for their having supported his brother Ptolemy VI (180–145). The 'exact sciences' made great progress there: Eratosthenes of Cyrene succeeded in measuring the earth's meridian. Aristarchus of Samos formulated the hypothesis that the earth revolved around the sun, only to be overridden by the authority of Aristotle: the world would have to wait for Copernicus. The calculation of areas and volumes made decisive progress with Apollonius of Perga, Pamphilia. In the second century Hipparchus of Nicaea founded trigonometry. In the field of medicine, in the third century, the *Hippocratic Corpus* was completed, containing the results of the research of the school of Cos (where Hippocrates was born in about 460). Herophilus of Chalcedon, considered by Galen to be 'the greatest anatomist of Antiquity', embarked upon dissection (which was practised by the Egyptians for mummification); he discovered the difference between arteries and veins and also the cause of the beat of the pulse. A study of the ethnic origins of these scholars proves that the Museum was truly international.

ARTISTS, ARCHITECTS AND ENGINEERS

There was no distinction between science (theoretical) and 'art' (*technè*, manual skill) to lead the Hellenes to despise their traditional 'know-how' which, unlike our own, drew no separation between artisan and artist, mason and architect, mechanic and engineer. Doctors were at once scientists and practitioners and sometimes men of letters too: Nicander of Colophon, a doctor at the court of Pergamum in the second century, composed hymns, a history of his city and two long poems, one on *Theriaka* (remedies to heal the bites of wild animals) and *Alexipharmaka* (antidotes to poisons).

In sculpture, there was no sign of any break with the models of the fourth century, Scopas and Praxiteles, whom Claude Mossé has described as an 'artistic *koinè*'. The features that characterize the Hellenistic period were already to be found on the red-figure Attic vases: emotive facial expressions, violent movement, the nudity of young bodies (for example, the *Aphrodite of Cnidus*, 'more woman than goddess'), realistic representations of suffering and old age. Here are a few examples: the *Statue of Demosthenes*, the work by Polyeuctus set up in 280 by the Athenians (a figure roughly covered in draperies clutched by two hands, with deep furrows scoring the cheeks and brow, and untidy hair) constitutes an exact plastic reflection of the epigram read by Plutarch, 'If your strength had equalled your determination, Demosthenes, the Macedonian Ares [the god of war] would never have ruled over the Greeks'; the *Weary Heracles* by

Lysippus of Sicyon, a contemporary of Alexander (Roman copy: the Farnese Hercules) is 'a prodigious mountain of flesh and bone' (F. Chamoux); the *Ludovisi Gaul* (a copy of the ex-voto dedicated in 283 by Attalus I of Pergamum, after his victory over the Galatians): the warrior is thrusting a sword into his throat, after killing his wife, who is stretched at his feet; the *Drunken Crone* by Myron of Pergamum (early second century) has an emaciated body and a distracted gaze, her hands gripping a capacious flask (*lagynos*). Along with the graceful 'Tanagra' and 'Nilotic' mosaic land-scapes, sometimes criticized as being excessively precious, all these works convey the same powerful emotion as do literary texts of the Hellenistic period. They manifest a profoundly unified Hellenism that has, as yet, lost none of its vigour.

The coins that were minted in the Hellenistic period display contrary tendencies, synthesized in the effigies of the sovereigns. The 'portrait of Alexander 'deifies' him, albeit with restraint (by associating him with the ram's horn of Zeus-Ammon or an elephant's scalp, to commemorate his Indian victories). Demetrius Poliorcetes sports a bull's horn in his hair, as does Seleucus I (whether young or old, both have long, pointed noses). The Ptolemies were innovative, in the Egyptian tradition, and placed along-side their own profile that of their sister-wife, as in the case of the two 'adelphi'; the fact that they had broken the taboo against incest was in itself enough to evoke their 'super-nature'.

Monumental architecture was part and parcel of the grandiose plans of urban development realized in the fourth century. The Halicarnassus mausoleum, 'justly considered the last truly classical artistic masterpiece' (G. Glotz), was conceived by Pytheus, the same architect who, in Alexander's day, was responsible for the temple of Athena Polias in Priene, completed in the second century. A number of ambitious urban developments re-flected the prosperity of the Hellenistic cities. They were to be found mainly in Asia Minor in the area under Ionian influence (which, already in the sixth century, under Achaemenid domination, could claim the two largest edifices in the Greek world known to Herodotus, the temple of Hera in Samos and the temple of Artemis in Ephesus). New temples, such as the temple of Apollo at Didyma (near Miletus) were built with compar-able dimensions. Here the original features were its forest of columns and the open-air courtyard that took the place of the *naos* in classical temples. Architects such as Pytheus, and Hermogenes in the second century, com-posed treatises on their mathematical research into proportions. The best-preserved theatres (such as those of Pergamum and Priene) and the spectacular dimensions of the Pharos of Alexandria, the Colossus of Rhodes and the altar of Zeus in Pergamum were impressive by reason of their gigantic proportions. But the only truly distinctive architectural feature of this period was the new concept of the agora, now designed as an enclosed precinct, bordered by a series of separate porticoes (as in the agora of Athens; see figure 58) or surrounded by an unbroken colonnade (the agora

Figure 57 Hellenistic royal coins: (a) Alexander with a ram's horn; (b) Alexander capped with an elephant's scalp; (c) Demetrius Poliorcetes with a bull's horn; (d) Seleucus I with a bull's horn; (e) Ptolemy I wearing the royal headband; (f) Ptolemy and Arsinoë Philadelphi (photo: Bibliothèque Nationale de France)

of the Italians in Delos; and the agora of Messina). From this time on this public space was inspired by the central courts of palaces or of the vast houses of important personages, such as those of Delos. Town planning and town manners now went hand in hand in new settlements, whatever their size: everywhere, in capitals, cities, military colonies, administrative centres and country towns, civic society strove to reproduce itself in identical fashion. Thus, according to L. Robert, on the site of Aï Khanum, close to the northern frontier of Afghanistan (possibly formerly Alexandria on the Oxus), in the independent Greek kingdom of Bactria, one finds a carefully irrigated civic territory, a town planned on a grid system and, engraved on a limestone plinth, an epigram and maxims copied from Delphi by an Aristotelian philosopher, Clearchus of Soli, Cilicia. One of these reads as follows: 'As a child, be well behaved; as a young man, be master of yourself; in middle life, be just; in old age, be wise; at your death, have no regrets.'

Let us conclude with one of the most sophisticated applications of Greek science, mechanics (that is, the art of using machinery, *mechanè*). Alexander was accompanied on his campaigns by many military engineers. The 'engineers' of Dionysius the Elder had studied and perfected the siege

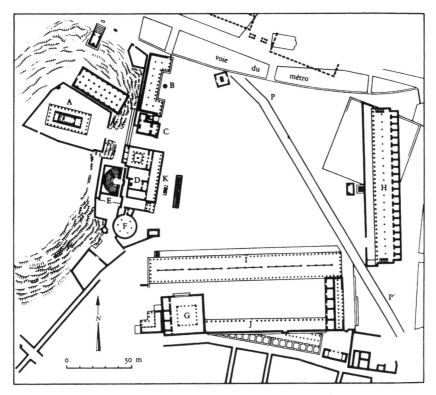

Figure 58 Athens: the agora in the second century BC. P–P¹ the Panathenaean Way; A temple of Hephaestus; B Portico of Zeus; C temple of Apollo Patrôos; D temple of the Mother of the Gods (archives); E Council Hall; F Prytaneum; G Theseion; H, I, J, K porticoes (from F. Chamoux, *La Civilisation hellénistique*, Paris, PUF, 1981)

machines of the Carthaginians. At the siege of Samos (430), Pericles employed the services of Artemon of Clazomenae, whose siege machines he greatly admired. For his expedition against the Scythians (512), Darius had got Mandrocles of Samos to throw a bridge of boats across the Bosphorus (in the temple of Hera in Samos, Mandrocles dedicated a picture of this construction). If we carried this retrospective ever further back, we should get to the mythical Daedalus and the fall of Icarus who 'being young, flew too high, and plunged into the sea when the sun melted the wax that held his wings together' (Diodorus). But the important point to note is that the Greeks had always been inventors of machines, which included the devices used by Euripides to produce spectacular effects (stages mounted on wheels, theatrical cranes to hoist actors aloft by means of ropes and pulleys): hence Aristophanes' parody in *Peace*, in which Trygeus flies off like Bellerophon on Pegasus , the winged horse: 'Now, whoa there, Pegasus! Oh, oh, I'm scared! Easy on, machine operator!' Again, it is all of a piece.

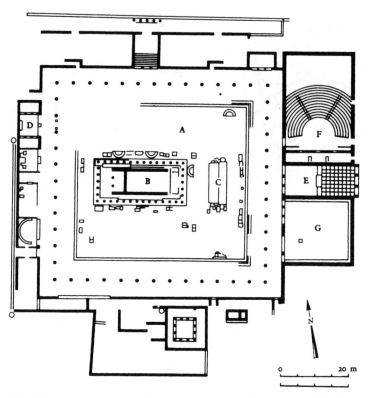

Figure 59 Messina: the agora. A square courtyard; B temple of Asclepius and Hygieia; C altar; D sanctuary of Artemis; E vestibule giving on to the agora; F auditorium with a hemicycle of stepped seats; G Council Chamber with seats along the walls (from F. Chamoux, *La Civilisation hellénistique*, Paris, PUF, 1981)

The builders of the great sixth-century Ionian temples used lifting machines, as is proved by the marks they left on the stones. The earliest Ionian philosophers, in particular Thales of Miletus, studied not only theoretical physics and mathematics but also, as Plato approvingly noted, the art of mechanics. The Pythagorean philosopher Archytas of Tarentum (late fifth century) and Eudoxus of Cnidus (mid-fourth century) seem to have been the first to research into the application of the sciences to the construction of machines and instruments for weighing things. The use of the pulley, the winch and the lever at this point became common in sailing, building in stone, the theatre and the operation of presses with levers and counter-weights in the production of wine and oil.

The earliest technical treatise to have been preserved is that of Aeneas Tacticus, *Siegecraft* (mid-fourth century). Historians such as Thucydides and Polybius took considerable interest in the military applications of new techniques, since victory depended as much upon these as upon the courage

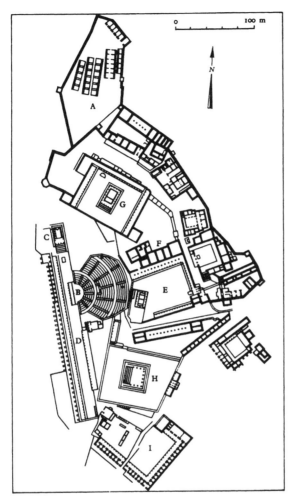

Figure 60 Pergamum: the Acropolis. A royal palace; B theatre; C temple of Dionysus; D terrace with three levels; E sanctuary of Athena; F library; G temple of Trajan; H Great Altar of Zeus; I agora (from F. Chamoux, *La Civilisation hellénistique*, Paris, PUF, 1981)

of the fighting men. Ancient authors attribute many discoveries to the most extensively talented inventor of the Hellenistic period, Archimedes of Syracuse (287–212), who lived at the court of Hiero II. To carry merchandise to Alexandria, he designed the *Syracusan*, with a tonnage greater than that of any other ship in Antiquity (about 2,000 metric tons), which he then presented to Ptolemy II Euergetes. Forced by circumstances to submit to the Roman protectorate, he bided his time and concentrated on preparing for his revenge, which never came. He was reputed to be the most absent-minded of scientists after Thales (after the death of Hiero, confident of his defensive machines, Archimedes failed to notice the development of the cabal that eventually resulted in his town being handed over to the Romans, and he himself disappeared in the massacre that followed). However, what we know of his long collaboration with Hiero shows that he was convinced that science had a great future, not only for the understanding of nature, but also for acquiring control over it (he dreamed of a lever that could lift up the world, if only it had somewhere upon which to rest . . .). The most zealous admirers and imitators of the Greek engineers and architects were the Romans, according to Vitruvius, who recorded their debt to the Greeks in his treatise *On Architecture*. When Scipio Aemilianus, the general who sacked Carthage, visited Egypt in 140, it was not simply as a tourist. He had been sent to the East 'to inspect the kingdoms of the allies' (Justin). The techniques of the Greeks were to be part of his booty. Before admiring 'a Roman achievement', it is always worth scratching the surface. What is usually uncovered is Hellenistic science.

Alexandrian science

300–290	Demetrius of Phalerum in Alexandria.
	Foundation of the Museum. Construction of the Pharos (lighthouse).
	Euclid, *The Elements of Geometry*.
	Strato of Lampsacus establishes the acceleration of falling bodies.
290–280	Foundation of the Library.
	The Egyptian priest, Manethon of Sebennytus, composes his *Chronicles of Egypt*, in Greek.
	Herophilus of Chalcedon, *On Dissections*.
	Aristarchus of Samos, *On the Size and Distance of the Sun and the Moon*.
280–270	Theocritus of Syracuse at the court.
	Callimachus draws up the catalogue of the Library.
270–250	Beginning of the translation of the Bible into Greek.
	Ctesibus of Alexandria invents the suction and force pump.
250–230	Eratosthenes of Cyrene calculates the circumference of the earth.
	Biton, *On the Construction of War Machines*.
	Scientific contacts between Syracuse and Alexandria.
230–200	Hermippus' commentary on the poems attributed to Zoroaster.
	Apollonius of Perga, *Conics*.
	Philon of Byzantium, *Mechanical Syntax*.
about 175	Aristobulus, *Explanation of the Writing of Moses*.
about 160	*The Epistle of Aristaeus to Philocrates*.
about 145	Ptolemy VIII Euergetes expels the Museum scholars.

THE DISCOVERY OF THE INNER MAN

A RELIGIOUS CRISIS?

The individualism for which Hellenistic man has been criticized was first diagnosed in religion and philosophy: was this a new symptom of 'crisis'? Apart from the cult of sovereigns, there is, to tell the truth, not much to be said about Hellenistic religion as such. It is true that the civic religion had been through a crisis, but that was during the Peloponnesian War and, at the cost of Socrates' death, it had been resolved at the beginning of the fourth century by a reconciliation between the erstwhile adversaries, the 'rationalists' and the 'traditionalists'. Those who see in the Hellenistic cults a formalism incapable of responding to new spiritual needs are also those who regard the Hellenistic city as 'an empty shell'. In their view, the 'shell' of civic religion from the fourth century on was filled by an influx of 'foreign cults' and 'religions of salvation' (we have already come across Asclepius, Bendis, Cybele, Sabazius and Adonis in Athens), then was smashed definitively by the victory of Christianity. But epigraphy provides a warning against jumping to such an erroneous conclusion: the Greek inscriptions testify to the vitality of the Hellenistic institutions right down to the point at which the Christian emperors of the fourth century AD closed down the temples, and the explanation for that was political and stemmed from Roman history.

By the fifth century a one-way assimilation between the gods of Greece and foreign gods was already under way: the latter were accepted in so far as they could be assimilated to the gods conceived in the image of man of Greek mythology. The process is complete by the time of Herodotus: Ammon *is* Zeus, Isis *is* Demeter, Osiris *is* Dionysus, the Ba'al of Tyre *is* Heracles, Astarte *is* Aphrodite. They are the same gods, whose names are translated into many different languages; furthermore, all of them are simply diverse manifestations of the divine, which is unique. The case that has attracted the most commentary is that of Sarapis, honoured since the time of Ptolemy I in the Sarapeion of Alexandria. It resulted from a fusion effected in Memphis, the religious capital of Egypt, between Osiris and the bull Hapi, which was deified after its death and embalmed (*Oser* + *Hapi* = Sarapis). In fact, though, the religious statue of Sarapis shed the animal reference that was essential to the Egyptian religion. If Ptolemy I's aim was really to bring Greeks and Egyptians together around a mixed god, protector of the dynasty, it failed: the new cult attracted only Hellenized Egyptians. In contrast, it spread spontaneously in the Greek world, where it was associated with Isis, particularly in Delos, from the third century on. Sarapis rivalled Asclepius as a healer god (who communicated his prescriptions through dreams). Isis too enjoyed a huge success that is not hard to understand. The hymns praising her ('aretalogies') proclaim that she can free men who are the prisoners of the mortal Fates (the *Moirai*), because she presides over the liquid element, the rivers and the seas where storms sweep men to their deaths. The perils of the sea symbolize human life, with all its predictable ups and downs. A goddess who was faithful to her husband Sarapis, full of motherly love for her son Horus, and was the incarnation of divine royalty and a universal protectress, beneficent exclusively to those who were just and good, was altogether reassuring, the more so given that she was all-powerful, which even Zeus never was. She satisfied a major need felt by the Hellenes in those troubled times.

There was nothing surprising or even particularly new about the vogue for mystery cults (such as the Mysteries of Eleusis) and for religious associations (such as the Dionysiac *thiasoi*). It was a response to the aspirations of people of this period with a taste for communities of a religious nature that mediated between the family and the city (particularly if they lived outside the city). Ever since the archaic period, the cult of Dionysus had been an integral part of the civic religion. Although certain aspects of him may strike us as foreign, for a long time he had no longer seemed foreign to the Greeks. The *thiasoi* and the brotherhoods of *orgeònes* (such as the devotees of Bendis in Piraeus) were not 'sects' that were marginal to the city (the word comes from *orgia*, which meant not 'orgy' but 'whatever is done in a cult'). These were mainstream cults, as can be seen from the Hellenistic inscriptions to be found in Athens and elsewhere. The taste for these practices should be regarded as extra proof of an already mentioned characteristic of Greek religion in general: an extraordinary richness that was capable of absorbing, transforming and diversifying human experience.

A NEW EXPERIENCE

The Hellenistic period did introduce a new experience into the religious domain, one that involved setting oneself at a certain distance from politics and society. 'For the experience of a truly internal dimension to take shape, there had first to have been the discovery of a mysterious and supernatural power within man himself, the *daimon-soul*' (J.-P. Vernant). The word *daimon* already existed in Homer, as did many other words that took on new meanings in the Hellenistic period (*laoi*, for example), and it had a very long history in Greek mythology. Since Socrates, the 'daimonic' had been understood as a breath that communicated dynamism to an individual, an immanent source of inspiration close enough to what might today be called one's 'genius' (from the Latin *ingenium*, from which the word 'engineer' also comes). As we have noticed, in the Hellenistic period an individual could be duplicitous in his social behaviour. He preserved that most elementary of fundamental liberties, the right to dissemble or disguise his thoughts. It was not so much a defensive reflex to protect his private interests or an obstinate attachment to the civic past, despite this having in many cases become no more than a façade. No, what man now discovered within himself was the reality of his invisible double. His religion became something it had never been in the classical period: a religion of the soul. It did not involve a rejection of the traditional cults or, as is sometimes claimed, an evasion, but rather prompted man to take a new look at himself, like turning over a card to see the other side. The power that he had always feared in the outside world and that he had tried to deflect in cults, by performing the appropriate rituals, was also present within himself. Let us call this individual energy the inner man. From it, the essential properties of human personality were later to emerge (*prosôpon*, in Latin *persona*, as yet designated only one's face, but next came to be used for a funerary image, a theatrical mask or the role played by an actor). But for the time being the soul appeared increasingly as a new dimension to man, one that it was important to liberate by turning away from the constraints imposed from outside. 'In a world subjected to political upheavals and sudden reversals of fortune, philosophy taught men how to resist the pressure of external circumstances and how to be independent of his own passions' (S. Said).

THE CYNICS

This unprecedented form of inner freedom made its appearance with Antisthenes (about 444–365). He was a disciple of Socrates, a little older than Plato. After the death of his master, he gathered his companions together at the Cynosarges gymnasium, in Athens (hence 'cynic'; the first part of the word means 'dog'). He chose to laugh at the society that had condemned Socrates to death, and mingled with those whom the Athenians called 'jokers', the public jesters. If people mocked him because he was a 'bastard' (his mother was said to be of Thracian origin), he riposted with a joke. After all, the god of gynmasia himself, Heracles, who had been admitted among the Olympians, was also a bastard, the son of Zeus and a mortal woman (Aristophanes uses the same point to raise a laugh in *The Birds*). And Cybele, the Mother of the Gods, honoured by the Athenians, herself came from Mount Ida, in Phrygia on the Hellespont. The divine was 'according to nature' but multiplied 'according to the laws', that is, through pure convention. And well-born people were those who practised virtue. A Cynic thus withdrew out of the limelight, to live 'according to nature'. Diogenes of Sinope (about 413–327), regarded by the Cynics as the model of a sage, who may have been responsible for the word *cosmopolitès*, 'citizen of the world', was said to have remarked to a pious pilgrim going into raptures over the number of offerings consecrated to the deities of Samothrace, the protectors of seafarers, 'There would be even more if those who were not saved had been able to make their offerings.' While mocking the common beliefs, his aim was to practise true piety. The Cynics were not anarchists. The Cynic poet Cercidas of

Megalopolis, Polybius' compatriot, who in his *Meliambics* deplored ostentatious wealth and the unequal division of property, was notwithstanding a friend of Aratus, the ambassador to the court of Antigonus Doson and commander of the infantry sent by his city to fight on the Macedonian side at the battle of Sellasia.

SCEPTICS AND EPICUREANS

The Cynics, who were street preachers, did not form a 'school' as other philosophers did, with a chief scholar designated by his predecessor. Yet, in common with other philosophers, they rejected Platonic idealism and followed the rule of confining themselves to knowledge acquired through the senses. E. Will has noted how they all converged on the concrete goal of philosophy, which was defined negatively as an absence of sorrow (*alypia*), anxiety (*atarxia*) and suffering (*apathia*). It was all a matter of liberating the inner man. The Sceptics (the name comes from a verb meaning 'to observe') refused to choose between the true and the false, as the criteria for doing so were not convincing. It was an old tradition, already encountered in the thinking of Xenophanes. They acceded to a state of tranquillity of soul by schooling themselves to indifference. Pyrrhon of Elis (about 360–270), the founder of this school, is said to have accompanied Alexander on his campaigns and to have encountered 'gymnosophists', that is, Hindu ascetics. His disciple, Timon of Phlius (about 320–230), whose remarks on 'the aviary of the Muses' are quoted above, is believed to have moved in the circles revolving around Antigonas Gonatas and Ptolemy II Philadelphus. The Sceptics eventually influenced the Platonic Academy, then headed by Carneades of Cyrene (215–129), who encouraged 'probabilism', the better to oppose the Stoics.

The 'Garden' of Epicurus (about 341–270) in Athens had very little in common with the meaning that 'Epicurean' has acquired in both French and English. Not that the Epicureans scorned sensual pleasures; but for them the supreme pleasure, the goal of Epicurean wisdom, was the enjoyment of total inaction, like that of the gods, who were unconcerned with the preoccupations of men and who existed in the spaces in between conglomerates of atoms in perpetual motion in the infinite void.

THE STOICS

Stoicism, which took its name from the *Stoa Poikilè*, the 'Painted Porch' on the agora of Athens, was quite different. Its founder Zeno of Citium, Cyprus (about 336–262), was originally a pupil of the Cynic Crates of Thebes, famous for his black humour. From him he retained the idea that a sage should live according to nature. The next leader of the school was Cleanthes of Assus (Mysia), until 232. One of his successors, Panaetius of Rhodes (about 185–109), lived for many years in Rome, a member of the circle surrounding Scipio Aemilianus where, according to Cicero, he met Polybius. Antigonus Gonatas met both Zeno and Cleanthes while living in Athens. Zeno composed a treatise on *The Republic*, and Cleanthes produced one on *Royalty*. Aratus of Soli (see above, p. 339) lived at the court of Pella. In his *Phainomena* he returned to the lesson of Aeschylus' *Prometheus Bound*, in which it is observed that even Zeus could not escape his destiny ('which is to reign forever'). An echo of this idea appears in an anecdote about Gonatas. He is said to have taught his son that 'the royalty of both of them was simply a glorious servitude.' Some scholars have detected a hint of Stoicism here. However, according to the system worked out by Stoicism, Zeus was not subject to destiny: he himself *was destiny*.

One striking feature of Stoicism is its systematic character, and no doubt the synthesis took some time to put together. However, the initial intuition and the coherence of its aims are evident in all its works (which mostly date from the Roman period). Stoicism strove hard to conciliate and reconcile all the contributions produced by Hellenism since the archaic period. The starting-point for Stoic thought was 'physics', as understood by the ancient Ionian philosophers who embarked upon the quest for a 'principle' (*archè*), that is, an initial force (natural, not mythical), the origin of sensible reality. Stoicism took over the doctrine of Heraclitus: the 'principle' is the 'ever-living fire', a primitive form of Reason (*Logos*), upon which the order of the world depends. But the secret of the world is to be found within oneself, and the goal that the sage sets himself is to remain master of himself in all circumstances. The sense of the adjective 'stoical' in French and in English expresses that ideal, which teaches the adult human being (and, most important, the great ones in this world) to be impassive in the face of adversity. In short, the systematic side of the *paideia* is extended into a 'continuous training'.

The motivating nerve-centre of the system (the Stoics compare their body of doctrines to a living organism) is the idea that the sensible world (the only true one) results from the interpenetration of two principles, the one passive, the other active, but both corporeal: 'The passive one is substance, indeterminate matter; the active one is the reason that resides within it, namely god.' The active principle that determines the physical chain of causes and effects is the Reason that is immanent in the world; the word 'god' is nothing other than the noun that designates *Logos*. Positioned in this manner at the active centre of the physical universe, Stoic logic (the science of reasoning) had no problem in taking over both religion 'according to the law' and myth 'according to the poets': all you had to do was accept that the 'ideas held in common' by all Greeks, such as their ancestral customs, were necessarily reasonable. In his *Hymn to Zeus*, Cleanthes identifies 'Zeus with a thousand names' with the active principle, which is thus given all the traditional attributes of the supreme god of the Greek pantheon, in particular the privilege of foreseeing the future. There was thus no difference between the activity of a 'physician' who looked for the first cause and a logician who proved its rationality, or a diviner who deduced the will of god by studying the omens.

Ethics likewise stemmed from immanent Reason. It was up to the sage to fight not only his own passions, which reflected the passive principle, but also all opinions contrary to reason. Cleanthes was said to have wanted to have Aristarchus of Samos (see above, p. 342) tried for impiety, as he considered him guilty of 'meddling with the health of the world' by suggesting that perhaps the earth moved round the sun. For man should follow the rules of reason. The sage's inner freedom consisted in deciding to do, not what was fixed for him by Destiny, but what his duty dictated to him, that is, to give each person his due. In this way the sage lived in conformity with the established order. For the Cynics, returning to nature was a means of freeing oneself from an intolerable social and political conformism. In contrast, Stoicism absorbed the individuality of a human being into the unity of the whole, and thereby helped him to be content with his lot, whatever that might be. A fine future for Stoicism in Rome seems to have been predictable. That was scant consolation for Athens which, however, remained and continued throughout Antiquity to remain the capital of philosophy.

Around the 220s

229 – The First Illyrian War

For a historian such as Polybius, who knew what happened later, the 220s marked as important a turning-point as the 350s had. The situation in the Adriatic was changing. The Illyrian kingdom, fast developing, had just inflicted a serious defeat upon a weakened Epirus (the battle of Phoenice, 230). After annexing Sicily at the end of the First Punic War (241), in 222 the Romans completed the integration of Italy by occupying Cisalpine Gaul (the Po delta). 'For Rome, the Adriatic Sea was now no longer a frontier, but a bridge.' In Illyria, the regent Teuta, Agron's widow, was allowing pirates to attack Italian traders, and occupied Corcyra. After she had rejected an ultimatum from them, the Romans landed in Corcyra, which surrendered without a fight. Apollonia, Epidamnus and the peoples of their hinterland returned 'to loyalty to the Roman people'. The Dalmatian islands did likewise and the Romans entrusted them to an Illyrian turncoat, Demetrius of Pharos. Teuta, defeated, was forced to abandon the coastal strip that included Apollonia, Epidamnus and the hinterland that had rallied to them. One has to admire the cleverness of this strategic choice: the Roman protectorate had projected a wedge between the Illyrians and the Epirots and now controlled all the trading ports of call along the route from the Otrante channel to the Po delta.

229 – The accession of Antigonus II Doson

At the time of the death of Demetrius II, Macedon was surrounded. Antigonus Doson, the son of Demetrius the Fair, was appointed guardian to the young Philip and king by the 'first of the Macedonians'. In a single summer, he repulsed the Dardanians and occupied southern Paeonia. The following year he recaptured Thessaly from the Aetolians, laid waste Doris and Phocis, then established a naval base at Opuntus.

227 – Revolution in Sparta

In 235 Cleomenes III, the new king of Sparta, took over the plans of Agis IV (executed in 240 upon his return from an expedition to help the Achaeans). Cleomenes' dream was shared by many cities at that time: it was to eject the Macedonians from Greece. His plan was to return to his city's legendary sources and restore it to the power that it had enjoyed in the fifth century and, to that end, to re-establish the community of the *Homoioi* by means of a radical reform of land-ownership; then to restore the Peloponnesian League. However, two of Sparta's rivals, Megalopolis in 235 and Argos in 229, had recently joined the Achaean federation. Because the Aetolians had handed several cities in eastern Arcadia over to Cleomenes, the Achaeans declared war on him. Cleomenes won a number of victories against Megalopolis, which was in an isolated situation. In 227, with the help of a few mercenaries, he seized full powers in Sparta, abolished the institution of the ephors and governed on his own. According to classical terminology, he was no longer a king but a tyrant. By incorporating the *perioikoi*, he increased the number of citizens to 4,000. They were each endowed with a *kleros* and were armed, and fought in the Macedonian fashion. Ptolemy III Euergetes, an ally of the Aetolians, transferred to Sparta the subsidies he had previously been giving the Achaeans.

224 – The foundation of the Hellenic League

Feeling threatened, Aratus, the *strategos* of the Achaeans, adopted a new policy: in 225 he signed a treaty with the Macedonians, to whom he returned Corinth. In 224 a new Hellenic League (or Symmachy) was formed at Aegion, the Achaeans' capital, under Macedonian hegemony. Its principal members were federated states that were at the peak of their power (the Achaeans, Thessalians, Epirots, Boeotians, Acarnanians and Phocidians). People began to dream: why should not the 'Macedonian exception' that seemed possible at the time of Antigonus Doson not have paved the way for a pan-Hellenic federation founded on general peace and freedom for all the federated states? But the opportunity was missed: directed against other Hellenes as it was, the new *symmachia* possessed no more consistency than the first League of Corinth had, on the eve of the Second Persian War.

To face up to this coalition, Cleomenes incorporated 6,000 helots, to whom he sold the rights of citizenship. Megalopolis was destroyed. The final confrontation took place during the summer of 222, at Sellasia, to the north of Sparta: it was a disaster for Cleomenes, who fled to Alexandria. For the first time in its history, Sparta was occupied by a garrison and governed by a Macedonian *epistatès*. At Doson's death, the new king of the Macedonians, Philip V (221–179) was, at the age of 17, in firm control of central Greece and the Peloponnese. Two other kings of barely 20 years of age had just succeeded to the Seleucid and Lagid thrones: Antiochus III (223–187) and Ptolemy IV Philopator (222–205). Perhaps this was a good omen. After all, Alexander had been only 20 years old at his accession.

220 – The war against Byzantium

Byzantium paid heavy tribute to the Celtic kingdom established in Thrace after 277. In 220 the Byzantines, at their wits' end, demanded toll dues from merchant vessels crossing the Bosphorus. Rhodes had no hesitation in making common cause with King Prusias of Bithynia against Byzantium. A small expedition proved enough to get the toll abolished. This marginal event coincided with what was happening in the Adriatic, where all problems of merchant navigation were being settled without any intervention from the Hellenistic monarchs. Rhodes and Rome were soon to clash, but at this point nobody foresaw that.

THE END OF GREEK HISTORY

RESISTANCE (220–188)

On the surface, everything seemed in order in the Mediterranean. Macedonia had recovered the means to exercise its Balkan hegemony. Antiochus III was to earn his title, 'the Great', in military exploits that momentarily gave the Seleucids greater territorial dominion than ever before. Egypt was to pull back within its continental frontiers and was not under threat.

However, one or two details had escaped the attention of the 'major powers': two cities, Rhodes and Rome (since the First Punic War) possessed the most powerful fleets at this time and hence also the ability to impose a Mediterranean thalassocracy; also, since the 'last adventure' of Pyrrhus, the Romans had had time to ponder upon the Hellenistic chequerboard and on the customary practices for maintaining the 'balance of powers'. Instead of confronting those powers with the arsenal of tactics that had enabled it to unify Italy and by means of which it would soon triumph definitively over Carthage, Rome had the intelligence to adapt to the purely Greek procedures of arbitaration and mediation which, for better or worse seemed to maintain that 'balance'. Flamininus was even to take over the worn-out old cry of 'liberty for the Hellenes' which, it is true, still had the power to stir hearts. E. S. Gruen has demonstrated the extent to which the Hellenistic States (kingdoms, federations and cities alike) were themselves responsible for becoming engaged in the process that led to their destruction. It was the very persistence of their international behaviour that occasioned the interventions of the Romans and determined their outcome. In fact, they literally committed suicide. And there was one more detail that only a historian spotted: 'From that point on [the 140th Olympiad, 220–216], the history of the world began to form one organic whole. Thenceforward the affairs of Italy and Africa became linked with those of Greece and Asia, and all things converged towards a single end' (Polybius). The history of historians thus (again according to Polybius) for the first time became 'worldwide', with the naive ambition, already embraced by the first Ionian cartographers, of covering the whole of the inhabited world (*oikoumene*). Through the force of circumstances, that history turned out to be *Roman*. For that reason, all that remains to be done here, to round off this *History of Greece*, is to recall to mind a number of events already considered elsewhere in this work, adopting as our cut-off date that suggested by Polybius, namely 146 BC, the year of the sacking of Carthage and Corinth.

THE WAR OF THE ALLIES (220–217)

The summer of 220 was marked by a new wave of brigandage and piracy. The Aetolians looted Phocis and Boeotia, captured a Macedonian ship off Cithera, landed at Patras in Achaea, and then laid waste Arcadia and Messenia. Demetrius of Pharos had, for his part, broken with the Romans in about 224, got himself appointed regent of the kingdom of Illyria and fought on the Macedonian side at the battle of Sellasia. In 220 he came to grief at Pylos, in Messenia, but seized quantities of loot in the Cyclades before being chased out by the Rhodian fleet. The fuse was in place. In the autumn the allies, convoked in Corinth by Philip V, declared war to 'liberate' Greece from the Aetolians.

In the spring of 219 the Roman Senate, which was preparing for a new war against Carthage in Spain and so could not afford the risk of being attacked from the rear in the Adriatic, decided on a rapid expedition (the Second Illyrian War). The Roman fleet ejected Demetrius of Pharos from the Dalmatian islands, which were attached to the southern Illyrian protectorate. The welter of detail recorded by Polybius (who detested the Aetolians) illustrates the volatile nature of a situation in which the actors, prisoners of past customs, failed to appreciate what was at stake in the seemingly 'one-off' decisions that they took to cope with the immediate circumstances. The Second Punic War (218–202) was to be the first example of what Polybius called a 'worldwide' conflict. The 'war of the allies' was marked by bloody reprisals and counter-reprisals (the Aetolians sacked the federal sanctuary of Dodona in Epirus, to which Philip V responded by sacking the sanctuary of Thermum in Aetolia). The peace concluded in Naupactus in 217 introduced no more than minor frontier adjustments. It was at this point that Philip V negotiated what was to prove the turning-point in his foreign policy. Learning of the successive victories of Hannibal's Carthaginians at Trebbia, Lake Trasimene (217) and Cannae (216), he decided to capitalize on them and eject the Romans from Illyria. In 215 he allied himself with Hannibal, then in Capua, who committed himself to getting the Romans to evacuate his Illyrian protectorate in return for Philip opening up a second front.

THE FIRST MACEDONIAN WAR (214–205)

Following a clumsy intervention at Messene (where Demetrius of Pharos was killed, shortly followed by Aratus), Philip tried to take Apollonia by attacking it from the sea (214). The Roman Calabrian fleet then also landed, taking the Macedonian camp by surprise in the middle of the night. The king burned his ships and returned to his capital by way of the mountains. Epirus had prudently opted for neutrality. In 213 Philip advanced with his army into northern Illyria. Unable to count on reinforcements (Hannibal having just captured Tarentum), the Roman praetor Valerius Laevinus logically enough entered into alliance with the Aetolians (212). The clauses of this alliance conformed with the customs of Hellenistic chancelleries: it was an alliance with a 'predetermined goal' that, in particular, fixed the spoils of war in advance (the Aetolians would acquire the conquered territories, while Rome would take the booty). Philip rushed from one front to the other, winning battle after battle, but without managing to alleviate the pressure from his adversaries. In 207 Hannibal was forced on to the defensive in southern Italy. The purpose of the deal struck with the Aetolians was achieved at little cost: the threatened fusion between the Carthaginians and the Macedonians never took place. Despairing of the promised help from the Romans, the by now exhausted Aetolians concluded a separate peace with Philip, with which the Romans then associated themselves (the Peace of Phoenice, 205).

THE SELEUCID REVIVAL (205–200)

The Lagids and the Seleucids were continuing their belligerent activities. Supported by his cousin Achaeus, who ejected Attalus I from Asia Minor (occupied since 226), Antiochus III put down the revolt of the eastern satrapies (222–220). Once back in Antioch, he learned that Achaeus had proclaimed himself king in Asia Minor. But there were more urgent matters to attend to (the Fourth Syrian War, 219–217). Seleuceia in Pieria was recaptured. The Seleucid army reached Sinai. Philopator's counsellors enrolled 30,000 Egyptians in the Lagid army, which was then victorious at Raphia (Tell Rafah), to the south of Gaza (June 217). The frontier was restored to the line drawn at the time of Philadelphus. Antiochus then treated with Pergamum, captured Achaeus in Sardis, had him executed, and finally won back Asia Minor.

What remained to be done was to re-establish the eastern frontier, if possible that of Seleucus I. In 220 the king of Atropatene Media (Azerbaijan) recognized Antiochus' suzerainty; in 212 the king of Armenia did likewise, followed in 209 by Arsaces II, the king of the Parthians. In 208 Antiochus III set out to put down a rebellion in Bactria, an independent Greek kingdom since 240. Having triumphed over King Euthydemus, whom he beseiged in his capital Bactra, he eventually (after two years) recognized Euthydemus as an allied king. He then crossed the Hindu Kush and symbolically received tribute from an Indian prince there. Feeling pleased with this, he set off on the return journey through Arachosia, Drangiana and Carmania, where he embarked for Gerrha (on the Arabian coast, opposite Bahrein), the terminus of the caravan route linking Gaza and the Persian Gulf. In return for a huge 'present' (silver, incense, myrrh), the Gerrheans got him to recognize their independence (205). Antiochus III was a man of determination. Upon his return to his capital, he learned that Ptolemy IV had just died, leaving a son, Ptolemy V Epiphanus (204–180) who was only 5 years old. Surely, this was his chance.

First, Antiochus concluded a pact of non-intervention with Philip: the latter would be free to act as he wished in Thrace while Antiochus seized Syria-Phoenicia (Fifth Syrian War, 202–200). The Seleucid troops advanced to Gaza, then withdrew to the sources of the river Jordan, where the victory of Panion (Banyas) at last procured them Palestine (200). The Seleucids' dream had become a reality.

THE SECOND MACEDONIAN WAR (200–194)

Philip took action immediately. In 202 he crossed Thrace and pushed on to the Straits, where he occupied Lysimacheia, Chalcedon and Chios, with the help of Prusias of Bithynia. In 201 it was the turn of Samos, which he captured from the Lagids. Next, he beat the Rhodian fleet and entered Miletus. However, he lost a land battle at Pergamum, then another at sea, off Chios, against a coalition of the fleets of Rhodes, Pergamum, Chios and Byzantium, all of which – not unreasonably – considered such aggression in peace-time as pure piracy. At this point Athens, with singularly thoughtless timing, chose to go to war against the Acarnanians, who were members of the Hellenic League. Philip despatched troops to lay waste Attica, while Attalus' fleet came to the aid of Athens.

Rome, having by now won the Second Punic War (201), was able, at the request of Rhodes and Pergamum, to launch its second Macedonian War without having to fight on two fronts. The procedure that Rome then followed should have given Philip's advisers pause for thought. Senatorial legates delivered the king an ultimatum similar to that received by the regent queen Teuta in 229: if he made war on any Greek people or laid a finger on Ptolemaic possessions, he would be at war with Rome. In the autumn of 200 a Roman army established rearguard bases in Illyria and Corcyra so as to isolate Philip V, who was busy laying siege to Athens. Early in 198 the newly elected consul T. Quinctius Flamininus landed in Illyria and sent Philip an ultimatum even sterner than the last one: the king was to evacuate all the land in his possession apart from Macedonia proper, leaving Greece free. Philip met this with a refusal and withdrew to Thessaly. The Achaeans, who were engaged in fighting against Nabis, the tyrant of Sparta, entered into alliance with first Pergamum, then Rhodes. Nabis and the Boeotians rallied to the Romans. Philip clashed with Flamininus at Cynoscephalae (near Pherae, in Thessaly). The outcome was a disaster for him that Polybius attributed to the manipulatory tactics of the legions (June 197). Philip, who had lost 13,000 men (8,000 of them killed), now accepted even heavier peace conditions: the evacuation of all his Greek possessions in both Europe and Asia; the surrender of his fleet; the restitution of all the ships he had seized from Rome, Rhodes and Pergamum; and a war indemnity of 1,000 talents.

There were still 'the affairs of Greece to be settled'. The task was entrusted to a commission of ten legates. The text of the senatus-consultum that they brought with them indicated the various stages by which this operation should proceed. In the long term, it declared, 'All the Greeks generally, those of Asia as well as those of Europe, are to be free and to govern themselves according to their own laws.' In the shorter term, the territories evacuated by the Macedonians were to be handed over to the Romans before the Isthmian Games. The senatorial commission would then arbitrate between the no doubt conflicting claims of Rome's allies. The Roman Senate was very conscious that its reference to the Greeks of Asia constituted an affront to Antiochus III, whose power was then at its peak. But they were at home with the diplomatic customs of Greece, which they applied with assurance, complementing them with a number of afterthoughts worthy of the Sparta of 404 and the Great King in 386.

At the Isthmian Games of July 196, a herald read out an impeccably drafted proclamation: 'The Senate of the Romans and Titus Quinctius [Flamininus] recognize the freedom of the following peoples, which will not suffer the imposition of troops of occupation or tributes and may govern themselves according to their own laws: the Corinthians, the

Phocidians, the Achaeans of Phthiotis, the Magnetes, the Thessalians, and the Pherrebians.' It was a limited list, for it named only the European peoples formerly subject to Macedonia, in fact, not even all of them. The text made no other general provisions. Rome laid on the table only the cards that it actually held at the time, reserving the right to reveal its full hand when the right moment came. The 'varied reactions' (acclamation from the naive, dissatisfaction from the rest, in particular the Aetolians) that were elicited by the herald's repeat reading, upon which the audience insisted, were too reminiscent of those that had followed the proclamation of the 'Macedonian Peace' at the Olympic Games of 324 (see above, p. 281) for Polybius not to have been thinking of them as he penned his account. Although fulsome in his praise of the magnanimity of the Romans in these solemn circumstances, he did have this to add: 'But most remarkable of all was that Fortune never crossed their designs and that everything, without exception, combined to bring about this unique moment.' Whatever the 'sentiments' and 'intentions' of the Senate, in which oligarchic rules insisted upon contradictory debates, the vice was in place. For the 'liberty of the Greeks' to disappear altogether, all that was necessary was to tighten it little by little.

THE WAR AGAINST NABIS (195–192)

After Cleomenes III was exiled in 222, the Spartans, led by tyrants who had no connections with any of the royal dynasties, had been party to the peace of Naupactus (217). Since 204 Nabis had been in power. Like others in the past, he dreamed of restoring his country to its former splendour, but this time in the form of a Hellenistic kingdom. He dared to do what nobody before him had: he gave the *perioikoi* and helots citizens' rights. Through force of habit, he laid waste the territory of Megalopolis and set supporters of his in authority in Messene (204). A new conflict then broke out against the Achaeans, who were led by the *strategos* Philipoemen, at whose side Lycortas, Polybius' father, fought. It was an indecisive war in which Argos took Nabis' side (197). In 195 Flamininus applied his principles: after a short campaign in Laconia, he forced Nabis to hand over Argos to him, along with any other possessions outside the strictly Spartan territory. That same year Hannibal, fleeing from Carthage, found refuge at the court of Antiochus III; meanwhile, his conqueror Scipio Africanus was consul. In 194 the Senate nevertheless decided to recall the legions. By the end of the year not a single Roman soldier remained on Greek soil.

The Achaeans now felt they had a free hand. In 193 they set about settling the Spartan question according to *their* principles. Nabis received Aetolian reinforcements, who made the most of the situation to assassinate him and loot the royal palace. The Spartan assembly accepted the conditions formulated by Philipoemen and joined the Achaean federation, leaving the social reforms in place (192). The final move came in 188, when Philipoemen exiled or sold as slaves all the 'new citizens' created by the tyrant. The Achaean federation now incorporated the whole of the Peloponnese, which the Romans called 'Achaea'.

THE ROMANO-AETOLIAN CONFLICT (192–188)

The destruction of Macedonian power had suited Antiochus III very well. In 196 he had landed at Lysimacheia. In response to the Roman embassy that arrived to order him and his army to evacuate Europe, he replied that he would content himself with recuperating a territory won by Seleucus I from Lysimachus in 281 (see above, p. 293). The trial of strength did not take place until 192, when it took the form of the Romano-Aetolian War. Dissatisfied with the results of Roman arbitration, the Aetolians asked Antiochus to come and liberate Greece from the Romans. It was exactly what Antiochus had been waiting for. The Aetolians assured him that the whole of Greece 'would flock to the coast as soon as his fleet was sighted'; so he landed at Demetrias. Philip loyally sided with the Romans. In the spring of 191 the consular army landed in Thessaly. The battle was fought at Thermopylae. The Romans, well-informed as usual, in their turn employed the manoeuvre used by the Persians in 480: Antiochus was surrounded and roundly beaten. He returned to Asia with his 500 remaining men. The Aetolians continued to resist until the autumn of 189, at which point they surrendered. The Romano-Aetolian treaty of 189 was the first permanent unequal treaty of alliance concluded by Rome in Greece, on the Hellenistic model perfected by the diadochi.

The Seleucid question was soon to be settled. The Roman fleet, assisted by the fleets of Rhodes and Pergamum, prevented the Phoenician fleet, commanded by Hannibal in person, from entering the Aegean Sea. The decisive battle was fought at Magnesia-ad-Sipylum (on the river Hermus, which flows into the sea to the north of Smyrna). Despite its numerical superiority (72,000 men against 40,000), the Seleucid army was crushed (January 189). Peace was concluded at Apamea, on the upper Meander (188). The treaty forbade the king to pass westward beyond the line of the Taurus (he thus retained Cilicia). The cities that were already free would remain so. The rest would be placed under the domination of either Pergamum or Rhodes: Rhodes received Lycia and Caria as far as the Meander; Pergamum recovered the territories lost in 226 (see above, p. 297). The Senate kept its distance from the game being played out in the East. By the end of 188 the victorious Roman army evacuated Asia. As for Philip V, he now devoted himself to Macedonia's geopolitical mission, by defending his northern frontier. He even made some progress in Thrace, where he recaptured Philippopolis (Plovdiv) before handing his throne on to his son Perseus (179).

IMPOTENCE (188–146)

Where Greece was concerned, after the peace of Apamea Rome found itself in the position of Philip II after Chaeronea: no Greek state was now powerful enough to predominate by military force. Tradition dictated that Rome should oversee a 'common peace'; and it looked as though the Senate was prepared to assume the normal consequences of this *de facto* situation, in the Greek manner: Rome's allies had divided the spoils of the two kings; the procedures for mediation were functioning correctly through arbitrators, the choice of whom was agreed by common consent of the parties involved; and senatorial missions of enquiry were seeking amicable solutions. But each time a new issue arose, the Senate was content simply to offer its good offices, and this was the source of a misunderstanding that would soon turn into resentment. It was not out of concern for its fine principles or out of passivity that the Senate abided by the letter of the senatus-consultum of 196; rather it was for reasons of economy, for a permanent Roman military presence would have been too costly. The flood of complaints from the East (which, as the Romans saw it, now included mainland Greece) increased the dependence of the Greeks quite enough to ensure their own preponderance at the least cost. Probably the Romans were also inspired by their own particular religious concept of peace. Whereas the Greeks thought of political order as an ever-shifting balance of forces, the Romans conceived it as a primary given fact that regulated relations with their neighbours that were normally pacific. Armed conflict could thus arise only as a result of external aggression. If it did, the Romans would legitimately defend themselves, after issuing an ultimatum warning the potential enemy that major interests of the Roman people were now at stake. Once peace was restored by victory, those under obligation to Rome had to shoulder their own responsibilities in the main-tenance of order. If they failed to do so, they were suspected of failing to honour the obligations that existed between 'friends' (to the great aston-ishment of the Rhodians in 167).

THE THIRD MACEDONIAN WAR (171–168)

When Perseus acceded to the throne he was 33 years old, had acquired considerable military experience at his father's side on the northern frontier and possessed a kingdom that was now in good demographic and eco-nomic shape. He had no difficulty in repulsing the two invasions that inevitably now took place, one by the Dardanians, the other by the Thracians. Unfortunately for him, the Dardanians asked for Roman aid, and Pergamum took a close interest in Thrace. Nevertheless, Perseus managed to get the Senate to renew the alliance of 196. But the Macedonian recovery was resented. Denunciations were soon pouring into the offices of the Senate, which proceeded to despatch two commissions of enquiry, in 173 and

172. Eumenes II of Pergamum (197–159) testified in person before the Senate, which then declared war on Perseus, accusing him of having 'borne arms against allies of the Roman people' (meaning the Dardanians and the Thracians). This time it was clearly to be a preventive war.

In the summer of 171 a consular army of 28,000 infantry and 1,400 cavalry marched through Epirus and entered Thessaly. Perseus mustered an army the like of which Macedon had not seen since Alexander's day (21,000 hoplites, making a total of 39,000 infantrymen including mercenaries, and 4,000 cavalry). He halted the Romans in the Tempe valley, and tried to negotiate with them during the winter, but without success. During the summer of 170 some of the Epirots revolted, cutting communications between Apollonia and the Roman army in Thessaly. The following summer, the Romans managed to restore communciations but achieved nothing else. At this point the Senate entrusted L. Aemilius Paullus with a large army (100,000 men, according to Plutarch) to fight Perseus and his allies (by now joined by Genthius, the king of the Illyrians). The last battle was fought in the heart of Macedonia, at Pydna (June 168). It took little over an hour to annihilate the Macedonian army (there are references to 20,000 dead and over 10,000 prisoners). Perseus fled to Samothrace, where he was captured by the Roman fleet. According to Plutarch, L. Aemilius Paullus deposited in the Treasury so much money raised by the booty that the Roman people paid no further taxes until the war between Antony and Octavian (43). After receiving Genthius' capitulation, the Roman army entered Epirus, meeting with virtually no resistance. The Senate ordered extermination: seventy strongholds were dismantled and in all 150,000 inhabitants sold as slaves (archaeology testifies to the extent of the destruction). Epirus was left to the tyranny of one of Rome's unconditional supporters, Charops. Illyria and Macedonia were declared 'free', that is, they were carved up, Illyria into three, Macedonia into four 'autonomous republics' – so autonomous that they were allowed no common institutions at all.

THE SIXTH SYRIAN WAR (170–168)

In thirty years the sovereigns had changed, but ambitions remained the same. Antiochus III had been succeeded by first Seleucus IV (187–175), then Antiochus IV Epiphanes (175–164), Ptolemy V by Ptolemy IV Philometor (180–145) who, through his mother Cleopatra, the daughter of Antiochus III, was the nephew of Antiochus IV. After a first victory at Pelusium (169), Antiochus IV had himself proclaimed king of Egypt in Memphis, then marched on Alexandria. It was at this point, in the suburb of Eleusis, to the west of the capital, that the famous incident took place in which the legate Popilius Laenas (who had just heard the news of the victory at Pydna) presented Antiochus IV with a senatus-consultum pressing him to evacuate Egyupt, drew a circle around the king, and insisted on a reply from him before he stepped outside it. Antiochus promised to do as the Senate wished: never again to pass beyond the 'Egyptian torrent' (Wadi el-Arish), which separated Sinai from Palestine. Rome took similar action with Eumenes II of Pergamum. Under threat from the Galatians in 168, he had annexed their territory. Not long after, a senatus-consultum restored the Galatians' autonomy, on condition that they remained inside their own frontiers.

The Third Macedonian War led to a more important change. For the senatorial majority in Rome, the dividing line was drawn no longer between separate Greek states but inside those states, between those who openly defended Roman interests and those who did not. Neutrality was no longer good enough. Rome demanded unconditional collaborators. That, at any rate, was the view of Polybius, who specifically condemned Charops in Epirus, Lyciscus in Aetolia, Mnasippus in Boeotia, Chremas in Acarnania and, above all, Callicrates in Achaea (a political opponent of his father Lycortas, who favoured a prudent neutrality). Even the Rhodians became victims of their traditional neutrality, which in the past had enabled them to safeguard their independence. After prolonged reflection, they had eventually despatched six warships against Perseus, which the Romans had scornfully returned to them. Their luke-warm attitude was severely punished: the Rhodians were forced to evacuate all the territories in Asia Minor that had come into their possession since 188. Athens, as a reward for its servility, recuperated Delos, which became an open port. The effect of this was to transfer there all passing merchant ships, along with the port taxes that they paid, which used to make Rhodes so rich (167).

We know of the systematic purging of the ruling classes through the high-quality testimony of Polybius. As a result of being denounced by Callicrates, he was himself sent to Italy in a group of 1,000 Achaeans, in principle to be brought to trial there. In fact, though, they were held as hostages. Thanks to the protection of the two sons of L. Aemilius Paullus, Polybius was allowed to remain in Rome. These hostages were not liberated until 150, when the surviving 300 returned to Achaea. Upon his return to his homeland, Polybius could see that the dissatisfaction provoked by Callicrates had created among the Achaeans a party of extremists who were determined at all costs to throw off the Roman yoke. He was relieved to be called upon as a military expert to join the last Roman expedition against Carthage (the Third Punic War, 150–146). In 147 he was at Scipio Aemilianus' side when, after being elected consul on the understanding that his mission was to destroy the rival city, Scipio in effect did so (April 146).

THE ACHAEAN WAR (149–146)

E. Will's comments on the Rhodians, quoted below, are applicable to all the moderates who, like Polybius, suffered for their views without understanding why and preferred to lay the blame, not upon the Romans, but (not without reason) upon their political opponents. 'Accustomed as they were to treat with the Senate as they did with the Hellenistic sovereigns, some thought they could continue to protect the interests of their city by manoeuvring between a resuscitated Macedonia and a still hesitant Rome: however much Rome denounced their ingratitude and treachery, they paid no heed.' By 150 Rome no longer had anything to fear from the world of the cities. Two symptoms indicated that there were still spasmodic signs of life in it: the internal conflicts resulting from a social and economic crisis the gravity of which Polybius underlines (a demographic decrease, the growth of, on one hand, huge fortunes and, on the other, abject poverty, and the shortsightedness of demagogues); and the petty squabbles over frontiers in which each side slaughtered as many of its opponents as possible, as in the 'good old days' (the war between Athens and Oropus in 155 is one example).

In Macedonia an unknown by the name of Andriscus passed himself off as Philip, the son of Perseus, who had died in Italy soon after his father. In 149 he roused the poorest inhabitants against the Romans, first in Macedonia, then in Thessaly. The rebellion was crushed in 148. The Senate resigned itself to a change of policy: according to one inscription, it was to the great relief of the richest of the Macedonians that Macedonia now became a Roman province placed under the authority of a proconsul resident in Thessalonika, where he was supported by a legion. Not long after this, work began on the construction of the Via Egnatia (named after the proconsul, Cn. Egnatius): two roads, the one from Epidamnus, the other from Apollonia, met before crossing the old Macedonian frontier and passed on towards Pella, Thessalonika and the Hebrus (the frontier of Thrace, now ruled by a protégé of Rome by the name of Cotys). The direction taken by this military road left no doubts as to the intentions of its creators: they were thinking in terms of a continental empire and were taking over the historic task previously undertaken by the Macedonians at the frontiers of Hellenism. The Roman empire did not yet exist, but the *Pax Romana* already did.

The last convulsion was to be the 'Achaean War', which came at a bad time for the Romans, who were already occupied in both Macedonia and Africa. This war was 'a secular conflict between Sparta and Megalopolis over a scrap of territory' (C. Préaux) that was presented as a juridical problem. Did the members of the federal Achaean State have the right to complain to the Senate about one another? The Senate proposed its good offices, but somewhat reluctantly. This time the delegate from Sparta was a supporter of Rome, but Callicrates died on the journey and was then replaced by a partisan of resistance to Rome, Diaius. The Senate appointed a commission of enquiry, which pressed the Achaeans to restore autonomy not only to Sparta but also to Corinth, Argos and a number of other small cities. The Achaeans were led by Critolaus, their elected *strategos*, Diaius, and their partisans, 'the most detestable citizens of all, enemies of the gods and corrupters of the nation, whom you would have imagined to be chosen deliberately from amongst the worst rogues in each of the cities, who ... with their left hands grabbed whatever the Romans offered with their right and, worse still, totally misunderstood their intentions,' wrote Polybius who, in this context, explained to his readers why he could not remain indifferent to the misfortunes of his country. Critolaus also made use of the old formulae of civil wars, declaring that the Achaeans' real enemies were neither the Romans nor the Spartans, but the Achaeans who were betraying the interests of their beleaguered country. His words were followed by actions: the military magistrates were granted full powers; and a moratorium on debts and imprisonment for debt was declared until such time as victory was won.

Instead of attacking Sparta, Critolaus went off to tackle and be beaten by the proconsul O. Caecilius Metellus, near Thermopylae, and died in the battle. Diaius replaced him, enrolled the slaves and levied extraordinary taxes from the wealthy. He was defeated on the isthmus by the consul L. Mummius, and fled to Megalopolis, where he killed his wife, set fire to his house and then committed suicide by taking poison. Corinth, evacuated by its Achaean garrison, surrendered without a fight (September 146). Despite this, on the orders of the Senate, it was looted and burned to the ground. It was a practice for which there were plenty of purely Greek precedents (for example, the sack of Plataea by the Thebans and the sack of Thebes by Alexander). Polybius saw paintings thrown to the ground and soldiers sitting on them to play at dice. All he could obtain from the commission responsible for restoring order in the cities that had revolted was that the statues of Achaeus, Aratus and Philopoemen should be spared. Rome had thus completed a full clear round. It was 'the end of Greek history' (E. Will). The disappearance of the Hellenistic world is part of Roman history.

CONCLUSION

Je suis né pour te connaître
Pour te nommer,
Liberté.
(I was born to know and name you, Liberty).

Paul Eluard

When the curtain falls on a play in the theatre, one of the actors sometimes appears in front of it to ask the public for its reactions. Upon completing a history of ancient Greece that from start to finish is a tragedy of violence and blood shed in the name of liberty, it is customary to seek a link with the present day. For the spectacle continues. Of course, Greece is still alive, seeking its place at the far end of the Balkan peninsula and perhaps also in the hearts of all of us, who have learned of liberty from it. So we could proceed to quote from memory Horace's words about 'the vanquished Greece that vanquished its ferocious victor' and, as some old textbooks do, list 'all that we owe to Greece' ('a modest material contribution, a major intellectual legacy, and an essential political inheritance' [Maller and Isaac]). Instead though, let us turn to Polybius, the great historian who himself witnessed what happened in 146 BC. He begins his epilogue as follows: 'Let me address a prayer to the gods: may I remain in the favour of the Roman people, and retain its trust. For I know full well that Fortune is prompt to show its jealousy of human beings and manifests its power particularly when one is tempted to rate oneself happy and believe that one's life has been a success.'

If he wished to pray to the gods and to drop his historian's mask and stand before us simply as a man, he was free to do so. And he had the right to raise a disturbing question. But we should like to understand. Should we invoke the title, *The Right Use of Treachery*, as P. Vidal-Naquet does when he likens Polybius to another of the 'Romans' collaborators', the Jew Flavius Josephus? Powerless, both men witnessed the death-throes of their respective countries, torn apart by civil war. Both, without conviction, invoked the tactical superiority of the Roman legions in order to 'understand the machine that had conquered them'. And both posed the question: 'Who *really* deserve to be considered traitors?' There is no easy answer in a situation in which a minority seizes power in a legal fashion but

368

then, through its proscriptions, destroys the very foundations of the city. An apparent traitor may well later be 'honoured as the benefactor and saviour of the country'. In this connection, Polybius blamed Demosthenes 'for having lightly and without discernment hurled the most stinging insults at the most remarkable men in Greece . . . for having entered into alliance with Philip' (see above, p. 265, a citation from the same fragment). Yet 'real' traitors did exist: 'Except on rare occasions, every time that the services of a traitor were needed, there was one to be found. One would normally be tempted to conclude that man, who passes for the cleverest of animals, may from many points of view be considered as the most stupid.'

We have no difficulty understanding the influence exerted by Hellenism on a barbarian West peopled by looters (as Thucydides, for whom the 'West' began to the west of Delphi, remarked). But the question that Polybius raises is more complicated: why and how did the Romans assimilate those whom they had conquered? Yet surely it is, in fact, comprehensible that a few men on the banks of the Tiber should have seized their chance so readily, and had the intelligence to mould themselves in the likeness of the Hellenistic cities, meanwhile sacrificing none of their own liberty. For was it not 'Greece's destiny' to spread its influence without proselytizing, to be a teacher without being a tyrant? In the early third century, the leading circles of the Roman people, already since the preceding century provided with the basic institutions that so fascinated Polybius, became Hellenized without the slightest regret. With what result? They became aware of themselves. Their counter-acculturation developed along with their acculturation, the one counterbalancing the other. The mid-third century saw the flowering of 'the first generation of Latin literature' (P. Grimal). Cultivated Romans, like other Hellenized peoples, were bilingual – but without ceasing to be themselves and without systematically fostering a hatred of 'others'. Perhaps that is why, in Greece, they eventually rallied, not 'traitors' in the real sense of the term, but men such as Polybius, who were despairing in the face of their own inability to realize their ideal.

We have noted the consummate efficiency with which the senatorial elite handled the language of diplomacy. It unearthed numerous legendary kin, going back to before the Trojan War (but all on the Trojan side). It appreciated the Greek civilization to the point of making it the basis of classical culture; and it imitated the cities so closely that no sooner was Greece captured than, with the Gracchi, Rome likewise embarked upon a century of civil wars. Yet one difference certainly separated the Romans from the Athenians: far from clinging, as the latter did, to an impossible autochthony, the Romans were to define themselves as refugees. The 'Town' (*Urbs*) was founded at a precise date, with the rites suited to the foundation of a colony. Their annals tell of an unflinchingly defensive history, in which the sword was used alongside the ploughshare. In order to live in peace, they were constantly obliged to fight against their aggressors. And so it was that (in order to preserve those two things that proved impossible in Greece: peace and liberty) they eventually found themselves in a sense constrained and forced to be the masters of the world!: masters endowed with such a gift of integration that the ancestors of the French people, the Gauls, even came to forget their maternal tongue . . .

The above digression was necessary to allow us to react to Polybius' prayer more calmly. By the time that he formulated it, all Polybius wanted was to live in peace. As he saw it, peace combined with liberty turned liberty into a new concept, for the first time available, albeit at the price of a catastrophe, to the entire inhabited world. Of course, for him those two words could only form a pair in an aristocratic regime. The fact was that ancient liberty presupposed servitude for the majority even – or rather particularly – in Athens, where liberty and slavery developed in parallel. The idea of liberty came into being during an aristocratic period, when it was coupled with equality or, to be more accurate, parity between 'those who were the same'. Liberty was not something 'given' from the start. It was a liberation, something that had to be won. To point out that at the beginning of history some men held power over others is to state the obvious; liberty came later, constituting a triumph over despotism. It developed in units of all sizes, country towns, other towns, peoples, an empire such as that of Rome, but was always the privilege of the few, of the warriors who, with the blessing of the religious authorities, offered peace in exchange for toil. And always the social body was represented as a community in which it was good to live together, like a banquet in which you feasted together, talking of literature or philosophy, admiring works of art, savouring all the pleasures of leisure, meanwhile as far as possible forgetting the other side of the coin, the world of work.

It goes without saying that this idea of liberty is no longer our own, because the world in which we have lived since the Industrial Revolution is a world of work. The movements tearing apart the social body that we have experienced since that time only make sense in the light of the first article in the 1789 declaration of human rights: 'Men are born and remain free and with equal rights.' We belong to a different world. So it is pointless to apply to the history of Antiquity the concepts that help us more or less to understand our own history, as was the tendency at the beginning of the twentieth century, based on the assumption that history was history. All the same, if the aim is not only to establish facts with total objectivity, but also to understand them and help others to understand them, no historian can manage without his or her maternal tongue and the logic of his or her own time (hence the quotation from Eluard at the beginning of this conclusion). And that has certainly been our aim in the present work.

THE SOURCES

Historians studying the ancient Greek world have at their disposal far fewer sources than those available for other periods, and if the number of documents is slowly increasing that is solely thanks to archaeology: the discovery and excavation of new sites bring to light inscriptions and objects that make it possible to be more precise about certain aspects of civilization and history and sometimes – very rarely – even to write an absolutely new page of history. The literary texts, on the other hand, have long been known, although a few new fragments of papyrus sometimes produce new data, as did the one discovered in 1962 near a tomb to the north-west of Salonika (known as the Derveni papyrus), which revealed a philosophical commentary on an Orphic theogony of the late fourth or early third century.

Below is a synthesis of the various types of sources available, but each of these needs to be set in its historical context by being related to the main body of this work, particularly in the case of the ancient authors who have already been cited or studied.

On the sources as a whole, see M. Cary, *The Documentary Sources of Greek History* (Oxford, 1927); Michael Crawford (ed.), *Sources for Ancient History* (Cambridge, 1983); G. F. Hill, R. Meiggs and A. Andrewes, *Sources for Greek History between the Persian and Peloponnesian Wars*, 2nd edn (Oxford, 1951).

THE LITERARY SOURCES

The literary texts that have come down to us represent only a fraction of the texts written in Greek Antiquity. They owe their survival to the goodwill of men of later ages who copied them out. Hardly any manuscripts go right back to the Greek classical or Hellenistic periods. Those that are available for us to read are the result of a process of sifting carried out by societies different from ours, which passed on whatever they regarded as important and whatever was to the taste of the age, meanwhile consigning to oblivion or simply omitting to copy texts that would undoubtedly have been very useful for our own knowledge of Greek history; some of the titles of lost texts are known to us from having been cited in some list or other. Furthermore, in Antiquity itself many of the libraries in which thousands of texts were kept were destroyed, the Library of Alexandria for one, burnt down in 47 BC. In other words, even if the literary texts that we possess are representative of a particular age and culture, they can never provide us with an exhaustive view of Greek civilization and history. Greek history is riddled with gaps.

Historians of today read texts that have been tidied up, criticized, . . . in short, 'established' after philologists, that is, specialists in language, have read all the existing manuscripts; and their work is indispensable. Although the dividing lines between the different literary genres are not always clear, for convenience's sake let us distinguish between a number of major types of texts.

HISTORIES

We have described the beginnings of the historical genre in Greece, with Hecataeus of Miletus. Next Herodotus, the author of *The Histories*, retraces part of the history of the archaic Greek world and creates a fresco of the non-Greek peoples known in his day alongside his central project, namely an account of the Persian Wars (see p. 166). Thucydides, in *The Peloponnesian War*, also recalls the earliest times in Greece before giving a virtually day-by-day history of part of the fifth century, along with a commentary on it (see p. 168). The string of 'classical' historians comes to an end with Xenophon's *Hellenica* (see p. 252) and its account of the battle of Mantinea (362). Not that the Greeks at that point stopped recording the sequence of memorable events in writing. Through extracts preserved from the fourth century and later, we know of many writers who continued the genre and were not without talent. Theopompus of Chios, who decribed the high deeds of Philip of Macedonia; Ephorus of Cyrene, whose general history spanned the years from the arrival of the Dorians down to 340, and Timaeus of Tauromenium, who wrote of the Greek West, stopping at the First Punic War. But the only work sufficiently well preserved to serve as a framework is that of Polybius (and even in this case the missing books have to be compensated for by consulting Livy). It is pointless to bewail the missing links in the chain, those that referred to Philip, Alexander and their successors (see p. 268). It is possible to reconstruct the broad lines of the framework of events from authors who were writing several centuries later but who refer copiously to their sources. Diodorus Siculus is one: his account begins with the Trojan War and continues down to the conquest of Gaul; another is Justinus, whose summary of Pompeius Trogus covers both East and West from the time of the Assyrians down to the Emperor Tiberius; and another is Plutarch, whose *Lives* belong to a literary genre that goes back to Xenophon. Then there are also Strabo of Amaseia, who composed a continuation of Polybius' work, some of which he repeats in his *Geography*, and Pausanias, whom it would be mistaken to regard simply as a tourists' guide, for the information that he provides, much of which is confirmed by archaeology, touches upon many areas of history.

On the historians, see: T. S. Brown, *The Greek Historians* (Lexington, MA, 1973); C. W. Fornara, *The Nature of History in Ancient Greece and Rome* (Berkeley, CA, and London, 1983); Simon Hornblower (ed.), *Greek Historiography* (Oxford, 1994); L. Pearson, *The Greek Historians of the West* (Atlanta, GA, 1987); Christopher Pelling, *Literary Texts and the Greek Historian* (London, 1999); Rosalind Thomas, *Oral Tradition and Written Record in Classical Athens* (Cambridge, 1989); H. Verdin, G. Schlepens and E. de Keyser (eds), *Purposes of History: Studies in Greek Historiography from the 4th to the 2nd Centuries BC* (Louvain, 1990)

Modern historians are interested in every aspect of the past and there is hardly a single literary text that does not provide some kind of data for their enquiries. However, literary texts can be used in this way on only one condition, namely that one respects the genre that each belongs to, for epic, poetry, drama and philosophy cannot be treated as though they constituted historical chronicles. One needs to learn how to slip inside a literary text, understand the particular way in which it works, and respect the kind of discourse that it produces before one can proceed to construct any historical investigation.

POETRY

The first great written Greek texts, the *Iliad* and the *Odyssey*, attributed to Homer, belong to the genre of epic poetry, and we have noted the problems that arise when they are used as historical documents (see pp. 28f.) In about 700 Hesiod provided a framework for Greek religious thought with his *Theogony* and his *Works and Days* (see pp. 210f.) Other archaic poets, such as Theognis of Megara, bear witness to the political crises of their time, and the legislator Solon left elegies that set out the broad lines of his reforms. Pindar, at the beginning of the fifth century, is a valuable source of information on the mythical traditions of the cities, as are some Hellenistic poets, such as Callimachus.

On poetry, see: Alan Cameron, *Callimachus and his Critics* (Princeton, NJ, 1995); D. E. Gerber (ed.), *A Companion to the Greek Lyric Poets* (Leiden, 1997); J. B. Hainsworth, *The Idea of Epic* (Berkeley, CA, 1991); W. R. Johnson, *The Idea of Lyric* (Berkeley, CA, 1982); J. K. Newman, *The Classical Epic Tradition* (Madison, WI, 1986).

THEATRICAL WORKS

It should again be stressed both how important and how difficult it is for historians to make use of the Athenian tragic and comic theatre of the fifth century as historical documents (see p. 169). The plays of Aeschylus, Sophocles, Euripides and Aristophanes, put on during religious festivals entirely organized by the city, really are among the documents in our possession that best enable us to understand how a civic community reflected on its own practices, judged its political life, and conceived of its relations with the gods. This period of intense theatrical creativity, limited to Athens, was very short and was over by the beginning of the fourth century, with Aristophanes' last play being performed in 388. After that, Menander is the only author of whom we possess more than citations taken out of context. The Hellenistic authors are full of metaphysical questioning and comic details.

On the theatre, see: E. Csapo and W. J. Slater, *The Context of Ancient Drama* (Ann Arbor, MI, 1995); Gregory W. Dobrov (ed.), *The City as Comedy: Society and Representation in Athenian Drama* (Chapel Hill, NC, 1997); P. E. Easterling (ed.), *The Cambridge Companion to Greek Tragedy* (Cambridge, 1997); J. R. Green, *Theatre in Ancient Greek Society* (London and New York, 1994); David Konstan, *Greek Comedy and Ideology* (Oxford, 1995); Christopher Pelling (ed.), *Greek Tragedy and the Historian* (Oxford, 1997); R. Seaford, *Reciprocity and Ritual: Homer and Tragedy in the Developing City-State* (Oxford, 1994); J. J. Winkler and F. Zeitlin (eds), *Nothing to do with Dionysus? Athenian Drama in its Social Context* (Princeton, NJ, 1990)

SPEECHES AND POLITICAL PAMPHLETS

In the mid-fifth century, political and judicial eloquence produced a new literary prose genre, rhetoric (see pp. 249f.). From 419 to about 322, a number of orators published their speeches. From these ten 'Attic orators' were selected, being considered as the very best models in the Roman period. Two-thirds of these works consist of legal speeches, which present an instantaneous 'snapshot' view of contemporary events in Athens. Many of them are extremely graphic and of a partiality seldom to be found elsewhere.

Political pamphlets constituted a literary genre in prose (long before, Solon had used the poetic form for the same purposes) that prolonged and developed the art of oratory, with the *ecclesia* as audience. The pamphlets were aimed at enlightened public opinion, that is to say anyone with the means to acquire a copy of the text. The most ancient specimen is *The Republic of the Athenians* (about 420), wrongly attributed to Xenophon, the author of which is known as 'the old oligarch'. The most important of these pamphlets are those by Isocrates. They were followed, in the Hellenistic period, by a number of pale essays that hardly rate the description 'philosophical' (such as *On royalty*).

On speeches, see: W. Robert Connor, *The New Politicians of Fifth-Century Athens* (Princeton, NJ, and London, 1971); George Kennedy, *The Art of Persuasion in Greece* (Princeton, NJ, and London, 1963); L. Pearson, *The Art of Demosthenes* (Meisenheim am Glan, 1976); R. Sealey, *Demosthenes and his Time* (Oxford, 1993); Too, Yun Lee, *The Rhetoric of Identity in Isocrates: Text, Power, Pedagogy* (Cambridge, 1995).

PHILOSOPHICAL ESSAYS

For Socrates and his disciples, thought on the perfect city formed a natural framework for moral philosophy. Some texts by Plato, Xenophon and Aristotle constitute fundamental sources for historians. Of course, one needs to distinguish between the ideology peculiar to the respective philosophers themselves and the wealth of verifiable data that these texts communicate in a perfectly honest fashion (for example, in Plato's *Laws*). Later philosophers testify to the profound changes in ways of thinking that took place from the mid-fourth century on.

On philosophy, see: Jonathan Barnes (ed.), *The Cambridge Companion to Aristotle* (Cambridge, 1995); John Dillery, *Xenophon and the History of his Times* (London, 1995); J. J. Keaney, *The Composition of Aristotle's* Athenaion Politeia: *Observation and Explanation* (Oxford and New York, 1992); D. Keyt and F. Miller (eds), *A Companion to Aristotle's "Politics"* (Cambridge, MA, 1991); Richard Kraut (ed.), *The Cambridge Companion to Plato* (Cambridge, 1992).

SCIENTIFIC AND SCHOLARLY TREATISES

From the time of the Presocratic philosophers of the archaic period on, scientific reflection was an important part of Greek thought on the world. The Hippocratic Corpus of the late fifth and the fourth centuries continued that tradition when it laid the foundations of medicine. Later, the culture of Alexandria produced erudition in all fields of knowledge. Lexicography sprang from the catalogues of Callimachus and continued to develop until the end of the Byzantine period. It gave rise to two kinds of works: glosses (or 'scholia'), brief notes introduced in the margins of classical works and later collected in volumes of their own; and dictionaries or 'lexicons', which provided explanations for ancient or little-known words and names, set out in alphabetical order. The same concern for accuracy is evident in all kinds of works that are still useful for historians seeking to correct ready-made ideas (on strategy, medicine, architecture and so on; see pp. 337f.).

On literary sources in general, see: Jonathan Barnes, *Early Greek Philosophy* (Harmondsworth, 1989); P. M. Fraser, *Ptolemaic Alexandria*, 3 vols (Oxford, 1972); G. S. Kirk, J. E. Raven and M. Schofield, *The Presocratic Philosophers*, 2nd edn (Cambridge, 1983); James Longrigg, *Greek Rational Medicine* (London, 1993); Rudolf Pfeiffer, *History of Classical Scholarship: From the Beginnings to the End of the Hellenistic Age* (Oxford, 1968); N. G. Wilson, *Scholars of Byzantium* (London, 1983).

PRIMARY SOURCES

Herodotus himself saw some of the monuments of which he writes: sanctuaries, altars, votive offerings, funerary monuments, public edifices; he himself visited some of the sites he mentions, for example, the battlefields of Marathon, Thermopylae and Plataea; and he himself examined twenty-four inscriptions, half of them written in foreign languages. What he valued was direct contact with the material vestiges of the past, because they constituted so many proofs for or against the local traditions. Archaeologists are always thrilled by that kind of direct contact. Primary sources appear in layers, like cards in a game of patience (for example, at Delphi, Delos and Xanthus in Lycia). Sometimes it is difficult to place them in a chronological sequence of general history. The fascinating but laborious disciplines of archaeology are clearly not 'auxiliary sciences'. They are an essential part of the profession of the historian.

EPIGRAPHY

Inscriptions engraved in stone are constantly providing us with new knowledge. Their growing number is explained by the fact that the ancient Greeks used this means of publication far more frequently than we do (the figure of 20,000 Attic inscriptions is sometimes cited). Epigraphists thus have the chance to read laws and decrees, treaties, frontier agreements, legal agreements, agreements of *isopoliteia* and *sympoliteia*, lists of debtors to the public treasury and innumerable honorific decrees. The sanctuaries constitute mines with a rich range of seams: sacred laws, votive offerings, dedications, expressions of gratitude for asylum addressed to kings, cities or confederations, oracular tablets, lists of all kinds, certificates of the affranchisement of slaves. To these may be added funerary inscriptions, graffiti and *ostraca* (short texts written in ink on pottery shards, not forgetting the Mycenaean tablets, which at a stroke set the dates of the most ancient texts known back a whole six centuries (see pp. 18f.). On the slopes of the Acropolis of Athens, archaeologists have discovered over 10,000 *ostraca*, used between 487 and 416 in the annual procedure of ostracism. In Upper Egypt, thousands of tax receipts inscribed on *ostraca* have been dug up. We also possess a hundred or more bronze plaques used to identify the heliasts when they collected their *misthos*.

In the Hellenistic period, inscriptions in Greek and also in local languages became even more numerous in the Cyclades, Asia Minor, Syria, Babylonia and Egypt, where important hieroglyphic inscriptions have been discovered (for example, the Pithom stele, in the Nile delta) and a number of bilingual or trilingual stelae in the synods of Egyptian priests: in 1822 one of these, the Rosetta stone, enabled Champollion to decipher hieroglyphics.

Newly discovered inscriptions are published in periodicals and subsequently added to some corpus, usually in accordance with a geographical classification (there is a corpus of Attic inscriptions, for example), but sometimes with a thematic classification. As a rule they are not translated, but nowadays a number of selections of translated inscriptions, with commentaries, are available. Each year the *Revue des Etudes Grecques* carries a record of new inscriptions: the epigraphical report.

On epigraphy, see: B. F. Cook, *Greek Inscriptions* (London, 1987); M. L. Lang, *The Athenian Agora 25: Ostraka* (Princeton, NJ, 1990); R. Meiggs and D. M. Lewis (eds), *A Selection of Greek Historical Inscriptions to the End of the Fifth Century* BC (Oxford, 1969); F. Miller, 'Epigraphy' in Michael Crawford (ed.), *Sources for Ancient History* (Cambridge, 1983); M. Ventris and J. Chadwick, *Documents in Mycenaean Greek*, 2nd edn (Cambridge, 1973); A. G. Woodhead, *The Study of Greek Inscriptions*, 2nd edn (Bristol, 1992).

PAPYROLOGY

Not all official documents were published on stelae. Public archives were stored in special buildings (in Athens, in the Metrôon, dedicated to the Mother of the Gods, on the agora). They included, for instance, Draco's laws on homicide and also the laws of Solon. At first they were transcribed on small wooden tablets (*sanides*) or larger ones (*axones*), later on papyrus or parchment (the latter being widely used in Pergamum and in Syria from the third century on), all of which were perishable materials. In 411 the Athenians were, for that reason, unable to lay their hands on the original laws of Cleisthenes. The number of rolls of papyrus (*chartai*) used in the Greek world during what has been dubbed 'the papyrological millennium' (from the fourth century BC to the sixth century AD) has been estimated to run into millions, but unfortunately many succumbed to either the damp or the appetite of rats. By a lucky chance, several thousand have nevertheless been recovered from Middle and Upper Egypt, from ancient villages buried in the desert sand, such as Philadelphia or Tebtunis in the Fayyum. Most had been reused as stable litter by the peasants or else as wrappings for mummies. In Egypt papyrus was so cheap that it was used as packing paper. Its sale was, of course, subject to a special tax. Not only has papyrology restored to the light of day many literary texts, even in little towns where nobody had imagined they would find readers of Homer, but it has revealed the daily lives of those whom history usually forgets. Even allowing for the uniqueness of Egypt, the economic, social and cultural information recorded on these papyri helps us to gain a better understanding of the phenomenon of Hellenization.

On papyrology, see: Roger S. Bagnall, *Reading Papyri, Writing Ancient History* (London and New York, 1995); Italo Gallo, *Greek and Latin Papyrology* (London, 1986); Naphtali Lewis, *Papyrus in Classical Antiquity* (Oxford, 1974); C. H. Roberts, *Greek Literary Hands 350 BC–AD 400*

(Oxford, 1956); E. G. Turner, *Greek Manuscripts of the Ancient World*, 2nd edn (London, 1987); E. G. Turner, *Greek Papyri*, 2nd edn (Oxford, 1980)

NUMISMATICS

Many coins have been recovered from excavations – of either a clandestine or an archaeological nature – often in the form of hoards buried by their owners. When carefully classified into different types and series, these constitute a (sometimes unique) source of documentation for those who know how to decipher them. It is thus that something of the astonishing destinies of the Graeco-Bactrian and Graeco-Indian kingdoms is known to us from the magnificent coins minted there down to the point when they disappeared, in the mid-first century BC. The circulation of coins, their values and their areas of diffusion all provide valuable data for economic analyses. The minting of coins bearing the effigies of sovereigns, which began in the Achaemenid empire with 'darics' and then became current under the diadochi, provides a fine gallery of portraits, either realistic or idealized, for historians to reflect upon. In some cases the deification of the king is discreetly indicated by some symbol adorning his head (see p. 344).

On numismatics, see: I. Carradice, *Greek Coins* (London, 1995); I. Carradice and M. J. Price, *Coinage in the Greek World* (London, 1988); C. Howgego, *Ancient History from Coins* (London, 1995); G. K. Jenkins, *Ancient Greek Coins*, 2nd edn (London, 1990); C. M. Kraay, *Archaic and Classical Greek Coins* (London, 1976); Otto Mørkholm, *Early Hellenistic Coinage from the Accession of Alexander to the Peace of Apamea (336–188 BC)* (Cambridge, 1991)

ARCHAEOLOGY

Archaeology is the study of material, as opposed to written sources, and all historians of Antiquity, if not themselves archaeologists, frequently need to turn to archaeological publications. The scope of the present work rules out any description of the techniques and methods used in Greek archaeology, but it must be pointed out that they have been affected by many new developments over the past fifty years and have played their part in revealing new problems for the historians to tackle. Let us consider a few examples. While excavation is always indispensable for an accurate knowledge of a site, archaeological prospection now makes it possible to study rural zones that are hardly built on at all and even, in the future, to understand more about the exploitation of a city territory as a whole. The development of prospection goes hand in hand with the recent interest taken by historians in open spaces, the landscape, the environment. Here now is a second example: the quantitative as well as qualitative study of the pots discovered on a particular site is fundamental to the revival of the history of economic exchanges and contacts between different regions of the Greek world in the archaic period: for historians of the economy, shards (the fragments of broken pots) hold as much interest as does an intact cup painted in a famous Athenian workshop. And here is a third example: the excavation of tombs in necropolises is now concerned not solely with digging up the finest objects there but also with the funerary furnishings as a whole and with the slightest traces of rituals. It can now throw light on the social context of burials or even make it possible to distinguish the broad lines of the lives of the living. Many of the most recent hypotheses that historians have produced about the Dark Ages are based on the study of tombs. It would be easy to supply many other examples showing the close connection between the advances made in archaeology and the new questions now being tackled by historians.

The structure of towns – the plan of archaic Smyrna comes to mind, or that of fifth-century Miletus or Priene, one century later – ranging from settlements of basic neolithic huts to the Hellenistic houses richly decorated with frescoes and mosaics of Delos or Ephesus, and including the palaces of Knossos and Mycenae, the edifices consecrated to the gods and their cults, altars, temples, treaure stores, theatres . . . the places for public life (agora, official buildings, gymnasia, banqueting halls): this whole scene of ruins provides the material background to a history which, without their presence, would be totally disembodied. But archaeology does more than simply reveal this background; it provides the keys to the techniques and skills of all those involved in creating it, from the architect down to the stone-mason; it reminds us of the priorities of societies that invested huge sums for their gods and competed with one another in erecting edifices flanking both sides of the sacred ways leading to sanctuaries, some of which were financed by donors rich enough to offer porticoes and gymnasia, societies that also erected ramparts and towers. As has repeatedly been pointed out in the first part of this book, archaeology, a source for all periods of Antiquity, just as important as the texts that survive, is the sole source for periods that antedate the appearance and use of writing.

Archaeology also brings to light objects that, in their turn, themselves become sources for historians: coins (see above), pots, and statues, among others.

On archaeology, see: William R. Biers, *The Archaeology of Greece: An Introduction*, 2nd edn (New York, 1987); Paul MacKendrick, *The Greek Stones Speak: The Story of Archaeology in Greek Lands*, 2nd edn (New York, 1982); I. Morris (ed.), *Classical Greece: Ancient Histories and Modern Archaeologies* (Cambridge, 1994); C. Renfrew and P. Bahn, *Archaeology: Theories, Methods and Practice* (London, 1991); A. M. Snodgrass, *An Archaeology of Greece: The Present State and the Future Scope of a Discipline* (Berkeley, CA, and London, 1987); Brian G. Trigger, *A History of Archaeological Thought* (Cambridge, 1989).

ICONOGRAPHY

For a long time historians regarded images painted on vases or sculpted in stone as illustrations that could, to some extent, confirm the data they had established on the basis of texts. Today, historians have learned to recognize the status of images as such, to study every painted or sculpted representation for itself, exactly as they would a text, and to take into account all its distinctive features and its own particular way of interpreting reality. The formidable collection of images created by the Greeks thus becomes an object of history in itself, one that frequently makes it possible to formulate traditional questions in a new way, opening up new fields of investigation. Extremely useful handbooks have classified images according to their mythological themes: recent syntheses focus upon, for instance, the iconography of sacrifice, the rituals relating to Dionysus, hunting, warfare, women. These have made it possible to rethink the themes of historical anthropology and they provide keys to the understanding of a Greek world that may have been just as much a civilization of images as it was a civilization of words.

On iconography, see: J. J. Pollitt, *Art in the Hellenistic Age* (Cambridge, 1986); Tom Rasmussen and Nigel Spivey (eds), *Looking at Greek Vases* (Cambridge, 1991); G. M. A. Richter, *The Sculpture and the Sculptors of the Greeks*, 4th edn (New Haven, CT, 1970); G. M. A. Richter, *Handbook of Greek Art*, 8th edn (Oxford and New York, 1983); C. Rolley, *Greek Bronzes* (London, 1986); Andrew Stewart, *Faces of Power: Alexander's Image and Hellenistic Politics* (Berkeley, CA, 1993).

CHRONOLOGICAL TABLE

	Events	Culture
Bronze Age 3000–2000	Early Helladic or Bronze Age Arrival of peoples speaking a proto-Greek	Cycladic art: idols
2000–1550	Middle Helladic or Bronze Age	First Cretan palaces, Linear A; A and B circles of shaft tombs in Mycenae
1550–1075	Late Helladic or Bronze Age or Mycenaean period	
1550–1500		Construction of the first *tholoi*
1500–1400	Mycenaean control of Crete	First documents written in Linear B. Palaces of Mycenae, Tiryns, Pylos
1375	Destruction of Knossos	
1325–1200	Peak of Mycenaean civilization	Construction of huge fortresses
about 1200	Destructions in Greece; Pylos abandoned; migrations westward	
1125–1075	Mainland settlements abandoned	
Iron Age 1050–900		Protogeometric pottery
900–700		Geometric pottery (appearance of first animal, then human figures peaking around 770–750, Dipylon); Lefkandi site (Euboea): princely tombs; major sanctuaries: offerings of bronze objects (tripods . . .)
about 800	The Spartans settle in Laconia	
776		First Olympic Games
775	Beginning of emigration eastward: Pithecussae Foundation of many new cities	Development of major sanctuaries: Thermon, Perachora, Delphi, Delos,

	Events	Culture
	in the West	Dodona, Ephesus; and of heroic cults
750–700		Alphabetic writing
		Homer, *Iliad* and *Odyssey*
about 740	Lelantine War in Euboea between Chalcis and Eretria	Late eighth: Hesiod, *Theogony, Works and Days*
	First Messenian War	
	Beginning of emigration to the Hellespont	
747–657	Corinth: oligarchy of the Bacchiads	
740–720	Sparta: First Messenian War	
700–550		Orientalizing period in pottery and sculpture; bronze basins
650–620	Sparta: Second Messenian War	
657–585	Corinth: Cypselid tyranny (Cypselus, Periander)	
about 650		Archilocus of Paros
late 7th		Semonides of Amorgos, Tyrtaeus and Alcman of Sparta
650–600		Sculpture: dedalic art
		Temples of Hera in Samos, Artemis in Ephesus; the first Greek coins: Aegina, Athens, Corinth. Thales (640–550?)
632	Athens: Megacles has Cylon and his friends massacred	
	Exile of Alcmaeonid family	
621–620	Athens, Draco: criminal legislation	
610–600		Statues: *Kouroi* of Sunium, *Kouros* of Dipylon
		Anaximander, then Anaximenes
620–540		Corinthian pottery
600–550		Laconian cups
about 600		Beginning of black-figure Attic pottery
		Heraion temple at Olympia
early 6th		Theognis of Megara; Sappho and Alceus in Mytilene; Anacreon in Teos
612	Athens seizes Salamis from Megara	
600–590	First Sacred War (over Delphi)	Temple of Artemis in Corcyra (about 590)
594–593	Athens: Solon is archon	

CHRONOLOGICAL TABLE

	Events	Culture
582		Delphi: First Pythian Games
573		Nemea: First Nemean Games
		Xenophanes of Colophon (570–475)
566		Athens: organization of the Great Panathenaea festival
561	Pisistratus, tyrant (d. 528)	Temple C at Selinus
550–525		Athens, potters and painters, Amasis and Exekias
540	Battle of Alalia: Carthaginians defeat Phocians	Anacreon of Teos, monodic poet
		Temple of Apollo in Corinth, treasure stores of Olympia; Pythagoras, born in Samos, lived in Crotona; Heraclitus of Ephesus (about 540–480)
534		Athens: first Dionysia tragic competition
530	Polycrates tyrant of Samos (d. 522)	First temple of Hera (Basilica) in Paestum
		Athens: first red-figure pottery
		Aeschylus (526–456)
522	Darius king of the Persians (d. 486)	Pindar: *Epicinies* (518–438)
		Parmenides of Elea (515–450)
		Delphi: (Alcmaeonid) temple of Apollo
		Temple G in Selinus
510	Fall of tyrant Hippias in Athens Croton destroys Sybaris	Temple of Athena in Marmaria,
		Temple of Olympian Zeus, Agrigentum
508	Cleisthenes in Athens: reforms	Late 6th: Antenor, Athenian sculptor
after 500		Construction of Athenian treasure store in Delphi
498–494	Revolt of Ionia	Anaxagoras born in Ionia, lived in Athens
		Sophocles (496–406)
494	Fall of Miletus War between Athens and Aegina	
493	Themistocles, archon in Athens	
490	First Persian War. Marathon	Temple of Aphaia in Aegina Empedocles of Agrigentum

	Events	Culture
489	Aristides archon in Athens	
486	Xerxes king of Persians (d. 461)	
485	Gelon tyrant of Syracuse	Herodotus (485–420)
		First comedy competition in Athens
483–482	Themistocles' naval law	
480–478	Second Persian War (Salamis, Plataea, Mycale)	Critius and Nesiotes: tyrannocides group
		Euripides (480–406)
478	Formation of Delian League	Hippodamus of Miletus: plan of Piraeus
about 470		Phidias, sculptor in Athens
472	Ostracism of Themistocles	Polygnotus of Thasos (painter)
	Cimon's importance	Tholos on agora of Athens
		Socrates (469–399)
468	Battle of the Eurymedon	
462–461	Ephialtes in Athens: reforms	Temple of Zeus, Olympia
	Ostracism of Cimon	(468–456)
		Hippocrates of Cos (b. 460?)
		Thucydides (460?–396?)
		Democritus of Abdera (460?–370?)
454	Transfer of the treasury of the Delian League to Athens	Mid-5th, importance in education of the Sophists: Gorgias, Protagoras, Antiphon
450		Second temple of Hera in Paestum
		Myron: the *Discobolos*
449	Peace of Callias: end of war against Persians	
449–447	Second Sacred War (Delphi)	
446–445	Thirty-Year Peace (between Athens and Sparta)	Aristophanes (b. about 445)
444–443	Foundation of Thurii in southern Italy	Construction of Parthenon with Ictinus and Callicrates (447–438)
443	Pericles, *strategos* (until 429)	
	Ostracism of Thucydides	
440		Lysias (b. about 440)
		Polycletes: the *Cupbearer*
		Temple 'of Concord' in Agrigentum
438		Phidias' statue of *Athena Parthenos*
436		Isocrates (436–338)
		Construction of Propylaea

	Events	Culture
		of the Acropolis (Mnesicles)
431	Beginning of Peloponnesian War (until 404)	
430	Plague in Athens	
429	Death of Pericles	Plato (429–347) Aristophanes' first comedy Late 5th-early 4th: Hippocratic treatises Xenophon (about 428–354)
427		Temple of Athena Nike on the Acropolis (427–424) Late 5th: temple of Apollo at Phigalie (Bassae)
425	Athens captures Sphacteria, role played by Cleon	
421	Peace of Nicias	
421–405		Erechtheum built on Acropolis
420	Alcibiades *strategos*	Paeonius: Nike of Olympia
415–413	Sicilian expedition	
415		Mutilation of the hermes, parody of the Mysteries of Eleusis
411–410	Oligarchic regime of the Four Hundred in Athens	
406	Battle of Arginusae, Athenian *strategoi* sentenced to death	Deaths of Sophocles and Euripides
405	Aegospotami: naval victory won by Lysander over Athens Dionysius the Elder (405–367) in Syracuse	
404	Artaxerxes II Mnemon (404–359) Capitulation of Athens; regime of the Thirty	
403	Restoration of democracy in Athens	*Against Eratosthenes* by Lysias (about 440–360)
401	Expedition of the Ten Thousand	
400		Monument to the Nereids in Xanthos
399	Death of Socrates Agesilaus (399–360) in Sparta	*On the Mysteries* by Andocides (about 440–390) Antisthenes the Cynic (444–365?) Hippocrates of Cos (b. 460?)

	Events	Culture
397	Conspiracy of Cinadon in Sparta	
396	Agesilaus in Asia Minor	
395	Corinthian War (395–386)	
392		*Olympic speech* by Gorgias (about 483–385)
391		*On the Peace* by Andocides
390		*Anabasis* by Xenophon (430–350?)
388		*Olympic speech* by Lysias *Plutus*, Aristophanes' last comedy
387		Plato founds the Academy
386	The King's Peace	
385	Jason of Pherae (385–370) in Thessaly	
382	Olynthian War (382–379)	
380		*Panegyric*, by Isocrates (436–338?) Scopas of Paros (early 4th)
377	Second Athenian confederation Mausolus (377–353) in Caria	
376	Pelopidas and Epaminondas in Thebes	
375		*The Republic*, by Plato
371	Battle of Leuctra	Praxiteles (b. Athens about 390)
369	Alexander of Pherae (369–358) in Thessaly Foundation of Messene	
368	Foundation of Megalopolis	
367	Dionysius the Younger (367–344) in Syracuse	Temple of Asclepius in Epidaurus
364	Battle of Cynocephalae	
362	Battle of Mantinea	
360	Archidamus II (360–338) in Sparta	
359	Philip II (359–336) in Macedonia	
358	Artaxerxes III Ochos (358–338)	Asclepeion in Athens
357	War of the allies against Athens (357–355) Amphipolis taken by Macedonians	Foundation of the new Priene
356	Sacred War against the Phocidians (356–346)	*On Peace*, by Isocrates
354	Eubulus' administration in Athens (354–346)	*Areopagiticus*, by Isocrates

	Events	Culture
351		*First Philippic*, by Demosthenes (384–322)
349		*Olynthians*, by Demosthenes *The Laws*, by Plato
348	Macedonians take Olynthus	
346	Peace of Philocrates	
344	Timoleon (344–337) in Syracuse	
343		Aeschines/Demosthenes, *On the Embassy* *Siegecraft*, by Aeneas Tacticus Mausoleum of Halicarnassus Eudoxus of Cnidus (400–350?) Diogenes the Cynic (413–327?)
342	Archidamus III in Italy (342–338)	
340		Temple of Zeus in Nemea
339	Sacred War against Amphissa	
338	Battle of Chaeronea Administration of Lycurgus in Athens (338–326)	
337	League of the Hellenes founded	
336	Darius II Codoman (336–330) Alexander III (336–323) in Macedonia	
335	Sack of Thebes. Antipater regent in Europe	Aristotle (384–322) founds Lyceum Lysippus, sculptor
334	Battle of the Granicus Alexander I of Epirus in Italy (334–331)	
333	Battle of Issus	
332	Fall of Tyre and Gaza	
331	Alexandria founded Battle of Gaugamela	
330	Agis' War Shortages in Athens Fire of Persepolis Death of Darius III	Tholos of Epidaurus Theatre of Epidaurus Phippeion of Olympia *On the Crown*, by Demosthenes *Against Ctesiphon* by Aeschines Theatre of Dionysus in Athens
329	Conquest of the eastern satrapies	
326	Alexander in India	
325	Revolt in Bactria	

	Events	Culture
324	Letter on recall of those banished	
323	Death of Alexander	Aristotle leaves Lyceum to
	Compromise of Babylon	Theophrastus
	Philip III Arridheus and Alexander IV made kings	
	Lamian War	
	Ptolemy satrap of Egypt	
322	Battle of Crannon	Deaths of Demosthenes,
	Oligarchy in Athens	Hyperides and Aristotle
	First War of the diadochi (322–321)	
321	Conference of Triparadisus	First comedy of Menander
	Seleucus satrap of Babylonia	(342–293)
		Pyrrhon of Elis (about 360–270)
320		Metroon of Olympia
		First period of construction at Ai Khanun
319	Second War of the diadochi (319–316)	
	Polyperchon succeeds Antipater	
317	Cassander in Greece	
	Assassination of Philip III	
	Execution of Olympias	
	Demetrius of Phalerum in Athens (317–307)	
	Agathocles (317–289) in Syracuse	
316	Third War of the diadochi (316–311)	
315	Foundation of Islanders' League	Construction of new Didymeion begins
314	Delos independent (314–166)	
312	Battle of Gaza	
311	Peace treaty between diadochi	
310	Assassination of Alexander IV and Roxane	Temple of Apollo in Clarus
309	Areus I (309–265) in Sparta	
	Athens liberated by Demetrius Poliorcetes	
	Pyrrhus (307–302, 297–272) in Epirus	
306/305	'Year of the Kings'	Foundation of 'Garden' of Epicurus (about 342–271)
305	Siege of Rhodes	
303	Treaty between Seleucus I and Chandragupta	Mauryas dynasty; Indo-Greek contacts

	Events	Culture
301	Battle of Ipsus	
300	Antioch-on-the-Orontes and many other cities founded by Seleucus I	*Elements*, by Euclid Foundation of Museum of Alexandria Construction of 'Colossus' of Rhodes and 'Lighthouse' of Alexandria
297	Death of Cassander	
294	Demetrius Poliorcetes (294–286) in Macedonia	
290		Library of Alexandria founded
287		Strato of Lampsacus heads Lyceum
285	Lysimachus (285) in Macedonia	Zeno of Kition (about 336–262)
284	Reconstitution of Achaean federation	Temple of Athena in Pergamum
283	Philetaerus (282–263) in Pergamum	
282	Ptolemy II (282–246) in Egypt	
281	Battle of Courupedium Antiochus I (281–261) in Syria Ptolemy Ceraunus (281–279) in Macedonia	
280	Pyrrhus in Italy (280–275)	Callimachus and Theocritus in Alexandria
279	Gauls in Delphi Victory of Lysimacheia	*Phainomena* by Aratus of Soli (315–240) Philetas of Cos (b. about 320) Cleanthes of Assus (about 331–232)
277	Antigonus Gonatas (277–275, 272–239) in Macedonia	
274	First Syrian War (274–271) Pyrrhus in Macedonia and Thessaly	
272	Alexander II (272–252) in Epirus Tarentum captured by Romans	
268	Hiero II (268–215) in Syracuse	Ashoka (268–232); Graeco-Buddhist inscriptions
267	Chremonidian War (267–262)	
263	Eumenes I (263–241) in Pergamum	
262	Capitulation of Athens; Macedonian garrison	

	Events	Culture
261	Antiochus II (261–246) in Syria	
260	Second Syrian War (260–253)	Painted stelae of Demetrias
		Argonautica by Apollonius Rhodius (about 295–215)
		Hippocratic Corpus completed
		Herophilus of Chalcedon in Alexandria
		Cercidas of Megalopolis (about 290–220)
251	Aratus integrates Sicyon into Achaean federation	
250		Portico of Antigonus in Delos
247	Arcases I (247–210), king of independent Parthia	
246	Ptolemy III (246–222) in Egypt	
	Seleucus II (246–225) in Syria	
	Third Syrian War (246–241)	
244	Agis IV (244–241) in Sparta	
241	Attalus I (241–197) in Pergamum	
240	Secession of Bactria	Beginning of construction of Asclepeion of Cos
239	Demetrius II (239–229) in Macedonia	
235	Cleomenes III (235–222) in Sparta	
232	Abolition of royalty in Epirus	
230	Illyro-Epirot War	Attalus' portico in sanctuary of Athena, Pergamum
229	Antigonus Doson (229–221) in Macedonia	Monument of the Galatians in Pergamum
	Athens liberated from Macedonian garrison	
	First Illyrian War	
	War against Sparta	
224	Hellenic League founded	
223	Antiochus III (223–187) in Syria	
222	Battle of Sellasia	
	Ptolemy IV (222–205) in Egypt	
221	Philip V (221–179) in Macedonia	
220	War of the Allies (220–217)	
219	Fourth Syrian War (219–217)	
215	Alliance of Philip V and Hannibal	Improvements to Acropolis of Lindos
214	First Macedonian War (214–205)	
212	Romano-Aetolian alliance	Death of Archimedes (about 287–212)
	Syracuse taken by the Romans	

	Events	Culture
211	Romano-Pergamumian alliance	Polybius of Megalopolis (about 210–125)
205	Nabis (205–192) in Sparta	
204	Ptolemy V (204–180) in Egypt	
202	Fifth Syrian War (202–200)	
200	Second Macedonian War (200–197)	Pergamum theatre improved
197	Battle of Cynocephalae Eumenes II (197–159) in Pergamum	Theatre of Segesta
196	Senatus-consultum on the 'liberty of the Greeks'	Myron of Pergamum (early 2nd)
192	Sparta joins the Achaean federation Romano-Aetolian War (192–188)	
191	Antiochus III defeated at Thermopylae	
190		Portico of Philip V in Delos
189	Antiochus III defeated at Magnesia on the Sipylus	
188	Peace of Apamea	
185		Victory of Samothrace
180	Ptolemy VI (180–145) in Egypt	Great altar in Pergamum Carneades of Cyrene
179	Perseus (179–168) in Macedonia	
175	Antiochus IV (175–164) in Syria	
171	Third Macedonian War (171–168)	
170	Sixth Syrian War (170–168)	Nicander of Colophon (2nd century)
168	Battle of Pydna	
167	Delos, free port and Athenian colony	
160		Agoras of Pergamum
159	Attalus II (159–138) in Pergamum	
155		New temple of Magnesia on the Meander by Hermogenes Panaetius of Rhodes (185–109?) *Stoa* of Attalus II in Athens
150		Attalid constructions in Delphi
149	Revolt of Andriscus in Macedonia	
148	Macedonia a Roman province	
146	Achaean War Sack of Corinth	

LEXICON

Agogè Name of the Spartan education system organized by the city.

Agon Competition, contest, e.g. the Olympic competition, inaccurately known as the 'Games'.

Agora 'Gathering', hence 'place for gathering': a vast open space, later, in the Hellenistic period, enclosed, generally by porticoes; the centre of the *polis*, from the classical period on, also the market-place. The magistrate responsible for policing the markets was the *agoranome*.

Amphictionia An association of peoples or cities centred on a sanctuary that they administered together, e.g. the Pylaio-Delphic group of twelve peoples of northern and central Greece centred on the sanctuaries of Apollo in Delphi and Demeter in Anthela, near Thermopylae.

Anachoresis In Lagid Egypt, the abandonment of one's place of work in order to elude the pressure of taxation and penal sanctions.

Andreion Name of the shared meal that daily brought citizens together in Crete, and also of the building in which they gathered.

Andron 'Men's room', an essential part of a Greek house.

Apella Assembly of the people (in Sparta in particular).

Apoikia Colony.

Aporos (plural *aporoi*) One who has nothing, a 'poor' man.

Archè That which comes first, beginning, principal; hence primacy, command, authority; hence public post, magistracy; also dominion, empire.

Archegetès Founder of a new city which, in many cases, then set up a cult of him.

Archon The word for a magistrate in many cities. In Athens there were nine of them.

Areopagus The council formed by all ex-archons in Athens, the function of which was to administer justice. It sat on the hill of Ares, hence its name.

Aristocracy Power in the hands of the 'best'.

Aristos The best one.

Astu or *asty* The town as a built-up space, inseparable from the *chôra*, together with which it formed the *polis*. In Athens this was one of the three areas upon which Cleisthenes' reforms focused. An *astynome* was a magistrate who belonged to a college that was responsible for supervising order, decency and cleanliness on the streets.

Asylia A privilege that a city could grant either to an individual or to another city. It afforded protection against reprisals (*sylai*) against both persons and property. The asylum that sanctuaries were recognized to afford protected suppliants within the sacred precinct.

Atelia   Exemption from taxation.

Atimia   The withdrawal of political rights.

Autokrator   'One who depends on himself alone', a *strategos* or ambassador who was exceptionally granted full powers, plenipotentiary. In the Hellenistic period he would be given freedom of action, usually reserved for the *Ecclesia*, in the diplomatic field.

Autonomia   A State (city, kingdom, *ethnos*) regulated by its traditional customs. The term was sometimes synonymous with independence.

Banker (*trapezites*, from *trapeza*, the 'table' of a money-changer).   A banker changed money, received deposits of sums of money or precious articles, served as an intermediary between two clients in the operations for setting up loans with interest. In Lagid Egypt, royal banks also handled Treasury operations.

Barbarian   Someone who did not speak Greek.

Basileus (plural, *basileis*)   King.

Basilikogrammatès   In Lagid Egypt, a royal scribe responsible for public writing at the level of the nome.

Bômos   Altar, indispensable for the Greek rite of sacrifice.

Boulè   Council in Athens, composed of 500 members or *bouletes*, from the time of Cleisthenes onward. The *bouleterion* was the building in which it met.

Cheirotonia   A vote by show of hands.

Chiliarch   'Leader of the one thousand'; in the Achaemenid empire, the leading figure after the king. This post was kept on by Alexander, but disappeared at the time of the diadochi.

Chlamys   A short, rectangular cloak worn by the cavalry and the ephebes.

Chôra   Rural territory; *chôra politiké*, civic land, dependent on a city; *chôra basiliké*, royal domain.

Choregia   Liturgy, assumed by a *choregos*, which consisted in paying all the costs of a chorus in a dramatic competition during the Dionysia festival in Athens.

Companion (*hetairos*)   A Macedonian noble serving in the cavalry.

Cosme   A Cretan magistrate.

Demagogue   A leader of the *dèmos*, often used in a pejorative sense to designate a politician who was abusing his powers of persuasion over the citizens.

Deme   A small territorial unit that was the basis of the entire political system in Athens (a member of a deme was a *demote*, the leader of a deme was a demarch; Athenians were known by their demotic names, that is, the names of their demes).

Demiourgos   'One who works for the people', the word used in particular for craftsmen in the Homeric period.

Democracy   'The power of the *dèmos*'.

Dèmos (or *damas*)   The people, in particular the citizen body.

Diagramma   'Circular'; a royal decision on a particular matter (economic, fiscal, civil, penal or administrative).

Dikasterion   A court of law.

Diké   Justice.

Dioketès   'Organizer'. In Lagid Egypt, the minister of finance, who inherited the functions of a high Egyptian dignitary known as early as the sixth century, who was responsible for forecasting agricultural resources.

Dokimasia   The examination of all candidates for citizenship and for magistracies in Athens.

Dôrea   'Gift', in Lagid Egypt an agricultural domain the use of which was allowed to a high-ranking dignitary.

Doulos   Slave.

Dromos   Corridor, a passage by which a tomb was entered.

Ecclesia   The assembly of the people in Athens.

Eisangelia   'Denunciation'. Public charges brought either before the *Boulè* against a magistrate, or before the *Ecclesia* against anyone accused of treason, corruption or conspiracy against the democracy. They could be punished by the death sentence.

Eisphora   A tax, originally levied only in exceptional circumstances, such as war. By the fourth century, however, it was being levied regularly, particularly from the wealthy.

Eleutheria   'Liberty'.

Eleutheros   Free. Said of an individual of free status, as opposed to a slave; of citizens not subject to the domination of a tyrant; and of a political community not subject to an empire.

Emporion   Port. A trading post for two communities with different structures and ways of life.

Emporos   Wholesaler, ship-owner (importer or exporter), as opposed to a *kapelos*, merchant.

Ephebe   A young man or boy between 18 and 20 years of age, learning to defend the city and, more generally, how to be a citizen.

Ephebeia   An institutionalized system of military and ideological training for boys before they became members of the citizen body, well attested in Athens.

Ephemeridai   Daily records, accounts; also the official diary of a reign.

Ephor   A magistrate in Sparta.

Epikleros   A daughter who inherited her father's land (*kleros*) in the absence of any sons, and who passed it on to her own sons.

Epicinian ode   A poem composed to commemorate a victory.

Epistatès   'The one with the top position'; in Athens, the president of the *Boulè* or the *Ecclesia*. In some other cities, a member of the college responsible for supervising public works; in the Hellenistic period, the king's representative in a city.

Epistolè   A letter from a Hellenistic head of state that had the force of law in the territories under his authority, or a letter addressed to another head of state.

Epistrategos   In Lagid Egypt, a military governor with authority over several nomes.

Eschatia   The border regions of a city territory.

Ethnos (plural, *ethnè*)   A people, an ethnic group.

Euporos   A 'have' (as opposed to a 'have-not'), hence a rich man.

Euthynai   The accounts rendered by an Athenian official at the end of his mandate.

Euergetes   'Benefactor', a title that a city granted by decree in gratitude for benefits received, sometimes accompanied by certain honours agreed upon by the assembly's vote.

Exedra   A meeting hall equipped with benches; or an open-air hemicircle.

Funerary furnishings   All the objects placed in a tomb with a corpse.

Gènos   Family, a social group that recognized a common ancestor and practised a common cult.

Gerousia   'Council of elders', the name of the Council in Sparta.

Graphè paranomion   A public charge of illegality against the author of a proposed decree.

Gumnos   Naked, that is to say 'without arms'.

Gymnasium   A public edifice frequented by adult athletes training for competitions, by ephebes training for hoplite combat, and by children placed in the charge of a *paidonomos* (supervisor) and a *paidotribes* (trainer). From the fourth century on and throughout the Hellenistic period, a centre of intellectual culture.

Gymnasiarch   The head of a gymnasium, the figure responsible for the order, maintenance and running of the gymnasium.

Gymnetes   Non-free, rural dependent in Argos.

Hectemoroi   Poor Athenian peasants subjected to paying heavy farming rent in kind by a wealthier landowner. In Athens, the system was abolished by Solon.

Hegemony   Being the head, holding the primary position; within the framework of an alliance, it referred to the power to command any military operations.

Heliaea   An Athenian court (an amalgamation of several courts of justice) that any citizen of over 30 years of age, a heliast, could attend.

Herôon   The sanctuary of a hero, in many cases close to his tomb.

Hestia   Hearth; *hestia koinè*, the common hearth of a city, in the prytaneum.

Hiereos   Priest.

Hieron   Sacred place, sanctuary.

Helot   A non-free rural dependent in Sparta.

Historiè   Enquiry.

Holocaust   A sacrifice in which the entire offering was burned.

Homoios (plural, *homoioi*)   An 'equal'. The citizens of Sparta referred to themselves as the *homoioi*.

Hoplite   An infantryman armed with a round shield (*hoplon*).

Hupomnèma   An *aide-mémoire* succinctly noting engagements and instructions; a hypomnematograph was a member of the royal entourage who was responsible for archives and *ephemeridai*.

Hypostyle   A stone supported by columns.

Idia   'Particularity', administrative identity, place of residence.

Indo-Europeans   Peoples speaking related languages, all with a common origin.

Isonomia   'Equal sharing', equality in political rights.

Isopoliteia   'Equal citizenship', a privilege exchanged between two cities that allowed the citizens of the one who settled in the other to enjoy citizens' rights upon request.

Isos   Equal.

Kaloskagathos   'Fine and good', the description of a perfect citizen.

Kleros   An allotment of land.

Komè   Peasant community (village, country town); a basic sociological and administrative unit in the *chôra*. In the Achaemenid and Hellenistic East, a country town (possibly fortified) would be headed by a comarch, 'village chief', assisted in Lagid Egypt by *komogrammatès*, 'village secretary'.

Korè   A girl. Also the name of a type of statue characteristic of the archaic period.

Kouros   A boy or youth; likewise a type of archaic statue.

Kratos   Power.

Kurios (or *Kyrios*)   Master, a woman's guardian.

Laos   A people; in Homeric epic, the body of warriors; in the Hellenistic period the word designated former dependents who had been given their liberty, organized in villages and represented by elders.

*Lawagetas   'Leader of the troops', one of the important figures in a Mycenaean palace.

Linear   The name of a type of writing used in the Second Millennium: Linear A, still not deciphered, preceded Linear B, which has been deciphered and transcribed into Greek.

Liturgy   A rich individual's obligation to finance enterprises in the public interest, such as the maintenance of triremes (trierarchy), the organization of public meals and so on.

Logos   Word, reason, account (in both senses).

Mantiké   Divination.

Megaron   The principal hall in a Mycenaean palace.

Metic   'One who lives with', the word for a foreigner domiciled in Athens, who benefited from certain guarantees.

Metoikion   A due that any resident foreigner had to pay in order to live in Attica.

Metropolis   'Mother-city'.

Minoan   Relating to Crete in the Second Millennium.

Misthos   An allowance paid to citizens participating in the political and judicial business of the Athenian city.

Misthosis   A leasing contract for agricultural land or houses belonging to private individuals, a sanctuary, a religious association or the royal estate.

Money (*nomisma*) or coins   Pieces of metal of standard value with legal currency in a political community. The monetary unit varied according to the metal chosen as standard (gold, electron, bronze, iron) and its weight (in Athens, a one drachma coin on average weighed 4.36 g of silver; in the Ptolemaic possessions, 3.69; in Pergamum after 188, 3.2 g). The most common models were the talent = 6,000 drachmas, the mine = 100 drachmas, the tetradrachma = 4 drachmas, the drachma = 6 obols, and the obol. The talent and the mine were accountancy units. One Attic talent weighed about 26.2 kg.

Mycenaean   Relating to mainland Greece in the Second Millennium BC. The model site is Mycenae itself.

Mystes (*ai*)   An initiate of a particular cult.

Mystery (mystery cult)   A cult for which there was an initiation and which sometimes required the faithful to keep secret the nature of that initiation.

Myth   A story that has an explanatory function and may relate to various areas of social and symbolic experience.

Mythology   A collection of mythical stories.

Naos   Temple.

Navarch   An admiral in command of a fleet of warships.

Necropolis   'Town of the dead', cemetery.

Nome   One of the territorial divisions in Egypt. The head of a nome was a nomarch.

Nomos (plural *nomoi*)   Law. In the fourth century it was opposed to *psephisma*: decree. *Nomos* often has the much wider sense of 'custom', 'tradition', but also 'constitution'.

Nomothetès (plural *nomothetai*)   Legislator. In fourth-century Athens, the member of a commission responsible for examining proposals for laws and voting for them by a show of hands. He would be selected by lot, for one day.

Oikiste   The leader of an expedition to found a new city.

Oikos   Household (designates both a community of human beings and a collection of possessions or property).

Oikoumene   The known Greek world as a whole.

Oligarchy   The power of a small number of men, the type of political regime most common in the cities.

Ostracism   A procedure, voted by the Ecclesia, that exiled an Athenian from the city for ten years.

Paideia   Education.

Palestra (from *palè*, fight)   A covered building where wrestlers practised.

Panegyrios A gathering.

Pantheon The group of gods honoured by a community.

Parthenos Girl, young woman.

Patris Ancestral land, the place of a family's origin.

Pedagogue The man (probably a slave) who took a child to his various teachers.

Pedonome A magistrate in Sparta, responsible for education.

Peltast A lightly-armed soldier (the *pelte* was his shield).

Penestès A rural dependent in Thessaly.

Peraeia 'Land situated on the other side', territory on the mainland belonging to an island city.

Periegesis 'World tour', the name for a particular kind of account.

Perioikos 'One who lives in the neighbourhood', the name in Sparta for a member of the free population without citizens' rights.

Peristyle A colonnade surrounding a hall or temple.

Phalanx A formation consisting of rows of hoplites.

Phoros 'Burden', the tribute paid to Athens by its allied cities in the fifth century; the dues paid by rural dependents; farm rent paid to the king or to some other individual for a lease.

Phratry A group of people who recognized a common ancestor, and on that account called themselves 'brothers'.

Phroura Garrison.

Phrourarch The commander of a garrison.

Polemarch A commander of troops.

Polemos War.

Poliad The adjective describing a deity who was patron of a city, e.g. Athena in Athens.

Polis City.

Politeia Constitution, political regime, citizens' rights; *patrios politeia*, ancestral constitution.

Politès Citizen.

Politography The inscription of new citizens of Greek origin in cases where the citizen body was shrinking.

Pompe Procession.

Probouleuma A proposal for a decree.

Proedros President.

Proedria The right to a front-row seat for all competitions organized by the city.

Propylaea 'That which is in front of the door'. A monumental entrance, for instance of a sanctuary, e.g. the *propylaea* of the Acropolis in Athens.

Proskynesis 'Prostration', the mark of respect shown to the sovereign by the Persians; an honour reserved for the gods by the Greeks.

Prostagma An order, a decree of either general or limited effect, issued in person by someone with authority in any matters regarding public or private law.

Prostatès   The guarantor of a foreigner in Athens.

Proxenos   Someone responsible in his own city for looking after the interests of individuals from other cities.

Prytanis   A name frequently used in the cities for a magistrate. In Athens, new *prytaneis* were set up by Cleisthenes' reforms.

Prytaneum   The place where a city's common hearth was frequently situated.

Psephisma   Decree.

Quorum   The minimal number of people required to be present at a deliberative assembly for its decisions on certain subjects to be valid.

Rhetor   An orator, later a politician, a master of eloquence or a *logograph* (a writer of speeches).

Rhetra   Constitutional law.

Satrap   The title of a man at the head of an administrative division of the Persian empire.

Sekos   The wall separating the *naos* from its peristyle in a temple.

Seisachteia   'Rejection of the burden', the measure attributed to Solon to resolve the agrarian crisis.

Somatophylakes   'Bodyguard', a high dignitary close to Alexander the Great; later, an honorific title in a Hellenistic royal court.

Sophist   An intellectual who taught how to manipulate rhetoric.

Stade   A unit of length of 600 feet. The track on which a race of one or several stades was run was called a *dromos*.

Stasis   Civil war.

Stenochoria   Lack of land.

Strategos   The name for a magistrate in many cities; in Athens there was a college of ten *strategoi*.

Symbolon (plural *symbola*)   A mark of recognition (an object broken in two); a counter handed out to citizens as they entered the Ecclesia, and exchanged when they left for the *misthos*; a legal agreement between two cities.

Symmachia   A coalition, league, confederation or military alliance sealed by an exchange of oaths.

Symmoria   A number of citizens grouped together for the payment of a tax (the *eisphora*) or to perform a liturgy in fourth-century Athens.

Sympoliteia   The union of two or more cities, instituting common citizenship.

Sympósion   The second phase of a Greek banquet, for drinking, talking and singing; the acme of high-class sociability.

Synedrion   'Session', an assembly with either deliberative or only consultative powers; royal council; war council; federal council in a *koinon*, or a confederal council in a *symacchia*.

Synegeneia   'Kinship'; officially recognized solidarity between two cities, based on common origins, either ethnic (between colonies founded by the same metropolis) or mythological (genealogical links with heroes or gods).

Synoecism   The gathering of a number of communities into a single one, a process that frequently led to the creation of a city.

Syntaxis   'Contribution', freely agreed financial participation (as opposed to the imposed *phoros*).

Syssition   The daily communal meal of the citizens of Sparta.

Tage   A Thessalian magistrate.

Technè   Manual skill, art, technique.

Temenos   Land reserved for a chief, king or god.

Tetrarch   The head of one of the four regions of Thessaly.

Thalassocracy   Power at sea. The term used for the assumed power of the Cretan world over the Mediterranean in the Second Millennium, and in the fourth century for the Athenian 'empire'.

Theogony   The genesis of the gods, an account of the establishment of the Greek pantheon.

Theoros   Ambassador.

Theoria   Embassy, delegation sent from one city to another, or from a city to a sanctuary.

Theos   Deity.

Themosthetès   'One who establishes the law', a legislator.

Thiasos   A group of the faithful celebrating a cult.

Tholos   A circular building. *Tholos* (or beehive) tombs are topped by a cupola; the meeting-place for the *prytaneis* in Athens was a *tholos*.

Tribe (*phylè*)   A political subdivision that was traditional in an *ethnos*.

Tributary   Describes an economic and social system in which the producers had to make contributions in kind to the ruling class.

Trierarch   The man in command of a trireme. In Athens, the triarch was the *leitourgos* (a man liable for a liturgy) who guaranteed part of the funds needed for a trireme to function.

Trireme   A warship with three levels of oarsmen.

Tyrant   An individual who seized or held on to power illegally.

Xenia   Hospitality.

Xenos   Depending on the context, a stranger, an enemy or a guest.

*Wanax   The head of a Mycenaean palace.

Zeugite   'One who possesses a team of oxen', the word for members of the third census class in the system attributed to Solon.

GUIDE TO FURTHER READING

GENERAL

REFERENCE WORKS

Cartledge, Paul. *The Greeks: A Portrait of Self and Others.* London, 1993.
Cary, M. *The Geographic Background of Greek and Roman History.* Oxford, 1949.
Crawford, Michael (ed.). *Sources for Ancient History.* Cambridge, 1983.
Hammond, N. G. L., *A History of Greece to 322 BC.* 3rd edn. Oxford, 1986.
Hammond, N. G. L. (ed.). *Atlas of the Greek and Roman World in Antiquity.* Park Ridge, NJ, 1981.
Hornblower, Simon and Spawforth, Antony (eds). *The Oxford Classical Dictionary.* 3rd edn. Oxford, 1986.
Stillwell, R., MacDonald, W. L. and McAllister, M. G. (eds). *The Princeton Encyclopedia of Classical Sites.* Princeton, NJ, 1976.

GENERAL STUDIES

Boardman, John et al. *The Oxford History of Greece and the Hellenistic World.* Oxford, 1991.
Boardman, J., Griffin, J. and Murray, O. (eds). *The Oxford History of the Greek World.* Oxford, 1991.
Cambridge Ancient History. 3rd edn, vols II–VII. Cambridge, 1973–95.
de Ste Croix, G. E. M. *The Class Struggle in the Ancient Greek World; From the Archaic Age to the Arab Conquests.* London, 1981.
Easterling, P. E. and Knox, B. M. W. (eds), *Greek Literature.* Vol. 1 of *The Cambridge History of Classical Literature.* Cambridge, 1985.
Finley, Moses I. *Politics in the Ancient World.* Cambridge and New York, 1991.
Grmek, Mirko D. and Muellner, Leonard. *Diseases in the Ancient Greek World.* Baltimore, MD, 1991.
Hall, Jonathan M. *Ethnic Identity in Greek Antiquity.* Cambridge, MA, 1997.
Herman, Gabriel. *Ritualized Friendship and the Greek City.* Cambridge, 1987.
Hansen, Mogens H. (ed.). *The Ancient Greek City-State.* Copenhagen, 1993.
Kuhrt, Amélie. *The Ancient Near East, c.3000–330 BC.* London, 1995.
Lloyd, G. E. R. *The Revolutions of Wisdom. Studies in the Claims and Practice of Early Greek Science.* Berkeley, CA, 1988.
Mallory, J. P. *In Search of the Indo-Europeans: Language, Archaeology and Myth.* London, 1989.
Mitchell, Lynette and Rhodes, P. J. *The Development of the Polis in Archaic Greece.* London and New York, 1997.

Murray, Oswyn and Price, Simon (eds). *The Greek City: From Homer to Alexander.* Oxford, 1990.

Renfrew, Colin, *Archaeology and Language. The Puzzle of Indo-European Origins,* Cambridge and New York, 1988.

Sallares, Robert, *Ecology of the Ancient Greek World.* London, 1991.

Snodgrass, A. *An Archaeology of Greece: The Present State and Future Scope of a Discipline.* Berkeley, Los Angeles and London, 1987.

Van Andel, T. H. and Runnels, Curtis. *Beyond the Acropolis: A Rural Greek Past.* Stanford, CA, 1987.

Vernant, Jean-Pierre. *Mortals and Immortals: Collected Essays.* ed. Froma I. Zeitlin. Princeton, NJ, 1992.

Vernant, Jean Pierre et al. *The Greeks.* Trans. Charles Lambert and Teresa Lavender Fagan. Chicago, 1995.

Vidal-Naquet, Pierre. *Politics Ancient and Modern.* Trans. Janet Lloyd. London, 1996.

Whittaker, C. R. (ed.). *Pastoral Economies in Classical Antiquity.* Cambridge, 1988.

WARFARE

Pritchett, W. K. *The Greek State at War.* Vols. 2–5. Berkeley, CA, 1975–91.

RELIGION

Alcock, Susan E. and Osborne, Robin (eds), *Placing the Gods: Sanctuaries and Sacred Space in Ancient Greece.* Oxford, 1996.

LAW

Bonner, R. J. and Smith, G. *The Administration of Justice from Homer to Aristotle.* 2 vols. Chicago, 1930.

ECONOMY AND TRADE

Austin, M. M. and Vidal-Naquet, Pierre. *Economic and Social History of Ancient Greece: An Introduction.* London, 1977.

Casson, Lionel. *Ancient Trade and Society.* Detroit, 1984.

Duncan, C. and Tandy, David (eds). *From Political Economy to Anthropology. Situating Economic Life in Past Societies.* Montreal, 1994.

Finley, Moses I. (ed.). *Classical Slavery.* London, 1987.

Garnsey, Peter, Hopkins, Keith and Whittaker, C. R. (eds). *Trade in the Ancient Economy.* Berkeley and Los Angeles, 1983.

Whittaker, C. R. (ed.). *Pastoral Economies in Classical Antiquity.* Cambridge, 1988.

AGRICULTURE

Burford, Allison. *Land and Labor in the Greek World.* Baltimore, MD, 1993.

Gallant, Thomas. *Risk and Survival in Ancient Greece.* Stanford, CA, 1991.

Garnsey, Peter. *Famine and Food Supply in the Graeco-Roman World. Responses to Risk and Crisis.* Cambridge, 1988.

Hanson, Victor Davis. *The Other Greeks: The Family Farm and the Agrarian Roots of Western Civilization.* New York, 1995.
Isager, S. and Skydsgaard, J. *Ancient Greek Agriculture.* London, 1992.
Wells, B. (ed.). *Agriculture in Ancient Greece.* Stockholm, 1992.

WOMEN AND THE FAMILY

Fantham, Elaine et al. *Women in the Classical World.* New York and Oxford, 1994.
Hawley, R. and Levick, B. (eds). *Women in Antiquity.* London, 1995.
Okin, Susan Moller. *Women in Western Political Thought.* Rev. edn. Princeton, NJ, 1992.
Rabinowitz, Nancy and Richlin, Amy (eds). *Feminist Theory and the Classics.* London, 1993.
Schmitt Pantel, P. (ed.). *A History of Women in the West I.* Cambridge, MA, 1992.

LITERATURE, INTELLECTUAL LIFE AND PHILOSOPHY

Guthrie, W. K. C. *A History of Greek Philosophy.* Vols. 1–5. Cambridge, 1979–86.

ART AND ARCHITECTURE

Hurwit, Jeffrey. *The Art and Culture of Early Greece, 1100–480 BC.* Ithaca, NY, 1985.

THE EARLY AEGEAN

GENERAL STUDIES

Bouzek, J. *Greece, Anatolia and Europe: Interrelations during the Early Iron Age.* Stockholm, 1997.
Burkert, Walter. *The Orientalizing Revolution: Near Eastern Influence on Greek Culture in the Early Archaic Age.* Cambridge, MA, 1992.
Chadwick, John. *The Mycenaean World.* London, 1976.
Desborough, V. R. d'A. *The Greek Dark Ages.* London, 1972.
—— *The Last Mycenaeans and their Successors.* Oxford, 1964.
Dickinson, O. P. T. K. *The Aegean Bronze Age.* Cambridge, 1994.
Drews, Robert. *The Coming of the Greeks: Indo-European Conquests in the Aegean and the Near East.* Princeton, NJ, 1988.
—— *The End of the Bronze Age: Changes in Warfare and the Catastrophe ca. 1200.* Princeton, NJ, 1993.
Finley, Moses I. *The World of Odysseus.* 2nd edn. Harmondsworth, 1978.
Foxhall, L. and Davies. J. K. (eds). *The Trojan War, Its Historicity and Context: Papers of the First Greenbank Colloquium.* Bristol, 1984.
Mellink, Machteld (ed.). *Troy and the Trojan War.* Bryn Mawr, PA, 1986.
Murray, Oswyn. *Early Greece.* 2nd edn. Cambridge, 1993.
Osborne, Robin. *Greece in the Making, 1200–479 BC.* London, 1996.
Renfrew, Colin and Cherry, J. (eds). *Peer Polity Interaction and Socio-Political Change.* Cambridge, 1986.

Sandars, N. K., *The Sea Peoples: Warriors of the Ancient Mediterranean, 1250–1150 BC*. London, 1987.

Simpson, R. Hope. *Mycenaean Greece*. London, 1982.

Snodgrass, A. M. *The Dark Age of Greece*. Edinburgh, 1971.

—— *Archaic Greece. The Age of Experiment*. Berkeley and Los Angeles, 1980.

Vermeule, Emily. *Greece in the Bronze Age*. Chicago, 1964.

WARFARE

Anderson, J. K. *Ancient Greek Horsemanship*. Berkeley and Los Angeles, 1961.

Bugh, G. R. *The Horsemen of Athens*. Princeton, NJ, 1985.

Garlan, Yvon. *Warfare in the Ancient World: A Social History*. New York, 1975.

Greenhalgh, P. A. L. *Early Greek Warfare*. Cambridge, 1973.

Hanson, V. D. *The Western Way of War: Infantry Battle in Classical Greece*. New York, 1989.

Pritchett, W. K. *The Greek State at War*. Berkeley and Los Angeles, 1974.

Wees, H. van. *Status Warriors: Violence and Society in Homer and History*. Amsterdam, 1992.

SOCIAL LIFE

Fisher, N. R. E. *Hybris: A Study in the Values of Honour and Shame in Ancient Greece*. Warminster, 1992.

RELIGION

Marinatos, Nanno and Hägg, Robin. *Greek Sanctuaries: New Approaches*. London, 1993.

ART AND ARCHITECTURE

Beazley, J. D. and Ashmole, Bernard. *Greek Sculpture and Painting*. Cambridge, 1932.

Langdon, Susan (ed.). *From Pasture to Polis. Art in the Age of Homer. With an Essay by Jeffrey M. Hurwit*. Columbia, MO, 1993.

Rasmussen, Tom and Spivey, Nigel (eds). *Looking at Greek Vases*. Cambridge, 1991.

THE ARCHAIC WORLD

GENERAL STUDIES

Aubet, Maria Eugenia. *The Phoenicians and the West. Politics, Colonies and Trade*. Cambridge, 1993.

Boardman, John. *The Greeks Overseas*. 2nd edn. London, 1982.

Coldstream, J. N. *Geometric Greece*. London, 1977.

Dougherty, Carol and Kurke, Leslie, *Cultural Politics in Archaic Greece. Cult, Performance, Politics*, Cambridge, 1993.

Graham, A. J. *Colony and Mother City in Ancient Greece*. 2nd edn. Chicago, 1983.

Hägg, R. *The Greek Renaissance of the Eighth Century BC.: Tradition and Innovation.* Stockholm, 1983.

McGlew, James F. *Tyranny and Political Culture in Ancient Greece.* Ithaca, NY, 1993.

Morris, Ian. *Burial and Ancient Society: The Rise of the Greek City State.* Cambridge, 1987.

Polignac, François de. *Cults, Territory, and the Origins of the Greek City-State.* Trans. Janet Lloyd. Chicago, 1995.

Ridgway, David. *The First Western Greeks.* Cambridge, 1992.

Whitley, A. J. M. *Style and Society in Dark Age Greece.* Cambridge, 1991.

REGIONAL HISTORIES

Andrewes, A. *The Greek Tyrants.* London, 1956.

Braund, David. *Georgia in Antiquity. A History of Colchis and Transcaucasian Iberia 550 BC–AD 562.* Oxford, 1994.

Cartledge, Paul. *Sparta and Laconia: A Regional History 1300–362 BC.* London, 1979.

Finley, Moses I. *Ancient Sicily to the Arab Conquest.* London, 1968.

Lambert, S. D. *Phratries of Attica.* Ann Arbor, 1996.

Manville, Philip Brook. *Origins of Citizenship in Ancient Athens.* Princeton, NJ, 1997.

Salmon, J. B. *Wealthy Corinth.* Oxford, 1984.

Shipley, Gordon. *A History of Samos, 800–188 BC.* New York, 1987.

LAW

Gagarin, Michael, *Early Greek Law*, Berkeley, Los Angeles and London, 1986.

WARFARE

Lazenby, J. F. *The Spartan Army.* Warminster, 1985.

LITERATURE, INTELLECTUAL LIFE AND PHILOSOPHY

Barnes, Jonathan (ed.). *Early Greek Philosophy.* Harmondsworth, 1989.

Foley, Helene Peet. *The Homeric Hymn to Demeter.* Princeton, NJ, 1994.

Richardson, N. J. *The Homeric Hymn to Demeter.* Oxford, 1974.

Williamson, Margaret. *Sappho's Immortal Daughters.* Cambridge, MA, 1996.

RELIGION

Burkert, Walter. *Greek Religion: Archaic and Classical.* Berkeley, 1985.

Morgan, Catherine A. *Athletes and Oracles. The Transformation of Olympia and Delphi in the Eighth Century BC.* Cambridge, 1990.

ART AND ARCHITECTURE

Boardman, John. *Athenian Black Figure Vases.* London, 1974.

—— *Athenian Red Figure Vases: The Archaic Period.* London, 1975.

—— *Greek Sculpture: The Archaic Period.* London, 1975.

THE CLASSICAL PERIOD

FIFTH CENTURY

GENERAL STUDIES

Badian, E. *From Plataea to Potidaea. Studies in the History and Historiography of the Pentecontaetia.* Baltimore, MD, 1993.

de Ste. Croix, G. E. M. *The Origins of the Peloponnesian War.* London, 1972.

Harris, William. *Ancient Literacy.* Cambridge, MA, 1989.

Hornblower, Simon. *The Greek World, 479–323 BC.* London, 1983.

Lazenby, John Francis. *The Defence of Greece 490–479 BC.* Warminster, 1993.

Lewis, D. M. *Sparta and Persia.* Leiden, 1977.

Meiggs, Russell. *The Athenian Empire.* Oxford, 1979.

Miller, Margaret Christina. *Athens and Persia in the Fifth Century BC.* Cambridge, 1997.

Morris, Ian (ed.). *Classical Greece: Ancient Histories and Modern Archaeologies.* Cambridge, 1994.

REGIONAL HISTORIES: ATHENS

Boegehold, Alan L. and Scafuro, Adele C. (eds), *Athenian Identity and Civic Ideology.* Baltimore, MD, 1994.

Connor, W. R., *The New Politicians of Fifth Century Athens.* Princeton, NJ, 1971.

Hansen, Mogens Herman. *The Athenian Ecclesia: A Collection of Articles 1976–83.* Copenhagen, 1983.

Loraux, Nicole. *The Invention of Athens: The Funeral Oration in the Classical City.* Trans. Alan Sheridan. Cambridge, MA, 1986.

Mattingly, Harold. *Athenian Empire Restored: Epigraphic and Historical Studies.* Ann Arbor, MI, 1996.

McGregor, Malcolm Francis. *Athenians and Their Empire.* London, 1987.

Osborne, Robin. *Demos. The Discovery of Classical Attica.* Cambridge, 1985.

Osborne, Robin and Hornblower, Simon (eds). *Ritual, Finance, Politics. Athenian Democratic Accounts Presented to David Lewis.* Oxford, 1994.

Powell, Anton. *Athens and Sparta.* London, 1988.

Rhodes, P. J. *The Athenian Boule.* Rev. edn. Oxford, 1985.

Traill, J. S. *The Political Organization of Attica.* Princeton, NJ, 1975.

Whitehead, David. *The Demes of Attica.* Princeton, NJ, 1986.

WARFARE

Gabrielsen, Vincent. *Financing the Athenian Fleet.* Baltimore, MD, 1994.

Fornara, Charles. *The Athenian Board of Generals from 501 to 404.* Wiesbaden, 1971.

Hanson, Victor Davis. *Warfare and Agriculture in Classical Greece.* Pisa, 1982.

—— *Hoplites.* London and New York, 1991.

Lazenby, J. F. *The Defence of Greece 490–479 BC.* Warminster, 1993.

Spence, I. G. *The Cavalry of Classical Greece: A Social and Military History with Particular Reference to Athens.* Oxford, 1994.

SOCIAL LIFE

Cohen, David. *Law, Society and Sexuality: The Enforcement of Morals in Classical Athens.* Cambridge, 1991.
Garlan, Yvon. *Slavery in Ancient Greece.* Ithaca, NY, 1988.
Golden, Mark. *Children and Childhood in classical Athens.* Baltimore, MD, 1993.
Hall, Edith. *Inventing the Barbarian: Greek Self-Definition through Tragedy.* Oxford, 1989.
Hunter, Virginia. *Policing Athens.* Princeton, NJ, 1994.
Mitchell, Lynette G. *Greeks Bearing Gifts: The Public Use of Private Relationships in the Greek World, 435–323 BC.* Cambridge, 1998.
Morris, Ian. *Death-Ritual and Social Structure in Classical Antiquity.* 1992.
Strauss, Barry S. *Fathers and Sons in Athens: Ideology and Society in the Era of the Peloponnesian War.* Princeton, NJ, 1997.

RELIGION

Bruit Zaidman, L. and Schmitt Pantel, P. *Religion in the Ancient Greek City.* Cambridge, 1992.
Easterling P. E. and Muir, J. V. (eds). *Greek Religion and Society.* Cambridge and New York, 1985.
Garland, Robert. *Introducing New Gods: The Politics of Athenian Religion.* London, NC, 1992.
Mikalson, Jon D. *Athenian Popular Religion.* Chapel Hill, NC, 1987.
Parker, Robert. *Athenian Religion: A History.* Oxford, 1997.

LITERATURE, INTELLECTUAL LIFE AND PHILOSOPHY

Dodds, E. R. *The Greeks and the Irrational.* Berkeley and Los Angeles, 1951.
Easterling, P. E. *The Cambridge Companion to Greek Tragedy.* Cambridge, 1997.
Guthrie, W. K. C. *A History of Greek Philosophy.* Cambridge, 1965–9.
Kennedy, George. *The Art of Persuasion in Greece.* London, 1963.
Kerferd, G. B. *The Sophistic Movement.* Cambridge, 1981.
Konstan, David. *Greek Comedy and Ideology.* Oxford, 1995.
Nussbaum, Martha. *The Fragility of Goodness: Luck and Ethics in Greek Tragedy and Philosophy.* Cambridge, 1986.
Padel, Ruth. *In and Out of the Mind: Greek Images of the Tragic Self.* Princeton, NJ, 1992.
Pickard-Cambridge, A. W. *Dithyramb, Tragedy, and Comedy.* 2nd edn, rev. T. B. L. Webster. Oxford, 1962.
—— *The Dramatic Festivals of Athens.* 2nd edn, rev. John Gould and D. M. Lewis. Oxford, 1968.
Rose, Peter. *Sons of the Gods, Children of Earth: Ideology and Literary Form in Ancient Greece.* Ithaca, NY, 1992.
Seaford, Richard. *Reciprocity and Ritual. Homer and Tragedy in the Developing City-State.* Oxford, 1994.
Wardy, Robert. *The Birth of Rhetoric: Gorgias, Plato, and Their Successors.* London, 1996.

Yunis, Harvey. *Taming Democracy: Models of Political Rhetoric in Classical Athens.* Ithaca, NY, 1996.

Zeitlin, Froma I. *Playing the Other: Essays on Gender and Society in Classical Greek Literature.* Princeton, NJ, 1995.

HISTORIANS AND HISTORIOGRAPHY

Connor, W. R. *Thucydides.* Princeton, NJ 1984.

Crane, Gregory. *Thucydides and the Ancient Simplicity: The Limits of Political Realism.* Berkeley, CA, 1998.

Gould, John. *Herodotus.* London, 1989.

Hartog, François. *The Mirror of Herodotus: The Representation of the Other in the Writing of History.* Berkeley, CA, 1988.

Hornblower, Simon (ed.). *Greek Historiography.* Oxford, 1994.

—— *A Commentary on Thucydides.* 2 vols. Oxford, 1991–6.

Kallet-Marx, Lisa. *Money, Expense, and Naval Power in Thucydides' History 1–5.24.* Berkeley, CA, 1993.

Lateiner, Donald. *The Historical Method of Herodotus.* Toronto, 1992.

Thomas, Rosalind. *Oral Tradition and Written Record in Classical Athens.* Cambridge, 1989.

LAW

Harrison, A. R. W. *The Law of Athens.* 2 vols. Oxford, 1968–71.

MacDowell, Douglas Maurice. *The Law in Classical Athens* London, 1991.

ECONOMY AND TRADE

Cohen, Edward E. *Athenian Economy and Society: A Banking Perspective.* Princeton, NJ, 1997.

Fisher, N. *Slavery in Classical Greece.* Bristol, 1993.

AGRICULTURE

Osborne, Robin. *Classical Landscape with Figures: The Ancient Greek City and its Countryside.* London, 1987.

Wood, Ellen Meiksins. *Peasant-Citizen and Slave: The Foundations of Athenian Democracy.* London, 1988.

WOMEN AND THE FAMILY

Demand, Nancy. *Birth, Death, and Motherhood in Classical Greece.* Baltimore, MD, 1994.

ART AND ARCHITECTURE

Ashmole, Bernard. *Architect and Sculptor in Classical Greece.* London and New York, 1972.

Ashmole, Bernard and Yalouris, N. *Olympia. The Sculptures of the Temple of Zeus.* London, 1967.

Bérard, C. (ed.). *A City of Images.* Princeton, NJ, 1989.

Boardman, John. *Athenian Red Figure Vases: The Classical Period.* London, 1978.

Boardman, John and Finn, D. *The Parthenon and its Sculptures.* London, 1985.

Brommer, Frank. *The Sculptures of the Parthenon.* London, 1979.

Burford, Allison. *Greek Temple Builders at Epidauros.* Liverpool, 1969.

Coulton, J. J. *Greek Architects at Work. Problems of Structure and Design.* London, 1977.

Dinsmoor, W. B. *The Architecture of Ancient Greece.* 3rd edn. London and New York, 1950.

Pickard-Cambridge, A. W. *The Theatre of Dionysos in Athens.* Oxford, 1946.

Pollitt, J. J. *The Ancient View of Greek Art.* London and New Haven, 1974.

—— *Art and Experience in Classical Greece.* Cambridge, 1972.

Robertson, D. C. *Greek and Roman Architecture.* 2nd edn. Cambridge, 1959.

Robertson, Martin. *The Art of Vase-Painting in Classical Athens.* Cambridge, 1992.

Travlos, John. *Pictorial Dictionary of Ancient Athens.* London and New York, 1971.

Ward-Perkins, J. B. *Cities of Ancient Greece and Italy: Planning in Classical Antiquity.* New York, 1974.

Wycherley, R. E. *The Stones of Athens.* Princeton, NJ, 1978.

POLITICS AND GOVERNMENT

Loraux, Nicole and Zeitlin, Froma. *The Children of Athena: Athenian Ideas about Citizenship and the Division Between the Sexes.* Trans. Caroline Levine. Princeton, NJ, 1994.

Ober, Josiah. *The Athenian Revolution: Essays on Ancient Greek Democracy and Political Theory.* Princeton, NJ, 1997.

Rhodes, P. J. *A Commentary on the Aristotelian 'Athenaion Politeia.'* Oxford, 1981.

Saxonhouse, Arlene W. *Fear of Diversity: The Birth of Political Science in Ancient Greek Thought.* Chicago, 1992.

Stockton, David L. *The Classical Athenian Democracy.* Oxford, 1990.

FOURTH CENTURY

GENERAL STUDIES

Borza, Eugene N. *In the Shadow of Olympus: The Emergence of Macedon.* Princeton, NJ, 1990.

—— *MAKEDONIKA.* Claremont, 1995.

Hammond, N. G. L. *A History of Macedonia.* 2 vols. Oxford, 1972–9.

—— *The Macedonian State.* Oxford, 1989.

—— *Philip of Macedon.* Baltimore, MD, 1994.

Sealey, Raphael. *Demosthenes and his Time: A Study in Defeat.* New York, 1993.

Veyne, Paul. *Bread and Circuses: Historical Sociology and Political Pluralism.* Trans. Brian Pearce. London, 1992.

REGIONAL HISTORIES

Buckler, J. *The Theban Hegemony 371–362.* Cambridge, MA, 1980.
Cartledge, Paul. *Agesilaus and the Crisis of Sparta.* London, 1987.
Caven, Brian. *Dionysius I: Warlord of Sicily.* New Haven, CT, 1990.
Hamilton, Charles D. *Sparta's Bitter Victories.* London, 1979.
—— *Agesilaus and the Failure of Spartan Hegemony.* Ithaca, NY, and London, 1991.
Sanders, L. J. *Dionysius I of Syracuse and Greek Tyranny.* London, 1988.
Westlake, H. D. *Thessaly in the Fourth Century BC.* London, 1935.

WARFARE

Munn, Mark H. *The Defense of Attica: The Dema Wall and the Boiotian War of 378–375 BC.*
Ober, Josiah. *Fortress Attica: Defense of the Athenian Land Frontier, 404–322 BC.* Leiden, 1985.

SOCIAL LIFE

Dover, K. J. *Greek Popular Morality in the Time of Plato and Aristotle.* Oxford, 1974.
Garnsey, Peter. *Ideas of Slavery from Aristotle to Augustine.* London, 1996.
Ober, Josiah. *Mass and Elite in Democratic Athens: Rhetoric, Ideology, and Power of the People.* 1991.

LITERATURE, INTELLECTUAL LIFE AND PHILOSOPHY

Ackrill, J. L. *A New Aristotle Reader.* Princeton, NJ, 1988.
Barnes, Jonathan. *Aristotle.* Oxford, 1983.
Barnes, Jonathan (ed.). *The Cambridge Companion to Aristotle.* Cambridge, 1995.
Kennedy, George. *Aristotle on Rhetoric: A Theory of Civic Discourse.* Oxford, 1991.
Kraut, Richard. *The Cambridge Companion to Plato.* Cambridge, London, 1992.
Lear, Jonathan. *Aristotle. The Desire to Understand.* Cambridge, 1988.
Too, Yun Lee. *The Rhetoric of Identity in Isocrates: Text, Power, Pedagogy.* Cambridge, 1995.

HISTORIANS AND HISTORIOGRAPHY

Dillery, John. *Xenophon and the History of His Times.* London, 1995.
Gray, Vivienne. *The Character of Xenophon's Hellenica.* Baltimore, MD, 1989.

THE HELLENISTIC PERIOD

GENERAL STUDIES

Bickerman, Elias J. *The Jews in the Greek Age.* Cambridge, MA, 1990.
Bosworth, A. B. *Conquest and Empire.* Cambridge, 1988.
Cartledge, Paul, Garnsey, Peter and Gruen, Erich (eds). *Hellenistic Constructs: Essays in Culture, History, and Historiography.* Berkeley and Los Angeles, 1997.

Grainger, John D. *The Cities of Seleucid Syria.* Oxford, 1990.
—— *Hellenistic Phoenicia.* Oxford, 1991.
Green, Peter, *Alexander of Macedon, 356–323 BC.* Rev. edn. Berkeley, Los Angeles and London, 1991.
—— *Alexander to Actium.* Berkeley and Los Angeles, 1993.
Green, Peter (ed.). *Hellenistic History and Culture.* Berkeley and Los Angeles, 1993.
Griffith, G. T., *Alexander the Great: The Main Problems.* Cambridge and New York, 1966.
Gruen, Erich S. *The Hellenistic World and the Coming of Rome.* Berkeley, 1986.
—— *Studies in Greek Culture and Roman Policy.* Berkeley, Los Angeles and London, 1996.
Kuhrt, Amélie and Sherwin-White, Susan. *Hellenism in the East: Greek and Non-Greek Civilizations from Syria to Central Asia After Alexander.* Berkeley and Los Angeles, 1988.
Sherwin-White, Susan and Kuhrt, Amélie. *From Samarkand to Sardis: A New Approach to the Seleucid Empire.* London, 1993.

REGIONAL HISTORIES

Bilde, Per (ed.). *Centre and Periphery in the Hellenistic World.* Aarhus, 1993.
Bowman, Alan K. *Egypt After the Pharaohs 332 BC–AD 642.* Berkeley and Los Angeles, 1986.
Downey, Susan B. *Hellenistic Religious Architecture: Alexandria through the Parthians.* Princeton, NJ, 1988.
Goudriaan, Koen. *Ethnicity in Ptolemaic Egypt.* Aarhus, 1992.
Haas, Christopher. *Alexandria in Late Antiquity.* Baltimore, MD, 1997.
Habicht, Christian. *Athens from Alexander to Antony.* Trans. Deborah Lucas Schneider. Cambridge, MA, 1997.
Holt, Frank Lee. *Thundering Zeus: The Making of Hellenistic Bactria.* Berkeley and Los Angeles, (forthcoming).
Johnson, Janet H. (ed.). *Life in a Multi-Cultural Society: Egypt from Cambyses to Constantine and Beyond.* Chicago, 1992.
Lewis, Naphtali. *Greeks in Ptolemaic Egypt.* Oxford, 1986.
Pomeroy, Sarah B. *Women in Hellenistic Egypt: From Alexander to Cleopatra.* 2nd edn. New York, 1990.
Potts, D. T. *The Arabian Gulf in Antiquity.* 2 vols. Oxford, 1990.
Samuel, Alan E. *The Shifting Sands of Interpretation: Interpretations of Ptolemaic Egypt.* Lanham, MD, 1989.
Thompson, Dorothy J. *Memphis Under the Ptolemies.* Princeton, NJ, 1988.

RELIGION

Burkert, Walter. *Ancient Mystery Cults.* Cambridge, MA, 1989.

LITERATURE, INTELLECTUAL LIFE AND PHILOSOPHY

Cameron, Alan. *Callimachus and His Critics.* Princeton, NJ, 1995.
Hunter, Richard. *Theocritus and the Archaeology of Greek Poetry.* Cambridge, 1996.

ART AND ARCHITECTURE

Fowler, Barbara Hughes. *The Hellenistic Aesthetic*. Madison, WI, 1990.

Pollitt, J. J. *Art in the Hellenistic Age*. Cambridge, 1986.

Stewart, Andrew. *Faces of Power: Alexander's Image and Hellenistic Politics*. Berkeley and Los Angeles, 1993.

INDEX

Note: Page numbers in *italics* refer to illustrations or tables